American Government and Politics Today: The Essentials

1996–1997 Edition

American Government and Politics Today: The Essentials

Barbara A. Bardes
University of Cincinnati

Mack C. Shelley II
Iowa State University

Steffen W. Schmidt
Iowa State University

West Publishing Company

Saint Paul/Minneapolis ■ New York ■ Los Angeles ■ San Francisco

COPY EDITOR	Mary Berry
COMPOSITION	Parkwood Composition Service
INDEX	Bob Marsh
COVER PHOTOGRAPH	© Peter Gridley, FPG International
TEXT PHOTOGRAPHS	Photo credits appear following the index

WEST'S COMMITMENT TO THE ENVIRONMENT

In 1906, West Publishing Company began recycling materials left over from the production of books. This began a tradition of efficient and responsible use of resources. Today, up to 95 percent of our legal books and 70 percent of our college and school texts are printed on recycled, acid-free stock. West also recycles nearly 22 million pounds of scrap paper annually—the equivalent of 181,717 trees. Since the 1960s, West has devised ways to capture and recycle waste inks, solvents, oils, and vapors created in the printing process. We also recycle plastics of all kinds, wood, glass, corrugated cardboard, and batteries, and have eliminated the use of Styrofoam book packaging. We at West are proud of the longevity and the scope of our commitment to the environment.

PRODUCTION, PREPRESS, PRINTING AND BINDING
BY WEST PUBLISHING COMPANY.

British Library Cataloguing-in-Publication Data. A catalogue record for this book is available from the British Library.

COPYRIGHT © 1986, 1988, 1990, 1992, 1994 BY WEST PUBLISHING COMPANY
COPYRIGHT © 1996 BY WEST PUBLISHING COMPANY
610 Opperman Drive
P.O. Box 64526
St. Paul, MN 55164–0526

03 02 01 00 99 98 97   8 7 6 5 4

Library of Congress Cataloging in Publication Data

ISBN 0–314–06948–8 (soft)
ISSN: 1084–9742
1996–1997 Essentials Version

Contents in Brief

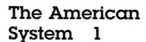

Contents

CHAPTER 2

The Constitution 31

CHAPTER 3

Federalism   65

PART TWO

Civil Rights and Liberties 99

CHAPTER 4

Civil Liberties 101

CHAPTER 5

Civil Rights   137

WHAT IF...WE HAD UNRESTRICTED IMMIGRATION?   138

African Americans and the Consequences of Slavery in the United States   139

PART THREE

People and Politics   187

CHAPTER 6

Public Opinion   189

WHAT IF...POLITICAL POLLS WERE BANNED?   190

How Powerful Is Public Opinion?   191

Defining and Measuring Public Opinion   192

The Qualities of Public Opinion   193
Intensity   193
Fluidity   193

CHAPTER 7

Interest Groups   221

CHAPTER 8

Political Parties   253

CHAPTER 9

Campaigns, Elections, and the Media 285

PART FOUR

Political Institutions 337

CHAPTER 10

The Congress 339

CHAPTER 11

The Presidency   385

**WHAT IF...THE VICE PRESIDENT SERVED AS THE PRESIDENT'S
CHIEF OF STAFF?   386**

CHAPTER 12
The Bureaucracy 423

POLITICS AND THE LAW:
Judicial Review—*Marbury v. Madison* (1803) 460

POLITICS AND THE LAW:
The Office of the Special Prosecutor 465

POLITICS AND CULTURAL DIVERSITY:
Does Our Legal System Reflect Our Diversity? 475

POLITICS: THE HUMAN SIDE:
William H. Rehnquist, Chief Justice of the Supreme Court 478

PART FIVE

Public Policy   489

CHAPTER 14

The Politics of Economic and Domestic Policymaking   491

POLITICS: THE HUMAN SIDE:
Carol Browner, Administrator of the EPA 511

POLITICS AND DIVERSITY:
The Fed Has a Cultural Diversity Problem 521

POLITICS AND COMPARATIVE PUBLIC DEBTS:
How the U.S. Public Debt Compares with That of Other Nations 523

GETTING INVOLVED:
The Importance of Government in Your Life 526

CHAPTER 15

Foreign and Defense Policy 531

WHAT IF...THE UN ENFORCED HUMAN RIGHTS WORLDWIDE? 532

What Is Foreign Policy? 533

POLITICS: THE HUMAN SIDE:
Warren Christopher, Secretary of State   539

POLITICS AND ETHICS:
The Demands of Ethnic Nationalism   560

Preface

At a point in its history when the United States has one of the strongest economies in the world and its former adversary, the Soviet Union, no longer exists, it is surprising that the nation has such an uncertain outlook for its future. Clearly aware that the United States is the sole remaining military superpower, the American people and their leaders seem unable to decide on what role we should play on the world stage.

The domestic political arena also appears to be unsettled and unpredictable, with both political parties striving to create new majorities. The 1992 election of Bill Clinton, who defeated both the incumbent president George Bush and the independent candidate Ross Perot, was widely seen as the beginning of a new political age, one that would be dominated by the demands and experiences of a new generation of leadership. Clinton's reputation as a moderate southern governor, his vice-presidential choice, Al Gore, Jr., and his young campaign team brought a freshness to American politics. He promised a "new covenant" with the American people. Clinton's victory, however, may have had within it the seeds of the 1994 electoral defeat for the Democratic party. Nineteen percent of the voters in 1992 cast their ballots for Ross Perot, the independent candidate for president who promised a totally new style of politics. The voters who were swayed by Perot were young, not affiliated with either party, and very unhappy with politics as usual.

Clinton's first two years in office were quite successful—apart from his initiative to reform the health-care system. The majority Democratic Congress passed a number of bills that Bush had vetoed, including the Brady Bill, the Family and Medical Leave Act, and a deficit-reduction bill that raised the taxes on upper-income Americans. Bill and Hillary Clinton, however, made health reform the centerpiece of their first two years. After a year of congressional hearings and consideration of the Clinton plan and many other plans, health-care reform was dropped from the agenda because there was no emerging consensus on how to reform such a massive sector of the nation's economy.

The 1994 congressional elections astonished most observers. The Republicans swept seats at every level of government, gaining control of both the House and the Senate, as well as many state governorships and legislatures. A fairly unknown firebrand Republican named Newt Gingrich became speaker of the House of Representatives, and, by enforcing party discipline, brought to the floor of the House all of the bills he had included in the Contract with America. The same observers who hailed the Clinton election as the beginning of a new age of moderate Democratic politics wondered if the American public was, instead, embracing the anti-government sentiments of the conservative Republicans. Is it possible that the Republicans will become the majority party, a place they have not held since the 1920s? Only future elections will tell.

It may seem paradoxical that although the American people and their political leaders are at present unable to find a consistent direction on many national issues, the degree to which people support certain basic political principles and get involved in local politics is unchanged. Most studies show that the majority of Americans are extremely patriotic and wish to see their nation, their states, and their local communities prosper. How the American people will be able to channel their desires and demands for political action through the political system is one of the topics addressed in this book.

A TOTAL LEARNING/TEACHING PACKAGE

This text, along with its numerous supplements, constitutes what we believe to be a total learning/teaching package. Specifically, the text itself contains numerous pedagogical aids and high-interest additions, such as the following:

1. *A Preview of Contents to Each Chapter.* To give the student an understanding of what is to come, each chapter starts out with a topical outline of its contents.

2. *What If . . .* To stimulate student interest in the chapter topics, each chapter begins with a hypothetical situation that we call *What If . . .* Some important *What If . . .* examples follow:

- "What If . . . The Constitution Were Easier to Amend?" (Chapter 2)
- "What If . . . We had Unrestricted Immigration?" (Chapter 5)
- "What If . . . Independent Voters Were the Majority?" (Chapter 8)
- "What If . . . Congresspersons Were Limited to Two Terms?" (Chapter 10)

3. *Margin Definitions.* Because terminology is often a stumbling block to understanding, each important term is printed in boldface, and a definition of the term appears in the margin adjacent to the boldfaced term. To help students locate these important terms quickly when reviewing the chapter materials, we list each boldfaced term and the page number on which it can be found in the *Key Terms* list at the end of the chapter. Additionally, all of the boldfaced terms and their definitions are contained in the *Glossary* at the end of the text, in which the terms are listed alphabetically.

4. *Did You Know . . . ?* Throughout the text, in the margins, are various facts and figures that we call *Did You Know . . . ?* They add relevance, humor, and a certain amount of fun to the student's task of learning about American government and politics. The following are examples of this feature:

- Did You Know . . . That the Democrats and Republicans each had exactly one woman delegate at their conventions in 1900? (Chapter 8)
- Did You Know . . . That in 1962, Representative Clem Miller, a California Democrat, was reelected to his congressional seat over challenger Don Clause despite the fact that Miller had died more than a month earlier in a plane crash? (Chapter 9)
- Did You Know . . . That in 1994, 1,500 civil servants in Charleston County, South Carolina, opened their tax information envelopes and discovered that they were legally dead because of a computer error, thereby

leaving only a half a dozen people deemed alive in that county's government? (Chapter 14)
■ Did You Know . . . That including those killed in the Civil War, more than one million American soldiers have been killed in the nation's wars? (Chapter 15).

5. *Profiles.* Every chapter is enlivened with a profile of a key individual who has made unique contributions to the American political system. These features are labeled *Politics: The Human Side.*

6. *Politics and . . .* Every chapter is further enlivened with special features entitled *Politics and . . .* , in which we take a closer look at some of the interesting aspects of topics discussed in the chapter. The following list shows some of these boxes:

■ *Politics and Cultural Diversity:* The Impact of Immigration (Chapter 1).
■ *Politics and Race:* From Integration Back to Segregation (Chapter 5).
■ *Politics and Political Parties:* The Republican Wave of 1994 (Chapter 8).
■ *Politics and People:* Attacking the Federal Government (Chapter 12).

7. *Getting Involved.* Because we believe that the best way for students to get a firmer understanding of the American political system is by direct participation, we offer suggestions on ways for them to get involved in the system. At the end of each chapter, there are suggestions on where to write, whom to call, and what to do. Some examples of this feature follow:

■ Your Civil Liberties: Searches and Seizures (Chapter 4).
■ Be a Critical Consumer of Opinion Polls (Chapter 6).
■ Influencing the President (Chapter 11).

8. *Point-by-point Chapter Summaries.* At the end of each chapter, the essential points in the chapter are presented in a point-by-point format for ease of review and understanding.

9. *Questions for Review and Discussion.* To elicit student interest and discussion in and out of class, there are two to five questions for review and discussion at the end of each chapter.

10. *Logging On—Suggestions for Using the Internet.* In keeping with the electronic age, we are providing students with suggestions on how to access the "information superhighway" by using the Internet. We describe the Internet and how it can be accessed in the *Logging On* feature at the end of Chapter 1. Then, in the *Logging On* section at the end of each subsequent chapter, we give appropriate suggestions for how to find information on special topics covered in the chapter.

11. *Selected References.* Important and understandable references are given at the end of each chapter. Each reference is annotated to indicate its usefulness and the area that it covers.

12. *Tables, Charts, and Photographs.* As you can readily see, the text uses tables and charts, as well as photographs, to summarize and illustrate important institutional, historical, and economic facts.

EMPHASIS ON CRITICAL THINKING

Whenever feasible, we have gone beyond mere factual narrative to discuss the rationale underlying specific political decisions and the likely consequences of those decisions in the future. For example, in Chapter 3, when discussing fiscal federalism, we not only describe federal mandates but also analyze the effects of unfunded federal mandates on already strained state budgets. This analysis provides a background for understanding the significance of the legislation enacted by Congress in 1995 to curb such mandates. As another example, in Chapter 14, on the politics of economic and domestic policymaking, we analyze policy problems in terms of which groups in society receive the benefits of particular policy decisions.

If the student uses our accompanying booklet, *Handbook on Critical Thinking and Writing in American Politics,* with the exercises in critical thinking, he or she will have a strong basis for analyzing not only American politics but all other college subjects as well.

THE ANNOTATED U.S. CONSTITUTION AND OTHER APPENDICES

So that this book can serve as a reference, we have included important documents for the student of American government to have close at hand. Of course, every college American government text includes the U.S. Constitution. We believe that this document—and students' understanding of it—is so important that we have included a fully annotated U.S. Constitution as Appendix B. Although our brief summaries of constitutional provisions should not be thought of as a substitute for a word-for-word analysis, they will help the student understand the finer points within each part of our Constitution.

In addition to the U.S. Constitution and a special new appendix on survival skills (see the next section), we have also included the following appendices:

- *The Declaration of Independence.*
- *The Presidents of the United States.*
- *Federalist Papers #10 and 51.*
- *How to Do Research in Political Science.*
- *Justices of the U.S. Supreme Court.*
- *Spanish Equivalents for Important Terms in American Government and Political Science.*

A SPECIAL APPENDIX ON SURVIVAL SKILLS

Students, as citizens, need certain survival skills. We include in this edition a special appendix called *A Citizen's Survival Guide.* It contains the following sections:

- You and the Political System.
- You and the Justice System.
- You and Your Personal Protection.
- You and Your Employer.

A FULL SUPPLEMENTAL PACKAGE

In conjunction with a number of our colleagues, we have developed a supplementary teaching materials package that we believe is the best available today.

Study Guide

The student *Study Guide* was written by James McElyea of Tulsa Junior College, Tulsa, Oklahoma. Each chapter provides learning objectives, a topical outline, a list of terms and concepts, and a variety of self-study questions. The *Study Guide* also contains an essay describing how students can develop and improve their study skills for the American government course. The *Study Guide* is available for student purchase.

Instructor's Manual

The *Instructor's Manual* was written by Michael Dinneen of Tulsa Junior College, Tulsa, Oklahoma, and includes learning objectives and annotated chapter outlines, as well as numerous teaching suggestions, examples, ideas for presentation, and supplemental lecture ideas. In the *Instructor's Manual* are suggested answers to the exercises in critical thinking found at the end of each *Critical Perspective* in the text.

Test Bank

The test bank was written by Michael Dinneen of Tulsa Junior College, Tulsa, Oklahoma. It contains over 1,300 test items. The test items are a mixture of multiple-choice, short-answer, and essay questions. Answers to the test items are page referenced.

Computerized Instructor's Manual

The entire *Instructor's Manual* is now available on disk in ASCII format. It can be coded for practically any word-processing program that you are using. You can modify the *Instructor's Manual* to meet your own needs and specifications.

Computerized Testing

A computerized testing program, WESTEST, containing the test questions from the test bank, is available with this text. WESTEST may be obtained for the IBM PC and compatible computers or the Apple Macintosh family of microcomputers. WESTEST allows instructors to create new tests, modify existing tests, change the questions from West's original test bank, and print tests in a variety of formats. Instructors can add questions of their own to the test bank. Instructors should contact their West sales representative to inquire about acquiring WESTEST.

A Book of Readings

Accompanying the book is a reader consisting of nineteen chapters keyed to the book's topics. Each chapter has from two to four short, interesting, timely, and thought-provoking articles taken from recent sources. The articles focus on subjects discussed in the book and provide the students with additional depth on these topics. Examples include political correctness and free speech, euthanasia, the influence of the media, and health-care reform. Each section has a short introduction that provides the student with a summary and overview. There are also study and discussion questions at the end of each chapter.

A Handbook on Critical Thinking and Writing

In keeping with the emphasis on critical thinking in this edition, we have written a handbook entitled *An Introduction to Critical Thinking and Writing in American Politics*. This handbook introduces students to a series of critical-thinking techniques that will allow them to make better use of the information they receive about the political sphere from campaign speeches, the mass media, and privately sponsored publications. Although the examples used in the handbook relate specifically to American politics, the techniques in critical thinking presented can be of value to the students in all their college courses, as well as in their day-to-day activities.

Handbooks of Selected Court Cases and Legislation

The decisions of the United States Supreme Court play an important role in American political developments, and for that reason, numerous significant Supreme Court decisions are discussed or cited in *American Government and Politics Today*. To further the student's understanding of the Supreme Court's reasoning, a special supplement on Supreme Court cases accompanies the 1996–1997 edition. The *Handbook of Selected Court Cases,* which contains thirty-two of the Supreme Court cases mentioned in the text, allows students to read the Court's own words on selected issues. Each case in the *Handbook* opens with a brief statement, in the author's own words, that describes the essential issue or issues before the Court. Then a summary of the case as it appears on WESTLAW is presented. Following this summary appear the actual words of the Court, excerpted directly from the Court's written opinion on the case. To assist the student in deciphering the meaning of certain legal terms and case citations, a preface to the *Handbook* provides a guide to legal citations and terminology.

Also included as a supplement for this edition is a separate *Handbook of Selected Legislation*. This pamphlet contains excerpts from many of the statutes referred to in this text.

College Survival Guide

The *College Survival Guide,* written by Bruce Rowe, offers tips for students on how they can succeed in college. The guide includes suggestions on how to finance an education, manage time effectively, prepare for and take examinations, improve concentration, and use the credit/no-credit option. The author also discusses cooperative-education programs and the importance of a liberal arts education. The *College Survival Guide* is especially helpful for first-year college students, students who are reentering college, and students from other countries.

An Analysis of the Breakup of the Soviet Union: *The Rise and Fall of the Soviet Union, 1917–1991*

To give students the background that they need to understand the challenges that face the United States in carrying out a foreign policy, a free student booklet about the dissolution of the Soviet Union is available to adopters. It is called *The Rise and Fall of the Soviet Union, 1917–1991.*

Videotapes

We are pleased to announce that *American Government and Politics Today* was selected as the recommended text for the Dallas County Community College District telecourse "Government by Consent," which began in 1990. The telecourse is distributed through Dallas Telecourse and the PBS Adult Learning Service to educational institutions.

All qualified adopters of *American Government and Politics Today* are able to select three special half-hour videotapes from this exciting telecourse. The program is devoted to topics central to the study of American government and includes interviews with major contemporary decision makers. Qualified adopters may also choose videos from West's Political Science Video Library. A list of tapes is available upon request.

Videodisc

The latest teaching technology involves the use of the videodisc. Similar to the familiar compact disc, a videodisc allows you to find instantly material that you need to illustrate points in the lecture. You can easily go exactly to the spot on the disc that you want. You can also still-frame for as long as you wish. *West's American Government Videodisc* includes, for example, Bill Moyers talking about the Bill of Rights and then interviewing citizens to get their opinions about that important document (in Unit Two) and David Frost interviewing past presidents (in Unit Five).

In addition to the motion sequences, there are hundreds of still frames that can be used in place of overhead transparencies. *West's American Government Videodisc* also has accompanying software, called The Lecture Builder™, as mentioned below.

Interactive Videodisc Learning—Interest Groups and Political Action Committees

A special interest for student learning is the interactive videodisc that we offer. It covers two lessons—interest groups and political action committees (PACs). Students can interact with the videodisc by answering questions at appropriate spots in the motion-video sequences. This system can be used with any videodisc player that can be controlled by one of the numerous consumer computer systems.

Software

Three software systems are available for the 1996–1997 edition of this text.

Your Research: Data Analysis for *American Government and Politics Today*.   Prepared by Eric Plutzer and Kenneth Heinz, this special software package can be used either by instructors for classroom demonstration or by students in conjunction with their homework. The software provides students with an opportunity to analyze political data in a user-friendly format.

The Lecture Builder™.   Those who use *West's American Government Videodisc* will find that The Lecture Builder™ software allows for complete customization of each separate lecture.

Interactive Software.   Interactive software allows students to interact with the videodisc that covers interest groups and political action committees.

Transparency Acetates

A set of approximately fifty full-color transparency acetates of key graphs, tables, and diagrams found in the text is available to adopters of this text.

FOR USERS OF PREVIOUS EDITIONS

As always, we want to thank you for your past support. Here we wish to let you know what changes have been made in the 1996–1997 edition. Basically, we have rewritten and updated more materials in this edition than in any other. You will find throughout, in every chapter, that the references to examples and political analysis reflect the work that has been done by our colleagues in the 1990s. We, of course, have replaced many of the features with new ones. The following summarizes the changes for this edition:

1. International coverage is integrated throughout the text.
2. There is even more political analysis.
3. The *Politics and . . .* (with some of the listings already given in this Preface) emphasize more political analysis than in the last edition.
4. The following *What If . . .* features are new:

■ "What If . . . We Had an Electronic Direct Democracy?" (Chapter 1).
■ "What If . . . The Constitution Were Easier to Amend?" (Chapter 2).
■ "What If . . . Independent Voters Were the Majority?" (Chapter 8).
■ "What If . . . The Federal Income Tax Became a Consumption Tax?" (Chapter 14).

Of course, all of the remaining *What If . . .* features from the previous edition have been updated.

5. We have made hundreds of changes and updates to the chapters of this book for the 1996–1997 edition. Here we list just a few of these revisions:

■ Chapter 1 ("America in a World of Change") has been substantially re-written to include information on the changing makeup of the U.S. population and the various political subcultures.

■ Chapter 2 ("The Constitution") contains a substantially revised discussion of the Articles of Confederation and a new section on the national convention as a means of amending the Constitution.

■ Chapter 3 ("Federalism") presents an updated discussion of federal mandates, their cost to the states, and recent legislation curbing unfunded federal mandates. A new exhibit on federal grants-in-aid is also included.

■ Chapter 4 ("Civil Liberties") now offers a clearer distinction between civil liberties and civil rights, contains additional information on the clear and present danger test and prior restraint, and includes a discussion of the 1988 Indian Gaming Regulatory Act and gambling on Indian reservations.

■ Chapter 5 ("The Rights of Minorities and Women") includes a virtually rewritten section on busing and a more thorough treatment of the Civil Rights Act of 1968 and discrimination in housing. The chapter also has been thoroughly revised to update and expand the discussions of sexual harassment, age discrimination in employment, the civil rights of juveniles, and the rights of gay males and lesbians.

■ Chapter 10 ("The Congress") has been substantially revised to reflect the impact of the 1994 elections on the makeup of Congress. A new feature has been added examining the "winners" and the "losers" of the 1994 elections, and a new section analyzes the accomplishments of the Republican-controlled Congress during the "first one hundred days." The names of party leaders and committee chairs in the 104th Congress are also included. Additionally, the chapter presents a substantially rewritten section on "How a Bill Becomes a Law," using the Brady Bill (the Handgun Violence Prevention Act of 1993) as an example, and an expanded discussion of redistricting and the courts' scrutiny of this issue.

■ Chapter 11 ("The Judiciary") contains a new section dealing with the powers of the courts (in addition to the power of judicial review) and information on recent appointments to the United States Supreme Court.

■ Chapter 14 ("The Politics of Economic and Domestic Policymaking") has been extensively revised and now presents a substantially rewritten section on the policymaking process, using the 1994 crime bill to illustrate the process; a new section on crime ("The Cold War of the 1990s"), including an examination of the prison "population bomb", extensively revised sections on taxes subsidies, and proposed balanced-budget amendments.

6. We have added to this edition a new chapter-ending feature. At the end of each chapter, we indicate to the student that politics is a process rather than a set of facts and institutions. Consequently, we have labeled these chapter-ending sections "America's Politics: Unfinished Work"; "The Constitution: Unfinished Work"; "Federalism: Unfinished Work"; and so on. These sections are forward looking in that they present ideas to the student-reader about what problems have yet to be solved in these various areas.

7. In this edition, we have listed (with page references) at the end of each chapter the terms that were boldfaced and defined in the margins of the chapter pages. The *Key Terms* list appears just before the *Chapter Summary*.

8. *Logging On* sections have been added at the end of each chapter in the 1996–1997 edition. These sections, which appear just before the *Selected*

References, give students suggestions on how they can use the Internet to access information on a wide variety of topics.

   9. The following appendices are new to this edition:

- *Justices of the U.S. Supreme Court.*
- *Spanish Equivalents for Important Terms in American Government and Political Science.*
- *A Citizen's Survival Guide.*

10. The *College Survival Guide,* a new supplement accompanying the 1996–1997 edition.

11. The new supplement entitled *Handbook of Selected Legislation.*

12. A new software program—Your Research: Data Analysis for *American Government and Politics Today*—also accompanies the 1996–1997 edition.

   Of course, all textual materials—text, figures, tables, features, and so on—have been revised as necessary to reflect the political developments that occurred since the last edition. This book has also been extensively updated to reflect the results of the November 1994 election and the impact of a Republican-controlled Congress on policymaking.

ACKNOWLEDGMENTS

Since we started this project a number of years ago, a sizable cadre of individuals has helped us in various phases of the undertaking. The following academic reviewers offered numerous constructive criticisms, comments, and suggestions during the preparation of all previous editions:

Danny M. Adkison
Oklahoma State University

Sharon Z. Alter
William Rainey Harper College,
Illinois

Kevin Bailey
North Harris Community College,
Texas

Dr. Charles T. Barber
University of Southern Indiana,
Evansville, Indiana

Clyde W. Barrow
Texas A&M University

Lynn R. Brink
North Lake College, Irving, Texas

Barbara L. Brown
Southern Illinois University at
Carbondale

Ralph Bunch
Portland State University, Oregon

Carol Cassell
University of Alabama

Frank J. Coppa
Union County College,
Cranford, New Jersey

Robert E. Craig
University of New Hampshire

Doris Daniels
Nassau Community College,
New York

Carolyn Grafton Davis
North Harris County College, Texas

Marshall L. DeRosa
Louisiana State University,
Baton Rouge, Louisiana

Michael Dinneen
Tulsa Junior College, Oklahoma

Gavan Duffy
University of Texas at Austin

George C. Edwards III
Texas A&M University

Mark C. Ellickson
Southwestern Missouri State
University, Springfield, Missouri

Elizabeth N. Flores
Del Mar College, Texas

Joel L. Franke
Blinn College, Brenham, Texas

William A. Giles
Mississippi State University

Donald Gregory
Stephen F. Austin State University,
Nacogdoches, Texas

Forest Grieves
University of Montana

Dale Grimnitz
Normandale Community College,
Bloomington, Minnesota

Stefan D. Haag
Austin Community College, Texas

Jean Wahl Harris
University of Scranton,
Scranton, Pennsylvania

David N. Hartman
Rancho Santiago College,
Santa Ana, California

Robert M. Herman
Moorpark College, California

Paul Holder
McClennan Community College,
Waco, Texas

Michael Hoover
Seminole Community College,
Sanford, Florida

J. C. Horton
San Antonio College, Texas

Willoughby Jarrell
Kennesaw College, Georgia

Loch K. Johnson
University of Georgia

Donald L. Jordan
United States Air Force Academy,
Colorado

John D. Kay
Santa Barbara City College,
California

Bruce L. Kessler
Shippensburg University,
Pennsylvania

Dale Krane
Mississippi State University

Charles W. Kegley
University of South Carolina

Samuel Krislov
University of Minnesota

Ray Leal
Southwest Texas State University,
San Marcos, Texas

Sue Lee
Center for Telecommunications,
Dallas County Community College
District

Carl Lieberman
University of Akron, Ohio

Orma Linford
Kansas State University

James D. McElyea
Tulsa Junior College, Oklahoma

William P. McLauchlan
Purdue University, Indiana

William W. Maddox
University of Florida

S. J. Makielski, Jr.
Loyola University, New Orleans

Jarol B. Manheim
George Washington University

J. David Martin
Midwestern State University, Texas

Bruce B. Mason
Arizona State University

Steve J. Mazurana
University of Northern Colorado

Thomas J. McGaghie
Kellogg Community College,
Michigan

Stanley Melnick
Valencia Community College,
Florida

Robert Mittrick
Luzurne County Community
College, Pennsylvania

Helen Molanphy
Richland College, Texas

Stephen Osofsky
Nassau Community College,
New York

John P. Pelissero
Loyola University of Chicago

Michael A. Preda
Midwestern State University, Texas

Charles Prysby
University of North Carolina

Donald R. Ranish
Antelope Valley College, California

Curt Reichel
University of Wisconsin

Russell D. Renka
Southeast Missouri State University

Eleanor A. Schwab
South Dakota State University

Len Shipman
Mount San Antonio College,
California

Scott Shrewsbury
Mankato State University,
Minnesota

Carol Stix
Pace University, Pleasantville, New
York

Gerald S. Strom
University of Illinois at Chicago

John R. Todd
North Texas State University

B. Oliver Walter
University of Wyoming

Thomas L. Wells
Old Dominion University, Virginia

Jean B. White
Weber State College, Utah

Allan Wiese
Mankato State University,
Minnesota

Robert D. Wrinkle
Pan American University, Texas

The 1996–1997 edition of this text is the result of our working closely with reviewers who each offered us penetrating criticisms, comments, and suggestions for how to improve the text. Although we haven't been able to take account of all requests, each of the reviewers listed below will see many of his or her suggestions taken to heart.

William Arp III
Louisiana State University

Kenyon D. Bunch
Fort Lewis College, Durango,
Colorado

John W. Epperson
Simpson College, Indianola,
Indiana

Daniel W. Fleitas
University of North Carolina at
Charlotte

Barry D. Friedman
North Georgia College

Robert S. Getz
SUNY–Brockport, New York

Kristina Gilbert
Riverside City College

Donald Gregory
Stephen F. Austin State University,
Nacogdoches, Texas

Richard J. Herzog
Stephen F. Austin State University,
Nacogdoches, Texas

Nancy B. Kral
Tomball College

Harry D. Lawrence
Southwest Texas Junior College,
Uvaide, Texas

Eileen Lynch
Brookhaven College

Keith Nicholls
University of Alabama

Neil A. Pinney
Western Michigan University

Paul Rozycki
Charles Stewart Mott Community
College, Flint, Michigan

Gilbert K. St. Clair
University of New Mexico

Benjamin Walter
Vanderbilt University, Tennessee

Many individuals helped during the research and editorial stages of this edition. We wish to thank Keith Hitch, William Eric Hollowell, Sherry Downing-Alfonso, Lavina Miller, Suzanne Jasin, Barbara Curtiss, and Sarah Davenport. Marie-Christine Loiseau also aided in proofreading. Clyde Perlee, Jr., our untiring editor at West Publishing Company, continued to offer strong support and guidance at every phase of this edition. Our project editor, Bill Stryker, helped us in this new design and photo research program. He remains the object of our sincere appreciation, as does Jan Lamar for her extensive developmental guidance and her ability to get all the teaching supplements out on time.

Any errors that remain are our own. We welcome any and all comments from instructors and students alike. Comments that we have received on previous editions have helped us improve this text. Nonetheless, we know that we need to continue to make changes as the needs of instructors and students change.

Barbara Bardes
Mack Shelley
Steffen Schmidt

PART ONE

The American System

1
America in a World of Change

 CHAPTER OUTLINE

WHAT IF . . .
We Had an Electronic Direct Democracy?

The technological means are here to support the creation of a direct democracy in the United States. In a direct democracy, not only do the people rule, or control the government, but the people also vote directly on the officials, laws, and policies of government. Imagine the consequences of using electronic means to make direct voting available for all citizens of the United States. Consider the possibility of each U.S. citizen eighteen years old or older voting on proposed laws or policies. For example, Americans could vote directly on whether U.S. military forces should be used to enforce peace in Bosnia, or citizens could choose among proposed health-care plans.

Upon turning eighteen, each American would register with a national board of election (local election boards would become obsolete). The voter's Social Security number would then be entered into a computerized data bank. Each individual would then create a private personal identification number (PIN) to go with that Social Security number. When the time would come to cast a vote on a national policy or issue, or in an election, the voter would dial an 800 number, enter his or her Social Security number and PIN, and be verified as an eligible voter. The numbers on the touch-tone telephone would be used to indicate choices or answers to recorded questions on the issues, or the system could use a remote television device. Because the entire process would be computerized, results could be tabulated virtually instantly.

The possibility of having an electronic direct democracy raises a number of issues. First, there are

technological issues, which probably all could be resolved. One is how to determine the legitimate identity of voters and how to avoid an individual's allowing a family member or friend to use his or her Social Security and PIN to vote. In fact, if that problem were not quickly resolved, buying and selling votes could be a lucrative business.

Of course, there would have to be some time period designated for campaigning and debate, as well as a closing date for voting. Polls could close simultaneously across the United States: midnight on the East Coast would be 9:00 P.M. in California. This would eliminate the possibility of the polls closing earlier in one part of the country and of individuals on the West Coast knowing the eastern or national results before they made their choices.

Finally, the technological innovations required for a direct electronic democracy raise the question of preserving the anonymity of the individual voter. In elections held with paper ballots, punch cards, or computer card ballots, the individual's identification is removed from the actual ballot when it is deposited in the ballot box. With electronic voting, however, the computer could easily keep track of who voted for which candidate. Therefore, it would be necessary to install safeguards to ensure that once the voter's identification was cleared, that number would not be "attached" to the electronic voting record. Without such a safeguard, voters might not trust the system.

Electronic direct democracy also would complicate the representation of interests in the United States. One of the major tasks of

the U.S. Congress is to balance the interests of various parts of the country. The give and take of legislation, the bargaining that occurs among representatives and senators, and the lengthy debates over the details of legislation are often attempts to provide some fairness in the legislative process to the many "publics" represented in Congress. Electronic direct democracy would make such a "balancing of interests" impossible.

Remember, for example, the legislation to provide billions of dollars for earthquake relief to California in 1994? It is very likely that almost all Californians who were eligible to vote in an electronic direct democracy would approve that legislation. Citizens in other parts of the nation, however, might not be as interested in that policy or might not pay such close attention to it. Therefore they might not be inclined to "turn out," or pick up their telephones and vote. The result would be legislation that favored one group or region—California. This characteristic of direct voting would be reinforced by media campaigns put on by private interest groups to convince individuals that it was important to vote for or against a particular issue. Such a "media circus" might convince us that our much-criticized legislatures constitute a better forum for lawmaking than would a direct democracy.

---

1. Would an electronic direct democracy increase citizen interest in government and policy issues?
2. How could the media best be used to promote public discussion of policies or laws that are being brought up for a direct vote?

The study of politics is often the study of changing political arrangements—changing how the society is ordered and how decisions affecting the people are made. While voters in the United States may consider changes in public campaign financing, changes in the electoral college, or even, as suggested in the opening *What If . . . ,* changing to an electronic direct democracy, people throughout the world are struggling to establish new forms of government for their nations. For more than seventy years, the Soviet Union appeared to be a monolithic nation with strong central authority and political processes that Western government regarded as undesirable or threatening. In the last five years, the Soviet Union has disappeared. It has fragmented into a commonwealth made up of loosely linked states and several states that no longer have political ties to Russia, once the central governing partner in the coalition. Some of these new states now have active political parties, hold elections, and have democratically elected governments. In other former Soviet republics, socialist parties have been elected to hold office through democratic elections. New political parties seem to form almost daily in the former Soviet republics, and old political parties assume new names in an attempt to convince voters that they are part of the new system.

In the last decade, a number of nations in Latin America threw off their former military governors or authoritarian regimes and moved toward establishing democratic systems. The same movement has taken place in nations in Asia, Africa, and much of the rest of the developing world. Few in the world who had the opportunity to watch television in the past decade can forget the image of the Berlin Wall coming down and opening the way to the reunification of Germany and the end of the Soviet Union. Many people remember the violent clash in Beijing's Tienanmen Square between the government and youthful Chinese demonstrators, who favored different paths to reform in the People's Republic of China.

The first biracial elections were held in South Africa in 1994. Prior to that, the officially supported system of racial segregation—apartheid—prevented black South Africans from participating in the political process. Racial segregation and the supremacy of whites had been traditionally accepted in South Africa even prior to the passage of the legal basis for apartheid in 1948. Throughout the 1970s and 1980s, unions, churches, and students organized protests against apartheid. In 1991, then president De Klerk announced a repeal of the acts that were the legal basis for apartheid. In March 1992, South African whites voted to end their minority rule.

POLITICAL CHANGE IN THE UNITED STATES

Voters in the United States demonstrated their desire for change in the 1992 presidential election. They denied reelection to George Bush (the Republican candidate who had occupied the presidency for only one term) and elected Bill Clinton (the first Democrat to be elected to the presidency in twelve years). About 19 percent of the voters cast their ballots for H. Ross Perot, the independent candidate for president, who ran on an antiparty, anti–big government platform.

As president, Bill Clinton embarked on a series of policy initiatives that were intended to change American government. He was successful in getting Congress to approve the Family and Medical Leave Act, in passing a deficit reduction bill, in appointing Ruth Bader Ginsburg, a supporter of women's rights, to the Supreme Court, and in gaining congressional approval of the North American Free Trade Agreement (NAFTA). The president and Mrs. Clinton also led the failed effort to design a massive health-care reform bill.

Just two years after the election of Bill Clinton, the voters again voted for change, overwhelmingly electing Republicans to the House, to the Senate, and to governorships and state legislatures throughout the country. As the results of the ballots were tallied, it became clear that not only did the Republicans win back control of the Senate but they also won a majority of the seats in the House, controlling the Congress for the first time in forty years. Representative Newt Gingrich from Georgia became the speaker of the House. He pledged to lead the Republican majority to reform government, including the passage of a balanced-budget amendment to the Constitution, a reduction in government programs, and a moderate reform of the health-care system rather than a major overhaul.

The willingness of Americans to debate these new initiatives and to demand changes in the way the government works is at the core of our democratic nation. Change—even revolutionary change—is a tribute to the success of a political system. As Abraham Lincoln put it, "This country with all its institutions, belongs to the people who inhabit it. Whenever they shall grow weary of the existing government, they can exercise their Constitutional right of amending it, or the revolutionary right to dismember or overthrow it."[1]

In the chapters that follow, we will look more closely at the **institutions** of our government and how they have changed over the decades. We will examine how the political processes of the nation work to accomplish those changes. To begin, we will look at why political institutions and processes are necessary in any society and what purposes they serve.

INSTITUTION
A long-standing, identifiable structure or association that performs functions for society.

WHAT IS POLITICS?

Why do nations and people struggle so hard to establish a form of government and continue to expend so much effort in **politics** to keep that gov-

POLITICS
According to David Easton, the "authoritative allocation of values" for a society; according to Harold Lasswell, "who gets what, when, and how" in a society.

---

1. *Oxford Dictionary of Quotations*, 3d ed. (Oxford, England: Oxford University Press, 1980), p. 314.

ernment functioning? Politics and forms of government are probably as old as human society. There are many definitions of *politics,* but all try to explain how human beings regulate conflict within their society. As soon as humans began to live in groups, particularly groups that were larger than their immediate families, there arose the need to establish rules about behavior, property, the privileges of individuals and groups, and how people would survive together. Politics can be best understood as the process of, as Harold Lasswell put it, "who gets what, when, and how."[2] To another social scientist, David Easton, politics should be defined as the "authoritative allocation of values."[3] Politics, then, is the struggle or process engaged in by human beings to decide which members of society get what benefits or privileges and which members are excluded from certain benefits or privileges.

In the early versions of human society, the tribe or village, politics was relatively informal. Tribal elders or hereditary chiefs were probably vested with the power to decide who married whom, who was able to build a hut on the best piece of land, and which young people succeeded them into the positions of leadership. Other societies were "democratic" from the very beginning, giving their members some form of choice in regard to leadership and rules. Early human societies rarely had the concept of property, so few rules were needed to decide who owned or inherited a given parcel of property. The concepts of property and inheritance are much more modern. As society became more complex and humans became settled farmers rather than hunters and gatherers, the problems of property, inheritance, sales and exchanges, kinship, and rules of behavior became important to resolve. Politics developed into the process by which some of these questions were answered.

Inevitably, conflicts arise in society, because members of different groups have unique needs, values, and perspectives. At least three different kinds of conflicts that may require the need for political processes to arise in a society:

1. People may differ over their beliefs, either religious or personal, or over basic issues of right and wrong. The kind of debate that has taken place in recent years on abortion is an example of this kind of conflict.

2. Members of a society may differ greatly in their perception of what the society's goals should be. In early society, that debate may have been over whether the group should move to a new territory or stay settled in its current situation. Today, Americans differ over whether the reform of health care should be the most important item on the public agenda, or whether finding a way to reduce crime and violence in our cities is the most important issue.

3. Individuals compete for scarce resources; jobs, income, and property are examples. The question of who might pay for a national health-care program is really a discussion of whether wealthier people would pay for the health care of the disadvantaged individuals in the society or whether all persons would pay on a more or less equal footing for national health care.

DID YOU KNOW . . .
That the word *politikos* (pertaining to citizen or civic affairs) was used by the Greeks thousands of years ago and that the English word *politics* entered the language around 1529?

---

2. Harold Lasswell, *Politics: Who Gets What, When and How* (New York: McGraw-Hill, 1936).
3. David Easton, *The Political System* (New York: Knopf, 1953).

THE NEED FOR GOVERNMENT AND POWER

GOVERNMENT
A permanent structure (institution) composed of decision makers who make society's rules about conflict resolution and the allocation of resources and who possess the power to enforce them.

If *politics* refers to conflict and conflict resolution, **government** refers to the structures by which the decisions are made that resolve conflict or allocate values. In early human societies, such as families and small tribes, there was no need for formal structures of government. Decisions were made by acknowledged leaders in those societies. In families, all members may meet together to decide values and priorities. Where there is a community that makes decisions and allocates values through informal rules, politics exists—but not government. Within most contemporary societies, these activities continue in many forms. For example, when a church decides to build a new building or hire a new minister, that decision may be made politically, but there is in fact no government. Politics can be found in schools, social groups, and other organized groups. When a society, however, reaches a certain level of complexity, it becomes necessary to establish a permanent or semipermanent group of individuals to act for the whole, to become the government.

Governments range in size from the volunteer city council and one or two employees of a small town to the massive and complex structures of the U.S. government or those of any other large, modern nation. Generally, governments not only make the rules but also implement them through the use of police, judges, and government officials. Some governments may be relatively limited in their power to make rules about the conduct of the individuals in the society. Other governments may have the power not only to decide public laws but also, as in the former Soviet Union, to control all enterprises within the society.

Authority and Legitimacy

AUTHORITY
The features of a leader or an institution that compel obedience, usually because of ascribed legitimacy. For most societies, government is the ultimate authority in the allocation of values.

LEGITIMACY
A status conferred by the people on the government's officials, acts, and institutions through their belief that the government's actions are an appropriate use of power by a legally constituted governmental authority following correct decision-making procedures. These actions are regarded as rightful and entitled to compliance and obedience on the part of citizens.

In addition to instituting and carrying out laws regulating individual behavior, such as traffic laws and criminal laws, most modern governments also attempt to carry out public policies that are intended to fulfill specific national or state goals. For example, a state may decide that its goal is to reduce teenage consumption of alcohol and the automobile accidents caused by such behavior. To do that, the state may institute extremely strong penalties for underage drinking, along with a statewide education program for teenagers and younger children about the dangers of drinking and driving. The U.S. government has instituted and attempted to implement a series of environmental laws meant to improve air and water quality. Environmental policies have required citizens to follow certain laws, such as those requiring the use of unleaded gasoline. Such policies also have forced citizens to buy only certain types of automobiles and to pay higher costs for electricity in order to reimburse the utility companies for the equipment they have installed to control emissions.

Why do citizens obey these laws and subject themselves to these regulations? One reason citizens obey the government is because the government has the **authority** to make such laws. By authority, we mean the ultimate right to enforce compliance with decisions. Americans also believe the laws should be obeyed because they possess **legitimacy**—that is, they are appropriate and rightful. The laws have been made according to the correct and accepted political process by representatives of the people. Therefore, the laws are accepted by the people as legitimate and having political authority.

The Question of Power

Another and perhaps more basic answer as to why we comply with the laws and rules of the government is because we understand that government has the **power** to enforce the law. We obey environmental laws and pay taxes in part because we acknowledge the legitimacy of the law. We also know that the government has the power to coerce our compliance with the law. Governments differ in the degree to which they must rely on coercion to gain **compliance** from their citizens. In authoritarian nations, the use of force is far more common than in democratic nations, in which most citizens comply with the law because they accept the authority of the government and its officials. In authoritarian or **totalitarian regimes**, the will of the government is imposed frequently and is upheld by the use of force.

The concept of power also involves the ability of one individual or group to influence the actions of another individual or group of individuals. We frequently speak of the power of the president to convince Congress to pass laws or the power of the American Association of Retired Persons to influence legislation. We also speak frequently of the power of money to influence political decisions. These uses of power are informal, including the use of rewards for compliance rather than the threat of coercion. More often than not, political power in the government is a matter of influence and persuasion rather than coercion.

POWER
The ability to cause others to modify their behavior and to conform to what the power holder wants.

COMPLIANCE
Accepting and carrying out authorities' decisions.

TOTALITARIAN REGIME
A form of government that controls all aspects of the political and social life of a nation. All power resides with the government. The citizens have no power to choose the leadership or policies of the country.

WHO GOVERNS?

One of the most fundamental questions of politics is which persons or groups of people control society through the government. Who possesses the power to make decisions about who gets what and how the benefits of the society are distributed among the people?

Sources of Political Power

At one extreme is a society governed by a totalitarian regime. In such a political system, a relatively small group of leaders or perhaps a single individual—a dictator—makes all political decisions for the society. Every aspect of political, social, and economic life is controlled by the government. The power of the ruler is total (thus, the term *totalitarianism*).

Many of our terms for describing the distribution of political power are derived from the ancient Greeks, who were the first Western people to study politics systematically. A society in which political decisions were controlled by a small group was called an **oligarchy**, meaning rule by a few members of the **elite**, who generally benefited themselves. Another form of rule by the few was known as **aristocracy**, meaning rule by the most virtuous, the most talented, or the best suited to the position. Later, in European history, *aristocracy* meant rule by the titled or the upper classes. In contrast to such a top-down form of control was the form known as **anarchy**, or the

OLIGARCHY
Rule by a few members of the elite, who generally make decisions to benefit their own group.

ELITE
An upper socioeconomic class that controls political and economic affairs.

ARISTOCRACY
Rule by the best suited, through virtue, talent, or education; in later usage, rule by the upper class.

ANARCHY
The condition of having no government and no laws. Each member of the society governs himself or herself.

DEMOCRACY
A system of government in which ultimate political authority is vested in the people. Derived from the Greek words *demos* ("the people") and *kratos* ("authority").

DIRECT DEMOCRACY
A system of government in which political decisions are made by the people directly, rather than by their elected representatives; probably possible only in small political communities.

LEGISLATURE
A government body primarily responsible for the making of laws.

INITIATIVE
A procedure by which voters can propose a law or a constitutional amendment.

REFERENDUM
An act of referring legislative (statutory) or constitutional measures to the voters for approval or disapproval.

condition of no government. Anarchy exists when each individual makes his or her own rules for behavior, and there are no laws and no government.

The Greek term for rule by the people was **democracy**. Although most Greek philosophers were not convinced that democracy was the best form of government, they understood and debated the possibility of such a political system. Within the limits of their culture, some of the Greek city-states operated as democracies.

The Athenian Model of Direct Democracy

The government of the ancient Greek city-state of Athens is often considered to be the historical model for a **direct democracy**. In fact, the system was not a pure system of direct democracy, because the average Athenian was not a participant in every political decision. Nonetheless, all major issues, even if decided by the committees of the ruling council, were put before the assembly of all citizens for a vote. The most important feature of Athenian democracy was that the **legislature** was composed of all of the citizens. (Women, foreigners, and slaves were excluded, because they were not citizens). Direct democracy in Athens is considered to have been an ideal form of democracy, because it demanded a high level of participation from every citizen.

Direct democracy also has been practiced in some Swiss cantons and, in the United States, in New England town meetings and in some midwestern township meetings. New England town meetings, which include all of the voters who live in the town, continue to make important decisions for the community—such as levying taxes, hiring city officials, and deciding local ordinances—by majority vote. Some states provide a modern adaptation of direct democracy for their citizens: In thirty-nine states, representative democracy is supplemented by the **initiative** or the **referendum**—a process by which the people may vote directly on laws or constitutional amend-

This town meeting in New Hampshire allows every citizen of the town to vote directly and in person for elected officials, for proposed policies, and, in some cases, for the town budget. To be effective, such a form of direct democracy requires that the citizens stay informed about local politics and devote time to discussion and decision making.

ments. The **recall** process, which is available in over a dozen states, allows the people to vote to remove an incumbent from state office.

The Dangers of Direct Democracy

Although they were aware of the Athenian model, the framers of the U.S. Constitution—for the most part—were opposed to such a system. For many centuries preceding this country's establishment, any form of democracy was considered to be dangerous and to lead to instability. But in the eighteenth and nineteenth centuries, the idea of a government based on the **consent of the people** gained increasing popularity. (See the discussion of one of the proponents of this idea, Thomas Jefferson, in this chapter's *Politics: The Human Side.*) Such a government was the main aspiration of the American and French revolutions, as well as of many subsequent ones. The masses, however, were considered to be too uneducated to govern themselves, too prone to the influence of demagogues (political leaders who manipulate popular prejudices), and too likely to abrogate minority rights.

James Madison defended the new scheme of government set forth in the U.S. Constitution, while warning of the problems inherent in a "pure democracy":

> A common passion or interest will, in almost every case, be felt by a majority of the whole . . . and there is nothing to check the inducements to sacrifice the weaker party or an obnoxious individual. Hence it is that such democracies have ever been spectacles of turbulence and contention, and have ever been found incompatible with personal security or the rights of property; and have in general been as short in their lives as they have been violent in their deaths.[4]

Like many other politicians of his time, Madison feared that pure, or direct, democracy would deteriorate into mob rule. What would keep the majority of the people, if given direct decision-making power, from abusing the rights of minority groups?

Representative Democracy

The framers of the U.S. Constitution attempted to craft a system of government that would ensure the continuation of a **republic**, meaning a government in which the power rests with the people, who elect representatives to govern them and to make the laws and policies. To eighteenth-century Americans, the idea of a republic also meant a government based on common beliefs and virtues that would be fostered within small communities. The rulers were to be amateurs—good citizens—who would take turns representing their fellow citizens, in a way similar to the Greek model.[5]

The U.S. Constitution creates a form of republican government known as a **representative democracy.** The people hold the ultimate power over the government through the election process, but policy decisions are all made by national officials. Even this distance between the people and the

RECALL
A procedure allowing the people to vote to dismiss an elected official from state office before his or her term has expired.

CONSENT OF THE PEOPLE
The idea that governments and laws derive their legitimacy from the consent of the governed.

REPUBLIC
The form of government in which sovereignty rests with the people, who elect agents to represent them in lawmaking and other decisions.

REPRESENTATIVE DEMOCRACY
A form of government in which representatives elected by the people make and enforce laws and policies.

---

4. James Madison, in Alexander Hamilton, James Madison, and John Jay, *The Federalist Papers,* No. 10 (New York: Mentor Books, 1964), p. 81. See Appendix D.
5. See the discussion of the founders' ideas in Gordon S. Wood, *The Radicalism of the American Revolution* (New York: Knopf, 1992).

POLITICS: THE HUMAN SIDE
Thomas Jefferson, President and Scholar

"I have sworn upon the altar of God eternal hostility against every form of tyranny over the mind of man."

BIOGRAPHICAL NOTES

Thomas Jefferson was born in Shadwell, Virginia, on April 13, 1743. He studied law, science, and philosophy at the College of William and Mary in colonial Virginia before beginning life as a planter at his plantation, Monticello. By the age of thirty, Jefferson had become a political activist. He was elected to the Continental Congress and, during the spring of 1776, drafted the Declaration of Independence. He returned to Virginia to take a seat in the Virginia House of Delegates that same year. He was elected governor of Virginia three years later.

After the conclusion of the American Revolution, Jefferson returned to Congress. He was appointed minister to France in 1785 and secretary of state in 1789. In 1796, Jefferson ran for president. He lost to John Adams but, as the Constitution decreed, became Adams's vice president. In the election of 1800, Jefferson and Aaron Burr received equal numbers of electoral votes. Alexander Hamilton threw his support to Jefferson in the House, and Jefferson became president. In 1809, after serving two terms, Jefferson retired to Monticello and lived there until he died on July 4, 1826, the same day that John Adams died.

POLITICAL CONTRIBUTIONS

The influence of Thomas Jefferson on the history and the political system of the United States cannot be overstated. As a young political radical, he drafted the Declaration of Independence, a document whose principles have become the heart of American political culture. Within his native Virginia, Jefferson influenced the writing of the state constitution and served in its legislature and governor's office.

Jefferson was widely recognized as a superb statesman and diplomat. Like his predecessor, Benjamin Franklin, Jefferson was able to convince the Europeans that the United States was a sovereign nation with a real possibility of surviving. Later, as president, he relied on his knowledge of European politics to try to keep the United States out of the Napoleonic wars.

When Jefferson became president in 1800, he brought a new set of political ideas to the White House. Disagreeing with the Federalists and their ideas of a strong central government with an elitist leadership, Jefferson ran on the ticket of the Democratic-Republican party, which later evolved into the contemporary Democratic party. Jefferson believed strongly in the idea of a citizen-politician, seeing the independent small farmer and small businessperson as essential to the continuation of democracy in this country. Like Thomas Paine, he believed that most men were able to hold and express political views and to participate in governing their nation.

Jefferson also believed in active presidential leadership. He put his own supporters in as many offices and judgeships as he could. He worked to support members of his new party in Congress, thus building a coalition to back his decisions. When the opportunity came to negotiate the Louisiana Purchase with France, Jefferson made the decision through an executive order, writing, "The less said about the constitutional difficulties, the better." The deal doubled the geographic size of the United States and opened the West for development.

After his retirement to Monticello, Jefferson continued his correspondence with many of his old political competitors. He and John Adams, the man he had opposed in 1796, exchanged political observations for almost twenty years. Both admitted that they had come to agreement on many issues. Adams, as well as most of his contemporaries, regarded Jefferson as one of the most brilliant men of his time. It has been said that the greatest assemblage of intellectual talent that ever gathered in the White House occurred when Thomas Jefferson dined there alone.

government was not sufficient. Other provisions in the Constitution made sure that the Senate and the president would be selected by political elites rather than by the people, although later changes to the Constitution allowed the voters to elect members of the Senate directly. This modified form of democratic government came to be accepted throughout the Western world as a compromise between the desire for democratic control and the needs of the modern state.

Principles of Democratic Government.   All representative democracies rest on the rule of the people as expressed through the election of government officials. In the twentieth century, **universal suffrage** is the rule. In the 1790s, only free white males were able to vote, and in some states they had to be property owners as well. Women did not receive the right to vote in national elections in the United States until 1920, and the right to vote was not really secured by African Americans until the 1960s.

Granting every person the right to participate in the election of officials recognizes the equal voting power of each citizen. This emphasis on the equality of every individual before the law is central to the American system. Because everyone's vote counts equally, the only way to make fair decisions is by some form of **majority** will. But to ensure that **majority rule** does not become oppressive, modern democracies also provide guarantees of minority rights. If certain democratic principles did not protect minorities, the majority might violate the fundamental rights of members of certain groups, especially groups that are unpopular or dissimilar to the majority population. In the past, the majority has imposed such limitations on African Americans, Native Americans, and Japanese Americans, to name only a few.

One way to guarantee the continued existence of a representative democracy is to hold free, competitive elections. Thus, the minority always has the opportunity to win elective office. For such elections to be totally open,

UNIVERSAL SUFFRAGE
The right of all adults to vote for their representatives.

MAJORITY
More than 50 percent.

MAJORITY RULE
A basic principle of democracy asserting that a numerical majority (usually 51 percent) in a political unit has the power to make decisions binding on the unit.

Volunteers register voters in the Spanish Harlem section of New York City. By setting up a table in the neighborhood, the election officials make registration more convenient for voters as well as less threatening. Both political parties often conduct voter registration drives in the months before general elections.

freedom of the press and speech must be preserved so that opposition candidates may present their criticisms of the government.

Constitutional Democracy. Another key feature of Western representative democracy is that it is based on the principle of **limited government.** Not only is the government dependent on popular sovereignty, but the powers of the government are also clearly limited, either through a written document or through widely shared beliefs. The U.S. Constitution sets down the fundamental structure of the government and the limits to its activities. Such limits are intended to prevent political decisions based on the whims or ambitions of individuals in government rather than on constitutional principles.

LIMITED GOVERNMENT
A form of government based on the principle that the powers of government should be clearly limited either through a written document or through wide public understanding; characterized by institutional checks to ensure that government serves the public rather than private interests.

DO WE HAVE A DEMOCRACY?

The sheer size and complexity of American society seem to make it unsuitable for direct democracy on a national scale. Some scholars suggest that even representative democracy is difficult to achieve in any modern state. They point to the low level of turnout for presidential elections and the even lower turnout for local ones. Polling data have shown that many Americans are neither particularly interested in politics nor well informed. Few are able to name the persons running for Congress in their district, and even fewer can discuss the candidates' positions. Members of Congress claim to represent their constituents, but few constituents follow the issues, much less communicate their views to their representatives. For the average citizen, the national government is too remote, too powerful, and too bureaucratic to be influenced by one vote.

Democracy for the Few

If ordinary citizens are not really making policy decisions with their votes, who is? One answer suggests that elites really govern the United States. Proponents of **elite theory** see society much as Alexander Hamilton did, who stated,

> All communities divide themselves into the few and the many. The first are the rich and the wellborn, the other the mass of the people. . . . The people are turbulent and changing; they seldom judge or determine right. Give therefore to the first class a distinct, permanent share in the government. They will check the unsteadiness of the second, and as they cannot receive any advantage by a change, they therefore will ever maintain good government.

ELITE THEORY
A perspective holding that society is ruled by a small number of people who exercise power in their self-interest.

Elite theory describes an American mass population that is uninterested in politics and willing to let leaders make the decisions. Some versions of elite theory posit a small, cohesive elite class that makes almost all the important decisions regarding the nation,[6] whereas others suggest that voters choose among competing elites. New members of the elite are recruited through the educational system so that the brightest children of the masses allegedly have the opportunity to join the elite stratum.

---

6. Michael Parenti, *Democracy for the Few*, 6th ed. (New York: St. Martin's Press, 1993).

Elites may have far more power and influence on the political system than do voters from the lower and middle classes. Because they share an educational background from selective schools, a higher income level, and common lifestyles, they are more likely to see government policy makers on a social basis and to form friendships with elected officials.

In such a political system, the primary goal of the government is stability, because elites do not want any change in their status. Major social and economic change takes place only if elites see their resources threatened. This selfish interest of the elites does not mean, however, that they are necessarily undemocratic or always antiprogressive. Political scientists Thomas Dye and Harmon Ziegler propose that American elites are more devoted to democratic principles and rights than are most members of the mass public.[7]

Elite theory can neither be proved nor disproved, because it is not possible to identify with certainty the members of the ruling elite. Some governmental policies, such as tax loopholes for the wealthy, may be perceived as elitist in nature, whereas other policies benefit many members of the public.

Democracy for Groups

A different school of thought looks at the characteristics of the American electorate and finds that our form of democracy is based on group interests. Even if the average citizen cannot keep up with political issues or cast a deciding vote in any election, the individual's interests will be protected by groups that represent him or her.

Theorists who subscribe to **pluralism** as a way of understanding American politics believe that people are naturally social and inclined to form associations. In the pluralists' view, politics is the struggle among groups to gain benefits for their members. Given the structures of the American political system, group conflicts tend to be settled by compromise and accommodation so that each interest is satisfied to some extent.[8]

PLURALISM
A theory that views politics as a conflict among interest groups. Political decision making is characterized by bargaining and compromise.

7. Thomas Dye and Harmon Ziegler, *The Irony of Democracy*, 9th ed. (Duxbury, Mass.: Wadsworth, 1993).
8. David Truman, *The Governmental Process* (New York: Knopf, 1951); and Robert Dahl, *Who Governs?* (New Haven, Conn.: Yale University Press, 1961).

HYPERPLURALISM
A situation that arises when interest groups become so powerful that they dominate the political decision-making structures, rendering any consideration of the greater public interest impossible.

Pluralists see public policy as resulting from group interactions carried out within Congress and the executive branch. Because there are a multitude of interests, no one group can dominate the political process. Furthermore, because most individuals have more than one interest, conflict among groups does not divide the nation into hostile camps.

There are a number of flaws in some of the basic assumptions of this theory. Among these are the relatively low number of people who formally join interest groups, the real disadvantages of pluralism for the poorer citizens, and pluralism's belief that group decision making always reflects the best interests of the nation.

With these flaws in mind, critics see a danger that groups may become so powerful that all policies become compromises crafted to satisfy the interests of the largest groups. The interests of the public as a whole, then, cannot be considered. Critics of pluralism have suggested that a democratic system can be virtually paralyzed by the struggle between interest groups. This struggle results in a condition sometimes called **hyperpluralism,** meaning that groups and their needs control the government and decision making rather than the government's acting for the good of the nation.

Both pluralism and elite theory attempt to explain the real workings of American democracy. Neither approach is complete, nor can either be proved. The perspective viewing the United States as run by elites reminds us that the founders were not great defenders of the mass public and suggests that people need constant motivation to stay involved in the political system. In contrast, the pluralist view underscores both the advantages and the disadvantages of Americans' inclination to join, to organize, and to pursue benefits for themselves. It points out all of the places within the American political system in which interest groups find it comfortable to work. With this knowledge, the system can be adjusted to keep interest groups within the limits of the public good.

IDEAS AND POLITICS: POLITICAL CULTURE

In spite of its flaws and weaknesses, most Americans are proud of their political system and support it with their obedience to the laws, their patriotism, or their votes. Given the diverse nature of American society and the wide range of ethnic groups, economic classes, and other interests, what gives Americans a common political heritage? One of the forces that unites Americans is the **political culture,** which can be defined as a patterned set of ideas, values, and ways of thinking about government and politics. For Americans, the political culture includes such symbolic elements as the flag, the Statue of Liberty, and the Lincoln Memorial. It includes such ideas as the belief that one is innocent until proven guilty. Political culture also encompasses deeply held values, including equality, liberty, and the right to hold property.

POLITICAL CULTURE
The collection of beliefs and attitudes toward government and the political process held by a community or nation.

POLITICAL SOCIALIZATION
The process through which individuals learn a set of political attitudes and form opinions about social issues. The family and the educational system are two of the most important forces in the political socialization process.

The degree to which Americans subscribe to a single set of values is surprising if you consider that virtually all U.S. citizens are descended from immigrants. The process by which such beliefs and values are transmitted to individuals is known as **political socialization.** Historically, the political parties played an important role in teaching new residents how to participate in the system in return for their votes. Frequently, the parties also provided the first economic opportunity in the form of jobs to immigrants and their families.

A fundamental source of political socialization is, of course, the family. The beliefs and attitudes transmitted to children by their parents play a large role in the formation of political views and values. Yet another major force for the socialization of Americans—past and present—has been the school system. The educational process continues to socialize the children of both immigrants and native-born Americans by explicitly teaching such basic political values as equality and liberty and by emphasizing patriotism.

A Political Consensus

Usually, the more homogeneous a population, the easier it is to have a political culture that is based on consensus. One of the reasons that Great Britain can maintain a limited government without a written constitution is that there exists substantial agreement within the population with respect to the political decision-making process of government. Even in a nation that is heterogeneous in geography and ethnic background, such as the United States, it is possible for shared cultural ideas to develop. We have already discussed one of the most fundamental ideas in American political culture—democracy. There are other concepts related to the notion of democracy that are also fundamental to American political culture, although individual Americans may interpret their meaning quite differently. Among these are liberty, equality, and property.

Liberty. The term **liberty** can be defined as the greatest freedom of individuals that is consistent with the freedom of other individuals in the society. In the United States, liberty includes religious freedom—both the right to practice whatever religion one chooses and freedom from any state-imposed religion. The basic guarantees of liberty are found not in the body of the U.S. Constitution but in the Bill of Rights, the first ten amendments

DID YOU KNOW . . .
That the 1990 U.S. census estimated that there may be at least 3.7 million illegal immigrants living in the United States?

LIBERTY
The greatest freedom of individuals that is consistent with the freedom of other individuals in the society.

Certain groups within the United States insist on maintaining their own cultural beliefs and practices. The Amish, pictured here, are descended from German religious sects and live in close communities in Pennsylvania, Ohio, Indiana, and Illinois, as well as in other states. The more conservative Amish groups do not use modern conveniences, such as automobiles or electricity, and have resisted immunizations and mandatory schooling for their children.

EQUALITY
A concept that all people are of equal worth.

INALIENABLE RIGHTS
Rights held to be inherent in natural law and not dependent on government; as asserted in the Declaration of Independence, the rights to "life, liberty, and the pursuit of happiness."

PROPERTY
Anything that is or may be subject to ownership. As conceived by the political philosopher John Locke, the right to property is a natural right superior to human law (laws made by government).

POPULAR SOVEREIGNTY
The concept that ultimate political authority rests with the people.

FRATERNITY
From the Latin *fraternus* (brother), a term that came to mean, in the political philosophy of the eighteenth century, the condition in which each individual considers the needs of all others; a brotherhood. In the French Revolution of 1789, the popular cry was "liberty, equality, and fraternity."

to the Constitution. The process of ensuring liberty for all Americans did not end with the adoption of the Bill of Rights but has continued through the political struggles of groups such as African Americans, women, and those who hold unpopular opinions.

The concept of liberty has both personal and political dimensions. Most Americans feel that each individual has the right to free expression and to choose whatever path he or she might want to take, economically, socially, and politically. The idea of liberty also has a specific meaning in the political process. Freedom of speech, freedom of the press, and the freedom to organize groups for political action are essential to maintaining competition for office and for the free and open discussion of political issues.

Equality. The Declaration of Independence states, "All men are created equal." Today, that statement has been amended by the political culture to include groups other than white males—women, African Americans, Native Americans, Asian Americans, and others. The definition of **equality**, however, has been disputed by Americans since the revolution.[9] Does equality mean simply political equality—the right to register to vote, to cast a ballot, and to run for political office? Does equality mean equal opportunity to develop one's talents and skills? If the latter is the meaning of equality, what should the United States do to ensure equal opportunities for those who are born poor, disabled, or female? Most Americans believe strongly that all persons should have the opportunity to fulfill their potential, but many disagree about whether it is the government's responsibility to eliminate economic and social differences.

Property. Many Americans probably remember that the **inalienable rights** asserted in the Declaration of Independence are the rights to "life, liberty, and the pursuit of happiness." The inspiration for that phrase, however, came from the writings of an English philosopher, John Locke, who stated clearly that people's rights were to life, liberty, and **property.** In American political culture, the pursuit of happiness and property are considered to be closely related. Americans place great value on owning land, on acquiring material possessions, and on the monetary value of jobs. Property can be seen as giving its owner political power and the liberty to do whatever he or she wants. At the same time, the ownership of property immediately creates inequality in society. But the desire to own property is so widespread among all classes of Americans that socialist movements, which advocate the redistribution of wealth and property, have had a difficult time securing a wide following in the United States.

Democracy, liberty, equality, and property—these concepts lie at the core of American political culture. Other issues—such as majority rule, **popular sovereignty**, and **fraternity**—are closely related to them. These fundamental principles are so deeply ingrained in U.S. culture that most Americans rarely think consciously about them.

---

9. Richard J. Ellis, "Rival Visions of Equality in American Political Culture," *Review of Politics,* Vol. 54 (Spring 1992), p. 254.

The Stability of the Culture

Political culture plays an important role in holding society together, because the system of ideas at the core of that culture must persuade people to support the existing political process through their attitudes and participation. If people begin to doubt the ideas underlying the culture, they will not transmit those beliefs to their children or support the existing political processes. As the number of immigrants to the United States continues to rise, especially on the East and West Coasts, and as society gives more recognition to the cultures of the groups within it, we might expect that the old cultural beliefs, especially beliefs in the importance of individualism and self-determination, might be eroded.

Consider that some subgroups, such as Native Americans and the Amish, have made concerted efforts to preserve their language and cultural practices. Many immigrant groups, including Hispanics, Asian Americans, and Caribbean Americans, maintain their language and cultural values within American cities and states. The question is whether these subgroups also subscribe to the values of the American political culture.

Recent polling data provide strong evidence that they do. Everett C. Ladd asserts that "the populace at large [is] distinguished by strong attachments to individualism, but these attachments are remarkably uniform across

DID YOU KNOW . . .
That approximately 87 percent of people in the United States call themselves Christians, and that three of the last four presidents—Jimmy Carter, Ronald Reagan, and George Bush—have all said they were born-again Christians?

Hispanic Americans join together to support a political candidate. Like other ethnic groups, these Hispanic voters seek to have their concerns heard by the candidates. In return, political candidates try to show their appreciation for the culture of the ethnic voters by delivering a speech in their language or promising more benefits for the group.

FIGURE 1-1

Patriotism of Different Groups in the United States

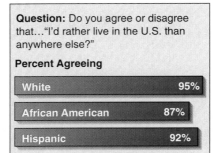

Question: Do you agree or disagree with the following statement..."I am very patriotic?"

Percent Agreeing

White	89%
Nonwhite	89%
College Graduate	89%
Some College	88%
High School Graduate	89%
Less than High School	89%

SOURCE: Survey by Times Mirror, May 1990.

social lines."[10] Ladd's data show that 66 percent of the people believe that one gets ahead by personal hard work rather than lucky breaks or help from others. Different ethnic groups within the society almost all have the same view: 69 percent of Hispanics, 71 percent of Native Americans, and 60 percent of African Americans say that hard work makes the difference. When asked whether they were very proud to be an American, 96 percent of all respondents answered in the affirmative. Again, there were virtually no differences between ethnic groups, age groups, or income groups. As Figures 1–1 and 1–2 show, patriotism and pride in living in the United States are high for almost all Americans. Ladd concludes that such evidence suggests that the basic beliefs and symbols of the political culture still command loyalty from Americans regardless of their other conflicts. (For a discussion of Americans' religious beliefs and their effects on the political scene, see this chapter's *Politics and Values*.)

THE CHANGING FACE OF AMERICA

The face of America is changing as its citizens age, become more diverse, and generate new needs for laws and policies. Long a nation of growth, the United States has become a middle-aged nation with a low birthrate and an increasing number of older citizens who want services from the government. The 1990 census showed that between 1980 and 1990, the U.S. population grew only 9.8 percent, the second lowest rate of growth in the history of taking such measurements.

Several aspects of this population trend have significant political consequences. The population is aging quickly; the median age (the age in reference to which half the people are older and half are younger) will reach thirty-five by the year 2000. Even more startling is the fact that almost 13 percent of the population is now sixty-five years old or older. By the year 2030, more than 21 percent of the population will be retired or approaching retirement. If the current retirement and pension systems remain in place, including Social Security, a very large proportion of each worker's wages will be deducted to support benefits for the retired.

Ethnic Change

The ethnic character of the United States is also changing. Whites have a very low birthrate, whereas African Americans and Hispanics have more children per family. As displayed in Table 1–1, including the effects of immigration, the proportion of whites has decreased, and the proportions of Hispanics, African Americans, and Asian Americans have increased even within the last decade.

Immigrants are also likely to shape American politics in the future. Few Americans think of the current period in our history as being as volatile as the early years of the twentieth century, when millions of Europeans immigrated to the United States. Yet, as Figure 1–3 shows, the percentage of population growth attributed to immigration was almost as high in the past decade as it was before World War I. In 1994, more than 1.7 million persons

FIGURE 1-2

How Different Groups Feel about Living in the United States

Question: Do you agree or disagree that..."I'd rather live in the U.S. than anywhere else?"

Percent Agreeing

White	95%
African American	87%
Hispanic	92%

SOURCE: Survey by ABC News, April 8–9, 1992, as reprinted in *Public Perspective*, March/April 1992.

10. Everett C. Ladd, "*E Pluribus Unum* Still: The Uniting of America," *Public Perspective*, May/ June 1992, pp. 3–5.

TABLE 1-1

Resident Population Distribution by Race and Hispanic Origin, 1980 to 1990

RACE/HISPANIC ORIGIN[a]	1980 NUMBER	1980 PERCENTAGE	1990 NUMBER	1990 PERCENTAGE	Change NUMBER	Change PERCENTAGE
Total population	**226,545,805**	**100.0%**	**248,709,873**	**100.0%**	**22,164,068**	**9.8%**
White	188,371,622	83.1	199,686,070	80.3	11,314,448	6.0
Black	26,495,025	11.7	29,986,060	12.1	3,491,035	13.2
American Indian, Eskimo, or Aleut	1,420,400	0.6	1,959,234	0.8	538,834	37.9
Asian or Pacific Islander	3,500,439	1.5	7,273,662	2.9	3,773,223	107.8
Other race	6,758,319	3.0	9,804,847	3.9	3,046,528	45.1
Hispanic origin	14,608,673	6.4	22,354,059	9.0	7,745,386	53.0

[a]Persons of Hispanic origin may be of any race.

SOURCE: U.S. Bureau of the Census release, 1991, as cited in *Universal Almanac 1996* (Kansas City, Mo.: Andrews and McMeel, 1996).

immigrated to the United States legally, with the greatest number coming from Mexico, but sizable numbers from Asian nations as well. These changes may place a strain on the cohesiveness of U.S. political culture and on the willingness of citizens to support the political structures of the nation.

Other Demographic Trends

Other changes in the face of America have more to do with our changing society. More Americans continue to fill the urban places of the nation in comparison with rural areas. By 1995, more than 75 percent of the population lived in an urban environment. Women continued to increase their participation in the educational system. By 1991, as many women as men had completed their high school educations, and the percentage of women who had completed college continued to grow.

FIGURE 1-3

Immigration as a Percentage of Total U.S. Population Growth, 1901 to 1990

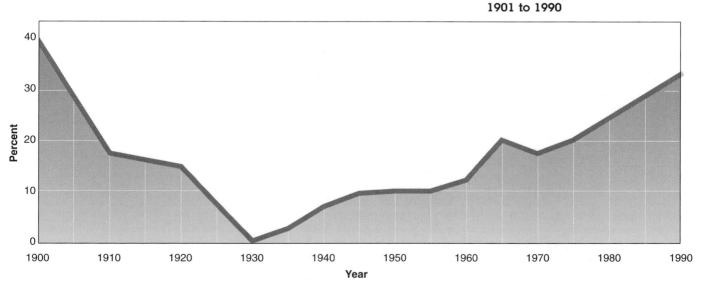

SOURCE: U.S. Immigration and Naturalization Service, Population Reference Bureau, *Population Bureau (1986)*, and U.S. Bureau of the Census, *1990 Census Profile (1991)*, as cited in *Universal Almanac 1994* (Kansas City, Mo.: Andrews and McMeel, 1994).

POLITICS AND VALUES
Americans and Religion

Given the strongly religious origins of the original thirteen colonies in the seventeenth and eighteenth centuries, it may not seem surprising that U.S. culture today is replete with religious symbols and practices. These practices spill over into the political arena in many ways. Our coins and paper currency bear the motto "In God We Trust," daily sessions of Congress begin with a prayer, and presidents take the oath of office resting one hand on the Bible.

In fact, Americans continue to express a high degree of association with religion and religious groups—more than that expressed by any other Western nation. Recent Gallup polls showed the following attitudes toward religion: 57 percent of respondents agreed that "religion can answer all or most of today's problems," whereas just 23 percent felt that "religion is largely old-fashioned and out of date." Although more than 60 percent of Americans claimed to be formally affiliated with a religious group, only 40 percent actually attended any religious service during a week.

According to one survey, almost one in three white Americans is affiliated with an evangelical church, believes that the Bible contains no errors, or reports being born again. Many scholars define as truly fundamentalist or evangelical those who report both being born again and believing in the Bible as being without error. That group would include about 20 percent of white American adults.

Given such widespread avowals of religious belief, it is not surprising that religion has influenced American culture and politics. Most Americans believe that the government or state should be kept separate from politics, but the deep religious strains in American culture make this difficult. Many Americans believe that prayer should be allowed in schools, but the Supreme Court has ruled that such practices violate the Constitution. Cities and school districts struggle to find appropriate ways to celebrate religious holidays, but pressure to celebrate the holidays of the majority group—Christians—leads to protests both from other religious bodies and from those who feel that no public entity should recognize religion in any way.

Religious views and leaders have also played a direct role in the American political arena. In recent decades, the strongest force for the insertion of religion into American politics has come from the political right. President Jimmy Carter himself sought support as a born-again, or evangelical, Christian, although his political positions were not in agreement with those enunciated by many fundamentalist groups. Pat Robertson, a fundamentalist minister with a large following from his television show "The 700 Club," campaigned for the Republican presidential nomination in 1988 but met with limited success.

What will be the future impact of religious beliefs on the political scene? Clyde Wilcox and Ted Jelen suggest that the Christian right is still politically powerful, but it is concentrating on winning control of political party machinery at the state and local level.* They also point out that movements such as Pat Robertson's have to struggle with the fact that Americans generally believe that their private and public lives should be kept separate. Religion and religious beliefs are considered private, and convincing members of a denomination to take those views to the public sphere of politics is not easily done.

*Ted Jelen and Clyde Wilcox, "The Christian Right in the 1990s," *Public Perspective*, March/April 1993, p. 11.

Change also continues in the structure of American families, although the traditional two-parent family is still very strong. Just twenty years ago, more than 85 percent of children lived in a two-parent family. Today, 71 percent of children under age eighteen live in two-parent families, and 25 percent live with only one parent. About one-fourth of the children of one-parent families live in poverty.

Other changes also have consequences for social policies. Although the national government has been committed to ending poverty since the mid-1960s, 13.5 percent of all Americans still live in households that have in-

Each year thousands of immigrants are sworn in as new U.S. citizens. The U.S. Constitution in Article I, Section 8, declares that Congress shall have the power to "establish a uniform Rule of Naturalization." Naturalization is the process by which individuals who are not yet citizens become U.S. citizens. Such individuals are called naturalized citizens as opposed to native-born citizens. There are myriad requirements to become a naturalized citizen. Because it is often difficult to do so, many immigrants remain in this country without proper documentation.

comes below the official poverty line. Although this number is large, it is below the 22 percent figure recorded in 1960. Far more alarming is the trend in prison populations. Since 1980, the number of persons incarcerated in state and federal prisons has increased from about 329,000 to over 1,000,000, an increase of over 200 percent. Finally, recent national surveys have found that about one-fifth of all Americans are barely literate and have difficulty dealing with simple documents. Each of these statistics raises political questions for the society as a whole. These facts challenge voters and their representatives to change policies in order to reduce poverty, crime, and illiteracy—if society can agree on how to accomplish these tasks.

IDEAS AND POLITICS: IDEOLOGY

An **ideology** is a closely linked set of beliefs about the goal of politics and the most desirable political order. True ideologies are well-organized theories that can guide virtually every decision that an individual or society can make. As discussed in this chapter's *Politics and Ideology,* the major ideologies of our time are usually represented as a continuum from far left to far right according to their views of the power of government. Few Americans, however, derive their views on politics from the more extreme ideologies. In fact, the U.S. political spectrum has been dominated for decades by two relatively moderate ideological positions: **liberalism** and **conservatism.**

American liberals believe that government should take strong positive action to solve the nation's economic and social problems. They believe that it is the obligation of the government to enhance opportunities for the economic and social equality of all individuals. Liberals tend to support programs to reduce poverty, endorse progressive taxation to redistribute income from wealthier classes to the poorer, and rely on government regulation to guide the activities of business and the economy.

IDEOLOGY
A comprehensive and logically ordered set of beliefs about the nature of people and about the institutions and role of government.

LIBERALISM
A set of beliefs that includes the advocacy of positive government action to improve the welfare of individuals, support for civil rights, and tolerance for political and social change.

CONSERVATISM
A set of beliefs that includes a limited role for the national government in helping individuals, support for traditional values and lifestyles, and a cautious response to change.

POLITICS AND IDEOLOGY
Competing Visions of Power

Political ideologies offer their adherents well-organized theories. These theories propose goals for the society and the political means by which those goals can be achieved. At the core of every political ideology is a set of values that guides its theory of governmental power. If we compare political ideologies on the basis of how much power the government should have within a society, we can array them on a continuum from left to right, as shown in the first box below.

For each of these ideological positions, the amount of power granted to the government is intended to achieve a certain set of goals within the society, and the perfect society would completely achieve these values. The values are arrayed in the second box below.

In the United States, there are adherents of each of these ideological positions. Given widely shared cultural values, however, only two of these belief systems consistently have played a central part in American political debates: liberalism and conservatism.

How Much Power Should the Government Have?

MARXISM-LENINISM	SOCIALISM	LIBERALISM *Moderate*	CONSERVATISM	LIBERTARIANISM
Central control of economy and political system.	Active government control of major economic sectors.	Positive government action to achieve economic and social goals.	Positive government action to support capitalism; action to uphold certain values.	Government action only for defense; no regulation of economy or individual behavior.

What Values Should the Government Pursue?

MARXISM-LENINISM	SOCIALISM	LIBERALISM	CONSERVATISM	LIBERTARIANISM
Total equality and security; unity and solidarity.	Economic equality; community.	Political liberty; economic security; equal opportunity.	Political liberty; economic liberty; order.	Total political and economic liberty for individuals.

Conservatives take a quite different approach to the role of government in the economy. Believing that the individual is primarily responsible for his or her own well-being, conservatives are less supportive of government initiatives to redistribute income or to craft programs that will change the status of individuals.

In the moral sphere, conservatives tend to support more government regulation of social values and moral decisions than do liberals. Thus, conservatives tend to oppose gay rights legislation and propose stronger curbs on pornography. Liberals usually support wider tolerance of different life choices and oppose government attempts to regulate personal behavior and morals.

Individuals in the society may not accept the full range of either liberal or conservative views. It is not unusual for Americans to be quite liberal on economic issues and supportive of considerable government intervention in the economy while holding conservative views on moral and social issues. Such a mixture of views makes it difficult for American political parties to identify themselves solely with either a conservative or liberal viewpoint, because such a position may cost them votes on specific issues.

There are also smaller groups of Americans who consider themselves to be communists, socialists, or libertarians, but these groups play a minor role in the national political arena. The limited role played by these and other alternative political perspectives is reinforced by the fact that they receive little positive exposure in classrooms, the media, or public discourse.

AMERICA'S POLITICS: UNFINISHED WORK

Although the U.S. government is one of the oldest democratic regimes in the world and its Constitution remains relatively unchanged more than two hundred years after it was written, the U.S. political system has been dynamic since its founding. As you will read in the chapters that follow, Americans have changed their ideas about who votes and who controls the government, constantly expanded their list of rights and liberties, originated and then revised a number of political parties, and significantly altered their view of the role of the national government in their lives and businesses.

Like the people of the nations of Eastern Europe and the former Soviet republics, the citizens of the United States have often pressed to make their government more responsive to the needs of the society and more effective in its functioning. What makes Americans different from the people of those other nations is a long and stable history that encourages them to try to modify the political structures and processes rather than invent totally new ones. Changing the political machinery has brought changes in the past—witness the social legislation of the New Deal in the 1930s and the Great Society in the 1960s—and Americans generally believe that change can occur again.

What are some of the American political tasks that remain unfinished? Clearly, Americans struggle to keep a cohesive society as people become more diverse in terms of ethnic and racial backgrounds, generational expectations, and economic level. How can a wider range of Americans participate in the political process and make the process work for them? What kinds of institutions and policies can meet the demands of world markets, the needs of an aging population, the expectations of a society with instant media access, and the hopes of the youngest generations for jobs and opportunities similar to those given to their parents and grandparents? Many alternatives are up for debate: new approaches to welfare and education reform, reductions in government spending, legal reform, an information superhighway to connect all Americans, and hundreds more.

The remainder of this book will examine the roots and structures of contemporary American government and politics, with particular attention to the ways in which they have changed over time. At the end of each chapter, we will consider the unfinished business of the subject at hand—whether it is the expansion of civil liberties or the attempts to curb the power of interest groups. Without a doubt, there is enough unfinished business to last many decades. Also without a doubt, Americans will make political changes as they see fit.

GETTING INVOLVED
Seeing Democracy in Action

One way to begin understanding the American political system is to observe a legislative body in action. There are thousands of elected legislatures in the United States at all levels of government. You might choose to visit the city council, a school board, the township board of trustees, the state legislature, or the U.S. Congress. Before attending a business session of the legislature, try to find out how the members are elected. Are they chosen by the "at-large" method of election so that each member represents the whole community, or are they chosen by specific geographic districts or wards? Some other questions you might want to ask are these: Is there a chairperson or official leader of the body who controls the meetings and who may have more power than the other leaders? What are the responsibilities of this legislature? Are the members paid political officials, or do they volunteer their services? Do the officials serve as full-time or part-time employees?

When you visit the legislature, keep in mind the theory of representative democracy. The legislators or council members are elected to represent their constituents. Observe how often the members refer to the voters, to their constituents, or to the special needs of their community or electoral district. Listen carefully for the sources of conflict within a community. If there is a debate, for example, over a zoning decision that involves the issue of land use, try to figure out why some members oppose the decision. Perhaps the greatest sources of conflict in local government are questions of taxation and expenditure. It is important to remember that the council or board is also supposed to be working toward the good of the whole; listen for discussions of the community's priorities.

If you want to follow up on your visit and learn more about representative government in action, try to get a brief interview with one of the members of the council or board. In general, legislators are very willing to talk to students, particularly students who also are voters. Ask the member how he or she sees the job of representative. How can the wishes of the constituents be identified? How does the representative balance the needs of the ward or district with the good of the whole community? You also might ask the member how he or she keeps in touch with constituents and informs them of the activities of the council or board.

After your visit to the legislative body, think about the advantages and disadvantages of representative democracy. Do you think the average citizen would take the time to consider all of the issues that representatives must debate? Do you think that, on the whole, the elected representatives act responsibly for their constituents?

To find out when and where the local legislative bodies meet, look up the number of the city hall or county building in the telephone directory, and call the clerk of council. For information on the structure of your local government, contact the local chapter of the League of Women Voters.

KEY TERMS

anarchy 9	hyperpluralism 16	pluralism 15
aristocracy 9	ideology 23	political culture 16
authority 8	inalienable rights 18	political socialization 16
compliance 9	initiative 18	politics 6
consent of the people 11	institution 6	popular sovereignty 18
conservatism 23	legislature 10	power 9
democracy 10	legitimacy 8	property 18
direct democracy 10	liberalism 23	recall 11
elite 9	liberty 17	referendum 10
elite theory 14	limited government 14	representative democracy 11
equality 18	majority 13	republic 11
fraternity 18	majority rule 13	totalitarian regime 9
government 8	oligarchy 9	universal suffrage 13

 CHAPTER SUMMARY

1. The willingness of Americans to debate new initiatives and to demand changes in the way the government works is at the core of our democratic nation. Americans worked hard to establish this form of government and continue to expend effort in politics to keep it functioning. *Politics* was defined by Harold Lasswell as the process of "who gets what, when, and how" in a society. David Easton defined it as the "authoritative allocation of values" in a society. The prerogative of government to make allocative decisions is based on authority, legitimacy, and power.

2. In a direct democracy, political decisions are made by the people directly. Fearing the problems of a direct democracy, the framers of the Constitution set up a representative, or indirect, democracy. The people control the government through the election of representatives. Decisions are made by majority rule, although the rights of minorities are protected.

3. Some scholars believe that most of the power in our society is held by elite leaders who actively influence political decisions, while the masses are apathetic. The pluralist viewpoint, in contrast, suggests that groups that represent the different interests of the people struggle for political power. In pluralist theory, the political process is characterized by bargaining and compromise between groups.

4. The American political system is characterized by a set of cultural beliefs that includes liberty, equality, and property. These beliefs are passed on to each generation of Americans through the process of political socialization. Additionally, the demographic make-up of the population is changing—it is growing older and more diverse, and includes more immigrants.

5. Americans' ideas about how government should act in their lives vary widely. These views may be included in liberal, conservative, or other ideological positions.

 QUESTIONS FOR REVIEW AND DISCUSSION

1. How do the groups that you belong to govern themselves? How does your church, fraternity, sorority, or club choose officers and make decisions? To what extent are the principles of democracy accepted by that group? If your group is not democratically organized, how is its decision-making power structured?

2. Given the great diversity of the population of the United States in terms of ethnic origin, religion, age, and region, how are common beliefs created and shared with new generations? What institutions—school, church, the family, or the community—shaped your own beliefs about politics and government?

3. How is your personal life shaped by government? How do the policies decided and implemented by the national and state governments place limits on your personal liberty? To what extent do those policies improve the quality of your life and its opportunities? Do you feel that you or your family had a part in deciding those policies?

 # Logging On: Welcome to the Internet, the On-Line Highway to Everywhere

A few years ago, only computer fanatics even knew about the Internet. Today over 20 million people use it (by 1998, it is projected to be 100 million worldwide). Over 60,000 networks are connected to the Internet, and the number is exploding.

The Internet—which is now a web of educational, corporate, and research computer networks around the world—started as a research and development link for the military-industrial complex. It now has many uses, including transmitting weather reports, doing library searches, and finding addresses of university faculty thousands of miles away. On the Internet, you'll find discussion groups, news groups, electronic publications (you can get the *Wall Street Journal* on your computer screen), and electronic mail (E-mail), the most common use of Internet.

Your college or university is probably connected directly to the Internet and pays thousands of dollars a year for this hookup. (If it is not, start a group to lobby for a hookup. That's your first political project!) Faculty, administrators, and students can get an E-mail address and password. The address is just like a mailbox at which you receive electronic information. Addresses differ depending on the gateway that leads from your computer through another computer to the person or address you want to reach. Each chapter of this book ends with Internet addresses and activities that you may find useful.

Get yourself an address now. Pick up a copy of the handout given to new users, and start playing with E-mail. A good starting point is to roam through the user-friendly **gopher** menus.

Open your connection the way you would to send or receive mail. Type **gopher** and hit the return key. You will be presented with a first-level menu of choices. Pick one by moving the arrow up or down to the item you want to open (at the blinking cursor, type in the number of your choice). When you are done playing, type **Q.** You may also want to contact the ''mother of all gopher'' sites, the University of Minnesota, by logging in, typing

gopher, and then typing **tc.umn.edu.** (Alternatively, you can get there by navigating through several levels of finding other information servers.)

SELECTED REFERENCES

Chiswick, Barry R., ed. *Immigration, Language, and Ethnicity: Canada and the United States.* Lanham, Md.: AEI Press, 1992. This collection of essays reviews the history of immigration policies in Canada and the United States, and it also gives an excellent portrait of the demographic and social characteristics of recent immigrants. Additionally, it discusses some of the issues raised by immigration with regard to language and wage policies.

Dahl, Robert A. *Modern Political Analysis,* 5th ed. Englewood Cliffs, N.J.: Prentice-Hall, 1990. Dahl's book contains definitions and explanations of politics and political analysis, political influence, political systems, and political socialization.

Dionne, E. J., Jr. *Why Americans Hate Politics.* New York: Simon & Schuster, 1991. Dionne argues that the two political ideologies, liberal and conservative, have not provided real solutions to the problems of crime, educational decline, race relations, and other pressing issues. He argues for a new "politics of the center" that will stimulate new participation and leadership.

Elazar, Daniel J. *The American Mosaic: The Impact of Space, Time, and Culture on American Politics.* Boulder, Colo.: Westview Press, 1994. Continuing his work on the development of regional cultures in the United States, Elazar investigates the influence of place and time on the political culture of specific regions. He proposes that an individual's specific location in the nation at a particular time will shape his or her political culture, as well as define an outlook on national politics.

Greider, William. *Who Will Tell the People: The Betrayal of American Democracy.* New York: Simon & Schuster, 1992. According to the author, a governing elite in Washington is running the United States and running it into the ground. The elite is made up of corporate lobbyists and lawyers, think-tank gurus, and aging political parties that have alienated the average American.

King, Anthony, ed. *The New American Political System.* Lanham, Md.: AEI Press, 1990. In this collection of essays, well-known and knowledgeable authors discuss their viewpoints on various aspects of the American political system.

Lapham, Lewis H. *The Wish for Kings.* New York: Grove Press, 1993. In a very controversial essay, Lapham criticizes the U.S. political system for having lapsed into an oligarchy ruled by elected officials who behave arrogantly and are supported by the ruling class. The public is apathetic and generally fearful about its own interests and admiring of media stars. Lapham suggests that a monarchy might be a more honest route to the goals of government than are elected politicians.

Lasswell, Harold. *Politics: Who Gets What, When and How.* New York: McGraw-Hill, 1936. This classic work defines the nature of politics.

Peterson, Steven A. *Political Behavior: Patterns in Everyday Life.* Newbury Park, Calif.: Sage, 1990. Peterson, in an unconventional approach to the topic of political behavior, stresses the effect of institutions and everyday experiences on people's perceptions of politics.

Stanley, Harold W., and Richard G. Niemi. *Vital Statistics on American Politics,* 4th ed. Washington, D.C.: Congressional Quarterly Press, 1994. This valuable reference work contains over two hundred tables and figures on a wide range of topics covering almost all aspects of American politics.

Tocqueville, Alexis de. *Democracy in America.* Edited by Phillips Bradley. New York: Vintage Books, 1945. Life in the United States as described by a French writer who traveled through the nation in the 1820s.

Wilcox, Clyde. *God's Warriors: The Christian Right in Twentieth-Century America.* Baltimore: Johns Hopkins University Press, 1992. Wilcox examines the history of the Christian Right movement in the United States and its recent rise to political prominence on national issues. He provides an extensive analysis of the types of individuals who share the beliefs of the Christian Right and suggests the potential for more political activity by that movement.

Wilson, Richard W. *Compliance Ideologies: Rethinking Political Culture.* New York: Cambridge University Press, 1992. Wilson describes the interaction between a country's politics and its culture and how that interaction can strengthen the state.

2
The Constitution

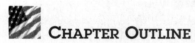
CHAPTER OUTLINE

31

WHAT IF . . .
The Constitution Were Easier to Amend?

The U.S. Constitution is the oldest living written constitution in the world. It has survived for more than two hundred years. This remarkably short document has not gotten much longer during that lengthy period. Indeed, it contains only twenty-seven amendments. As you will read in this chapter, passing an amendment to the Constitution requires great effort on the part of those who wish to do so. In spite of the over seven thousand amendments that Congress has considered, only thirty-three have been submitted to the states after having been passed by Congress.

What if it were easier to amend the Constitution? One thing is certain: There would be more amendments. How many and what kind are unknown, of course. At a minimum, we can look at what has happened in states that have relatively easy constitutional amendment procedures.

The U.S. Constitution is about 7,000 words long. The average state constitution is more than three times as long as the federal Constitution. For example, the Louisiana Constitution of 1921 (which was replaced by a new constitution in 1974) contained over 250,000 words. Nineteen states have constitutions that have been amended 100 times or more. Consider that the citizens of Alabama by 1996 had been asked to approve over 650 amendments, of which they adopted over 450!

Additionally, state legislators seem to have a difficult time distinguishing between constitutional law and statutory law. (Normally, constitutions provide only general principles.) The Louisiana Constitution has an amendment declaring Huey Long's birthday a legal holiday. The South Dakota Constitution has an amendment authorizing a cordage and twine plant at the state penitentiary. The Alabama Constitution has an amendment establishing the Alabama Heritage Trust Fund.

Clearly, the easier it is for a constitution to be amended, the more this process will be used. When a constitution can be amended easily, we get constitutional amendments; simple legislation requires a laborious process to pass. Furthermore, in states that allow their constitutions to be amended easily, constitutional amendments often are proposed in an attempt to override unfavorable state court decisions.

Thus, if the U.S. Constitution could be amended more easily, it possibly would become more similar to state constitutions and would become quite long. Organized special interest groups would lobby Congress to amend the Constitution rather than simply to pass new laws. The basic and relatively limited powers and rights outlined in the U.S. Constitution perhaps would lose some of their importance if they became part of a lengthier and more complicated document.

---

1. What is the distinction between constitutional law and the statutes that Congress normally passes?
2. Who has benefited from the difficulty of amending the U.S. Constitution?
3. What would be the benefit of making the amending process for the U.S. Constitution less difficult?

We the People of the United States, in Order to form a more perfect Union, establish Justice, insure domestic Tranquility, provide for the common defence, promote the general Welfare, and secure the Blessings of Liberty to ourselves and our Posterity, do ordain and establish this Constitution for the United States of America.

Every schoolchild in America has at one time or another been exposed to these famous words from the Preamble to the U.S. Constitution. The document itself is remarkable: As this chapter's *What If . . .* just pointed out, the U.S. Constitution, compared with others in the states and in the world, is relatively short. And, because amending it is difficult (as you will see later in this chapter), it has relatively few amendments. Perhaps even more remarkable is the fact that it has remained largely intact for over two hundred years.

How and why this Constitution was created is a story that has been told and retold. It is worth repeating, because the historical and political context in which this country's governmental machinery was formed is essential to understanding American government and politics today. The Constitution was not the result of completely creative thinking. Many of its provisions were grounded in contemporary political philosophy. The delegates to the Constitutional Convention in 1787 brought with them two important sets of influences: their political culture and their political experience. In the years between the first settlements in the New World and the writing of the Constitution, Americans had developed a political philosophy about how people should be governed and had tried out numerous forms of government. These experiences gave the founders the tools with which they constructed the Constitution.

INITIAL COLONIZING EFFORTS

The first British outpost in North America was set up by Sir Walter Raleigh in the 1580s for the purpose of harassing the Spanish treasure fleets. The

The first British settlers who landed on the North American continent faced severe tests of endurance. This woodcut depicts a cold existence for the settlers in the late 1500s and early 1600s.

group, known as the Roanoke Island Colony, stands as one of history's great mysteries: After a three-year absence to resupply the colony, Raleigh's captain, John White, returned in 1590 to find signs that the colony's residents apparently had moved north to Chesapeake Bay. White was unable to search further, and no verifiable evidence of the fate of the "lost colony" has ever been recorded. Local legends in North Carolina maintain that the lost colonists survived and intermarried with the Native Americans, and that their descendants live in the region today.

In 1607, the British government sent over a group of farmers to establish a trading post, Jamestown, in what is now Virginia. The Virginia Company of London was the first to establish successfully a permanent British colony in the Americas. The king of England gave the backers of this colony a charter granting them "full power and authority" to make laws "for the good and welfare" of the settlement. The Jamestown colonists instituted a **representative assembly**, setting a precedent in government that was to be observed in later colonial adventures.

Jamestown was not a commercial success. Of the 105 men who landed, 67 died within the first year. But 800 new arrivals in 1609 added to their numbers. By the spring of the next year, frontier hazards had cut their numbers to 60. Of the 6,000 people who left England for Virginia between 1607 and 1623, 4,000 of them perished. The historian Charles Andrews has called this the "starving time for Virginia."[1]

Separatists, The *Mayflower*, and the Compact

The first New England colony was established in 1620. A group of mostly extreme Separatists, who wished to break with the Church of England, came over on the ship *Mayflower* to the New World, landing at Plymouth (Massachusetts). Before going on shore, the adult males—women were not con-

REPRESENTATIVE ASSEMBLY
A legislature composed of individuals who represent the population.

1. Charles M. Andrews, *The Colonial Period of American History*, Vol. 1 (New Haven, Conn.: Yale University Press, 1934), p. 110.

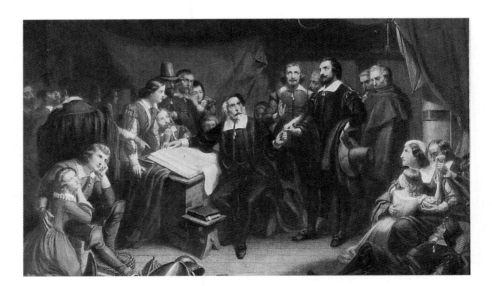

The signing of the compact aboard the *Mayflower*. In 1620, the Mayflower Compact was signed by almost all of the men aboard the ship *Mayflower*, just before disembarking at Plymouth, Massachusetts. It stated, "We . . . covenant and combine ourselves together into a civil body politick . . . ; and by vertue hearof to enacte, constitute, and frame such just and equal laws . . . as shall be thought [necessary] for the generall good of the Colonie."

sidered to have any political status—drew up the Mayflower Compact, which was signed by forty-one of the forty-four men aboard the ship on November 21, 1620. The reason for the compact was obvious: This group was outside the jurisdiction of the Virginia Company of London, which had chartered their settlement in Virginia, not Massachusetts. The Separatist leaders feared that some of the *Mayflower* passengers might conclude that they were no longer under any obligations of civil obedience. Therefore, some form of public authority was imperative. As William Bradford (a printer and editor in Philadelphia) recalled in his accounts, there were "discontented and mutinous speeches that some of the strangers amongst them had let fall from them in the ship; That when they came a shore they would use their owne libertie; for none had power to command them."[2]

The compact was not a constitution. It was a political agreement in which the signers agreed to submit to majority-rule government, pending the receipt of a royal charter. The Mayflower Compact's historical and political significance is twofold: It depended on the consent of the affected individuals, and it served as a prototype for similar compacts in American history. According to Samuel Eliot Morison, the compact proved the determination of the English immigrants to live under the rule of law, based on the *consent of the people*.[3]

More Colonies, More Government

Another outpost in New England was set up by the Massachusetts Bay Colony in 1630. Then followed Rhode Island, Connecticut, New Hampshire, and others. By 1732, the last of the thirteen colonies, Georgia, was established. During the colonial period, Americans developed a concept of limited government, which followed from the establishment of the first colonies under Crown charters. Theoretically, London governed the colonies. In practice, owing partly to the colonies' distance from London, the colonists exercised a large measure of self-government. The colonists were able to make their own laws, as in the Fundamental Orders of Connecticut in 1639. The Massachusetts Body of Liberties in 1641 supported the protection of individual rights and was made a part of colonial law. In 1682, the Pennsylvania Frame of Government was passed. Along with the Pennsylvania Charter of Privileges of 1701, it established the rationale for our modern Constitution and Bill of Rights. All of this legislation enabled the colonists to acquire crucial political experience. After independence was declared in 1776, the states quickly set up their own constitutions.

BRITISH RESTRICTIONS AND COLONIAL GRIEVANCES

The Navigation Acts of 1651 were the earliest general restrictions on colonial activity. These acts imposed the condition that only English ships (including

---

MILESTONES IN EARLY U.S. POLITICAL HISTORY

1585 British outpost set up in Roanoke.

1607 Jamestown established; Virginia Company lands settlers.

1620 Mayflower Compact signed.

1630 Massachusetts Bay Colony set up.

1639 Fundamental Orders of Connecticut adopted.

1641 Massachusetts Body of Liberties adopted.

1682 Pennsylvania Frame of Government passed.

1701 Pennsylvania Charter of Privileges written.

1732 Last of thirteen colonies established.

1756 French and Indian War declared.

1765 Stamp Act; Stamp Act Congress meets.

1770 Boston Massacre.

1774 First Continental Congress.

1775 Second Continental Congress; Revolutionary War begins.

1776 Declaration of Independence signed.

1777 Articles of Confederation drafted.

1781 Last state signs Articles of Confederation.

1783– "Critical period" in U.S.
1789 history; weak national government.

1786 Shays' Rebellion.

1787 Constitutional Convention.

1788 Ratification of Constitution.

1791 Ratification of Bill of Rights.

---

2. John Camp, *Out of the Wilderness: The Emergence of an American Identity in Colonial New England* (Middleton, Conn.: Wesleyan University Press, 1990).
3. See Morison's "The Mayflower Compact" in Daniel J. Boorstin, ed., *An American Primer* (Chicago: University of Chicago Press, 1966), p. 18.

King George III (1738–1820) was king of Great Britain and Ireland from 1760 until his death on January 29, 1820. Under George III, the first attempt to tax the American colonies was made. Ultimately, the American colonies, exasperated at renewed attempts at taxation, proclaimed their independence on July 4, 1776.

FIRST CONTINENTAL CONGRESS
The first gathering of delegates from twelve of the thirteen colonies, held in 1774.

SECOND CONTINENTAL CONGRESS
The 1775 congress of the colonies that established an army.

ships of its colonies) could be used for trade within the British Empire. The Proclamation of 1763 declared that no colonial settlement could be established west of the Appalachians. In 1764, the Sugar Act was passed, in part to pay for the French and Indian War. Many colonists were unwilling to pay the required tax.

Further regulatory legislation was to come. In 1765, the British Parliament passed the Stamp Act, providing for internal taxation, or, as the colonists' Stamp Act Congress assembled in 1765 called it, "taxation without representation." The colonists boycotted the Stamp Act. The success of the boycott (the Stamp Act was repealed a year later) generated a feeling of unity within the colonies. The British, however, continued to try to raise revenues in the colonies. When duties on glass, lead, paint, and other items were passed in 1767, the colonists boycotted the purchase of English commodities in return. The colonists' fury over taxation climaxed in the Boston Tea Party: Colonists dressed as Mohawk Indians dumped almost 350 chests of British tea into the Boston Harbor as a gesture of tax protest. In retaliation, the British Parliament passed the Coercive Acts (the "Intolerable Acts") in 1774, which closed Boston Harbor and placed the government of Boston under direct British control. The colonists were outraged—and they responded.

THE COLONIAL RESPONSE: THE CONTINENTAL CONGRESSES

New York, Pennsylvania, and Rhode Island proposed the convening of a colonial congress. The Massachusetts House of Representatives requested that all colonies hold conventions to select delegates to be sent to Philadelphia for such a congress. The **First Continental Congress** was held at Carpenter's Hall on September 5, 1774. It was a gathering of delegates from twelve of the thirteen colonies (Georgia did not attend until 1775). At that meeting, there was little talk of independence. The Congress passed a resolution requesting that the colonies send a petition to King George III expressing their grievances. Resolutions were also passed requiring that the colonies raise their own troops and boycott British trade. The British government condemned the Congress's actions, treating them as open acts of rebellion.

The delegates to the First Continental Congress declared that in every county and city, a committee was to be formed whose mission was to spy on the conduct of friends and neighbors and to report to the press any violators of the trade ban. The formation of these committees was an act of cooperation among the colonies, which represented a step toward the creation of a national government.

By the time the **Second Continental Congress** met in May 1775 (this time all the colonies were represented), fighting already had broken out between the British and the colonists. One of the main actions of the Second Congress was to establish an army. It did this by declaring the militia that had gathered around Boston an army and naming George Washington as commander in chief. The participants in that Congress still attempted to reach a peaceful settlement with the British Parliament. One declaration of the Congress stated explicitly that "we have not raised armies with ambitious designs of separating from Great Britain, and establishing independent states.'' But by the beginning of 1776, military encounters had become increasingly frequent.

Public debate was acrimonious. Then Thomas Paine's *Common Sense* appeared in Philadelphia bookstores. The pamphlet was a colonial best-seller.[4] Many agreed that Paine did make common sense when he argued that

> a government of our own is our natural right: and when a man seriously reflects on the precariousness of human affairs, he will become convinced, that it is infinitely wiser and safer, to form a constitution of our own in a cool and deliberate manner, while we have it in our power, than to trust such an interesting event to time and chance.[5]

Students of Paine's pamphlet point out that his arguments were not new—they were common in tavern debates throughout the land. Rather, it was the near poetry of his words—which were at the same time as plain as the alphabet—that struck his readers.

DECLARING INDEPENDENCE

The Resolution of Independence

On April 6, 1776, the Second Continental Congress voted for free trade at all American ports for all countries except Great Britain. This act could be interpreted as an implicit declaration of independence. The next month, the Congress suggested that each of the colonies establish state governments unconnected to Britain. Finally, on July 2, the Resolution of Independence was adopted by the Second Continental Congress:

> RESOLVED, That these United Colonies are, and of right ought to be free and independent States, that they are absolved from allegiance to the British Crown, and that all political connection between them and the state of Great Britain is, and ought to be, totally dissolved.

The actual Resolution of Independence was not legally significant. On the one hand, it was not judicially enforceable, for it established no legal rights or duties. On the other hand, the colonies were already, in their own judgment, self-governing and independent of Britain. Rather, the Resolution of Independence and the subsequent Declaration of Independence were necessary to establish the legitimacy of the new nation in the eyes of foreign governments, as well as in the eyes of the colonists themselves. What the new nation needed most was supplies for its armies and a commitment of foreign military aid. Unless it appeared in the eyes of the world as a political entity separate and independent from Britain, no foreign government would enter into a contract with its leaders. (Many historians believe that Paine, in a series of articles written in 1778 and collectively called *The Crisis*, was the first to use the term *United States*.)[6]

"You know, the idea of taxation with representation doesn't appeal to me very much either."

Drawing by Handelsman; © 1970 The New Yorker Magazine, Inc.

---

4. To do relatively as well today, a book would have to sell between eight and ten million copies in its first year of publication.

5. *The Political Writings of Thomas Paine*, Vol. 1 (Boston: J. P. Mendum Investigator Office, 1870), p. 46.

6. A. J. Ayer, *Thomas Paine* (New York: Atheneum, 1988), p. 42.

NATURAL RIGHTS
Rights held to be inherent in natural law, not dependent on governments. John Locke stated that natural law, being superior to human law, specifies certain rights of "life, liberty, and property." These rights, altered to become "life, liberty, and the pursuit of happiness," are asserted in the Declaration of Independence.

July 4, 1776—The Declaration of Independence

By June 1776, Thomas Jefferson already was writing drafts of the Declaration of Independence in the second-floor parlor of a bricklayer's house in Philadelphia. On adoption of the Resolution of Independence, Jefferson had argued that a declaration putting forth clearly the causes that compelled the colonies to separate from England was necessary. The Second Congress assigned the task to him, and he set to work, enumerating the major grievances. Some of his work was amended to gain unanimous acceptance (for example, his condemnation of the slave trade was eliminated to satisfy Georgia and North Carolina), but the bulk of it was passed intact on July 4, 1776. On July 19, the modified draft became "the unanimous declaration of the thirteen United States of America." On August 2, it was signed by the members of the Second Continental Congress.

A revolutionary concept of the Declaration was the assumption, inspired by the ideas of John Locke, that people have **natural rights** ("unalienable Rights"), including the rights to "life, liberty, and the pursuit of happiness." Governments are established to secure these rights, and governments derive their power "from the consent of the governed."[7] The Declaration claimed that whenever any form of government "becomes destructive to these ends, it is the Right of the People to alter or to abolish it, and to institute a new government."

THE RISE OF REPUBLICANISM

Not everyone had agreed with the notion of independence. There were recalcitrant colonists in the middle and lower southern colonies who de-

---

7. Not all scholars were truly influenced by Locke. For example, Jay Fliegelman states that "Jefferson's fascination with Homer, Ossian, Patrick Henry, and the violin is of greater significance than his indebtedness to Locke." Jay Fliegelman, *Declaring Independence: Jefferson, Natural Language, and the Culture of Performance* (Stanford, Calif.: Stanford University Press, 1993).

Members of the Second Continental Congress signed the Declaration of Independence on July 4, 1776. Minor changes were made in the document in the following two weeks. On July 19, the modified draft became the "unanimous declaration of the thirteen United States of America." On August 2, the members of the Second Continental Congress signed it. The first official printed version carried only the signatures of the Congress's president, John Hancock, and its secretary, Charles Thompson.

manded that independence be preceded by the formation of a strong central government. But the anti-Royalists in New England and Virginia, who called themselves Republicans, were against a strong central government. They opposed monarchy, executive authority, and virtually any form of restraint on the power of local groups. These so-called Republicans were a major political force from 1776 to 1780. Indeed, they almost prevented victory over the British by their unwillingness to cooperate with any central authority.

During this time, all the states adopted written constitutions. Eleven of the constitutions were completely new. Two of them—those of Connecticut and Rhode Island—were old royal charters with minor modifications. Republican sentiment led to increased power for the legislatures. In Pennsylvania and Georgia, **unicameral** (one-body) **legislatures** were unchecked by executive or judicial authority. Basically, the Republicans attempted to maintain the politics of 1776. In almost all states, the legislature was predominant.

THE ARTICLES OF CONFEDERATION: OUR FIRST FORM OF GOVERNMENT

The fear of a powerful central government led to the passage of the Articles of Confederation. The term **confederation** is important; it means a voluntary association of *independent* **states**, in which the member states agree to only limited restraints on their freedom of action. As a result, confederations seldom have an effective executive authority.

On June 6, 1776, Richard Henry Lee proposed that a confederation be established. So the Second Continental Congress appointed thirteen men to a drafting committee. Satisfied that progress was occurring, on August 20, 1776, the Second Continental Congress agreed to proceed with the second draft of what would become the Articles of Confederation. Four issues remained for settlement: (1) the equal representation of all states in the Congress, (2) the basis for the apportionment of common expenses, (3) the grant of powers to the central government over western lands, and (4) the distribution of power between the states and the central legislative body to define the precise location of sovereignty. This last point was resolved in favor of each individual state.

The final form of the Articles of Confederation was achieved by November 15, 1777. It was not until March 1, 1781, however, that the last state, Maryland, agreed to ratify what was called the Articles of Confederation and Perpetual Union. Well before the final ratification of the articles, there was in fact implementation of many of them: The Continental Congress and the thirteen states conducted American military, economic, and political affairs by the standards, and in the form specified by, the Articles.[8]

Under the Articles, the thirteen original colonies, now states, established on March 1, 1781, a government of the states—the Congress of the Confederation. The Congress was a unicameral assembly of so-called ambassadors from each state, with each state possessing a single vote. Each year, the Congress would choose one of its members as its president, but the Articles

UNICAMERAL LEGISLATURE
A legislature with only one legislative body, as compared with a bicameral (two-house) legislature, such as the U.S. Congress. Nebraska is the only state in the union with a unicameral legislature.

CONFEDERATION
A political system in which states or regional governments retain ultimate authority except for those powers they expressly delegate to a central government. A voluntary association of independent states, in which the member states agree to limited restraints on their freedom of action.

STATE
A group of people occupying a specific area and organized under one government; may be either a nation or a subunit of a nation.

8. Robert W. Hoffert, *A Politics of Tensions: The Articles of Confederation and American Political Ideas* (Niwot, Colo.: University Press of Colorado, 1992).

■

FIGURE 2–1   ■

The Structure of the Confederal Government under the Articles of Confederation

Congress

Congress had one house. Each state had two to seven members, but only one vote. The exercise of most powers required approval of at least nine states. Amendments to the Articles required the consent of all the states.

Committee of the States

A committee of representatives from all the states was empowered to act in the name of Congress between sessions.

Officers

Congress appointed officers to do some of the executive work.

The States

did not provide for a president of the United States. The Congress was authorized in Article X to appoint an executive committee of the states "to execute in the recess of Congress, such of the powers of Congress as the United States, in Congress assembled, by the consent of nine [of the thirteen] states, shall from time to time think expedient to vest with them." The Congress was also allowed to appoint other committees and civil officers necessary for managing the general affairs of the United States. The Articles did not establish a separate judicial institution, although Congress had certain judicial functions. In addition, the Congress could regulate foreign affairs and establish coinage and weights and measures. But it lacked an independent source of revenue and the necessary executive machinery to enforce its decisions throughout the land. Figure 2–1 illustrates the structure of the government under the Articles of Confederation; Table 2–1 summarizes the powers—and the lack of powers—of Congress under that system.

Article II of the Articles of Confederation guaranteed each state its sovereignty:

> Each state retains its sovereignty, freedom and independence, and every power, jurisdiction, and right, which is not by this Confederation expressly delegated to the United States in Congress assembled.

Accomplishments under the Articles

Although the Articles of Confederation had many defects, there were also some accomplishments during the eight years of their existence. Certain states' claims to western lands were settled. Maryland had objected to the

TABLE 2–1   ■

Powers of the Congress of the Confederation

CONGRESS HAD POWER TO	CONGRESS LACKED POWER TO
■ Declare war and make peace.	■ Provide for effective treaty-making power and control foreign relations; it could not compel states to respect treaties.
■ Enter into treaties and alliances.	
■ Establish and control armed forces.	
■ Requisition men and money from states.	■ Compel states to meet military quotas; it could not draft soldiers.
■ Regulate coinage.	■ Regulate interstate and foreign commerce; it left each state free to set up its own tariff system.
■ Borrow money and issue bills of credit.	
■ Fix uniform standards of weight and measurement.	■ Collect taxes directly from the people; it had to rely on states to collect and forward taxes.
■ Create admiralty courts.	
■ Create a postal system.	■ Compel states to pay their share of government costs.
■ Regulate Indian affairs.	
■ Guarantee citizens of each state the rights and privileges of citizens in the several states when in another state.	■ Provide and maintain a sound monetary system or issue paper money; this was left up to the states, and monies in circulation differed tremendously in value.
■ Adjudicate disputes between states upon state petition.	

claims of Massachusetts, New York, Connecticut, Virginia, the Carolinas, and Georgia. It was only after these states consented to give up their land claims to the United States as a whole that Maryland signed the Articles of Confederation. Another accomplishment under the Articles was the passage of the Northwest Ordinance of 1787, which established a basic pattern of government for new territories north of the Ohio River.

Finally, the Articles created a sort of "first draft" for the Constitution of the United States that was to follow. In a sense, it was an unplanned experiment applying some of the principles of government set forth in the Declaration of Independence.

Weaknesses of the Articles

Although Congress had the legal right to declare war and to conduct foreign policy, it did not have the right to demand revenues from the states. It could only *ask* for them. Also, the actions of Congress required the consent of nine states. Any amendments to the Articles required the unanimous consent of the Congress and confirmation by every state legislature. Further, the Articles did not create a national system of courts.

Basically, the functioning of the government under the Articles depended on the goodwill of the states. Article III of the Articles simply established a "league of friendship" among the states—no national government was intended.

Probably the most fundamental weakness of the Articles, and the most basic cause of their eventual replacement by the Constitution, concerned the lack of power to raise money for the militia. The Articles lacked any language giving Congress coercive power to raise money (by levying taxes) to provide adequate support for the military forces controlled by Congress. When states refused to send money to support the government (not one state met the financial requests made by Congress under the Articles), Congress resorted to selling off western lands to speculators or issuing bonds that sold for less than their face value. Due to a lack of resources, the Continental Congress was forced to disband the army, even in the face of serious Spanish and British military threats.

Shays' Rebellion and the Need for Revision of the Articles

By 1786, in Concord, Massachusetts, the scene of one of the first battles of the Revolution, there were three times as many people in prison for debt as there were for all other crimes combined. In Worcester County, Massachusetts, the ratio was even higher—twenty to one. Most of the prisoners were small farmers who could not pay their debts owing to the disorganized state of the economy.

In August 1786, mobs of musket-bearing farmers led by former revolutionary captain Daniel Shays seized county courthouses and disrupted the trials of the debtors in Springfield, Massachusetts. Shays and his men then launched an attack on the federal arsenal at Springfield, but they were repulsed. Shays' Rebellion demonstrated that the central government could not protect the citizenry from armed rebellion or provide adequately for the public welfare.

DRAFTING THE CONSTITUTION

The Annapolis Convention

The Virginia legislature called for a meeting of all the states to be held at Annapolis, Maryland, on September 11, 1786—ostensibly to discuss commercial problems only. It was evident to those in attendance (including Alexander Hamilton and James Madison) that the national government had serious weaknesses that had to be addressed if it were to survive. Among the important problems to be solved were the relationship between the states and the central government, the powers of the national legislature, the need for executive leadership, and the establishment of policies for economic stability.

At this Annapolis meeting, a call was issued to all the states for a general convention to meet in Philadelphia in May 1787 "to consider the exigencies of the union." When the Republicans, who favored a weak central government, realized that the Philadelphia meeting would in fact take place, they approved the convention in February 1787. But they made it explicit that the convention was "for the sole and express purpose of revising the Articles of Confederation." Those in favor of a stronger national government—the Federalists, as they were to be called—had different ideas.

The Philadelphia Convention

The designated date for the opening of the convention was May 14, 1787. Because few of the delegates had actually arrived in Philadelphia by that time, however, it was not formally opened in the East Room of the Pennsylvania State House until May 25.[9] By then, fifty-five of the seventy-

---

9. The State House was later named Independence Hall. This was the same room in which the Declaration of Independence had been signed eleven years earlier.

George Washington presided over the Constitutional Convention of 1787. Although the convention was supposed to have started on May 14, 1787, few of the delegates had actually arrived in Philadelphia by that date. It formally opened in the East Room of the Pennsylvania State House (later named Independence Hall) on May 25. Only Rhode Island did not send any delegates.

four delegates chosen for the convention had arrived. (Of those fifty-five, only about forty played active roles at the convention.) Rhode Island was the only state that refused to send delegates.

Not a Commoner among Them

Who were the fifty-five delegates to the Constitutional Convention? They certainly did not represent a cross section of eighteenth-century American society. Indeed, most were members of the upper class. Consider the following facts:

1. Thirty-three were members of the legal profession.
2. Three were physicians.
3. Almost 50 percent were college graduates.
4. Seven were former chief executives of their respective states.
5. Six were large plantation owners.
6. Eight were important businesspersons.

They were also relatively young by today's standards: James Madison was thirty-six, Alexander Hamilton was only thirty-two, and Jonathan Dayton of New Jersey was twenty-six. The venerable Benjamin Franklin (see this chapter's *Politics: The Human Side*), however, was eighty-one and had to be carried in on a portable chair borne by four prisoners from a local jail. Not counting Franklin, the average age was just over forty-two.

Additionally, all of the delegates were white and male. In contrast, some of the demographics of the 535 members of the 104th Congress, which took office in January 1995, are as follows: 40 are African Americans, 18 are Hispanics, and 57 are women.

The Working Environment

The conditions under which the delegates worked for 115 days were far from ideal and were made even worse by the necessity of maintaining total secrecy. The framers of the Constitution felt that if public debate were started on particular positions, delegates would have a more difficult time compromising or backing down to reach agreement. Consequently, the windows were usually shut in the East Room of the State House. Summer quickly arrived, and the air became heavy, humid, and hot by noon of each day. Also, when the windows were open, flies swarmed into the room. The delegates did, however, have a nearby tavern and inn to which they retired each evening. The Indian Queen became the informal headquarters of the delegates.

Factions among the Delegates

We know much about the proceedings at the convention because James Madison kept a daily, detailed personal journal. A majority of the delegates were strong nationalists—they wanted a central government with real power, unlike that of the central government under the Articles of Confederation. George Washington and Benjamin Franklin preferred limited national authority based on a separation of powers. But they were apparently willing to accept any type of national government, as long as the other

DID YOU KNOW . . .
That certain delegates to the Philadelphia Convention, Alexander Hamilton among them, wanted to eliminate state governments entirely, giving Congress "indefinite authority" and making the states administrative shells?

POLITICS: THE HUMAN SIDE
Benjamin Franklin, Statesman and Scientist

"We must indeed all hang together, or, most assuredly, we shall all hang separately."

BIOGRAPHICAL NOTES

Benjamin Franklin was born in 1706, the son of a Boston candle-maker and one of seventeen children. Family funds were insufficient for him to aim for Harvard, so he turned his hand to printing and went to Philadelphia in 1723. He decided that London was the place to perfect his printing and writing knowledge, and he spent two years there. His simple writing style and great clarity of expression began to be rewarded. *Poor Richard's Almanac,* published annually between 1732 and 1757, was one of Franklin's most profitable enterprises, selling ten thousand copies a year. When he was twenty-three years old, Franklin wrote his first treatise on economics: *A Modest Inquiry into the Nature of Necessity of a Paper Currency* (1729). Perhaps it was not co-incidental that Franklin was the first to print Pennsylvania paper currency.

Franklin was a crusader for learning and also a good businessman. He introduced printing and news publications to many communities throughout the colonies. He also helped start the present University of Pennsylvania in 1751. In 1753, he was named deputy postmaster general of the colonies. He died in 1790.

POLITICAL CONTRIBUTIONS

Franklin was a Radical member of the Pennsylvania Assembly from 1751 to 1764. During this time, as agent for the Assembly, he visited England, where he increased his stature in both social and scientific circles. From 1764 to 1775, he mediated quarrels between England and the American colonies. He was instrumental in securing the repeal of the Stamp Act in 1766.

Upon his return to America, he played a leading part in the fight for independence. During the war, he sat in the Second Continental Congress. Franklin helped draft the Declaration of Independence, which he also signed. That same year, he went to Paris to enlist French financial aid and later became the new nation's minister there. The French called him "the crafty old chameleon" because of his ability to extract millions of dollars from King Louis XVI, which supposedly hastened the downfall of that European monarch, as well as others.

Franklin signed the first U.S. treaty of alliance with France in 1778. He then helped negotiate, and subsequently became one of the signatories of, the Treaty of Paris in 1783, by which American independence was finally recognized by Great Britain. Franklin attended the Constitutional Convention and was named to the key committee that developed the details of the "Great Compromise." Shortly after the Constitutional Convention, Franklin was asked, "What sort of government have you given us?" He replied, "A republic, if you can keep it."

Of Franklin, John Adams once said that his "reputation was more universal than that of Leibniz, Newton, or Voltaire, and he was the first civilized American."

delegates approved it. A few advocates of a strong central government, led by Gouverneur Morris of Pennsylvania and John Rutledge of South Carolina, distrusted the ability of the common people to engage in self-government.

Among the nationalists were several monarchists, including Alexander Hamilton, who was chiefly responsible for the Annapolis Convention's call for the Constitutional Convention. In a long speech on June 18, he presented his views: "I have no scruple in declaring . . . that the British government is the best in the world and that I doubt much whether anything short of it will do in America." Hamilton wanted the American president to hold office for life and to have absolute veto power over the legislature.

Another important group of nationalists were of a more democratic stripe. Led by James Madison of Virginia and James Wilson of Pennsylvania, these democratic nationalists wanted a central government founded on popular support.

Still another faction consisted of nationalists who were less democratic in nature and who would support a central government only if it were founded on very narrowly defined republican principles. This group was made up of a relatively small number of delegates, including Edmund Randolph and George Mason of Virginia, Elbridge Gerry of Massachusetts, and Luther Martin and John Francis Mercer of Maryland.

Most of the other delegates from Maryland, New Hampshire, Connecticut, New Jersey, and Delaware were concerned about only one thing—claims to western lands. As long as those lands became the common property of all states, they were willing to support a central government.

Finally, there was a group of delegates who were totally against a national authority. Two of the three delegates from New York quit the convention when they saw the nationalist direction of its proceedings.

Politicking and Compromises

The debates at the convention started on the first day. James Madison had spent months reviewing European political theory. When his Virginia delegation arrived ahead of most of the others, it got to work immediately. By the time George Washington opened the convention, Governor Edmund Randolph of Virginia was immediately able to present fifteen resolutions. In retrospect, this was a masterful stroke on the part of the Virginia delegation. It set the agenda for the remainder of the convention—even though, in principle, the delegates had been sent to Philadelphia for the sole purpose of amending the Articles of Confederation. They had not been sent to write a new constitution.

The Virginia Plan.   Randolph's fifteen resolutions proposed an entirely new national government under a constitution. It was, however, a plan that not surprisingly favored the large states, including Virginia. Basically, it called for the following:

1. A **bicameral** (two-house) **legislature**, with the lower house chosen by the people and the smaller upper house chosen by the lower house from nominees selected by state legislatures. The number of representatives would be proportional to a state's population, thus favoring the large states. The legislature could void any state laws.
2. The creation of an unspecified national executive, elected by the legislature.
3. The creation of a national judiciary appointed by the legislature.

It did not take long for the smaller states to realize they would fare poorly under the Virginia plan, according to which Virginia, Massachusetts, and Pennsylvania would form a majority in the national legislature. The debate on the plan dragged on for a number of weeks. It was time for the small states to come up with their own plan.

The New Jersey Plan.   On June 15, lawyer William Paterson of New Jersey offered an alternative plan. After all, argued Paterson, under the

Elbridge Gerry (1744–1814), from Massachusetts, was a patriot during the Revolution. He was a signatory of the Declaration of Independence and later became governor of Massachusetts (1810–1812). He became James Madison's new vice president when Madison was reelected in December 1812.

BICAMERAL LEGISLATURE
A legislature made up of two chambers, or parts. The U.S. Congress, composed of the House of Representatives and the Senate, is a bicameral legislature.

SUPREMACY DOCTRINE
A doctrine that asserts the superiority of national law over state or regional laws. This principle is rooted in Article VI of the Constitution, which provides that the Constitution, the laws passed by the national government under its constitutional powers, and all treaties constitute the supreme law of the land.

GREAT COMPROMISE
The compromise between the New Jersey and the Virginia plans that created one chamber of the Congress based on population and one chamber that represented each state equally; also called the Connecticut Compromise.

Articles of Confederation all states had equality; therefore, the convention had no power to change this arrangement. He proposed the following:

1. The fundamental principle of the Articles of Confederation—one state, one vote—would be retained.
2. Congress would be able to regulate trade and impose taxes.
3. All acts of Congress would be the supreme law of the land.
4. Several people would be elected by Congress to form an executive office.
5. The executive office would appoint a Supreme Court.

Basically, the New Jersey plan was simply an amendment of the Articles of Confederation. Its only notable feature was its reference to the **supremacy doctrine,** which was later included in the Constitution.

The "Great Compromise."   The delegates were at an impasse. Most wanted a strong national government and were unwilling even to consider the New Jersey plan. But when the Virginia plan was brought up again, the small states threatened to leave. It was not until July 16 that the **Great Compromise** was achieved. Roger Sherman of Connecticut proposed the following:

1. A bicameral legislature in which the House of Representatives would be apportioned according to the number of free inhabitants in each state, plus three-fifths of the slaves.
2. An upper house, the Senate, which would have two members from each state elected by the state legislatures.

This plan, often called the Connecticut Compromise because of the role of the Connecticut delegates in the proposal, broke the deadlock. It did exact a political price, however, because it permitted each state to have equal representation in the Senate. Having two senators represent each state in effect diluted the voting power of citizens living in more heavily populated states and gave smaller states disproportionate political powers. But the Connecticut Compromise resolved the large-state/small-state controversy. In addition, the Senate acted as part of a checks-and-balance system against the House, which many feared would be dominated by, and responsive to, the masses.

The Great Compromise also settled another major issue—how to deal with slaves in the representational scheme. Slavery was legal everywhere except in Massachusetts, but it was concentrated in the South. The South wanted slaves to be counted equally in determining representation in Congress. But equal representation meant equal taxation, and the South wanted to avoid equal taxation. Sherman's three-fifths compromise solved the issue, satisfying those northerners who felt that slaves should not be counted at all and those southerners who wanted them to be counted as free whites. Actually, Sherman's Connecticut plan spoke of three-fifths of "all other persons" (and that is the language in the Constitution itself). It is not hard to figure out, though, who those other persons were.

Slavery and Other Issues.   The slavery issue was not completely eliminated by the three-fifths compromise. Many delegates were opposed to slavery and wanted it banned entirely in the United States. Charles Pinckney of South Carolina led strong southern opposition to the idea of a ban on slav-

An American slave market from a painting by Taylor. The writers of the Constitution did not ban slavery in the United States but did agree to limit the importing of new slaves after 1808. Nowhere are the words *slavery* or *slaves* used in the Constitution. Instead, the Constitution uses such language as "no person held in service" and "all other persons."

ery. Finally, the delegates agreed that Congress could limit the importation of slaves after 1808. The compromise meant that the issue of slavery itself was never addressed. The South won twenty years of unrestricted slave trade and a requirement that escaped slaves in free states be returned to their owners in slave states.

The agrarian South and the mercantile North were in conflict. The South was worried that the northern majority in Congress would pass legislation unfavorable to its economic interests. Because the South depended on exports of its agricultural products, it feared the imposition of export taxes. In return for acceding to the northern demand that Congress be given the power to regulate commerce among the states and with other nations, the South obtained a promise that export taxes would not be imposed. Even today, such taxes are prohibited. The United States is one of the few countries that does not tax its exports.

There were other disagreements. The delegates could not decide whether to establish only a Supreme Court or to create lower courts as well. They deferred the issue by mandating a Supreme Court and allowing Congress to establish lower courts. They also disagreed over whether the president or the Senate would choose the Supreme Court justices. A compromise was reached, with the agreement that the president would nominate the justices and the Senate would confirm the nomination.

These compromises, as well as others, resulted from the recognition that if one group of states refused to ratify the Constitution, it was doomed.

Working toward Final Agreement

The Connecticut Compromise was reached by mid-July. The makeup of the executive branch and the judiciary, however, was left unsettled. The remaining work of the convention was turned over to a five-man Committee

SEPARATION OF POWERS
The principle of dividing governmental powers among the executive, the legislative, and the judicial branches of government.

MADISONIAN MODEL
The model of government devised by James Madison in which the powers of the government are separated into three branches: executive, legislative, and judicial.

CHECKS AND BALANCES
A major principle of the American governmental system whereby each branch of the government exercises a check on the actions of the others.

of Detail, which presented a rough draft of the Constitution on August 6. It made the executive and judicial branches subordinate to the legislative branch.

The Madisonian Model.   The major issue of **separation of powers** had not yet been resolved. The delegates were concerned with structuring the government to prevent the imposition of tyranny—either by the majority or by a minority. It was Madison who devised a governmental scheme—sometimes called the **Madisonian model**—to achieve this: The executive, legislative, and judicial powers of government were to be separated so that no one branch had enough power to dominate the others. The separation of powers was by function, as well as by personnel, with Congress passing laws, the president enforcing and administering laws, and the courts interpreting laws in individual circumstances.

Each of the three branches of government would be independent of the others, but they would have to cooperate to govern. Figure 2–2 outlines these **checks and balances.** The president has veto power over congressional acts. Congress controls the budget, and the Senate must approve pres-

FIGURE 2–2
Checks and Balances

The major checks and balances among the three branches are illustrated here. Some of these checks are not mentioned in the Constitution, such as judicial review—the power of the courts to declare federal or state acts unconstitutional—or the president's ability to refuse to enforce judicial decisions or congressional legislation. Checks and balances can be thought of as a confrontation of powers or responsibilities. Each branch checks the action of another; two branches in conflict have powers that can result in balances or stalemates, requiring one branch to give in or both to reach a compromise.

The Supreme Court can declare presidential actions unconstitutional.

The president nominates federal judges; the president can refuse to enforce the Court's decisions; the president grants pardons.

THE JUDICIARY

The Supreme Court can declare congressional laws unconstitutional.

Congress can rewrite legislation to circumvent the Court's decisions; the Senate confirms federal judges; Congress determines the number of judges.

THE PRESIDENCY

The president proposes laws and can veto congressional legislation; the president makes treaties, executive agreements, and executive orders; the president can refuse, and has refused, to enforce congressional legislation; the president can call special sessions of Congress.

The Congress makes legislation and can override a presidential veto of its legislation; the Congress can impeach and remove a president; the Senate must confirm presidential appointments and consent to the president's treaties based on a two-third's concurrence; the Congress has the power of the purse and provides funds for the president's programs.

THE CONGRESS

idential appointments. The Supreme Court consists of judges appointed by the president but with the advice and consent of the Senate.[10] Madison also wanted to prevent the branches from abdicating their power to other branches. Note that our Constitution forces cooperation between at least two branches. But with checks and balances, we see simultaneous protection of the independence of each branch, yet forced dependence. For example, Congress can pass a law, but the executive branch must enforce and administer it.

The Executive.   Some delegates favored a plural executive made up of representatives from the various regions. This was abandoned in favor of a single chief executive. Some argued that Congress should choose the executive. To make the presidency completely independent of the proposed Congress, however, an **electoral college** was adopted, probably at James Wilson's suggestion. To be sure, the electoral college created a cumbersome presidential election process. It could even result in a candidate who came in second in the popular vote becoming president by being the top vote getter in the electoral college. The electoral college insulated the president, however, from direct popular control. The seven-year single term that some of the delegates had proposed was replaced by a four-year term and the possibility of reelection.

ELECTORAL COLLEGE
A group of persons called electors selected by the voters in each state and Washington, D.C.; this group officially elects the president and vice president of the United States. The number of electors in each state is equal to the number of each state's representatives in both houses of Congress. The Twenty-third Amendment to the Constitution permits Washington, D.C., to have as many electors as a state of comparable population.

THE FINAL DOCUMENT

On September 17, 1787, the Constitution was approved by thirty-nine delegates. Of the fifty-five who had attended originally, only forty-two remained. Only three delegates refused to sign the Constitution. Others disapproved of at least parts of it but signed anyway to begin the ratification debate.

The Constitution that was to be ratified established the following fundamental principles:

1. Popular sovereignty, or control by the people.
2. A republican government in which the people choose representatives to make decisions for them.
3. Limited government with written laws, in contrast to the powerful monarchical English government against which the colonists had rebelled.
4. Separation of powers, with checks and balances among branches to prevent any one branch from gaining too much power.
5. A federal system that allowed for states' rights, because the states feared too much centralized control.

THE MOTIVES OF THE FRAMERS

Despite the sweeping pronouncements of the Constitution, scholars continue to debate its purpose. Was it designed to protect all the people against

---

10. After *Marbury v. Madison* in 1803 (1 Cranch 137; see the appendix at the end of this chapter, which discusses legal citations), the Supreme Court became part of this checks-and-balances system through judicial review and the limited right to declare the policies of the other two branches of government unconstitutional. See Chapter 13.

the power of government and their own excesses? Or was it written to serve the interests of the people and groups that wielded economic power in the United States after the Revolution?

In 1913, historian Charles Beard published *An Economic Interpretation of the Constitution of the United States,* charging that the Constitution had been produced primarily by wealthy property owners who desired a stronger government able to protect their property rights.[11] Beard also claimed that the Constitution had been imposed by undemocratic methods to prevent democratic majorities from exercising real power. He pointed out that there was never any popular vote on whether to hold a constitutional convention in the first place. Furthermore, most people in the country (white males without property, women, and slaves) were not even eligible to vote on the Constitution, and only about one-sixth of adult white males actually voted for ratification.

Beard's critics respond that Beard greatly exaggerated the undemocratic nature of early American society. Most white males, contrary to Beard's assertion, were in fact eligible to vote. Beard's critics also point out that the enduring—fundamentally republican—ideology of the American Revolution prevented the emergence of a domineering elite.

THE DIFFICULT ROAD TO RATIFICATION

RATIFICATION
Formal approval.

The founders knew that **ratification** of the Constitution was far from certain. Indeed, because it was almost guaranteed that many state legislatures would not ratify it, the delegates agreed that each state should hold a special convention. Elected delegates to these conventions would discuss and vote on the Constitution. Further departing from the Articles of Confederation, the delegates agreed that as soon as nine states (rather than all thirteen) approved the Constitution, it would take effect, and Congress could begin to organize the new government.

The Federalists Push for Ratification

FEDERALIST
The name given to one who was in favor of the adoption of the U.S. Constitution and the creation of a federal union. The Federalists favored a strong central government.

ANTI-FEDERALIST
An individual who opposed the ratification of the new Constitution in 1787.

The two opposing forces in the battle over ratification were the Federalists and the Anti-Federalists. The **Federalists**—those in favor of a strong central government and the new Constitution—had an advantage over the **Anti-Federalists**, who wanted to prevent the Constitution (in its then-current form) from being ratified. In the first place, the Federalists had assumed a positive name, leaving their opposition the negative label of *Anti*-Federalist. More important, the Federalists had attended the Constitutional Convention and knew of all the deliberations that had taken place. Their opponents had no such knowledge, because those deliberations had not been open to the public. Thus, the Anti-Federalists were at a disadvantage in terms of information about the document. The Federalists also had time, power, and money on their side. Communications were slow. Those who had access to the best communications were Federalists—mostly wealthy bankers, lawyers, plantation owners, and merchants living in urban

---

11. Charles A. Beard, *An Economic Interpretation of the Constitution of the United States* (New York: Macmillan, 1913; New York: Free Press, 1986).

areas, where communication was better. The Federalist campaign was organized relatively quickly and effectively to elect Federalists as delegates to the state ratifying conventions.

The Anti-Federalists, however, had at least one strong point in their favor: They stood for the status quo. In general, the greater burden is placed on those advocating change.

The Federalist Papers.   In New York, opponents of the Constitution were quick to attack it. Alexander Hamilton answered their attacks in newspaper columns over the signature "Caesar." When the Caesar letters had little effect, Hamilton switched to the pseudonym Publius and secured two collaborators—John Jay and James Madison. In a very short time, those three political figures wrote a series of eighty-five essays in defense of the Constitution and of a republican form of government. These widely read essays appeared in New York newspapers from October 1787 to August 1788 and were reprinted in the newspapers of other states. Although we do not know for certain who wrote every one, it is apparent that Hamilton was responsible for about two-thirds of the essays. These included the most important ones interpreting the Constitution, explaining the various powers of the three branches, and presenting a theory of judicial review. Madison's *Federalist Paper* No. 10 (see Appendix D), however, is considered a classic in political theory; it deals with the nature of groups—or factions, as he called them. In spite of the rapidity with which *The Federalist Papers* were written, they are considered by many to be perhaps the best example of political theorizing ever produced in the United States.[12]

The Anti-Federalist Response.   The Anti-Federalists used such pseudonyms as Montezuma and Philadelphiensis in their replies. Many of their attacks against the constitution were also brilliant. They claimed that it was a document written by aristocrats and would lead to aristocratic tyranny. More important, the Anti-Federalists believed that the Constitution would create an overbearing and overburdening central government inimical to personal liberty. (The Constitution said nothing about liberty of the press, freedom of religion, or any other individual liberty.) They wanted to include a list of guaranteed liberties, or a bill of rights. Finally, the Anti-Federalists decried the weakened power of the states.

The Anti-Federalists cannot be dismissed as a bunch of unpatriotic extremists. They included such patriots as Patrick Henry and Samuel Adams. They were arguing what had been the most prevalent view of the time. This view derived from the French political philosopher Montesquieu, who believed that liberty was only safe in relatively small societies governed by direct democracy or by a large legislature with small districts. The Madisonian view favoring a large republic, particularly expressed in *Federalist Papers* No. 10 and No. 51 (see Appendix D), was actually the more *un*popular view of the time. Madison was probably convincing because citizens were already persuaded that a strong national government was necessary to combat foreign enemies and to prevent domestic insurrections. Still, some researchers

DID YOU KNOW . . .
That term limits were included among the fifteen resolutions of the Virginia plan submitted to the Constitutional Convention in Philadelphia, but they were put aside "as entering too much into detail for general propositions"?

---

12. Some scholars believe that *The Federalist Papers* played only a minor role in securing ratification of the Constitution. Even if this is true, they still have lasting value as an authoritative explanation of the Constitution.

believe it was mainly the bitter experiences with the Articles of Confederation, rather than Madison's arguments, that created the setting for the ratification of the Constitution.[13]

The March to the Finish

The struggle for ratification continued. Strong majorities were procured in Delaware, Pennsylvania, New Jersey, Georgia, and Connecticut. After a bitter struggle in Massachusetts, ratification passed by a narrow margin on February 6, 1788. By the spring, Maryland and South Carolina had ratified by sizable majorities. Then on June 21 of that year, New Hampshire became the ninth state to ratify the Constitution. Although the Constitution was formally in effect, this meant little without Virginia and New York, the latter not ratifying for yet another month. (See Table 2–2.)

It is interesting to note here that the "mother" country, Britain, did not have a written constitution at the time, nor does it have one today. (See this chapter's *Politics and Comparative Systems* for a discussion of Britain's unwritten constitution.)

Was the Constitution Truly Favored by the Majority?

Political scientists and historians still debate whether the Constitution actually was favored by a popular majority. The delegates at the various state ratifying conventions had been selected by only 150,000 of the approximately 4 million citizens of that time. That does not seem very democratic—at least not by today's standards. (On election day in 1992, for example, 104 million persons—of 190 million people of voting age—voted in the presidential election.) Even Federalist John Marshall believed that in some of the

13. Of particular interest is the view of the Anti-Federalist position contained in Herbert J. Storing, *What the Anti-Federalists Were For* (Chicago: University of Chicago Press, 1981). Storing also edited seven volumes of the Anti-Federalist writings, *The Complete Anti-Federalist* (Chicago: University of Chicago Press, 1981). See also Josephine F. Pacheco, *Antifederalism: The Legacy of George Mason* (Fairfax, Va.: George Mason University Press, 1992).

TABLE 2–2
Ratification of the Constitution

STATE	DATE	VOTE FOR–AGAINST
Delaware	Dec. 7, 1787	30–0
Pennsylvania	Dec. 12, 1787	46–23
New Jersey	Dec. 19, 1787	38–0
Georgia	Jan. 2, 1788	26–0
Connecticut	Jan. 9, 1788	128–40
Massachusetts	Feb. 6, 1788	187–168
Maryland	Apr. 28, 1788	63–11
South Carolina	May 23, 1788	149–73
New Hampshire	June 21, 1788	57–46
Virginia	June 25, 1788	89–79
New York	July 26, 1788	30–27
North Carolina	Nov. 21, 1789*	187–77
Rhode Island	May 29, 1790	34–32

*Ratification was originally defeated on August 4, 1788, by a vote of 184–84.

POLITICS AND COMPARATIVE SYSTEMS
The "Unwritten" British Constitution

Great Britain has no single written document that serves as its constitution. Therefore, it is difficult to obtain a clear outline, in the form of a central body of constitutional rules, that indicates how the British government operates and how the rights of its citizens are protected. In the place of one document, Britain has a collection of customs and practices, as well as judicial decisions handed down in numerous court cases. In fact, what is regarded as making up the British constitution today is actually statutes, judicial decisions, conventions, constitutional commentaries, authoritative opinions, letters, and works of scholarship. These include the Magna Carta (1215), the 1689 Bill of Rights, the Reform Act of 1832, laws passed by Parliament, and various charters.

Perhaps, then, the distinction between the British "unwritten" constitution and our own is simply that the British constitution is uncodified, existing in written fragments. The U.S. Constitution is aggregated, whereas the British constitution is disaggregated. In Great Britain, the lack of a single document that can be called a constitution is offset by the government's unitary and political party–based constitutional monarchy. Britain's government is more cohesive than the American government, which is more fluid and decentralized.

adopting states a majority of the people opposed the Constitution.[14] We have to realize, however, that the adoption of the Constitution was probably as open a process as was reasonable at that time. Transportation and communication were rudimentary and slow. It would have been difficult to discover the true state of popular opinion, even if the leaders of the new nation had been concerned to do so. In any event, as soon as the Constitution was ratified, the movement to place limits on the power of the national government began.

THE BILL OF RIGHTS

Bills of rights had been included in state constitutions at least as early as 1776, when George Mason of Virginia wrote the Virginia Declaration of Rights. That document was modeled on the traditional rights established in England and present in the British Bill of Rights of 1689.

Ratification of the U.S. Constitution in several important states could not have proceeded if the Federalists had not assured the states that amendments to the Constitution would be passed to protect individual liberties against incursions by the national government. Many of the recommendations of the state ratifying conventions included specific rights that were considered later by James Madison as he labored to draft what became the Bill of Rights.

Ironically, a year earlier Madison had told Jefferson, "I have never thought the omission [of the Bill of Rights] a material defect" of the Constitution. But Jefferson's enthusiasm for a bill of rights apparently influenced Madison, as did his desire to gain popular support for his election to Congress. He promised in his campaign letter to voters that, once elected, he would force

LET'S SEE NOW ...WE'LL GIVE THEM FREEDOM, BUT NOT TOO MUCH FREEDOM; LIBERTY BUT NOT TOO MUCH LIBERTY; DEMOCRACY, BUT NOT TOO MUCH DEMOCRACY...

Copyright 1985 Sidney Harris.

---

14. Beard, *An Economic Interpretation of the Constitution,* p. 299.

DID YOU KNOW . . .

That some of the framers of the Constitution were influenced by Native-American political values, particularly those of the Iroquois Confederacy? The Iroquois concluded a treaty in 1520 that contained wording ("We, the people, to form a union, to establish peace, equity, and order . . .") very similar to the Preamble of the U.S. Constitution.

Congress to "prepare and recommend to the states for ratification, the most satisfactory provisions for all essential rights."

Madison had to cull through more than two hundred state recommendations. It was no small task, and in retrospect he chose remarkably well. (One of the rights appropriate for constitutional protection that he left out was equal protection under the laws—but that was not commonly regarded as a basic right at that time. It wasn't until 1868 that an amendment guaranteeing that no state shall deny equal protection to any person was ratified. The Supreme Court has applied this guarantee to certain actions of the federal government as well.)

The final number of amendments that Madison and a specially appointed committee came up with was seventeen. Congress tightened the language somewhat and eliminated five of the amendments. Of the remaining twelve, two—dealing with the apportionment of representatives and the compensation of the members of Congress—were not ratified immediately by the states. Eventually, Supreme Court decisions led to legislative reforms relating to apportionment. The amendment relating to compensation of members of Congress was ratified 203 years later—in 1992!

On December 15, 1791, the national Bill of Rights was adopted when Virginia agreed to ratify the ten amendments. The basic structure of American government had already been established. Now the fundamental rights of individuals were protected, at least in theory, at the national level. The proposed amendment that Madison characterized as "the most valuable amendment in the whole lot"—which would have prohibited the *states* from infringing on the freedoms of conscience, press, and jury trial—had been eliminated by the Senate. Thus, the Bill of Rights as adopted did not limit state power, and individual citizens had to rely on the guarantees contained in the particular state constitution or state bill of rights. The country had to wait until the violence of the Civil War before significant limitations on state power in the form of the Fourteenth Amendment became part of the national Constitution.

ALTERING THE CONSTITUTION: THE FORMAL AMENDMENT PROCESS

The U.S. Constitution is short (see Appendix B). One of the reasons it is short is that the framers intended it to be only a framework for governing, to be interpreted by succeeding generations. One of the reasons it has remained short is because the formal amending procedure does not allow for changes to be made easily. Article V of the Constitution outlines the way in which amendments may be proposed and ratified (see Figure 2–3).

Two formal methods of proposing an amendment to the Constitution are available: (1) a two-thirds vote in each house of Congress or (2) a national convention called by Congress at the request of two-thirds of the state legislatures.

Ratification can occur by one of two methods: (1) by a positive vote in three-fourths of the legislatures of the various states or (2) by special conventions called in the states for the specific purpose of ratifying the proposed amendment and a positive vote in three-fourths of them. The second method has been used only once, to repeal Prohibition. That situation was

FIGURE 2-3

The Formal Constitutional Amending Procedure

There are two ways of proposing amendments to the U.S. Constitution and two ways of ratifying proposed amendments. Among the four possibilities, the usual route has been proposal by Congress and ratification by state legislatures. Only in the case of the ratification of the Twenty-first Amendment in 1933, which repealed the Eighteenth Amendment (Prohibition), was ratification by state conventions used. The Constitution has never been amended by two-thirds of the states requesting a national convention to be called by Congress and then having the proposed amendment ratified by the legislatures of three-fourths of the states or by state conventions in three-fourths of the states.

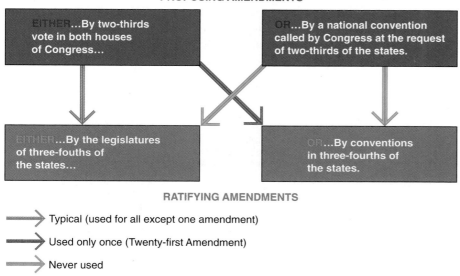

PROPOSING AMENDMENTS

EITHER...By two-thirds vote in both houses of Congress...

OR...By a national convention called by Congress at the request of two-thirds of the states.

EITHER...By the legislatures of three-fouths of the states...

OR...By conventions in three-fourths of the states.

RATIFYING AMENDMENTS

Typical (used for all except one amendment)

Used only once (Twenty-first Amendment)

Never used

exceptional because it involved an amendment (the Twenty-first) to repeal an amendment (the Eighteenth, which had created Prohibition). State conventions were necessary for repeal of the Eighteenth Amendment because the "pro-dry" legislatures in the more conservative states would never have passed the repeal. (Note that Congress determines the method of ratification to be used by all states for each proposed constitutional amendment.)

Many Amendments Proposed, Few Accepted

Congress has considered more than seven thousand amendments to the Constitution. Only thirty-three have been submitted to the states after having been passed by Congress, and only twenty-seven have been ratified (see Table 2–3). It should be clear that the process is much more difficult than a graphic depiction like Figure 2–3 can indicate. Because of competing social and economic interests, the requirement that two-thirds of both the House and Senate approve the amendments is difficult to achieve. Thirty-four senators, representing only seventeen sparsely populated states, could block any amendment. For example, the Republican-controlled House passed the Balanced Budget Amendment within the first one hundred days of the 104th Congress, but it was defeated in the Senate by one vote.

After approval by Congress, the process becomes even more arduous. Three-fourths of the state legislatures must approve the amendment. Only those amendments that have wide popular support across parties and in all regions of the country are likely to be approved.

Why was the amendment process made so difficult? The framers feared that a simple amendment process could lead to a tyranny of the majority, which could pass amendments to oppress disfavored individuals and groups.

Limits on Ratification

A reading of Article V of the Constitution reveals that the framers of the Constitution specified no time limit on the ratification process. The Supreme Court has held that Congress can specify a time for ratification as long as it is "reasonable." Since 1919, most proposed amendments have included a

TABLE 2–3

Amendments to the Constitution

AMENDMENTS	SUBJECT	YEAR ADOPTED	TIME REQUIRED FOR RATIFICATION
1st–10th	The Bill of Rights	1791	2 years, 2 months, 20 days
11th	Immunity of states from certain suits	1795	11 months, 3 days
12th	Changes in electoral college procedure	1804	6 months, 3 days
13th	Prohibition of slavery	1865	10 months, 3 days
14th	Citizenship, due process, and equal protection	1868	2 years, 26 days
15th	No denial of vote because of race, color, or previous condition of servitude	1870	11 months, 8 days
16th	Power of Congress to tax income	1913	3 years, 6 months, 22 days
17th	Direct election of U.S. senators	1913	10 months, 26 days
18th	National (liquor) prohibition	1919	1 year, 29 days
19th	Women's suffrage	1920	1 year, 2 months, 14 days
20th	Change of dates for congressional and presidential terms	1933	10 months, 21 days
21st	Repeal of the Eighteenth Amendment	1933	9 months, 15 days
22d	Limit on presidential tenure	1951	3 years, 11 months, 3 days
23d	District of Columbia electoral vote	1961	9 months, 13 days
24th	Prohibition of tax payment as a qualification to vote in federal elections	1964	1 year, 4 months, 9 days
25th	Procedures for determining presidential disability, presidential succession, and filling a vice presidential vacancy	1967	1 year, 7 months, 4 days
26th	Prohibition of setting minimum voting age above eighteen in any election	1971	3 months, 7 days
27th	Prohibition of Congress's voting itself a raise that takes effect before the next election	1992	203 years

requirement that ratification be obtained within seven years. This was the case with the proposed Equal Rights Amendment. When three-fourths of the states had not ratified in time, Congress extended the limit for an additional three years and three months. That extension expired on June 30, 1982, and the amendment had still not been ratified. Another proposed amendment, which would have guaranteed congressional representation to the District of Columbia, fell far short of the thirty-eight state ratifications needed before its August 22, 1985, deadline.

On May 7, 1992, the Michigan state legislature became the thirty-eighth state to ratify the Twenty-seventh Amendment (on congressional compensation)—one of the two "lost" amendments of the twelve that originally were sent to the states in 1789. Because most of the amendments proposed in recent years have been given a time limit of only seven years by Congress, it was questionable for a while whether the amendment would become effective even if the necessary number of states ratified it. Is 203 years too long a lapse of time between the proposal and the final ratification of an amendment? It apparently was not, because the amendment was certified as legitimate by archivist Don Wilson of the National Archives on May 18, 1992.

The National Convention Provision

The Constitution provides that a national convention requested by the legislatures of two-thirds of the states can propose a constitutional amendment. Congress has received approximately 400 convention applications since the Constitution was ratified; every state has applied at least once. Less than 20 applications were submitted during the Constitution's first 100 years, but more than 150 have been filed in the last two decades. No national convention has been held since 1787, and many national political and judicial leaders are uneasy about the prospect of convening a body that could propose any amendment whatsoever, even one calling for a new form of government. The state legislative bodies that originate national convention applications, however, appear not to be uncomfortable with such a constitutional modification process; more than 230 state constitutional conventions have been held. The major national convention campaigns have reflected dissatisfaction, as one scholar has noted, "of a conservative and rural hue, with the social and economic policies associated with the federal government."[15]

The Constitution is silent about many of the procedures that would be required at a national convention, and significant questions abound about the nature and process of such a convention: Does Congress have wide or narrow discretion in determining the acceptability and/or validity of applications? If sufficient numbers of applications are submitted, but Congress refuses to call a convention, do the states have any other recourse? Is a vote of Congress necessary to authorize the issuance of a call for a national convention? Can the president veto such an action? When and where would the convention meet? How would the delegates be elected? Would they represent the states or the people as an aggregate? Can the convention be limited to one specific issue? Does Congress have any legal authority to set

---

15. Russell L. Caplan, *Amending the Constitution by National Convention* (New York: Oxford University Press, 1988).

convention ground rules? Members of Congress have proposed legislation that would provide constitutional convention procedural controls, but no such act has been passed.

INFORMAL METHODS OF CONSTITUTIONAL CHANGE

Formal amendments are one way of changing our Constitution, and, as is obvious by their small number, they have not been resorted to very frequently. If we discount the first ten amendments (the Bill of Rights), which passed soon after the ratification of the Constitution, there have been only seventeen formal alterations of the Constitution in the more than two hundred years of its existence.

But looking at the sparse number of formal constitutional changes gives us an incomplete view. The brevity and ambiguity of the original document has permitted great changes in the Constitution by way of changing interpretations over time. As the United States grew, both in population and territory, new social and political realities emerged. Congress, presidents, and the courts found it necessary to interpret the Constitution's provisions in light of these new realities. The Constitution has proved to be a remarkably flexible document, adapting itself time and again to new events and concerns.

Congressional Legislation

The Constitution gives the Congress broad powers to carry out its duties as the nation's legislative body. For example, Article I, Section 8, of the Constitution gives Congress the power to regulate foreign and interstate commerce. Although there is no clear definition of foreign commerce or interstate commerce in the Constitution, Congress has cited the *commerce clause* as the basis for passing thousands of laws that have defined the meaning of foreign and interstate commerce. Similarly, Article III, Section 1, states that the national judiciary shall consist of one supreme court and "such inferior courts, as Congress may from time to time ordain and establish." Through a series of acts, Congress has used this broad sanction to establish the federal court system of today.

Presidential Actions

Even though the Constitution does not expressly authorize the president to propose bills or even budgets to Congress, presidents since the time of Woodrow Wilson (who served as president from 1913 to 1921) have proposed hundreds of bills to Congress each year. Presidents have also relied on their Article II authority as commander in chief of the nation's armed forces to send American troops abroad into combat, although the Constitution provides that Congress has the power to declare war. Presidents have also conducted foreign affairs by the use of **executive agreements**, which are legally binding documents made between the president and a foreign head of state. The Constitution does not mention such agreements.

EXECUTIVE AGREEMENT
A binding international agreement made between chiefs of state that does not require legislative sanction.

Judicial Review

Another way of changing the Constitution—or of making it more flexible—is through the power of **judicial review.** In the landmark case of *Marbury v. Madison,*[16] decided in 1803, the Supreme Court ruled a provision of an act of Congress to be unconstitutional. Chief Justice John Marshall declared that it is "the province and duty of the Judiciary department to say what the law is." Although the case was primarily concerned with the power of the Supreme Court in relation to the other two branches of the federal government, the principle of judicial review itself opened the way for Congress and the executive branch to test the elasticity of the Constitution—that is, it allowed them to see how far and in what ways it could be "stretched" without breaking.

Through the process of judicial review, the Supreme Court adapts the Constitution to modern situations. Electronic technology, for example, did not exist when the Constitution was ratified. Nonetheless, in this century the Supreme Court used the Fourth Amendment guarantees against unreasonable searches and seizures to place limits on wiretapping and other electronic eavesdropping methods by government officials. Additionally, the Supreme Court has changed its interpretation of the Constitution in accordance with changing times. It ruled in 1896 that "separate-but-equal" public facilities for African Americans were constitutional; but by 1954 the times had changed, and the Supreme Court reversed that decision.[17]

Woodrow Wilson summarized the Supreme Court's work when he described it as "a constitutional convention in continuous session." Basically, the law is what the Supreme Court says it is at any point in time.

Interpretation, Custom, and Usage

The Constitution has also been changed through its interpretation by both Congress and the president. Originally, the president had a staff consisting of personal secretaries and a few others. Today, because Congress delegates specific tasks to the president and the chief executive assumes political leadership, the executive office staff alone has increased to several thousand persons. The executive branch provides legislative leadership far beyond the intentions of the Constitution.

Changes in the ways of doing political business have also altered the Constitution. The Constitution does not mention political parties, yet these informal, "extraconstitutional" organizations make the nominations for offices, run the campaigns, organize the members of Congress, and in fact change the election system from time to time. The emergence and evolution of the party system, for example, has changed the way of electing the president. The Constitution calls for the electoral college to choose the president. Today, the people vote for electors who are pledged to the candidate of their party, effectively choosing the president themselves. Perhaps most strikingly, the Constitution has been adapted from serving the needs of a small, rural republic with no international prestige to providing a framework of government for an industrial giant with vast geographic, natural, and human resources.

JUDICIAL REVIEW
The power of the Supreme Court or any court to declare unconstitutional federal or state laws and other acts of government.

---

16. 1 Cranch 137 (1803). See Chapter 13.
17. *Brown v. Board of Education of Topeka,* 347 U.S. 483 (1954).

THE CONSTITUTION: UNFINISHED WORK

The U.S. Constitution has been called a "living" constitution because the framers embodied it with sufficient flexibility so that its meaning and application could change as the nation and its people changed. As we fully develop the age of technology, information, and communication, this inherent flexibility undoubtedly will be pushed to its limits at times. As you will see in the remaining chapters of this text, major issues are already arising with respect to the "information highway" that is developing at this very instant. The federal government is attempting to impose a standard on communications encryption software that would allow the government access to even the most highly encrypted telephone, facsimile, or computer messages when the U.S. government believes that national security is at stake. But the users of electronic mail and the like are claiming that the Constitution protects them from such potential "eavesdropping" by the U.S. government.

As we mentioned earlier in this chapter, the issue of a constitutional convention may well need to be faced. Given that the Constitution is relatively silent about the mechanics of such a convention, certainly new work will have to be performed in order to undertake such a historic action.

Throughout the years to come, the U.S. Constitution will be tested time and again. Ultimately, the courts, the Congress, and the president, as well as the citizens jointly, will determine the prevailing interpretation of that document.

GETTING INVOLVED
How Can You Affect the U.S. Constitution?

The Constitution is an enduring document that has survived more than two hundred years of turbulent history. It is also a changing document, however. Twenty-seven amendments have been added to the original Constitution. How can you, as an individual, actively help to rewrite the Constitution?

One of the best ways is to work for (or against) a constitutional amendment. At the time of this writing, national coalitions of interest groups are supporting or opposing proposed amendments concerning limitations on the size of the government and anti-abortion laws. If you want an opportunity to change the Constitution—or to assure that it is not changed—you could work for or with one of the alliances of groups interested in the fate of these amendments.

The following contacts should help you get started on efforts to affect the U.S. Constitution directly.

GOVERNMENT REFORM

An organization whose goal is to "reduce the size and cost of federal government to those functions specified in the U.S. Constitution" is the Liberty Amendment Committee of the U.S.A., P.O. Box 20888, El Cajon, CA 92021. The ultimate goal of LACUSA is to see the so-called Liberty Amendment (now pending in Congress) ratified and then to abolish the income tax.

An even more general goal—namely, to encourage Congress to call a constitutional convention (the most open-ended way to change the Constitution)— is pursued by Conservatives for a Constitutional Convention, P.O. Box 582, Desert Hot Springs, CA 92240.

The Movement for Economic Justice, 1638 R St. N.W., Washington, DC 20029, is an activist organization seeking grass-roots involvement. Its goals are to encourage greater government responsiveness in such areas as revenue sharing, inflation, and "fundamental economic reform." It conducts programs and training conferences and issues newsletters.

ABORTION—BOTH SIDES

One of the organizations whose primary goal is to secure the passage of the Human Life Amendment is the American Life Lobby, Route 6, Box 162-F, Stafford, VA 22554 (703-659-4193). The Human Life Amendment would recognize in law the "personhood" of the unborn, secure human rights protections for the fetus from the time of fertilization, and prohibit abortion under any circumstances.

The National Abortion and Reproductive Rights Action League, 1156 15th St. N.W., Suite 700, Washington, DC 20005 (202-973-3000), is a political action and information organization working on behalf of "pro-choice" issues—that is, the right of women to have control over reproduction. The organization has roughly 150,000 members.

KEY TERMS

Chapter Summary

1. An early effort by Great Britain to establish North American colonies was unsuccessful. The first English colonies were established at Jamestown in 1607 and Plymouth in 1620. The Mayflower Compact created the first formal government. By the mid-1700s, other British colonies had been established along the Atlantic seaboard from Georgia to Maine.

2. In 1763, the British tried to reassert control over their increasingly independent-minded colonies through a series of taxes and legislative acts. The colonists responded with boycotts of British products and protests. Representatives of the colonies formed the First Continental Congress in 1774. The delegates sent a petition to the king of England expressing their grievances. The Second Continental Congress established an army in 1775 to defend colonists against attacks by British soldiers.

3. On July 4, 1776, the Second Continental Congress approved the Declaration of Independence. Perhaps the most revolutionary aspects of the Declaration were its assumptions that people have natural rights to life, liberty, and the pursuit of happiness; that governments derive their power from the consent of the governed; and that people have a right to overthrow oppressive governments. During the Revolutionary War, however, all of the colonies adopted written constitutions that severely curtailed the power of executives, thus giving their legislatures predominant powers. By the end of the Revolutionary War, the states had signed the Articles of Confederation, creating a weak government with few powers. The Articles proved to be unworkable because the national government had no way to assure compliance by the states with such measures as securing tax revenues.

4. General dissatisfaction with the Articles of Confederation prompted delegates to call the Philadelphia Convention in 1787. Although the delegates originally convened with the idea of amending the Articles, the discussions soon focused on creating a constitution for a new form of government. The Virginia plan and the New Jersey plan were offered but did not garner widespread support. A compromise offered by the state of Connecticut helped to break the large-state/small-state disputes dividing the delegates. The final version of the Constitution provided for the separation of powers and for checks and balances.

5. Fears of a strong central government prompted the addition of the Bill of Rights to the Constitution. The Bill of Rights secured a wide variety of freedoms for Americans, including the freedoms of religion, speech, and assembly. It was initially applied only to the federal government, but amendments to the Constitution following the Civil War made it clear that the Bill of Rights also applied to the states.

6. An amendment to the Constitution may be proposed by either a two-thirds vote in each house of Congress or by a national convention called by Congress at the request of two-thirds of the state legislatures. Ratification can occur by either a positive vote in three-fourths of the legislatures of the various states or by special conventions called in the states for the specific purpose of ratifying the proposed amendment and a positive vote in three-fourths of these state conventions. Informal methods of constitutional change include congressional legislation, presidential actions, judicial review, and changing interpretations of the Constitution.

Questions for Review and Discussion

1. Under the Articles of Confederation, Congress had no power to regulate interstate commerce. The absence of this power encouraged the states to engage in a certain type of legislation. What type of legislation was this, and what effect do you think it had on economic growth?

2. The writing of the Constitution can be seen as the first real working of group interest, or pluralism, in the United States. What kinds of bargains or compromises were struck in the writing of this document? How were the various interests in the thirteen colonies protected by the provisions of the Constitution?

3. Although the Constitution calls for separation of powers, a more accurate description of the system might be one of "separate branches sharing powers." What provisions of the Constitution require that the branches cooperate, or "share," power in order for the government to function?

4. In this chapter, there are four subsections under the heading "Informal Methods of Constitutional

Change." Of the four methods, which do you think is most important, and why? Give examples to back up your argument.

5. The Anti-Federalists expressed many fears in their writings. Two of the most important involved taxation and the centralization of government. With respect to taxation, they feared that the central government would expand its taxing power slowly and would end up restricting how much the states and cities could tax because the federal government would be taking so much. Do you think this prediction was accurate? Why or why not? The second major fear of the Anti-Federalists was that the capital city would cause the central government to lose touch with its constituents. Have members of Congress lost touch with their home states by living in Washington, D.C.? Why or why not?

 ## LOGGING ON: THE CONSTITUTION

If you would like more information on the U.S. Constitution, one good way to find it is to look at a news group that can be reached through the address

alt.politics.usa.constitution

If you want to subscribe to news groups like this, contact your university computer center for details on how to do it. Every university or college access system is different, so get local help.

Another interesting source of information is the Internet Wiretap On-line Library. The address is

wiretap.spies.com

Why do these groups use weird names like this? We don't know, but this address gives you a menu of things to roam through, including the U.S. Constitution, the Articles of Confederation, and constitutions from other countries. This library also contains other electronic texts.

Access this through **gopher** (See Chapter 1) or FTP (File Transfer Protocol; if you haven't used this, get local help). In using FTP, at the prompt, type **dir.** There will be a list of files and directories. Type **dir** again, and you'll see a directory entitled World. Type **cd World** (Capitalize the *W* in *World*). Type **dir,** and you'll get a long list of constitutions.

If you want to download one of these, type **get** and the file name for the one you want. The file should now be in your home directory. Have fun.

 ## SELECTED REFERENCES

Beard, Charles A. *An Economic Interpretation of the Constitution of the United States.* New York: Macmillan, 1913; New York: Free Press, 1986. This classic interpretation of the motives of the founders of the republic emphasizes the founders' economic interests in the success of the nation.

Beeman, Richard, Stephen Botein, and Edward C. Carter II, eds. *Beyond Confederation: Origins of the Constitution and American National Identity.* Chapel Hill, N.C.: University of North Carolina Press, 1987. This collection of essays discusses the debate over the intentions of the framers of the Constitution.

Calvi, James V., and Susan Coleman. *Cases in Constitutional Law: Summaries and Critiques.* Englewood Cliffs, N.J.: Prentice-Hall, 1994. This text summarizes and critiques over one hundred of the most significant constitutional cases that the Supreme Court has decided.

Hamilton, Alexander, James Madison, and John Jay. *The Federalist Papers*. Cambridge, Mass.: Harvard University Press, 1961. The complete set of columns from the *New York Packet* defending the new Constitution is presented.

Nathanson, Steven. *Should We Consent to Be Governed?* Belmont, Calif.: Wadsworth, 1992. The author examines the issues of natural rights, limited government, and the republican form of government.

Pacheco, Josephine F., ed. *Antifederalism: The Legacy of George Mason*. Fairfax, Va.: George Mason University Press, 1992. A collection of essays that examines the concept of antifederalism as it exists today and how the persistence of this political idea has been instrumental in shaping our nation.

Simmons, A. John. *On the Edge of Anarchy: Locke, Consent, and the Limits of Society*. Princeton, N.J.: Princeton University Press, 1993. The author explores Locke's view of the nature of limits on political relations among individuals.

Snowiss, Sylvia. *Judicial Review and the Law of the Constitution*. New Haven, Conn.: Yale University Press, 1990. An examination of the nature and extent of judicial review.

Storing, Herbert J. *The Complete Anti-Federalist*. 7 vols. Chicago: University of Chicago Press, 1981. The views of those opposed to the Constitution are examined.

Wood, Gordon S. *The Radicalism of the American Revolution*. New York: Knopf, 1992. This study of the American revolution puts it in the perspective of other revolutions. The author examines the meaning of the American Revolution in today's context.

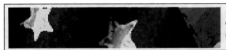

APPENDIX TO CHAPTER TWO: How to Read Case Citations and Find Court Decisions

Many important court cases are discussed in references in footnotes throughout this book. Court decisions are recorded and published. When a court case is mentioned, the notation that is used to refer to, or to cite, the case denotes where the published decision can be found.

State courts of appeals decisions are usually published in two places, the state reports of that particular state and the more widely used *National Reporter System* published by West Publishing Company. Some states no longer publish their own reports. The *National Reporter System* divides the states into the following geographic areas: Atlantic (A. or A.2d, where *2d* refers to *Second Series*), South Eastern (S.E. or S.E.2d), South Western (S.W. or S.W.2d), North Western (N.W. or N.W.2d), North Eastern (N.E. or N.E.2d), Southern (So. or So.2d), and Pacific (P. or P.2d).

Federal trial court decisions are published unofficially in West's *Federal Supplement* (F.Supp.), and opinions from the circuit courts of appeals are reported unofficially in West's *Federal Reporter* (F., F.2d, or F.3d). Opinions from the United States Supreme Court are reported in the *United States Reports* (U.S.), the *Lawyers' Edition of the Supreme Court Reports* (L.Ed.), West's *Supreme Court Reporter* (S.Ct.), and other publications. The *United States Reports* is the official publication of United States Supreme Court decisions. It is published by the federal government. Many early decisions are missing from these volumes. The citations of the early volumes of the *U.S. Reports* include the names of the actual reporters, such as Dallas, Cranch, or Wheaton. *McCulloch v. Maryland*, for example, is cited as 17 U.S. (4 Wheat.) 316. Only after 1874 did the present citation system, in which cases are cited based solely on their volume and page numbers in the *United States Reports*, come into being. An unofficial and more complete edition of Supreme Court decisions, the *Lawyers' Edition of the Supreme Court Reports*, is published by the Lawyers Cooperative Publishing Company of Rochester, New York. West's *Supreme Court Reporter* is an unofficial edition of decisions dating from October 1882. These volumes contain headnotes and numerous brief editorial statements of the law involved in the case.

State courts of appeals decisions are cited by giving the name of the case; the volume, name, and page number of the state's official report (if the state publishes its own reports); the volume, unit, and page number of the *National Reporter;* and the volume, name, and page number of any other selected reporter. Federal court citations are also listed by giving the name of the case and the volume, name, and page number of the reports. In addition to the citation, this textbook lists the year of the decision in parentheses. Consider, for example, the case *United States v. Curtiss-Wright Export Co.*, 299 U.S. 304 (1936). The Supreme Court's decision of this case may be found in volume 299 of the *United States Reports* on page 304. The case was decided in 1936.

3
Federalism

CHAPTER OUTLINE

WHAT IF . . .
We Had a National Police Force?

The U.S. Constitution reserves all powers to the states that are not expressly delegated to the federal government. The primary motivation for limiting the national government's powers was to prevent it from encroaching on the rights of the states. But this structure was also adopted because many of the delegates to the 1787 Philadelphia Convention believed that certain governmental functions could be performed more capably by the states.

Nearly every municipality in the United States maintains a police force responsible for protecting its residents. Every state also maintains a police force, such as a state highway patrol, that enforces the laws along highways such as the interstate system. The federal government operates the Federal Bureau of Investigation (FBI). The FBI handles only those types of crimes that are under the jurisdiction of the federal government, such as counterfeiting, interstate auto theft, and smuggling. The FBI often cooperates with state and local officials in such actions as drug seizures.

What if all of the nation's police forces—on the local, state, and national levels—were merged into a single force? Such an arrangement would be similar to that found in many nations such as France. If the United States had a similar system of government, we would expect to see a centralization of authority and power in Washington, D.C. The decisions of local police chiefs could then be overruled by the national office in Washington. Because a national police force would probably be funded by Congress, state and local offices would have less freedom to decide how to respond to what used to be purely local matters. Any failure to follow the directions of the national government could be punished by cutting off funding and demoting or firing local officials.

A national police force might be more efficient, because there would no longer be any problems with disputes over jurisdiction. But this gain might be offset by the need for actions on purely local matters to be approved by the national office. If a murder takes place in Dallas, for example, the Dallas Police Department is primarily responsible for conducting the investigation and coordinating the efforts to catch the murderer. In a national police system, however, the Dallas Police Department's efforts would be overseen by the national office.

One efficiency of a national police force might be a common computer database listing all persons having criminal records in the country. This would be a significant improvement over the present situation, in which national, state, and local officials often cannot easily track the movements of a criminal because comprehensive databases do not exist. In addition, having a single police force would make it possible to formulate a single strategy to capture a felon, as opposed to the current situation in which local, state, and federal officials may operate at cross-purposes with one another.

What is the likelihood that we will ever have a national police force? The chances are remote at best. People distrust the federal government in general. They also believe it is too far removed from the local scene to be able to respond effectively to purely local crimes such as bicycle thefts and vandalism. Moreover, many people do not believe that the federal government is better able to solve crimes than are local police agencies, nor do they feel that the operational efficiency of these local agencies would be improved if most major decisions had to be made in Washington, D.C. Most important is the issue of accountability. The residents of a municipality would have little influence over the choice of the police chief if the nation had a single police force. In addition, many people would be concerned that a national police force could pose a political threat to the independence of the government itself.

---

1. How might the operational inefficiencies of the present system be reduced without merging all local, state, and national agents into a single police force?

2. Is a national police force more appropriate for a geographically compact country such as France than for a larger country such as the United States? Why or why not?

The United States has no one national police force, as you saw in this chapter's opening *What If . . . .* Instead, there are literally thousands of separate police forces. This should not be surprising, because there are many separate governments in this country. One national government and fifty state governments, plus local governments, create a grand total of more than 85,000 governments in all! The breakdown can be seen in Table 3–1. Those 85,000 governments contain about 500,000 elected officeholders.

Visitors from France or Spain are often awestruck by the complexity of our system of government. Consider that a criminal action can be defined by state law, by national law, or by both. Thus, the alleged criminal can be prosecuted in the state court system or in the federal court system (or both). Often, economic regulation over exactly the same matter exists at the local level, the state level, and the national level—generating multiple forms to be completed, multiple procedures to be followed, and multiple laws to be obeyed. Numerous programs are funded by the national government but administered by state and local governments.

There are various ways of ordering relations between central governments and local units. *Federalism* is one of these ways. Understanding federalism and how it differs from other forms of government is important in understanding the American political system.

THREE SYSTEMS OF GOVERNMENT

There are basically three ways of ordering relations between central governments and local units: (1) a unitary system, (2) a confederal system, and (3) a federal system. The most popular, both historically and today, is the unitary system.

TABLE 3–1
The Number of Governments in the United States Today

With more than 85,000 separate governmental units in the United States today, it is no wonder that intergovernmental relations in the United States are so complicated. Actually, the number of school districts has decreased over time, but the number of special districts created for single purposes, such as flood control, has increased from only about 8,000 during World War II to over 30,000 today.

Federal government		1
State governments		50
Local governments		86,692
Counties	3,043	
Municipalities (mainly cities or towns)	19,296	
Townships (less extensive powers)	16,666	
Special districts (water, sewer, etc.)	33,131	
School districts	14,556	
	86,692	
TOTAL		86,743

SOURCE: U.S. Department of Commerce, *Statistical Abstract of the United States* (Washington, D.C.: U.S. Government Printing Office, 1994).

A Unitary System of Government

A **unitary system** of government is the easiest to define: Unitary systems allow ultimate governmental authority to rest in the hands of the national, or central, government. Consider a typical unitary system—France. There are departments and municipalities in France. Within the departments and the municipalities are separate government entities with elected and appointed officials. So far, the French system appears to be very similar to the United States system, but the similarity is only superficial. Under the unitary French system, the decisions of the governments of the departments and municipalities can be overruled by the national government. Also, the national government can cut off the funding of many departmental and municipal government activities. Moreover, in a unitary system such as that in France, all questions related to education, police, the use of land, and welfare are handled by the national government.[1] Great Britain, Sweden, Israel, Egypt, Ghana, and the Philippines also have unitary systems of government, as do most countries today.

A Confederal System

You were introduced to the elements of a **confederal system** of government in Chapter 2, when we examined the Articles of Confederation. A confederation is the opposite of a unitary governing system. It is a league of independent states in which a central government or administration handles only those matters of common concern expressly delegated to it by the member states. The central governmental unit has no ability to make laws directly applicable to individuals unless the member states explicitly support such laws. The United States under the Articles of Confederation and the Confederate States during the American Civil War were confederations.

There are few, if any, confederations in the world today that resemble those that existed in the United States between 1781 and 1788. Switzerland is a confederation of twenty-three sovereign cantons, and several republics of the former Soviet Union formed the Commonwealth of Independent States. Countries have formed confederations with one another for limited purposes: military/peacekeeping, as in the case of the North Atlantic Treaty Organization or the United Nations; or economic, as in the case of the European Union (formerly the European Community) or the economic unit created by the North American Free Trade Agreement.

A Federal System

Between the unitary and confederal forms of government lies the **federal system**. In this system, authority is divided, usually by a written constitution, between a central government and regional, or subdivisional, governments (often called constituent governments). The central government and the constituent governments both act directly on the people through laws and through the actions of elected and appointed governmental officials. Within each government's sphere of authority, each is supreme in theory.

---

1. In the past decade, legislation has altered somewhat the unitary character of the French political system.

Contrast a federal system to a unitary one in which the central government is supreme and the constituent governments derive their authority from it. Australia, Canada, Mexico, India, Brazil, and Germany are examples of nations with federal systems. See Figure 3–1 for a comparison of the three systems.

The Historical Reasons for American Federalism

There are historical, as well as practical, reasons why the United States developed in a federal direction. Some of these reasons are discussed below.

Political Pragmatism.   As you saw in Chapter 2, the historical basis of the federal system was laid down in Philadelphia at the Constitutional Convention, where strong national government advocates (see this chapter's *Politics: The Human Side* on Alexander Hamilton) opposed equally strong states' rights advocates. This dichotomy continued through to the ratifying conventions in the several states. The resulting federal system was a compromise. The supporters of the new constitution were political pragmatists—they realized that without a federal arrangement, there would be no ratification of the new constitution. The appeal of federalism was that it retained state traditions and local power while establishing a strong national government capable of handling common problems.

Size and Regional Isolation.   At the time of the Philadelphia Convention, the thirteen colonies taken together were geographically larger than England or France. Slow travel and communication combined with geographic spread contributed to the isolation of many regions within the colonies. It could, for example, take up to several weeks for all of the colonies to be informed about one particular political decision. Even if the colonial leaders had agreed on the desirability of a unitary system, the problems of size and regional isolation would have made such a system operationally difficult.

FIGURE 3–1

The Flow of Power in Three Systems

In a unitary system, the flow of power is from the central government to the local and state governments. In a confederal system, the flow of power is in the opposite direction—from the state and local governments to the central government. In a federal system, the flow of power is, in principle, both ways.

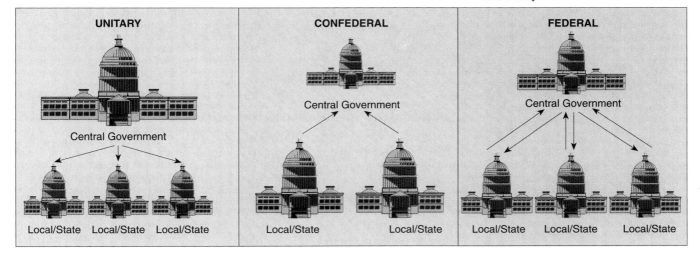

POLITICS: THE HUMAN SIDE
Alexander Hamilton, Statesman

"The more close the union of the states, and the more complete the authority of the whole, the less opportunity will be allowed the stronger states to injure the weaker."

BIOGRAPHICAL NOTES

Alexander Hamilton was born in the West Indies in (we think) 1757, the illegitimate son of a Scottish merchant. He was sent to New York for his studies. He later became the aide and confidential secretary to George Washington from 1779 to 1781. Hamilton was a commander in the field during the Revolutionary War, after which he established a successful law practice in New York. He was appointed by Washington as his first secretary of the treasury. He died in 1804 after a duel with his rival, Aaron Burr.

POLITICAL CONTRIBUTIONS

Hamilton was a delegate to the Philadelphia Constitutional Convention. He later led the forces in favor of ratification of the Constitution at the New York state convention. Hamilton's successful politicking for ratification in that state was highlighted by a series of eighty-five public letters, which were printed in New York City newspapers from October 27, 1787, to August 16, 1788. The letters, which represented the joint work of Hamilton, James Madison, and John Jay, have come to be known as *The Federalist Papers*. About two-thirds of them are attributable to Hamilton.

Hamilton's admiration for a strong and energetic national government is evident in *The Federalist Papers*. He wrote that "the vigor of government is essential to the security of liberty" and that the fledgling nation confronted the alternatives of "adoption of the new Constitution or a dismemberment of the Union." History and common sense showed that "if these States should either be wholly disunited, or only united in partial confederacies, the subdivisions into which they might be thrown would have frequent and violent contests with each other." A divided nation of sovereign states would also be easy prey for the divide-and-conquer tactics of other nations. "A firm Union will be of the utmost moment to the peace and liberty of the States as a barrier against domestic faction and insurrection," whereas weak confederations would lead to "incurable disorder and imbecility in the government." The Constitution was not designed to abolish state governments, but to make them "constituent parts of the national sovereignty" by congressional representation.

A vigorous national government working for a common interest would also provide economic benefits from "an active commerce, an extensive navigation, [and] a flourishing marine," and the nation would be able to compete against European commercial power. "An unrestricted intercourse between the States themselves will advance the trade of each by an interchange of their respective productions, not only for the supply of reciprocal wants at home, but for exportation to foreign markets."

Sectionalism and Political Subcultures.   The American way of life has always been characterized by a number of political subcultures, which divide along the lines of race, wealth, education, and, more recently, age, degree of religious fundamentalism, and sexual preference. Subcultures associated with geography naturally developed because different groups of individuals became concentrated in different regions. The agricultural society of the South generated a traditionalist subculture, stressing the family and community. The middle Atlantic states appeared to engender an individualist subculture in which politics was viewed simply as another business.

The existence of diverse political subcultures would appear to be at odds with a political authority concentrated solely in a central government. Had the United States developed into a unitary system, the various political subcultures certainly would have been less able to influence government behavior (relative to their own regions and interests) than they have been, and continue to be, in our federal system.

Other Arguments for Federalism

The arguments for federalism in the United States and elsewhere involve a complex set of factors, some of which we have already noted. First, for big countries, such as the United States, India, and Nigeria, federalism allows many functions to be "farmed out" by the central government to the states or provinces. The lower levels of government, accepting these responsibilities, can thereby become the focus of political dissatisfaction rather than the national authorities. Second, even with modern transportation and communications systems, the sheer geographic or population size of some nations makes it impractical to locate all political authority in one place. Finally, federalism brings government closer to the people. It allows more direct access to, and influence on, government agencies and policies, rather than leaving the population restive and dissatisfied with a remote, faceless, all-powerful central authority. In the United States, federalism historically has had benefits as well as drawbacks. State governments have long been a training ground for future national leaders. Presidents Ronald Reagan and Bill Clinton made their political mark as state governors.

The states themselves have been testing grounds for new government initiatives such as unemployment compensation, which began in Wisconsin, and air-pollution control, which was initiated in California. Of course, some actions pioneered at the state level, such as Prohibition, were disastrous.

Arguments against Federalism

Not everyone thinks federalism is such a good idea. Some see it as a way for powerful state and local interests to block progress and impede national plans. Others see dangers in "creeping," or expanding, federalism. President Ronald Reagan said, "The Founding Fathers saw the federalist system as constructed something like a masonry wall. The States are the bricks, the national government is the mortar. . . . Unfortunately, over the years, many people have increasingly come to believe that Washington is the whole wall."[2]

Smaller political units are more likely to be dominated by a single political group, and the dominant groups in some cities and states have resisted implementing equal rights for all minority groups. (This was essentially the argument that James Madison put forth in *Federalist Paper* No. 10, which

---

2. Text of the address by the president to the National Conference of State Legislatures, Atlanta, Georgia (Washington, D.C.: The White House, Office of the Press Secretary, July 30, 1981), as quoted in Edward Millican, *One United People, The Federalist Papers and the National Idea* (Lexington, Ky.: The University Press of Kentucky, 1990).

you can read in Appendix D to this text.) Others point out, however, that the dominant factions in other states have been more progressive than the national government in many areas, such as the environment.

THE CONSTITUTIONAL BASIS FOR AMERICAN FEDERALISM

No mention of the designation "federal system" can be found in the U.S. Constitution. Nor is it possible to find a systematic division of governmental authority between the national and state governments in that document. Rather, the Constitution sets out different types of powers (see Figure 3–2). These powers can be classified as (1) the delegated powers of the national government, (2) the reserved powers of the states, (3) concurrent powers, and (4) prohibited powers.

Powers Delegated to the National Government

The powers delegated to the national government include both expressed and implied powers, as well as resulting powers and the special category of inherent powers.

Expressed Powers. Most of the powers expressly delegated to the national government are found in Article I, Section 8, of the Constitution. Some expressly delegated powers include setting standards for weights and measures, making uniform naturalization laws, admitting new states, establishing post offices, and declaring war.

Resulting Powers. Sometimes several expressed powers are added together, and they are called **resulting powers.** For example, consider the printing of paper money as legitimate currency for trade and purchasing. The Constitution gives Congress the expressed power to coin money, as well as to borrow money and to regulate interstate commerce. The resulting power gives the national government the authority to designate the money it produces as legitimate currency for the payment of debts.

RESULTING POWERS
The accumulation of several expressed powers that results in a specific power of the federal government.

Implied Powers. Article I, Section 8, also states that the Congress shall have the power

> To make all laws which shall be necessary and proper for carrying into Execution the foregoing Powers, and all other Powers vested by this Constitution in the Government of the United States, or in any Department or Officer thereof.

ELASTIC CLAUSE, OR NECESSARY AND PROPER CLAUSE
The clause in Article I, Section 8, that grants Congress the power to do whatever is necessary to execute its specifically delegated powers.

This clause is sometimes called the **elastic clause,** or the **necessary and proper clause,** because it provides flexibility to our constitutional system. It gives Congress all those powers that can be reasonably inferred but that are not expressly stated in the brief wording of the Constitution. The clause was first used in the Supreme Court decision of *McCulloch v. Maryland*[3] (discussed later in this chapter) to develop the concept of implied powers.

---

3. 4 Wheaton 316 (1819). See the appendix to Chapter 2 for more information about how court decisions are referenced.

Through this concept, the national government has succeeded in strengthening the scope of its authority to meet the numerous problems that the framers of the Constitution did not, and could not, anticipate.

Inherent Powers.   A special category of national powers that is not implied by the necessary and proper clause consists of what have been labeled the inherent powers of the national government. These powers derive from the fact that the United States is a sovereign power among nations, and as such, its national government must be the only government that deals with other nations. Under international law, it is assumed that all nation-states, regardless of their size or power, have an *inherent* right to ensure their own

FIGURE 3–2

The American Federal System— Division of Powers between the National Government and the State Governments

Here we look at the constitutional powers of both the national government and the state governments together. Then we look at the powers denied by the Constitution to each level of government.

SELECTED CONSTITUTIONAL POWERS

National Government	National and State Governments	State Governments
IMPLIED "To make all Laws which shall be necessary and proper for carrying into Execution the foregoing Powers, and all other Powers vested by this Constitution in the Government of the United States, or in any Department or Officer thereof." (Article 1, Section 8, Clause 18)	CONCURRENT ■ To levy and collect taxes ■ To borrow money ■ To make and enforce laws ■ To establish courts ■ To provide for the general welfare ■ To charter banks and corporations	RESERVED TO THE STATES ■ To regulate intrastate commerce ■ To conduct elections ■ To provide for public health, safety, and morals ■ To establish local governments ■ To ratify amendments to the federal constitution ■ To establish a state militia
EXPRESSED ■ To coin money ■ To conduct foreign relations ■ To regulate interstate commerce ■ To levy and collect taxes ■ To declare war ■ To raise and support the military ■ To establish post offices ■ To establish courts inferior to the Supreme Court ■ To admit new states		

SELECTED POWERS DENIED BY THE CONSTITUTION

National Government	National and State Governments	State Governments
■ To tax articles exported from any state ■ To violate the Bill of Rights To change state boundaries To suspend the right of *habeas corpus* To make *ex post facto* laws To subject officeholders to a religious test	■ To grant titles of nobility ■ To permit slavery ■ To deny citizens the right to vote because of race, color, or previous servitude To deny citizens the right to vote because of sex	■ To tax imports or exports ■ To coin money ■ To enter into treaties ■ To impair obligations of contracts ■ To abridge the privileges or immunities of citizens or deny due process and equal protection of the laws

■

When the Los Angeles earthquake destroyed billions of dollars of property, the state government looked to the federal government for financial aid for the quake's victims. Proponents of a strong central government argued that the states alone cannot handle significant local emergencies and that is why the federal government must step in.

survival. To do this, each nation must have the ability to act in its own interest among and with the community of nations—by, for instance, making treaties, waging war, seeking trade, and acquiring territory.[4] The national government has these powers whether or not they have been enumerated in the Constitution. Some constitutional scholars categorize inherent powers as a third type of power, completely distinct from the delegated powers (both expressed and implied) of the national government.

Reserved Powers of the State Governments

The Tenth Amendment states that the powers not delegated to the United States by the Constitution, nor prohibited by it to the states, are reserved to the states, or to the people. These are the reserved powers that the national government cannot deny to the states. Because these powers are not expressly listed—and because they are not limited to powers that are expressly listed—there is sometimes a question as to whether a certain power is delegated to the national government or reserved to the states. State powers have been held to include each state's right to regulate commerce within its borders and to provide for a state militia. States also have the reserved power to make laws on all matters not prohibited to the states by the national or state constitutions and not expressly, or by implication, delegated to the national government. The states also have **police power**—the authority to legislate for the protection of the health, morals, safety, and welfare of the people.

The ambiguity of the Tenth Amendment is illustrated by the fact that, on occasion, states have used their power to pass discriminatory legislation,

POLICE POWER
The authority to legislate for the protection of the health, morals, safety, and welfare of the people. In the United States, most police power is a reserved power of the states.

---

4. See especially *United States v. Curtiss-Wright Export Co.*, 299 U.S. 304 (1936), which upheld the validity of a joint resolution of Congress delegating the power to the president to prohibit arms shipments to foreign belligerents.

such as laws prohibiting interracial marriages. These laws were passed on the assumption that because the Constitution did not grant such regulatory power to the national government, that power was reserved to the states acting through their legislatures. But such laws were declared to be unconstitutional and immediately became unenforceable by the states.[5]

Concurrent Powers

In some areas, the Constitution gives national and state governments an equal right to pass legislation and to regulate certain activities. These are called **concurrent powers.** Most concurrent powers are not specifically stated in the Constitution; they are only implied. An example of a concurrent power is the power to tax. The types of taxation are divided between the levels of government. States may not levy a tariff (a set of taxes on imported goods); the federal government may not tax real estate; and neither may tax the facilities of the other. If the state governments did not have the power to tax, they would not be able to function other than on a ceremonial basis.

Other concurrent powers include the power to borrow money, to establish courts, and to charter banks and corporations. Concurrent powers are normally limited to the geographic area of the state and to those functions not preempted by the Constitution or by the national government—such as the coinage of money and the negotiation of treaties.

The foregoing discussion might give the impression that the power of the states today is derived solely from the Constitution. This would be a mistake, for the independence of the states rests, in large part, on the commitment of American citizens to the idea of local self-government. In addition, and perhaps more important, members of the national legislature—senators and representatives—are elected by their local constituencies. Except for the president, politicians in the national government have obtained their power by satisfying those local constituencies, rather than by satisfying some ill-defined, broad national constituency. Even the president must appeal to local constituencies to some degree, however, because the presidential candidate receiving the largest popular vote in a state wins all of that state's electoral votes (with some exceptions). Furthermore, many of the programs paid for and undertaken by the national government are carried out by the state and local governmental units—for example, the interstate highway system, most of the welfare system, job-creation programs, and environmental clean-up programs.

Prohibited Powers

The Constitution prohibits or denies a number of powers to the national government. For example, the national government has expressly been denied the power to impose taxes on goods sold to other countries (exports). Moreover, any power not delegated expressly or implicitly to the federal government by the Constitution is prohibited to it. For example, the national government cannot create a national public school system.

The states are also denied certain powers. These are found in Article I, Section 10, as well as in the Thirteenth, Fourteenth, Fifteenth, Nineteenth,

DID YOU KNOW . . .
That Abraham Lincoln, the "Great Emancipator," claimed on taking office that he would not attack slavery as an institution and that he even wanted a constitutional amendment to make the right to own slaves irrevocable?

CONCURRENT POWERS
Powers held jointly by the national and state governments.

---

5. *Loving v. Virginia*, 388 U.S. 1 (1967).

Twenty-fourth, and Twenty-sixth Amendments. For example, no state is allowed to enter into a treaty on its own with another country.

HORIZONTAL FEDERALISM

So far we have examined only the relationship between central and state governmental units. But, of course, the states have numerous commercial, social, and other dealings among themselves. These interstate activities, problems, and policies make up what can be called **horizontal federalism.** The national Constitution imposes certain "rules of the road" on horizontal federalism, which have had the effect of preventing any one state from setting itself apart from the other states. The three most important clauses in the Constitution relating to horizontal federalism, all taken from the Articles of Confederation, require that

1. Each state give full faith and credit to every other state's public acts, records, and judicial proceedings.
2. Each state extend to every other state's citizens the privileges and immunities of its own citizens.
3. Each state agree to render persons who are fleeing from justice in another state back to their home state when requested to do so.

The Full Faith and Credit Clause

Article IV, Section 1, of the Constitution provides that "Full Faith and Credit shall be given in each State to the public Acts, Records, and judicial Proceedings of every other State." This clause applies only to civil matters. It ensures that rights established under deeds, wills, contracts, and the like in one state will be honored by other states. It also ensures that any judicial decision with respect to such property rights will be honored, as well as enforced, in all states. The **full faith and credit clause** was originally put

HORIZONTAL FEDERALISM
Activities, problems, and policies that require state governments to interact with one another.

FULL FAITH AND CREDIT CLAUSE
A section of the Constitution that requires states to recognize one another's laws and court decisions. It ensures that rights established under deeds, wills, contracts, and other civil matters in one state will be honored by other states.

The only indication that a motorist has crossed a state boundary on Interstate 95 is the "Welcome to Maine" sign posted there. There are no border posts, and no visa, passport, or special permission is needed to change states. Different traffic laws may apply, however.

in the Articles of Confederation to promote mutual friendship among the people of the different states. In fact, it has contributed to the unity of American citizens, because it protects their legal rights as they move about from state to state. This is extremely important for the conduct of business in a country with a very mobile citizenry.

Privileges and Immunities

Privileges and immunities are defined as special rights and exemptions provided by law. Article IV, Section 2, indicates that "The Citizens of each State shall be entitled to all Privileges and Immunities of Citizens in the se veral States." This clause indicates that states are obligated to extend to citizens of other states protection of the laws, the right to work, access to courts, and other privileges they grant their own citizens. It means, quite simply, that a resident of Alabama cannot be treated as an alien (noncitizen) when that person is in California or New York. He or she must have access to the courts of each state, to travel rights, and to property rights.[6]

Interstate Extradition

Article IV, Section 2, states that "[a] person charged in any State with Treason, Felony, or another Crime who shall flee from Justice and be found in another State, shall on Demand of the executive Authority of the State from which he fled, be delivered up, to be removed to the State having jurisdiction of the Crime." The language here appears clear, yet governors of one state were not legally required to **extradite** (render to another state) a fugitive from justice until 1987. Furthermore, the federal courts will not order such an action; it is rather the moral duty of the governor to extradite. (In October 1993, however, because of an interstate compact, a federal court ordered convicted murderer Thomas Grasso to be extradited from Oklahoma to New York. In Oklahoma, Grasso was awaiting execution, whereas in new York he had been sentenced to twenty years in prison. The governor of Oklahoma, David Walters, claimed that then New York governor Mario Cuomo, an outspoken opponent of the death penalty, was trying to keep "Oklahoma from exercising its right to capital punishment.")

The Peaceful Settlement of Differences between States

States are supposed to settle their differences peacefully. In so doing, they may enter into agreements called **interstate compacts**—if consented to by Congress. In reality, congressional consent is necessary only if such a compact increases the power of the contracting states relative to other states (or to the national government). Typical examples of interstate compacts are the establishment of the Port of New York Authority by the states of New York and New Jersey and the regulation of the production of crude oil and natural gas by the Interstate Oil and Gas Compact of 1935. Sometimes states are unable to reach agreement on important issues, however, as you can see in this chapter's *Politics and the Environment.*

PRIVILEGES AND IMMUNITIES
Special rights and exceptions provided by law. Article IV, Section 2, of the Constitution requires states not to discriminate against one another's citizens. A resident of one state cannot be treated as an alien when in another state; he or she may not be denied such privileges and immunities as legal protection, access to courts, travel rights, or property rights.

EXTRADITE
To surrender an accused or convicted criminal to the authorities of the state from which he or she has fled; to return a fugitive criminal to the jurisdiction of the accusing state.

INTERSTATE COMPACT
An agreement between two or more states. Agreements on minor matters are made without congressional consent, but any compact that tends to increase the power of the contracting states relative to other states or relative to the national government generally requires the consent of Congress. Such compacts serve as a means by which states can solve regional problems.

---

6. Out-of-state residents have been denied lower tuition rates at state universities, voting rights, and immediate claims to welfare benefits. Actually, the courts have never established a precise meaning of the term *privileges and immunities*.

POLITICS AND THE ENVIRONMENT
Las Vegas Wants Other States' Water

Las Vegas is in the middle of a desert. Nonetheless, it has artificial waterfalls, artificial lakes, and water amusement parks. It only receives 4 inches of rain a year, so it must obtain its water from elsewhere. Las Vegas has been operating under an old seven-state compact that allocates Colorado water to 40 million Americans living in the West.

Rather than curtail growth and the use of water, Las Vegas has told its neighboring states that they must increase that city's allocation from the Colorado River . . . or else. The "or else" would involve Las Vegas's running more than 1,200 miles of pipes into a network of underground basins, which would then take water from more than 20,000 square miles of wilderness, national parks, and ranching country. Las Vegas also wants to take water from the Virgin River, which flows through parts of Utah and Arizona as well as Nevada.

Of course, surrounding states are claiming that Las Vegas is trying to make a "water grab" that would kill much of the surrounding desert

Although Las Vegas is in the middle of a desert, water is used as if it were cheap. In fact it is cheap because the state obtains much of its water relatively cheaply from the Colorado River. Because other states use water from that river, there is an issue about how it should be allocated.

ecology. So Las Vegas has yet another proposal: a new Colorado River interstate compact. Las Vegas water authority personnel point out that too much water from the Colorado River is going to farmers in California (and at prices well below what the water is worth). Las Vegans believe that the current Colorado River seven-state compact has to be redone, because the West is the fastest growing urbanized area in the United States today, with 40 million people.

THE SUPREMACY OF THE NATIONAL CONSTITUTION

SUPREMACY CLAUSE
The constitutional provision that makes the Constitution and federal laws superior to all conflicting state and local legislation.

The supremacy of the national constitution over subnational laws and actions can be found in the **supremacy clause** of the Constitution. The supremacy clause (Article VI, Paragraph 2) states the following:

> This Constitution and the Laws of the United States which shall be made in Pursuance thereof; and all Treaties made . . . under the Authority of the United States, shall be the supreme Law of the Land; and the Judges in every State shall be bound thereby, any Thing in the Constitution or Laws of any State to the Contrary notwithstanding.

In other words, states cannot use their reserved or concurrent powers to thwart national policies. All national and state officers, as well as judges, must be bound by oath to support the Constitution. Hence, any legitimate exercise of national governmental power supersedes any conflicting state action.[7] Of course, deciding whether a conflict actually exists is a judicial matter, as you will soon read about in the case of *McCulloch v. Maryland.*

Some political scientists believe that national supremacy is critical for the longevity and smooth functioning of a federal system. Nonetheless, the application of this principle has been a continuous source of conflict. Indeed, the most extreme result of this conflict was the Civil War, which we explore in more detail later.

MILESTONES IN NATIONAL GOVERNMENT SUPREMACY

Numerous court decisions and political events, and even more numerous instances of bureaucratic decision making, have given our national government significant political power. Such was not the case during the early days of the American republic. Historically, there are at least four milestones on the route to today's relatively more powerful national government. They are as follows:

1. The Supreme Court case of *McCulloch v. Maryland*[8] (1819), in which the doctrine of implied powers of the national government was clarified.
2. The Supreme Court case of *Gibbons v. Ogden*[9] (1824), in which the national government's power over commerce was defined for the first time in an expansive way.
3. The Civil War (1861 to 1865).
4. The Supreme Court case of *Brown v. Board of Education* (1955), in which the federal government exerted control over the implementation of local school district integration plans (discussed at length in Chapter 5).

McCulloch v. Maryland (1819)

The U.S. Constitution says nothing about establishing a national bank. Article I, Section 8, gives Congress the power "[t]o coin Money, regulate the Value thereof, and of foreign Coin, and fix the Standard of Weights and Measures." Nonetheless, at different times Congress chartered two banks—the First and Second Banks of the United States—and provided part of their initial capital; they were thus national banks.

The government of Maryland imposed a tax on the Second Bank's Baltimore branch. It was an attempt to put that branch out of business. The branch's cashier, James William McCulloch, refused to pay the Maryland tax. Maryland took McCulloch to its state court. In that court, the state of Maryland won. Because similar taxes were being levied in other states, the national government appealed the case to the Supreme Court, then headed by Chief Justice John Marshall.

The Constitutional Questions.   The questions before the Supreme Court were of monumental proportions. The very heart of national power

7. An excellent example of this is President Dwight Eisenhower's disciplining of Arkansas governor Orval Faubus by federalizing the National Guard to enforce the court-ordered desegregation of Little Rock High School.
8. 4 Wheaton 316 (1819).
9. 9 Wheaton 1 (1824).

under the Constitution, as well as the relationship between the national
government and the states, was at issue. Congress has the authority to make
all laws that are "necessary and proper" for the execution of Congress's
expressed powers. Strict constitutional constructionists looked at the word
necessary and contended that the national government had only those powers *indispensable* to the exercise of its designated powers. To them, chartering
a bank and contributing capital to it were not necessary, for example, to coin
money and regulate its value. Nothing was specifically stated in the Constitution about the creation by the national government of a national bank.

Loose constitutional constructionists disagreed. They believed that the
word *necessary* could not be looked at in its strictest sense. If one were to
interpret the necessary and proper clause literally, it would have no practical
effect. As Hamilton once said, "It is essential to the being of the national
Government, that so erroneous a conception of the meaning of the word
necessary should be exploded." The other important question before the Court
was the following: If the bank was constitutional, could a state tax it?

Marshall's Decision.   Three days after hearing the arguments in the
case, Chief Justice John Marshall announced the decision of the Court.
(Some suspect that Marshall probably made his decision in this case even
before he heard the opposing arguments.) Marshall's Federalist views are
evident in his decision. It is true, Marshall said, that Congress's power to
establish a national bank was not expressed in the Constitution. He went
on to say, however, that if establishing such a national bank aided the national government in the exercise of its designated powers, then the authority to set up such a bank could be implied. To Marshall, the necessary
and proper clause embraced "all means which are appropriate" to carry out
"the legitimate ends" of the Constitution. Only when such actions are forbidden by the letter and spirit of the Constitution are they thereby unconstitutional. There was nothing in the Constitution, according to Marshall,
"which excludes incidental or implied powers; and which requires that
everything granted shall be expressly and minutely described." It would be
impossible to spell out every action that Congress might legitimately take—
the Constitution "would be enormously long and could scarcely be embraced by the human mind."

In perhaps the single most famous sentence ever uttered by a Supreme
Court justice, Marshall said, "[W]e must never forget it is a constitution we
are expounding." In other words, the Constitution is a living instrument
that has to be interpreted to meet the "practical" needs of government.
Having established this doctrine of implied powers, Marshall then answered
the other important question before the Court and established the doctrine
of national supremacy. Marshall stated that no state could use its taxing
power to tax an arm of the national government. If it could, "the declaration
that the Constitution . . . shall be the supreme law of the land, is empty and
unmeaning declamation."

Marshall's decision became the basis for strengthening the national government's power from that day on. The Marshall Court enabled the national
government to grow and to meet problems that the Constitution's framers
were unable to foresee. Today, practically every expressed power of the national government has been expanded in one way or another by use of the
necessary and proper clause.

John Marshall (1755–1835) was the
fourth chief justice of the Supreme
Court. When Marshall took over, the
Court had little power and almost no
influence over the two other branches
of government. Some scholars have
declared that Marshall is the true architect of the American constitutional
system, because he single-handedly
gave new power to the Constitution.
Early in his career, he was an attorney and was elected to the first of
four terms in the Virginia Assembly.
He was instrumental in the fight to
ratify the Constitution in Virginia. Prior
to being named to the Supreme
Court, he won a seat in Congress in
1799 and in 1800 became secretary
of state to John Adams.

Gibbons v. Ogden (1824)

One of the more important parts of the Constitution included in Article I, Section 8, is the so-called **commerce clause**, in which Congress is given the power "[t]o regulate Commerce with foreign Nations, and among the several States, and with the Indian Tribes." What exactly does "to regulate commerce" mean? What does "commerce" entail? The issue here is essentially the same as that raised by *McCulloch v. Maryland:* How strict an interpretation should be given to a constitutional phrase? As can be expected, because Marshall interpreted the necessary and proper clause liberally in *McCulloch v. Maryland,* he also, five years later, used the same approach in interpreting the commerce clause.

COMMERCE CLAUSE
The section of the Constitution in which Congress is given the power to regulate trade among the states and with foreign countries.

The Issue before the Court.   Robert Fulton, inventor of the steamboat, and Robert Livingston, American minister to France, secured a monopoly of steam navigation on the waters in New York State from the New York legislature in 1803. They licensed Aaron Ogden to operate steam-powered ferryboats between New York and New Jersey. Thomas Gibbons decided to compete with Ogden, but he did so without New York's permission. Ogden sued Gibbons. The New York state courts granted Ogden an **injunction,** prohibiting Gibbons from operating in New York waters. Gibbons appealed to the Supreme Court.

INJUNCTION
An order issued by a court to compel or restrain the performance of an act by an individual or government official.

Marshall's Decision.   Marshall defined *commerce* as all commercial intercourse—that is, all business dealings. The Court ruled against Ogden's monopoly, thus reversing the injunction against Gibbons. Marshall used this opportunity not only to expand the definition of commerce but also to validate and increase the power of the national legislature to regulate commerce. Said Marshall, "What is this power? It is the power . . . to prescribe the rule by which commerce is to be governed. This power, like all others vested in Congress, is complete in itself." In other words, the power of the national government to regulate commerce has no limitations, other than those specifically found in the Constitution.

As a result of Marshall's decision, the commerce clause allowed the national government to exercise increasing authority over all areas of economic affairs throughout the land. Some scholars believe that Marshall's decision in *Gibbons v. Ogden* welded the people of the United States into a unit by the force of their commercial interests. Although Congress did not immediately exploit this broader grant of power, today few areas of economic activity remain outside the regulatory power of the national legislature.

The Civil War

We usually think of the Civil War simply as the fight to free the slaves. The facts are quite different. Freedom for the slaves was an important aspect of the Civil War, but not the only one, and certainly not the most important one, say many scholars. At the heart of the controversy that led to the Civil War was the issue of national government supremacy versus the rights of the separate states. The Civil War brought to an ultimate and violent climax the ideological debate that had been outlined by the Federalist and

The Civil War was not fought over just the question of slavery. Rather, the supremacy of the national government was at issue. Had the South won, presumably any state or states would have the right to secede from the Union.

Anti-Federalist parties in the early years of the nation. This debate was sparked anew by the passage of a tariff in 1828. The state of South Carolina attempted to nullify the tariff, claiming that in cases of conflict between a state and the national government, the state should have the ultimate authority over its citizens.

Nullification and Secession.   Defending the concept of **nullification** was a well-educated and articulate senator from South Carolina, John C. Calhoun. Not a newcomer to politics, Calhoun had served the national government in several capacities—as vice president, as secretary of state, and as secretary of war. Calhoun viewed the federal system as simply a compact (as in the Articles of Confederation) among sovereign states. The national government was not the final judge of its own power—the ultimate sovereign authority rested with the several states. It followed that the national government could not force a state and its citizens to accept a law against their will. In such cases, Calhoun argued, the state had the right to declare a national law *null and void* and therefore not binding on its citizens. This theory of nullification uses the concept of **interposition**, in which a state places itself between its citizens and the national government as a protector, shielding its citizens from any national legislation that may be harmful to them.[10]

Calhoun also espoused the political doctrine of the **concurrent majority.** He maintained that democratic decisions could be made only with the concurrence of all segments of society affected by the decision. Without that agreement, a decision should not be binding on those whose interests it violates.

Calhoun's concurrent-majority thesis was used by others later as a justification for the **secession** of the southern states from the Union. The ultimate defeat of the South, however, permanently ended any idea that a state within the Union can successfully claim the right to secede. We live in "the

NULLIFICATION
The act of nullifying, or rendering void. John C. Calhoun asserted that a state had the right to declare a national law to be null and void and therefore not binding on its citizens, on the assumption that ultimate sovereign authority rested with the several states.

INTERPOSITION
The act in which a state places itself between its citizens and the national government as a protector, shielding its citizens from any national legislation that may be harmful to them. The doctrine of interposition has been rejected by the federal courts as contrary to the supremacy clause in Article VI of the Constitution.

CONCURRENT MAJORITY
A principle advanced by John C. Calhoun whereby democratic decisions could be made only with the concurrence of all segments of society affected by the decision. Without their concurrence, a decision should not be binding on those whose interests it violates.

SECESSION
The act of formally withdrawing from membership in an alliance; the withdrawal of a state from the federal union.

---

10. Thomas Jefferson and James Madison also used the theory of interposition in the Kentucky and Virginia Resolutions of 1799, written to protest the Alien and Sedition Acts of 1798.

POLITICS AND THE STATES
Breaking Up Is Hard to Do, or Northern versus Southern California

When the South tried to break away from the other states in the last century, the North was willing to engage in a civil war to ensure national supremacy. Could northern California secede from the state of California? Or would a civil war be fought over the supremacy of the state government?

Actually, there have been many attempts by parts of states to secede and form a new state. For example, "Winston" was formed in 1862 by the inhabitants of Winston County, Alabama, and it even issued its own money. It sought neutrality during the Civil War, but Confederate troops made that prospect impossible.

But what about the northern part of California seceding from the nation's most populous state? Since the mid-1800s, there have been at least twenty-five attempts to separate northern and southern California. When a nonbinding question was placed on the June 1992 ballot of thirty-one out of California's fifty-eight counties, twenty-seven counties voted in favor of the proposal. (When voters were allowed to express their opinion in creating three separate states of North, Central, and Southern California the following year, however, the majority of voters were against the idea.)

The political impetus behind the desire of some northern counties to secede from California is their belief that they are deprived of power in the state. After all, 93 percent of the state's population is found south of the state's capital in Sacramento. But 47 percent of the counties are located from Sacramento up to the northern border with Oregon. Consequently, northern residents believe that their needs are being sacrificed for those of the urban centers. For example, the state has mandated that counties and municipalities provide a variety of services, including increased welfare payments and more criminal courts. Between 85 and 90 percent of the average California county's budget is dictated by mandates from the state government in Sacramento. The state government, however, has not financed these mandated services. The result is that sparsely populated rural counties in northern California are in a fiscal bind, some approaching bankruptcy. Officials in these counties believe that they could do better on their own.

indestructible union of indestructible states," as the Supreme Court has said. It is not without irony that the Civil War, brought about in large part because of the South's desire for increased states' rights, in fact resulted in the opposite—an increase in the political power of the national government. (Are states "indestructible"? That is the subject of this chapter's *Politics and the States*.)

War and Growth of the National Government.   Thousands of new employees were hired to run the Union war effort and to deal with the social and economic problems that had to be handled in the aftermath of war. A billion-dollar ($1.3 billion, which is over $11 billion in today's dollars) national government budget was passed for the first time in 1865 to cover the increased government expenditures. The first (temporary) income tax was imposed on citizens to help pay for the war. Both the increased national government spending and the nationally imposed income tax were precursors to the expanded role of the national government in the American federal system.[11] Civil liberties were curtailed in the Union and in the Confederacy in the name of the wartime emergency. The distribution of

---

11. The future of the national government's powerful role was cemented with the passage of the Sixteenth Amendment (ratified in 1913), which authorized the federal income tax. Annual federal government expenditures now exceed one-fifth of annual national economic output.

pensions and widow's benefits also boosted the national government's social role. The North's victory set the nation on the path to a modern industrial economy and society.

THE CONTINUING DISPUTE OVER THE DIVISION OF POWER

As we have noted, *McCulloch v. Maryland* expanded the implied powers of the federal government. The dispute, and its ultimate outcome, can be viewed as part of a continuing debate about the boundaries between federal and state authority, with the Supreme Court as the boundary setter, or referee. As we might expect, the character of the referee will have an impact on the ultimate outcome of any boundary dispute. While John Marshall was chief justice of the Supreme Court, he did much to permit the increase in the power of the national government and the reduction in that of the states. During the Jacksonian era (1829–1837), a shift back to states' rights began. In particular, the business community preferred state regulation (or, better yet, no regulation) of commerce. The question of the regulation of commerce became one of the major issues in federal-state relations.

The issue was often resolved in favor of the states under U.S. Supreme Court Justice Roger Taney, who headed the Court from 1836 until 1864. Taney's goal was to shift the constitutional emphasis from the national level and return power to the states. He was particularly concerned with shoring up state power in the regulation of business and other activities within state borders, such as public health, safety, and morals. Under Taney, the police power of the states became the basic instrument through which property was controlled in the "public interest."

The continuing dispute over the division of power between the national government and the states can be looked at in terms of the historical phases of federalism in the United States: dual federalism, cooperative federalism, and the new federalism.

Dual Federalism

DUAL FEDERALISM
A system of government in which the states and the national government each remain supreme within their own spheres. The doctrine looks on nation and state as coequal sovereign powers. It holds that acts of states within their reserved powers could be legitimate limitations on the powers of the national government.

ECONOMIC REGULATION
The regulation of business practices by government agencies.

The doctrine of **dual federalism** emphasized a distinction between federal and state spheres of government authority, particularly in the area of **economic regulation.** The distinction between *intra*state commerce (which was not under the control of the national government) and *inter*state commerce (which was under the control of the national government) became of overriding importance. For example, in 1918, the Supreme Court ruled that a 1916 federal law banning child labor was unconstitutional, because it was a local problem, and the power to deal with it was reserved to the states.[12] Even as recently as 1976, the Court held that a federal law regulating wages and overtime pay could not be applied to state government employees, as that would damage the states' ability to function effectively and would violate state sovereignty.[13] A 1985 Supreme Court decision over-

12. *Hammer v. Dagenhart,* 247 U.S. 251 (1918). This decision was overruled in *United States v. Darby,* 312 U.S. 100 (1940).
13. *National League of Cities v. Usery,* 426 U.S. 833 (1976); altered by *Equal Employment Opportunity Commission v. Wyoming,* 460 U.S. 226 (1982).

In the 1800s, very young children worked in coal mines. Today, child labor laws prohibit employers from hiring such young Americans. Some argue that even in the absence of child-labor laws, few, if any, children would still be working in the mines, because the United States is a much richer country than it was a hundred years ago. Presumably, today's parents, no longer at subsistence income levels, would opt to have their children go to school.

turned this ruling and stated that Congress, rather than the courts, should decide which state activities the federal government can regulate.[14]

For most of this century, however, when Congress has chosen to regulate an activity, the courts have upheld the regulation against any challenge that the activity does not involve interstate commerce. This has been true even if the activity does not appear to involve commerce between places in different states. A notable exception to this trend occurred in 1995. In *United States v. Lopez,*[15] the Supreme Court ruled that the federal Gun-Free School Zones Act, which made it a federal offense to possess firearms in school zones, was unconstitutional. The Court held that Congress, in passing the act, had exceeded its authority under the commerce clause, because the possession of a gun in a local school zone was not an economic activity that substantially affected interstate commerce.

Cooperative Federalism

Franklin D. Roosevelt was inaugurated on March 4, 1933, as the thirty-second president of the United States. In the previous year, nearly 1,500 banks had failed (and 4,000 more would fail in 1933). Thirty-two thousand businesses closed down, and one-fourth of the labor force was unemployed. The national government had been expected to do something about the disastrous state of the economy. But for the first three years of the Great Depression, the national government did very little. That changed with the new Democratic administration's energetic intervention in the economy. FDR's "New Deal" included numerous government spending and welfare programs, in addition to voluminous regulations relating to economic activity. The U.S. Supreme Court, still abiding by the legal doctrine of dual

---

14. *Garcia v. San Antonio Metro,* 469 U.S. 528 (1985).
15. 115 S.Ct. 1624 (1995).

COOPERATIVE FEDERALISM
The theory that the states and the national government should cooperate in solving problems.

federalism, rejected as an unconstitutional interference in state powers virtually all of Roosevelt's national regulation of business. It was not until 1937 that the Court, responding to Roosevelt's Court-packing threat and worsening economic conditions (including the outbreak of violent labor disputes), ruled that manufacturing could be regulated as interstate commerce by the national government.[16]

Some political scientists have labeled the era since 1937 as an era of **cooperative federalism**, in which the states and the national government cooperate in solving complex common problems. Others see the Supreme Court's 1937 decision as the beginning of an era of national supremacy, in which the power of the states has been consistently diminished. In particular, Congress can pass virtually any law that regulates almost any kind of economic activity, no matter where that activity is located. For all intents and purposes, the doctrine of dual federalism has been dead for quite some time, although there were attempts at reviving it during the Reagan administration (1981–1989). Many members of racial and ethnic minorities have expressed a preference for cooperative federalism and national supremacy, believing that their rights are better protected when the federal government has oversight of state government actions.

The Growth of National-Level Powers

Even if the Great Depression had not occurred, we probably still would have witnessed a growth of national-level powers as the country became increasingly populated, industrial, interdependent with other countries, and a world power. This meant that problems and situations that once were treated locally would begin to have a profound impact on Americans hundreds or even thousands of miles away.

---

16. *National Labor Relations Board v. Jones & Laughlin Steel Corp.*, 301 U.S. 1 (1937). For a different view of the historical significance of this decision, see Morton Grodzins, "Centralization and Decentralization in the American Federal System," in Robert A. Goldwin, ed., *A Nation of States: Essays on the American Federal System* (Chicago: Rand McNally, 1963).

This mural in San Francisco was one of the many projects sponsored by the New Deal's Works Progress Administration (WPA) in the 1930s. The federal government's efforts to alleviate unemployment (in this case, among artists) during the Great Depression signaled a shift from dual federalism to cooperative federalism.

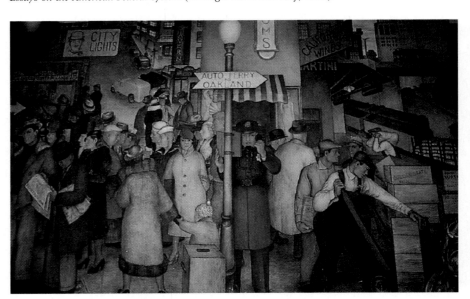

For example, if one state is unable to maintain an adequate highway system, the economy of the entire region may suffer. If another state maintains a substandard educational system, the quality of the work force, the welfare rolls, and the criminal justice agencies in other states may be affected. So the death of dual federalism and the ascendancy of national supremacy had a very logical and very real set of causes. Our more mobile, industrial, and increasingly interdependent nation demanded more uniform and consistent sets of rules, regulations, and governmental programs.

Nowhere can the shift toward a greater role for the central government in the United States be seen better than in the shift toward increased central government spending as a percentage of total government spending. Figure 3–3 shows that in 1929, on the eve of the Great Depression, local governments accounted for 60 percent of all government outlays, whereas the federal government accounted for only 17 percent. After Roosevelt's New Deal had been in place for several years during the Great Depression, local governments gave up half their share of the government spending pie, dropping to 30 percent, and the federal government increased its share to 47 percent. Estimates are that in 1996, the federal government accounts for about 66 percent of all government spending.

The New Federalism

The third phase of federalism, which began in 1969, was labeled by President Richard Nixon as the **new federalism.** Its goal was to reduce the restrictions attached to federal grants—that is, to allow local officials to make the decisions about how the money is to be spent. Under Nixon's program, money was given directly to states and localities without any strings attached. This program, which was known as *revenue sharing,* lasted through 1986.

With President Ronald Reagan's election in 1980, the administration took steps to privatize various federal programs, including low-cost housing, prisons, and hospitals. Reassigning government programs to the private sector

> **DID YOU KNOW . . .**
> That local governments, which can be created as well as abolished by their state, have no independent existence according to the Constitution, unlike the state and national governments?

> **NEW FEDERALISM**
> A plan to limit the national government's power to regulate, as well as to restore power to state governments. Essentially, the new federalism was designed to give the states greater ability to decide for themselves how government revenues should be spent.

FIGURE 3–3

The Shift toward Central Government Spending

Before the Great Depression, local governments accounted for 60 percent of all government spending, with the federal government accounting for only 17 percent. By 1960, federal government spending was up to 64 percent, local governments accounted for only 19 percent, and the remainder was spent by state governments. The estimate for 1995 is that the federal government accounts for 66 percent and local governments for 15.5 percent.

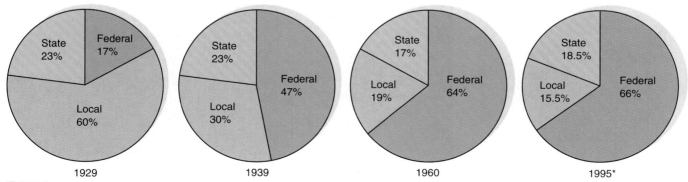

*Estimated
SOURCE: U.S. Department of Commerce, Bureau of the Census, *Government Finances* (Washington, D.C.: U.S. Government Printing Office, 1994).

seemed to go well beyond the new federalism. But even with more traditional shifting of money to states, analysis shows that the new federalism was probably more talk than action. The politics behind this inaction are relatively straightforward.

Take the case of the revenue-sharing program, in which the federal government simply gave back to the state and local governments a certain portion of federal taxes. This process generated specific constituencies among governments, but not among voters. Consequently, there were no well-organized groups of people lobbying Congress to increase revenue sharing. So, when the federal government budget continued to be in the red in the 1980s, it was relatively easy for the members of Congress to let the program die. Also, under the Reagan, Bush, and Clinton administrations, the number of **federal mandates** to the states in the areas of health, pollution control, and welfare increased dramatically, a topic to which we return later in this chapter.

FEDERAL MANDATE
A requirement in federal legislation that forces states and municipalities to comply with certain rules.

FISCAL FEDERALISM: FEDERAL GRANTS

Today, the national government collects over 60 percent of all tax dollars. As part of our system of cooperative federalism, the national government gives back to the states (and local governments) a significant amount—an estimated $245 billion in fiscal year 1996. Federal grants of money are one way that the Tenth Amendment to the U.S. Constitution can be bridged. In other words, even when the activity at hand is clearly reserved to the states because the involved powers are *not* delegated to the federal government, the federal government can still influence those activities through its award of federal grants.

Currently there are two predominant methods by which the national government returns nationally collected tax dollars to state and local governments: categorical grants-in-aid and block grants.

Under cooperative federalism, the federal and the state governments attempt to solve society's problems together. This mass transportation project is being jointly undertaken by the Massachusetts Bay Transportation Authority and the U.S. Department of Transportation. In other words, there is joint funding for a project that will help solve a problem in a specific geographic location.

Categorical Grants-in-Aid

Grants, usually called grants-in-aid, from the national government to the states occurred even before the ratification of the Constitution. Some students reading this book may be attending a land-grant college. These are state universities that were built with the proceeds from the sale of land grants given by the national government to the states. Cash grants-in-aid started in 1808, when Congress gave money to the states to pay for the state militia. It was not until the twentieth century that the federal grants-in-aid program became significant, however. The major growth began in the 1960s, when the dollar amount of grants-in-aid quadrupled.

The major category of grants-in-aid to the states is labeled **categorical grants-in-aid** because these grants are used for specific programs. Currently, there are over four hundred categories for these types of grants. The restrictions and regulations that accompany categorical grants-in-aid started to mushroom during the administration of Franklin D. Roosevelt (1933–1945). The number and scope of the categorical grants also expanded further as part of the Great Society programs of President Lyndon Johnson (1963–1969). Grants became available in the fields of education, pollution control, conservation, recreation, and highway construction and maintenance.

For some of the categorical grant programs, the state and local governments must put up a share of the money, usually called **matching funds.** For other types of programs, the funds are awarded according to a formula that takes into account the relative wealth of the state, a process known as **equalization.** As you can see in Figure 3–4, federal grants-in-aid grew rapidly during the Nixon and Ford administrations, as well as during the Carter administration. The rate of growth slowed considerably during the Reagan administration, only to speed up again under Presidents Bush and Clinton.

CATEGORICAL GRANTS-IN-AID
Federal grants-in-aid to states or local governments that are for very specific programs or projects.

MATCHING FUNDS
For many categorical grant programs, money with which the state must "match" the federal funds. Some programs only require the state to raise 10 percent of the funds, whereas others approach an even share.

EQUALIZATION
A method for adjusting the amount of money that a state must put up to receive federal funds. The formula used takes into account the wealth of the state or its ability to tax its citizens.

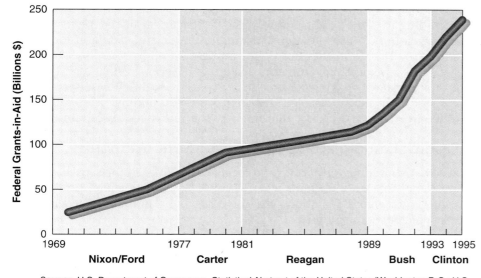

FIGURE 3–4

Federal Grants-in-Aid

SOURCE: U.S. Department of Commerce, *Statistical Abstract of the United States* (Washington D.C.: U.S. Government Printing Office, 1994). Data for 1995 are projected.

BLOCK GRANTS
Federal programs that provide funding to the state and local governments for general functional areas, such as criminal justice or mental-health programs.

Block Grants

As part of the new federalism, governors and mayors succeeded in convincing Washington that fewer restrictions should be placed on the grants-in-aid. No state or local official ever liked all of the strings attached to myriad grants-in-aid. The solution was to group a number of categorical grants under one broad purpose. Thus, the **block grant** was born in 1966 in the field of health. Out of the numerous block grants that were proposed from 1966 until the election of Ronald Reagan in 1980, only five were actually legislated. At the Reagan administration's urging, Congress increased the number to nine. By the beginning of the 1990s, such block grants accounted for over 10 percent of all federal aid programs.

Governors and mayors have generally preferred block grants because they give the states more flexibility in how the money is spent. Congress, however, generally has preferred categorical grants so that the expenditures are targeted according to congressional priorities, including programs for disadvantaged groups and individuals. Governors and state legislators argue that the people and governments in the states know best how to serve their constituents.

With the Republican sweep of Congress in the 1994 elections, block grants became the center of attention again. Republicans proposed reforming welfare and a number of other federal programs by transforming the categorical grants-in-aid to block grants and transferring more of the policymaking authority to the states. Many governors praised these proposals for vesting more power in the states and at the same time reducing the burden of federal bureaucracy. Others, however, cautioned that a completely decentralized system would mean that individuals with the same needs could receive quite different treatment and benefits depending on their state of residence. Whether the movement to increase block grants continues probably will depend on the degree to which Republicans maintain their control of Congress and the legislatures in many states.

FEDERAL MANDATES

According to some political observers, the remainder of the 1990s will see an increasing conflict between Washington, D.C., and state and local governments. This conflict concerns the burden placed by *federal mandates* on state and municipal governments. Examples of recent federal mandates are minimum water purity requirements for specific localities; requirements for access by physically disabled persons to public buildings, sidewalks, and other areas; and mandatory minimum prison sentences for certain crimes.

Preemption of Federal Laws over State Authority

Federal mandates *preempt* state and local laws or rules in the sense that congressional legislation prevails when it conflicts with state and local laws or regulations. Figure 3–5 shows the increase in the number of federal laws that preempt state authority.

Some of the Costs of Federal Mandates

No accurate analysis exists of the overall costs to state and local governments incurred as a result of federal mandates. Certain mandates, however, clearly

FIGURE 3–5

Federal Laws That Preempt State Laws

This graph shows the number of federal laws that preempt state authority. As you can see, the greatest growth in federal preemption is in laws regulating the environmental, health, or safety areas. Laws affecting commerce, energy, labor, and transportation run a close second.

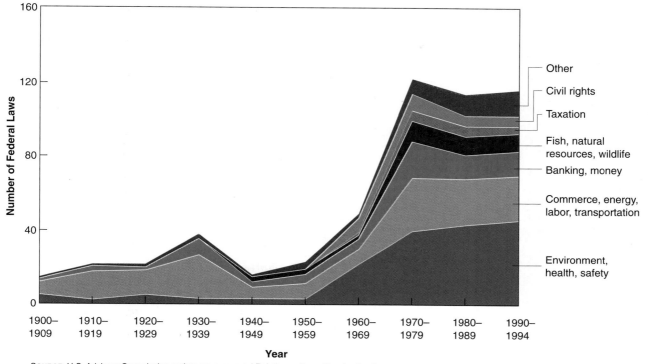

SOURCE: U.S. Advisory Commission on Intergovernmental Relations, plus authors' estimates.

are very costly. One mandate involves eligibility for Medicaid. Medicaid is the federally subsidized, state-run health-care program for low-income Americans. The estimated cost of the program for the states is $60 billion in 1995. It is difficult to obtain cost estimates for federal mandates, but some researchers have made an attempt. The National Association of Towns and Townships estimated that in fiscal year 1993, federal mandates cost taxpayers in cities more than $6.5 billion. In Table 3–2, you see projected total costs for unfunded federal mandates from 1994 through 1998.

One of the major "planks" in the Republican platform of 1994 was a promise to end unfunded mandates to state and local governments. By March 1995, the Republican-controlled 104th Congress had indeed succeeded in passing a bill to regulate the use of such federal mandates. The bill requires the Congressional Budget Office (CBO) to prepare cost estimates for any new mandate that would impose more than $50 million in costs on state and local governments or more than $100 million on the private sector. On the basis of CBO estimates, a member of Congress may make a point of order challenging the mandate.

On close analysis, however, the 1995 legislation was mostly symbolic; it accomplished little actual change in the use of unfunded federal mandates.

TABLE 3–2

The Projected Cost of Federal Mandates to the States through 1998

MANDATE	FISCAL YEARS 1994–1998 PROJECTED TOTAL COSTS (IN BILLIONS OF DOLLARS)
Underground storage tank regulations	1.041
Clean Water Act/wetlands	29.303
Clean Air Act	3.652
Solid waste disposal	5.476
Safe Drinking Water Act	8.644
Asbestos removal	.747
Lead-based paint	1.628
Endangered species	.189
Americans with Disabilities Act	2.196
Fair Labor Standards Act*	1.122
TOTAL	53.998

*Exempt employee & other costs.
SOURCE: National Association of Towns and Townships.

For example, a congressional point of order can be overridden by a simple majority vote—rather than the larger majority (such as three-fifths) proposed by several legislators. Furthermore, although the Republicans had sought to repeal previously legislated mandates dealing with such matters as civil rights and discrimination, the compromise bill that President Clinton signed exempts these matters. The act also exempts legislation concerning such issues as constitutional rights, voting rights, and national security. In short, the act exempts the matters that account for many of the unfunded mandates imposed on state and local governments during the last decade.

FEDERALISM: UNFINISHED WORK

Catastrophic events in the United States emphasize the relationship between state governments and the national government. Los Angeles experienced massive riots in the spring of 1992. That summer, southern Florida sustained $30 billion in damages inflicted by Hurricane Andrew. Midwestern residents experienced widespread losses because of flooding in the summer of 1993, and heavy damages were sustained in the Los Angeles earthquake in January 1994. In the face of catastrophic events, state and local governments argue that they have insufficient resources to meet the needs of the affected areas. Should the federal government step in?

Most observers seem to argue in favor of such federal funding for natural disasters, but others point out that the federal government budget deficit is hundreds of billions of dollars a year. In an attempt to mitigate the fiscal problems facing the federal government, lawmakers in Washington, D.C., have reduced the rate of growth of funding to the states while at the same time increasing federal control over states' affairs. In essence, Washington, D.C., has been creating more social programs but imposing the costs directly on the states. After the 1994 elections, Republicans in Congress attempted to reverse this trend by enacting legislation regulating the use of unfunded federal mandates.

At both the state and local levels, relations with the federal government are often acrimonious and may continue to be so. There is even a growing acrimony between local governments and their state capitals. The issue concerns state mandates that require local governments to undertake certain actions, such as spending a specified amount on certain types of welfare recipients.

The financial issue is perhaps the most important issue in the unfinished work of federalism. Increasingly, attempts by one level of government to force another level of government to pay directly for such social programs will create conflict.

GETTING INVOLVED
Writing Letters to the Editor

Just about every day an issue concerning federalism is discussed in the media. Advocates of decentralization—a shift of power from federal to state or local governments—argue that we must recognize the rights of states to design their own destinies and master their own fates. Advocates of centralization—more power to the national government—see the shift in power under decentralization as undermining the national purpose, common interests, and responsibilities that bind us together in pursuit of national goals.

The big question is how much the national government should do for the people. Is it within the power of the national government to decide what the law should be on abortion? Before 1973, each state set its own laws without interference from the national government. Who should be responsible for the homeless? Should the national government subsidize state and local efforts to help them?

You may have valid, important points to make on these or other issues. One of the best ways to make your point is by writing an effective letter to the editor of your local newspaper (or even to a national newspaper such as the *New York Times*). First, you should familiarize yourself with the kinds of letters that are accepted by the newspapers to which you want to write. Then, follow these rules for writing an effective letter:

1. Use a typewriter, and double-space the lines. If possible, use a word processor with a spelling checker and grammar checker.
2. Your lead topic sentence should be short, to the point, and powerful.
3. Keep your thoughts on target—choose only one topic to discuss in your letter. Make sure it is newsworthy and timely.
4. Make sure your letters are concise; never let your letter exceed a page and a half in length (double-spaced and typewritten).
5. If you know that facts were misstated or left out in current news stories about your topic, supply the facts. The public wants to know.
6. Don't be afraid to express moral judgments. You can go a long way by appealing to the readers' sense of justice.
7. Personalize the letter by bringing in your own experiences.
8. With appropriate changes, send your letter to the editors of more than one newspaper or magazine. Make sure, however, that the letters are not exactly the same.
9. Sign your letter, and give your address and your telephone number. If your letter is not published, try again. Eventually, one will be.

KEY TERMS

block grant   90

categorical grant-in-aid   89

commerce clause   81

concurrent majority   82

concurrent powers   75

confederal system   68

cooperative federalism   86

dual federalism   84

economic regulation   84

elastic clause   72

equalization   89

extradite   77

federal mandate   88

federal system   68

full faith and credit clause   76

horizontal federalism   76

injunction   81

interposition   82

interstate compact   77

matching funds   89

necessary and proper
    clause   72

new federalism   87

nullification   82

police power   74

privileges and immunities   77

resulting powers   72

secession   82

supremacy clause   78

unitary system   68

 CHAPTER SUMMARY

1. There are three basic models for ordering relations between central governments and local units: (a) a unitary system, (b) a confederal system, and (c) a federal system. A unitary system, such as in France, is one in which the national government has ultimate authority. This system is the most common. A confederal system is a league of independent states, each state having essentially sovereign powers. The central government handles only matters of common concern that have been expressly delegated to it by member states. Somewhere between the unitary and the confederal forms of government lies the federal system. In a federal system, authority is divided between the central government and the regional, or subdivisional, governments.

2. Federalism is probably the best arrangement in large countries because of their size and consequent regional differences and political subcultures. A division of power between local and national governments brings government closer to the people and allows government to meet the local needs of its citizens. State governments in the United States have also served as testing grounds for future national leaders and new initiatives.

3. The Constitution expressly delegated certain powers to the national government in Article I, Section 8. In addition to these expressed powers, the national government has implied and inherent powers. Implied powers are those that are reasonably necessary to carry

out the powers expressly delegated to the national government. Inherent powers are those held by the national government by virtue of its being a sovereign state with the right to preserve itself.

4. The Tenth Amendment to the Constitution states that powers not delegated to the United States by the Constitution, nor prohibited by it to the states, are reserved to the states, or to the people. In certain areas, the Constitution provides for concurrent powers, which are powers that are held jointly by the national and state governments. The classic example of a concurrent power is the power to tax.

5. The three most important clauses in the Constitution relating to horizontal federalism require that (a) each state give full faith and credit to every other state's public acts, records, and judicial proceedings; (b) each state extend to every other state's citizens the privileges and immunities of its own citizens; and (c) each state agree to return persons who are fleeing from justice to another state back to their home state when requested to do so.

6. The supremacy clause of the Constitution states that the Constitution, congressional laws, and national treaties are the supreme law of the land. States cannot use their reserved or concurrent powers to override national policies.

7. *McCulloch v. Maryland* (1819) enhanced the implied power of the federal government through Chief

Justice John Marshall's broad interpretation of the "necessary and proper" clause of Article I of the Constitution.

8. *Gibbons v. Ogden* (1824) enhanced and consolidated national power over commerce. Chief Justice Marshall interpreted the commerce clause of the Constitution broadly and held that the commerce power was complete in itself, with no limitations other than those found specifically in the Constitution. The regulation of commerce became one of the major issues in federal-state relations.

9. At the heart of the controversy that led to the Civil War was the issue of national government supremacy versus the rights of the separate states. The notion of nullification eventually led to the secession of the Confederate states from the Union. But the effect of the South's desire for increased states' rights and the subsequent Civil War was an increase in the political power of the national government.

10. In dual federalism, each of the states and the federal government remain supreme within their own spheres. The era since the Great Depression has sometimes been labeled as one of cooperative federalism, in which states and the national government cooperate in solving complex common problems. Others view it as the beginning of an era of national supremacy. Another phase of federalism was labeled the *new federalism* by President Nixon and was revived by President Reagan. The goal of the new federalism was to decentralize federal programs, giving more responsibility to the states.

11. There are basically two separate methods by which the national government returns nationally collected tax dollars to state and local governments: categorical grants-in-aid and block grants.

12. Federal government mandates have placed a heavy burden on state and local governments, which do not always have sufficient resources to pay the costs incurred by implementing the mandates.

 ## QUESTIONS FOR REVIEW AND DISCUSSION

1. The Advisory Commission on Inter-governmental Relations (ACIR) has, among other things, recommended that Congress and the states consider a constitutional amendment that would give two-thirds of the states the power to declare null and void an act of Congress. If such an amendment were passed, what might be some of the results?

2. At the time of the framing of the Constitution, state governments existed as sovereign political units. All but Rhode Island sent delegates to the Constitutional Convention. Does this mean that the state governments formally helped to create the Constitution? The Constitution was ratified through ratification conventions composed of citizens of each state. Does this therefore mean that the approval of the Constitution was made by, and rests with, the people?

3. "The federal government, because it is more efficient, can collect taxes more easily than can the combination of all fifty state governments. Therefore, the federal government should do so and remit taxes to the states in the form of revenue sharing." Do you agree with this statement? Why or why not?

4. How would our system of government differ if there were no division of powers between the national government and the states?

5. Population has been shifting from the colder northern states to the warmer southern and western states. Why does this population movement necessarily result in a regional conflict within the national government?

 ## LOGGING ON: FEDERALISM

A federalism-related topic that is probably of interest to you, as a student, is that of education. For a discussion of educational policy, there is a mailing list you may want to subscribe to called EDPOLYAR. For more information, access

glass@asu.edu

Education may also be of particular interest to you, as a computer user, because computers and computer networks will have a huge impact on the way we teach and learn in the future. One example of a pioneer in education is Cynthia Denton, who uses her personal computer in Hobson, Montana, to teach students in rural locations. For more information on her project, you can contact her at

cynthia@bigsky.dillon.mt.us

There is a mailing list for those of you who are interested in the fairness of state and federal government programs. To subscribe, contact

fairness-request@mainstream.com

Perhaps you are looking for discussions on various civil rights issues and how federal and state governments do and should play a role in them. If so, you may want to investigate

clari.news.issues.civil rights

There are even discussion groups out there for the most radical groups. For discussions of what society would be like without rulers and government, access

alt.society.anarchy

Or for those of you who are fed up with government and are planning to overthrow the existing system, here is a source for discussion and helpful tips on how to carry out your revolution:

alt.society.revolution

SELECTED REFERENCES

Beer, Samuel H. *To Make a Nation: The Rediscovery of American Federalism.* Cambridge, Mass.: Harvard University Press, 1993. This study of the purpose of American federalism begins with European political thought. The author discusses the originality of American federalism in both theory and practice. He contrasts the nation-centered federalism of the Constitution's framers and the state-centered federalism of their opponents.

Bensel, Richard F. *Yankee Leviathan: The Origins of Central State Authority.* New York: Cambridge University Press, 1990. In this analysis of state formation, Bensel looks closely at the changes in political structure caused by the Civil War.

Fix, Michael, and Daphne A. Kenyon, eds. *Coping with Mandates: What Are the Alternatives?* Lanham, Md.: University Press of America, 1990. This excellent examination of the mandates issue focuses on the history of mandates and their relationship to policy goals, the burden that mandates place on state and local governments, and the potential of alternative approaches to the mandates issue.

Hamilton, Alexander, John Jay, and James Madison. *The Federalist: A Collection of Essays Written in Favor of the New Constitution.* Edited by George W. Carey and James McClellan. Dubuque, Ia.: Kendall/Hunt, 1990. This student-oriented edition makes these classic essays accessible to this generation and includes an introduction, analytical notes, a glossary, and an index.

Ottosen, Garry K. *Making American Government Work: A Proposal to Reinvigorate Federalism.* Lanham, Md.: University Press of America, 1992. The author contends that the divided responsibilities and fragmented power between the states and the national government have made American government unworkable. He believes that the solution to this problem is to reinvigorate federalism. He examines the critical issue of competition between and among the states.

Pickvance, C. G., and E. Preteceille. *State and Locality: A Comparative Perspective on State Restructuring.* Irvington, N.Y.: Columbia University Press, 1991. The authors offer an insightful comparative study of the relationship between central and local governments in several nations, including the United States.

Rich, Michael J. *Federal Policymaking and the Poor: National Goods, Local Choices, and Distributional Outcomes.* Princeton, N.J.: Princeton University Press, 1993. This is a study of the impact of federal programs designed to help needy people. There is an extensive analysis of the Community Development Block Grant Program, the principal federal program for aiding cities. The author points out that the redistributive power of federal programs depends on choices made by local government officials.

Riker, William H. *Federalism.* Boston: Little, Brown, 1964. This classic discussion of federalism offers a highly critical account of the American version of this form of government.

Zimmerman, Joseph F. *Federal Preemption: The Silent Revolution.* Ames, Ia.: Iowa State University Press, 1991. A consultant to the U.S. Advisory Commission on Intergovernmental Relations analyzes federal preemption. Included is a chapter on the role of the federal courts in adjudicating preemption disputes. The author points to the many problems in federal preemption and argues that preemption really means mandates on state and local governments without compensation.

PART TWO

Civil Rights and Liberties

4 Civil Liberties

 CHAPTER OUTLINE

WHAT IF . . .
The *Miranda* Rules Were Eliminated?

Since the mid-1960s, the criminal justice process in the United States has been governed largely by what have come to be known as the *Miranda* rules. These rules, established by a 1966 Supreme Court decision, hold that criminal suspects must be treated in such a manner as to decrease the probability that they will be convicted wrongly of crimes they did not commit. The *Miranda* rules include four warnings and a waiver. Before being interrogated, a person in police custody must be informed of the following: (1) The person has the right to remain silent. (2) Anything the person says can be used against him or her in court. (3) The person has the right to an attorney. (4) If the person cannot afford an attorney but wants one, then one will be appointed. The person in custody must waive these rights before any statement he or she makes during the interrogation will be admitted as evidence.

There are some exceptions to the *Miranda* rules. For instance, a confession will be admitted as evidence, even if it is given before a suspect is informed of his or her rights, if the suspect also confesses after being informed. A probationer's confession to his or her probation officer without the warnings is admissible. If the warnings are given, a confession will be admitted, even if the police lie to the suspect's lawyer or fail to tell the suspect that the lawyer wants to see him or her.

What might happen if the *Miranda* rules were eliminated? It is very difficult to know for certain. But some outcomes can be guessed at from the American experience with criminal justice pro-

cedures that were in general use before the introduction of the *Miranda* rules. It was once common, and might be again, for suspects to be subjected to the "third degree," which ranged from mild psychological pressure to violent physical and mental torture. The past record includes both allegations and proved instances of beatings, threats of severe punishment, denial of access to legal counsel, incarceration without formal charges being filed, sleep deprivation, suspects' being kept in handcuffs (sometimes with their arms wrapped around radiators), and other violations of what we today regard as the rights of criminal suspects. These actions and worse ones are common in other countries today that do not have *Miranda*-type protections for their citizens.

If you were arrested in a future America that did not have the *Miranda* rules, what kind of treatment could you expect? The odds are that many, if not most, police officers and prosecutors would behave decently and with respect for your constitutional rights. But without a doubt there would be a strong incentive for law-enforcement officers to go out of their way to get a conviction. If you were ensnared in such a system, whether you were guilty or not, any of the following might happen. Depending on the seriousness of the offense with which you were charged, you might be arrested in the middle of the night without being told why. Your arms might be handcuffed or tied very uncomfortably, and you would be compelled to accompany the arresting officers to the police station. Once in detention,

you probably would not have the automatic right to make a telephone call to a lawyer who could give you legal advice or to contact your family to let them know what had happened to you.

There are reasons to expect that many of the excesses of the past might not be repeated if the *Miranda* rules were repealed. Educational levels among police officials are higher than before, and many are college-trained in the social sciences and related disciplines that encourage sensitivity to human rights. Furthermore, experienced law-enforcement officers would have become used to *Miranda*-governed procedures and trained in the proper treatment of criminal suspects, and those habits would take some time to break.

The incidents of police brutality that are reported today indicate that methods of interrogation employed in the pre-*Miranda* past might be used again, however. Also, most public opinion polls indicate a hardening of popular attitudes toward crime and alleged criminals, and many Americans are demanding harsher treatment of drug dealers, rapists, child pornographers, and murderers. In such a climate, police and the public might not make a clear distinction between those who actually are guilty of such offenses and those who may be merely suspected of committing crimes.

---

1. Which groups would fare worse in the United States without the *Miranda* rules, and why?
2. What are the costs to society of retaining the *Miranda* rules?

The right to be informed of your rights if you are ever arrested (as discussed in this chapter's opening *What If . . .*) is so well known that it shows up in movies and television series constantly. Americans have many other rights that relate to individual freedom. Most Americans believe that they have more individual freedom than virtually any other people on earth. For the most part, this opinion is accurate. The freedoms that we take for granted—religion, speech, press, and assembly—are relatively unknown in some parts of the world. In some nations today, citizens have little chance of living without government harassment if they choose to criticize openly, through speech or print, the government or its actions. Indeed, if the United States suddenly had the same rules, laws, and procedures about verbal and printed expression that exist in certain other countries, American jails would be filled overnight with transgressors.

CIVIL LIBERTIES AND THE FEAR OF GOVERNMENT

Without government, people live in a state of anarchy. With unbridled government, men and women may end up living in a state of tyranny. The framers of the Constitution wanted neither extreme. As was pointed out in Chapter 2, the Declaration of Independence was based on the idea of natural rights. These are rights discoverable in nature and history, according to such philosophers as John Locke and John Dickinson, who wrote that natural rights "are born with us; exist with us; and cannot be taken away from us by any human power."[1]

Linked directly to the strong prerevolutionary sentiment for natural rights was the notion that a right was first and foremost a *limitation* on any government's ruling power. To obtain ratification of the Constitution by the necessary nine states, the Federalists had to deal with the colonists' fears of a too-powerful national government. The **Bill of Rights** was the result. These first ten amendments to the U.S. Constitution were passed by Congress on September 25, 1789, and ratified by three-fourths of the states by December 15, 1791. When we speak of civil liberties in the United States, we are referring mostly to the specific limitations on government outlined in the Bill of Rights (although there are such limitations in the Constitution's main text itself, including the prohibition against *ex post facto* laws and others found in Section 9 of Article I).

Here we must make a distinction between the technical definitions of *civil liberties* and *civil rights*. **Civil liberties** represent something that the government *cannot do,* such as abridge a freedom by, for example, taking away someone's freedom of speech. In contrast, **civil rights** represent something that the government *must do,* such as guaranteeing to individuals a power or privilege. The right to vote is one such civil right. In this chapter we will examine civil liberties, and in the following chapter, civil rights.

THE BILL OF RIGHTS

The First Amendment to the Constitution is, for many, the most significant part of the Bill of Rights, as well as the mainstay of the statement in the

BILL OF RIGHTS
The first ten amendments to the U.S. Constitution. They contain a listing of the freedoms that a person enjoys and that cannot be infringed upon by the government, such as the freedoms of speech, press, and religion.

CIVIL LIBERTIES
Those personal freedoms that are protected for all individuals and generally that deal with individual freedom. Civil liberties typically involve restraining the government's actions against individuals.

CIVIL RIGHTS
Those powers or privileges that are guaranteed to individuals or protected groups and that are protected from arbitrary removal by government or by individuals.

---

1. As quoted in Bernard Bailyn, *The Ideological Origins of the American Revolution* (Cambridge, Mass.: Harvard University Press, 1967), p. 77.

That one of the proposed initial constitutional amendments—"No State shall infringe the equal rights of conscience, nor the freedom of speech, nor of the press, nor of the right of trial by jury in criminal cases"—was never sent to the states for approval because the states' rights advocates in the First Congress defeated this proposal?

Declaration of Independence that all people should be able to enjoy life, liberty, and the pursuit of happiness. It is in the First Amendment that our basic freedoms of religion, speech, the press, assembly, and the right of petition are set forth. The first part of this chapter examines each of these freedoms in detail.

The Nationalization of the Bill of Rights

Most citizens do not realize that, as originally presented, the Bill of Rights limited only the power of the national government, not that of the states. In other words, a citizen in the state of Virginia in 1795 could not sue successfully in federal court against a law passed in Virginia that violated one of the amendments in the Bill of Rights. Each state had (and still has) its own constitution with its own bill of rights.

Whereas the states' bills of rights were similar to the national one, there were some differences, and perhaps more important, each state's judicial system interpreted the rights differently. A citizen in one state effectively had a different set of civil rights from a citizen in another state. It was not until the Fourteenth Amendment was ratified in 1868 that our Constitution explicitly guaranteed to everyone due process of the law. Section 1 of that amendment provides that

> [n]o State shall make or enforce any law which shall abridge the privileges or immunities of citizens of the United States; nor shall any State deprive any person of life, liberty, or property, without due process of law; nor deny to any person within its jurisdiction the equal protection of the laws.

Section 5 of the amendment explicitly gives Congress the power to enforce by appropriate legislation the provisions of the amendment. Note the use of the terms *citizen* and *person*. *Citizens* have political rights, such as voting and running for office. But no *person*, citizen or alien, can be denied civil liberties (speech, press, and religion) nor have his or her property taken without equal recourse to the legal system.[2]

The Incorporation Issue

The Fourteenth Amendment was passed as a standard that would guarantee both due process and equal protection under the laws for all persons. The courts did not agree. Many jurists still believed, as John Marshall stated in the *Barron v. Mayor of Baltimore* decision, that the states were "distinct governments framed by different persons and for different purposes."[3] Marshall's statement in the *Barron* decision was plain: the Bill of Rights limits only the national government and not the state governments. The *Barron* decision is still the general rule of law. We shall see, though, that it has been modified greatly in practice through later interpretations of the Fourteenth Amendment.

In 1873, in the *Slaughter-House Cases*, the U.S. Supreme Court upheld the principle of **dual citizenship**, arguing that to deprive states of their author-

DUAL CITIZENSHIP
The condition of being a citizen of two sovereign political units; being a citizen of both a state and the nation.

2. Section 2 of the amendment, which concerns voting rights, contains the first use in the Constitution of the word *male*. At the time of the amendment's adoption, women were not allowed to vote.
3. 7 Peters 243 (1833).

ity and their identity would "fetter and degrade state governments."[4] The Court refused to apply the guarantees of the Bill of Rights to the states under the Fourteenth Amendment's privileges and immunities clause. A Louisiana law prohibited livestock yards and slaughterhouses within New Orleans, except for the Crescent City Company's operation. Butchers and others adversely affected sought to have the law declared void, in part under the Fourteenth Amendment. The Supreme Court held that the Fourteenth Amendment creates two types of citizenship—federal and state—and that the privileges and immunities clause extends federal constitutional protection only to the privileges and immunities of national citizenship. The Court reasoned that the Louisiana statute did not infringe on any of the privileges and immunities of national citizenship.

Only gradually, and never completely, did the Supreme Court accept the **incorporation theory**—that no state could act in violation of the U.S. Bill of Rights. By holding that those rights are protected against actions of the states, as well as of the national government, the Court has made their meanings uniform. Table 4–1 shows the rights that the Court has incorporated into the Fourteenth Amendment and the case in which it first applied each protection. The practical implementation of the Fourteenth Amendment has taken place relatively slowly.

The last hundred years of Supreme Court decisions have bound the fifty states to accept for their respective citizens most of the guarantees that are contained in the U.S. Bill of Rights. The exceptions usually have involved

INCORPORATION THEORY
The view that most of the protections of the Bill of Rights are incorporated into the Fourteenth Amendment's protection against state governments.

---

4. 16 Wall 36 (1873).

TABLE 4–1   ■

Incorporating the Bill of Rights into the Fourteenth Amendment

YEAR	ISSUE	AMENDMENT INVOLVED	COURT CASE
1925	Freedom of speech	I	*Gitlow v. New York*, 268 U.S. 652.
1931	Freedom of the press	I	*Near v. Minnesota*, 283 U.S. 697.
1932	Right to a lawyer in capital punishment cases	VI	*Powell v. Alabama*, 287 U.S. 45.
1937	Freedom of assembly and right to petition	I	*De Jonge v. Oregon*, 299 U.S. 353.
1940	Freedom of religion	I	*Cantwell v. Connecticut*, 310 U.S. 296.
1947	Separation of state and church	I	*Everson v. Board of Education*, 330 U.S. 1.
1948	Right to a public trial	VI	*In re Oliver*, 333 U.S. 257.
1949	No unreasonable searches and seizures	IV	*Wolf v. Colorado*, 338 U.S. 25.
1961	Exclusionary rule	IV	*Mapp v. Ohio*, 367 U.S. 643.
1962	No cruel and unusual punishment	VIII	*Robinson v. California*, 370 U.S. 660.
1963	Right to a lawyer in all criminal felony cases	VI	*Gideon v. Wainwright*, 372 U.S. 335.
1964	No compulsory self-incrimination	V	*Malloy v. Hogan*, 378 U.S. 1.
1965	Right to privacy	I	*Griswold v. Connecticut*, 381 U.S. 479.
1966	Right to an impartial jury	VI	*Parker v. Gladden*, 385 U.S. 363.
1967	Right to a speedy trial	VI	*Klopfer v. North Carolina*, 386 U.S. 213.
1969	No double jeopardy	V	*Benton v. Maryland*, 395 U.S. 784.

the right to bear arms, the right to refuse to quarter soldiers, and the right to a grand jury hearing. Thus, for all intents and purposes, the national Bill of Rights must be applied uniformly by individual state governments to their laws and practices.

Just as judicial interpretation of the Fourteenth Amendment required more than a hundred years to "nationalize" the Bill of Rights, judicial interpretation has shaped the true nature of those rights as they apply to individuals in the United States. As we shall see in the following pages, there have been numerous conflicts over the meaning of such simple phrases as *freedom of the press* and *freedom of religion*. To understand what freedoms we actually have, we have to examine some of those conflicts.

FREEDOM OF RELIGION

In the United States, freedom of religion consists of two principal precepts as they are presented in the First Amendment. The first has to do with the separation of church and state, and the second guarantees the free exercise of religion.

The Separation of Church and State

ESTABLISHMENT CLAUSE
The part of the First Amendment prohibiting the establishment of a church officially supported by the national government. It is applied to questions of state and local government aid to religious organizations and schools, questions of the legality of allowing or requiring school prayers, and questions of the teaching of evolution versus fundamentalist theories of creation.

The First Amendment to the Constitution states, in part, that "Congress shall make no law respecting an establishment of religion." In the words of President Jefferson, the **establishment clause** was designed to create a "wall of separation of Church and State."[5] Perhaps Jefferson was thinking about the religious intolerance that characterized the first colonies. Although

_____

5. The impenetrability of this wall has been called into question by a book that got a warm endorsement from President Bill Clinton. In *The Culture of Disbelief* (New York: Basic Books, 1993), Yale professor Stephen Carter argues that American law and politics have suffered by excluding religion from public discourse.

Fundamentalists Vicki Frost and her husband challenged certain textbooks as being too secular and violating their freedom of religion. Other people have argued that public schools cannot teach about religion because that would be a violation of the establishment clause.

many of the American colonies were founded by groups in pursuit of religious freedom, they were quite intolerant nonetheless of religious nonconformity within their own communities. Jefferson undoubtedly was also aware that state religions were the rule; among the original thirteen American colonies, nine of them had official religions.

As interpreted by the Supreme Court, the establishment clause in the First Amendment means at least the following:

> Neither a state nor the federal government can set up a church. Neither can pass laws which aid one religion, aid all religions, or prefer one religion over another. Neither can force nor influence a person to go to or to remain away from church against his will or force him to profess a belief or disbelief in any religion. No person can be punished for entertaining or professing religious beliefs or disbeliefs, for church attendance or nonattendance. No tax in any amount, large or small, can be levied to support any religious activities or institutions, whatever they may be called, or whatever form they may adopt to teach or practice religion. Neither a state nor the federal government can, openly or secretly, participate in the affairs of any religious organizations or groups and vice versa.[6]

The establishment clause covers all conflicts about such matters as the legality of allowing or requiring school prayers, the teaching of evolution versus fundamental theories of creation, and state and local government aid to religious organizations and schools.

The Issue of School Prayer.   Do the states have the right to promote religion in general, without making any attempt to establish a particular religion? That is the question in the issue of school prayer and was the precise question presented in 1962 in *Engel v. Vitale,* the so-called Regents' Prayer Case in New York.[7] The State Board of Regents of New York had suggested that a prayer be spoken aloud in the public schools at the beginning of each day. The recommended prayer was as follows:

> Almighty God, we acknowledge our dependence upon Thee,
> And we beg Thy blessings upon us, our parents, our teachers, and our Country.

Such a prayer was implemented in many New York public schools.

The parents of a number of students challenged the action of the regents, maintaining that it violated the establishment clause of the First Amendment. At trial, the parents lost. The Supreme Court, however, ruled that the regents' action was unconstitutional because "the constitutional prohibition against laws respecting an establishment of a religion must mean at least that in this country it is no part of the business of government to compose official prayers for any group of the American people to recite as part of a religious program carried on by any government."[8] The Court's conclusion was based in part on the "historical fact that governmentally established religions and religious persecutions go hand in hand."[9] In 1963, the Supreme Court outlawed daily readings of the Bible and recitation of the Lord's Prayer in public schools.[10]

---

6. *Everson v. Board of Education,* 330 U.S. 1 (1947).
7. 370 U.S. 421 (1962).
8. *Engel v. Vitale,* 421.
9. *Engel v. Vitale,* 421.
10. *Abington School District v. Schempp,* 374 U.S. 203 (1963).

Children pray in school. Such in-school prayer is in violation of Supreme Court rulings based on the First Amendment. A Supreme Court ruling does not necessarily carry with it a mechanism for enforcement everywhere in the United States, however.

Although the Supreme Court has ruled repeatedly against officially sponsored prayer and Bible-reading sessions in public schools, other means for bringing some form of religious expression into public education have been attempted. In 1983, the Tennessee legislature passed a bill requiring public school classes to begin each day with a minute of silence. Alabama also had a similar law. In 1985, the Supreme Court struck down as unconstitutional the Alabama law authorizing one minute of silence in all public schools for prayer or meditation. The majority of the Court concluded that because the law specifically endorsed prayer, it appeared to support religion.[11]

Recently, courts have dealt with cases involving prayer in public schools outside the classroom. The Supreme Court, in *Lee v. Weisman*, said that a prayer that had been made a part of graduation ceremonies violated the establishment clause.[12] In another case, *Jones v. Clear Creek Independent School District*, however, a U.S. circuit court of appeals concluded that a graduation prayer was allowable when requested by a majority of seniors.[13] In 1993, the Supreme Court decided not to hear an appeal in the *Jones* decision and, in *Lamb's Chapel v. Central Moriches Union Free School District*, held that the after-hours use of public school facilities by a church did not violate the establishment clause.[14] It is certainly possible that by the time you read this book, another school-prayer case will have reached the Supreme Court. Some states have reintroduced one or two minutes of silence at the beginning of each school day in order to allow students to pray. As of 1995, a number of states either had bills pending or had passed some type of school moment-of-silence legislation.

Forbidding the Teaching of Evolution.   Certain religious groups have attempted to forbid the teaching of evolution in public schools. One such law was passed in Arkansas, only to be struck down by the Supreme Court in the 1968 *Epperson v. Arkansas* case.[15] The Court held that the Arkansas legislation violated the establishment clause, for it imposed religious beliefs on students. The Arkansas legislature then passed a law requiring the teaching of the biblical story of the Creation alongside the teaching of evolution. In 1982, the Supreme Court declared this law unconstitutional.

Louisiana enacted a similar law—the Louisiana Balanced Treatment for Creation-Science and Evolution-Science in Public School Instruction Act. In 1987, the Supreme Court declared that this law was also unconstitutional, in part because it had as its primary purpose the promotion of a particular religious belief.[16]

Aid to Church-Related Schools.   Throughout the United States, all property owners except religious, educational, fraternal, literary, scientific, and similar nonprofit institutions must pay property taxes. A large part of the proceeds of such taxes goes to support public schools. But not all school-

---

11. *Wallace v. Jaffree*, 472 U.S. 38 (1985).
12. 112 S.Ct. 2649 (1992).
13. 977 F.2d 963 (1992).
14. 113 S.Ct. 2141 (1993).
15. 393 U.S. 97 (1968).
16. *Edwards v. Aguillard*, 482 U.S. 578 (1987).

age children attend public schools. Fully 12 percent attend private schools, of which 85 percent have religious affiliations. Numerous cases have reached the Supreme Court in which the Court has tried to draw a fine line between permissible public aid to students in church-related schools and impermissible public aid to religion.

It is at the elementary and secondary levels that these issues have arisen most often. In a series of cases, the Supreme Court has allowed states to use tax funds for lunches, textbooks, diagnostic services for speech and hearing problems, standardized tests, and transportation for students attending church-operated elementary and secondary schools.[17] In a number of cases, however, the Supreme Court has held state programs helping church-related schools to be unconstitutional. In *Lemon v. Kurtzman,* the Court ruled that direct state aid could not be used to subsidize religious instruction.[18] The Court in the *Lemon* case gave its most general statement on the constitutionality of government aid to religious schools, stating that the aid had to be secular in aim, that it could not have the primary effect of advancing or inhibiting religion, and that the government must avoid "an excessive entanglement with religion." All laws under the establishment clause are now subject to the three-part *Lemon* test. In other cases, the Court has denied state reimbursements to religious schools for field trips and for developing achievement tests.

The Free Exercise of Religious Beliefs

The First Amendment constrains Congress from prohibiting the free exercise of religion. Does this **free exercise clause** mean that no type of religious practice can be prohibited or restricted by government? Certainly, a person can hold any religious belief that he or she wants; or a person can have no religious belief. When, however, religious *practices* work against public policy and the public welfare, the government can act. For example, regardless of a child's or parent's religious beliefs, the government can require certain types of vaccinations. Similarly, public school students can be required to study from textbooks chosen by school authorities. The sale and use of marijuana for religious purposes has been held illegal, because a religion cannot make legal what would otherwise be illegal. Conducting religious rites that result in beheaded and gutted animals being left in public streets normally is not allowed.

The courts and lawmakers are constantly faced with a dilemma. On the one hand, no law may be made that requires someone to do something contrary to his or her religious beliefs or teachings, because this would interfere with the free exercise of religion. On the other hand, if certain individuals, because of their religious beliefs, are exempted from specific laws, then such exemptions might tend to favor religion and be contrary to the establishment clause. The original view of the Court was that although religious beliefs are protected by the law, acting on those beliefs may not be.

FREE EXERCISE CLAUSE
The provision of the First Amendment guaranteeing the free exercise of religion.

---

17. See *Everson v. Board of Education,* 330 U.S. 1 (1947); *Meek v. Pittenger,* 421 U.S. 349 (1975); and *Committee for Public Education v. Regan,* 444 U.S. 646 (1980).
18. 403 U.S. 602 (1971).

For instance, children of Jehovah's Witnesses are not required to say the Pledge of Allegiance at school,[19] but their parents cannot prevent them from accepting medical treatment (such as blood transfusions) if in fact their lives are in danger. The current view of the Court is that in all but a few situations, a state is free to require everyone to comply with a law that is generally valid. In other words, states can punish or deny benefits to people whose religious practices violate a law. In *Employment Division, Department of Human Resources of Oregon v. Smith,* the Court stated that a state can make exceptions to the establishment clause for religious practices, but the Constitution does not require it to do so.[20]

In November 1993, President Clinton signed the Religious Freedom Restoration Act, which requires that laws that infringe in any way on the free exercise of religion in public places be justified by a "compelling state interest." Some scholars have suggested that this act legislatively reverses the decision of the Supreme Court in *Smith.* In 1993, the Supreme Court unanimously found that a municipality could not ban animal sacrifices conducted as part of established religious practices.[21]

FREEDOM OF EXPRESSION

Perhaps the most frequently invoked freedom that Americans have is the right to free speech and a free press without government interference. These rights guarantee each person a right of free expression by all means of communication and ensure all persons a full discussion of public affairs. Each of us has the right to have our say, and all of us have the right to hear what others say. For the most part, Americans can criticize public officials and their actions without fear of reprisal or imprisonment by any branch of government.

Permitted Restrictions on Expression

At various times, restrictions on expression have been permitted. A description of several such restrictions follows.

Clear and Present Danger.   When a person's remarks present a clear and present danger to the peace or public order, they can be curtailed constitutionally. Justice Oliver Wendell Holmes used this reasoning in 1919 when examining the case of a socialist who had been convicted for violating the Espionage Act. Holmes stated:

> The question in every case is whether the words are used in such circumstances and are of such a nature as to create a *clear and present danger* that they will bring about the substantive evils that Congress has a right to prevent. It is a question of proximity and degree. [Emphasis added.][22]

Thus, according to the **clear and present danger test**, expression may be restricted if evidence exists that such expression would cause a condition,

CLEAR AND PRESENT DANGER TEST
The test proposed by Justice Holmes for determining when government may restrict free speech. Restrictions are permissible, he argued, only when speech provokes a "clear and present danger" to the public order.

19. *West Virginia State Board of Education v. Barnette,* 319 U.S. 624 (1943).
20. 494 U.S. 872 (1990).
21. *Church of Lukumi Babalu Aye v. Hialeah,* 113 S.Ct. 2217 (1993).
22. *Schenck v. United States,* 249 U.S. 47 (1919).

actual or imminent, that Congress has the power to prevent. Commenting on this test, Justice Louis D. Brandeis in 1920 said, "Correctly applied, it will reserve the right of free speech . . . from suppression by tyrannists, well-meaning majorities, and from abuse by irresponsible, fanatical minorities."[23] A related test is the **preferred-position test.** Only if the government is able to show that limitations on speech are absolutely necessary to avoid imminent, serious, and important evils are such limitations allowed. Another test is called the **sliding-scale test.** The courts must examine the facts of each individual case carefully before restricting expression.

The Supreme Court modified the clear and present danger test in the early 1950s. At the time, there was considerable tension between the United States and the Soviet Union. The Soviet Union's government was run by the Communist party. Twelve members of the American Communist party were convicted of violating a statute that made it a crime to conspire to teach, advocate, or organize the violent overthrow of any government in the United States. The Supreme Court affirmed the convictions, significantly modifying the clear and present danger test in the process. The Court applied a "grave and probable danger rule." Under this rule, "the gravity of the 'evil' discounted by its improbability, justifies such invasion of free speech as is necessary to avoid the danger." This rule gave much less protection to free speech than did the clear and present danger test.[24]

The Bad-Tendency Rule.   According to the **bad-tendency rule,** speech or other First Amendment freedoms may be curtailed if there is a possibility that such expression might lead to some "evil." In *Gitlow v. New York,* a member of a left-wing group was convicted of violating New York state's criminal anarchy statute when he published and distributed a pamphlet urging the violent overthrow of the U.S. government.[25] In its majority opinion, the Supreme Court held that although the First Amendment afforded protection against state incursions on freedom of expression, Gitlow could be punished legally in this particular instance because his expression would tend to bring about evils that the state had a right to prevent.

No Prior Restraint.   Restraining an activity before that activity has actually occurred is referred to as **prior restraint.** It involves censorship, as opposed to subsequent punishment. Prior restraint of expression would require, for example, a permit before a speech could be made, a newspaper published, or a movie or TV show exhibited. Most, if not all, Supreme Court justices have been especially critical of any governmental action that imposes prior restraint on expression:

> A prior restraint on expression comes to this Court with a "heavy presumption" against its constitutionality. . . . The government thus carries a heavy burden of showing justification for the enforcement of such a restraint.[26]

One of the most famous cases concerning prior restraint involved the so-called Pentagon Papers. On June 13, 1971, the *New York Times* carried its

---

PREFERRED-POSITION TEST
A court test used in determining the limits of free expression guaranteed by the First Amendment. Under this test, limitations on speech are permissible if they are necessary to avoid imminent, serious, and important evils.

SLIDING-SCALE TEST
A test that requires the courts to examine the facts of each individual case carefully before restricting expression.

BAD-TENDENCY RULE
A rule stating that speech or other First Amendment freedoms may be curtailed if there is a possibility that such expression might lead to some "evil."

PRIOR RESTRAINT
Restraining an action before the activity has actually occurred. It involves censorship, as opposed to subsequent punishment.

---

23. *Schaefer v. United States,* 251 U.S. 466 (1920).
24. *Dennis v. United States,* 341 U.S. 494 (1951).
25. 268 U.S. 652 (1925).
26. *Nebraska Press Association v. Stuart,* 427 U.S. 539 (1976). See also *Near v. Minnesota,* 283 U.S. 697 (1931).

first article about the forty-seven-volume, classified *U.S. Government History of American Policy in Vietnam from 1945 to 1967*. The *Washington Post* also began a similar series on the secret study, based on documents it had secured. The U.S. attorney general obtained a court order suspending the publication of these materials by both the *Times* and the *Post*. Both cases reached the Supreme Court within days, and the justices were deeply divided on the constitutional issues. Did Americans have the right to know (and the press the right to inform them) of information that the government claimed might endanger national security? Would such publication jeopardize U.S. national security in the long run? The Court ruled six to three in favor of the newspapers' right to publish the information.[27] This case affirmed the no prior restraint doctrine.

The Protection of Symbolic Speech

Symbolic Speech
Nonverbal expression of beliefs, which is given substantial protection by the courts.

Not all expression is in words or in writing. Gestures, movements, articles of clothing, and so on may be considered **symbolic**, or nonverbal, **speech.** Such speech is given substantial protection today by our courts. During the Vietnam War (1964–1973), when students around the country began wearing black armbands in protest, a Des Moines, Iowa, school administrator issued a regulation prohibiting students in the Des Moines school district from wearing them. The U.S. Supreme Court ruled that such a ban violated the free speech clause of the First Amendment. It reasoned that the school district was unable to show that wearing the black armbands had disrupted normal school activities. Furthermore, the school's ruling was discriminatory, as it selected certain forms of symbolic speech for banning. Lapel crosses and fraternity rings, for instance, symbolically speak of a person's affiliations, but these were not banned.[28]

In 1989, in *Texas v. Johnson,* the Supreme Court ruled that state laws that prohibited the burning of the American flag as part of a peaceful protest also violated the freedom of expression protected by the First Amendment. Congress responded by passing the Flag Protection Act of 1989, which was ruled unconstitutional by the Supreme Court in June 1990.[29] Congress and President Bush immediately pledged to work for a constitutional amendment to "protect our flag." More recently, courts in Ohio ruled that the Ku Klux Klan could erect a Klan cross, saying that "freedom of speech would be meaningless if it did not apply equally to all groups, popular and unpopular alike." Freedom of speech can also apply to group-sponsored events. In 1995, the Supreme Court held that forcing the organizers of Boston's St. Patrick's Day parade to include gays and lesbians violated the organizers' freedom of speech.

The Protection of Commercial Speech

Commercial Speech
Advertising statements, which have increasingly been given First Amendment protection.

Commercial speech is usually defined as advertising statements. Can advertisers use their First Amendment rights to prevent restrictions on the

---

27. *New York Times Company v. United States* and the *United States v. The Washington Post,* 403 U.S. 713 (1971).
28. *Tinker v. Des Moines School District,* 393 U.S. 503 (1969).
29. *United States v. Eichman,* 496 U.S. 310 (1990).

Mary Beth Tinker and her brother John display the armbands they wore to protest the Vietnam War. Their school principal tried to prevent them from wearing such bands while at school. The Supreme Court, however, ruled that the armbands constituted symbolic speech that was protected by the First Amendment. In a later case involving a principal's censorship of a school newspaper, however, the Supreme Court ruled that "school officials may impose reasonable restrictions on the speech of students." The Court noted that students' rights "are not automatically coextensive with the rights of adults in other settings."

content of commercial advertising? Until the 1970s, the Supreme Court held that such speech was not protected by the First Amendment. By the mid-1970s, however, more and more commercial speech was brought under First Amendment protection. According to Justice Harry A. Blackmun, "Advertising, however tasteless and excessive it sometimes may seem, is nonetheless dissemination of information as to who is producing and selling what product for what reason and at what price."[30] If consumers are to make more intelligent marketplace decisions, there must be a "free flow of commercial information," according to Blackmun and the Court. Thus, for example, the federal government cannot prohibit the mailing of unsolicited advertisements (so-called junk mail), a state cannot prohibit the advertising of drug prices by pharmacies, and a town cannot prohibit the use of "for sale" signs by sellers of homes.

Generally, the Court has considered a restriction on commercial speech valid as long as it (1) seeks to implement a substantial government interest, (2) directly advances that interest, and (3) goes no further than necessary to accomplish its objective. In 1993, the Court held that a Cincinnati law prohibiting the distribution of commercial handbills on public property, although allowing the installation of racks for newspapers, ran afoul of the First Amendment.[31] The city had asserted that the elimination of commercial handbills was necessary to maintain safety and improve the attractiveness of the city. The Court, however, said that such a ban placed too much importance on the distinction between commercial and noncommercial speech and that the distinction bore no relationship to the safety and attractiveness of the city.

---

30. *Virginia State Board of Pharmacy v. Virginia Citizens Consumer Council, Inc.,* 425 U.S. 748 (1976).
31. *City of Cincinnati v. Discovery Network, Inc.,* 113 S.Ct. 1505 (1993).

Nonadvertising "speech" by businesses has also achieved First Amendment protection. In *First National Bank v. Belotti,* the Supreme Court examined a Massachusetts statute prohibiting corporations from spending money to influence "the vote on any question submitted to the voters, other than one materially affecting any of the property, business, or assets of the corporation."[32] That statute was struck down as unconstitutional because it unnecessarily restrained "free speech." Similarly, the Court has held that a law forbidding a corporation from using bill inserts to express its views on controversial issues violates the First Amendment.[33] Laws banning the financing of advertisements supporting specific political candidates with money drawn from a corporation's general funds, however, do not violate the First Amendment.[34]

Unprotected Speech: Obscenity

Numerous state and federal statutes make it a crime to disseminate obscene materials. All such state and federal statutes prohibiting obscenity have been deemed constitutional if the definition of obscenity conforms with that of the then-current U.S. Supreme Court. Basically, the courts have not been willing to extend constitutional protections of free speech to what they consider obscene materials. For example, in *Roth v. United States,* the Supreme Court stated, "Obscenity is not within the area of constitutionally protected speech or press."[35]

But what is obscenity? Justice Potter Stewart once said that even though he could not define obscenity, "I know it when I see it."[36] The problem, of course, is that even if it were agreed on, the definition of obscenity changes with the times. Victorians deeply disapproved of the "loose" morals of the Elizabethan Age. The works of Mark Twain and Edgar Rice Burroughs have at times been considered obscene (after all, Tarzan and Jane were not legally wedded).

The Supreme Court has grappled from time to time with the problem of specifying an operationally effective definition of obscenity. In the *Roth* case in 1957, the Court coined the phrase "utterly without redeeming social importance." Since then, Supreme Court justices have viewed numerous films to determine if they met this criterion. By the 1970s, the justices had recognized the failure of the *Roth* definition. In *Miller v. California,* Chief Justice Warren Burger created a formal list of requirements, known as the *Roth-Miller* test of obscenity, that currently must be met for material to be legally obscene. Under this test, material is obscene if (1) the average person finds that it violates contemporary community standards; (2) the work taken as a whole appeals to a prurient interest in sex; (3) the work shows patently offensive sexual conduct; and (4) the work lacks serious redeeming literary, artistic, political, or scientific merit.[37]

The problem, of course, is that one person's prurient interest is another person's artistic pleasure. The Court went on to state that the definition of

The Constitution does not specifically protect pornography, but rather guarantees freedom of speech in general. Local laws differ considerably concerning what is and is not pornographic and therefore in what is and is not legal.

---

32. 435 U.S. 765 (1978).
33. *Consolidated Edison Co. v. Public Service Commission,* 447 U.S. 550 (1980).
34. *Austin v. Michigan Chamber of Commerce,* 494 U.S. 652 (1990).
35. 354 U.S. 476 (1957).
36. *Jacobellis v. Ohio,* 378 U.S. 184 (1964).
37. 413 U.S. 5 (1973).

prurient interest would be determined by the community's standards. The Court avoided presenting a definition of obscenity, leaving this determination to local and state authorities. Consequently, the *Miller* case has had widely inconsistent applications. Obscenity is still a constitutionally unsettled area, whether it deals with speech or printed or filmed materials. Some women's rights activists, often in alliance with religious fundamentalists, have begun a drive to enact new antipornography laws on the basis that pornography violates women's rights. In 1982, the Supreme Court upheld state laws making it illegal to sell material showing sexual performances by minors. In 1990, the Court ruled that states can outlaw the possession of child pornography in the home. The Court reasoned that the ban on private possession is justified because owning the material perpetuates commercial demand for it and for the exploitation of the children involved.[38]

Unprotected Speech: Slander

Can you say anything you want about someone else? Not really. Individuals are protected from **defamation of character,** which is defined as wrongfully hurting a person's good reputation. The law has imposed a general duty on all persons to refrain from making false, defamatory statements about others. Breaching this duty orally involves the wrongdoing called **slander.**[39]

Legally, slander is the public uttering of a statement that holds a person up for contempt, ridicule, or hatred. Slanderous public uttering means that the defamatory statements are made to, or within the hearing of, persons other than the defamed party. If one person calls another dishonest, manipulative, and incompetent when no one else is around, that does not constitute slander. The message is not communicated to a third party. If, however, a third party accidentally overhears defamatory statements, the courts have generally held that this constitutes a public uttering and therefore slander, which is prohibited.

Fighting Words and Hecklers' Veto

The Supreme Court has prohibited types of speech "which by their very utterance inflict injury or intend to incite an immediate breach of peace that governments may constitutionally punish."[40] The reference here is to a prohibition on public speakers from using **fighting words.** These may include racial, religious, or ethnic slurs that are so inflammatory that they will provoke the "average" listener to fight.

Under the Supreme Court leadership of Chief Justice Warren Burger, fighting words were more and more narrowly construed. For example, a four-letter word used in reference to the draft and emblazoned on a sweater is not considered a fighting word unless it is directed at a specific person. In 1992, the Court struck down a St. Paul, Minnesota, ordinance that banned cross burnings and other expressions of racial bias on the ground that these activities were protected speech.[41]

DEFAMATION OF CHARACTER
Wrongfully hurting a person's good reputation. The law has imposed a general duty on all persons to refrain from making false, defamatory statements about others.

SLANDER
The public uttering of a statement that holds a person up for contempt, ridicule, or hatred. This means that the defamatory statement is made to, or within the hearing of, persons other than the defamed party.

FIGHTING WORDS
Words that, when uttered by a public speaker, are so inflammatory that they could provoke the average listener to violence; the words are usually of a racial, religious, or ethnic type.

---

38. *Osborne v. Ohio,* 495 U.S. 103 (1990).
39. Breaching it in writing involves the wrongdoing called *libel,* which is discussed in the next major section.
40. *Cohen v. California,* 403 U.S. 15 (1971).
41. *R.A.V. v. City of St. Paul, Minnesota,* 112 S.Ct. 2538 (1992).

HECKLERS' VETO
Boisterous and generally disruptive behavior by listeners of public speakers that, in effect, vetoes the public speakers' right to speak.

Members of a crowd listening to a speech are prohibited from exercising a **hecklers' veto.** The boisterous and disruptive behavior of hecklers poses the threat of disruption or violence, so hecklers are vetoing the essential rights of the speaker.

Free Speech and Violence

In recent years, some state universities have challenged the boundaries of the protection of free speech provided by the First Amendment with the issuance of campus speech and behavior codes. Such codes are designed to prohibit so-called "hate speech"—abusive speech attacking persons on the basis of their ethnicity, race, or other criteria. For example, a University of Michigan code banned "any behavior, verbal or physical, that stigmatizes or victimizes an individual on the basis of race, ethnicity, religion, sex, sexual orientation, creed, national origin, ancestry, age, marital status, handicap or Vietnam-era veterans status." A federal court found that the code violated students' First Amendment rights.[42] Although many people assert that such codes are necessary to stem violence on American campuses, the courts generally have held, as in the University of Michigan case, that they are unconstitutional restrictions on the right to free speech.

In a June 1995 speech, Senate Majority Leader and presidential hopeful Bob Dole focused public attention on another free-speech issue when he delivered a stinging critique of the film and music industry. Dole maintained that the entertainment industry stretched the limits of free speech too far by permitting the American public, and particularly American youth, to be exposed to extremely violent films and song lyrics. He claimed that the leaders of the industry should not be allowed to "hide behind the lofty language of free speech in order to profit from the debasing of America." Following this speech, Dole was chided by some for being so tardy in jumping on the moral bandwagon and criticized by others for advocating censorship.

Both campus speech and behavior codes and recent criticisms of the film and music industry raise a controversial issue: whether rights to free speech can (or should) be traded off to reduce violence in America.

FREEDOM OF THE PRESS

Freedom of the press can be regarded as a special instance of freedom of speech. Of course, at the time of the framing of the Constitution, the press meant only newspapers, magazines, and perhaps pamphlets. As technology has modified the ways in which we disseminate information, so too have the laws touching on freedom of the press been modified. But what can and cannot be printed still occupies an important place in constitutional law.

Defamation in Writing

LIBEL
A written defamation of a person's character, reputation, business, or property rights. To a limited degree, the First Amendment protects the press from libel actions.

ACTIONABLE
Furnishing grounds for a lawsuit. Actionable words, for example, in the law of libel are such words that naturally imply damage to the individual in question.

Libel is defamation in writing. As with slander, libel is an **actionable** wrong only if the defamatory statements are observed by a third party. If one person

_____
42. *Doe v. University of Michigan,* 721 F.Supp. 852 (1989).

writes another a private letter wrongfully accusing him or her of embezzling funds, that does not constitute libel. It is interesting that the courts have generally held that dictating a letter to a secretary constitutes communication of the letter's contents to a third party, and therefore, if defamation has occurred, the wrongdoing of libel is actionable.

Newspapers are often involved in libel suits. *New York Times Co. v. Sullivan*[43] explored an important question about public officials and libel. Sullivan, a commissioner of the city of Montgomery, Alabama, sued the *New York Times* for libel because it had printed an advertisement critical of the actions of the Montgomery police during the civil rights movement. Under Alabama law, the jury found that the statements were in fact libelous on their face, so that damages could be awarded to Sullivan without proof of the extent of any injury to him. The jury awarded him a half-million dollars, and the Alabama Supreme Court upheld the judgment.

The U.S. Supreme Court, however, unanimously reversed the judgment. It found that Alabama's libel laws as applied to public officials in the performance of their duty deprived critics of their rights of free speech under the First and Fourteenth Amendments.[44] Speaking for the Court, Justice William J. Brennan, Jr., stated that libel laws such as those in Alabama would inhibit the unfettered discussion of public issues. The Court indicated that only when a statement was made with **actual malice** against a public official could damages be obtained. If the Court had upheld the Alabama judgment, virtually any criticism of public officials could be suppressed.

A Free Press versus a Fair Trial: Gag Orders

Another major freedom of the press issue concerns newspaper reports of criminal trials. Amendment VI of the Bill of Rights guarantees a fair trial. In other words, the accused have rights. But the Bill of Rights also guarantees freedom of the press. What if the two appear to be in conflict? Which one prevails?

Jurors certainly may be influenced by reading news stories about the trial in which they are participating. In the 1970s, judges increasingly issued **gag orders**, which restricted the publication of news about a trial in progress or even a pretrial hearing. A landmark case was decided by the Supreme Court in 1976, based on the trial of E. C. Simants, who was charged with the murder of a neighboring family.[45] Because the murder occurred in the course of a sexual assault, details of the crime were lurid. A local Nebraska judge issued an order prohibiting the press from reporting information gleaned in a pretrial hearing. Because there were only 860 people in the town, the judge believed that such publicity would prejudice potential jurors. The Supreme Court unanimously ruled that the Nebraska judge's gag order had violated the First Amendment's freedom of the press clause. Chief Justice Warren Burger indicated that even pervasive adverse pretrial publicity did not necessarily lead to an unfair trial and that prior restraints on

ACTUAL MALICE
Actual desire and intent to see another suffer by one's actions. Actual malice involves a condition of mind that prompts a person to do a wrongful act willfully (that is, on purpose) to the injury of another, or to do intentionally a wrongful act toward another without justification or excuse. Actual malice in libel cases generally consists of intentionally publishing, without justifiable cause, any written or printed matter that is injurious to the character of another.

GAG ORDER
An order issued by a judge restricting the publication of news about a trial in progress or a pretrial hearing in order to protect the accused's right to a fair trial.

---

43. 376 U.S. 254 (1964).
44. Remember that the Supreme Court has held that the Fourteenth Amendment "nationalizes" most of the liberties listed in the Bill of Rights.
45. *Nebraska Press Association v. Stuart*, 427 U.S. 539 (1976).

publication were not justified. Some justices even went so far as to indicate that gag orders are never justified.

In spite of that *Nebraska Press Association* ruling, the Court has upheld certain types of gag orders. In *Gannett Company v. De Pasquale,* the highest court held that if a judge found a reasonable probability that news publicity would harm a defendant's right to a fair trial, the court could impose a gag rule: "Members of the public have no constitutional right under the Sixth and Fourteenth Amendments to *attend* criminal trials."[46]

The *Nebraska* and *Gannett* cases, however, involved pretrial hearings. Could a judge impose a gag order on an entire trial, including pretrial hearings? In *Richmond Newspapers, Inc. v. Virginia,* the Court ruled that actual trials must be open to the public except under unusual circumstances.[47]

Confidentiality and Reporters' Work Papers

By the 1980s, the courts had begun to rule in cases concerning the press's responsibility to law-enforcement agencies. In one case, Myron Farber, a *New York Times* reporter who had possession of extensive notes relating to a murder case, was jailed in 1978 in New Jersey for not turning this material over to law-enforcement officials. The Supreme Court refused to review the case.[48]

Moreover, in several cases the police were permitted to search newspaper offices for documents related to cases under investigation. In general, the courts have moved in the direction of requiring the press to cooperate in criminal investigations to a much greater degree than it had before. These cases obviously raise a serious question about the confidentiality of working papers and background information that reporters obtain in the course of doing stories or investigative reporting.

One important case concerned the *Stanford Daily.*[49] The campus newspaper of Stanford University had its offices searched by police officers with a search warrant. They were looking for photographs that would identify demonstrators who may have been responsible for injuries to the police. In this particular case, in 1978, the Court ruled that the protection of confidentiality, and therefore the protection of the First Amendment's guarantee of a free press, was less important under the specific circumstances than the needs of law-enforcement agencies to secure information necessary for prosecution. Congress responded to the *Stanford Daily* case by enacting the Privacy Protection Act of 1980.[50] This law applies to state as well as federal law-enforcement personnel. It limits their power to obtain evidence from the news media by means of a search warrant and in many instances requires that they use a subpoena.

More recently, a federal appeals court broadened the conditions required to force the media to give up notes and other material. The court said newspaper and television reporters had to relinquish their notes and videotape outtakes of interviews with a lawyer who represented an alleged Mafia boss,

---

46. 443 U.S. 368 (1979).
47. 448 U.S. 555 (1980).
48. *New York Times Co. v. Jascalevich,* 439 U.S. 1317 (1978).
49. *Zurcher v. Stanford Daily,* 436 U.S. 547 (1978).
50. 42 U.S.C. Sections 2000aa to 2000aa-12.

John Gotti. The court's ruling indicated that a reporter's material only had to be "relevant" to a case in order for it to be required to be relinquished to parties in a federal criminal trial.[51]

More than half the states have enacted so-called shield laws. These laws protect reporters against having to reveal their sources and other confidential information.

Other Information Channels: Motion Pictures, Radio, and TV

The framers of our Constitution could not have imagined the ways in which information is disseminated today. Nonetheless, they fashioned the Constitution into a flexible instrument that could respond to social and technological changes. First Amendment freedoms have been applied differently to newer forms of information dissemination.

Motion Pictures: Some Prior Restraint.   The most onerous of all forms of government interference with expression is prior restraint. As was noted, the Supreme Court has not declared all forms of censorship unconstitutional, but it does require an exceptional justification for such restraint. Only in a few cases has the Supreme Court upheld prior restraint of published materials.

The Court's reluctance to accept prior restraint is less evident in the case of motion pictures. In the first half of the twentieth century, films were routinely submitted to local censorship boards. In 1968, the Supreme Court ruled that a film can be banned only under a law that provides for a prompt hearing at which the film is shown to be obscene. Today, few local censorship boards exist. Instead, the film industry regulates itself primarily through the industry's rating system.

Radio and TV: Limited Protection.   Of all forms of communication, television is perhaps the most influential, and radio runs a close second. Radio and television broadcasting has the most limited First Amendment protection. In 1934, the national government established the Federal Communications Commission (FCC) to regulate electromagnetic wave frequencies. No one has a right to use the airwaves without a license granted by the FCC. The FCC grants licenses for limited periods and imposes numerous regulations on broadcasting.

Although Congress has denied the FCC the authority to censor what is transmitted, the FCC can impose sanctions on those radio or TV stations broadcasting "filthy words," even if the words are not legally obscene.[52] From 1993 through 1995, the FCC fined some radio stations that broadcast the talk show hosted by Howard Stern a total of over $1.5 million for what the agency considered to be indecent radio programs. Also, the FCC has occasionally refused to renew licenses of broadcasters who presumably have not "served the public interest."

---

51. *United States v. Cutler*, 6 F.3d 67 (2d Cir. 1993).
52. *Federal Communications Commission v. Pacifica Foundation*, 438 U.S. 726 (1978).

Radio "shock jock" Howard Stern apparently offended the sensitivities of the Federal Communications Commission (FCC). That regulatory body fined Stern's radio station owner hundreds of thousands of dollars for Stern's purported obscene outbursts on radio. The extent to which the FCC can regulate speech over the air involves the First Amendment. Today, both on the radio and on TV, what is considered permissive and acceptable would probably have been considered "obscene" three decades ago.

FAIRNESS DOCTRINE
An FCC regulation affecting broadcasting media, which required that fair or equal opportunity be given to legitimate opposing political groups or individuals to broadcast their views.

Perhaps one of the more controversial of the FCC's rulings was its **fairness doctrine**, which imposed on owners of broadcast licenses an obligation to present "both" sides of significant public issues. In 1987, the FCC repealed the fairness doctrine. The FCC determined that the doctrine was unconstitutional because it violated broadcasters' freedom of speech under the First Amendment.

THE RIGHT TO ASSEMBLE AND TO PETITION THE GOVERNMENT

The First Amendment prohibits Congress from making any law that abridges "the right of the people peaceably to assembly and to petition the Government for a redress of grievances." Inherent in such a right is the ability of private citizens to communicate their ideas on public issues to government officials, as well as to other individuals. The Supreme Court has often put this freedom on a par with the freedom of speech and the freedom of the press. Nonetheless, it has allowed municipalities to require permits for parades, sound trucks, and demonstrations, so that public officials may control traffic or prevent demonstrations from turning into riots.[53] This became a major issue in 1977 when the American Nazi party wanted to march through the largely Jewish suburb of Skokie, Illinois. The American Civil Liberties Union (see this chapter's *Politics: The Human Side*) defended the Nazis' right to march (in spite of its opposition to the Nazi philosophy). The Supreme Court let stand a lower court's ruling that the city of Skokie had violated the Nazis' First Amendment guarantees by denying them a permit to march.[54]

---

53. *Davis v. Massachusetts,* 167 U.S. 43 (1897).
54. *Collin v. Smith,* 439 U.S. 916 (1978).

POLITICS: THE HUMAN SIDE
Ira Glasser, Executive Director, American Civil Liberties Union

"The Bill of Rights protects liberty precisely by limiting what the majority may do to minorities. Free speech, for example, is protected because the First Amendment prohibits Congress from passing any laws that abridge what people say or think, no matter how unpopular their views may be."

BIOGRAPHICAL NOTES

Ira Glasser has headed the American Civil Liberties Union (ACLU) since 1978. He received a bachelor's degree in mathematics at Queens College in 1959 and a master's degree in mathematics from Ohio State University in 1960. He went on to do graduate study in sociology and philosophy at the New School for Social Research in New York City. After professorships at Queens College and Sara Lawrence University, in 1964 Glasser became a research associate at the University of Illinois. During this time, he was also associate editor and then editor of *Current* magazine. He later became associate director of the New York Civil Liberties Union in 1967 and served as its executive director from 1970 to 1978. Glasser has been given the Gavel Award by the American Bar Association, has received the Martin Luther King Award, and has been named a member of the board of directors of the Asian-American Legal Defense and Educational Fund.

POLITICAL CONTRIBUTIONS

Ira Glasser, as head of the ACLU, is continuing the work of this country's most well-known champion of civil liberties. The ACLU was founded by Roger Baldwin, Jane Addams, Helen Keller, and Norman Thomas in New York City in 1920 with the expressed goal of defending "the rights of [men and women] set forth in the Declaration of Independence and the Constitution." In addition to issuing public statements and organizing protests, the ACLU initiates test cases in the courts and also writes supporting briefs in other cases. The ACLU has committees on due process, equality, free speech, church-state issues, and academic freedom, among others. Currently, the ACLU has about 275,000 members.

Besides overseeing the operation of the ACLU, Glasser has written extensively about civil liberties and related issues since he wrote "Are You Being Bugged? The Case against Privacy Invasion" in *Manhattan East* in 1967. He was particularly critical of the invasion of privacy that occurred during the Nixon administration in an article on the Constitution and the courts in a book entitled *What Nixon Is Doing to Us* in 1973. Glasser was also critical of the Reagan administration. He wrote "The Coming Assault on Civil Liberties," which appeared in the book *What Reagan Is Doing to Us*. In addition, he wrote a variety of other articles that appeared in books critical of the Reagan years.

Today Glasser continues to champion a strict interpretation of the Bill of Rights for every American. As in the past, Glasser's leadership of the ACLU will find the organization participating directly or indirectly in almost every major civil liberties case that will be contested in American courts.

The right to assemble has been defined broadly. For example, municipal and state governments do not have the right to require any organization to publish its membership list. This was decided in *NAACP v. Alabama*.[55] The state of Alabama had required the National Association for the Advancement of Colored People (NAACP) to publish a list of its members. The Supreme Court held that the requirement was unconstitutional because it violated

---

55. 357 U.S. 499 (1958).

With their right to assemble and demonstrate protected by the Constitution, members of the modern Ku Klux Klan march in Wilmington, North Carolina. The police escort is charged with making sure that neither the marchers nor the observers provoke any violence.

the NAACP's right of assembly, which the Court addressed in terms of freedom of association.

The courts generally have interpreted the right to parade and protest more narrowly than pure forms of speech or assembly. The Supreme Court has generally upheld the right of individuals to parade and protest in public places, but it has ruled against parades and protests when matters of public safety were at issue. In *Cox v. New Hampshire,* for example, the Court ruled that sixty-eight Jehovah's Witnesses had violated a statute prohibiting parading without a permit and upheld the right of a municipality to control its public streets.[56]

MORE LIBERTIES UNDER SCRUTINY: MATTERS OF PRIVACY

During the past several years, a number of civil liberties that relate to the right to privacy have become important social issues. Among the most important are the right to sexual freedom, the right to have an abortion, and the right to die.

The Right to Privacy

No explicit reference is made anywhere in the Constitution to a person's right to privacy. The courts did not take a very positive approach toward the right to privacy until relatively recently. For example, during Prohibition, suspected bootleggers' telephones were routinely tapped, and the information obtained was used as a legal basis for prosecution. In *Olmstead v. United States,* the Supreme Court upheld such an invasion of privacy.[57] Jus-

---

56. 312 U.S. 569 (1941).
57. 277 U.S. 438 (1928). This decision was overruled later in *Katz v. United States,* 389 U.S. 347 (1967).

tice Louis Brandeis, a champion of personal freedoms, strongly dissented to the majority decision in this case. He argued that the framers of the Constitution gave every citizen the right to be left alone. He called such a right "the most comprehensive of rights and the right most valued by civilized men."

In the 1960s, the highest court began to modify the majority view. In *Griswold v. Connecticut,* in 1965, the Supreme Court overthrew a Connecticut law that effectively prohibited the use of contraceptives, holding that the law violated the right to privacy.[58] Justice William O. Douglas formulated a unique way of reading this right into the Bill of Rights. He claimed that the First, Third, Fourth, Fifth, and Ninth Amendments created "penumbras, formed by emanations from those guarantees that help give them life and substance," and he went on to talk about zones of privacy that are guaranteed by these rights. When we read the Ninth Amendment, we can see the foundation for his reasoning: "The enumeration in the Constitution of certain rights, shall not be construed to deny or disparage others retained by the people." In other words, just because the Constitution, including its amendments, does not specifically talk about the right to privacy does not mean that this right is denied to the people.

In a reversal of this trend, the Supreme Court ruled in 1986 (by a vote of five to four) that the right to privacy does not protect homosexual acts between consenting adults. It ruled that a Georgia law prohibiting sodomy—oral or anal sex—was constitutional.[59] About half the states have sodomy laws, which are generally intended to restrict homosexual activities.

An important privacy issue, created in part by new technology, is the amassing of information on individuals by government. The average American citizen has personal information filed away in dozens of agencies—such as the Social Security Administration and the Internal Revenue Service. Because of the threat of indiscriminate use of private information by nonauthorized individuals, Congress passed the Privacy Act in 1974. This was the first law regulating the use of federal government information about private individuals. Under the Privacy Act, every citizen has the right to obtain copies of personal records collected by federal agencies and to correct inaccuracies in such records.

The Right to Have an Abortion

Historically, abortion was not a criminal offense before the "quickening" of the fetus (the first movement of the fetus in the uterus, usually between the sixteenth and eighteenth weeks of pregnancy). During the last half of the nineteenth century, however, state laws became more severe. By 1973, performance of an abortion was a criminal offense in most states—the government controlled reproductive rights. In *Roe v. Wade,* the United States Supreme Court accepted the argument that the laws against abortion violated "Jane Roe's" right to privacy under the Constitution.[60] The Court did not answer the question about when life begins. It simply said that "the right to privacy is broad enough to encompass a woman's decision whether or not to terminate her pregnancy." The Court did not say that such a right

---

58. 381 U.S. 479 (1965).
59. *Bowers v. Hardwick,* 478 U.S. 186 (1986).
60. 410 U.S. 113 (1973). Jane Roe was not the real name of the woman in this case. It is a common legal pseudonym used to protect a person's privacy.

Both pro-choice and antiabortion groups have repeatedly exercised the right to assemble and protest government action. Here, pictures show pro-choice groups protesting outside the Supreme Court building in Washington, D.C., and antiabortion groups picketing outside the 1992 Republican National Convention. The main purpose of such protests is to gain media attention and gather support for their positions.

was absolute. Instead, it asserted that any state could impose certain regulations that would safeguard the health of the mother and protect potential life after the first three months of pregnancy.

Thus, the Court balanced different interests when it decided that during the first trimester (three months) of pregnancy, abortion was an issue solely between a woman and her doctor. The state could not limit abortions except to require that they be performed by licensed physicians. During the second trimester, to protect the health of the mother, the state was allowed to specify the conditions under which an abortion could be performed. During the final trimester, the state could regulate or even outlaw abortions except when necessary to preserve the life or health of the mother.

After *Roe,* the Supreme Court issued decisions in a number of cases defining and redefining the boundaries of state regulation of abortion. Twice the Court has struck down laws that required a woman who wished to have an abortion to undergo counseling designed to discourage abortions.[61] The Court has held, however, that the government can prohibit doctors in medical clinics that receive federal funding from discussing abortion with their patients.[62]

In 1989, the Supreme Court announced its decision in *Webster v. Reproductive Health Services,* a case that challenged very restrictive state laws on abortion.[63] In a narrow five-to-four majority, the Court upheld the restrictions that Missouri placed on the performing of abortions, opening the way for many other states to enact similar or more restrictive laws. Specifically, the ruling allowed states to pass laws that, like the Missouri statute, ban the use of public hospitals or other taxpayer-supported facilities from performing abortions; bar public employees, including doctors and nurses, from assisting in abortions; and require the performance of viability tests on any fetus thought to be at least twenty weeks old. Although the *Webster* decision did not overturn the right to have an abortion, the Court's ruling was a

61. *Thornburgh v. American College of Obstetricians and Gynecologists,* 476 U.S. 747 (1986); *City of Akron v. Akron Center for Reproductive Health, Inc.,* 462 U.S. 416 (1983).
62. *Rust v. Sullivan,* 500 U.S. 173 (1991).
63. 492 U.S. 490 (1989).

major victory for antiabortion forces. The ultimate effect of the *Webster* decision was to make obtaining an abortion more difficult in some states than in others.

In 1990, the territory of Guam banned all abortions except those necessary to save a woman's life or to preserve her health. Similar laws making abortion a crime have been passed in Louisiana and Utah. These laws are seen as direct challenges to *Roe v. Wade*. A federal district court refused to enforce the Guam law, and a federal appeals court affirmed the decision.[64] Supporters of the law argued that recent Supreme Court decisions have effectively nullified the principles announced in *Roe*. The appeals court emphasized that the Supreme Court has never expressly overruled *Roe*.

The Pennsylvania Abortion Control Act, parts of which were similar to the Missouri law considered by the Supreme Court in *Webster* in 1989, came before the Court in 1992 in *Planned Parenthood v. Casey*.[65] The act required that a woman who wished to have an abortion receive specific counseling and wait twenty-four hours. A married woman was required to notify her husband. Unmarried girls under the age of eighteen and not self-supporting were required by the act to obtain the consent of one of their parents or the permission of a state judge. A federal appeals court upheld all of the act's provisions except the husband-notification requirement. In a five-to-four decision, the Supreme Court also upheld these provisions of the Pennsylvania law. Recently, the Supreme Court ruled that abortion protesters could be prosecuted under laws governing racketeering.[66] But it also ruled that an injunction restricting certain antiabortion activities at a clinic violated First Amendment rights.[67]

The Right to Die

The question of whether the right to privacy includes the right to die is now a major point of controversy. Suicide and **euthanasia**, or mercy killing, are both illegal; but many extremely ill people do not want their lives prolonged through expensive artificial measures. These situations often end up in court, because hospitals and doctors sympathetic to the patient's wishes do not want to be legally or morally responsible for giving the order to stop treatment, even with the patient's and family's consent.

The 1976 case involving Karen Ann Quinlan was one of the first publicized right-to-die cases.[68] The parents of Quinlan, a young woman who had been in a coma since age twenty-one and kept alive by a respirator, wanted her respirator removed. The New Jersey Supreme Court ruled that the right to privacy includes the right of a patient to refuse treatment and that patients unable to speak can exercise that right through a family member or guardian. In its ruling on a 1985 case, the New Jersey Supreme Court set some clear guidelines for when care could be withheld for patients who cannot express their own wishes.[69] Care can be withheld if (1) the patient

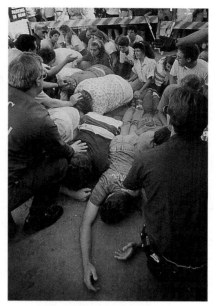

Antiabortion forces increased their demonstration throughout the 1990s. The clash between the pro-choice and the antiabortion forces have resulted in several individuals being killed. The courts imposed restrictions on what antiabortion forces could do in their demonstrations around abortion clinics.

EUTHANASIA
Killing incurably ill people for reasons of mercy.

---

64. *Guam Society of Obstetricians and Gynecologists v. Ada*, 962 F.2d 1366 (9th Cir. 1992). Upon appeal to the United States Supreme Court, the Court refused to hear the case.
65. 112 S.Ct. 2791 (1992).
66. *National Organization of Women v. Joseph Scheidler*, 114 S.Ct. 36 (1993).
67. *Madsen v. Women's Health Center Inc.*, 114 S.Ct. 907 (1994).
68. *In re Quinlan*, 70 N.J. 10, 355 A.2d 647 (1976).
69. *In re Conroy*, 98 N.J. 321, 486 A.2d 1209 (1985).

definitely would have refused treatment, (2) evidence suggests that treatment would have been refused, and (3) the burdens of continuing care are greater than the benefits.

In 1992, the state of Washington considered legalizing euthanasia, but the voters rejected the idea. Essentially, the new law would have allowed physicians to assist terminally ill patients "in dying with dignity." Mentally competent patients certified by two doctors as having less than six months to live could have requested assisted death. Patients in comas or vegetative states could have been removed from life-sustaining machines and artificial food and water tubes. Similar measures have been considered in California, Oregon, and the European Union. In the 1990s, the activities of Michigan doctor Jack Kevorkian in assisting people to die focused the public's attention on this issue.

THE GREAT BALANCING ACT: THE RIGHTS OF THE ACCUSED VERSUS THE RIGHTS OF SOCIETY

The United States has one of the highest violent crime rates in the world. It is not surprising, therefore, that many citizens have extremely strong opinions about the rights of those accused of criminal offenses. When an accused person, especially one who has confessed to some criminal act, is set free because of an apparent legal "technicality," many people may feel that the rights of the accused are being given more weight than the rights of society and of potential or actual victims. Why, then, give criminal suspects rights? The answer is partly to avoid convicting innocent people, but mostly because all citizens have rights, and criminal suspects are citizens.

The courts and the police must constantly engage in a balancing act of competing rights. At the basis of all discussions about the appropriate balance is, of course, the U.S. Bill of Rights. The Fourth, Fifth, Sixth, and Eighth Amendments deal specifically with the rights of criminal defendants.

Rights of the Accused

The basic rights of criminal defendants are outlined below. When appropriate, the specific amendment on which a right is based also is given.

Limits on the Conduct of Police Officers and Prosecutors

- No unreasonable or unwarranted searches and seizures (Amend. IV).
- No arrest except on probable cause (Amend. IV).
- No coerced confessions or illegal interrogation (Amend. V).
- No entrapment.
- Upon questioning, a suspect must be informed of his or her rights.

Defendant's Pretrial Rights

WRIT OF *HABEAS CORPUS*
Habeas corpus means, literally, "you have the body." A writ of *habeas corpus* is an order that requires jailers to bring a person before a court or judge and explain why the person is being held in prison.

- **Writ of *habeas corpus*** (Article I, Section 9).
- Prompt arraignment (Amend. VI).
- Legal counsel (Amend. VI).
- Reasonable bail (Amend. VIII).
- To be informed of charges (Amend. VI).
- To remain silent (Amend. V).

Trial Rights

- Speedy and public trial before a jury (Amend. VI).
- Impartial jury selected from a cross section of the community (Amend. VI).
- Trial atmosphere free of prejudice, fear, and outside interference.
- No compulsory self-incrimination (Amend. V).
- Adequate counsel (Amend. VI).
- No cruel and unusual punishment (Amend. VIII).
- Appeal of convictions.
- No double jeopardy (Amend. V).

Extending the Rights of the Accused: *Miranda v. Arizona*

In 1963, near Phoenix, Arizona, a young woman was kidnapped and raped. A twenty-three-year-old, mentally disturbed suspect, Ernesto Miranda, was arrested soon after the crime took place. After two hours of questioning, he confessed and was later convicted. Miranda's lawyer appealed his conviction. The lawyer argued that the police had never informed Miranda that he had the right to remain silent and the right to be represented by counsel. In 1966, in a five-to-four decision, the United States Supreme Court ruled in Miranda's favor:

> Prior to any questioning, the person must be warned that he has a right to remain silent, that any statement he does make may be used against him, and that he has a right to the presence of an attorney, either retained or appointed.[70]

The majority voted to reverse the conviction on the basis of the Fifth and Sixth Amendments, but the minority complained that the majority was distorting the Constitution by placing the rights of criminal suspects above the rights of society as a whole. The balancing act was again in question. Police officials sided with the minority view, but many agreed with the majority that criminal law enforcement would be more reliable if it were based on independently secured evidence rather than on confessions obtained under coercive interrogation conditions in the absence of counsel.

Another extension of the rights of the accused was made by the Court in the case of Clarence Earl Gideon, described in this chapter's *Politics and Criminal Justice*.

Recent Rulings and Their Impact on *Miranda*

The Supreme Court under Chief Justice Warren Burger did not expand the *Miranda* ruling but rather reduced its scope and effectiveness. Also, Congress in 1968 passed the Omnibus Crime Control and Safe Streets Act. This act provided—among other things—that in federal cases, a voluntary confession could be used as evidence even if the accused was not informed of his or her rights.

Today, juries can accept confessions without being convinced they

---

70. *Miranda v. Arizona*, 384 U.S. 436 (1966).

This individual is being read his *Miranda* rights by the arresting officer. These rights were established in the 1966 case *Miranda v. Arizona*. The rights concern minimum procedural safeguards. They are also known as the *Miranda* warnings and include informing arrested persons prior to questioning (1) that they have the right to remain silent, (2) that anything they say may be used as evidence against them, and (3) that they have the right to the presence of an attorney.

POLITICS AND CRIMINAL JUSTICE
The Case of Clarence Earl Gideon

In 1962, Clarence Earl Gideon sent a petition to the Supreme Court to review his most recent conviction, which was for breaking into a pool hall and stealing some money in Panama City, Florida. That petition would not only change Gideon's life but would become a landmark case in constitutional law as well.

Clarence Gideon had been in trouble with the law during much of his life and in jail at least four times before for various minor crimes. Those who knew him, including his jailers, found him rather likeable and relatively harmless.

Gideon claimed in his petition that his conviction and sentencing to a five-year term in prison violated the due process clause of the Fourteenth Amendment to the Constitution, which says that "no state shall . . . deprive any person of life, liberty, or property, without due process of the law." Gideon reported that at the time of his trial,

when he asked for the assistance of a lawyer, the court refused this aid. The heart of Gideon's petition lay in the notion that "to try a poor man for a felony without giving him a lawyer was to deprive him of due process of law."

The problem with Gideon's argument was that the Supreme Court had established a precedent twenty

years earlier in *Betts v. Brady*, when it held that criminal defendants were not automatically guaranteed the right to have a lawyer present when they were tried in court except in capital cases.*

Gideon was successful, with the help of his court-appointed lawyer, Abe Fortas (who later was named to the Supreme Court by President Lyndon B. Johnson). In the case of *Gideon v. Wainwright*, the court decided in Gideon's favor, saying that persons who can demonstrate that they are unable to afford to have a lawyer present and are accused of felonies must be given a lawyer at the expense of the government.† Gideon was retried, represented by an attorney appointed by the court. He was found innocent of the charges.

*316 U.S. 455 (1942).
†372 U.S. 335 (1963).

were voluntary.[71] Even in cases that are not tried in federal court, confessions made by criminal suspects who have not been completely informed of their legal rights may be taken into consideration.[72] In 1984, the Supreme Court added another exception to the *Miranda* rule by allowing the introduction of evidence into the courtroom that was voluntarily given by the suspect before he had been informed of his rights. The Court held that when "public safety" required action (in this case, to find a loaded gun), police could interrogate the suspect before advising him of his right to remain silent.[73]

The Exclusionary Rule

EXCLUSIONARY RULE
A policy forbidding the admission at trial of illegally seized evidence.

At least since 1914, judicial policy has prohibited the admission of illegally seized evidence at trials in federal courts. This is the so-called **exclusionary rule.** Improperly obtained evidence, no matter how telling, could not be used by prosecutors. This includes evidence obtained by police in violation

71. See especially *Lego v. Twomey*, 404 U.S. 477 (1972).
72. *Michigan v. Tucker*, 417 U.S. 433 (1974).
73. *New York v. Quarles*, 467 U.S. 649 (1984).

of the Fourth Amendment. The Fourth Amendment protects against unreasonable searches and seizures and requires that a search warrant may be issued by a judge to a police officer only on probable cause (a demonstration of facts that permit a reasonable belief that a crime has been committed). The question that must be determined by the courts is what constitutes an "unreasonable" search and seizure.

The reasoning behind the exclusionary rule is that it forces police officers to gather evidence properly, in which case their due diligence will be rewarded by a conviction. There have always been critics of the exclusionary rule who argue that it permits guilty persons to be freed because of innocent errors.

This rule was first applied to state courts in the 1961 Supreme Court decision *Mapp v. Ohio*.[74] In this case, the Court overturned the conviction of Dollree Mapp for the possession of obscene materials. Police found pornographic books in her apartment after searching it without a search warrant despite her refusal to let them in.

In a 1984 case, the Court seemed to be loosening the severity of the exclusionary rule. A Boston police officer suspected a man of murder and wished to search his residence. The officer used a technically incorrect search warrant form. The Massachusetts Appeals Court threw out the conviction because of this technical defect. But the U.S. Supreme Court held that the officer acted in good faith and thereby created the "good faith exception."[75] In the summer of 1994, a judge involved in the O. J. Simpson case, Kathleen Kennedy-Powell, refused to suppress evidence obtained without a warrant. She declared that the Los Angeles police detectives were "acting for a benevolent purpose."

Capital Punishment: Cruel and Unusual?

Amendment VIII prohibits cruel and unusual punishment. Throughout history, "cruel and unusual" referred to punishments that were more serious than the crimes—the phrase referred to torture and to executions that prolonged the agony of dying. The Supreme Court never interpreted "cruel and unusual" to prohibit all forms of capital punishment in all circumstances. Indeed, a number of states had imposed the death penalty for a variety of crimes and allowed juries to decide when the condemned could be sentenced to death. But many believed, and in 1972 the Supreme Court agreed, that the imposition of the death penalty was random and arbitrary.[76]

The Supreme Court's 1972 decision stated that the death penalty, as then applied, violated the Eighth and Fourteenth Amendments. It ruled that capital punishment is not necessarily cruel and unusual if the criminal has killed or attempted to kill someone. In its opinion, the Court invited the states to make more precise laws so that the death penalty would be applied more consistently. A majority of states have done so. In the 1990s, an increasing number of states are executing death-row inmates. Indeed, although there were almost no executions in the 1970s, during the 1980s and

---

74. 367 U.S. 643 (1961).
75. *Massachusetts v. Sheppard,* 468 U.S. 981 (1984).
76. *Furman v. Georgia,* 408 U.S. 238 (1972).

Capital punishment became a viable alternative after a 1972 Supreme Court ruling. In 1992, Arizona executed its first inmate in twenty-nine years, Delaware its first in forty-six years, and California its first in twenty-five years.

1990s there have been as many as 37 in one year. Since 1976, there have been over 230 executions nationwide. (Also, soon there may be federal executions. See this chapter's feature on *Politics and the Death Penalty*.)

Issues surrounding the sanity of death-row inmates have come up in the last decade. In 1986, the Supreme Court ruled that the U.S. Constitution bars states from executing convicted killers who have become insane while waiting on death row *(Ford v. Wainwright)*.[77] Despite this ruling, in 1989 (in *Penry v. Lynaugh*), the Supreme Court held that mentally retarded persons may be executed for murder.[78] In the same year, the Court found that defendants who were as young as sixteen could be executed if they had committed a murder.[79] Finally, in *Murray v. Giarratano*, the Court held that indigent death-row inmates have no constitutional right to a lawyer for a second round of state court appeals.[80]

The Supreme Court also must wrestle with issues involving racial discrimination and the death penalty. When the Court considered statistical evidence regarding one state's death-sentencing process, which the defendant claimed was racially discriminatory, the Court held that some disparities are an inevitable part of the criminal justice system and do not necessarily violate the Constitution.[81] In Georgia, in 1978, the defendant, a black man, was convicted of armed robbery and murder—shooting a white police officer in the face during the robbery of a store. The jury recommended the death penalty, and the trial court followed the recommendation. On appeal, the defendant presented a statistical study based on more than two thousand

---

77. 477 U.S. 399 (1986).
78. 492 U.S. 302 (1989).
79. *Stanford v. Kentucky*, 492 U.S. 361 (1989).
80. 492 U.S. 1 (1989).
81. *McCleskey v. Kemp*, 481 U.S. 279 (1987).

POLITICS AND THE DEATH PENALTY
Federal Crimes Punishable by Death

The death penalty was widely accepted when the Constitution and the Bill of Rights were written and ratified. At the time, the states made many offenses punishable by death. South Carolina, for example, classified 165 offenses as capital crimes. The federal government authorized capital punishment in fewer cases (notably, treason).

By the twentieth century, however, the number of crimes subject to the death penalty had dwindled. From the 1930s to the 1960s, almost 90 percent of the cases in which the death penalty was applied involved murder; most of the rest involved rape. Kidnapping, aircraft piracy, espionage, and treason were involved in only 1 percent of the cases. Today, virtually all death sentences are for murder.

State prosecutors have always been more vigorous than federal prosecutors in seeking the death penalty for capital crimes. In fact, the federal government had not executed anyone in almost thirty years when, in 1988, Congress amended the Continuing Drug Enterprises Act (the "Drug Kingpin Act"). The amendment authorized the death penalty for a killing associated with a "continuing criminal enterprise," such as drug trafficking. In 1992, federal prosecutors began to seek the death penalty vigorously in such cases. In 1994, in Terre Haute, Indiana, the Federal Bureau of Prisons built the first national execution chamber in U.S. history. The accompanying table indicates the number of federal cases from 1988 to 1995 in which the death penalty was initially sought and the subsequent disposition of those cases.

FEDERAL DEATH PENALTY, 1988–1995*

Total number of defendants against whom the death penalty was initially sought	48
Disposition of cases:	
—Sentenced to death (now pending on appeal)	6
—Sentenced to less than death (after jury/judge decided against death)	11
—Capital prosecution discontinued by the government	13
—Died prior to arrest	1
—Committed suicide during trial	1
—Awaiting trial on capital charges	16

SOURCE: NAACP Legal Defense Fund, Federal Death Penalty Resource Counsel Project, National Coalition to Abolish the Death Penalty.
*As of June 1995.

murder cases that occurred in Georgia during the 1970s. The study purported to show that the death sentence was imposed more often on black defendants convicted of killing whites than on white defendants convicted of killing blacks. The Supreme Court decided that the statistics did not prove that race enters into capital sentencing decisions or that it was a factor in the defendant's case. The Court stated that the unpredictability of jury decisions does not justify their condemnation, because it is the jury's function to make difficult judgments. The Court explained that any method for determining guilt or punishment has its weaknesses and the potential for misuse. Despite such imperfections, the Court concluded, constitutional guarantees are met when the method has been made as fair as possible.

Capital punishment remains one of the most debated aspects of our criminal justice system. Those in favor of it maintain that it serves as a deterrent to serious crime and satisfies society's need for justice and fair play. Those opposed to the death penalty do not believe it has any deterrent value and hold that it constitutes a barbaric act in an otherwise civilized society. Recent public opinion polls have demonstrated that a large majority of Americans favor using the death penalty more frequently.

CIVIL LIBERTIES: UNFINISHED WORK

During the 1950s, 1960s, and 1970s, the United States Supreme Court made numerous landmark decisions establishing new liberties for all Americans. During the 1980s and early 1990s, federal judges issued fewer important decisions regarding civil liberties. At the state level, though, the state supreme courts continued to expand civil liberties beyond what the federal courts were willing to do. We can expect this trend toward increased state authority and expanded civil liberties to continue and to serve as an example of the flexibility of the American system of government.

The courts certainly will have to grapple with free speech issues relating to what is and is not obscene. Also, the extent to which unpopular groups are allowed to express themselves will certainly be an ongoing issue with which the courts will have to deal. First Amendment issues undoubtedly will be brought to the fore as the political correctness movement continues to meet opposition from advocates of free speech.

Perhaps privacy issues will occupy the courts' calendars even more. No one quite knows where the "information highway" is going and how it will be built. What is certain is that increasing numbers of Americans will be able to have access to data banks in this country and throughout the world. Increasing numbers of Americans will communicate via E-mail over the information highway. More and more of what is found in print today will be available on the Internet and other computer networks. How much monitoring of the information highway should the government undertake? No one knows the answer to this critical question, but we can be certain that the courts will have to draft decisions about it.

The abortion issue as it relates to privacy and other constitutional matters has yet to be resolved and constitutes some of the major unfinished work in the area of civil liberties. Those for and against abortion can be expected to continue their aggressive lobbying on behalf of their respective positions. The Supreme Court in particular may be faced with difficult questions relating to this issue.

Finally, because crime continues to be a major problem in the United States, the rights of the accused will not remain unchallenged. As society looks for new ways to halt crime in this country, attempts will continue to be made to make it easier for police and prison officials to apprehend suspected individuals and to keep convicted criminals in prison longer.

GETTING INVOLVED
Your Civil Liberties: Searches and Seizures

What happens if you are stopped by members of the police force? Your civil liberties protect you from having to provide any other information than your name and address. Indeed, you are not really required to produce identification, although it is a good idea to show this to the officers. Normally, even if you have not been placed under arrest, the officers have the right to frisk you for weapons, and you must let them proceed. The officers cannot, however, check your person or your clothing further if, in their judgment, no weaponlike object is produced. The officers may search you only if they have a search warrant or probable cause that they will likely find incriminating evidence if the search is conducted. Normally, it is unwise to resist physically the officers' attempt to search you if they do not have probable cause or a warrant; it is usually best simply to refuse orally to give permission for the search, preferably in the presence of a witness. Also, it is usually advisable to tell the officer as little as possible about yourself and the situation that is under investigation. Being polite and courteous, though firm, is better than acting out of anger or frustration and making the officers irritable. If you are arrested, it is best to keep quiet until you can speak with a lawyer.

If you are in your car and are stopped by the police, the same fundamental rules apply. Always be ready to show your driver's license and car registration quickly. You may be asked to get out of the car. The officers may use a flashlight to peer inside if it is too dark to see otherwise. None of this constitutes a search. A true search requires either a warrant or probable cause. No officer has the legal right to search your car simply to find out if you may have committed a crime. Passengers in a car that has been stopped by the police are legally required only to give a name and address. Passengers are not even obligated to produce a piece of identification.

If you are in your residence and a police officer with a search warrant appears, you should examine the warrant before granting entry. A warrant that is correctly made out will state the exact place or persons to be searched, a description of the object sought, and the date of the warrant (which should be no more than ten days old), and it will bear the signature of a judge or magistrate. If the search warrant is in order, you should not make any statement. If you believe the warrant to be invalid, you should make it clear orally that you have not consented to the search, preferably in the presence of a witness. If the warrant later is proved to be invalid, normally any evidence obtained will be considered illegal.

Officers who attempt to enter your home without a search warrant can do so only if they are pursuing a suspected felon into the house. Rarely is it advisable to give permission for a warrantless search. You, as the resident, must be the one to give permission if any evidence obtained will be considered to be legal. The landlord, manager, or head of a college dormitory cannot give legal permission. A roommate, however, can give permission for a search of his or her room, which may allow the police to search those areas in which you have personal belongings.

If you find yourself a guest in a location that is being legally searched, you may be legally searched also. But unless you have been placed under arrest, you cannot be compelled to go to the police station or into a squad car.

If you would like to find out more about your rights and obligations under the laws of searches and seizures, you might wish to contact the following organizations:

The American Civil Liberties Union
22 East 40th St.
New York, NY 10016
212-725-1222

Legal Defense Fund
67 Winthrop St.
Cambridge, MA 02138
617-864-8680

KEY TERMS

actionable 117	defamation of character 115	hecklers' veto 116
actual malice 117	dual citizenship 104	incorporation theory 105
bad-tendency rule 111	establishment clause 106	libel 116
Bill of Rights 103	euthanasia 125	preferred-position test 111
civil liberties 103	exclusionary rule 128	prior restraint 111
civil rights 103	fairness doctrine 120	slander 115
clear and present danger	fighting words 115	sliding-scale test 111
test 110	free exercise clause 109	symbolic speech 112
commercial speech 112	gag order 117	writ of *habeas corpus* 126

 CHAPTER SUMMARY

1. To deal with American colonists' fears of a too-powerful national government, after the adoption of the U.S. Constitution, Congress proposed a Bill of Rights. These ten amendments to the Constitution were ratified by the states by the end of 1791. The amendments represent civil liberties—that is, they are limitations on government.

2. Originally, the Bill of Rights limited only the power of the federal government, not that of the states. Gradually, however, the Supreme Court accepted the incorporation theory under which no state can violate the Bill of Rights.

3. The First Amendment protects against government interference with the freedom of religion by requiring a separation of church and state and by guaranteeing the free exercise of religion. The separation of church and state is mandated in the establishment clause. Under this clause, the Supreme Court has ruled against officially sponsored prayer, Bible-reading sessions, and "meditation, prayer, or silent reflection" in public schools. The Court has also struck down laws forbidding the teaching of evolution or requiring the teaching of the biblical story of the Creation. The government can provide financial aid to religious schools if the aid is secular in aim, the aid does not have the primary effect of advancing or inhibiting religion, and the government avoids "an excessive entanglement with religion."

4. The First Amendment protects against government interference with the freedom of speech, which includes symbolic speech (wearing black armbands to protest a war, for example). Restrictions are permitted when expression presents a clear and present danger to the peace or public order, or when expression has a bad tendency (that is, when it might lead to some "evil"). Expression may be restrained before it occurs, but such prior restraint has a "heavy presumption" against its constitutionality. Commercial speech (advertising) and noncommercial speech by businesses have received First Amendment protection. Speech that has not received First Amendment protection includes expression judged to be obscene, utterances considered to be slanderous, and speech constituting fighting words or a hecklers' veto.

5. The First Amendment protects against government interference with the freedom of the press, which can be regarded as a special instance of freedom of speech. Speech by the press that does not receive protection includes libelous statements made with actual malice. Publication of news about a criminal trial may be restricted by a gag order under unusual circumstances. The press may be asked to cooperate in criminal investigations by revealing its sources or providing other evidence in response to subpoenas or search warrants. In most states, shield laws protect reporters from having to reveal their sources and confidential information.

6. The First Amendment protects the right to assemble peaceably and to petition the government. Permits may be required for parades, sound trucks, and demonstrations to maintain the public order, and a permit may be denied to protect the public safety. To avoid government interference with freedom of association, an organization cannot be required to publish a list of its members.

7. Under the Ninth Amendment, rights not specifically mentioned in the Constitution are not denied to the people. Among these unspecified rights is a right to privacy, which has been implied through the First, Third, Fourth, Fifth, and Ninth Amendments. This right has been used to strike down a law prohibiting the use of contraceptives and to protect a woman's right to control reproduction. The right to privacy has not been held to protect homosexual acts. Whether the right to privacy includes the right to die is an ongoing controversial issue.

8. The Constitution includes protections for the rights of persons accused of crimes. Under the Fourth Amendment, no one may be subject to an unreasonable search or seizure or arrested except on probable cause. Under the Fifth Amendment, an accused person has the right to remain silent. Under the Sixth Amendment, an accused person must be informed of the reason for his or her arrest. The accused also has the right to adequate counsel, even if he or she cannot afford an attorney, and the right to a prompt arraignment and a speedy and public trial before an impartial jury selected from a cross section of the community. Under the Eighth Amendment, cruel and unusual punishment is prohibited. The exclusionary rule forbids the admission in court of illegally seized evidence. There is a "good faith exception" to the exclusionary rule: Illegally seized evidence need not be thrown out owing to, for example, a technical defect in a search warrant. Whether the death penalty is cruel and unusual punishment continues to be debated.

QUESTIONS FOR REVIEW AND DISCUSSION

1. The Bill of Rights initially applied only to the federal government. Does this mean that the states' governments had an unlimited ability to bridle their citizens' basic civil liberties? Why or why not?

2. "If parents had the ability to choose freely which schools their children attended, the school prayer issue would be much less important." Do you agree or disagree with this statement? Explain your answer.

3. The Supreme Court has often made the distinction between free speech and less-protected commercial speech. Why do you think a distinction has been made between "regular" speech and commercial speech?

4. What is the trade-off between judges' issuing gag orders and the public's "right to know"? In other words, whose freedoms and liberties are at issue when a gag order is instituted by a judge?

5. Where in the Constitution is there a guaranteed right to privacy?

6. Today there are numerous "drug exceptions" to the Fourth Amendment's prohibition against unreasonable searches and seizures. What are the advantages and drawbacks involved in allowing such drug exceptions, which are typically used when the possibility of illegal drug manufacture, sale, or use is involved?

7. "As long as there is the possibility of one innocent person's being put to death under capital punishment laws, such laws should be deemed unconstitutional." Do you agree or disagree with this statement? Why?

LOGGING ON: CIVIL LIBERTIES

U.S. Department of State reports on human rights practices in various countries are available through **gopher** by searching for

U.S. Department of State Foreign Affairs Network (DOS FAN)

You could choose, for example, to look at the 1994 report for Burma, which can be found under East Asia and the Pacific.

On the topic of abortion, two news groups might be of interest if you like to debate. The first is

alt.abortion.inequity

The second news group is

talk.abortion

If the subject of censorship is close to your heart, you will certainly find Project Censored's list of the Top Ten Censored Stories to be a must read. Use **gopher** to log into

zippy.sonoma.edu

Once you're on, look for the Project Censored directory. In that directory you will find the Top Ten Censored Stories lists for the last several years. This is a very interesting project that is well worth investigating.

 ## SELECTED REFERENCES

Brownlie, Ian. *Basic Documents on Human Rights*. 3d ed. New York: Oxford University Press, 1993. This compact handbook gives a useful collection of sources on human rights throughout the world. It includes recent U.N. declarations; European conventions; and Latin American, African, and Asian human rights developments.

Calvi, James V., and Susan Coleman. *Cases in Constitutional Law: Summaries and Critiques*. Englewood Cliffs, N.J.: Prentice-Hall, 1994. Of the 122 significant Supreme Court cases involving the Constitution included in this book, dozens apply to civil liberties, including freedom of religion (Chapter 6); freedom of speech, press, and association (Chapter 7); and the rights of accused persons (Chapter 8).

Carroll, William A., and Normal B. Smith, eds. *American Constitutional Rights: Cases, Documents and Commentary*. Lanham, Md.: University Press of America, 1991. This casebook describes the fluctuation, growth, and decline in the constitutional rights of the individual throughout American history.

Cushman, Robert. *Cases in Civil Liberties*. 6th ed. Englewood Cliffs, N.J.: Prentice-Hall, 1994. This collection of Supreme Court cases includes introductory notes that place each opinion in its social, economic, and political context. The book includes cases involving the nationalization of the Bill of Rights, all First Amendment rights, and the power to protect individuals.

Lewis, Anthony. *Gideon's Trumpet*. New York: Vintage, 1964. This work is absolutely essential reading for understanding how criminal rights cases reach the Supreme Court.

Pacheco, Josephine S., ed. *To Secure the Blessings of Liberty: Rights in American History*. Lanham, Md.: University Press of America and Center for the Study of Constitutional Rights, 1993. The essays in this book examine the expanding concepts of liberty by demonstrating the relevance of the Bill of Rights in today's world.

Rauch, Jonathan. *Kindly Inquisitors: The New Attacks on Free Thought*. Chicago: University of Chicago Press, 1993. The author attempts to move beyond the First Amendment in defending morality. He examines fundamentalists' beliefs, intellectual egalitarian beliefs, and humanitarian beliefs, the latter involving the "political correctness" movement.

Shriffin, Steven H. *The First Amendment, Democracy, and Romance*. Cambridge, Mass.: Harvard University Press, 1990. In this highly readable and well-researched work, Shriffin argues that the First Amendment should be interpreted more broadly and that emotion, as well as logic, has its place in the law.

Stone, Geoffrey R., Richard A. Epstein, and Cass R. Sunstein, *The Bill of Rights in the Modern State*. Chicago: University of Chicago Press, 1992. This collection of essays written by prominent constitutional scholars explores some of today's most controversial constitutional issues. Such issues as freedom of religion, freedom of speech, and constitutional interpretation are discussed from a variety of perspectives.

Waldron, Jeremy. *Liberal Rights: Collected Papers 1981–1991*. New York: Cambridge University Press, 1993. The author deals with freedom, toleration, and neutrality in arguing for a robust conception of liberty. He defends the right of people to act in ways that others might not approve of. He also argues that the state should be neutral with respect to religious and ethical systems.

5
Civil Rights

 CHAPTER OUTLINE

WHAT IF . . .
We Had Unrestricted Immigration?

Until 1875, the United States was open to almost unlimited immigration. Only prostitutes and convicts were excluded. But government policy has undergone many permutations since that time, so by the mid-1990s American immigration laws have become a complicated mix of quotas and special provisions—over thirty different categories. These include quotas by region of the world, country, skill, and economic condition. Immigration quotas also apply to relatives of U.S. citizens, refugees, those seeking temporary political asylum, and seasonal laborers (migrant workers). Under a recent law, so-called employer sanctions impose fines and other penalties on persons (companies) knowingly hiring illegal aliens.

What if the United States were to return to an open immigration policy? The world in the 1990s is characterized by easy transportation; mobility; and rapid, sometimes simultaneous, worldwide communications. People in every corner of the world can learn about life in the United States. For many in countries torn by strife and plagued by poverty, the United States still seems a golden land of economic opportunity and political freedom. Moreover, the "American way of life," including its popular culture of emblematic blue jeans, hamburgers, rock music, and other distinctive characteristics, has an enormous allure for people in many other places. Thus, an open immigration policy, no questions asked, would clearly stimulate a huge number of people to come to the United States or to send their children or other relatives.

With open immigration, the arrival of these millions would have both negative and positive consequences. On the negative side, U.S. institutions would be challenged by the surge of new persons requiring education, housing, health care, and other services. A relatively unmonitored immigration policy no doubt would allow in some new criminals, human rights abusers, and drug dealers. The needs of sick persons seeking medical help and the poor, unskilled, and unemployable among the newcomers would place severe strains on cities, counties, states, and the federal government. Racially, ethnically, and religiously diverse immigrant groups might clash with one another and increase the tension in U.S. neighborhoods. This has happened with recent Vietnamese and Korean immigrants on the one hand and established African Americans, Hispanics, and European

Americans on the other, in New York City and other places.

There would, however, also be great advantages to open immigration. Entrepreneurs and others wishing to move away from places with an uncertain future (Hong Kong, for instance, which reverts to Chinese control in 1997) would bring their capital, skills, and energy, which would stimulate the economy. The new wave of immigrants also would bring their cultures and, in the manner of traditional immigrant groups, greatly enrich American music, art, dance, and a host of other cultural forms.

One thing is certain: With or without unrestricted immigration, America again is becoming a land of immigrants. Immigration in the 1980s increased the number of Americans for whom English was a foreign language. By the beginning of the 1990s, the number of U.S. residents for whom English was a foreign language was more than 32 million Americans. That represents one in seven of the over 230 million residents who are five years old or older. Indeed, the projections are that even without unrestricted immigration, minority groups will make up 47 percent of the U.S. population by the middle of the next century.

1. When did your family immigrate to the United States? From what country did they come?
2. Would they be able to immigrate to the United States today?
3. What did they do for a living when they arrived?

We hold these Truths to be self-evident, that all Men are created equal . . .

These are beautiful words, to be sure. But when they were written in 1776, the term *men* had a somewhat different meaning than it has today. It did not include slaves, women, or Native Americans. So individuals in these groups were not considered equal. It has taken this nation over two hundred years to approach even a semblance of equality among all Americans. Certainly, the issue of equality faces the many new immigrants that this nation welcomes each year. If the United States were to allow open immigration, as it did for much of this nation's history (as explained in this chapter's *What If . . .*), numerous political, legal, and social issues with respect to equality among all Americans would become even more important.

The struggle for equality has not been easy. It is a struggle perhaps best described as an effort to strengthen and to expand constitutional guarantees to *all* persons in our society. In this chapter we examine the rights of various minorities and groups: African Americans, Mexican Americans and other Hispanics, Native Americans, Asian Americans, women, gays, the elderly, and juveniles—to name just some of them.

Minority rights have often been called civil rights, and the quest for the expansion of minority rights has been called the civil rights movement. Because the modern civil rights movement started with the struggle for African-American equality, that story is told first.

AFRICAN AMERICANS AND THE CONSEQUENCES OF SLAVERY IN THE UNITED STATES

Article I, Section 2, of the U.S. Constitution states that congressional representatives and direct taxes are to be apportioned among the states according to their respective numbers. These numbers were to be obtained by adding to the total number of free persons "three fifths of all other Persons." The "other persons" were, of course, slaves. A slave was thus equal to three-fifths of a white person.[1] As Abraham Lincoln stated sarcastically, "All men are created equal, except Negroes." Before 1863, the Constitution thus protected slavery and made equality impossible in the sense we use the word today. African-American leader Frederick Douglass pointed out that "Liberty and Slavery—opposite as Heaven and Hell—are both in the Constitution."

The constitutionality of slavery was confirmed just a few years before the outbreak of the Civil War in the famous *Dred Scott v. Sanford*[2] case of 1857. The Supreme Court held that slaves were not citizens of the United States, nor were they entitled to the rights and privileges of citizenship. The Court also ruled that the Missouri Compromise, which banned slavery in the territories north of 36° 30' latitude (the southern border of Missouri), was unconstitutional. The *Dred Scott* decision had grave consequences. Most observers contend that the ruling contributed to making the Civil War inevitable.

---

1. It may seem ironic that the median wage of African Americans today is approximately three-fifths that of whites.
2. 19 Howard 393 (1857).

DID YOU KNOW . . .
That the original Constitution failed to describe the status of a citizen or how this status could be acquired?

This portrait is of Dred Scott (1795–1858), an American slave who was born in South Hampton County, Virginia. He was the nominal plaintiff in a test case that sought to obtain his freedom on the ground that he lived in the free state of Illinois. Although the Supreme Court ruled against him, he was soon emancipated and became a hotel porter in St. Louis.

With the emancipation of the slaves by President Lincoln's Emancipation Proclamation in 1863 and the passage of the Thirteenth, Fourteenth, and Fifteenth Amendments during the Reconstruction period following the Civil War, constitutional inequality was ended. The Thirteenth Amendment (1865) states that neither slavery nor involuntary servitude shall exist within the United States. The Fourteenth Amendment (ratified on July 9, 1868) tells us that *all* persons born or naturalized in the United States are citizens of the United States. It states, furthermore, "No State shall make or enforce any law which shall abridge the privileges or immunities of the citizens of the United States; nor shall any State deprive any person of life, liberty or property, without due process of law; nor deny to any person within its jurisdiction the equal protection of the laws." The Fifteenth Amendment seems equally impressive: "The right of citizens of the United States to vote shall not be denied or abridged by the United States or by any State on account of race, color, or previous condition of servitude." Pressure was brought to bear on Congress to include in the Fourteenth and Fifteenth Amendments a prohibition against discrimination based on sex, but with no success.

As we shall see, the words of these amendments had little immediate effect. Although slavery was legally and constitutionally ended, African-American political and social inequality has continued to the present time. In the following sections, we discuss several landmarks in the struggle of African Americans to overcome this inequality.

The Civil Rights Acts of 1865 to 1875

At the end of the Civil War, President Lincoln's Republican party controlled the national government and most state governments, and the so-called Radical Republicans, with their strong antislavery stance, controlled that party. The Radical Republicans pushed through the Thirteenth, Fourteenth, and Fifteenth Amendments to the Constitution (the "Civil War amend-

Abraham Lincoln reads the Emancipation Proclamation on July 22, 1862. The Emancipation Proclamation did not abolish slavery (that was done by the Thirteenth Amendment, in 1865), but it ensured that slavery would be abolished if and when the North won the Civil War. After the Battle of Antietam on September 17, 1862, Lincoln publicly announced the Emancipation Proclamation and declared that all slaves residing in states that were still in rebellion against the United States on January 1, 1863, would be freed once those states came under the military control of the Union Army.

ments"). From 1865 to 1875, they succeeded in getting Congress to pass a series of civil rights acts that were aimed at enforcing these amendments. Even Republicans who were not necessarily sympathetic to a strong anti-slavery position wanted to undercut Democratic domination of the South. What better way to do so than to guarantee African-American suffrage?

The first Civil Rights Act in the Reconstruction period that followed the Civil War was passed in 1866 over the veto of President Andrew Johnson. That act extended citizenship to anyone born in the United States and gave African Americans full equality before the law. The act further authorized the president to enforce the law with national armed forces. Many considered the law to be unconstitutional, but such problems disappeared in 1868 with the adoption of the Fourteenth Amendment.

Among the six other civil rights acts in the nineteenth century, one of the more important ones was the Enforcement Act of May 31, 1870, which set out specific criminal sanctions for interfering with the right to vote as protected by the Fifteenth Amendment and by the Civil Rights Act of 1866. Equally important was the Civil Rights Act of April 20, 1872, known as the Anti–Ku Klux Klan Act. This act made it a federal crime for anyone to use law or custom to deprive an individual of his or her rights, privileges, and immunities secured by the Constitution or by any federal law.

The last of these early civil rights acts, known as the Second Civil Rights Act, was passed on March 1, 1875. It declared that everyone is entitled to full and equal enjoyment of public accommodations, theaters, and other places of public amusement, and it imposed penalties for violators. This act, however, was virtually nullified by the *Civil Rights Cases* of 1883 discussed below.

The Ineffectiveness of the Civil Rights Acts

The Reconstruction statutes, or civil rights acts, ultimately did little to secure equality for African Americans in their civil rights. Both the *Civil Rights Cases* and the case of *Plessy v. Ferguson* effectively nullified these acts.

The *Civil Rights Cases*.   The Supreme Court invalidated the 1875 Civil Rights Act when it held, in the *Civil Rights Cases*[3] of 1883, that the enforcement clause of the Fourteenth Amendment (which states that "[n]o State shall make or enforce any law which shall abridge the privileges or immunities of citizens") was limited to correcting actions by states in their official acts; thus, the discriminatory acts of private citizens were not illegal. ("Individual invasion of individual rights is not the subject matter of the Amendment.") The 1883 Supreme Court decision met with widespread approval throughout most of the United States.

Twenty years after the Civil War, the nation was all too willing to forget about the Civil War amendments and the civil rights legislation of the 1860s and 1870s. The other civil rights laws that the Court specifically did not invalidate became dead letters in the statute books, although they were never repealed by Congress. At the same time, many former proslavery secessionists had regained political power in the southern states.

---

3. 109 U.S. 3 (1883).

DID YOU KNOW . . .
That by the end of the Civil War, 180,000 African-American troops were in arms for the North, rendering services that included occupying conquered territory, and that Lincoln said the war could never have been concluded without these occupying forces?

SEPARATE-BUT-EQUAL DOCTRINE
The doctrine holding that segregation in schools and public accommodations does not imply that one race is superior to another; rather, it implies that each race is entitled to separate-but-equal facilities.

***Plessy v. Ferguson:* Separate but Equal.**   A key decision during this period concerned Homer Plessy, a Louisiana resident who was one-eighth African American. In 1892, he was riding in a train from New Orleans when the conductor made him leave the car, which was restricted to whites, and directed him to a car for nonwhites. At that time, Louisiana had a statute providing for separate railway cars for whites and African Americans.

Plessy went to court, claiming that such a statute was contrary to the Fourteenth Amendment's equal protection clause. In 1896, the United States Supreme Court rejected Plessy's contention. The Court concluded that the Fourteenth Amendment "could not have been intended to abolish distinctions based upon color, or to enforce social . . . equality." The Court indicated that segregation alone did not violate the Constitution: "Laws permitting, and even requiring their separation in places where they are liable to be brought into contact do not necessarily imply the inferiority of either race to the other."[4] So was born the **separate-but-equal doctrine.**

The only justice to vote against this decision was John Marshall Harlan, a former slaveholder. He stated in his dissent, "Our Constitution is color-blind, and neither knows nor tolerates classes among citizens." Justice Harlan also predicted that the separate-but-equal doctrine would "in time prove to be . . . as pernicious as the decision . . . in the Dred Scott Case."

For more than half a century, the separate-but-equal doctrine was accepted as consistent with the equal protection clause in the Fourteenth Amendment. In practical terms, the separate-but-equal doctrine effectively nullified this clause. *Plessy v. Ferguson* became the judicial cornerstone of racial discrimination throughout the United States. Even though *Plessy* upheld segregated facilities in railway cars only, it was assumed that the Supreme Court was upholding segregation everywhere as long as the separate facilities were equal. The result was a system of racial segregation, particularly in the South, that required separate drinking fountains; separate seats in theaters, restaurants, and hotels; separate public toilets; and separate waiting rooms for the two races—collectively known as Jim Crow laws. "Separate" was indeed the rule, but "equal" was never enforced, nor was it a reality.

The End of the Separate-but-Equal Doctrine

A successful attack on the separate-but-equal doctrine began with a series of lawsuits in the 1930s to admit African Americans to state professional schools. By 1950, the Supreme Court had ruled that African Americans who were admitted to a state university could not be assigned to separate sections of classrooms, libraries, and cafeterias. In 1951, Oliver Brown decided that his eight-year-old daughter, Linda Carol Brown, should not have to go to an all-nonwhite elementary school twenty-one blocks from her home, when there was a white school only seven blocks away. The National Association for the Advancement of Colored People (NAACP), formed in 1909, decided to help Oliver Brown. The results were monumental in their impact on American society.

---

4. *Plessy v. Ferguson,* 163 U.S. 537 (1896).

Brown v. Board of Education of Topeka.   The 1954 unanimous decision in *Brown v. Board of Education of Topeka*[5] established that public school segregation of races violates the equal protection clause of the Fourteenth Amendment. Concluding that separate schools are inherently unequal, Chief Justice Warren stated that "to separate [African Americans] from others of similar age and qualifications solely because of their race generates a feeling of inferiority as to their status in the community that may affect their hearts and minds in a way unlikely ever to be undone." Warren said that separation implied inferiority, whereas the majority opinion in *Plessy v. Ferguson* had said the opposite.

"With All Deliberate Speed."   The following year, in *Brown v. Board of Education*[6] (sometimes called the second *Brown* decision), the Court asked for rearguments concerning the way in which compliance with the 1954 decision should be undertaken. The Supreme Court declared that the lower courts must ensure that African Americans would be admitted to schools on a nondiscriminatory basis "with all deliberate speed." The high court told lower federal courts that they had to take an activist role in society. The district courts were to consider devices in their desegregation orders that might include "the school transportation system, personnel, [and] revision of school districts and attendance areas into compact units to achieve a system of determining admission to the public schools on a nonracial basis."

Reactions to School Integration

One unlooked-for effect of the "all deliberate speed" decision was that the term *deliberate* was used as a loophole by some officials, who were able to delay desegregation by showing that they were indeed acting with all deliberate speed but still were unable to desegregate. Another reaction to court-ordered desegregation was "white flight." In some school districts, the public school population became 100 percent nonwhite when white parents sent their children to newly established private schools, sometimes known as "segregation academies."

The white South did not let the Supreme Court ruling go unchallenged. Arkansas's Governor Orval Faubus used the state's National Guard to block the integration of Central High School in Little Rock in September 1957. The federal court demanded that the troops be withdrawn. Finally, President Dwight Eisenhower had to federalize the Arkansas National Guard and send it to quell the violence. Central High became integrated.

The universities in the South, however, remained segregated. When James Meredith, an African-American student, attempted to enroll at the University of Mississippi in Oxford in 1962, violence flared there, as it had in Little Rock. Two men were killed, and a number of people were injured in campus rioting. President John Kennedy sent federal marshals and ordered federal troops to maintain peace and protect Meredith. One year later, George Wallace, governor of Alabama, promised "to stand in the schoolhouse door" to prevent two African-American students from enrolling at the University of Alabama

Jim Crow laws required the segregation of the races, particularly in public facilities such as this theater. The name "Jim Crow" originates from a nineteenth-century vaudeville character who was called Jim (which was a common name) Crow (for a black-colored bird). Thus, the name "Jim Crow" was applied to laws and practices affecting African Americans.

---

5. 347 U.S. 483 (1954).
6. 349 U.S. 294 (1955).

in Tuscaloosa. Wallace was forced to back down when Kennedy federalized the Alabama National Guard.

An Integrationist Attempt at a Cure: Busing

In most parts of the United States, the process of achieving racial balance in schools has been made difficult because of residential concentration by race. Although it is true that a number of school boards in northern districts created segregated schools by drawing school district lines arbitrarily, the residential concentration of African Americans and other minorities in well-defined geographic locations has contributed to the difficulty of achieving racial balance. This concentration results in *de facto* segregation.

Court-Ordered Busing. The obvious solution to both *de facto* and *de jure* segregation seemed to be transporting some African-American school-children to white schools and some white schoolchildren to African-American schools. Increasingly, the courts ordered school districts to engage in such **busing** across neighborhoods. Busing was unpopular with many groups. In the mid-1970s, almost 50 percent of African Americans interviewed were opposed to busing, and approximately three-fourths of the whites interviewed held the same opinion.[7] Nonetheless, through 1976, the Supreme Court fairly consistently came down on the side of upholding busing plans in the cases it decided.

Changing Directions. In an apparent reversal of previous decisions, the Supreme Court in June 1986 allowed the Norfolk, Virginia, public school

---

7. Diane Ravitch, "Busing: The Solution That Has Failed to Solve," *New York Times*, December 21, 1975, section 4, p. 3.

DE FACTO SEGREGATION
Racial segregation that occurs not as a result of laws but because of past social and economic conditions and residential patterns.

DE JURE SEGREGATION
Racial segregation that occurs because of laws or administrative decisions by public agencies.

BUSING
The transportation of public school students from areas where they live to schools in other areas to eliminate school segregation based on residential patterns.

After the *Brown* decision, aggressive white reaction followed for a number of years, particularly with respect to the attempt to desegregate the school system in Little Rock, Arkansas. After the local school board secured approval of the federal courts for desegregation, Governor Orval Faubus sent in the state's National Guard to preserve order when a handful of African-American students entered Little Rock Central High School on September 2, 1957. The National Guard was withdrawn after a few weeks and replaced by a white mob. President Dwight Eisenhower sent in five hundred soldiers on September 24, many of whom remained there for the rest of the school year. (The high school was closed in 1958).

To remedy *de facto* segregation, the courts often imposed busing requirements on school districts. Busing meant transporting children of white neighborhoods to nonwhite schools, and vice versa. Busing has been one of the most controversial domestic policies in the history of this country. Initially, bused students had to be escorted by police because of potential violence. This scene was photographed in Boston in the 1970s.

system to end fifteen years of court-ordered busing of elementary school-children.[8] The Norfolk school board supported the decision because of a drop in enrollment from 32,500 whites attending public schools in 1970, when busing was ordered, to fewer than 14,000 in 1985.

In 1991, the Supreme Court held, in *Board of Education v. Dowell,*[9] that a school board only needs to show that it has complied in "good faith" with a desegregation decree. In *Dowell,* the Supreme Court instructed a lower court administering the decree that if school racial concentration was a product of residential segregation that resulted from "private decision making and economics," its effects may be ignored entirely.

In *Freeman v. Pitts,*[10] decided in 1992, the Supreme Court also stressed the importance of "local control over the education of children." In *Freeman,* a Georgia school district, which had once been segregated by law and was operating under a federal district court-administered desegregation decree, was allowed to regain partial control over its schools, although it was judged to have not complied with certain aspects of the decree. In 1995, the Supreme Court ruled in *Missouri v. Jenkins* that the state of Missouri could stop spending money to attract a multiracial student body through major educational improvements. This decision dealt a potentially fatal blow to the use of magnet schools for racial integration.[11]

---

8. *Riddick v. School Board of City of Norfolk,* 627 F.Supp. 814 (E.D.Va. 1984); *certiorari* denied, 479 U.S. 938 (1986).
9. 498 U.S. 237 (1991).
10. 503 U.S. 467 (1992).
11. 115 S.Ct. 2038 (1995).

Lower federal courts have followed the Supreme Court's lead in allowing school districts to discontinue busing.[12] These and other cases hold that once a school district implements a plan to establish a racially neutral school system, the district is not responsible for any resegregation that results from changing demographics (such as "white flight"). Nevertheless, busing is still approved as a remedy for cases in which school districts are segregating students.[13]

The executive branch has also made significant changes in desegregation policy. The Reagan administration's Justice Department refused to enforce busing plans and supported congressional efforts, such as the Johnston-Helms Amendment, to restrict the power of federal district courts in ordering busing as a remedy.[14] (See this chapter's *Politics and Race* feature entitled "From Integration Back to Segregation" for a further discussion of this issue.)

Alternatives to Integrated Schools.   The integrationist approach to solving the problem of inequality in schools, which was the product of the *Brown* decision, has gradually lost support in favor of an approach that emphasizes school-funding equalization. By the end of 1994, several school-financing cases had been filed across the country, all basically alleging that poor conditions in urban schools violate state constitutional guarantees of equal educational opportunity. The goal of a racially balanced school, envisioned in the *Brown* decision, has given way to the goal of educated children. The city of Milwaukee has experimented with all-African-American, all-male schools. Some educators believe such schools provide a promising alternative to integrated public schools.

THE CIVIL RIGHTS MOVEMENT

The *Brown* decision applied only to public schools. Not much else in the structure of existing segregation was affected. In December 1955, a forty-three-year-old African-American woman, Rosa Parks, boarded a public bus in Montgomery, Alabama. When the bus became crowded and several white people stepped aboard, Parks was asked to move to the rear of the bus, the "colored" section. She refused, was arrested, and was fined $10; but that was not the end of the matter. For an entire year, African Americans boycotted the Montgomery bus line. The protest was headed by a twenty-seven-year-old Baptist minister, Dr. Martin Luther King, Jr. During the protest period, he went to jail, and his house was bombed.[15] In the face of overwhelming odds, however, King won. In 1956, the federal district court issued an injunction prohibiting the segregation of buses in Montgomery. The era of civil rights protests had begun.

The following year, in 1957, King formed the Southern Christian Leadership Conference (SCLC). King's philosophy of nonviolent civil disobedi-

---

12. See, for example, *Flax v. Potts,* 864 F.2d 1157 (5th Cir. 1989); and *Price v. Austin Independent School District,* 729 F.Supp. 533 (W.D.Tex. 1990).
13. *Keyes v. School District No. 1,* 895 F.2d 659 (10th Cir. 1990).
14. Lisa A. Stewart, "Another Skirmish in the Equal Education Battle," *Harvard Civil Rights–Civil Liberties Law Review,* Summer 1992.
15. Read King's "Letter from the Birmingham Jail" for a better understanding of this period.

POLITICS AND RACE
From Integration Back to Segregation

There have been many changes in the U.S. educational system since *Brown v. Board of Education of Topeka* in 1954. But instead of this nation's having an increasingly integrated school system, relatively recent evidence shows that there is a renewed growth of segregation in American schools. According to the National School Boards Association's report, "The Growth of Segregation in American Schools," the Northeast has the most segregated schools in the country and the

South, the most integrated. But even in the South, the trend is toward more segregation. At the beginning of the 1990s, less than 40 percent of African-American students attended predominantly white schools, compared with 44 percent in 1987.

Nationwide, one out of every three African-American and Hispanic students goes to a school with more than 90 percent minority enrollment. In the largest U.S. cities, fifteen out of sixteen African-

American and Hispanic students go to schools with almost no whites.

Has the cause been renewed racism? Not according to many observers. The major cause is that the relative proportion of whites who live in big cities has declined rapidly. Whites have left big cities, whereas immigration and high minority birth rates have increased the presence of minorities in those urban areas.

ence was influenced greatly by Henry David Thoreau's *On Civil Disobedience* and by Mahatma Gandhi's life and teachings. Gandhi had led Indian resistance to the British colonial system from 1919 to 1947. He used tactics such as demonstrations and marches, as well as purposeful, public disobedience to unjust laws, while remaining nonviolent. King's followers successfully used these methods to widen public acceptance of their case.

For the next decade, African Americans and sympathetic whites engaged in sit-ins, freedom rides, and freedom marches. In the beginning, such demonstrations were often met with violence, but the contrasting image of nonviolent African Americans and violent, hostile whites created strong public support for the civil rights movement. When African Americans in Greensboro, North Carolina, were refused service at a Woolworth's lunch counter, they organized a sit-in that was aided day after day by sympathetic whites and other African Americans. Enraged customers threw ketchup on the protestors. Some spat in their faces. But the sit-in movement continued to grow. Within six months of the first sit-in at the Greensboro Woolworth's, hundreds of lunch counters throughout the South were serving African Americans.

The sit-in technique was also used successfully to integrate interstate buses and their terminals, as well as railroads engaged in interstate transportation. Although buses and railroads that were engaged in interstate transportation were prohibited by law from segregating African Americans from whites, they stopped doing so only after the sit-in protests.[16]

---

16. See *Morgan v. Commonwealth of Virginia,* 328 U.S. 373 (1946); and *Henderson v. United States,* 339 U.S. 819 (1950).

POLITICS AND RACE
Martin Luther King, Jr.: "I Have a Dream"

On August 28, 1963, in the centennial year of the Emancipation Proclamation, a long-planned mass mobilization of civil rights supporters took place in the March on Washington for Jobs and Freedom. The march, in which 250,000 African-American and white men and women participated, was a major event in the civil rights movement and the leadership of Martin Luther King, Jr., head of the Southern Christian Leadership Conference. The March on Washington helped to generate the political momentum that resulted in the landmark civil rights legislation of 1964 and 1968. It also propelled King, an Atlanta Baptist minister, to the forefront of the civil rights movement.

The day's program included speeches by civil rights leaders John Lewis, Roy Wilkins, A. Philip Randolph, and Martin Luther King, Jr. The jobs, education, and antidiscrimination programs called for by earlier speakers were summarized in King's words:

There will be neither rest nor tranquility in America until the Negro is granted his citizenship rights. The whirlwinds of revolt will continue to shake the foundations of our nation until the bright day of justice emerges. . . . I have a dream that my

four little children will one day live in a nation where they will not be judged by the color of their skin but by the content of their character. . . . When we let freedom ring, when we let it ring from every village and every hamlet, from every state and every city, we will be able to speed up that day when all God's children, black men and white men, Jews and Gentiles, Protestants and Catholics, will be able to join hands and sing in the words of that old Negro Spiritual, "Free at last! Free at last! Thank God almighty, we are free at last!"

The contribution of Martin Luther King, Jr., to minority rights was officially recognized on October 20, 1983, when, after originally opposing the legislation, President Ronald Reagan signed into law an act establishing January 15, King's birthday, as a national holiday beginning in 1986.

SOURCE: David L. Lewis, *King: A Critical Bibliography* (New York: Praeger, 1970), pp. 210–232; and Lenwood G. Davis, *I Have a Dream . . . : The Life and Times of Martin Luther King, Jr.* (Westport, Conn.: Negro Universities Press, 1969), pp. 132–140.

The civil rights movement, with King at its head, gathered momentum in the 1960s. One of the most famous of the violence-plagued protests occurred in Birmingham, Alabama, in the spring of 1963, when Police Commissioner Eugene "Bull" Connor unleashed police dogs and used electric cattle prods against the protestors. The object of the protest had been to provoke a reaction by local officials so that the federal government would act. People throughout the country viewed the event on national television with indignation and horror, and such media coverage played a key role in the process of ending Jim Crow conditions in the United States. The ultimate result was the most important civil rights act in the nation's history, the Civil Rights Act of 1964 (to be discussed shortly).

MODERN CIVIL RIGHTS LEGISLATION AND ITS IMPLEMENTATION

In the wake of the Montgomery bus boycott, public sentiment for stronger civil rights legislation put pressure on Congress and President Dwight Eisenhower to act. The action taken was relatively symbolic. The Civil Rights Act of 1957 established a Civil Rights Commission and a new Civil Rights Division within the Justice Department.

The growing number of demonstrations and sit-ins successfully created further pressure for more legislation through the classic democratic politics of mobilization of public opinion, coordinated with the lobbying efforts of political leaders. The Civil Rights Act of 1960 was passed to protect voting rights. Whenever a pattern or practice of discrimination was documented, the Justice Department, on behalf of the voter, could bring suit, even against a state. The act also set penalties for obstructing a federal court order by threat of force and for illegally using and transporting explosives. But the 1960 Civil Rights Act, as well as that of 1957, had little substantive impact.

The same cannot be said about the Civil Rights Acts of 1964 and 1968 or the Voting Rights Act of 1965 (discussed in the next sections). Those acts marked the assumption by Congress of a leading role in the enforcement of the constitutional notion of equality for *all* Americans, as provided by the Fourteenth and Fifteenth Amendments.

The Civil Rights Act of 1964

As the civil rights movement mounted in intensity, equality before the law came to be "an idea whose time has come," in the words of conservative Senate Minority Leader Everett Dirksen. The Civil Rights Act of 1964, the most far-reaching bill on civil rights in modern times, forbade discrimination on the basis of race, color, religion, gender, and national origin.

In 1963, a historic civil rights bill was before Congress. Many opposed the bill as too radical. To galvanize senators and representatives to pass the bill, Martin Luther King, Jr., organized the March on Washington for Jobs and Freedom. On August 28, 1963, about 250,000 Americans appeared in Washington to call for its passage. At the time, it was the largest demonstration in the capital's history.

The major provisions of the act were as follows:

1. It outlawed arbitrary discrimination in voter registration.
2. It barred discrimination in public accommodations, such as hotels and restaurants, whose operations affect interstate commerce.
3. It authorized the federal government to sue to desegregate public schools and facilities.
4. It provided for the withholding of federal funds from programs administered in a discriminatory manner.
5. It established the right to equality of opportunity in employment.

Several factors led to the passage of the 1964 act. As noted earlier, there had been a dramatic change in the climate of public opinion owing to violence perpetrated against protesting African Americans and whites in the South. Second, the assassination of President John F. Kennedy in 1963, according to some, had a significant effect on the national conscience. Many believed the civil rights program to be the legislative tribute that Congress paid to the martyred Kennedy. Finally, the 1964 act could be seen partly as the result of President Lyndon B. Johnson's vigorous espousal of the legislation after his gradual conversion to the civil rights cause. The act was passed in Congress only after the longest **filibuster** in the history of the Senate (eighty-three days) and only after **cloture** was imposed for the first time to cut off a civil rights filibuster.

FILIBUSTER
In the Senate, unlimited debate to halt action on a particular bill.

CLOTURE
A method invoked to close off debate and to bring the matter under consideration to a vote in the Senate.

The Civil Rights Act of 1968 and Other Housing-Reform Legislation

Martin Luther King, Jr., was assassinated on April 4, 1968. Nine days after King's death, President Johnson signed the Civil Rights Act of 1968, which forbade discrimination in most housing and provided penalties for those attempting to interfere with individual civil rights (giving protection to civil rights workers, among others). Although the open-housing provision (called the Fair Housing Act) seemed important at the time, it was rendered superfluous by that summer, when the Supreme Court prohibited discrimination in the sale and rental of all housing, using as a precedent the Civil Rights Act of April 9, 1866.[17]

Employment and Affirmative Action

EQUAL EMPLOYMENT OPPORTUNITY COMMISSION (EEOC)
A commission established by the 1964 Civil Rights Act to (1) end discrimination based on race, color, religion, gender, or national origin in conditions of employment and (2) promote voluntary action programs by employers, unions, and community organizations to foster equal job opportunities.

Title VII of the Civil Rights Act of 1964 is the cornerstone of employment-discrimination law. It prohibits discrimination in employment based on race, color, religion, gender, or national origin. Under Title VII, executive orders were issued that banned employment discrimination by firms that received any federal funding. The 1964 Civil Rights Act created a five-member body, the **Equal Employment Opportunity Commission (EEOC)**, to administer Title VII.

The EEOC can issue interpretive guidelines and regulations, but these do not have the force of law. Rather, they give notice of the commission's enforcement policy. The EEOC also has investigatory powers. It has broad

---

17. *Jones v. Mayer*, 329 U.S. 409 (1968).

authority to require the production of documentary evidence, to hold hearings, and to **subpoena** and examine witnesses under oath.

To put teeth in the 1964 law, President Johnson applied the concept of **affirmative action** in 1965. Affirmative action can be defined as remedial steps taken to improve work opportunities for women, racial and ethnic minorities, and other persons considered to have been deprived of job opportunities in the past on the basis of their race, color, religion, gender, or national origin.

Backlash against Affirmative Action

By the early 1970s, Labor Department regulations imposing numerical employment goals and timetables had been applied to every company that did more than $10,000 worth of business of any sort with the national government. Affirmative action plans were also required whenever an employer had been ordered to develop such a plan by a court or by the EEOC because of past discrimination. Finally, labor unions that had been found to discriminate against women or minorities were required to follow affirmative action plans.

Many people became convinced that affirmative action plans had a negative impact on whites, especially white males, and such plans began to be challenged in the courts.

The *Bakke* Case. Alan Bakke, a Vietnam War veteran and engineer who had been turned down for medical school at the Davis campus of the University of California, discovered that his academic record was better than those of some of the minority applicants who had been admitted to the program. He sued the University of California regents, alleging **reverse discrimination.** The UC–Davis Medical School had held sixteen places out of one hundred for educationally "disadvantaged students" each year, and the administrators at that campus admitted to using race as a criterion for admission for these particular minority slots. At trial in 1974, Bakke said that his exclusion from medical school violated his rights under the Fourteenth Amendment's provision for equal protection of the laws.

On June 28, 1978, the Supreme Court handed down its decision in *Regents of the University of California v. Bakke*.[18] The Court did not actually rule against affirmative action programs but did hold that Bakke must be admitted to the UC–Davis Medical School because its admission policy had used race as the *sole* criterion for the sixteen "minority" positions. But Justice Lewis Powell, speaking for the Court, indicated that race can be considered "as a factor" among others in admissions (and presumably hiring) decisions. In other words, it is legal to give special consideration to "afflicted minority groups" in an effort to remedy past discrimination. Race can be one of many criteria for admission, but not the only one. So affirmative action programs, but not specific quota systems, were upheld as constitutional.

The *Weber* Case. In 1979, a claim of reverse discrimination in employment was addressed in *United Steelworkers of America v. Weber*.[19] At issue in

---

18. 438 U.S. 265 (1978).
19. 443 U.S. 1963 (1979).

SUBPOENA
To serve with a legal writ requiring a person's appearance in court to give testimony.

AFFIRMATIVE ACTION
A policy in job hiring that gives special consideration or compensatory treatment to traditionally disadvantaged groups in an effort to overcome present effects of past discrimination.

REVERSE DISCRIMINATION
The charge that affirmative action programs requiring preferential treatment or quotas discriminate against those who do not have minority status.

that case was Brian F. Weber's complaint that as a white employee in Kaiser Aluminum and Chemical Corporation's plant in Gramercy, Louisiana, he was denied his rightful place in a training program that would have raised his salary had he successfully completed it. Because of the affirmative action program in his union, he was passed over in favor of African Americans with less seniority.

The Supreme Court held against Weber. The Court stated that the prohibition against racial discrimination in Title VII must be read against the background of the legislative history of Title VII calling for voluntary or local resolution of the discrimination problems as well as against the historical context from which the 1964 Civil Rights Act arose. In other words, the union apprenticeship program at Kaiser Aluminum violated the words of the Civil Rights Act of 1964, but not its spirit. Essentially, any form of reverse discrimination—even explicit quotas—is permissible provided that it is the result of a legislative, executive, or judicial finding of past discrimination.

The Court's More Recent Record on Reverse Bias

In 1984, in *Firefighters Local Union No. 1784 v. Stotts,*[20] the Supreme Court said that layoffs of Memphis firefighters had to be done on the basis of seniority unless there were African-American employees who could prove they were victims of racial bias. In 1986, however, in *Wygant v. Jackson Board of Education,*[21] the Court sent the signal that affirmative action could apply to hiring but not to layoffs. This mixed message came from a case brought by a group of white teachers in Jackson, Michigan. The case challenged a labor contract that called for laying off three white teachers for every faculty member belonging to a minority group in order to preserve the school system's racial and ethnic ratios. In a 5-to-4 vote, the Court's majority said that the Jackson plan violated the Fourteenth Amendment's guarantee of equal protection of the laws.

In 1989, the Supreme Court considered whether whites could challenge employment decisions made on the basis of an earlier judgment that included goals for hiring African Americans as firefighters in the city of Birmingham, Alabama. White firefighters who had not been parties in the earlier proceedings alleged that because of their race, they were being denied promotions in favor of less-qualified African Americans. The Supreme Court held that the white firefighters could challenge those employment decisions.[22] In another 1989 decision, the Court overturned a local government minority-preference program, signaling to dozens of cities and states that hundreds of affirmative action programs might also be invalid.[23]

In regard to racial discrimination, the Court made it harder for minority workers to sue employers.[24] In another ruling, racial harassment was exempted from a widely used antibias law.[25] The Court also held that

---

20. 467 U.S. 561 (1984).
21. 476 U.S. 267 (1986).
22. *Martin v. Wilks,* 490 U.S. 755 (1989).
23. *Richmond v. J. A. Croson Co.,* 488 U.S. 469 (1989).
24. *Wards Cove Packing Co. v. Atonio,* 490 U.S. 642 (1989).
25. *Patterson v. McLean Credit Union,* 491 U.S. 164 (1989).

employment-discrimination laws do not apply outside the territorial limits of the United States.[26]

The Civil Rights Act of 1991

By 1990, civil rights activists were arguing that the conservative rulings of the Supreme Court made it difficult for victims of employment discrimination to prove their cases. Believing that the courts could not be counted on to expand civil rights protections, some activists turned to Congress. Congress responded with the Civil Rights Act of 1991, which effectively overturned the conservative rulings and made it easier for workers to sue employers. Another section of the act includes racial harassment under the widely used antibias law from which the Supreme Court had exempted it. Also, the act bars challenges to earlier judgments that include goals for hiring minorities by persons in the same circumstances as the firefighters in the Birmingham case—thus overruling the Supreme Court's 1989 decision on this issue. Finally, the act provides for the recovery of money damages, including punitive damages, in intentional discrimination cases and provides for jury trials in cases under Title VII of the Civil Rights Act of 1964.

Affirmative Action under Scrutiny

The momentum of affirmative action programs was reversed in 1994 and 1995. First, after the elections of 1994 gave Republicans control of Capitol Hill, it was clear that the civil rights laws were likely to be scrutinized and amended to weaken affirmative action provisions. Then, President Bill Clinton announced that he would order an internal review of affirmative action to see if the programs were working and to examine the question of whether the programs were discriminating against nonminorities. Many liberals were taken aback by this initiative from a Democratic president who had been very supportive of the rights of minorities, including women and gay men and lesbians.

   In June 1995, the Supreme Court addressed the issue of affirmative action in *Adarand Constructors, Inc. v. Pena.*[27] The case involved a minority set-aside program for federal highway contracts. A white contractor, the low bidder on the work, had charged that he had been discriminated against when the minority contractor, with a higher bid, was selected for the work. The Supreme Court, in a bitterly divided, five-to-four decision, held that federal government programs that classify people by race are presumed to be unconstitutional—even if the programs are designed for benign purposes, such as expanding opportunities for minority groups—unless a "compelling government interest" can be demonstrated. How this ruling will ultimately affect affirmative action programs is difficult to predict.

THE VOTING RIGHTS ACT OF 1965

The Fourteenth Amendment, ratified on July 9, 1868, provided for equal protection of the laws. The Fifteenth Amendment, ratified on February 3,

26. *Equal Employment Opportunity Commission v. Arabian American Oil Co.,* 499 U.S. 244 (1991).
27. 115 S.Ct. 2097 (1995).

1870, stated that "[t]he right of citizens of the United States to vote shall not be denied or abridged by the United States or by any State on account of race, color, or previous condition of servitude." Immediately after the adoption of those amendments, African Americans in the South began to participate in political life—but only because of the presence of federal government troops and northern Radical Republicans who controlled the state legislatures.

Historical Barriers to African-American Political Participation

The brief enfranchisement of African Americans ended after 1877, when southern Democrats regained control of state governments after the federal troops that occupied the South during the Reconstruction era were withdrawn. Social pressure, threats of violence, and the terrorist tactics of the Ku Klux Klan combined to dissuade African Americans from voting. Southern politicians, using everything except race as a formal criterion, passed laws that effectively deprived African Americans of the right to vote.

White Primaries and Grandfather Clauses.   By using the ruse that political party primaries were private, southern whites were allowed to exclude African Americans. The Supreme Court, in *Grovey v. Townsend*,[28] upheld such exclusion. Indeed, it was not until 1944, in *Smith v. Allwright*,[29] that the highest court finally found the **white primary** to be a violation of the Fifteenth Amendment. The Court reasoned that the political party was actually performing a state function in holding a primary election, not acting as a private group. By being denied a vote in the primary, African Americans had been prevented from participating in the selection of public officials from the end of Reconstruction until World War II. The **grandfather clause** restricted the voting franchise to those who could prove that their grandfathers had voted before 1867. Most African Americans were automatically disenfranchised by this provision. In *Guinn v. United States*, in 1915, the Supreme Court held that grandfather clauses were unconstitutional.[30]

Poll Taxes and Literacy Tests.   Another device to prevent African Americans from voting was the **poll tax**, requiring the payment of a fee to vote. This practice ensured the exclusion of poor African Americans from the political process. It wasn't until the passage of the Twenty-fourth Amendment, in 1964, that the poll tax as a precondition to voting was eliminated. That amendment, however, applied only to national elections. In *Harper v. Virginia State Board of Elections*,[31] in 1966, the Supreme Court declared that the payment of any poll tax as a condition for voting in any election is unconstitutional.

Literacy tests also were used to deny the vote to African Americans. Such tests asked potential voters to read, recite, or interpret complicated texts, such as a section of a state constitution, to the satisfaction of local registrars.

WHITE PRIMARY
A state primary election that restricts voting to whites only; outlawed by the Supreme Court in 1944.

GRANDFATHER CLAUSE
A device used by southern states to exempt whites from state taxes and literacy laws originally intended to disenfranchise African-American voters. It restricted the voting franchise to those who could prove that their grandfathers had voted before 1867.

POLL TAX
A special tax that must be paid as a qualification for voting. The Twenty-fourth Amendment to the Constitution outlawed the poll tax in national elections, and in 1966 the Supreme Court declared it unconstitutional in all elections.

LITERACY TEST
A test administered as a precondition for voting, often used to prevent African Americans from exercising their right to vote.

---

28. 295 U.S. 45 (1935).
29. 321 U.S. 649 (1944).
30. 238 U.S. 347 (1915).
31. 383 U.S. 663 (1966).

By the 1960s, the distribution of seats in state legislatures among state voting districts had become another obstacle to African Americans' political participation. The frequent use of area instead of population as a basis for voting districts led to the domination of state legislatures by (white) rural representatives. In 1962, the Supreme Court decided that federal courts could hear cases involving state districting,[32] and in 1964, the Court ruled that population is the only acceptable basis for the distribution of seats in a legislative body.[33]

The Struggle for Voting Rights.   As late as 1960, only 29.1 percent of African Americans of voting age were registered in the southern states, in stark contrast to 61.1 percent of whites. In 1965, Martin Luther King, Jr., took action to change all that. Selma, the seat of Dallas County, Alabama, was chosen as the site to dramatize the voting-rights problem. In Dallas County, only 2 percent of eligible African Americans had registered to vote by the beginning of 1965. King organized a fifty-mile march from Selma to the state capital in Montgomery. He didn't get very far. Acting on orders of Governor George Wallace to disband the marchers, state troopers did so with a vengeance—with tear gas, night sticks, and whips.

Once again the national government was required to intervene to force compliance with the law. President Lyndon Johnson federalized the National Guard, and the march continued. During the march, the president went on television to address a special joint session of Congress urging passage of new legislation to ensure African Americans the right to vote. The events during the Selma march and Johnson's dramatic speech, in which he invoked the slogan of the civil rights movement ("We shall overcome"), were credited for the swift passage of the Voting Rights Act of 1965.

Provisions of the Voting Rights Act of 1965

The Voting Rights Act of 1965 had two major provisions. The first one outlawed discriminatory voter-registration tests. The second major section authorized federal registration of persons and federally administered voting procedures in any political subdivision or state that discriminated electorally against a particular group.[34] The act targeted counties, mostly in the South, in which less than 50 percent of the eligible population was registered to vote. Federal voter registrars were sent to these areas to register African Americans who had been restricted by local registrars. Within one week after the act was passed, forty-five federal examiners were sent to the South. A massive voter-registration drive covered the country.

In 1970, the Voting Rights Act was extended to August 1975. In 1975, Congress extended the act to August 1982, and it was again extended in 1983. The act originally brought federal supervision to areas of the country known for discriminating against African Americans in the voter-registration process. But in 1970 and in 1975, the law was extended to other states and to other groups, including Spanish-speaking Americans, Asian Americans,

The Ku Klux Klan, or KKK, is well known for its burning-cross symbol. The KKK, which first met in Nashville's Maxwell House in April 1867, was organized during the Reconstruction period after the Civil War for the purpose of preventing former slaves from benefiting from the civil rights guaranteed by postwar federal legislation and constitutional amendments. After World War I, the KKK also became anti-Catholic and anti-Semitic.

---

32. *Baker v. Carr,* 369 U.S. 186 (1962).
33. *Reynolds v. Sim,* 377 U.S. 533 (1964).
34. In addition, the act indicated that in Congress's opinion, the state poll tax was unconstitutional.

and Native Americans, including Alaskan natives. As a result of this act, its extensions, and the large-scale voter-registration drives in the South, the number of African Americans registered to vote climbed dramatically. By 1980, 55.8 percent of African Americans of voting age in the South were registered.

By 1986, the number of registered African-American voters nationally was more than 11 million. By 1996, there were more than 7,500 African-American elected officials in the United States, including the mayors of Atlanta, Dallas, Detroit, and the District of Columbia. In 1984, the Reverend Jesse Jackson became the first African-American candidate to compete seriously for the Democratic presidential nomination. In 1988, a renewed effort to register thousands more African Americans and other minority voters helped Jackson achieve an impressive total primary and caucus vote. In 1989, Virginia became the first state to elect an African-American governor. In 1991, Clarence Thomas, an African American generally considered to be politically conservative, became a justice of the Supreme Court, replacing Thurgood Marshall, the first African-American justice.

HISPANICS IN AMERICAN SOCIETY

The second largest minority group in America can be classified loosely as Hispanics—or individuals from Spanish-speaking backgrounds. Even though this minority group represents over 8 percent of the American population, its diversity and geographic dispersion have hindered its ability to achieve political power, particularly at the national level. Mexican Americans constitute the majority of the Hispanic population. The next largest group is Puerto Ricans, followed by Cubans, and finally Hispanics from Central and South America.

Economically, Hispanics in the United States are less well off than non-Hispanic whites but a little better off than African Americans. About 27 percent of them live in poverty. Unlike the economic situation of African Americans, that of Hispanics is worsening. The percentage of their population below the poverty level rose over 3 percentage points between 1982 and 1992. The unemployment rate for Hispanics decreased less than the rate for any other group, and their real median income actually dropped during that period. Hispanic leaders have attributed these declines to language barriers and lack of training (which lead to low-paying jobs), as well as to continuing immigration (which deflates statistical progress).

Politically, Hispanics are gaining power in some states. By the early 1990s, at least 5 percent of the members of the state legislatures of Arizona, California, Colorado, Florida, New Mexico, and Texas were of Hispanic ancestry.

Mexican Americans

During the early 1800s, Mexico owned California, as well as Arizona, New Mexico, Texas, Utah, Nevada, parts of Wyoming and Oklahoma, and most of Colorado. By 1853, these territories had all been acquired by the United States (by purchase or by war) and were settled mainly by Anglos. The treaty ending the Mexican War in 1848 explicitly guaranteed for all former citizens of Mexico then living in U.S. territory the same liberties, protections, and rights as any other American citizens. They did not receive this treatment, though. These Mexicans' rights were frequently violated as Anglos appropriated their land.

Mexicans have continued to settle in the United States, immigrating to this country primarily for economic reasons. Some Mexicans look to the United States for employment and a chance to better their lives. Since 1820, slightly more than 8 percent of all immigrants into the United States have been of Mexican origin. Most Mexican Americans still live in the southwestern United States, but many have moved to Indiana, Illinois, Pennsylvania, and Ohio.

Mexican Americans, as well as other Hispanics in the United States, have a comparatively low level of political participation in elections. The lower overall participation rate is related to the lower overall socioeconomic status among Hispanics. The gap among ethnic groups has narrowed in recent years, however. Currently, the voting participation rate of Hispanic citizens is only about 10 percentage points less than the national average. Further, when citizens of equal incomes and educational backgrounds are compared, the Hispanic citizens' participation rate is higher than average.

Mexican Americans also have had some success in sending their own representatives to Congress. In 1976, the Hispanic caucus in the House of Representatives consisted of five people—a California Mexican American, two Texas Mexican Americans, the resident commissioner from Puerto Rico, and a Puerto Rican from New York City. In the 104th Congress, in 1995, the number of Hispanics had risen to 18. Also, the members of President Bill Clinton's cabinet include two Hispanic Americans—Henry Cisneros, who serves as the secretary of housing and urban development, and Federico Peña, the secretary of transportation. Mexican Americans have also gained political clout in local politics.

Spanish-language billboards in Miami, Florida, demonstrate the pervasiveness of Spanish-speaking cultures in some sections of the United States. Indeed, southern Florida leads the nation in the number of Americans who speak a language other than English at home. In Dade County, 57 percent of the residents do not speak English at home. In the adjacent city of Hialeah, the figure is 90 percent.

Puerto Ricans

Because Puerto Rico is a U.S. commonwealth, its inhabitants are American citizens. As such, they may move freely between Puerto Rico and the United States. In recent years, more Puerto Ricans have emigrated from the United States to Puerto Rico than from the island to the mainland. Currently, Puerto Ricans constitute about 12 percent of the Hispanic population in the United States. Most of them who come to the continental United States reside in the New York–New Jersey area.

In Puerto Rico, Puerto Ricans use U.S. currency, U.S. mails, and U.S. courts. They are also eligible for U.S. welfare benefits and food stamps, but they pay no federal taxes unless they move to the continental United States. By 1996, almost three-fourths of Puerto Ricans living in Puerto Rico were eligible for food stamps. Those who come to the mainland do not fare much better, owing to economic and language barriers and racial discrimination.

Puerto Ricans have had few political successes on the mainland. There are more than a million Puerto Ricans living in New York City, constituting at least 10 percent of the city's population, but only about 30 percent of them are registered to vote. Other statistics show that currently there are only a few Puerto Rican city council members and only one Puerto Rican member of Congress. In New York City's massive bureaucracy, only a small percentage of the administrators are Puerto Rican.

Cuban Americans

About 5 percent of the Hispanics in the United States are Cubans or Cuban Americans. Unlike their Hispanic brothers and sisters from Mexico and Puerto Rico, Cuban Americans chose to come to the United States for political, as well as economic, reasons. They left Cuba because they opposed the communist government of Fidel Castro. Many of the émigrés came from the educated middle class, and although they had to leave most of their financial assets behind, their education and training helped them to become established economically with relative ease. In Miami, for example, one can find numerous examples of former Cuban professionals who started out as taxi drivers and today own banks, retail stores, and law practices.

A majority of Cuban Americans reside in southern Florida, although some live in New York City and elsewhere. Economically, they constitute a major force in the southern Florida region. Politically, they have been very successful in gaining power within city and county governments. Cuban-American members of Congress include Ileana Ros-Lehtinen and Lincoln Diaz-Balart, both elected as Republicans to the House of Representatives from districts in southern Florida. The political influence of Cuban Americans will certainly rise as their percentage of the population increases. In Dade County, Hispanics, particularly Cubans, now constitute the majority of the county's population.

As a group, Cuban Americans are known for being staunchly anticommunist, and they strongly oppose any attempts of the American government to improve relations with communist Cuba. Militant Cuban-American organizations have actually denounced, threatened, or even bombed individuals and institutions in southern Florida that they feel are pro-Castro or procommunist.

FIGURE 5–1

Native-American and White Family Earnings Compared

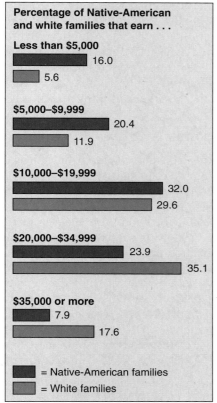

Percentage of Native-American and white families that earn . . .

Less than $5,000
16.0
5.6

$5,000–$9,999
20.4
11.9

$10,000–$19,999
32.0
29.6

$20,000–$34,999
23.9
35.1

$35,000 or more
7.9
17.6

■ = Native-American families
▢ = White families

SOURCE: U.S. Department of Commerce.

NATIVE AMERICANS

When the New World was "discovered," there were about ten million Native Americans, or "Indians," living there. It is estimated that they had inhabited areas from the north slope of Alaska to the southern tip of South America for at least thirty thousand years before Europeans arrived. By 1996, the number of full-blooded Native Americans in the continental United States had declined to less than half a million, owing to the effects of war and diseases brought to the continent by European immigrants. In the latest census, about two million individuals identified themselves as Native Americans. The five states with the largest Native-American populations are Oklahoma, Arizona, California, New Mexico, and Alaska.

Native Americans have not fared well economically, as is evident in Figure 5–1. From the point of view of health, Native Americans are even worse off than their economic status shows. Table 5–1 shows that the death rates per 100,000 of the population are two and sometimes three or more times the national average.

The Appropriation of Native-American Lands

When the Confederation Congress passed the Northwest Ordinance in 1787, it stated that "the utmost good faith shall always be observed towards the Indians; their lands and property shall never be taken from them without their consent; and in their property, rights, and liberty, they shall never be invaded or disturbed, unless in just and lawful wars authorized by congress." In 1789, Congress designated the Native-American tribes as foreign nations to enable the government to sign land and boundary treaties with them.

During the next hundred years, many agreements were made with the Native-American tribes; however, many were broken by Congress, as well as by individuals who wanted Native-American lands for settlement or exploration. In 1830, Congress instructed the Bureau of Indian Affairs to remove all Native-American tribes to lands west of the Mississippi River to free land east of the Mississippi for white settlement. From that time on, Native

TABLE 5–1

Native Americans: Death Rates per 100,000 Population, 1993

	NATIVE AMERICANS (INCLUDING ALASKANS)	ALL RACES
Motor-vehicle accidents	43.1	17.0
All other accidents	36.7	16.2
Alcoholism	30.0	9.0
Diabetes	29.1	10.0
Homicide	15.4	9.0
Pneumonia, influenza	13.1	10.1
Suicide	17.5	11.4
Tuberculosis	3.7	0.7

SOURCE: Indian Health Service, Center for Disease Control, 1994.

Americans who refused to be "removed" to whatever lands were designated for them were moved forcibly. During the resettlement of the Cherokee tribe in 1838 and 1839, on a forced march known as the "Trail of Tears," nearly four thousand out of fifteen thousand Cherokees died.

With the passage of the Dawes Act (General Allotment Act) of 1887, the goal of Congress became the "assimilation" of Native Americans into American society. Each family was allotted acreage within the reservation to farm, and the rest was sold to whites. The number of acres in reservation status was reduced from 140 million to about 47 million acres. Tribes that refused to cooperate with this plan lost their reservations altogether.

Native-American Political Response

Native Americans have been relatively unsuccessful in garnering political power. This is partly because the tribes themselves have no official representation in government and partly because the tribes are small and scattered. In the 1960s, the National Indian Youth Council (NIYC) was the first group to become identified with Indian militancy. At the end of the 1960s, a small group of persons identifying themselves as Indians occupied Alcatraz Island, claiming that the island was part of their ancestral lands. In 1972, several hundred Native Americans marched to Washington and occupied the Bureau of Indian Affairs (BIA). (Founded in 1824 as part of the War Department, today the BIA runs the Indian reservation system with the tribes.) They arrived in a caravan labeled "The Trail of Broken Treaties." In 1973, supporters of the American Indian Movement (AIM) took over Wounded Knee, South Dakota, which had been the site of the massacre of at least 150 Sioux Indians by the U.S. Army in 1890.[35] The goal of these demonstrations

---

35. This famous incident was the subject of Dee Brown's best-selling book, *Bury My Heart at Wounded Knee* (New York: Holt, Rinehart, and Winston, 1971), published two years before the modern siege.

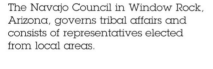

The Navajo Council in Window Rock, Arizona, governs tribal affairs and consists of representatives elected from local areas.

was to protest federal policy and to dramatize injustices toward Native Americans.

Native Americans today face the continuing problem of dealing with a divided BIA. Some BIA bureaucrats want to maintain the dependency of the Native Americans on the reservation system run by the agency. Recently, however, the BIA has let more and more tribes control the police, job-training, educational, and social programs that the BIA used to manage. Nonetheless, there are still numerous conflicts between Indian tribes and the BIA, as well as between them and state governments. Native Americans face the additional problem of being a fragmented political group now that large numbers of their population do not live on reservations.

Compensation for Past Injustices

As more Americans have become aware of the concerns of Native Americans, Congress has started to compensate for past injustices. In the Native American Languages Act of 1990, for example, Congress declared that Native-American languages are unique and serve an important role in maintaining Indian culture and continuity. Under the act, the government shares responsibility with the Indian community for the survival of native languages and native cultures. Courts, too, have shown a greater willingness to recognize Native-American treaty rights. For example, cases dealing with the right of present-day Native Americans to a share of the annual salmon harvest in Washington involved, in part, enforcement of nineteenth-century treaty provisions.[36] In a decision that may open the way for other long-standing Native-American claims, the Supreme Court ruled that three tribes of Oneida Indians could claim damages for the use of tribal land that had been unlawfully conveyed in 1795.[37] Lower court cases decided since this ruling may limit recovery on other similar claims, however.[38]

In 1988, Congress passed the Indian Gaming Regulatory Act, allowing Native Americans to have profit-making gambling operations on their land. This has had a rapid and profound effect on economic and social aspects of reservation life and has affected non–Native-American public authorities significantly as well. For example, Connecticut Governor Lowell Weicker allowed slot machines at a Mashantucket Pequot casino in his state in exchange for a pledge by the tribe to contribute $100 million a year in gambling profits to a state fund that aids troubled cities and towns.[39] Gambling on Native-American property has, in the words of the *New York Times*, "become a multibillion-dollar industry that fuels a renaissance of American Indian tribal fortunes and culture; the trend is reversing a population exodus from reservations."[40] The rapid expansion of reservation gambling (involving at least seventeen states and fifty-two tribes) concerns some authorities. A petition signed by forty-nine state governors has been delivered to

DID YOU KNOW . . .
That Native Americans were not made citizens of the United States until an act of Congress on June 15, 1924?

---

36. *United States v. Washington*, 384 F.Supp. 312 (W.D. Wash. 1974); affirmed 520 F.2d 676 (9th Cir. 1975); substantially affirmed, *Washington v. Washington State Commercial Passenger Fishing Vessel Association*, 443 U.S. 548 (1979).

37. *County of Oneida v. Oneida Indian Nation*, 470 U.S. 226 (1985).

38. See, for example, *Yankton Sioux Tribe of Indians v. South Dakota*, 796 F.2d 241 (9th Cir. 1986).

39. *New York Times*, April 17, 1993, p. I1.

40. *New York Times*, January 31, 1993, p. I1.

Congress requesting tighter definition and regulation of Native-American casinos.[41]

ASIAN AMERICANS

Because Asian Americans have a relatively high median income, they are typically not thought of as being victims of discrimination. This certainly was not always the case. The Chinese Exclusion Act of 1882 prevented persons from China and Japan from coming to the United States to prospect for gold or to work on the railroads or in factories in the West. Japanese-American students were segregated into special schools after the 1906 San Francisco earthquake so that white children could use their buildings.

The 1941 Japanese bombing of Pearl Harbor intensified the fear of the Japanese. Executive Order 9066, signed by President Franklin D. Roosevelt on February 19, 1942, set up "relocation" camps for virtually all Japanese Americans living in the United States. The Japanese were required to dispose of their property, usually at below-market prices. The Japanese Americans were subjected to a curfew, excluded from certain "military areas," and finally ordered to report to "assembly" centers, from which they were evacuated to the relocation camps. The Supreme Court upheld the curfew, the exclusion order, and the order to report to assembly centers.[42] It wasn't until 1944 and 1945 that the relocation camps were closed and the prisoners freed, after a December 18, 1944, Supreme Court ruling deemed such activity illegal. Three Japanese Americans who had been jailed for resisting relocation during World War II successfully sued the United States in 1983. They won damages, and their 1942 convictions were overturned because of their claim that the army lied about the possibility of security threats. In 1988, Congress provided funds to compensate former camp inhabitants or their survivors—$1.25 billion for 65,000 people.

Recently, a new group of Asians has had to fight discrimination—those from Southeast Asia. More than a million Indochinese war refugees, most of them from Vietnam, have come into the United States in the last twenty-five years. Like their predecessors, the newer immigrants have quickly increased their median income; only about one-third of all such households receive welfare of any sort. Most have come with families and have been sponsored by American families or organizations, so they have had good support systems to help them get started. As with Chinese Americans and Japanese Americans, once they become established, they are seen as economic threats by those who believe they are being displaced by the new immigrants.

WOMEN'S POSITION IN SOCIETY: EARLY POLITICAL MOVEMENTS

In 1776, Abigail Adams reminded her husband, John Adams, to "remember the women." Despite this reminder, women, although considered citizens

---

41. *New York Times,* March 23, 1993, p. A22.
42. *Hirabayashi v. United States,* 320 U.S. 81 (1943); and *Korematsu v. United States,* 323 U.S. 214 (1944).

in the early years of the nation, had no political rights. The first political cause in which women became actively engaged was the slavery abolition movement.

In 1848, Lucretia Mott and Elizabeth Cady Stanton organized the first women's rights convention in Seneca Falls, New York. The three hundred people who attended approved a Declaration of Sentiments: "We hold these truths to be self-evident: that all men *and women* are created equal." In the following twelve years, groups of feminists held seven conventions in different cities in the Midwest and East. With the outbreak of the Civil War, however, advocates of women's rights were urged to put their support behind the war effort, and most agreed.

The Suffrage Issue and the Fifteenth Amendment

"The right of citizens of the United States to vote shall not be denied or abridged by the United States or by any State on account of race, color, or previous condition of servitude." So reads Section 1 of Amendment XV to the Constitution, which was ratified in 1870. The campaign for the passage of this amendment split the women's **suffrage** movement. Militant feminists wanted to add "sex" to "race, color, or previous condition of servitude." Other feminists, along with many men, opposed this view; they wanted to separate African-American suffrage and women's suffrage to ensure the passage of the amendment. So, although the African-American press supported the women's suffrage movement, it became separate from the racial equality movement. Still, some women attempted to vote in the years following the Civil War. One, Virginia Louisa Minor, was arrested and convicted in 1872. She appealed to the Supreme Court, but the Court upheld her conviction.[43]

---

43. *Minor v. Happersett,* 21 Wall. 162 (1874). The Supreme Court reasoned that the right to vote was a privilege of state, not federal, citizenship. The Court did not consider privileges of state citizenship to be protected by the Fourteenth Amendment.

Elizabeth Cady Stanton (1815–1902) was a social reformer and a women's suffrage leader. At her wedding in 1840 to Henry B. Stanton, she insisted on dropping the word *obey* from the marriage vows. She wrote *The History of Women's Suffrage,* which was published in 1886.

SUFFRAGE
The right to vote; the franchise.

The words of Susan B. Anthony are still used today by those who work for women's political equality.

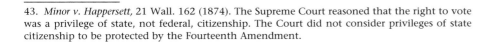

Susan B. Anthony (1820–1906) was a leader of the women's suffrage movement who was also active in the anti-alcohol and antislavery movements. In 1869, with Elizabeth Cady Stanton, she founded the National Suffrage Association. In 1888, she organized the International Council of Women and, in 1904, the International Women's Suffrage Alliance, in Berlin.

Women's Suffrage Associations

Susan B. Anthony and Elizabeth Cady Stanton formed the National Suffrage Association in 1869. According to their view, women's suffrage was a means to achieve major improvements in the economic and social situation of women in the United States. In other words, the vote was to be used to obtain a larger goal. Lucy Stone, however, felt that the vote was the only major issue. Members of the American Women's Suffrage Association, founded by Stone and others, traveled to each state, addressed state legislatures, wrote, published, and argued their convictions. They achieved only limited success. In 1890, the two organizations quit battling and joined forces. The National American Women's Suffrage Association had only one goal—the enfranchisement of women—but it made little progress.

By the early 1900s, small radical splinter groups were formed, such as the Congressional Union, headed by Alice Paul. This organization worked solely for the passage of an amendment to the U.S. Constitution. Willing to use "unorthodox" means to achieve its goal, this group and others took to the streets. There were parades, hunger strikes, arrests, and jailings. Finally, in 1920, seventy-two years after the Seneca Falls convention, the Nineteenth Amendment was passed: "The right of citizens of the United States to vote shall not be denied or abridged by the United States or by any State on account of sex." Women were thus enfranchised. Although today it may seem that the United States was slow to give women the vote, it was really not too far behind the rest of the world (see Table 5–2).

WOMEN'S CONTINUED STRUGGLE FOR EQUAL STATUS

Obviously, the right to vote does not guarantee political power. It has been more than half a century since women obtained the right to vote in most countries of the Western world, yet the number of women who have held high political positions are few.

The Struggle in the United States

In the United States, of the more than ten thousand members who have served in the House of Representatives, only 1 percent have been women. In Congress, the men's club atmosphere prevails, although the elections of 1992 brought substantially more women to the 103d Congress than either the Senate or the House had seen before. Six women were seated in the Senate in January 1993; the Senate had never before had more than two women at one time. The House had an average of twenty-three women between 1981 and 1992; forty-seven were seated in 1993. After the 1994 election, there were forty-nine women in the House and eight in the Senate.

Women have also been represented meagerly in federal political appointments, although this situation is changing. President Franklin Roosevelt appointed the first woman to a cabinet post—Frances Perkins, who was secretary of labor from 1933 to 1945. President Gerald Ford (1974–1977), appointed a woman as secretary of housing and urban development. President Jimmy Carter (1977–1981) had three women in his cabinet and appointed many female judges. President Ronald Reagan (1981–1989)

TABLE 5–2 ■

Years, by Country, in Which Women Gained the Right to Vote

COUNTRY	YEAR
New Zealand	1893
Australia	1902
Finland	1906
Norway	1913
Denmark	1915
Germany	1919
United States	1920
United Kingdom	1928
Switzerland*	1971

*With the exception of one canton (confederal unit), Appenzell Inner Rhoden, in which, in April 1990, men voted to continue to bar women from voting at all.

SOURCE: Data derived from Marilyn French, *The War Against Women* (New York: Summit Books, 1992); and Anne Phillips, *Engendering Democracy* (University Park, Pa.: Pennsylvania State University Press, 1991).

appointed women to two major cabinet posts and to head the U.S. delegation to the United Nations. He is also credited with a historical first in his appointment of Sandra Day O'Connor to the Supreme Court in 1981. President George Bush appointed two women to cabinet posts, and a woman served as his international trade negotiator. President Bill Clinton named three women to cabinet posts and appointed Ruth Bader Ginsburg to the Supreme Court. Despite these changes, however, women have yet to be appointed to any of the "inner" cabinet posts—secretary of state, secretary of the treasury, and secretary of defense.

The representation of women in political office does not reflect their participation as voters. As Table 5–3 indicates, the absolute turnout of female voters nationally is higher than that of male voters.

The National Organization for Women (NOW)

Although often identified as a middle-class movement, the modern women's movement seeks to define sexism and to eradicate it from all spheres of life for all women. One of the most prominent of the organizations associated with the women's movement is the National Organization for Women (NOW). NOW was formed in 1966 by writer Betty Friedan and others who were dissatisfied with the lack of aggressive action against sex discrimination by the then-largest women's organizations—the National Federation of Business and Professional Women's Clubs and the League of Women Voters. The specific issue around which NOW coalesced was the failure of the Equal Employment Opportunity Commission (EEOC) to enjoin newspapers from running separate want ads for men and women (including ads run in separate columns for men and women, ads addressed "men only," or ads stating "women need not apply"). In June 1966, at the third annual Conference of State Commissions on the Status of Women, the attendees demanded a resolution condemning such sex discrimination in employment. They were told that the conference "was not allowed to pass such a resolution"—or to take any action, for that matter. NOW was formed and immediately sent telegrams to the EEOC. After a series of tough battles, in 1968 NOW won its war against sex-segregated want ads.

NOW elected Betty Friedan as its first president and adopted a blanket resolution designed "to bring women into full participation in the mainstream of American society *now*, exercising all the privileges and responsibilities

DID YOU KNOW . . .
That the African-American abolitionist Frederick Douglass was invited to speak at the first women's rights convention, in 1848 in Seneca Falls, New York, and that he was among the thirty-two men who signed the convention's Declaration of Sentiments?

TABLE 5–3

Voting and Registration

Voting participation by females has recently been equal to, or greater than, voting participation by males. In both percentage and absolute terms, more females than males voted and registered in 1992.

	PERSONS OF VOTING AGE (MILLIONS)	PERSONS REPORTING THEY REGISTERED (MILLIONS)	PERSONS REPORTING THEY VOTED (PERCENTAGE)
Male	88.6	66.9	60.2
Female	97.1	69.3	62.3

SOURCE: U.S. Department of Commerce, *Statistical Abstract of the United States* (Washington, D.C.: U.S. Government Printing Office, 1995).

thereof in truly equal partnership with men." NOW grew from its 300 members in 1966 to over 280,000 members in 1996. It has continued to be one of the leading pressure groups in the struggle for women's rights.

The Supreme Court and Sex Discrimination

Laws that include different provisions for men and women are not always struck down by the Supreme Court. The Court has established standards for determining whether gender classifications are acceptable. Laws with racial classifications are always "suspect" and are invalidated unless the government can prove that the classifications are "necessary to a compelling objective" (in fact, laws with racial classifications have been invalidated in almost every case). Laws that classify by gender are permissible if they "substantially relate to important governmental interests." For example, a law punishing males but not females for statutory rape is valid because of the important governmental interest in preventing teenage pregnancy in those circumstances.[44] A law granting a husband, as "head and master" of the house, the right to unilaterally sell or give away property owned jointly with his wife is not valid.[45] This standard for evaluating the acceptability of gender classifications was established by the Court in 1971 in *Reed v. Reed*, a case involving an Idaho law that gave men preference over women in administering estates of dead relatives.[46] In 1973, the Supreme Court struck down a federal law providing that servicemen's wives automatically receive certain benefits but servicewomen's husbands receive these benefits only if they demonstrate a certain degree of need.[47] In this case, some of the justices unsuccessfully tried to apply to gender cases the "suspect" standard applied to race cases.

The Equal Rights Amendment

The Equal Rights Amendment (ERA) states:

> Equality of rights under the law shall not be denied or abridged by the United States or by any state on account of sex.

The ERA, the proposed amendment, was first introduced in Congress in 1923 by leaders of the National Women's Party, who felt that getting the vote would not be enough to change women's status. After years during which the amendment was not even given a hearing in Congress, it was finally approved by both chambers and was sent to the state legislatures for ratification on March 22, 1972.

As was noted in Chapter 2, any constitutional amendment must be ratified by the legislatures (or conventions) in three-fourths of the states before it can become law. The states at first responded enthusiastically and, as some observers have noted, ratified with little deliberation. Most of the twenty-two states that ratified the ERA in 1972 did so without holding the customary hearings. Hawaii ratified the same day Congress passed the amendment.

---

44. *Michael M. v. Superior Court,* 450 U.S. 464 (1981).
45. *Kirchberg v. Feenstra,* 450 U.S. 455 (1981).
46. 404 U.S. 71 (1971).
47. *Frontiero v. Richardson,* 411 U.S. 677 (1973).

At the same time, opposing forces were becoming organized and militant, and the remaining states began to approach the amendment more warily. Between January 1, 1973, and March 22, 1979, fifteen additional states had ratified, and five had rescinded.

Opposition to the ERA gained strength rapidly. Although such opposition became broadly based, initially it was made up of elements from the political margins. In 1972, the platform of the American party (which had nominated former segregationist Alabama governor George Wallace for president in 1968) denounced the ERA as a "socialistic plan to destroy the home."

The necessary thirty-eight states failed to ratify the amendment within the seven-year period specified by Congress, in spite of the support given to the ERA in numerous national party platforms, by six presidents, and by both houses of Congress. NOW boycotted nonratifying states. Nonetheless, the anti-ERA campaign was successful.

FEDERAL RESPONSES TO SEX DISCRIMINATION IN THE WORKPLACE

Although the ERA did not pass, several efforts were made by the federal government to eliminate sex discrimination in the labor market both before and after the introduction of the amendment.

Sex Discrimination

Sex was included as a prohibited basis for discrimination in the job market under Title VII of the Civil Rights Act of 1964, although Title VII does not cover discrimination based on sexual preferences. Since its enactment, Title VII has been used to strike down so-called protective legislation, which prevents women from undertaking jobs deemed "too dangerous or strenuous by the state." In practice, such protective legislation often "protected" women from higher-paying jobs. Under the Equal Employment Opportunity Commission (EEOC) guidelines, such state statutes may not be used as a defense to a charge of illegal **sex discrimination.**

Sexual Harassment

Sexual harassment has also been outlawed by Title VII. In April 1980, the EEOC issued its first guidelines on the subject. Under the guidelines, all unwelcome sexual advances, requests, or other physical or verbal conduct of a sexual nature constitutes illegal sexual harassment if submission to them is a condition of employment or a basis of pay, of promotion, or of other employment decisions. Also, if such unwanted conduct interferes with an employee's job performance or creates an intimidating, hostile, or offensive environment, it is illegal.

The courts have gone so far as to hold the employer liable for illegal sexual harassment by supervisors. EEOC guidelines go one step further—they hold an employer liable for a supervisor's conduct regardless of the employer's knowledge of such conduct or even when the employer has a policy forbidding such conduct.

SEX DISCRIMINATION
Overt behavior in which people are given differential or unfavorable treatment on the basis of sex; any practice, policy, or procedure that denies equality of treatment to an individual or to a group because of gender.

SEXUAL HARASSMENT
Harassment on the basis of sex, in violation of Title VII of the Civil Rights Act of 1964. This includes unwanted physical or verbal conduct or abuse of a sexual nature that interferes with a recipient's job performance or carries with it an implicit or explicit threat of adverse employment consequences.

That in 1922, at age eighty-seven, Rebecca Latimer Felton was the first and oldest woman to serve in the U.S. Senate—although she was appointed as a token gesture and was allowed to serve only one day?

Furthermore, the EEOC says that an employer "should take all steps necessary to prevent sexual harassment from occurring, such as affirmatively raising the subject, expressing strong disapproval, developing appropriate sanctions, informing employees of their right to raise and how to raise the issue of harassment . . . and developing methods to sensitize all concerned." EEOC guidelines say that the recipient of unwanted sexual advances must make known clearly that such conduct is objectionable and unwelcome.[48]

The number of sexual-harassment complaints filed through the Equal Employment Opportunity Commission has increased in recent years, from about five thousand in 1985 to about eight thousand in 1995. The issue of sexual harassment received national attention in 1991, when charges of improper behavior were leveled at U.S. Supreme Court nominee Clarence Thomas by law professor Anita Hill. According to Hill, Thomas had sexually harassed her in the early 1980s when they both worked at the EEOC. Although Hill's charges caused a national furor, Thomas's nomination was approved.[49]

In 1993, investigations surrounding the "Tailhook" scandal forced the resignation of several top U.S. Navy officers. At a naval aviation convention in 1991, during an after-hours party, several women were pushed through a "gauntlet" of drunken, groping male aviators. Some of the women said later that no one intervened to help them.

In November 1991, President George Bush signed into law the Civil Rights Act of 1991, which greatly expanded the remedies for victims in sexual harassment cases. The act states specifically that victims can seek compensatory and punitive damages in addition to the back pay and other remedies previously available.

Pension Fund Contributions

In 1978, in a Title VII–based decision, the Supreme Court ruled that an employer (the city of Los Angeles) could not require female employees to make higher pension-fund contributions than male employees earning the same salaries.[50] This and similar cases involving differential life insurance premiums for males and females (prohibited by a 1983 ruling) represent another set of issues on which Americans have been slowly redefining gender-based discrimination.[51]

Fetal Protection Policies

Fetal protection policies prevent fertile women from working in jobs in which they could be exposed to hazardous substances that could harm them or their unborn children. Men were not usually affected by these restrictions, even though medical studies have revealed that male reproductive systems may also be damaged from prolonged exposure to hazardous ma-

Paula Jones brought a lawsuit against President Clinton in 1994. Jones was unable to bring a suit for sexual harassment, because the statute of limitations had run out. Nonetheless, she accused Clinton of violating her civil rights when she was an employee of the state of Arkansas and he was the governor. She claimed that he made unwanted sexual advances and acted in an obscene manner. Her lawsuit has been stayed until Clinton leaves office.

48. See Joel Friedman *et al., Sexual Harassment: What It Is, What It Isn't, What It Does to You and What You Can Do about It* (Deerfield Beach, Fla.: Health Communications, 1992).
49. For views of the Thomas-Hill controversy from two completely different perspectives, see David Brock, *The Real Anita Hill: The Untold Story* (New York: Free Press, 1993), and Timothy M. Phelps and Helen Winternitz, *Capitol Games* (New York: Hyperion, 1992).
50. *Los Angeles v. Manhart,* 435 U.S. 702 (1978).
51. Congressional Quarterly, *Guide to the U.S. Supreme Court* (Washington, D.C., 1979).

terials, such as lead. The policies were regarded as a way to avoid later suits in which mothers or children would accuse a company of having failed to take precautions that might have protected them from harm.

One of the most extreme fetal protection policies was adopted in 1982 by Johnson Controls, Inc., the country's largest producer of automobile batteries. The Johnson policy required all women of childbearing age working in jobs that entailed periodic exposure to lead or other hazardous materials to prove that they were infertile or to transfer to other positions. Women who agreed to transfer often had to accept cuts in pay and reduced job responsibilities. At least one woman who refused to accept a safer job agreed to be sterilized. Employees and their union, United Auto Workers, brought a suit against Johnson, claiming that the fetal protection policy violated Title VII. The Supreme Court agreed that the policy was discriminatory: "Women as capable of doing their jobs as their male counterparts may not be forced to choose between having a child and having a job."[52]

The Equal Pay Act of 1963

The Equal Pay Act was enacted in 1963 as an amendment to the Fair Labor Standards Act of 1938. Since 1979, it has been administered by the EEOC. Basically, the act prohibits sex-based discrimination in the wages paid for equal work on jobs when their performance requires skill, effort, and responsibility under similar conditions. It is job content rather than job description that controls in all cases. For the equal pay requirements to apply, the act requires that male and female employees must work at the same establishment.

With equal-pay questions, the issue focuses more on the jobs performed by two employees and whether they are substantially equal than on the equivalence of employees' skills and training. A wage differential for equal work is justified if it is shown to be because of (1) seniority, (2) merit, (3) a system that pays according to quality or quantity of production, or (4) any factor other than sex.[53]

Comparable Worth, or Pay Equity

The concept of **comparable worth,** or pay equity, is that women should receive equal pay not just for equal (that is, the same) work, but also for work requiring comparable skill, effort, and responsibility. This is an effort to redress the effects of traditional "women's work" being undervalued and underpaid. Indeed, four out of five women hold jobs that have largely become women's work—for example, secretary (99 percent female), telephone operator (88 percent female), and nurse (94 percent female).

In 1981, the Supreme Court ruled that female workers could sue under Title VII even if they were not performing the same jobs as men. In this case, a group of female prison guards given the title "matrons," in Washington County, Oregon, claimed that they did not receive the same salaries as male prison guards, known as "deputy sheriffs." Their jobs differed from the men's in that they had fewer prisoners to guard and they also performed

Women took part in Operation Desert Storm in 1991 as officers and enlisted personnel. Although a congressional act restricts women from holding combat positions, they often performed their jobs in combat zones.

COMPARABLE WORTH
The idea that compensation should be based on the worth of the job to an employer and that factors unrelated to the worth of a job, such as the sex of the employee, should not affect compensation. Supporters of the comparable-worth doctrine argue that women should be entitled to comparable wages for doing work that is different from, but of comparable worth and value to, work done by higher-paid men.

52. *United Auto Workers v. Johnson Controls, Inc.,* 499 U.S. 187 (1991).
53. Paul England, *Comparable Worth: Theories and Evidence* (New York: Walter de Gruyter, 1992).

The "Willmar 8"—female bank employees picket for equal pay. The question of equal pay for equal work has not been fully resolved with the passage of federal legislation. Women still earn, on average, 30 percent less than their male counterparts.

clerical tasks. The Court ruled that they could sue on the basis of sex discrimination.[54]

Defendants in equal-pay cases have relied successfully upon a stipulation that they were only following market wages in their failure to pay women's jobs the same amount as men's jobs. In both *American Federation of State, County, and Municipal Employees v. State of Washington*[55] and *American Nurses Association et al. v. State of Illinois*,[56] the courts allowed the market wage defense to defeat the plaintiffs' claims of intentional discrimination. Some observers have noticed a "conservative drift," beginning in 1980, in court decisions regarding sex-based wage discrimination.

THE STATUS OF OLDER AMERICANS

Americans are getting older. In colonial times, about half the population was under the age of sixteen. In 1990, the number of people under the age of sixteen was fewer than one in four, and half were thirty-three or older. By the year 2050, at least half could be thirty-nine or older.

Today, the median age of the population of the United States is almost thirty-three, and 32 million Americans (13 percent of the population) are sixty-five or over. As can be seen in Figure 5–2, it is estimated that by the year 2020, this figure will have reached 53.6 million. From 2010 to 2030, the Bureau of the Census predicts that the portion of the population over age sixty-five will grow 76 percent, while the population under age sixty-five will increase only 6.5 percent (see Figure 5–2).

---

54. *Washington County, Oregon v. Gunther,* 452 U.S. 161 (1981).
55. 770 F.2d 1401 (1985).
56. 783 F.2d 716 (1986).

FIGURE 5–2 ■

Population Projections: Persons Age 65 and Older (in Millions)

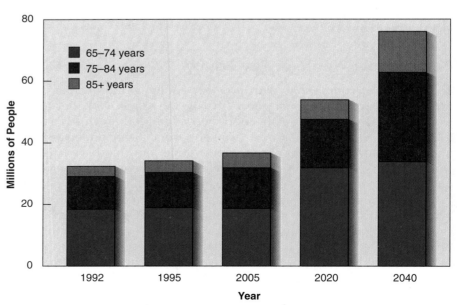

SOURCE: U.S. Department of Commerce, *Statistical Abstract of the United States* (Washington, D.C.: U.S. Government Printing Office, 1994).

Age Discrimination in Employment

A news anchor who subsequently sued her employer for discriminatory employment practices heard the following words at the time of her removal from the air: "Christine, our viewer research results are in and they are really devastating. The people of Kansas City don't like watching you anchor the news because you are too old, too unattractive, and you are not sufficiently deferential to men."[57] Age discrimination has been the subject of judicial and legislative actions, beginning most prominently with the Age Discrimination in Employment Act of 1967 (ADEA). The unstated policies of many companies not to hire and to demote or dismiss people they felt to be "too old" have made it extremely difficult for such workers to succeed in their jobs or continue with their careers. In spite of their proven productivity, older workers have suffered from discrimination in employment for many years. One of their major problems has been **mandatory retirement.**

Congressional Actions.   Age was not included within the protections of the 1964 Civil Rights Act. Congress, therefore, directed the secretary of labor to prepare a report on the problem of age discrimination. In 1965, that report, *The Older American Workers—Age Discrimination in Employment,* documented widespread discrimination. The report served as the impetus for passage of the Age Discrimination in Employment Act of 1967. The act, which applies to employers, employment agencies, and labor organizations and covers individuals over the age of forty, prohibits discrimination against individuals on the basis of age unless age is shown to be a bona fide occupational qualification reasonably necessary to the normal operation of the particular business.

Specifically, it is against the law to discriminate by age in wages, benefits, hours worked, or availability of overtime. Employers and unions may not discriminate in providing fringe benefits, such as education or training programs, career development, sick leave, and vacations. It is a violation of the act to publish notices or advertisements indicating an age-preference limitation or discrimination based on age. Even advertisements that imply a preference for youthful workers over older workers are in violation of the law. Requesting age on an application is not illegal but may be closely scrutinized in light of the employer's hiring practices.

The Age Discrimination in Employment Act of 1967 was amended in 1974 to include state and local governments and to furnish protection to most federal employees. More important, in 1978, Congress made extensive amendments to the 1967 act, prohibiting mandatory retirement of most employees under age seventy. Many states had already passed similar statutes. In 1986, mandatory retirement rules were finally outlawed, except for a few selected occupations. The act's protection was extended to individuals over age seventy to whom it had not previously been available.

Court Actions.   Mandatory retirement laws for government employees may result in many otherwise qualified people losing their jobs and thus may not promote efficiency in government. But the laws have been upheld in the courts. In 1976, the Supreme Court, in *Massachusetts Board of*

DID YOU KNOW . . .
That those eighty-five years of age or older constitute the most rapidly growing segment of the U.S. population, and that by the year 2040, this group will constitute 8 percent of the total population?

MANDATORY RETIREMENT
Forced retirement when a person reaches a certain age.

---

57. Christine Craft, *Too Old, Too Ugly, and Not Deferential to Men* (Rocklin, Calif.: Prima Publishing & Communications, 1988).

Lovola West Burgess is president of the American Association of Retired People (AARP). This powerful lobbying group started small but has become perhaps the largest such group in the nation. Anyone over 50 is eligible. All that is required is a small payment for dues (currently $15 a year). In exchange, AARP members obtain relatively lower priced insurance, special air fares and vacation deals, and other benefits. The AARP can effectively counter proposed legislation that will affect its membership. It does so with letter writing campaigns and personal calls by its members to members of Congress.

Retirement v. Murgia, upheld a Massachusetts law requiring state troopers to retire at age fifty.[58] The Court said that age could not be considered a "suspect" classification. In 1985, however, in *Johnson v. Mayor of Baltimore,* the Court held that a federal statute requiring certain government employees to retire at a specified age (such as requiring federal firefighters to retire at age fifty-five) does not mean that a similar mandatory retirement age can be imposed on employees of other governmental units or similar private-sector employees.[59]

Age and Government Benefits

Americans over the age of sixty-five receive a disproportionate share of government spending. Almost half the entire federal budget is spent on Medicare and Social Security. Medicare costs recently have risen at about twice the rate of inflation for the economy as a whole. Many entitlement programs, like Medicare and Social Security, have been tied legislatively to external factors so that spending on them has become, to a large degree, uncontrollable and automatic.

Given the higher levels of political participation by older Americans (they rank first in voter registration and voter turnout), the number of political leaders that are or will soon be over sixty-five, and the population "bulge" of baby boomers who are approaching retirement age, it seems very likely that the administration of entitlement programs increasingly could become the predominant responsibility of the U.S. government. This likelihood, coupled with the prospect of a constitutional amendment forcing a balanced budget, has prompted one writer to forecast that "the government will, over time, become merely a giant transfer payment pump, a gray source of stipends from familiar entitlement programs for an aging population, and especially for the population that includes Bill Clinton, who was born in 1946, Year One of the baby boom."[60]

THE RIGHTS OF PERSONS WITH DISABILITIES

By the 1970s, persons with disabilities were becoming a political force. Congress passed the Rehabilitation Act in 1973, which prohibited discrimination against persons with disabilities in programs receiving federal aid. The Department of Health, Education, and Welfare, or HEW (now Health and Human Services, or HHS), however, was slow to issue regulations needed to implement this act. When these regulations still had not been issued by April 1977, members of the American Coalition of Citizens with Disabilities staged a "wheel-in" by occupying several Washington HEW offices. A few weeks after this event, HEW passed the necessary regulations.

There was still disagreement, however, about what constituted discrimination. People with disabilities wanted the right to physical access so that they could compete more effectively in the marketplace. This meant modifying physical structures so that people who needed to do so could avoid the curbs, stairways, and other obstacles that make mobility difficult for

58. 427 U.S. 307 (1976).
59. 472 U.S. 353 (1985).
60. George Will, *Washington Post,* February 10, 1994.

them. A 1978 amendment to the Rehabilitation Act of 1973 established the Architectural and Transportation Barriers Compliance Board. Regulations for ramps, elevators, and the like in all federal buildings were implemented.

Congress passed the Education for All Handicapped Children Act in 1975. Unofficially, this act has been referred to as the "bill of rights for handicapped youth." It guarantees that all children with disabilities will receive an "appropriate" education.

In 1990, Congress passed new legislation to provide expanded access to public facilities, including transportation. The Americans with Disabilities Act of 1990 (ADA) (the "handicapped's bill of rights") prohibits job discrimination against the 43.6 million Americans with physical and mental disabilities, including those with acquired immune-deficiency syndrome (AIDS), and it requires access to public buildings and public services. Physical access means ramps; handrails; wheelchair-accessible restrooms, counters, drinking fountains, telephones, and doorways; and more accessible mass transit. In addition, other steps must be taken to comply with the act: Car-rental companies must provide cars with hand controls for disabled drivers. Telephone companies are required to have operators pass on messages from the speech-impaired who use telephones with keyboards. (See this chapter's feature entitled *Politics and Americans with Disabilities* for a discussion of how these modifications provide more than physical access.)

One group active in the fight for rights for persons with disabilities is Americans Disabled for Accessible Public Transit, or Americans Disabled for Attendant Programs Today (ADAPT). Formed in 1983 to fight for wheelchair lifts on public buses, ADAPT achieved its goal with the inclusion in the Americans with Disabilities Act of 1990 of a provision that all new buses be equipped with hydraulic lifts for people in wheelchairs. ADAPT's other objectives include Medicaid funding for attendants for disabled persons, allowing them to live relatively independently. Currently, Medicaid pays for

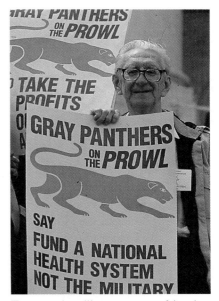

These senior citizens are marching to save government-provided medical services. Medical expenses are a major problem for older Americans. A rising percentage of government spending goes, however, for medical care to the aged.

President George Bush signs the 1990 Americans with Disabilities Act. The law requires corporations and public institutions to implement access for persons with disabilities.

nursing home care only. ADAPT asks that 20 percent of Medicaid funds paid to nursing homes be diverted to attendant programs. (See this chapter's *Politics: The Human Side* for information on another group that champions the cause of Americans with disabilities.)

Such legislation highlights the question of the economic trade-offs that have to be made when resources are allocated to benefit specially selected groups in society. It is not enough to state simply that persons with disabilities (or older citizens or any other disadvantaged group) should be given better treatment in the United States. We must also ask who will bear the costs of this improved treatment. This is both an economic and a political question.

THE RIGHTS AND STATUS OF JUVENILES

Approximately seventy-six million Americans—30 percent of the total population—are under twenty-one years of age. The definition of *children* ranges from persons under age sixteen to persons under age twenty-one. However defined, children form a large group of individuals in the United States and have the fewest rights and protections. For example, children do not have the same rights to freedom of expression in the schools as adults have elsewhere.

The reason for this lack is the common presumption of society and its lawmakers that children are basically protected by their parents. This is not to say that children are the exclusive property of the parents. Rather, an overwhelming case in favor of *not* allowing parents to control the actions of their children must be presented before children can be given authorization to act without parental consent or before the state can act be given authorization to on children's behalf without regard to their parents' wishes.

Supreme Court decisions affecting children's rights of today began a process of slow evolution with *Brown v. Board of Education of Topeka,* the landmark civil rights case of 1954.[61] In *Brown,* the Court granted children the status of rights-bearing persons. In 1967, the court expressly held that children have a constitutional right to be represented by counsel at the government's expense in a criminal action.[62] Five years later, the Court acknowledged that, "children are 'persons' within the meaning of the Bill of Rights. We have held so over and over again."[63]

Supreme Court decisions affecting the rights of children have also touched upon another very controversial issue: abortion. In 1976, the Court recognized a girl's right to have an abortion without consulting her parents.[64] More recently, however, the Court has allowed state laws to dictate whether consent must be obtained by the child. In 1993, the Court refused to review a case involving a state law that required girls under the age of eighteen to obtain the consent of both parents or a judge prior to an abortion.[65] In effect, then, the state law was upheld.

---

61. 347 U.S. 483 (1954).
62. *In re Gault,* 387 U.S. 1 (1967).
63. *Wisconsin v. Yoder,* 406 U.S. 205 (1972).
64. *Planned Parenthood of Central Missouri v. Danforth,* 428 U.S. 52 (1976).
65. *Barnes v. Mississippi,* 114 S.Ct. 468 (1993).

POLITICS AND AMERICANS WITH DISABILITIES
Special Treatment

Twenty percent of the population of the United States has some form of disability, and there are hundreds of different disabilities. All persons with disabilities share a common experience, however: discrimination. The United States Supreme Court has recognized "invidious discrimination against the handicapped"—discrimination that is often the product of "thoughtlessness and indifference," causing persons with disabilities "to live among society shunted aside, hidden, and ignored."*

This discrimination motivated the movement to push for the enactment of the Americans with Disabilities Act (ADA) of 1990. It has also prompted many of those with disabilities to change the way they are perceived by society. "We don't want to be dependent any more. We want to be part of society in every way," says Lex Friedan of the Institute for Rehabilitation and Research Foundation. In other words,

*Alexander v. Choate, 469 U.S. 287 (1985).

disabled persons share not only a common experience but also a common desire: to be treated like everyone else.

Being treated like everyone else does not mean the total absence of special treatment. Persons with disabilities do want special treatment in the form of regulations mandated by the ADA. They want special treatment in the form of expenditures by government and business. Special treatment is not unique to persons with disabilities—business firms and others receive special treatment in the same forms. Broadly, special treatment for persons with disabilities is designed to give them the opportunity to live without allowing a disability to define them or dominate their lives.

Businesses see persons with disabilities as a source of customers and employees. On the whole, however, business has been afraid of the increased costs associated with the special treatment required by the ADA. One of the purposes of the

ADA is to make disabilities irrelevant in employment decisions.

Generally, an employer complies with the ADA if an applicant for employment is considered on the basis of his or her ability to do the job with reasonable accommodation. As a rule, persons with disabilities are to be judged on the basis of the average level of performance by their peers. An employer violates the ADA if an applicant is rejected on the basis of stereotypes or generalizations about his or her disability or disabilities in general. There is a dispute over what constitutes "reasonable accommodation" and what it will cost. The dispute may be settled only in the courts.

Perhaps a better way to view the provisions of the ADA is to consider what they will *not* cost. The ADA reduces the dependency of persons with disabilities on federal and state funds and opens a way for persons with disabilities to earn a living and pay taxes like everyone else.

Voting Rights and the Young

The Twenty-sixth Amendment to the Constitution, ratified on July 1, 1971, reads as follows:

> The right of citizens of the United States, who are eighteen years of age or older, to vote shall not be denied or abridged by the United States or by any State on account of age.

Before this amendment, the age at which citizens could vote was twenty-one. But why did the Twenty-sixth Amendment specify age eighteen? Why not seventeen or sixteen? And why did it take until 1971 to allow those between the ages of eighteen and twenty-one to vote?

There are no easy answers to such questions. One cannot argue simply that those under twenty-one, or those under eighteen, are "incompetent." Incompetent at what? Certainly, one could find a significant number of seventeen-year-olds who can understand the political issues presented to

POLITICS: THE HUMAN SIDE
Jesse Brown, Secretary, Department of Veterans Affairs

"I am proud of my family and my faith. I am proud to be a black man with a rich cultural heritage. I am proud to have served in the U.S. Marines, and I am proud that I am an advocate for veterans. And let the record show that I shall be a secretary for veterans affairs, not a secretary of veterans affairs."

BIOGRAPHICAL NOTES

Jesse Brown, born on March 27, 1944, spent his teens and early adult years in and around Chicago. He was an honors graduate of Chicago City College and also attended Roosevelt University in Chicago, as well as Catholic University in Washington, D.C. Brown enlisted in the Marine Corps in 1963 and was wounded during combat in 1965 while patrolling in the Danang area of Vietnam. The gunshot wounds that he suffered left his right arm partially paralyzed. He is a member of the Veterans of Foreign Wars, the Military Order of the Purple Heart, and the Marine Corps League.

POLITICAL CONTRIBUTIONS

While Brown lived in Chicago, he served as vice president of the Vietnam Civil Council, as well as the Mayor's Committee on Employment of the Handicapped. He then started a long professional career with the Disabled American Veterans (DAV). He joined the staff of the DAV in 1967 as a National Service Officer trainee in Chicago and then supervised the National Service Office in Washington, D.C., from 1973 until he was promoted to supervisor of the National Appeals staff. He became the DAV's executive director in 1989, when he took over the group's Washington office. He championed that organization's advocacy efforts with the federal executive branch and Congress on behalf of disabled veterans and their families. He also supervised the legislative, national service, employment, and volunteer programs.

On January 22, 1993, Brown was sworn in by President Bill Clinton as the secretary of veterans affairs. In this position, Brown oversees nationwide programs of health care, assistant services, and national cemeteries. Today, there are over 26 million living veterans, as well as another 45 million dependents and survivors of deceased veterans who are eligible for Veterans Administration (VA) services and benefits. Indeed, there are still children of Civil War veterans who draw VA benefits. Brown is in charge of a budget of over $35 billion.

As secretary of veterans affairs, Brown will continue to face criticism of the largest health-care system in the nation. The VA health-care system includes over 170 medical centers, over 360 outpatient and outreach clinics, and over 150 nursing homes and related units. Prior to Brown's taking over the department, criticism of VA hospitals reached a high point after Oliver Stone's film, *Born on the Fourth of July,* appeared with Tom Cruise in the role of a paralyzed Vietnam veteran who received indifferent care at a VA hospital. Brown and his successors also face a declining veteran population and one that promises to decline even further as the size of the military is reduced.

them as well as can many adults eligible to vote. One of the arguments used for granting suffrage to eighteen-year-olds was that, because they could be drafted to fight in the country's wars, they had a stake in public policy. At the time, the example of the Vietnam War was paramount.

Have eighteen- to twenty-year-olds used their right to vote? Yes and no. Immediately after the passage of the Twenty-sixth Amendment, the percentage of eighteen- to twenty-year-olds registering to vote was 58 percent (in 1972), and 48.4 percent reported that they had voted. In the 1992 presidential election, of the 9.7 million Americans in the eighteen-to-twenty voting age bracket, 48.2 percent were registered, and 38.5 percent reported that they had voted.

The Rights of Children in Civil and Criminal Proceedings

Children today have limited rights in civil and criminal proceedings in our judicial system. Different procedural rules and judicial safeguards apply in civil and criminal laws. **Civil law** relates in part to contracts among private individuals or companies. **Criminal law** relates to crimes against society that are defined by society acting through its legislatures.

Civil Rights of Juveniles.   Children are defined exclusively by state law with respect to private contract negotiations, rights, and remedies. The legal definition of **majority** varies from eighteen to twenty-one years of age, depending on the state. If an individual is legally a minor, as a rule, he or she cannot be held responsible for contracts entered into. In most states, only contracts entered into for so-called **necessaries** (things necessary for subsistence, as determined by the courts) can be enforced against minors. Also, when minors engage in negligent behavior, typically their parents are liable. If, for example, a minor destroys a neighbor's fence, the neighbor may bring suit against the child's parent but not against the child.

Civil law encompasses an area that has recently broken new ground in children's rights: child custody. Child custody rulings have traditionally given little weight to the wishes of the child. Courts have maintained their right to act on behalf of the child's "best interests"[66] but have sometimes been constrained from doing so by the "greater" rights possessed by adults. For instance, a widely publicized Michigan Supreme Court ruling awarded legal custody of a two-and-a-half-year-old Michigan resident to an Iowa couple.[67] The court clearly and somewhat regretfully said that the law had allowed it to consider only parents' rights and not the child's best interests.

Children's rights and their ability to articulate their rights for themselves in custody matters were strengthened, however, by several well-publicized rulings in which older children were involved. In 1992, an eleven-year-old Florida boy filed suit in his own name, assisted by his own privately retained legal counsel, to terminate his relationship with his biological parents and to have the court affirm his right to be adopted by foster parents. The court granted his request.[68] In 1992, a New York court recognized the rights of an eleven-year-old boy to dismiss a court-appointed attorney and retain a lawyer of his own choosing to represent his interests in a court battle his parents were waging over his custody.[69]

Criminal Rights of Juveniles.   One of the main requirements for an act to be criminal is intent. The law has given children certain defenses against criminal prosecution because of their presumed inability to have

CIVIL LAW
The law regulating conduct between private persons over noncriminal matters. Under civil law, the government provides the forum for the settlement of disputes between private parties in such matters as contracts, domestic relations, and business relations.

CRIMINAL LAW
The law that defines crimes and provides punishment for violations. In criminal cases, the government is the prosecutor, because crimes are against the public order.

MAJORITY
Full age; the age at which a person is entitled by law to the management of his or her own affairs and to the full enjoyment of civil rights.

NECESSARIES
In contract law, necessaries include whatever is reasonably necessary for suitable subsistence as measured by age, state, condition in life, and so on.

---

66. *Kingsbury v. Buckner,* 134 U.S. 650 (1980).
67. *In re Clausen,* 442 Mich. 648 (1993).
68. *Kingsley v. Kingsley,* 623 So.2d 780 (Fla.App. 1993).
69. *New York Times,* November 10, 1992, p. 6.

COMMON LAW
Judge-made law that originated in England from decisions shaped according to prevailing customs. Decisions were applied to similar situations and thus gradually became common to the nation. Common law forms the basis of legal procedures in the United States.

criminal intent. Under the **common law**, children up to seven years of age were considered incapable of committing a crime, because they did not have the moral sense to understand that they were doing wrong. Children between the ages of seven and fourteen were also presumed to be incapable of committing a crime, but this presumption could be challenged by showing that the child understood the wrongful nature of the act. Today, states vary in their approaches. Most states retain the common law approach, although age limits vary from state to state. Other states have simply set a minimum age for criminal responsibility.

All states have juvenile court systems that handle children below the age of criminal responsibility who commit delinquent acts. The aim of juvenile courts is allegedly to reform rather than to punish. In states that retain the common law approach, children who are above the minimum age but are still juveniles can be turned over to the criminal courts if the juvenile court determines that they should be treated as adults. Children still do not have the right to trial by jury or to post bail. Also, parents can still commit their minor children to state mental institutions without allowing the child a hearing.

Although minors still do not usually have the full rights of adults in criminal proceedings, they have certain advantages. In felony, manslaughter, murder, armed robbery, and assault cases, juveniles are usually not tried as adults. They may be sentenced to probation or "reform" school for a relatively few years regardless of the seriousness of their crimes. Most states, however, allow juveniles to be tried as adults (often at the discretion of the judge) for certain crimes, such as murder. When they are tried as adults, they are treated to due process of law and tried for the crime, rather than being given the protective treatment reserved for the juvenile delinquent.

THE RIGHTS AND STATUS OF GAY MALES AND LESBIANS

Studies by sociologist Alfred Kinsey and his associates in the late 1940s and early 1950s, coupled with more recent research, indicate that between 3 and

This juvenile is being arrested in the same way as an adult would be, but he does not have the rights under criminal law of an adult. Juveniles normally receive less severe punishment than adults do for similar crimes, however.

15 percent of the American population may have some varying degree of homosexual orientation.[70] Gay males and lesbians therefore represent one of the most important minorities in the United States. Nonetheless, their rights did not surface as a major issue on the American political and legal scene until the late 1960s.

The Law and Public Attitudes

On June 27, 1969, patrons of the Stonewall Inn, a New York City bar popular with gay males and lesbians, responded to a police raid by throwing beer cans and bottles because they were angry at what they felt was unrelenting police harassment. In the ensuing riot, which lasted two nights, hundreds of gay males and lesbians fought with police. Before Stonewall, the stigma attached to homosexuality and the resulting fear of exposure had tended to keep most gay males and lesbians acquiescent. In the months immediately after Stonewall, however, "gay power" graffiti began to appear in New York City. The Gay Liberation Front and the Gay Activist Alliance were formed, and similar groups sprang up in other parts of the country.[71] Thus Stonewall has been called "the shot heard round the homosexual world."[72]

The status of gay males and lesbians again came to national attention in 1977, when Anita Bryant, of Florida orange juice and television commercial fame, organized a "Save Our Children" campaign. Its purpose was to rescind the law protecting the legal rights of gay males and lesbians in Dade County, Florida. The Dade County law protected them from discrimination in public accommodations, housing, and employment. Bryant's campaign against the gay community's effort to keep the law on the books was successful. In June 1977, Miami citizens voted 2 to 1 to repeal the law protecting gay males and lesbians. Similar laws were repealed in Eugene, Oregon; Wichita, Kansas; and St. Paul, Minnesota. In the 1990 primary, Broward County, Florida, voters defeated a proposal designed to give gay males and lesbians greater protection against discrimination (the so-called "human rights referendum") by a margin of 3 to 2. Voters in Colorado passed a state constitutional amendment that would prohibit state and local governments from passing laws to protect gay males and lesbians. This amendment was struck down, however, in 1993 by a judge hearing a suit brought by, among others, tennis star Martina Navratilova.

A major effort by the gay community in California to get a gay rights bill enacted into law was foiled when Governor Pete Wilson vetoed the bill in October 1991. Today, twenty-five states still have antihomosexual laws on the books. In the summer of 1986, the Supreme Court upheld by a five-to-four decision an antigay law in the state of Georgia that made homosexual conduct between two adults a crime. The defendant in the case was seen engaging in consensual homosexual activity in his bedroom. He was arrested by a police officer who had been looking for him because of an unpaid traffic ticket and had observed the defendant through a window. Justice Byron

Gay males and lesbians have become an important political force in American politics today. These demonstrators believe that constitutional civil rights and liberties, including equal protection of the laws, should extend to gay males and lesbians and that laws permitting discrimination against these groups should be repealed.

---

70. See Alfred Kinsey, *Sexual Behavior in the Human Male* (Philadelphia: Saunders, 1948) and *Sexual Behavior in the Human Female* (Philadelphia: Saunders, 1953); and Margaret Cruikshank, *The Gay and Lesbian Liberation Movement* (New York: Routledge, Chapman & Hall, 1992).

71. Wayne R. Dynes, ed., *Encyclopedia of Homosexuality* (New York: Garland, 1990), p. 1349.

72. Cruikshank, *Gay and Lesbian Liberation Movement.*

White, in a written opinion, said that "we are quite unwilling" to "announce . . . a fundamental right to engage in homosexual sodomy."[73]

Attitudes toward gay males and lesbians are changing, however. Recent Gallup polls show that 47 percent of Americans believe that private homosexual relations between consenting adults should not be considered illegal. Almost one hundred cities throughout the United States currently have laws prohibiting discrimination against homosexuals in the areas of housing, education, banking, labor union employment, and public accommodations. Since 1982, Wisconsin has had on its books a general law prohibiting all discrimination against gay males and lesbians. In 1989, Massachusetts passed a law specifically stating that the state does not endorse homosexuality nor recognize homosexual partnerships but that no discrimination against gay males or lesbians shall exist. In 1990, St. Paul, Minnesota, passed a new ordinance prohibiting discrimination on the basis of sexual orientation in housing, education, employment, and public accommodations. In a number of states and localities, laws against "hate crimes" include actions taken against homosexuals, even though the genesis of those laws was crimes against African Americans and Hispanics.

Gay Males and Lesbians in the Military

The U.S. Department of Defense traditionally has viewed homosexuality as incompatible with military service. As gay males and lesbians have become more vocal in recent years, this policy has been attacked and brought to the attention of the executive and judicial branches of government.

In July 1993, President Bill Clinton announced that a new policy, generally characterized as "don't ask, don't tell," would be in effect. It would allow gay males and lesbians to serve in the military as long as they did not commit homosexual acts. Enlistees would not be asked about their sexual orientation. Military officials endorsed the new policy, after opposing it initially, but gay rights leaders were not enthusiastic. Clinton had promised during his presidential campaign to repeal outright the long-standing ban.

The Gay Community and Politics

The number of organizations of gay males and lesbians grew from fifty in 1969 to more than a thousand by the end of the 1970s. These groups have been active in exerting political pressure on legislatures, the media, schools, and churches. In 1973, some of these organizations succeeded in having the American Psychiatric Association remove homosexuality from its list of disorders. During the 1970s and 1980s, half the states repealed sodomy laws. The Civil Service Commission eliminated its ban on the employment of gay males and lesbians. In 1980, the Democratic party platform included a gay rights plank. The largest gay rights groups today are the Human Rights Campaign Fund, which hopes to see federal gay rights laws passed, and the National Gay and Lesbian Task Force, which works toward the repeal of state antisodomy laws and the passage of state and local gay rights legislation.

Gay males and lesbians have been elected to public offices in increasing numbers. Public awareness of elected officials who were gay or lesbian was

---

73. *Bowers v. Hardwick*, 478 U.S. 186 (1986).

significantly heightened when, on November 27, 1978, San Francisco supervisor Harvey Milk—thought to be the first openly gay person elected to office in a major city—was assassinated, along with the city's mayor, George Moscone. The killer, a former supervisor, was angry at the mayor for refusing to reinstate him after he resigned and was unhappy with Milk for supporting the mayor. Many gay males and lesbians across the country, however, tended to view the highly publicized event as a "hate crime."

Two members of the 104th Congress, which took office in January 1995, are openly gay—Barney Frank and Gerry Studds, both of Massachusetts. Other liberal members of Congress have vigorously supported gay rights issues.

CIVIL RIGHTS: UNFINISHED WORK

To be sure, since the 1950s, the gains of African Americans, Hispanics, Native Americans, Asian Americans, women, children, gay males and lesbians, persons with disabilities, and older Americans have been impressive. Nonetheless, fear of people who are different, as well as a general fear of change, continues to exist. Consequently, we can be certain that controversy over the role that these groups play, or should play, in our society will continue to foster both private and public debate. What special benefits should be given to older citizens and persons with disabilities, for example? Have affirmative action programs for women and minorities gone too far? How much should society be worried about the rights of children when there is evidence that juvenile crime is increasing?

Certainly the expanding proportion of the American population that is over age sixty-five will lead to political and economic conflicts in the future. Today, federal government spending on children is only 14 percent of federal government spending on those over age sixty-five. As senior citizens become a larger percentage of the population, their political power will continue to grow. They will undoubtedly clash repeatedly with those who champion the spending of more resources on children in the United States and those who believe more resources should be spent on minorities who have been disadvantaged.

In the second half of the 1990s, women and minorities will certainly push to obtain more political power by being elected to more federal, state, and local offices. Gay males and lesbians will certainly fight for an increase in the number of antidiscrimination statutes at the state and local levels. African Americans and other racial and cultural minorities will assert the values of their histories and cultures.

Can racism and prejudice be overcome? How this question is answered may determine our future, because the nation will only increase in diversity.

GETTING INVOLVED
Dealing with Discrimination

When you apply for a job, you may be subjected to a variety of possibly discriminatory practices—based on your race, color, gender, religion, age, national origin, sexual preference, or disability. You may also be subjected to a battery of tests, some of which you may feel are discriminatory. At both state and federal levels, the government has continued to examine the fairness and validity of criteria used in job-applicant screening. If you believe that you have been discriminated against by a potential employer, you may wish to consider the following steps:

1. Evaluate your own capabilities, and determine if you are truly qualified for the position.
2. Analyze the reasons that you were turned down (or dismissed). Do you feel that others would agree with you that you have been the object of discrimination, or would they uphold your employer's claim?
3. If you still believe that you have been unfairly treated, you have recourse to several agencies and services.

You should first speak to the personnel director of the company and politely explain that you feel you have not been adequately evaluated. If asked, explain your concerns clearly. If necessary, go into explicit detail, and indicate that you feel that you may

have been discriminated against. If a second evaluation is not forthcoming, contact the local branch of your state employment agency. If you still do not obtain adequate help, contact one or more of the following agencies, usually found by looking in your telephone directory under "State Government" listings.

1. If a government entity is involved, a state ombudsman or citizen aide who will mediate may be available.
2. You may wish to contact the state civil rights commission, which will at least give you advice even if it does not wish to take up your case.
3. The state attorney general's office will normally have a division dealing with discrimination and civil rights.
4. There may be a special commission or department specifically set up to help you, such as a women's status commission or a commission on Hispanics or Asian Americans. If you are a woman or a member of such a minority, contact these commissions.
5. Finally, at the national level, you can contact the American Civil Liberties Union. You can also contact the most appropriate federal agency: the Equal Employment Opportunity Commission, 2401 E. St. N.W., Washington, DC 20506.

 KEY TERMS

affirmative action   151

busing   144

civil law   177

cloture   150

common law   178

comparable worth   169

criminal law   177

de facto segregation   144

de jure segregation   144

Equal Employment
   Opportunity Commission
   (EEOC)   150

filibuster   150

grandfather clause   154

literacy test   154

majority   177

mandatory retirement   171

necessaries   177

poll tax   154

reverse discrimination   151

separate-but-equal
   doctrine   142

sex discrimination   167

sexual harassment   167

subpoena   151

suffrage   163

white primary   154

CHAPTER SUMMARY

1. The civil rights movement started with the struggle by African Americans for equality. Before the Civil War, African Americans were slaves, and slavery was protected by the Constitution and the Supreme Court. In 1863 and during the years after the Civil War, the Emancipation Proclamation and the Thirteenth, Fourteenth, and Fifteenth Amendments (the "Civil War amendments") legally and constitutionally ended slavery. Politically and socially, however, African-American inequality continued. The *Civil Rights Cases* (1883) and *Plessy v. Ferguson* (1896) effectively nullified the civil rights acts that were passed between 1865 and 1875.

2. Legal segregation was declared unconstitutional by the Supreme Court in *Brown v. Board of Education of Topeka* (1954), in which the Court stated that separation implied inferiority. In *Brown v. Board of Education* (1955), the Supreme Court ordered federal courts to ensure that public schools were desegregated "with all deliberate speed." The Civil Rights Act of 1964 banned discrimination on the basis of race, color, religion, gender, or national origin in employment and public accommodations. The act created the Equal Employment Opportunity Commission and led to a presidential order for affirmative action to improve opportunities for those who had been deprived of them due to discrimination. Affirmative action programs were perceived by many whites as a form of reverse discrimination, and in recent years, such programs have come under close scrutiny.

3. Historically, African Americans had been excluded from the voting process through poll taxes, grandfather clauses, white primaries, and literacy tests. The Twenty-fourth Amendment (ratified in 1964) and a 1966 Supreme Court decision outlawed poll taxes. The Voting Rights Act of 1965 outlawed discriminatory voter-registration tests and authorized federal registration of persons and federally administered procedures in any state or political subdivision evidencing electoral discrimination or low registration rates.

4. Today, Hispanics make up the second largest minority group in the United States. Hispanics have faced discriminatory barriers to political participation. Several Hispanic political organizations have succeeded in removing barriers in public facilities, education, and employment, including the language barrier for those not fluent in English.

5. In 1787, Congress declared Native-American tribes to be foreign nations to enable the government to sign land and boundary treaties with them. Over the next century, many treaties were made, and most were broken. Native Americans were forced westward as white settlement expanded. Congress passed the Dawes Act (General Allotment Act) in 1887 to assimilate Native Americans. Generally, assimilation was forced on Native Americans so the government could acquire their land and resources. Partly because their numbers were so diminished and the tribes so scattered, Native Americans have been unsuccessful in attaining political power.

6. The Chinese Exclusion Act of 1882 prevented Chinese persons from coming to work in the western United States in certain occupations. In 1942, at a time of intensified fear of the Japanese because of the bombing of Pearl Harbor, the president ordered the relocation of West Coast residents of Japanese descent to internment camps. In 1988, Congress provided funds to compensate those Americans and their survivors.

7. In the early years of the United States, women were considered citizens, but they were citizens without political rights. After the first women's rights convention in 1848, the women's movement gained momentum. Progress was slow, however, and it was not until 1920, when the Nineteenth Amendment was passed, that Women gained the universal right to vote. The National Organization for Women (NOW) and other women's rights groups continue to work for equal rights for women in all spheres of life.

8. Federal government efforts to eliminate sex discrimination in the labor market include prohibiting sex as a basis for discrimination under Title VII of the Civil Rights Act of 1964. Under this act, the Supreme Court has upheld the right of women to be free also from sexual harassment on the job, from having to make higher pension-fund contributions than males earning the same salaries, and from fetal protection policies that discriminate against women. The Equal Pay Act of 1963 prohibits sex discrimination in wages paid for equal work at the same establishment. Women who are paid less than men for work of comparable skill, effort, and responsibility may sue under Title VII on the basis of sex discrimination.

9. Problems associated with aging and retirement are becoming increasingly important as the number of older persons in the United States increases. Medicare and Medicaid have ameliorated some of the problems of medical expenses for many older people. The Age Discrimination in Employment Act of 1967 prohibits job-related discrimination against individuals over the age of forty on the basis of age, unless an exception applies.

10. Persons with disabilities are protected under the Rehabilitation Act of 1973, which prohibits discrimination against persons with disabilities in programs receiving federal aid; the Education for All Handicapped Children Act of 1975, which provides that all children with disabilities receive an "appropriate" education; and the Americans with Disabilities Act of 1990, which prohibits job discrimination against persons with physical and mental disabilities and requires expanded access to public facilities, including transportation, and to services offered by such private concerns as car-rental and telephone companies.

11. Although children form a large group of Americans, they have the fewest rights and protections, in part because it is commonly presumed that parents protect their children. The Twenty-sixth Amendment grants the right to vote to those age eighteen or older. In most states, only contracts entered into for necessaries can be enforced against minors. When minors engage in negligent acts, their parents may be held liable. Minors have some defense against criminal prosecution because of their presumed inability at certain ages to have criminal intent. For those below the age of criminal responsibility, there are state juvenile courts. When minors are tried as adults, they receive all of the rights accorded to adults.

12. Gay rights did not surface as a major issue on the American political and legal scene until the late 1960s, despite the large number of people with some degree of homosexual orientation in the United States. Half of the states have antihomosexual laws, and a state law that made homosexual conduct between consenting adults a crime has been upheld by the Supreme Court. Many local governments and some state governments now prohibit discrimination against gay males and lesbians in education, housing, banking, employment, and public accommodations.

 ## QUESTIONS FOR REVIEW AND DISCUSSION

1. Why was the Supreme Court, during the first half of this century, able to conclude that the separate-but-equal doctrine was constitutionally acceptable, whereas during the second half it concluded that the doctrine was unconstitutional?

2. What were some of the ways in which African Americans were effectively excluded from the political process following the Reconstruction era?

3. Different minority groups in the United States have different socioeconomic situations. What are some of the possible explanations for such differences?

4. To what extent do you believe that legalized gambling on Native-American property will alter the culture of Native Americans?

5. What might be some of the possible negative effects that could result from an affirmative action program designed to increase the percentage of women in certain types of jobs?

6. Think about the concept of equal pay for comparable work. What kinds of jobs traditionally performed by men would be comparable in effort, skill, and worth to, say, an executive secretary or a switchboard operator? How would the economy be affected if the wages for many "women's jobs" were greatly increased?

 ## LOGGING ON: STRIVING FOR EQUALITY

The many interesting Usenet news groups include mainstream and alternative groups. One news group that covers the topics discussed in this chapter is

alt.discrimination

It deals with affirmative action, quotas, bigotry, and persecution, to name some of its topics.

A news group on women's issues can be reached at

alt.feminism

or at

soc.women

There is also a group that discusses men and their problems and relationships. You can reach this group at

soc.men

A group that discusses gay and lesbian rights is

alt.politics.homosexuality

An interesting news group dealing with African-American topics is

soc.culture.african.american

If you're interested in Native-American issues, you can explore the news group

alt.native

Asian-American topics can be found on the news group

soc.culture.asian.american

 ## SELECTED REFERENCES

Belz, Herman. *Equality Transformed: A Quarter-Century of Affirmative Action.* New Brunswick, N.J.: Transaction, 1990. Belz explores the changing nature of affirmative action policies over time.

Brown, Dee. *Bury My Heart at Wounded Knee.* New York: Holt, Rinehart & Winston, 1971. This book is an important examination of the treatment of Native Americans as the frontier pushed westward.

Bumiller, Kristin. *The Civil Rights Society.* Baltimore: Johns Hopkins University Press, 1992. In this provocative and insightful analysis of the effect of civil rights legislation on American minorities, Bumiller argues that laws prohibiting discrimination achieve an unintended result—they serve to reinforce the social identity of minorities as victims and thus enhance their sense of powerlessness in American society.

Burtless, Gary, ed. *Work, Health, and Income among the Elderly.* Washington, D.C.: Brookings Institute, 1987. This collection of papers examines the economic implications of changing patterns among older people.

Carmichael, Stokely, and Charles V. Hamilton. *Black Power: The Politics of Liberation in America.* New York: Vintage Books, 1967. This is a classic expression of the politics of racism in the United States and of the struggle to overcome white domination.

Cornell, Stephen. *The Return of the Native: American Indian Political Resurgence.* New York: Oxford University Press, 1988. Cornell's work is considered to be the best study of Native Americans as an important and increasingly politicized ethnic minority.

Duke, Louis Lovelace. *Women in Politics: Outsiders or Insiders?* Englewood Cliffs, N.J.: Prentice-Hall, 1993. In this volume, you will read about contemporary women's issues that are addressed in the current political process, as well as about how government institutions and processes influence the lives of American women.

Faludi, Susan. *Backlash: The Undeclared War against American Women.* New York: Crown, 1991. The author suggests that the women's movement is losing ground because the media and the new right of American politics have created a backlash against women's equality.

Kluger, Richard. *Simple Justice.* New York: Knopf, 1975. The history of the 1954 Supreme Court ruling on *Brown v. Board of Education of Topeka* and African Americans' struggle for equality is investigated.

Nieman, Donald G. *Promises to Keep: African-Americans and the Constitutional Order, 1776 to the Present.* New York: Oxford University Press, 1991. This historical and political account of the struggle for rights by African Americans emphasizes the social and political context of legal developments.

Paglia, Camille. *Sexual Personae: Art and Decadence from Nefertiti to Emily Dickinson.* New Haven, Conn.: Yale University Press, 1991. This is one of the most controversial books on gender to be published in recent years. Paglia, a feminist, stands on end most of the principles of politically correct feminism.

Schlesinger, Arthur. *The Disuniting of America.* New York: Norton, 1991. The author warns of the dangers of ethnic particularism, of the rejection by some minorities of "Eurocentrism" in culture and curriculum, and of the emergence of "political correctness" in the United States.

Sigelman, Lee. *Black Americans' Views of Racial Equality: The Dream Deferred.* New York: Cambridge University Press, 1991. Sigelman presents a statistical analysis, based on surveys, of African-American attitudes about racial inequality and injustice with respect to age, gender, and economic status.

Tate, Katherine. *From Protest to Politics: The New Black Voters in American Elections.* Cambridge, Mass.: Harvard University Press, 1993. The author argues that the struggle for African-American civil rights has moved into the voting booth. She argues that in the 1990s, resistance to addressing African-American needs will encourage African-American organizations to stress civil rights over economic development.

Vardin, Patricia A., and Ilene N. Brody, eds. *Children's Rights: Contemporary Perspectives.* New York: Teachers College Press, 1979. This is a valuable collection of essays on the rights of children in American society.

Woodward, C. Vann. *The Strange Career of Jim Crow.* New York: Oxford University Press, 1957. This is the classic study of segregation in the southern United States.

PART THREE

People and Politics

6
Public Opinion

 CHAPTER OUTLINE

WHAT IF . . .
Political Polls Were Banned?

Public opinion polls abound. They are commissioned by public agencies to help identify public needs or to measure public satisfaction with services. They are sponsored by private corporations to tap public attitudes toward their products. Newspapers, television stations, and entire networks either contract with commercial pollsters to gather data or, as the *New York Times* does, set up their own polling operations. Finally, political parties and candidates also commission polls to identify the public's preferences on policies and candidates.

Even relatively inattentive voters suspect that political candidates design their campaigns in reaction to polling data. If the polls show that the public thinks the candidate is too interested in international politics, then the candidate's stump speech suddenly focuses on domestic issues. Public discomfort with a candidate's personality traits may lead to deliberate attempts by the candidate to change his or her public image.

What would campaigns and elections be like if all such political polls were banned? Federal regulations might allow, for example, polls taken by public or other agencies that focus on policies or issues but ban polls that ask for opinions about individuals or parties. In particular, polls that ask how a person might vote would not be allowed.

Much of the information generated by polls would probably not be missed. As columnist Brian Dickinson put it, "What does it mean that 48 percent of the voters think that the Supreme Court is too conservative?" After all, the Court is not elected; the Constitution makes it perfectly clear that the president nominates candidates and the Senate confirms them. Besides, do voters mean that the Court is politically conservative, or too pro-business, or socially conservative? The likelihood that such polling data are based on a common set of definitions is extremely low.

Information generated by polls is often published to create a news story. If there were no daily or weekly readings on the president's popularity, would it change the way that Americans evaluate how the government is really performing? Probably not. Instead of leaning on the latest presidential popularity figures to decide whether to support presidential proposals, members of Congress would have to make their own judgments of the chief executive's initiatives.

The character of American elections, however, would be changed by a ban on political polling. Candidates would have to plan their campaigns and choose the issues they think are most crucial without regard to immediate public reaction. They would be unable to change their campaign strategy whenever the polls indicated that they were lagging behind in the "horse race." Journalists would not be able to issue daily reports on that same horse race. Instead, they might pay more attention to the candidates' speeches. Some journalists might try to find out what other public officials say about a candidate or analyze the feasibility of a candidate's proposals.

Finally, the voters would have to cast their votes without knowing which candidate was ahead in the polls. In some elections, the polls have found the race to be so close that no winner could be projected. Such elections tend to increase voter turnout because of the excitement of the contest. Banning polls might have a similar effect on voter participation, as well as limit some of the more manipulative campaign strategies.

---

1. Is polling the public just reporting the facts, like any other kind of news reporting? Should poll reporting be protected by the First Amendment?
2. How does knowing which candidate is ahead shape campaign strategy? How does knowing the latest poll results affect voters' decisions?

In an era of widespread public opinion polling, what role does public opinion play in the American political system? If the United States is a representative democracy, how powerful is the voice of the public, as it is expressed through polls, and how powerful should it be? Because our representatives in Washington and in our state legislatures must make decisions on policies and issues that affect the country throughout the year, it would seem that the views of the public, as measured by polls, would help politicians in voting on the laws.

Public opinion as expressed by polls, however, may be limited in its usefulness by its very character. After all, the pollster wrote the question, called the voters, and perhaps forwarded the results to the politicians. Public opinion, as gathered by commercial or academic polls, is not equivalent to constituents' writing to their representatives, nor does answering a poll require the effort that going out to vote does. In fact, public opinion polls normally include the views of many individuals who do not vote and, as this chapter's *What If . . .* suggests, may actually suppress voter turnout.

HOW POWERFUL IS PUBLIC OPINION?

At various times in the recent history of the United States, public opinion has played a powerful role in presidential politics. Beginning in 1965, public opinion became more divided over the war in Vietnam. Numerous public expressions of opposition to the war took place, as measured by the polls and demonstrations in many cities. By 1968, when Lyndon Johnson was preparing to run for another term, public opinion against the war was expressed through a surge of support for antiwar candidate Senator Eugene McCarthy in the New Hampshire primary. Faced with public disapproval, Johnson dropped out of the race.

As the scandal surrounding the 1972 **Watergate break-in** unfolded, revealing the role of President Richard Nixon through congressional hearings and tape recordings from his office, a similar groundswell of opinion against the president occurred. In this case, the disastrous fall in the president's approval ratings to less than 25 percent coincided with the decision by the House Judiciary Committee to initiate impeachment proceedings against the president. Nixon, facing an impeachment trial, resigned from office.

Both of these cases illustrate the power of public opinion when there is great public dissatisfaction with the government or with an official. Rarely, however, is public opinion expressed so strongly over a long period of time.

In most situations, public opinion is used by legislators, politicians, and presidents to shore up their own arguments. It provides a kind of evidence for their own point of view. If the results of polls do not support their position, they can either commission their own poll or ignore the polls. As debate began on President Bill Clinton's ill-fated health-insurance proposal, politicians could find a poll or a question within a poll to support every viewpoint. In the weeks before President George Bush ordered the beginning of the air war against Iraq, only about 50 percent of the public believed that the use of force was the right thing to do to drive Iraq out of Kuwait. Within a few days after the beginning of the air war, more than 85 percent of all Americans believed that Bush had acted correctly by attacking Iraq. In neither of these cases, however, was public opinion overwhelmingly

WATERGATE BREAK-IN
The 1972 illegal entry into the Democratic Campaign offices engineered by participants in Richard Nixon's reelection campaign.

Those who wish to have legislation passed often muster the forces of public opinion to help convince Congress to pass it. Here you see citizens voicing their opinion on health-care reform.

on one side or the other initially. Thus, elected officials, although aware of the polls, could carry on their politics with little fear of reprisal from the voters and, as in the case of Bush, with the hope that the public would rally to support them. Public opinion, then, is neither all powerful nor powerless.

DEFINING AND MEASURING PUBLIC OPINION

There is no one public opinion, because there are many different "publics." In a nation of more than 260 million people, there may be innumerable gradations of opinion on an issue. What we can do, though, is describe the distribution of opinions among the public about a particular question. Thus, we define **public opinion** as the aggregate of individual attitudes or beliefs shared by some portion of adults.

As the time approached for the congressional vote for the North American Free Trade Agreement (NAFTA), for example, opponents could claim that Americans did not approve the treaty. One month before the vote, however, an NBC/*Wall Street Journal* poll showed the following distribution of opinions: 29 percent of Americans supported the treaty; 33 percent opposed it; 34 percent felt they didn't know enough about the treaty to answer the question; and 4 percent had no opinion.[1]

How is public opinion made known in a democracy? In the case of the Vietnam War, it was made known by numerous antiwar protests, countless articles in magazines and newspapers, and continuing electronic media coverage of antiwar demonstrations. Normally, however, public opinion becomes known in a democracy through elections and, in some states, initiatives or referenda. Other ways are through lobbying and interest group activities, which are also used to influence public opinion.

Public opinion can be defined most clearly by its effect. As political scientist V. O. Key, Jr., said, public opinion is what governments "find it pru-

---

1. *Public Perspective* (November/December 1993), p. 76.

PUBLIC OPINION
The aggregate of individual attitudes or beliefs shared by some portion of adults. There is no one public opinion, because there are many different "publics."

Union members protest a cut in benefits. A strike can be seen as an expression of public opinions, but if the union does not get support from others, politicians will feel little effect.

dent to heed."[2] This means that for public opinion to be effective, enough people have to hold a particular view with such strong conviction that a government feels its actions should be influenced by that view.

An interesting question arises as to when *private* opinion becomes *public* opinion. Everyone probably has a private opinion about the competence of the president, as well as private opinions about more personal concerns, such as the state of a neighbor's lawn. We say that private opinion becomes public opinion when the opinion is publicly expressed and if the opinion concerns public issues. When someone's private opinion becomes so strong that the individual is willing to go to the polls to vote for or against a candidate or an issue—or is willing to participate in a demonstration, to discuss the issue at work, to speak out on local television, or to participate in the political process in any one of a dozen other ways—then that opinion becomes public opinion.

DID YOU KNOW . . .
That James Madison and others argued in *The Federalist Papers* that public opinion was potentially dangerous and should be diffused through a large republic with separation of government powers?

THE QUALITIES OF PUBLIC OPINION

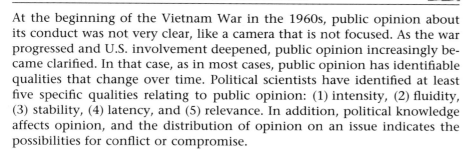

At the beginning of the Vietnam War in the 1960s, public opinion about its conduct was not very clear, like a camera that is not focused. As the war progressed and U.S. involvement deepened, public opinion increasingly became clarified. In that case, as in most cases, public opinion has identifiable qualities that change over time. Political scientists have identified at least five specific qualities relating to public opinion: (1) intensity, (2) fluidity, (3) stability, (4) latency, and (5) relevance. In addition, political knowledge affects opinion, and the distribution of opinion on an issue indicates the possibilities for conflict or compromise.

Intensity

How strongly people are willing to express their private opinions determines the **intensity** of public opinion. Consider an example that has been in the news regularly—the civil war in Bosnia. Most Americans who have opinions about this conflict do not have very strong opinions, because they find the situation difficult to understand. A small percentage of citizens have extremely intense convictions pro or con. But the average intensity is still quite mild. In contrast, public opinion about the Clarence Thomas/Anita Hill controversy (discussed in Chapter 5) was quite intense, on average. Most men and women held very strong opinions about whether Thomas had sexually harassed Hill. Intensity of public opinion is often critical in generating public action. Intense minorities can win on issues of public policy over less intense majorities.

INTENSITY
The strength of a position for or against a public policy or an issue. Intensity is often critical in generating public action; an intense minority can often win on an issue of public policy over a less intense majority.

Fluidity

Public opinion can change drastically in a very short period of time. When this occurs, we say that public opinion is fluid. At the end of World War II, for example, the American people were about evenly divided in their

2. V. O. Key, Jr., *Public Opinion and American Democracy* (New York: Knopf, 1961), p. 10.

opinions of the U.S. wartime ally, the Soviet Union. A 1945 Roper poll showed that about 39 percent of Americans saw the Soviets as peace loving, whereas 38 percent felt they were aggressive. During the years of the Cold War (1947 to, roughly, 1985), American opinion about the aims of the Soviet Union was very consistent. Between 13 and 17 percent of the American people believed that the Soviet Union was peace loving, and more than 60 percent saw it as aggressive.

Mikhail Gorbachev's leadership of the Soviet Union and his policy of openness toward the West, however, created an extremely fluid state of opinion among Americans. As Americans watched his attempts at internal reform and his willingness to allow the Eastern European nations to pull away from the Russian orbit, American opinion about the Soviet Union changed quickly. Between 1985 and 1990, the number of Americans who saw the Soviet Union as peace loving increased from 17 to 43 percent.[3] The **fluidity** of American opinion was a response to the rapidly changing conditions in the Soviet Union and world politics. Such fluidity in public opinion reflects public awareness of government policy and in turn influences government decision making.

Stability

Many individual opinions remain constant over a lifetime. Taken together, individual opinions that constitute public opinion also may be extremely stable, persisting for many years. Consider the effect of the Civil War on political attitudes in the South. It was the Republicans under Abraham Lincoln who, in the eyes of southerners, were responsible for the Civil War and the ensuing humiliations experienced by a defeated South. Consequently, the South became strongly Democratic. Until the post–World War II period, it was called the **Solid South**, because Democratic candidates nearly always won. We can say that public opinion in the South in favor of Democrats and against Republicans had great **stability**.

Latency

Not all political opinions are expressed by the holders of opinions. There may be potential political opinions—those not yet realized. Political scientists call these **latent**, or quiescent, **public opinions**. Some say, for example, that Adolf Hitler exploited the latent public opinion of post–World War I Germany by forming the National Socialist party. The public was ripe for a leader who would militarize Germany and put Germany back on its feet. Latent public opinion offers golden opportunities for political leaders astute enough to perceive it and act on it politically.

When average citizens are asked to respond to highly complex issues about which they have imperfect knowledge, their opinions may remain latent. This was true in the example of the NAFTA survey data given earlier. Because of the complexity of the issues involved, many Americans could not predict the future impact of the agreement on their own lives, much less on the economy of the nation. Even within a few weeks of the vote, almost 40

FLUIDITY
The extent to which public opinion changes over time.

SOLID SOUTH
A term describing the tendency of the post–Civil War southern states to vote for the Democratic party. (Voting patterns in the South have changed, though.)

STABILITY
The extent to which public opinion remains constant over time.

LATENT PUBLIC OPINION
Unexpressed political opinions that have the potential to become manifest attitudes or beliefs.

3. Alvin Richman, "The Polls: Changing American Attitudes toward the Soviet Union," *Public Opinion Quarterly*, Vol. 55 (1991), p. 144.

percent of the poll's respondents were unable to make a decision. What the views of those citizens would have been if they had been better informed is unknown. Poll questions dealing with views on foreign nations also produce a high proportion of responses indicating that many people rarely think about these kinds of issues.

Relevance

Relevant public opinion for most people is simply public opinion that deals with issues concerning them. If a person has a sick parent who is having trouble meeting medical bills, then public opinion that is focused on the issues of Medicare or Medicaid will be relevant for that person. If another person likes to go hunting with his or her children, gun control becomes a relevant political issue. Of course, **relevance** changes according to events. Public concern about inflation, for example, was at an all-time low during the late 1980s and early 1990s. Why? Because the United States had relatively little inflation during that period. Public opinion about the issue of unemployment certainly was relevant during the Great Depression in the 1930s, but not during the 1960s, when the nation experienced 102 months of almost uninterrupted economic growth from 1961 to 1969.

Certain popular books or spectacular events can make a particular issue relevant. The succession of violent crimes—ranging from the bombing of the Federal Building in Oklahoma City to the many kidnappings and murders of children—made crime and violence a top priority for citizens in 1995.

RELEVANCE
The extent to which an issue is of concern at a particular time. Issues become relevant when the public views them as pressing or of direct concern to daily life.

Political Knowledge

People are more likely to base their opinions on knowledge about an issue if they have strong feelings about the topic. Just as relevance and intensity are closely related to having an opinion, individuals who are strongly interested in a question will probably take the time to read about it.

Looking at the population as a whole, the level of political information is modest. Survey research tells us that slightly less than 29 percent of adult Americans can give the name of their congressperson, and just 25 percent can name both U.S. senators from their state. Only 34 percent of adults know that Congress declares war,[4] though almost 70 percent know the majority party in Congress. What these data tell us is that Americans do not expend much effort remembering political facts that may not be important to their daily lives.

Americans are also likely to forget political information quite quickly. Facts that are of vital interest to citizens in a time of crisis lose their significance after the crisis has passed. In the 1985 *New York Times*/CBS News Survey on Vietnam, marking the tenth anniversary of the end of that conflict, 63 percent of those questioned knew that the United States sided with the South Vietnamese in that conflict. Only 27 percent remembered, however, which side in that conflict launched the Tet offensive, which was a major political defeat for American and South Vietnamese forces.[5]

4. Michael X. Della Carpini and Scott Keeter, "The Public's Knowledge of Politics," in J. David Dennamar, ed., *Public Opinion, the Press, and Public Policy* (Westport, Conn.: Praeger, 1992), p. 29.
5. *New York Times*/CBS News Survey, February 23–27, 1985.

If political information is perceived to be of no use to an individual or is painful to recall, it is not surprising that facts are forgotten. What is more disturbing than forgetting the past is the inability of many citizens to give basic information about current issues. Polls on the U.S. military action in the Persian Gulf in 1991, for example, showed that most Americans tend to learn some basic facts about critical events, but only a few have detailed information. Studies showed that more than half of all Americans knew that the United States provided most of the troops in the Persian Gulf conflict and knew that Iraq's army outnumbered the U.S. forces there. Only 10 percent, however, knew that the United States imports only 10 percent of its oil from the Middle East.[6]

Consensus and Division

There are very few issues on which most Americans agree. The more normal situation is for opinion to be distributed among several different positions. Looking at the distribution of opinion can tell us how divided the public is on a question and give us some indication of whether compromise is possible. The distribution of opinion can also tell us how many individuals have not thought about an issue enough to hold an opinion.

When a large proportion of the American public appears to express the same view on an issue, we say that a **consensus** exists, at least at the moment the poll was taken. Figure 6–1 shows the pattern of opinion that might be called consensual. Issues on which the public holds widely differing attitudes result in **divisive opinion** (Figure 6–2). If there is no possible middle position on such issues, we expect that the division will continue to generate political conflict.

Figure 6–3 shows a distribution of opinion indicating that most Americans either have no information about the issue or are not interested enough in the issue to formulate a position. This figure illustrates latent, or quiescent, opinion. Politicians may feel that the lack of knowledge gives them more room to maneuver, or they may be wary of taking any action for fear that the opinion will crystallize after a crisis. It is possible that we would see the latent pattern most often if survey respondents were totally honest. Research has shown that some individuals will express fabricated opinions to an interviewer on certain topics rather than admit their ignorance.

MEASURING PUBLIC OPINION: POLLING TECHNIQUES

The History of Opinion Polls

Although some idea of public opinion can be discovered by asking persons we know for their opinions or by reading the "Letters to the Editor" sections in newspapers, most descriptions of the distribution of opinions are based on **opinion polls.** During the 1800s, certain American newspapers and magazines spiced up their political coverage by doing face-to-face straw polls

CONSENSUS
General agreement among the citizenry on an issue.

DIVISIVE OPINION
Public opinion that is polarized between two quite different positions.

OPINION POLL
A method of systematically questioning a small, selected sample of respondents who are deemed representative of the total population. These polls are widely used by government, business, university scholars, political candidates, and volunteer groups to provide reasonably accurate data on public attitudes, beliefs, expectations, and behavior.

---

6. Della Carpini and Keeter, "Public's Knowledge of Politics," p. 29.

FIGURE 6–1
Consensus Opinion

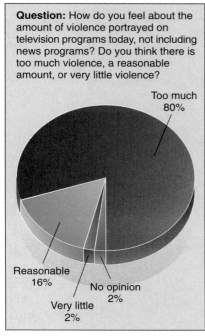

Question: How do you feel about the amount of violence portrayed on television programs today, not including news programs? Do you think there is too much violence, a reasonable amount, or very little violence?

Too much
80%

Reasonable
16%

No opinion
2%

Very little
2%

SOURCE: Times Mirror Media Monitor, as cited in *Gallup Poll Monthly*, August 1993, p. 18.

FIGURE 6–2
Divisive Opinion

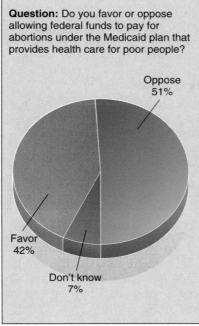

Question: Do you favor or oppose allowing federal funds to pay for abortions under the Medicaid plan that provides health care for poor people?

Oppose
51%

Favor
42%

Don't know
7%

SOURCE: PSR/*Newsweek*, April 8–9, 1993, as cited in *Public Perspective*, May/June 1993, p. 9.

FIGURE 6–3
Latent Opinion

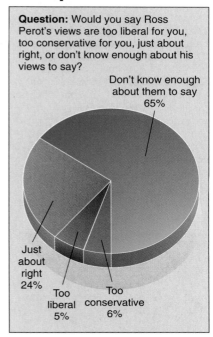

Question: Would you say Ross Perot's views are too liberal for you, too conservative for you, just about right, or don't know enough about his views to say?

Don't know enough
about them to say
65%

Just
about
right
24%

Too
liberal
5%

Too
conservative
6%

Note: Forty-five percent of Americans said they don't know enough about Bill Clinton's views to say, 31% felt that way about George Bush.

SOURCE: Survey by ABC News/*Washington Post*, June 3–7, 1992, as cited in *Public Perspective*, July/August 1993, p. 86.

(unofficial polls indicating the trend of political opinion) or mail surveys of their readers' opinions. In this century, the magazine *Literary Digest* further developed the technique of opinion polls by mailing large numbers of questionnaires to individuals, many of whom were its own subscribers. From 1916 to 1936, more than 70 percent of the magazine's election predictions were accurate.

Literary Digest, however, suffered a major setback in its polling activities when it predicted that Republican candidate Alfred Landon would win over Democratic candidate Franklin D. Roosevelt in 1936, based on more than two million returned questionnaires. Landon won in only two states. A major problem with the *Digest*'s polling technique was its continuing use of nonrepresentative respondents. In 1936, at the bottom of the Great Depression, those people who were the magazine's subscribers were, for one thing, considerably more affluent than the average American.

Several newcomers to the public opinion poll industry accurately predicted Roosevelt's landslide victory. The organizations of these newcomers are still active in the poll-taking industry today: the Gallup poll of George Gallup, and Roper and Associates founded by Elmo Roper. Gallup and Roper, along with Archibald Crossley, developed the modern polling techniques of market research. Using personal interviews with small samples of selected voters (less than a few thousand), they showed that they could predict with accuracy the behavior of the total voting population.

"Are you uninformed or apathetic?"
"I don't know and I don't care."

"Why Are Your Papers in Order?" © 1984 by Peter C. Vey.

This NBC news pollster conducts an interview with a "representative" American. Changes in public opinion are often measured on a regular basis by numerous polling organizations, such as this television network. Indeed, polling results have become ubiquitous. They are reported in newspapers and news magazines virtually every day of the year. TV commentators refer to them in the morning and evening news reports. Some contend that we have become a nation of percentages—X percent of Americans believe this and Y percent of Americans believe that.

Government officials during World War II were keenly interested in public opinion about the war effort and about the increasing number of restrictions placed on civilian activities. Improved methods of sampling were used, and by the 1950s, a whole new science of survey research was developed, which soon spread to Western Europe, Israel, and other countries. Survey research centers sprang up throughout the United States, particularly at universities. Some of these survey groups are the American Institute of Public Opinion at Princeton, New Jersey; the National Opinion Research Center at the University of Chicago; and the Survey Research Center at the University of Michigan.

Sampling Techniques

How can interviewing less than two thousand voters tell us what tens of millions of voters will do? Clearly, it is necessary that the sample of individuals be representative of all voters in the population. Consider an analogy. Let's say we have a large jar containing pennies of various dates, and we want to know how many pennies were minted within certain decades (1940–1949, 1950–1959, and so on). There are ten thousand pennies in the jar. One way to estimate the distribution of the dates on the pennies—without examining all ten thousand—is to take a representative sample. This sample would be obtained by mixing the pennies up well and then removing a handful of them—perhaps one hundred pennies. The distribution of dates might be as follows:

- *1940–1949: 5 percent.*
- *1950–1959: 5 percent.*
- *1960–1969: 20 percent.*
- *1970–1979: 30 percent.*
- *1980–present: 40 percent.*

If the pennies are very well mixed within the jar, and if you take a large enough sample, the resulting distribution would probably approach the actual distribution of the dates of all ten thousand coins.

The most important principle in sampling, or poll taking, is randomness. Every penny or every person should have a known chance, and especially an *equal chance,* of being sampled. If this happens, then a small sample should be representative of the whole group both in demographic characteristics (age, religion, race, living area, and the like) and in opinions. The ideal way to sample the voting population of the United States would be to put all voter names into a jar—or a computer—and randomly sample, say, two thousand of them. Because this is too costly and inefficient, pollsters have developed other ways to obtain good samples. One of the most interesting techniques is to choose a random selection of telephone numbers and interview the respective households. This technique produces a relatively accurate sample at a low cost.

To ensure that the random samples include respondents from relevant segments of the population—rural, urban, Northeast, South, and so on—most survey organizations randomly choose, say, urban areas that they will consider as representative of all urban areas. Then they randomly select their respondents within that area. A generally less accurate technique is known as *quota sampling.* For this type of poll, survey researchers decide how many persons of certain types they need in the survey—such as minorities, women, or farmers—and then send out interviewers to find the necessary number of these types. This method often not only is less accurate, but it also may be biased if, say, the interviewer refuses to go into certain neighborhoods or will not interview after dark.

Generally, the national survey organizations take great care to select their samples randomly, because their reputations rest on the accuracy of their results. Usually, the Gallup or Roper polls interview about 1,500 individuals, and their results have a very high probability (say, 95 percent) of being correct—within a margin of plus or minus 3 percentage points. The accuracy with which the Gallup poll has predicted national election results is reflected in Table 6–1.

Similar sampling techniques are used in many other, nonpolitical situations. For the Nielsen ratings of television programs, for example, representative households are selected by the A. C. Nielsen Company, and a machine is attached to each household's television set. The machine monitors viewing choices twenty-four hours a day and transmits this information to the company's central offices. A one-point drop in a Nielsen rating can mean a loss of revenue of millions of dollars to a television network. A one-point drop indicates that about 800,000 fewer viewers are watching a particular show. This means that advertisers are unwilling to pay as much for viewing time. Indeed, advertising rates are based in many cases solely on Nielsen ratings. When you consider that only about three thousand families have that little machine attached to their television sets, it is apparent that the science of selecting representative samples has come a long way—at least far enough to convince major advertisers to accept advertising fees based on the results of those samples.

Problems with Polls

Public opinion polls are, as noted above, snapshots of the opinions and preferences of the people at a specific moment in time and as expressed in response to a specific question. Given that definition, it is fairly easy to understand situations in which the polls are wrong. For example, opinion

DID YOU KNOW . . .
That for the 1984 presidential election between Ronald Reagan and Walter Mondale, the last preelection Gallup poll missed the actual percentage of Reagan's popular vote support by only 0.2 percentage points?

Interviewers who work for the Harris poll call survey respondents. Such telephone surveys have considerable accuracy, because the telephone numbers are selected at random.

TABLE 6–1
Gallup Poll Accuracy Record

YEAR	GALLUP FINAL SURVEY		ELECTION RESULTS		DEVIATION*
1994†	53.5%	Republican	53.5%	Republican	0.0
1992‡	49.0	CLINTON	43.2	CLINTON	+5.8
1990	54.0	Democratic	54.1	Democratic	−0.1
1988	56.0	BUSH	53.9	BUSH	−2.1
1984	59.0	REAGAN	59.1	REAGAN	−0.1
1982	55.0	Democratic	56.1	Democratic	−1.1
1980	47.0	REAGAN	50.8	REAGAN	−3.8
1978	55.0	Democratic	54.6	Democratic	+0.4
1976	48.0	CARTER	50.0	CARTER	−2.0
1974	60.0	Democratic	58.9	Democratic	+1.1
1972	62.0	NIXON	61.8	NIXON	+0.2
1970	53.0	Democratic	54.3	Democratic	−1.3
1968	43.0	NIXON	43.5	NIXON	−0.5
1966	52.5	Democratic	51.9	Democratic	+0.6
1964	64.0	JOHNSON	61.3	JOHNSON	+2.7
1962	55.5	Democratic	52.7	Democratic	+2.8
1960	51.0	KENNEDY	50.1	KENNEDY	+0.9
1958	57.0	Democratic	56.5	Democratic	+0.5
1956	59.5	EISENHOWER	57.8	EISENHOWER	+1.7
1954	51.5	Democratic	52.7	Democratic	−1.2
1952	51.0	EISENHOWER	55.4	EISENHOWER	−4.4
1950	51.0	Democratic	50.3	Democratic	+0.7
1948	44.5	TRUMAN	49.9	TRUMAN	−5.4
1946	58.0	Republican	54.3	Republican	+3.7
1944	51.5	ROOSEVELT	53.3	ROOSEVELT	−1.8
1942	52.0	Democratic	48.0	Democratic	+4.0
1940	52.0	ROOSEVELT	55.0	ROOSEVELT	−3.0
1938	54.0	Democratic	50.8	Democratic	+3.2
1936	55.7	ROOSEVELT	62.5	ROOSEVELT	−6.8

NOTE: No Congressional poll done in 1986.

*Average deviation for 29 national elections: 2.2 percent.

TREND IN DEVIATION:

Elections	Average Error
1936–1950	3.6
1952–1994	1.6

†Data based on national aggregate vote estimate computed by The Roper Center, with votes cast for minor party candidates removed.

‡The Ross Perot candidacy created an additional source of error in estimating the 1992 presidential vote. There was no historical precedent for Perot, an independent candidate who was accorded equal status to the major party nominees in the presidential debates and had a record advertising budget. Gallup's decision to allocate none of the undecided vote to Perot, based on past performance of third party and independent candidates, resulted in the overestimation of Clinton's vote.

SOURCE: *The Gallup Poll Monthly*, November 1994.

polls leading up to the 1980 presidential election showed President Jimmy Carter defeating challenger Ronald Reagan. Only a few analysts noted the large number of "undecided" respondents to poll questions a week before the election. Those voters shifted massively to Reagan at the last minute, and Reagan won the election.

Polls may also report erroneous results because the pool of respondents was not chosen in a scientific manner. That is, the form of sampling and the number of people sampled may be too small to overcome **sampling error,** which is the difference between the sample results and the true result

SAMPLING ERROR
The difference between a sample's results and the true result if the entire population had been interviewed.

President Harry S Truman holds up the front page of the *Chicago Daily Tribune* issue that predicted his defeat on the basis of a Gallup poll. The poll had indicated that Truman would lose the 1948 contest for his reelection by a margin of 55.5 to 44.5 percent. Gallup's poll was completed more than two weeks before the election, so it missed the undecided voters. Truman won the election with 49.9 percent of the vote.

if the entire population had been interviewed. The sample would be biased, for example, if the poll interviewed people by telephone and did not correct for the fact that more women than men answer the telephone and that some populations (college students and very poor individuals, for example) cannot be found so easily by telephone. Unscientific mail-in polls, telephone call-in polls, and polls completed by the workers in a campaign office are usually biased and do not give an accurate picture of the public's views.

As poll takers get close to election day, they become even more concerned about their sample of respondents. Some pollsters continue to interview eligible voters, meaning those over eighteen and registered to vote. Many others use a series of questions in the poll and other weighting methods to try to identify "likely voters" so that they can be more accurate in their election-eve predictions. When a poll changes its method from reporting the views of eligible voters to reporting those of likely voters, the results are likely to change dramatically.

Finally, it makes sense to expect that the results of a poll will depend on the questions that are asked (see this chapter's *Politics and Polls* entitled "Asking Real Questions"). Depending on what question is asked, voters could be said either to support a particular proposal or to oppose it. Furthermore, respondents' answers are also influenced by the order in which questions are asked, the types of answers they are allowed to choose, and in some cases, by their interaction with the interviewer. To some extent, people try to please the interviewer. They answer questions about which they have no information and avoid some answers to try to measure up to the interviewer's expectations.

The Polls and the 1992 Presidential Election

As the 1992 election drew near and the polls still showed President George Bush trailing Bill Clinton (see Figure 6–4), the president started referring to the myriad surveyors of the public as "those nutty pollsters" and insisted that their results did not reflect the true sentiments of the voters. Of course, Bush's campaign was well supplied with its own polling data, which showed

POLITICS AND POLLS
Asking Real Questions

As more and more organizations sponsor public opinion polls, Professor Phil Meyer has noted an increasing tendency in the media to report on what he describes as "hamster polls." Meyer recalls the elementary schoolteacher who holds up the class hamster and asks the students whether they think the hamster is a male or a female. The children express their opinion by a show of hands. This is the quintessential hamster poll—a poll that asks individuals to express an opinion without any knowledge whatsoever of the facts. In Meyer's view, many of the polls that are currently conducted ask respondents to make impossible judgments: Do you think that Russia will become a democracy or a dictatorship? Do you think that Miami is the most dangerous city in the nation? Do you think that California will be rocked by a massive earthquake this year? Such questions require the respondent to guess about the answer, because the answer requires either knowledge about the future or knowledge from research that is probably unavailable to the ordinary citizen.

about the same margins as the media polls. Bush's disparagement of the polls underlined how important they had become to the campaign plans of the candidates. At the same time, Clinton had become more cautious on the campaign trail, carefully protecting his lead in the states in which the polls showed him to be a clear winner. H. Ross Perot, in contrast, simply refused to discuss the polls and continued to fund lavishly his campaign for the presidency.

There were more polls commissioned and reported during the campaign in 1992 than in any prior presidential year. All of the major news organizations—NBC, ABC, CBS, and CNN—and the major national newspapers commissioned polls throughout the campaign. Many newspapers ran

FIGURE 6–4 ■

Tracking the *New York Times*/ CBS News Poll—Voters' Approval of Candidates

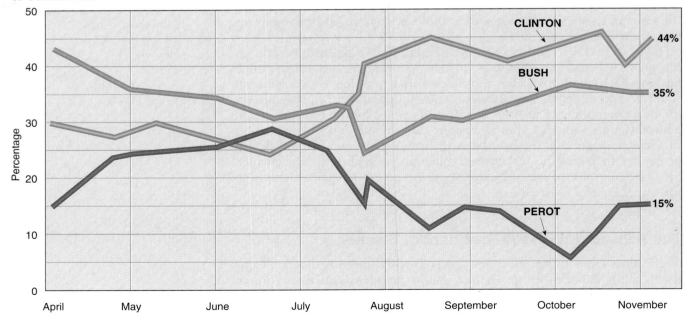

SOURCE: *New York Times*, October 25, 1992, p. 12; and *New York Times*, November 3, 1992, p. 9.

weekly features comparing the results of the most recent polls. Some journalists tried to avoid emphasizing the polling data and focused more on the issues behind the numbers, but the data won out in the last few weeks of the campaign. Polls were commissioned after every debate to report which candidate "won" the debate. The Bush campaign received a strong positive jolt when the CNN/*USA Today* poll reported that the president was quickly closing the gap on Bill Clinton ten days before the election. No other polling organization, however, could find the same phenomenon that weekend. Even the news anchors started discussing how the polls chose their respondents and how the results were tallied. (See this chapter's *Politics: The Human Side* for information on the president's pollster.)

HOW PUBLIC OPINION IS FORMED

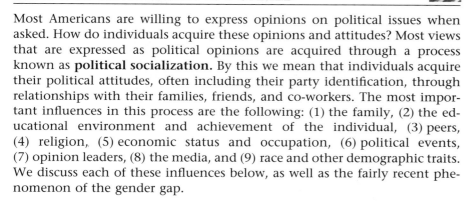

Most Americans are willing to express opinions on political issues when asked. How do individuals acquire these opinions and attitudes? Most views that are expressed as political opinions are acquired through a process known as **political socialization.** By this we mean that individuals acquire their political attitudes, often including their party identification, through relationships with their families, friends, and co-workers. The most important influences in this process are the following: (1) the family, (2) the educational environment and achievement of the individual, (3) peers, (4) religion, (5) economic status and occupation, (6) political events, (7) opinion leaders, (8) the media, and (9) race and other demographic traits. We discuss each of these influences below, as well as the fairly recent phenomenon of the gender gap.

POLITICAL SOCIALIZATION
The process by which individuals acquire political beliefs and attitudes.

"Glad you brought that up, Jim. The latest research on polls has turned up some interesting variables. It turns out, for example, that people will tell you any old thing that pops into their heads."

Drawing by Saxon © 1984 The New Yorker Magazine, Inc

POLITICS: THE HUMAN SIDE
Stan Greenberg, The President's Pollster

"I don't know whether [polling] is good for democracy, but I know it's good for the President."

BIOGRAPHICAL NOTES

Moving from the quiet of an academic life to the maelstrom of presidential politics may not have been the life plan of Stan Greenberg, but he seems to thrive in either environment. Born in Philadelphia in 1945, Stanley Greenberg proceeded through life as a scholar, earning his doctorate in political science at Harvard University and then beginning a teaching career at Yale University in 1970. He moved from teaching to research after about a decade and began a firm with another pollster, Celinda Lake, in his basement in New Haven, Connecticut, in 1980. Greenberg demonstrated his ability as a pollster in the 1980 senatorial election campaign of Christopher Dodd, working closely with Rosa DeLauro, one of Dodd's aides, who is also Greenberg's wife. Greenberg first met Bill and Hillary Rodham Clinton in 1988 while he was working on a children's project in Arkansas. Because of his success in the Clinton presidential campaign, he became the president's pollster after the inauguration. DeLauro is now a member of Congress, elected as a representative from Connecticut in 1990.

POLITICAL CONTRIBUTIONS

Greenberg's special value to the Clinton campaign and then to the presidential advisory team is his expertise in determining the attitudes and voting behavior of middle-class voters. According to DeLauro, he understands these voters well because he himself has a middle-class background. During the presidential campaign, he advised Bill Clinton to take positions that would appeal to Democrats who were disaffected from the party and to independents who were looking for reasons to vote against George Bush. To do this, Greenberg suggested that Clinton avoid appearing too close to traditional Democratic constituencies, such as African-American voters. For that reason, Clinton was willing to attack the Reverend Jesse Jackson for supporting a rap singer (Sister Souljah) who espoused violence in her music.

Greenberg, a quiet, congenial person, believed strongly that the party should listen to the needs of middle-class Americans. As he put it, "Even though I come from the left, I have always been uncomfortable with elitist liberalism, which I think is disdainful of the values of working-class Americans."*

*New York Times, October 27, 1992, p. A20.

As pollster to the president, Greenberg does not formally work for the White House but has, instead, a contract with the Democratic National Committee for approximately $1.6 million per year. His duties include polling on issues and political matters and reporting to the president. Usually, he meets with President Clinton once a week or more, giving him data from the polls and joining the team of presidential advisors. As Greenberg explains it, "My job is to keep people caught in the day-to-day action aware of what the mission is."†

Greenberg, like other pollsters who have preceded him—Bob Teeter for George Bush, Dick Wirthlin for Ronald Reagan, Pat Caddell for Jimmy Carter, and Louis Harris for John F. Kennedy—has a controversial role to play. Many critics believe that there is a tendency for presidents to suggest policies that are dictated by their polls. Others believe that polling is critical to keeping the support of the voters so that presidential policies will be approved by Congress.

†*Hartford Courant,* December 27, 1993, p. A1.

The Importance of the Family

The family is the most important force in political socialization. Not only do our parents' political attitudes and actions affect our adult opinions, but the family also links us to other socialization forces. We acquire our ethnic identity, our notion of social class, our educational opportunities, and our early religious beliefs from our families. Each of these factors can also influence our political attitudes.

How do parents transmit these attachments? Studies suggest that the influence of parents is due to two factors: communication and receptivity. Parents communicate their feelings and preferences to children constantly. Because children have such a strong need for parental approval, they are very receptive to their parents' views.[7]

The clearest legacy of the family is partisan identification. If both parents identify with one party, there is a strong likelihood that the children will begin political life with the same party preference. In their classic study of political attitudes among adolescents, M. Kent Jennings and Richard G. Niemi probed the partisan attachments of high school seniors and their parents during the mid-1960s.[8] They found that Democratic parents tend to produce Democratic children about two-thirds of the time and that Independent and Republican parents transmit their beliefs about parties only slightly less well. There is still a sizable amount of cross-generational slippage, however. In all, Jennings and Niemi found that 59 percent of the children agreed with their parents' party ties.

In a 1973 reinterview of the same children and their parents, Jennings and Niemi found that the younger people had become notably more independent of partisan ties, whereas their parents went through very little change.[9] By 1973, a majority of the children had deviated from their parents' partisanship.

Educational Influence on Political Opinion

Education is a powerful influence on an individual's political attitudes and on political behavior. From the early days of the republic, schools were perceived to be important transmitters of political information and attitudes. Children in the primary grades learn about their country mostly in patriotic ways. They learn to salute the flag, to say the Pledge of Allegiance, and to celebrate national holidays. Later, in the middle grades, children learn more historical facts and come to understand the structure of government and the functions of the president, judges, and Congress. By high school, students have a more complex understanding of the political system, may identify with a political party, and may take positions on issues.

Patriotism is instilled in children through the process of political socialization. The children in this picture know that their parents approve of this display of support for the flag, thus enhancing their patriotic feelings.

7. Robert S. Erikson, Norman R. Luttbeg, and Kent L. Tedin, *American Public Opinion: Its Origins, Content and Impact,* 4th ed. (New York: Macmillan, 1991), pp. 141–142.

8. M. Kent Jennings and Richard G. Niemi, *The Political Character of Adolescence: The Influence of Families and Schools* (Princeton, N.J.: Princeton University Press, 1974).

9. M. Kent Jennings and Richard G. Niemi, *Generations and Politics* (Princeton, N.J.: Princeton University Press, 1981).

DID YOU KNOW . . .
That young children first think of politics in terms of a benevolent president and a helpful police officer?

PEER GROUP
A group consisting of members sharing common relevant social characteristics. These groups play an important part in the socialization process, helping to shape attitudes and beliefs.

Generally, education is closely linked to political participation. The more education a person receives, the more likely it is that the person will be interested in politics, be confident in his or her ability to understand political issues, and be an active participant in the political process.

Peers and Peer Group Influence

Once a child enters school, the child's friends become an important influence on behavior and attitudes. As young children, and later as adults, friendships and associations in **peer groups** are influential on political attitudes. We must, however, separate the effects of peer group pressure on opinions and attitudes in general from peer group pressure on political opinions. For the most part, associations among peers are nonpolitical. Political attitudes are more likely to be shaped by peer groups when the peer groups are involved directly in political activities.

Individuals who join interest groups based on ethnic identity may find, for example, a common political bond through working for the group's civil liberties and rights. African-American activist groups may consist of individuals who join together to support government programs that will aid the African-American population. Members of a labor union may feel strong political pressure to support certain pro-labor candidates.

Religious Influence

Religious associations tend to create definite political attitudes, although why this occurs is not clearly understood. Surveys show that Roman Catholic respondents tend to be more liberal on economic issues than are Protestants. Apparently, Jewish respondents are more liberal on all fronts than either Catholics or Protestants. In terms of voting behavior, it has been observed that northern white Protestants are more likely to vote Republican, whereas northern white Roman Catholics more often vote Democratic; everywhere in the United States, Jews mostly vote Democratic.

These associations between religious background and political attitudes are derived partly from the ethnic background of certain religious groups and the conditions at the time their forebears immigrated to the United States. Germans who immigrated before the Civil War tend to be Republican regardless of their religious background, whereas Eastern European Catholics, who arrived in the late nineteenth century, adopted the Democratic identity of the cities in which they made their homes. The relationship between religion and party affiliation is shown in Figure 6–5.

Sometimes a candidate's religion enters the political picture, as it did in the 1960 presidential election contest between Democrat John Kennedy and Republican Richard Nixon. The fact that Kennedy was a Catholic—the second Catholic to be nominated by a major party—polarized many voters. Among northern whites, Kennedy was supported by 83 percent of voting Catholics and by 93 percent of Jewish voters but by only 28 percent of the Protestants who voted.

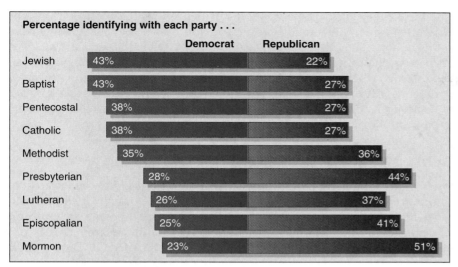

Percentage identifying with each party . . .

	Democrat	Republican
Jewish	43%	22%
Baptist	43%	27%
Pentecostal	38%	27%
Catholic	38%	27%
Methodist	35%	36%
Presbyterian	28%	44%
Lutheran	26%	37%
Episcopalian	25%	41%
Mormon	23%	51%

SOURCE: *New York Times,* April 10, 1991.

FIGURE 6–5
Religion and Party Affiliation

The Influence of Economic Status and Occupation

How wealthy you are and the kind of job you hold are also associated with your political views. Social-class differences emerge on a wide range of issues. Poorer people are more inclined to favor government social-welfare programs but are likely to be conservative on social issues such as abortion. The upper middle class is more likely to hold conservative economic views but to be tolerant of social change. People in lower economic strata also tend to be more isolationist on foreign-policy issues and are more likely to identify with the Democratic party and vote for Democratic candidates. Support for civil liberties and tolerance of different points of view tend to be greater among those with higher social status and lower among those with lower social status. Probably, it is educational differences more than the pattern of life at home or work that account for this.

The Influence of Political Events

People's political attitudes may be shaped by political events and the nation's reactions to them. In the 1960s and 1970s, the war in Vietnam—including revelations about the secret bombing in Cambodia—and the Watergate break-in and subsequent cover-up fostered widespread cynicism toward government. In one study of the impact of Watergate, Christopher Atherton found that schoolchildren changed their image of President Nixon from a "benevolent" to a "malevolent" leader as the scandal unfolded. Negative views also increased about other aspects of politics and politicians. Members of that age group moderated their views, however, as they matured.[10]

When events produce a long-lasting political impact, **generational effects** result. Voters who grew up in the 1930s during the Great Depression were likely to form life-long attachments to the Democratic party, the party of

GENERATIONAL EFFECT
A long-lasting effect of events of a particular time period on the political opinions or preferences of those who came of political age at that time.

---

10. Erikson, Luttbeg, and Tedin, *American Public Opinion*, p. 153.

Franklin D. Roosevelt. There was some evidence that the years of economic prosperity under Ronald Reagan during the 1980s may have influenced young adults to identify with the Republican party. A 1990 poll showed that 52 percent of thirteen- to seventeen-year-olds thought of themselves as Republicans, whereas 32 percent of this age group thought of themselves as Democrats. Although the number of younger voters identifying themselves as Republicans declined in 1992, the youngest voters still were more likely to be Republican then Democratic.[11]

Opinion Leaders' Influence

OPINION LEADER
One who is able to influence the opinions of others because of position, expertise, or personality. Such leaders help to shape public opinion either formally or informally.

We are all influenced by those with whom we are closely associated or whom we hold in great respect—friends at school, family members and other relatives, teachers, and so on. In a sense, these people are **opinion leaders**, but on an informal level; that is, their influence over us is not necessarily intentional or deliberate. We are also influenced by formal opinion leaders, such as presidents, lobbyists, congresspersons, or news commentators, who have as part of their jobs the task of swaying people's views. Their interest lies in defining the political agenda in such a way that discussions about policy options will take place on their terms.

Media Influence

MEDIA
The technical means of communication with mass audiences.

Newspapers, television, and other **media** act as sources of information, commentary, and images. Newspapers and news magazines (such as *Time* or *Newsweek*) are especially rich sources of knowledge about political issues. Some argue that newspaper editorials normally have a heavily pro-Republican and conservative slant, especially for presidential endorsements, and that columnists are often selected to reflect such biases. Journalists are perceived as having a counteracting Democratic and liberal bias. Television, the media source relied on by most Americans, conveys only limited political information about issues or candidates' qualifications. Although there is little evidence that the media directly influence opinions, many studies show how the media provide an agenda for the political process and filter the information that individuals receive about issues.[12]

The Influence of Demographic Traits

African Americans show a much stronger commitment than do whites to steady or more rapid racial desegregation. African Americans tend to be more liberal than whites on social-welfare issues, civil liberties, and even foreign policy. Party preference and voting among African Americans since the 1930s have supported the Democrats very heavily, and wealth has little impact on African-American attitudes.

It is somewhat surprising that a person's chronological age has comparatively little impact on political preferences. Still, young adults are somewhat more liberal than older people on most issues, and they are considerably

---

11. "Age, Generation, and Party ID," *Public Perspective* (July/August 1992), p. 16.
12. W. Russell Newman, Marion R. Just, and Ann N. Crigler, *Common Knowledge: News and the Construction of Political Meaning* (Chicago: University of Chicago Press, 1992).

more liberal on such issues as civil disobedience and racial and sexual equality.

Finally, attitudes vary from region to region, although such patterns probably are accounted for mostly by social class and other differences. Regional differences are relatively unimportant today. There is still a tendency for the South and the East to be more Democratic than the West and the Midwest. More important than region is a person's residence—urban, suburban, or rural. Big cities tend to be more liberal and Democratic because of their greater concentration of minorities and newer ethnic groups. Smaller communities are more conservative and, outside the South, more Republican.

The Gender Gap

Until the 1980s, there was little evidence that men's and women's political attitudes were very different. The election of Ronald Reagan in 1980, however, soon came to be associated with a **gender gap.** In a May 1983 Gallup poll, 43 percent of the women polled approved of Reagan's performance in office and 44 percent disapproved, versus 49 percent of men who approved and 41 percent who disapproved.[13]

In the 1988 election, the gender gap reappeared, but in a modified form. Although the Democrats hoped that women's votes would add significantly to their totals, a deep split between men and women did not occur. The final polls showed that 54 percent of the men voted for George Bush, as did 50 percent of the women. The 1992 presidential election again found women more likely than men to vote for the Democrats: 46 percent of women voted for Bill Clinton, compared with 41 percent of men. Additionally, women were less likely to vote for H. Ross Perot than were men.

Women also appear to hold different attitudes than their male counterparts on a range of issues other than presidential preferences. They are much more likely to oppose capital punishment, as well as the use of force abroad. A 1982 poll sponsored by the Chicago Council on Foreign Relations showed that only 34 percent of American women favored the government's selling military equipment to other nations, whereas 50 percent of men supported this strategy. Women's reluctance to support the use of force reinforced the gender gap in 1991. As the troop build-up in Saudi Arabia increased, women's approval of George Bush lagged 10 to 14 percentage points behind that of men. Other studies have shown that women are more concerned about risks to the environment, more supportive of social welfare, and more supportive of extending civil rights to gay men and lesbians than are men.[14] These differences of opinion appear to be growing and may become an important factor in future elections at national and local levels.

THE POLITICAL CULTURE OF AMERICANS

Americans are divided into a multitude of ethnic, religious, regional, and political subgroups. In many cases, members of these groups hold a particular set of opinions about government policies, about the goals of the

GENDER GAP
Most often used to describe the difference between the percentage of votes a candidate receives from women and the percentage the candidate receives from men. The term was widely used after the 1980 presidential election.

Reenacting in 1993 the March on Washington, which originally occurred in 1963.

---

13. *Gallup Report,* May 1983.
14. *Gallup Poll Monthly,* April 1993, p. 33.

POLITICAL CULTURE
That set of beliefs and values regarding the political system that are widely shared by the citizens of a nation.

POLITICAL TRUST
The degree to which individuals express trust in the government and political institutions. This concept is usually measured through a specific series of survey questions.

society, and about the rights of their group and the rights of others. Given the diversity of American society and the wide range of opinions contained within it, how is it that the political process continues to function without being stalemated by conflict and dissension?

One explanation is rooted in the concept of the **political culture,** which can be described as a set of attitudes and ideas about the nation and the government. As discussed in Chapter 1, our political culture is widely shared by Americans of many different backgrounds. To some extent, it consists of symbols, such as the American flag, the Liberty Bell, and the Statue of Liberty. One of the reasons that the renovation of the statue so strongly engaged the imagination of the citizens is because it symbolizes two major aspects of American political culture: the pursuit of liberty and the fact that most Americans are descended from immigrants who sought liberty and equality.

The elements of our political culture also include certain shared beliefs about the most important values in the American political system. Research by Donald Devine suggests there is a set of key values that is central to the political culture.[15] Among the most important are three of the values from the revolutionary period: (1) liberty, equality, and property; (2) support for religion; and (3) community service and personal achievement. The structure of the government—particularly federalism, the political parties, the powers of Congress, and popular rule—were also found to be important values.

The political culture provides a general environment of support for the political system. If the people share certain beliefs about the system and a reservoir of good feeling exists toward the institutions of government, the nation will be better able to weather periods of crisis, such as Watergate. This foundation of goodwill may combat cynicism and increase the level of participation in elections as well. During the 1960s and 1970s, survey research showed that the overall level of **political trust** declined steeply. A considerable proportion of Americans seemed to feel that they could not trust government officials and that they could not count on officials to care about the ordinary person. This index of political trust reached an all-time low in 1994, reflecting Americans' cynicism about the government and politicians generally (see Table 6–2).

15. Donald Devine, *Political Culture of the United States* (Boston: Little, Brown, 1972).

TABLE 6–2

Trends in Political Trust

QUESTION: How much of the time do you think you can trust the government in Washington to do what is right—just about always, most of the time, or only some of the time?

	1964	1968	1972	1974	1976	1978	1980	1982	1984	1986	1988	1990	1992	1994
Percentage saying:														
Always/Most of the time	76	61	53	36	33	29	25	32	46	42	44	27	23	22
Some of the time	22	36	45	61	63	67	73	64	51	55	54	73	75	78

SOURCE: *New York Times*/CBS News Surveys; the University of Michigan Survey Research Center, National Election Studies.

One way to determine whether Americans really believe in the values that are central to the political culture is to examine the degree of **political tolerance** they are willing to show toward those who hold views differing strongly from their own. Researchers asked Americans if they would be willing to permit demonstrations by a number of groups who espouse particular opinions.[16] More than 80 percent of those asked were willing to permit demonstrations opposing crime in the community and pollution. About 60 percent felt that it would be acceptable to permit African-American militants or radical students to demonstrate, whereas only 40 percent would support efforts to march for the legalization of marijuana. Although we do not find that all Americans are willing to extend political tolerance to groups indiscriminately, it appears that the political culture is strong enough to provide freedom for many points of view.

POLITICAL TOLERANCE
The degree to which individuals are willing to grant civil liberties to groups that have opinions differing strongly from their own.

PUBLIC OPINION ABOUT GOVERNMENT

A vital component of public opinion in the United States is the considerable ambivalence with which the public regards many major national institutions. Table 6–3 shows trends from 1973 to 1995 in Gallup public opinion polls asking respondents, at regularly spaced intervals, "how much confidence you, yourself, have" in the institutions listed. Over the years, military and religious organizations have ranked highest, but note the decline in confidence in churches following the numerous scandals concerning

16. David G. Lawrence, "Procedural Norms and Tolerance: A Reassessment," *American Political Science Review,* Vol. 70 (1976), p. 88.

TABLE 6–3

Confidence in Institutions Trend

QUESTION: I am going to read a list of institutions in American society. Would you please tell me how much confidence you, yourself, have in each one—a great deal, quite a lot, some, or very little?

	PERCENTAGE SAYING "GREAT DEAL" OR "QUITE A LOT"											
	1973	1975	1977	1979	1981	1983	1985	1987	1989	1991	1993	1995
Church or organized religion	66%	68%	65%	65%	64%	62%	66%	61%	52%	56%	53%	57%
Military	NA	58	57	54	50	53	61	61	63	69	67	64
U.S. Supreme Court	44	49	46	45	46	42	56	52	46	39	43	44
Banks and banking	NA	NA	NA	60	46	51	51	51	42	30	38	43
Public schools	58	NA	54	53	42	39	48	50	43	35	39	40
Congress	42	40	40	34	29	28	39	NA	32	18	19	21
Newspapers	39	NA	NA	51	35	38	35	31	NA	32	31	30
Big business	26	34	33	32	20	28	31	NA	NA	22	23	21
Television	37	NA	NA	38	25	25	29	28	NA	24	21	33
Organized labor	30	38	39	36	28	26	28	26	NA	22	26	26

NA = Not asked.
SOURCE: *The Gallup Poll News Service,* May 6, 1995, p. 2.

TABLE 6–4

Most Important Problem Trend, 1975–1995

Year	Problem
1995	Crime and violence
1994	Crime, violence, health care
1993	Health care, deficit
1992	Unemployment, budget deficit
1991	Economy
1990	War in Middle East
1989	War on drugs
1988	Economy, budget deficit
1987	Unemployment, economy
1986	Unemployment, budget deficit
1985	Fear of war, unemployment
1984	Unemployment, fear of war
1983	Unemployment, high cost of living
1982	Unemployment, high cost of living
1981	High cost of living, unemployment
1980	High cost of living, unemployment
1979	High cost of living, energy problems
1978	High cost of living, energy problems
1977	High cost of living, unemployment
1976	High cost of living, unemployment
1975	High cost of living, unemployment

SOURCE: *Gallup Report,* 1995.

television evangelists in the late 1980s. Note also the heightened regard for the military after the war in the Persian Gulf in 1991. The United States Supreme Court, which many people do not see as a particularly political institution, although it is clearly involved in decisions with vitally important consequences for the nation, also scored well, as did banks and banking until recently. A series of unpopular Supreme Court decisions from 1989 to 1991 and the savings and loan scandals of about the same time caused the public's confidence in both of those institutions to drop significantly by 1991. Even less confidence is expressed in newspapers, big business, television, and organized labor, all of which certainly are involved directly or indirectly in the political process. In 1991, following the check-kiting scandal and other embarrassments, confidence in Congress fell to a record low of 18 percent.

Although people may not have much confidence in government institutions, they nonetheless turn to government to solve what they perceive to be the major problems facing the country. Table 6–4, which is based on Gallup polls conducted over the years 1975 to 1995, shows that the leading problems clearly have changed over time. The public tends to emphasize problems that are immediate. It is not at all unusual to see fairly sudden, and even apparently contradictory, shifts in public perceptions of what government should do.

This gives rise to a critically important question: Is government really responsive to public opinion? A study by political scientists Benjamin I. Page and Robert Y. Shapiro suggests that in fact the national government is very responsive to the public's demands for action.[17] In looking at changes in public opinion poll results over time, Page and Shapiro show that when the public supports a policy change, policy changes in a direction congruent with the change in public opinion 43 percent of the time, policy changes in a direction opposite to the change in opinion 22 percent of the time, and policy does not change at all 33 percent of the time. So, overall, the national government could be said to respond to changes in public opinion about two-thirds of the time. Page and Shapiro also show, as should be no surprise, that when public opinion changes more dramatically—say, by 20 percentage points rather than by just 6 or 7 percentage points—government policy is much more likely to follow changing public attitudes.

POLITICAL IDEOLOGY

Political candidates and officeholders in the United States frequently are identified as liberals or conservatives. In recent years, variations on these labels include post–Cold War liberals and neoconservatives. These terms refer loosely to a spectrum of political beliefs that commonly are arrayed on a continuum from left to right. Each of the terms has changed its meaning from its origins and continues to change as the issues of political debate change. In the United States, however, the terms most frequently refer to sets of political positions that date from the Great Depression.

Liberals are most commonly understood to embrace national government solutions to public problems, to believe that the national government should intervene in the economy to ensure its health, to support social wel-

17. See the extensive work of Page and Shapiro in Benjamin I. Page and Robert V. Shapiro, *The Rational Public: Fifty Years of Trends in Americans' Policy Preferences* (Chicago: University of Chicago Press, 1992).

fare programs to assist the disadvantaged, and to be tolerant of social change. Today, liberals are often identified with pro–women's rights positions, pro–civil rights policies, and opposition to increased defense spending. California representative Ronald V. Dellums and Massachusetts senator Edward Kennedy are usually tagged as liberals.

In contrast, conservatives usually feel that the national government has grown too large, that the private sector needs less interference from the government, that social-welfare programs should be limited, that state and local governments should be able to make their own decisions, and that the nation's defense should be strengthened. Some conservatives express grave concerns about the decline of family life and traditional values in this country; they would not be tolerant of gay rights laws, for example. Arizona senator Barry Goldwater represented conservatism in the 1960s, whereas Senator Jesse Helms and 1992 presidential candidate Pat Buchanan are examples of today's variety.

When asked, Americans usually are willing to identify themselves on the liberal-conservative spectrum. More individuals are likely to consider themselves moderates than as liberals or conservatives. As Table 6–5 shows, the number of conservatives increased and the number of liberals declined in the early years of the Reagan administration, but by 1986, the proportions were about the same as ten years earlier.

Most Americans, however, do not fit into the categories as nicely as do Edward Kennedy or Pat Buchanan. Such political leaders, who are quite conscious of their philosophical views and who hold a carefully thought out and a more or less consistent set of political beliefs, can be described as **ideologues.** Partly because most citizens are not highly interested in all political issues and partly because Americans have different stakes in politics, most people have mixed sets of opinions that do not fit into one ideological framework. Election research suggests that only a small percentage of all

IDEOLOGUE
An individual whose political opinions are carefully thought out and relatively consistent with one another. Ideologues are often described as having a comprehensive world view.

TABLE 6–5

Ideological Self-Identification, 1976 to 1995

There has been relatively little change in the distribution of liberals and conservatives, even after the elections of self-described liberal or conservative presidents.

YEAR	LIBERAL	MODERATE	CONSERVATIVE	NO OPINION
1976	21%	41%	26%	12%
1977	21	38	29	12
1978	21	35	27	17
1979	21	42	26	12
1980	19	40	31	11
1981	18	43	30	9
1982	17	40	33	11
1984	17	41	31	11
1986	20	45	28	7
1988	18	45	33	4
1990	20	45	28	6
1992	19	41	34	6
1993	18	45	32	5
1994	18	48	34	0
1995	19	42	34	5

SOURCE: *Gallup Reports;* and *New York Times*/CBS News Surveys.

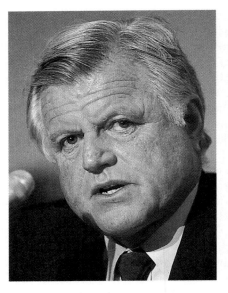

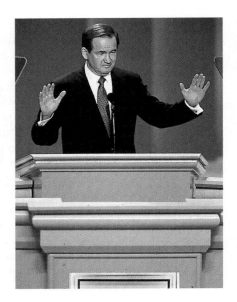

Senator Edward Kennedy (left) of Massachusetts has been a liberal voice throughout his tenure in Congress. Patrick Buchanan (right), who opposed President George Bush during the Republican presidential primaries in 1992, is an outspoken conservative. Buchanan has built a career in television as a political commentator.

Americans, perhaps less than 10 percent, could be identified as ideologues. The rest of the public conceives of politics more in terms of the parties or of economic well-being.

Some critics of the American political system have felt that elections would be more meaningful and that the nation could face important policy problems more effectively if Americans were more ideological in their thinking. Public opinion research suggests that for most Americans, political issues are not usually as important as events in their daily lives are. There is little evidence to suggest that forces are in place to turn Americans into highly motivated ideological voters.

PUBLIC OPINION AND THE POLITICAL PROCESS

Surveys of public opinion, no matter what fascinating questions they ask or how quickly they get the answers, are not equivalent to elections in the United States. Because not all Americans are equally interested in politics or equally informed, public opinion polls can suggest only the general distribution of opinion on issues. Many times, only a few citizens have formulated preferences, and these preferences will be changed by events. Such changing preferences are discussed in the *Politics and Polls* entitled "Health Reform in the Polls."

Politicians, whether in office or in the midst of a campaign, see public opinion as important to their careers. The president, members of Congress, governors, and other elected officials realize that strong support by the public as expressed in opinion polls is a source of power in dealing with other politicians. It is far more difficult for a senator to say no to the president if the president is immensely popular and if polls show approval of the president's policies. Public opinion also helps political candidates identify the most important concerns among the public and may help them shape their campaigns successfully.

Although opinion polls cannot give exact guidance on what the government should do in a specific instance, the opinions measured in polls do

POLITICS AND POLLS
Health Reform in the Polls

Polling early in 1992 revealed that the public felt that health care in the United States had become too expensive for most individuals and that many Americans either had no health insurance or were fearful that they would lose their insurance. Health-policy reform quickly became a leading campaign issue for all presidential candidates. Bill Clinton made it one of his top campaign issues and, after winning the election, announced that he would form a task force to recommend a new policy. He appointed his wife, Hillary Rodham Clinton, as the leader of the effort.

Polling on health-care reform became an industry. Polls were commissioned by the White House to find out whether the public would support a consumption tax, a kind of national sales tax, to pay for health care. Stanley Greenberg, the president's pollster, admitted that the White House looked for another type of funding after polls showed little public support for such a tax.*

Interest groups, including health-insurance companies, hospital corporations, labor unions, and pharmaceutical companies, commissioned polls to find out what the public supported and to acquire data that they could use in the debate. Polls sponsored by the news media tried to identify the parameters of public support, but the complexity of the issue made a clear understanding of public preferences very difficult. By the fall of

*New York Times, December 9, 1993, p. A20.

1993, a number of polls showed that a majority of Americans favored a plan that would guarantee health insurance to all Americans, even if it meant increasing taxes. In mid-November 1993, a CBS/New York Times poll found that 64 percent of Americans expressed a "willingness to pay higher taxes to provide health insurance to all Americans."

Opponents to the plan, however, began to build a case for alternative proposals, and the Clintons came under fire for the Whitewater development scheme. The resulting drop in the president's approval ratings undoubtedly weakened support for the Clinton health-insurance plan. By March 1994, a New York Times poll showed a drop in support for the Clinton plan. Although the public strongly supported health insurance that could never be canceled and that is accessible to every American, 57 percent believed that the Clinton plan would make their own health care more expensive, and only 44 percent thought that the plan would be fair to people like themselves.

In a more detailed study by a leading health-policy institute, 43.6 percent of the respondents were very satisfied with their own health care, but more than half (56 percent) believed that fundamental changes were needed in the system. Almost half (48 percent) were willing to pay higher taxes to cover all Americans, but few wanted to pay much more. Respondents generally supported taxes on alcohol, cigarettes, guns, and ammunition to

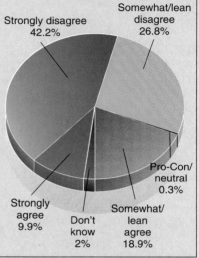

Question: Employers should be required to pay health insurance premiums for all their employees even if some employees need to be laid off because of the increased costs to the business…Do you agree or disagree?

Strongly disagree 42.2%

Somewhat/lean disagree 26.8%

Pro-Con/ neutral 0.3%

Somewhat/ lean agree 18.9%

Don't know 2%

Strongly agree 9.9%

SOURCE: National Health Survey, January, 1994, Institute for Health Policy and Health Services Research, University of Cincinnati Medical Center.

pay for the program but rejected any employer-paid plan that would cost jobs.† (See the accompanying figure for the results of part of this survey.)

What was the message to policymakers from all of these data? Americans want health insurance for all but are very concerned about cost. Policymakers will have to wrestle with the difficult choices.

†The National Health Survey, January 1994, Institute for Health Policy and Health Services Research, University of Cincinnati Medical Center.

Rally in Washington, D.C., for the
"Contract with America."

set an informal limit on government action. For example, consider the highly controversial issue of abortion. Most Americans are moderates on this issue; they do not approve of abortion as a means of birth control, but they do feel that it should be available under certain circumstances. Yet sizable groups of people express very intense feelings both for and against abortion. Given this distribution of opinion, most elected officials would rather not try to change policy to favor either of the extreme positions. To do so would clearly violate the opinion of the majority of Americans. In this case, as in many others, public opinion does not make public policy; rather, it restrains officials from taking truly unpopular actions. If officials do act in the face of public opposition, the consequences of such actions will be determined at the ballot box.

PUBLIC OPINION: UNFINISHED WORK

Public opinion is a vital part of the political process—it identifies issues for resolution, provides for a public debate on the issues, gives policymakers some idea of what the voters prefer, and sets boundaries on those same policymakers. The polling industry, however, may be close to putting itself out of business either through public distrust or government regulation.

The science of polling provides powerful information to private and governmental bodies to manipulate the public, to influence markets and the economy, and to shape the public agenda. Yet there is no mechanism to sort out "accurate" and "scientific" polls from marketing devices. The explosion of polls and poll results has also alienated the public. Refusal rates for polls have soared to above 40 percent in some instances. This means that certain groups within the public are no longer willing to cooperate with the pollsters, thus weakening the samples.

At the same time that the public is wearying of the polls and paying less attention to them, the media are increasing their expenditures on them, polling on almost every conceivable issue. The real danger is that deliberation

GETTING INVOLVED
Be a Critical Consumer of Opinion Polls

Americans are inundated with the results of public opinion polls. The polls, often reported to us through television news, the newspaper, *Time, Newsweek,* or radio, purport to tell us a variety of things: whether the president's popularity is up or down, whether gun control is more popular now than previously, or who is leading the pack for the next presidential nomination.

What must be kept in mind with this blizzard of information is that not all the poll results are equally good or equally believable. As a critical consumer, you need to be aware of what makes one set of public opinion poll results valid and other results useless or even dangerously misleading.

How were the people who were interviewed selected? Pay attention only to opinion polls that are based on scientific, or random, samples, in which a known probability was used to select every person who was interviewed. These *probability samples,* as they are also called, can take a number of different forms. The simplest to understand is known as a *random sample,* in which everybody had a known, and possibly an equal, chance of being chosen to be interviewed. As a rule, do not give credence to the results of opinion polls that consist of person-in-the-shopping-mall interviews broadcast on local television news segments. The main problem with this kind of opinion taking, which is a special version of a so-called *accidental sample,* is that not everyone had an equal chance of being in the mall when the interview took place. Also, it is almost certain that the people in the mall are not a reasonable cross section of a community's entire population (shopping malls would tend to attract people who are disproportionately younger, female, mobile, and middle class).

Probability samples are useful (and nonprobability samples are not) for the following reason: When you know the odds that the particular sample would have been chosen randomly from a larger population, you can calculate the range within which the real results for the whole population would fall if everybody had been interviewed. Well-designed probability samples will allow the pollster to say, for example, that he or she is 95 percent sure that 61 percent of the public, plus or minus 4 percentage points, supports national health insurance. It turns out that if you want to become twice as precise about a poll result, you would need to collect a sample four times as large. This tends to make accurate polls quite expensive and difficult to collect. Typically, national public opinion polls by, for example, the Gallup organization seldom interview more than about 1,500 respondents. With a sample of that size, Gallup is able to be correct to within about 3 percentage points of the probably true figures in 95 samples out of every 100.

There are other important points to keep in mind when you see opinion poll results. How were people contacted for the poll—by mail, by telephone, in person in their homes, or in some other way? By and large, because of its lower cost, polling firms have turned more and more to telephone interviewing. This method usually can produce highly accurate results. Its disadvantage is that telephone interviews typically need to be short and to deal with questions that are fairly easy to answer. Interviews in person are better for getting useful information about why a particular response was given to a question. They take much longer to complete, however, and are not as useful if results must be generated quickly. Results from mailed questionnaires should be taken with a grain of salt. Usually, only a small percentage of people complete them and send them back.

Be particularly critical of telephone "call-in" polls. When viewers or listeners of television or radio shows are encouraged to call in their opinions to an 800 telephone number, the call is free, but the polling results are useless. Only viewers who are interested in the topic will take advantage of calling in, and that group, of course, is not representative of the general public. Polls that use 900 numbers are perhaps even more misleading. The only respondents to those polls are those who care enough about the topic to pay for a call. Both types of polls are likely to be manipulated by interest groups or supporters of a political candidate, who will organize their supporters to make calls and reinforce their own point of view. Remember, when seeing the results of any poll, take a moment and try to find out how the poll was conducted.

on the real effects of policies and their impact on society will be drowned out by poll results that substitute for public debate. Whether the answer is to regulate polls, to outlaw polls before elections or at some other time, or just to allow the polls to exhaust themselves, any change undoubtedly will provoke strong opposition from the media, as well as from those who see a challenge to First Amendment freedoms.

 KEY TERMS

consensus 196	media 208	political trust 210
divisive opinion 196	opinion leader 208	public opinion 192
fluidity 194	opinion poll 196	relevance 195
gender gap 209	peer group 206	sampling error 200
generational effect 207	political culture 210	Solid South 194
ideologue 213	political socialization 203	stability 194
intensity 193	political tolerance 211	Watergate break-in 191
latent public opinion 194		

 CHAPTER SUMMARY

1. Public opinion is the aggregate of individual attitudes or beliefs shared by some portion of adults. It has at least five special qualities: (a) intensity—the strength of an opinion; (b) fluidity—the extent to which opinion changes; (c) stability—the extent to which opinion remains constant; (d) latency—quiescent opinions; and (e) relevance—the extent to which an issue is of concern at a particular time. Opinions are also affected by political knowledge and distributed among the public in different ways. Consensus issues are those on which most people agree, whereas divisive issues are those about which people strongly disagree.

2. Most descriptions of public opinion are based on the results of opinion polls. The accuracy of polls is based on sampling techniques that ensure randomness in the selection of respondents. Polls only measure opinions held on the day they are taken and will not reflect rapidly changing opinions. Certain methodological problems may reduce the accuracy of polls.

3. Opinions and attitudes are produced by a combination of socialization, information, and experience. Young people, for example, are likely to be influenced by their parents' political party identification. Education has an effect on opinions and attitudes, as do peer groups, religious affiliation, and economic status. Political events may have generational effects, shaping the opinions of a particular age group. Opinion leaders, the media, ethnicity, and gender also affect political views.

4. A political culture exists in the United States because so many Americans hold similar attitudes and beliefs about how the government and the political system should work. In addition, most Americans are able to identify themselves as liberals, moderates, or conservatives, even though they may not articulate a consistent philosophy of politics—that is, an ideology.

5. Public opinion can play an important part in the political system by providing information to candidates, by indicating support or opposition to the president and Congress, and by setting limits on government action through public pressure.

QUESTIONS FOR REVIEW AND DISCUSSION

1. Should public opinion polls be regulated so that consumers can be assured that these polls are accurate and complete? How much harm is done by the overuse of polls and the reporting of inaccurate poll data?
2. Should public opinion have more influence over public policy than do elections? To what extent should the president and the members of Congress consider public opinion when deciding on policies? What are

some of the limits on the value of public opinion as a way to decide public policy?
3. How are opinions formed on issues or on politicians? Think about your own opinions on health-care policy, for example. What factors—demographic, political, social, or informational—are influencing your thinking?

LOGGING ON

For those interested in expressing opinions or hearing the opinions of others, there is a discussion forum made just for you:

bit.listserv.politics

This news group is simply a forum in which people can discuss the political subjects of the day. It is a good way to get an informal sample of ''what America really thinks'' rather than relying on the network news to tell you.

Those interested in the more scholarly applications of public opinion can subscribe to the mailing list of *Public Opinion and Foreign Policy Journal.* To subscribe, simply send a letter via E-mail to

listserv@uga.cc.uga.edu

In the body of the letter, simply write

SUBSCRIBE POFP.J [your first name and last name]

SELECTED REFERENCES

Asher, Herbert. *Polling and the Public: What Every Citizen Should Know.* 3d ed. Washington, D.C.: Congressional Quarterly Press, 1995. This brief introduction to the science of polling pays special attention to the use of polls by the media and by political candidates.

Brehm, John. *The Phantom Respondents: Opinion Surveys and Political Representation.* Ann Arbor, Mich.: University of Michigan Press, 1993. This study examines who does not participate in polls and what difference it makes to the outcomes of polls.

De Mott, Benjamin. *The Imperial Middle Class: Why Americans Can't Think Straight about Class.* New York: Morrow,

1990. This interesting book explains why Americans do not accept social class as a relevant factor in identity; rather, the school experience and pop culture, especially television, are the crucial factors.

Donovan, Robert, and Ray Scherer. *Unsilent Revolution: Television News and American Public Life, 1948–1991.* New York: Cambridge University Press, 1992. The authors explore the effect that television has had on such institutions as politics, current events, and public opinion over the last half-century.

Erikson, Robert S., Norman R. Luttbeg, and Kent L. Tedin. *American Public Opinion: Its Origins, Content, and Impact.*

4th ed. New York: Macmillan, 1990. This book gives an overview of public opinion, its formation, and its distribution within the public. It also explores how public opinion influences public policy.

Herbst, Susan. *Numbered Voices: How Opinion Polling Has Shaped American Politics.* Chicago: University of Chicago Press, 1993. In this study, Herbst inquires into the American fascination with counting opinions and how opinion polls and their results have come to play such an important role in American politics.

McCombs, Maxwell, Edna Einsiedel, and David Weaver. *Contemporary Public Opinions: Issues and the News.* Hilldale, N.J.: Lawrence Erlbaum, 1991. The authors look at how the news media and other forms of information transmission influence the formation of public opinion.

Page, Benjamin I., and Robert Y. Shapiro. *The Rational Public: Fifty Years of Trends in Americans' Policy Preferences.* Chicago: University of Chicago Press, 1992. An examination of public opinion data over more than five decades leads to the conclusion that public opinions are fairly stable and rational and that opinions do have an influence on public policy over time.

Zaller, John R. *The Nature and Origins of Mass Opinion.* New York: Cambridge University Press, 1992. Zaller focuses on the role of the mass media in generating public opinion on public policy, civil rights issues, trust in government, presidential actions, and other matters.

7
Interest Groups

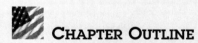

CHAPTER OUTLINE

The Role of Interest Groups

Major Interest Groups

Interest Group Strategies

Regulating Lobbyists

Why Interest Groups Have So Much Power

WHAT IF . . . Interest Groups' Contributions Were Limited to $100 per Candidate?

Suppose that the Realtors' Political Action Committee gives more than $3 million to congressional candidates to use in their 1996 election campaigns. Under the current campaign financing law, political action committees (PACs) representing interest groups can give up to $5,000 to each candidate for each election. Thus, the realtors could give contributions of $5,000 for both the primary and general elections to about three hundred incumbent legislators or their challengers.

What would the realtors expect to get for these contributions? With many interest groups in the PAC contribution game, it is unlikely that $5,000 will exert much influence on a congressperson for a particular vote. Most legislators agree, however, that such support from an interest group will guarantee access for the lobbyists of the organization, particularly if the candidate is in a tougher race than usual. PAC contributions may earn a polite hearing for the realtors' political needs.

How would the system for gaining access to legislators change if interest groups were limited in their campaign contributions to only $100 per candidate? In the case of the Realtors' Political Action Committee, the total expenditure for supporting every member of the House and his or her opponents would be about $87,000, down $2.9 million from the current situation. Obviously, with interest groups able to contribute far less than ordinary citizens, who are now able to give up to $1,000 per candidate per election (with an overall limit of $25,000 per election), PAC contributions would simply be symbolic, signifying the group's basic support for a legislator or challenger. No group could claim a position of special financial importance in a legislator's campaign, and it would be less likely that a group could gain a hearing for its views.

If the limits for the contributions of individuals to campaigns were not also changed, it is likely that interest groups would try to organize their members to make maximum contributions to legislators or candidates who were favorable to their causes. This would be a much harder task, and in the end, interest groups could not claim that the group itself was responsible for the contributions. It is also likely that interest groups would try to gain access to the legislators by providing other kinds of contributions to the campaign—such as individuals to work for the candidate at the grass-roots level or loaning the candidate an office.

Limiting interest group contributions to $100 could have a considerable impact on the usually very high reelection rate of incumbent legislators. No longer could incumbent committee chairpersons build campaign war chests through the traditional maximum PAC contributions. Currently, the greatest proportion of interest group contributions goes to incumbent legislators who hold positions of power in the majority party either as congressional leaders or as committee chairpersons. These PAC contributions are made to ensure access to the corridors of power regardless of whether or not the legislator faces a serious electoral challenge.

Limiting their contributions could so restrict interest group activities that groups might be willing to support public financing for congressional campaigns. Although public financing is already a reality for the general presidential election, Congress has been unable to agree on a public financing law for itself. Republicans have proposed an outright ban on PACs, coupled with a requirement that a majority of contributions come from individuals in a member's district. Democrats favored public financing for all candidates, but no source for the funding could be agreed upon.

In any event, a limit on PAC contributions would likely change the landscape of campaigning. Without the assurance of thousands of PAC dollars for each campaign, legislative candidates would have to forgo much of the media advertising that they use today. In making their choices, candidates and voters might have to rely on reading about candidates' positions and studying the issues rather than depending on television advertising. Many Americans might regard this as a healthy development.

---

1. What kinds of influence do interest groups gain from making campaign contributions to candidates?

2. Would reducing the size of contributions make interest groups more likely to support challengers rather than incumbent legislators?

THE ROLE OF INTEREST GROUPS

The passage of the North American Free Trade Agreement (NAFTA) in late 1993 gave President Bill Clinton a moment of real triumph during his first year in office. Although he had hesitated during the presidential campaign to support the treaty, which had been negotiated by the Bush administration, he later decided to commit himself and his administration to its passage.

Rarely in recent history has a piece of legislation fired such a conflict between **interest groups** and produced such strange political bedfellows. (An interest group is an organized group of individuals with common objectives who actively attempt to influence policymakers through direct and indirect methods.) While the general public was trying to follow the debate and was bombarded by about $10 million in advertising both for and against the treaty, interest groups, lobbyists, the president's own staff, and alliances of groups worked the halls of Congress. (See this chapter's *What If . . .* for a discussion on limiting the influence of interest groups.)

Among the interests that lined up against NAFTA were the labor unions, a number of environmental groups, some farm groups, civil rights groups, and some clergy and followers of H. Ross Perot. Some of these interests forged an alliance, called the Citizens Trade Committee, that rallied support at the grass roots. Republicans generally supported the pact, as did large and small business groups, most international companies, and some consumer groups that believed the treaty might bring lower prices to the public.

As the date of the vote drew near, some observers noted that the pro-NAFTA forces were working from an elegant conference room near the House floor with the aid of cellular phones and computers, whereas the anti-NAFTA forces were holed up in a basement office several blocks away with one telephone to share. Not only did it seem that the pro-NAFTA groups

INTEREST GROUP
An organized group of individuals sharing common objectives who actively attempt to influence policymakers (in all three branches of the government and at all levels) through direct and indirect methods, including the marshalling of public opinion, lobbying, and electioneering. Also called *pressure group* or *lobby*.

Lobbying activity becomes most intensive the day a vote is being taken on an important issue. Here lobbyists are working frantically on the day that the North American Free Trade Agreement vote was taken. Not surprisingly, lobbyists are often found in the lobbies of Congress.

had some clout in the House; they also had the president to lobby for extra votes. After the vote, opponents charged that the president "bought" the votes of many members through special agreements, such as trade protection for citrus fruit and an added retraining program for workers who lost their jobs as a result of the agreement.

The passage of NAFTA represented a battle of huge interest groups, highly paid lobbyists, and extraordinary pressure from the White House. Interests, however, are also likely to be represented by more ordinary people who make their points in Congress and the statehouses of America. When a small businesswoman contacts her state representative about a proposed change in law, she is lobbying the government. When farmers descend on Wash, D.C., in tractors or Americans with disabilities gather in the corridors of city hall, they are also interest groups lobbying their representatives. Protected by the First Amendment's guarantee of the right to assemble and petition the government for the redress of grievances, individuals have joined together in voluntary associations to try to influence the government since the Boston Tea Party, which involved, after all, an eighteenth-century trade issue.

How Widespread Are Interest Groups?

Alexis de Tocqueville observed in 1834 that "in no country of the world has the principle of association been more successfully used or applied to a greater multitude of objectives than in America."[1] But de Tocqueville probably could not have conceived of the more than 100,000 associations existing in the United States in the 1990s. It is estimated that about two-thirds of the U.S. population is formally associated with some type of group. Of course, the majority of these 100,000 groups do not strictly fit our definition of an interest group, because they are not actively seeking to change or influence government policy. But we can be sure that the purpose of the roughly 1,200 organizations whose names begin with the word *National* listed in the Washington, D.C. telephone directory is to do just that. To this list, we can add many of the 600 organizations listed in the D.C. telephone directory that begin with the word *American* or *Americans*. Currently, it is estimated that at least 80,000 individuals are employed in the nation's capital to influence government.[2]

The Benefits of Interest Groups

The structure of our political system makes it possible for individuals and groups to exert influence at many different points in the system. As the role of the government has expanded and touched more aspects of society, interest groups have multiplied to try to influence government action. Most American governments have legislative, executive, and judicial branches. If, for example, the state legislature passes a law that may hurt a local industry, then the representatives of that industry, the employees whose jobs may be

Alexis de Tocqueville (1805–1859), a French social historian and traveler, first commented on Americans' predilection for group action.

1. Alexis de Tocqueville, *Democracy in America,* Vol. 1, edited by Phillips Bradley (New York: Knopf, 1980), p. 191.
2. See Table 7–5 later in this chapter for the number of these lobbyists who are registered.

affected, and the citizens of the town in which the industry is located may well feel that they should express their dissatisfaction and try to have the law changed. They may attempt to influence the governor, who could veto the legislation, or they may concentrate on the bureaucracy to forestall the law's implementation. The newly formed interest group may try to block the legislation in the courts. At the next election, the group may try to defeat those representatives who voted for the bill. If it receives no satisfaction at the state level, the group may try to move the debate to the federal level. All of the institutions of government offer it similar access under the First Amendment to the Constitution, which guarantees citizens the right to assemble and petition the government for the redress of grievances.

Individuals join interest groups for a variety of reasons. Obviously, the proliferation of interest groups and the growth in their membership require a reciprocity of interests. An interest group must give individuals an incentive to become members of the group, and members of the group must have their needs satisfied through the group's activities, or they will no longer participate.

Solidary Incentives. Interest groups offer **solidary incentives** for their members. Solidary incentives include companionship, a sense of belonging, and the pleasure of associating with others. Although the National Audubon Society was founded originally to save the snowy egret from extinction, most members join today to learn more about birds and to meet and share their pleasure with other individuals who enjoy birdwatching as a hobby. Even though the incentive might be solidary for many members, the society nonetheless also pursues an active political agenda, working to preserve the environment and to protect endangered species. Most members may not play any part in working toward larger, more national goals unless the organization can convince them to take political action or unless some local environmental issue arises.

Material Incentives. For other individuals, interest groups offer direct **material incentives.** A case in point is the American Association of Retired Persons (AARP), which provides discounts, insurance plans, and organized travel opportunities for its members. Because of its exceptionally low dues ($15 annually) and the benefits gained through membership in AARP, it has become the largest—and a very powerful—interest group in the United States. AARP can claim to represent the interests of millions of senior citizens and can show that they actually have joined the group. For most seniors, the material incentives outweigh the membership costs.

Many other interest groups offer indirect material incentives for their members. Such groups as the American Dairy Association or the National Association of Automobile Dealers do not give discounts or freebies to their members, but they do offer indirect benefits and rewards by, for example, protecting the material interests of their members from government policy-making that is injurious to their industry or business.

Purposive Incentives. Interest groups also offer the opportunity for individuals to pursue political, economic, or social goals through joint action. Such **purposive incentives** offer individuals the satisfaction of taking action for the sake of their beliefs or principles. The individuals who belong to antiabortion or pro-choice groups have joined those groups because they

DID YOU KNOW . . .
That at least half of all lobbyists in Washington, D.C., are women?

SOLIDARY INCENTIVE
A reason or motive having to do with the desire to associate with others and to share with others a particular interest or hobby.

MATERIAL INCENTIVE
A reason or motive having to do with economic benefits or opportunities.

PURPOSIVE INCENTIVE
A reason or motive having to do with ethical beliefs or ideological principles.

are concerned about the issue of whether abortions should be made available to the public. People join such groups because they feel strongly enough about the issues to support the groups' work with money and time.

Interest Groups and Social Movements

SOCIAL MOVEMENT
A movement that represents the demands of a large segment of the public for political, economic, or social change.

Interest groups are often spawned by mass **social movements.** Such movements represent demands by a large segment of the population for change in the political, economic, or social system. Social movements are often the first expression of latent discontent with the contemporary system. They may be the authentic voice of weaker or oppressed groups in society that do not have the means or standing to organize as interest groups. For example, the women's movement of the mid-nineteenth century suffered social disapproval from most mainstream political and social leaders. Because women were unable to vote or take an active part in the political system, it was difficult for women who desired greater freedoms to organize formal groups. After the Civil War, when more women became active in professional life, the first real women's rights group, the National Suffrage Association, came into being.

African Americans found themselves in an even more disadvantaged situation after the end of the Reconstruction period. Not only were they unable to exercise political rights in many southern and border states, but also participation in any form of organization could lead to economic ruin, physical harassment, or even death. The civil rights movement of the 1950s and 1960s was clearly a social movement. Although there were several formal organizations that worked to support the movement—including the Southern Christian Leadership Conference, the National Association for the Advancement of Colored People, and the Urban League—only a social movement could generate the kinds of civil disobedience that took place in hundreds of towns and cities across the country.

President Clinton is shown here addressing the American Association of Retired People (AARP), which has become one of the most powerful lobbying groups in America. As the population ages, a larger percentage of Americans are over 55. Any president knows the importance of keeping such an important interest group happy. Through its lobbying effort, the AARP has been effective in preventing any significant reductions in the growth of Social Security benefits.

Social movements are often precursors of interest groups. They may generate interest groups with specific goals that successfully recruit members through the incentives the group offers. In the case of the women's movement of the 1960s, the National Organization for Women was formed out of a demand to end sex-segregated job advertising in newspapers.

MAJOR INTEREST GROUPS

Thousands of groups exist to influence government. Among the major types of interest groups are those that represent the main sectors of the economy—business, agricultural, and labor groups. In addition, there are many groups whose purpose is to protect the interests of public employees and professionals. In more recent years, a number of "public interest" organizations have been formed to represent the needs of the general citizenry, including some "single-issue" groups. The interests of foreign governments and foreign businesses are also represented in the American political arena. Table 7–1 lists some of the interest groups that were lobbying Congress in 1994 and the interests that they represented.

Business Interest Groups

Thousands of trade and business organizations attempt to influence government policies. Some groups target a single regulatory unit, whereas others try to effect major policy changes. Three big business pressure groups are consistently effective: (1) the National Association of Manufacturers (NAM), (2) the U.S. Chamber of Commerce, and (3) the Business Roundtable. The annual budget of the NAM is more than $8 million, which it collects in dues from about 14,000 relatively large corporations. Organized in Cincinnati in 1895 as an association made up predominantly of small businesses, the NAM became, during the Great Depression of the 1930s, primarily a proponent of the interests of large corporations. Of particular interest to the NAM is legislation that affects labor laws, minimum wage rates, corporate taxes, and trade regulations.

Sometimes called the National Chamber, the U.S. Chamber of Commerce represents more than 100,000 businesses. Dues from its members, which include upward of 3,500 local chambers of commerce, approach $30 million a year.

Two hundred of the largest corporations in the United States send their chief executive officers to the Business Roundtable. This organization is based in New York, but it does its lobbying in Washington, D.C. Established in 1972, the Roundtable was designed to promote a more aggressive view of business interests in general, cutting across specific industries. Dues paid by the member corporations are determined by the companies' wealth. Roundtable members include American Telephone and Telegraph, General Motors, USX Corporation, and International Business Machines. The Roundtable opposed common-site picketing legislation, the proposed Consumer Protection Agency, automobile emissions standards, and industrial pollution control.

Although business groups may share a common core of ideas, some interest groups may not agree on policies, even within their own organizations.

TABLE 7–1
Selected Lobby Registrations

The following groups, corporations, and individuals were among those registering with the Office of Records and Registration of the House of Representatives during one month in 1994.

LOBBY	TYPE	INTEREST
Alliance of American Insurers	Trade association	Health Security Act
American Chiropractic Association	Professional association	Health care
American Institute of Certified Public Accountants	Professional association	Modification of liability for accountants
Armour Pharmaceutical Co.	U.S. corporation	New technology in stabilizing blood supplies
Emily's List	Interest group	Campaign finance reform
General Atomics, Inc.	U.S. corporation	Funding of nuclear reactor research
Government of Mexico, Finance Ministry	Foreign government	Ratification of tax treaty
Independent Defense Contractors Association	Trade association	Small business
International Women's Health Coalition	Interest group	Women's reproductive health and rights issues in foreign aid
Leech Lake Tribal Council	Interest group	Agriculture
Major League Baseball Players Association	Labor organization	Antitrust exemption of major-league baseball
McDonnell Douglas Corp.	U.S. corporation	Defense authorization and appropriations
Pizza Hut, Inc.	U.S. corporation	Taxes and mandated benefits
U.S. Term Limits	Interest group	Limitation on terms of political office

SOURCE: *Congressional Quarterly*, February 12, 1995.

The NAM, for example, was badly divided over the NAFTA treaty because it would be beneficial to some businesses but not to all.

Agricultural Interest Groups

American farmers and their workers represent about 2 percent of the U.S. population. In spite of this, farmers' influence on legislation beneficial to their interests has been enormous. In 1995, American farmers received more than $25 billion in direct and indirect subsidies from the federal government. Programs designed to keep farm incomes high include price supports, target prices, soil conservation, and myriad other policies.

Farmers have succeeded in their aims because they have very strong interest groups and also because they are geographically dispersed and therefore have many representatives and senators to speak for them. The American Farm Bureau Federation, established in 1919, has 3 million members. It was instrumental in getting government guarantees of "fair" prices during the Great Depression in the 1930s.[3] In principle, the federation, controlled by wealthier farmers, is no longer in favor of government price supports. These farmers, who are engaged in large-scale farming, do not need government price supports to compete effectively.

Another important agricultural special interest organization is the National Farmers' Union (NFU). The NFU was founded in 1902 and claims a membership of more than a quarter of a million today. The oldest farm lobby organization is the National Grange, founded in 1867. With a membership of more than half a million, it finds its support among dairy farmers in New England, the Middle Atlantic states, and, to a lesser extent, the Pacific states. It champions basically the same causes as the NFU, including higher agricultural support prices.

Labor Interest Groups

LABOR MOVEMENT
Generally, the full range of economic and political expression of working-class interests; politically, the organization of working-class interests.

Interest groups representing the **labor movement** date back to at least 1886 with the formation of the American Federation of Labor (AFL). In 1955, the AFL joined forces with the Congress of Industrial Organizations (CIO). Today, the combined AFL-CIO is an enormous union with a membership exceeding 13 million workers. In a sense, the AFL-CIO is a union of unions.

The political arm of the AFL-CIO is the Committee on Political Education (COPE). COPE's activities are funded by voluntary contributions from union members. COPE has been active in state and national campaigns since 1956. In principle, it is used to educate workers and the general public on issues and candidates of interest to labor. Some critics of COPE allege that union members are pressured into making contributions to the organization. Other

---

3. The Agricultural Adjustment Act of 1933 (declared unconstitutional) was replaced by the 1937 Agricultural Adjustment Act and later changed and amended several times.

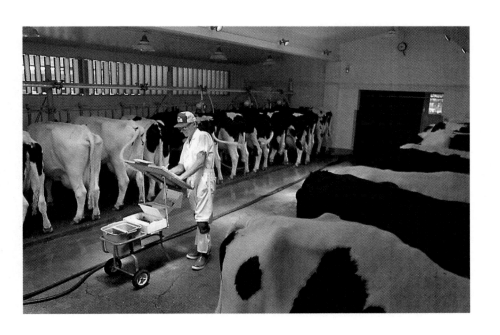

Dairy farmers are one of the best-organized agricultural interest groups. The distribution of milk with school lunches is but one of the ways that the government tries to support milk prices and protect the industry.

SERVICE SECTOR
The sector of the economy that provides services—such as food services, insurance, and education—in contrast to the sector of the economy that produces goods.

critics claim that its "education" is simply partisan political propaganda favorable to the Democratic party. The AFL-CIO, through COPE, has established policies on such issues as Social Security, housing, health insurance, and foreign trade.

Other unions are also active politically. One of the most widely known is the International Brotherhood of Teamsters, which was led by Jimmy Hoffa until his expulsion in 1967 because of alleged ties with organized crime. The Teamsters Union was established initially in 1903 and today has a membership of 1.4 million and an annual budget of $73 million.

Another independent union is the United Auto Workers, founded in 1935. It now has a membership of 840,000 and an annual budget of $230 million. Also very active in labor lobbying is the United Mine Workers union, representing about 200,000 members.

Labor group pressure on Congress has been only partly successful. Although unions successfully allied themselves with civil rights groups in the 1960s, they lost on such issues as the Taft-Hartley Act of 1948, which put some limits on the right to strike and the right to organize workers. They were also frustrated in their efforts in 1975 and 1977 to enact a bill designed to facilitate the picketing of construction sites. In 1994, Congress failed to adopt proposed legislation that would have made it more difficult for companies to hire replacements for striking workers.

The role of unions in American society has weakened in recent years, as witnessed by a decline in union membership from 34.7 percent of American workers in 1954 to 15.1 percent in 1995 (Figure 7–1). The strength of union membership traditionally lay with blue-collar workers. But in the age of automation and with the rise of the **service sector**, blue-collar workers in basic industries (autos, steel, and the like) represent a smaller and smaller percentage of the total working population. Because of this decline in the industrial sector of the economy, national unions are looking to nontraditional areas for their membership, including migrant farm workers, service

Union strikers line the streets outside the Caterpillar factory protesting the use of nonunion workers, or "scabs," to replace them on the assembly line.

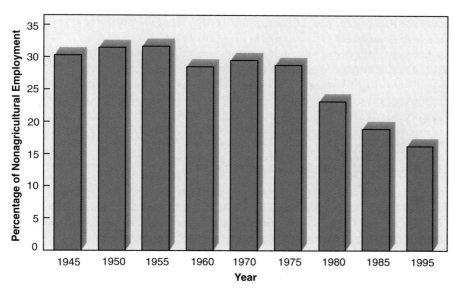

FIGURE 7–1 ■

Decline in Union Membership as a Percentage of Nonagricultural Employment from 1945 to 1995

SOURCE: Leo Troy and Neil Sheflin, *U.S. Union Sourcebook* (West Orange, N.J.: Industrial Relations Data and Information Services, 1985); and Bureau of Labor Statistics.

workers, and most recently, public employees—such as police officers; fire-fighting personnel; and teachers, including college professors.

Public Employee Interest Groups

The degree of unionization in the private sector has declined since 1965, but this has been offset by growth in the unionization of public employees. Table 7–2 shows the number of members in the three largest public employee unions, which grew more than 700 percent from 1960 to 1995. With a total work force of more than 6.6 million, these unions are likely to continue expanding.

Both the American Federation of State, County, and Municipal Employees and the American Federation of Teachers are members of the AFL-CIO's Public Employee Department. Originally, the public employee unions started out as social and professional organizations. Over the years, they have become quite militant and are often involved in strikes. Many of these

TABLE 7–2 ■

The Growth in Public Employee Unionism

UNION NAME	1960	1979	1995
American Federation of State, County, and Municipal Employees	185,000	889,000	1,285,000
American Federation of Government Employees	70,000	236,000	210,000
American Federation of Teachers	56,000	423,000	794,000
Total	311,000	1,548,000	2,289,000

SOURCE: Bureau of Labor Statistics, 1995.

strikes are illegal, because certain public employees do not have the right to strike and essentially sign a contract so stating.

A powerful interest group lobbying on behalf of public employees is the National Education Association (NEA), a nationwide organization of about 1.8 million administrators, teachers, and others connected with education. The NEA lobbies intensively for increased public funding of education. The NEA sponsors regional and national conventions each year and has an extensive program of electronic media broadcasts, surveys, and the like.

Interest Groups of Professionals

Numerous professional organizations exist, including the American Bar Association, the Association of General Contractors of America, the Institute of Electrical and Electronic Engineers, the Screen Actors Guild, and others. Some professional groups, such as those formed by lawyers and doctors, are more influential than others due to their social status. Lawyers have a unique advantage—a large number of members of Congress share their profession. In terms of money spent on lobbying, however, one professional organization stands out head and shoulders above the rest—the American Medical Association (AMA). Founded in 1947, it is now affiliated with more than 2,000 local and state medical societies, and has a total membership of 237,000 and an administrative staff of 1,000. Together with the American Dental Association, the AMA spent an estimated $3 million in 1994 congressional campaign contributions in its efforts to influence legislation.

The AMA's most notable, but largely unsuccessful, lobbying effort was against the enactment of Medicare, which provides health insurance coverage for the elderly. In the early 1960s, the AMA launched a national advertising campaign to convince the public that Medicare was tantamount to "socialized medicine" and that private plans would offer better protection. This indirect lobbying, combined with direct pressure on members of Congress, delayed passage of the legislation until 1965 and ensured that the bill's language would protect and enhance doctors' incomes. More recently, the AMA has lobbied against the fees for services established under Medicare and stringent medical-cost containment.

Environmental Groups

Environmental interest groups are not new. The Audubon Society was founded in 1905 to protect the snowy egret from the commercial demand for hat decorations. The patron of the Sierra Club, John Muir, worked for the creation of national parks more than ninety years ago. But the blossoming of national environmental groups with mass memberships is a relatively recent phenomenon. Since the first Earth Day, organized in 1972, many interest groups have sprung up to protect the environment in general or unique ecological niches. The groups range from the National Wildlife Federation, with a membership of more than 4.5 million and an emphasis on education, to the fairly elite Environmental Defense Fund, with a membership of 250,000 and a focus on influencing federal policy. Other groups include the Nature Conservancy, which seeks members' contributions so the organization can buy up threatened natural areas and either give them to state or local governments or manage them itself, and the more radical Greenpeace Society and Earth First.

The *Rainbow Warrior*, the flagship of Greenpeace, is both a symbol for the environmental interest group and a resource that can be used for actions at sea to protect the environment. The *Rainbow Warrior* has acted to save dolphins, to protest oil spills, and to stop Japanese and Russian whaling.

Greenpeace has become famous for its well-documented and widely disseminated efforts to stop Russian and Japanese whalers at sea, which put the lives of the group's members in jeopardy. At the most radical end of the spectrum is Earth First, an organization that has spiked redwood trees with large nails to stop lumbering. Although this practice makes the trees much less valuable to harvest, it has also caused serious injuries to loggers. The Sierra Club and the World Wildlife Fund have appealed to young upper-middle-class professionals who not only want to contribute to saving the environment but also to enjoy the groups' travel programs and merchandise offerings.

Public Interest Groups

Public interest is a difficult term to define because, as we noted earlier, there are many publics in our nation of more than 260 million. It is nearly impossible for one particular public policy to benefit everybody, which makes it practically impossible to define the public interest. Nonetheless, over the past few decades, a variety of law and lobbying organizations have been formed "in the public interest."

PUBLIC INTEREST
The best interests of the collective, overall community; the national good, rather than the narrow interests of a self-serving group.

Nader Organizations. The most well known and perhaps the most effective public interest groups are those organized under the leadership of consumer activist Ralph Nader. The story of Ralph Nader's rise to the top began after the publication, in 1965, of his book *Unsafe at Any Speed,* a lambasting critique of the purported attempt by General Motors (GM) to keep from the public detrimental information about GM's rear-engine Corvair. Partly as a result of Nader's book, Congress began to consider testimony in favor of an automobile safety bill. GM made a clumsy attempt to discredit Nader's background. Nader sued, the media exploited the story, and when GM settled out of court for several hundred thousand dollars, Nader became the recognized champion of consumer interests. Since then, Nader has turned over much of his income to the various public interest

Ralph Nader began the movement to create public interest groups through the publication, in 1965, of his book *Unsafe at Any Speed,* which criticized General Motors for underplaying the dangers of its Corvair automobile. Since that time, he has founded a number of not-for-profit public interest groups that track business and governmental actions in specific policy arenas.

groups he has formed or sponsored. Now, there are numerous national "Naderite" organizations promoting consumer interests.

Other Public Interest Groups.   Partly in response to the Nader organizations, numerous conservative public interest law firms have sprung up that are often pitted against the consumer groups in court. Some of these are the Mountain States Legal Defense Foundation, the Pacific Legal Foundation, the National Right-to-Work Legal Defense Foundation, the Washington Legal Foundation, and the Mid-Atlantic Legal Foundation.

One of the largest public interest pressure groups is Common Cause, founded in 1968, whose goal is to reorder national priorities toward "the public" and to make governmental institutions more responsive to the needs of the public. Anyone willing to pay dues of $15 a year can become a member. Members are polled regularly to obtain information about local and national issues requiring reassessment. Some of the activities of Common Cause have been (1) helping to ensure the passage of the Twenty-sixth Amendment (giving eighteen-year-olds the right to vote), (2) achieving greater voter registration in all states, (3) supporting the complete withdrawal of all U.S. forces from South Vietnam in the 1970s, and (4) promoting legislation that would limit campaign spending.

Other public interest pressure groups are active on a wide range of issues. The goal of the League of Women Voters, founded in 1920, is to educate the public on political matters. Although generally nonpartisan, it has lobbied for the Equal Rights Amendment and for government reform. The Consumer Federation of America is an alliance of about two hundred local and national organizations interested in consumer protection. The American Civil Liberties Union dates back to World War I, when, under a different name, it defended draft resisters. It generally enters into legal disputes related to Bill of Rights issues.

Single-Issue Groups

In recent years, a number of interest groups have formed that are focused on one issue. The abortion debate has created various antiabortion groups (such as Right to Life) and pro-choice groups (such as the National Abortion Rights Action League). Other single-issue groups are the National Rifle Association, the Right to Work Committee (an anti-union group), and the Hudson Valley PAC (a pro-Israel group).

Narrowly focused groups such as these may be able to call more attention to their respective causes because they have simple and straightforward goals and because their members tend to care intensely about the issues. Thus, they can easily motivate their members to contact legislators or to organize demonstrations in support of their policy goals. (See this chapter's *Politics: The Human Side* for information on another single-issue interest group.)

Foreign Governments

Home-grown interests are not the only players in the game. Washington, D.C., is also the center for lobbying by foreign governments as well as private foreign interests. Large research and lobbying staffs are maintained by governments of the largest U.S. trading partners, such as Japan, South Korea,

Tanya Metaksa, Executive Director of the National Rifle Association (NRA) Institute for Legislative Action, salutes the members at their national convention. After the bombing of the Federal Building in Oklahoma City, the NRA was embarrassed by a recruitment piece mailed to millions that referred to government agents as "jackbooted thugs." Former president George Bush resigned his membership in the organization as a protest against the mailing.

Canada, and the European Union (EU) countries (see this chapter's *Politics and Economics*). Even smaller nations, such as those in the Caribbean, engage lobbyists when vital legislation affecting their trade interests is considered. Frequently, these foreign interests hire former representatives or former senators to promote their positions on Capitol Hill.

INTEREST GROUP STRATEGIES

Interest groups employ a wide range of techniques and strategies to promote their policy goals. Although few groups are successful at persuading Congress and the president to endorse their programs completely, many are able to prevent legislation injurious to their members from being considered or at least to weaken such legislation. The key to success for interest groups is the ability to have access to government officials. To achieve this, interest groups and their representatives try to cultivate long-term relationships with legislators and government officials. The best of such relationships are based on mutual respect and cooperation. The interest group provides the official with excellent sources of information and assistance, and the official in turn gives the group opportunities to express its views.

The techniques used by interest groups may be divided into those that are direct and indirect. **Direct techniques** include all those ways in which the interest group and its lobbyists approach the officials personally to press their case. **Indirect techniques**, in contrast, include strategies that use the general public or individuals to influence the government for the interest group.

Direct Techniques

Lobbying, publicizing ratings of legislative behavior, and providing campaign assistance are the three main direct techniques used by interest groups.

DIRECT TECHNIQUE
An interest group activity that involves interaction with government officials to further the group's goals.

INDIRECT TECHNIQUE
A strategy employed by interest groups that uses third parties to influence government officials.

POLITICS: THE HUMAN SIDE
Marian Wright Edelman, Founder, Children's Defense Fund

"We must place our kids first in both our private actions and our public actions."

BIOGRAPHICAL NOTES

Marian Wright Edelman was born in 1939 in Bennettsville, South Carolina, the youngest of five children. Her father, Arthur Wright, was a Baptist minister who worked to improve the lives of African Americans in his small southern town. He stressed the need to persevere in achieving one's goals and especially, to get an education. Marian, who was named after the opera diva Marian Anderson, attended Spelman College in Atlanta and Yale Law School. She became the first female African American to be admitted to the bar in the state of Mississippi. During the civil rights movement, Marian Wright applied her legal talents to defend civil rights workers and to investigate poverty in the South for Senator Robert Kennedy. Later, she married Peter Edelman, a Kennedy assistant, whom she first met in Mississippi.

Edelman is the founder and leader of the Children's Defense Fund, a Washington-based research and lobbying organization that works for the interests of American children, particularly those from poor families. Known as a children's crusader, Edelman has spent twenty years directing research on the status of children in the United States, formulating policy proposals for government, and lobbying for the passage of legislation.

POLITICAL CONTRIBUTIONS

Edelman began her research and lobbying career with the Washington Research Project in 1968 and founded the Children's Defense Fund in 1973. Since that time, she has been tireless in her efforts to call attention to the extent of hunger, poverty, and illness among the nation's children. She has lobbied for better child care, for increased Head Start funds, and for education to prevent teenage pregnancy.

Voicing her philosophy, Edelman says that "parenting . . . nurturing the next generation is the most important function of this society. . . . We must place our kids first in both our private actions and our public actions. . . . We talk about family values but when we look at our policies, we don't do it."*

One way that the government can support the family is through access to good child care for all American families. A major proponent of the Act for Better Child Care, Edelman worked hard to push Democrats and Republicans, the National Education Association, and church groups to agree on a compromise measure that would both increase the number of child-care facilities and help low- and moderate-income families to pay for child care. The coalition did not hold, and a less comprehensive bill passed in 1990.

In spite of this setback, Edelman sees a bright future for child-care legislation because of the growing number of working women of all economic classes. She plans to continue her efforts to put the welfare of children first on the public agenda.

*Glen Elasser, "Lessons For Life," *Chicago Tribune*, May 10, 1992, Section 6, p. 3.

LOBBYING
The attempt by organizations or by individuals to influence the passage, defeat, or contents of legislation and the administrative decisions of government. The derivation of the term may be traced back to over a century ago, when certain private citizens regularly congregated in the lobby outside the legislative chambers before a session to petition legislators.

Lobbying Techniques.   As might be guessed, the term **lobbying** comes from the activities of private citizens regularly congregating in the lobbies of legislative chambers before a session to petition legislators. In the latter part of the nineteenth century, railroad and industrial groups openly bribed state legislators to pass legislation beneficial to their interests, giving lobbying a well-deserved bad name. Today, standard lobbying techniques still include buttonholing (detaining and engaging in conversation) senators and representatives in state capitols and in Washington, D.C., while they are moving from their offices to the voting chambers. Lobbyists, however, do more than that.

POLITICS AND ECONOMICS
American and Foreign Interests: A New Alliance

Foreign nations and corporations have employed lobbyists in the United States for many years, usually working for trade preferences and other economic benefits. Some former members of Congress have become lobbyists for these nations, working for Middle Eastern or Asian states. In recent years, the amount of money spent by foreign nations and corporations has continued to grow. The accompanying figure shows that Japan spends far more than any other nation in this effort, with Canada ranking second and Germany third.

With the increase in international trade and the growth of multinational corporations, lobbyists for U.S. corporations are now likely to be working in alliances with those representing foreign nations. Boeing Corporation, the manufacturer of aircraft, frequently works with representatives of the People's Republic of China for improvement of that nation's trade status, because China is such a strong customer for its products. Canadian timber interests found an ally in the U.S. home-building industry, and IBM often works with its Japanese business

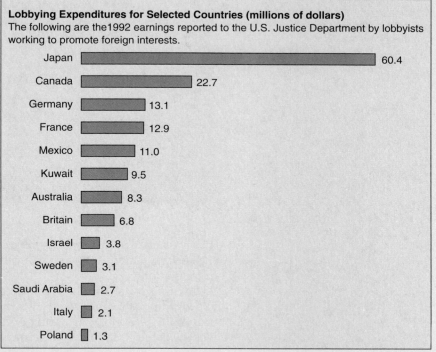

Lobbying Expenditures for Selected Countries (millions of dollars)
The following are the 1992 earnings reported to the U.S. Justice Department by lobbyists working to promote foreign interests.

Japan	60.4
Canada	22.7
Germany	13.1
France	12.9
Mexico	11.0
Kuwait	9.5
Australia	8.3
Britain	6.8
Israel	3.8
Sweden	3.1
Saudi Arabia	2.7
Italy	2.1
Poland	1.3

SOURCE: U.S. Justice Department.

partners. Sometimes a U.S. firm will take a position against another U.S. firm in trade negotiations or in lobbying for legislation that will help

it. The question arises as to whether U.S. firms might have a negative effect on the U.S. economy with these political partners.

Lobbyists engage in an array of activities to influence legislation. These include, at a minimum, the following:

1. Engaging in private meetings with public officials to make known the interests of the lobbyist's clients. Although acting on behalf of a client, often lobbyists furnish needed information to senators and representatives (and government agency appointees) that they could not hope to obtain on their own. It is to the lobbyist's advantage to provide accurate information so that the policymaker will rely on this source in the future.
2. Testifying before congressional committees for or against proposed legislation.
3. Testifying before executive rule-making agencies—such as the Federal Trade Commission or the Consumer Product Safety Commission—for or against proposed rules.

The job of a lobbyist never stops. This Washington lobbyist is trying to convince a member of a congressperson's staff to get the congressperson to vote a particular way. While many critics of lobbyists and interest groups argue that they distort the actions of our government, the First Amendment prohibits the government from regulating their speech.

4. Assisting legislators or bureaucrats in drafting legislation or prospective regulations. Often, lobbyists can furnish legal advice on the specific details of legislation.

5. Inviting legislators to social occasions such as cocktail parties, boating expeditions, and other events. Most lobbyists feel that contacting legislators in a more relaxed social setting is effective. The extent to which legislators feel obligated to lobbyists for entertaining them is hard to gauge.

6. Providing political information to legislators and other government officials. Often the lobbyists will have better information than the party leadership about how other legislators are going to vote. In this case, the political information they furnish may be a key to legislative success.

The Ratings Game.   Many interest groups attempt to influence the overall behavior of legislators through their rating systems. Each year, the interest group selects those votes on legislation that it feels are most important to the organization's goals. Each legislator is given a score based on the percentage of times that he or she voted in favor of the group's position. The usual scheme ranges from 0 to 100 percent. If a legislator has a score of, for example, 95 percent on the Americans for Democratic Action (ADA) rating, it means that he or she supported that group's position to a high degree (see Table 7–3). A legislator with such a high ADA score is usually considered to be very liberal. The groups that use rating systems range from the American Conservative Union to the League of Conservation Voters (an environmental group). Each year, the league identifies the twelve legislators having what it sees as the worst records on environmental issues and advertises them as the "Dirty Dozen." In 1992, Vice President Dan Quayle was given a "lifetime achievement" award by the League of Conservation Voters for his three years of opposing environmental regulations.[4]

---

4. Bureau of National Affairs, *Daily Report for Executives*, September 16, 1992.

Campaign Assistance.

Interest groups have additional strategies to use in their attempts to influence government policies. Groups recognize that the greatest concern of legislators is to be reelected, so they focus on their campaign needs. Associations with large memberships, such as labor unions or the National Education Association, are able to provide workers for political campaigns, including precinct workers to get out the vote, volunteers to put up posters and pass out literature, and people to staff telephone banks for campaign headquarters.

In many states where membership in certain interest groups is large, candidates vie for the groups' endorsements in the campaign. Gaining those endorsements may be automatic, or it may require that the candidates participate in a debate or interview with the interest groups. Endorsements are important because an interest group usually publicizes its choices in its membership publication and because the candidate can use the endorsement in his or her campaign literature. Traditionally, labor unions such as the AFL-CIO and the United Auto Workers have endorsed Democratic party candidates. Republican candidates, however, often try to persuade union locals at least to refrain from any endorsement. Making no endorsement can then be perceived as disapproval of the Democratic party candidate.

PACs and Political Campaigns.

In the last two decades, the most important form of campaign help from interest groups has become the political contribution from a group's **political action committee (PAC)**. The 1974 Federal Election Campaign Act and its 1976 amendments allow corporations, labor unions, and special interest groups to set up PACs to raise money for candidates. For a PAC to be legitimate, the money must be raised from at least fifty volunteer donors and must be given to at least five candidates in the federal election. As pointed out in this chapter's opening *What If . . .* feature, PACs can contribute up to $5,000 to each candidate in each election. Each corporation or each union is limited to one PAC. As you might imagine, corporate PACs obtain funds from executives in their firms, and unions obtain PAC funds from their members.

The number of PACs has grown astronomically, as has the amount they spend on elections. There were about 1,000 political action committees in 1976; by 1994 there were more than 4,600 (see Figure 7–2). Corporate PACs are increasing in number at a rate greater than other varieties. The total amount of spending by PACs grew from $19 million in 1973 to an estimated $400 million in 1991–1992. Of all of the campaign money spent by House candidates in 1994, about 32 percent came from PACs.[5]

Interest groups funnel PAC money to candidates who they think can do the most good for them. Frequently, they make the maximum contribution of $5,000 per election to candidates who face little or no opposition. The summary of PAC contributions given in Figure 7–3 shows that the great bulk of campaign contributions goes to incumbent candidates rather than to challengers. Table 7–4 shows the amounts contributed by the top twenty PACs in 1992. It is clear that some PACs balance their contributions between Democratic and Republican candidates. Corporations are particularly likely to give money to Democrats in Congress as well as to Republicans, because

---

TABLE 7–3

ADA Ratings for 1995

Americans for Democratic Action, a liberal political organization, tracks the votes of all senators and representatives on the set of issues that ADA thinks is most important. The "score" for each legislator is the percentage of "correct" votes from the ADA's point of view. Many other interest groups also engage in the ratings game.

SENATOR	HIGHEST RATING
Feingold, D., Wisconsin	100%
Harkin, D., Iowa	100
Moynihan, D., New York	100
Wellstone, D., Minnesota	100
Kerry, D., Massachusetts	95
Lauterberg, D., New Jersey	95
Leahy, D., Vermont	95
Pell, D., Rhode Island	95
Rockefeller, D., West Virginia	95
Sarbanes, D., Maryland	95
Simon, D., Illinois	95

	LOWEST RATING
Burns, R., Montana	0%
Craig, R., Idaho	0
Dole, R., Kansas	0
Helms, R., North Carolina	0
Kempthorne, R., Idaho	0
Pressler, R., South Dakota	0
Coats, R., Indiana	5
Coverdell, R., Georgia	5
Faircloth, R., North Carolina	5
Lott, R., Mississippi	5
McConnell, R., Kentucky	5
Nichols, R., Oklahoma	5
Smith, R., New Hampshire	5

SOURCE: *Americans for Democratic Action*, 1995.

POLITICAL ACTION COMMITTEE (PAC)

A committee set up by and representing a corporation, labor union, or special interest group. PACs raise and give campaign donations on behalf of the organizations or groups they represent.

---

5. Norman Ornstein, Thomas E. Mann, and Michael J. Malbin, *Vital Statistics on Congress, 1993–1994* (Washington, D.C.: Congressional Quarterly Press, 1994), p. 95.

FIGURE 7–2   ■

The Increase in PACs, 1974 to 1994

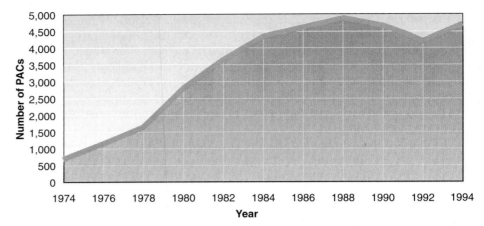

SOURCE: Larry Makinson, *Open Secrets: The Cash Constituents of Congress* (Washington, D.C.: Congressional Quarterly Press, 1994).

many Democratic incumbents chair important committees or subcommittees. Why, might you ask, would business leaders give to Democrats who may be more liberal than themselves? Interest groups see PAC contributions as a way to ensure access to powerful legislators, even if they may disagree with them some of the time. PAC contributions are, in a way, an investment in a relationship.

The campaign finance regulations clearly limit the amount that a PAC can give to any one candidate, but there is no limit on the amount that a PAC can spend on an independent campaign, either on behalf of a candidate or party or in opposition to one. During the 1970s and early 1980s, one of the

FIGURE 7–3   ■

PAC Contributions to Congressional Candidates, 1974–1994

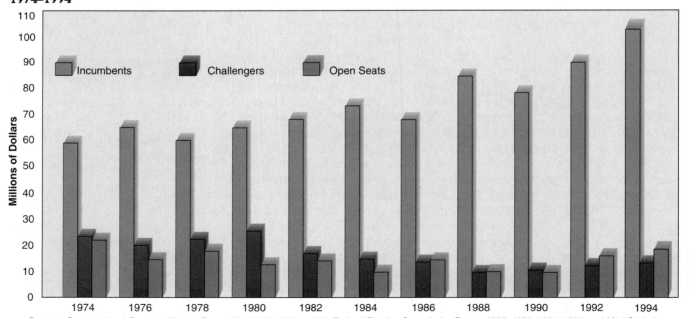

SOURCE: *Congressional Quarterly Weekly Report,* March 22, 1986, p. 657; *Federal Election Commission Report,* 1987, 1989, 1991, 1995; and *Vital Statistics on Congress, 1993–1994.*

TABLE 7–4

The Top Twenty PAC Contributors

RANK	CONTRIBUTOR	TOTAL	PAC %	DEM %	REP %	PRINCIPAL CATEGORY
1	National Association of Realtors	$3,094,228	100%	55%	44%	Real estate
2	American Medical Association	$2,647,981	100	49	51	Doctors
3	Teamsters Union	$2,438,184	99+	92	8	Teamsters
4	National Education Association	$2,334,715	99+	93	7	Teachers unions
5	United Auto Workers	$1,801,772	99+	99	1	Manufacturing unions
6	Letter Carriers Union	$1,755,478	99+	86	14	Postal unions
7	American Federation of State/County/Municipal Employees	$1,549,720	99+	98	2	Local government unions
8	National Association of Retired Federal Employees	$1,545,122	100	76	24	Federal worker unions
9	Association of Trial Lawyers of America	$1,539,550	100	87	13	Lawyers
10	Carpenters Union	$1,526,534	99+	96	4	Contruction unions
11	National Association of Life Underwriters	$1,487,800	100	51	49	Life insurance
12	Machinists/Aerospace Workers Union	$1,487,495	99+	98	1	Manufacturing unions
13	AT&T	$1,477,200	98	57	43	Long distance
14	American Bankers Association	$1,473,061	100	55	45	Commercial banks
15	National Association of Home Builders	$1,362,550	99+	48	52	Residential construction
16	Laborers Union	$1,359,119	99+	92	8	Construction unions
17	National Auto Dealers Association	$1,313,900	100	38	62	Auto dealers
18	International Brotherhood of Electrical Workers	$1,257,920	99+	97	2	Communication unions
19	Air Line Pilots Association	$1,167,797	100	81	19	Air transport unions
20	American Institute of CPAs	$1,089,294	99+	56	44	Accountants

SOURCE: Adapted from Larry Makinson, *Open Secrets: The Cash Constituents of Congress* (Washington, D.C.: Congressional Quarterly Press, 1992).

most prominent PACs in the United States was the National Conservative Political Action Committee, or NCPAC. This interest group espoused a conservative philosophy, opposing abortion, supporting prayer in school, and supporting a strong defense policy. NCPAC targeted specific senators and representatives for defeat, spending large sums of money against them in primary and general elections.

Indirect Techniques

Interest groups can try to influence government policy by working through third parties—which may be constituents, the general public, or other groups. Indirect techniques mask the interest group's own activities and make the effort appear to be spontaneous. Furthermore, legislators and government officials are often more impressed by contacts from constituents than from an interest group's lobbyist.

Generating Public Pressure. In some instances, interest groups try to produce a "groundswell" of public pressure to influence the government. Such efforts may include advertisements in national magazines and newspapers, mass mailings, television publicity, and demonstrations. Computers and satellite links make communication efforts even more effective (see this chapter's *Politics and Technology*). Interest groups may commission polls to find out what the public's sentiments are and then publicize the results. The intent of this activity is to convince policymakers that public opinion overwhelmingly supports the group's position.

Some corporations and interest groups also engage in a practice that might be called **climate control.** This strategy calls for public relations efforts that

CLIMATE CONTROL
The use of public relations techniques to create favorable public opinion toward an interest group, industry, or corporation.

That in the 1994 congressional elections, political action committees gave over 71 percent of their campaign funds to incumbents?

ACT UP, a group dedicated to increasing awareness of the AIDS epidemic, stages a protest in Albany, New York. ACT UP members try to focus the public's attention on the need to increase funding for research into the causes of and cures for the disease.

are aimed at improving the public image of the industry or group and not necessarily related to any specific political issue. Contributions by corporations and groups in support of public television programs, sponsorship of special events, and commercials extolling the virtues of corporate research are examples of climate control. By building a reservoir of favorable public opinion, groups believe it less likely that their legislative goals will be met with opposition by the public.

Using Constituents as Lobbyists.   One of the most effective interest group activities is the use of constituents to lobby for the group's goals. In the "shotgun" approach, the interest group tries to mobilize large numbers of constituents to write or phone their legislators or the president. Often, the group provides postcards or form letters for constituents to fill out and mail. These efforts are only effective on Capitol Hill when there is an extraordinary number of responses, because legislators know that the voters did not initiate the communication on their own.

A more influential variation of this technique uses only important constituents. Known as the "rifle" technique, or the "Utah plant manager's theory," the interest group contacts an influential constituent, such as the manager of a local plant in Utah, to contact the senator from Utah.[6] Because the constituent is seen as being responsible for many jobs or other resources,

6. Kay Lehman Schlozman and John T. Tierney, *Organized Interests and American Democracy* (New York: Harper & Row, 1986), p. 293.

POLITICS AND TECHNOLOGY
High-Tech Lobbying

Interest group activity has exploded in recent years. One particularly important aspect of lobbying in this new era is the use of modern technology to enhance the role of pressure groups.

Lobbying organizations have for many years employed "grass-roots" tactics for influencing the outcomes of government decisions. These tactics have included soliciting citizens to send letters to members of Congress, mobilizing protest movements, and endorsing or attacking candidates during election campaigns.

What is new, exciting, and potentially crucial is the availability of computer-based technology and expanded telecommunications facilities for communicating more effectively and more quickly with targeted segments of the population. Elected representatives may in fact not know which interest group was involved in a "write-your-congressperson" campaign. Groups also generate massive telephone call-in efforts with instructions to members to emphasize a slightly different aspect of an issue that most concerns them. The goal of such campaigns, made possible by computer-controlled mass mailings to targeted citizens, is to produce at least the appearance that the interest group has a massive, unified, intense, and growing block of supporters.

Not only computers, but also advanced television technology, has allowed pressure groups to increase their role in American politics. Such use is particularly striking in the case of the New Right groups on the conservative side of the political spectrum. Conservative activist Paul Weyrich has created National Empowerment Television (NET). NET is a satellite network that allows local groups to see public officials debate the issues and to ask questions through an interactive connection. NET broadcasts three shows per month. Weyrich believes that the impact on elected officials of his viewing groups and concerns is much stronger than the usual letters and telegrams. In fact, Weyrich claims that his program on Clarence Thomas's nomination to the Supreme Court forced two Democratic senators to vote for Thomas's confirmation.

Business pressure groups have adopted the tactics that have been so successful for the New Right. Apart from the more traditional efforts of soliciting letters, telegrams, and phone calls to elected officials, the National Chamber of Commerce has a major high-technology communications system available to send its interpretations of pending legislation and other matters to members; a monthly magazine (Nation's Business) with a circulation of 1.25 million; a weekly newsletter (Washington Report) that is sent to nearly a million members and friends of the group; a weekly television program ("It's Your Business") that is carried on more than one hundred stations; a radio show ("What's the Issue?") that discusses major national topics on more than four hundred stations; and Biznet, a closed-circuit, tax-exempt television network, which in theory would allow the Chamber of Commerce to mobilize its members and supporters in only a matter of hours. Future developments in high-tech lobbying will be limited only by the speed with which new technological innovations can be put in place.

the legislator is more likely to listen carefully to the constituent's concerns about legislation than to a paid lobbyist.

Building Alliances. Another indirect technique used by interest groups is to form an alliance with other groups concerned about the same legislation. Often, these groups will set up a paper organization with an innocuous name, such as the Citizens Trade Committee, to represent their joint concerns. In this case, the alliance, comprising environmental, labor, and consumer groups, opposed the passage of NAFTA. Members of such an alliance share expenses and multiply the influence of their individual groups by combining their efforts.[7] Other advantages of such an alliance are that it looks as if larger public interests are at stake, and it blurs the specific interests

7. *San Diego Union-Tribune*, December 4, 1993, p. C1.

of the individual groups involved. These alliances also are efficient devices for keeping like-minded groups from duplicating one another's lobbying efforts.

REGULATING LOBBYISTS

Congress made its first attempt to control lobbyists and lobbying activities through Title III of the Legislative Reorganization Act of 1946, otherwise known as the Federal Regulation of Lobbying Act. The act actually provided for public disclosure more than for regulation, and it neglected to specify which agency would enforce its provisions. Its specific provisions are as follows:

1. Any person or organization that receives money to be used principally to influence legislation before Congress must register.

2. Any individual lobbyist or a representative of a group who is registering must, under oath, give his or her name, address, place of employment, salary, amount and purpose of expenses, and duration of employment.

3. Every registered lobbyist must give quarterly reports on his or her activities; these reports are published in the *Congressional Record*.

4. Anyone failing to satisfy the specific provisions of the act can be fined up to $10,000 and receive a five-year prison term.

Drawing by Steiner © 1994 The New Yorker Magazine, Inc.

"A very special interest to see you, Senator."

In a famous case relating to the constitutionality of the 1946 lobbying act, the Supreme Court emphasized that the intention of the act was simply to enable Congress to discover "who is being hired, who is putting up the money, and how much."[8] The Court stated that the lobbying law does not violate due process, freedom of speech or press, or freedom to petition. But the Court narrowly construed the application of the act, holding that it applied only to those lobbyists who *directly* seek to influence federal legislation. Any lobbyist indirectly seeking to influence legislation simply through public opinion does not fall within the scope of the activities regulated by the act.

Currently, about seven thousand lobbyists are registered under the act (see Table 7–5). The act has probably had no effect on the amount of money spent on lobbying and the types of activities engaged in by lobbyists. No enforcement agency has been created by Congress, and the public is almost totally ignorant of the information disclosed in the quarterly reports. The problem facing Congress, of course, is that any stricter regulation of lobbying will run into constitutional problems because of the potential abridgement of First Amendment rights. Also, so long as the Supreme Court does not view indirect lobbying as falling under the purview of the act, lobbying will be difficult to control.

After the Watergate scandal in 1972, Congress attempted to pass a new bill that would make strict registration and reporting provisions concerning campaign contributions a requirement. By 1978, Congress had succeeded in passing legislation that addressed the problem of ethics in government. (See this chapter's *Politics and Ethics* for an account of a prosecution under the 1978 Ethics in Government Act.) Regulation of lobbyists, however, has been difficult for Congress to accomplish.

WHY INTEREST GROUPS HAVE SO MUCH POWER

It has been claimed that we are a nation of special interests. Organized interest groups have obtained special benefits for their members and blocked legislation that clearly seems to be supported by most citizens. The power of interest groups in the American political system probably results from a number of factors, some of which are inherent in the groups themselves and some of which are derived from the structure of our government.

---

8. *United States v. Harriss,* 347 U.S. 612 (1954).

TABLE 7–5
What Proportion of Lobbyists Are Registered?

Total number of registered lobbyists		6,880
Registered as congressional lobbyists	5,935	
Registered as foreign agents	785	
Registered as executive branch agents	160	
Estimated total number of persons lobbying in Washington		80,000

ANSWER: Fewer than 10% are registered.

SOURCE: *Wall Street Journal,* May 30, 1991, p. A16, updated by authors.

POLITICS AND ETHICS
Lobbying by Former Government Officials

In 1978, Congress passed the Ethics in Government Act as a reaction to the Watergate scandal during the Nixon administration. The main purpose of the act was to provide for independent investigations of present or former high-ranking government officials, unless the charges filed against an official are judged by the attorney general to be without merit. The act prohibits former senior government employees from lobbying their former agency on any matter for a year after leaving, from lobbying any department for two years on an issue in which they had a direct responsibility, and from lobbying for the rest of their lives on issues in which they participated "personally and substantially."

On May 29, 1986, Whitney North Seymour was appointed by a three-judge federal court to serve as a special prosecutor to investigate conflict-of-interest charges against former deputy White House chief of staff Michael K. Deaver. Deaver left the White House staff in May 1985 to become a highly paid lobbyist for foreign governments and business corporations. Deaver discussed with Robert McFarlane, the president's national security adviser at the time, some objections his client, the Commonwealth of Puerto Rico, had to a proposed revision in tax laws. This occurred about two or three months after Deaver left office, in violation of the one-year prohibition on direct lobbying of his former White House colleagues.

In addition to these incidents, Deaver's work on behalf of the Daewoo Corporation, a large steel company in South Korea, the U.S. defense contractor Rockwell International Corporation, and Canada was also examined. For his efforts, Deaver was paid well by his clients: $105,000 by Canada, $250,000 by Rockwell International, $250,000 by Daewoo, and an undisclosed amount by Puerto Rico.

After a seven-week trial in late 1987, Deaver was found guilty and became the first person convicted under the Ethics in Government Act. In January 1988, a federal appeals court voted to strike down the provision of the law that authorizes judges to appoint special prosecutors to investigate high-level executive-branch crimes. But on June 29, 1988, the U.S. Supreme Court upheld the validity of the special-prosecutor provisions.

Many other White House employees and members of Congress have become lobbyists. Former representative Willis D. Gradison retired from Congress in 1993 to become head of the Health Insurance Association of America, the major interest group for insurers. After a one-year hiatus, Gradison returned to Congress to lobby against the Clinton health-care proposal.

Not all interest groups have an equal influence on government. Each has a different combination of resources to use in the policymaking process. Some groups are composed of members who have high social status and enormous economic resources, such as the National Association of Manufacturers. Other groups, such as labor unions, derive influence from their large memberships. Still other groups, such as environmentalists, have causes that can claim strong public support even from those people who have no direct stake in the issue. Groups such as the National Rifle Association are well organized and have highly motivated members. This enables them to channel a stream of mail toward Congress with a few days' effort.

Even the most powerful interest groups do not always succeed in their demands. Whereas the National Chamber of Commerce may be accepted as having a justified interest in the question of business taxes, many legislators might feel that the group should not engage in the debate over the size of the federal budget deficit. In other words, groups are seen as having a legitimate concern in the issues closest to their interests but not necessarily in broader issues. This may explain why some of the most successful groups are those that focus on very specific issues—such as tobacco farming, the funding of abortions, or handgun control—and do not get involved in larger conflicts.

As pluralist theories suggest, the structure of American government also invites the participation of interest groups. The governmental system has many points of access or places in the decision-making process where interest groups may focus an attack. If a bill opposed by a group passes the Senate, the lobbying efforts shift to the House of Representatives or to the president to seek a veto. If, in spite of all efforts, the legislation passes, the group may even lobby the executive agency or bureau that is supposed to implement the law and hope to influence the way in which the legislation is applied. In some cases, interest groups carry their efforts into the court system, either by filing lawsuits or by filing briefs as "friends of the court." The constitutional features of separation of powers and checks and balances encourage interest groups in their efforts.

INTEREST GROUPS: UNFINISHED WORK

The role of interest groups in American politics has been in question since the writing of the Constitution. James Madison, among many others, worried about how to control the "mischiefs of faction" while recognizing that the very business of a democracy is to resolve the conflicts between interests. Today, the power of interest groups is probably greater than ever before: PACs sponsored by interest groups are able to raise and spend huge amounts of money to support candidates and parties; politicians admit that such support buys access, if not influence; groups use modern technology to rally their members; and Congress seems unable to get beyond the adjudication of interests to write policy for the good of all.

In the future, Americans will consider whether to limit the role that interest groups can play in campaigns and elections either by reducing the financial support these groups can give or by eliminating that influence altogether through some public financing scheme. Then, all taxpayers would support campaigns rather than special groups. It is unlikely that there will be any attempt to limit severely the contact that groups have with political decision makers, because their right to access is protected by the First Amendment to the Constitution. Lobbyists could, however, be required to report every contact publicly; interest groups could be required to make public the amount that they spend on their attempts to influence government; or the use of the media by specialized groups for their own interest could be regulated.

The existence of interest groups, nonetheless, has great advantages for a democracy. By participating in such groups, individual citizens are empowered to influence government in ways far beyond the ballot. Groups do increase the interest and participation of voters in the system. And, without a doubt, these groups can protect the rights of minorities through their access to all branches of the government. Thus, the future could see a continued expansion of interest groups, particularly among segments of society that have been left out of the debate. The political system might be reformed to encourage such participation, making the struggle among groups more inclusive rather than less. In any case, given the structure of the government with its pluralist enticements for group struggle, it is unlikely that these political associations will disappear soon.

GETTING INVOLVED
The Gun Control Issue

Is the easy availability of handguns a major cause of crime? Do people have a right to possess firearms to defend home and hearth? These questions are part of a long-term and heated battle between organized pro-firearm and anti-firearm camps. The disagreements run deeply and reflect strong sentiments on both sides. The fight is fueled by the one million gun incidents occurring in the United States each year—the murders, suicides, assaults, accidents, robberies, and injuries in which guns are involved. Proponents of gun control seek new restrictions on gun purchases—if not a ban on them entirely—while decreasing existing arsenals of privately owned weapons. Proponents of firearms are fighting back. They claim that firearms are a cherished tradition, a constitutional right, and a vital defense need for individuals. They contend that the problem lies not in the sale and ownership of the weapons themselves but in the criminal use of firearms.

The National Coalition to Ban Handguns favors a total ban, taking the position that handguns "serve no valid purpose, except to kill people." The National Rifle Association of America (NRA) opposes

James and Sarah Brady led the movement for handgun control after James Brady was seriously wounded in the assassination attempt on President Ronald Reagan in 1981.

a ban. The NRA claims, among other things, that a gun law won't reduce the number of crimes. It is illogical to assume, according to the NRA, that persons who refuse to obey laws prohibiting rape, murder, and other crimes will obey a gun law.

The debate is intense and bitter. Gun control proponents accuse their adversaries of being "frightened little men living in the pseudomacho myth." Gun control opponents brand the other side as "new totalitarians" intent on curbing individual freedom. The NRA, founded in 1871, is currently one of the most powerful single-issue groups on the American political scene, representing the 70 million gun owners in the United States.

In 1993, Congress passed a law instituting a five-day waiting period for all handgun purchases. Most observers saw this as a defeat for the NRA. That group, however, asserted that the law would have no effect on crime. If you agree with the NRA's position and want to get involved in its efforts in opposition to further gun control legislation, contact the NRA at the following address:

The National Rifle Association
1600 Rhode Island Ave. N.W.
Washington, DC 20036
202-828-6000

If, however, you are concerned with the increase in gun-related crimes and feel that stricter gun laws are necessary, you can get involved through these organizations:

Committee for the Study of Handgun Misuse
109 N. Dearborn St., Suite 704
Chicago, IL 60602
312-614-5593

The National Coalition to Ban Handguns
100 Maryland Ave. N.E.
Washington, DC 20002
202-544-7190

Handgun Control, Inc.
810 18th St. N.W., Suite 705
Washington, DC 20006
202-638-4723

KEY TERMS

climate control 241	lobbying 236	purposive incentive 225
direct technique 235	material incentive 225	service sector 230
indirect technique 235	political action committee	social movement 226
interest group 223	(PAC) 239	solidary incentive 225
labor movement 229	public interest 233	

 CHAPTER SUMMARY

1. An interest group is an organized group of individuals who share common objectives and who actively attempt to influence government policy. Interest groups proliferate in the United States because they can influence government at many points in the political structure and because they offer solidary, material, and purposive incentives to their members. Interest groups are often created out of social movements.

2. Major types of interest groups include business, agricultural, labor, public employee, professional, and environmental groups. Other important groups may be considered public interest groups. In addition, single-issue interest groups and foreign governments lobby the government.

3. Interest groups use direct and indirect techniques to influence government. Direct techniques include testifying before committees and rule-making agencies, providing information to legislators, rating legislators' voting records, and making campaign contributions. Contributions are often made through political action committees, or PACs. Most PAC money is given to incumbents to ensure access for the group. Indirect techniques to influence government include campaigns to rally public sentiment, letter-writing campaigns, influencing the climate of opinion, and using constituents to lobby for the group's interest.

4. The 1946 Legislative Reorganization Act was the first attempt to control lobbyists and their activities through registration requirements. The Supreme Court narrowly construed the act as applying only to lobbyists who directly seek to influence federal legislation.

 QUESTIONS FOR REVIEW AND DISCUSSION

1. Which interest groups seem to be among the most powerful in the United States? What characteristics—size, prestige, resources, geographic location, political position—seem to make them more influential than others?

2. Consider the possibility of removing all interest group influence from campaigns and elections—no contributions of money, assistance, workers, or other material help. How would candidates appeal to the voters' interests? How would the interactions between politicians and groups change after the election? Would the influence of interest groups in Washington, D.C., be lessened?

3. Imagine that you are a member of Congress considering an important legislative proposal, such as health-care reform. To which interest groups would you be likely to listen? Which of the techniques used by such groups would be likely to influence your attitudes and your decisions? Could you make up your mind without considering the voices of interest groups?

LOGGING ON: INTEREST GROUPS

The sources of information on interest groups are numerous. If you are interested in the exploration of outer space, you might want to look at the news group

sci.space.policy

Maybe you are more interested in environmental protection. If so, try the news group

rec.outdoors.national.parks

Or, if you are of a different persuasion, try

alt.kill.the whales

To get on a mailing list that discusses such topics as fathers' rights and equality, use the following E-mail address:

listserv@indycms.iupui.edu

In the body of the letter, type

SUBSCRIBE FREE-L (your first name and last name)

Finally, you can access the news group

alt.pave.the.earth

Its motto is ``One world, one people, one slab of asphalt.'' There seems to be a news group for everyone.

By the way, if you would like to give the Clinton-Gore administration a piece of your mind, you might join the news group

alt.dear.white house

which monitors open letters to the White House. Otherwise, contact Bill directly at

president@white house.gov

 ## SELECTED REFERENCES

Birnbaum, Jeffrey. *The Lobbyists.* New York: Times Books/Random House, 1993. This is an excellent account of the work of lobbyists in the halls of Congress as reported by a journalist. Birnbaum reports on some of the conflicts between interest groups and industries, as well as on the exchange of staff between Congress and the associations.

Cigler, Allan J., and Burdette A. Loomis. *Interest Group Politics,* 4th ed. Washington, D.C.: Congressional Quarterly Press, 1995. This collection of essays deals with interest groups in general and with the politics of specific groups such as the environmental movement, religious groups, abortion groups, and agricultural groups.

Clawson, Dan, Alan Neutstadtl, and Denise Scott. *Money Talks: Corporate PACs and Political Influence.* New York: Basic Books, 1992. How corporations set up PACs, how they decide which candidates to support, and the goals of that support are covered in this excellent investigation.

Greider, William. *Who Will Tell the People? The Betrayal of American Democracy.* New York: Simon & Schuster, 1992. Greider argues that the American political process has degenerated into a "grand bazaar" in which interest groups' money is exchanged for political power and influence.

Makinson, Larry. *Open Secrets: The Cash Constituents of*

Congress. Washington, D.C.: Congressional Quarterly Press, 1992. This extensive reference book on PACs and Congress includes the actual contributions of the major PACs to the members of congressional committees and to the members of Congress.

Rosenthal, Alan. *The Third House: Lobbyists and Lobbying in the States.* Washington, D.C.: Congressional Quarterly Press, 1993. Interest groups and lobbyists have proliferated not only at the national level but also within states and cities. This study examines the growth of lobbying efforts and interest groups at the state level using comparative data and interviews with lobbyists and state government officials.

Rothenberg, Lawrence S. *Linking Citizens to Government: Interest Group Politics at Common Cause.* New York: Cambridge University Press, 1992. This in-depth exploration and analysis of one of the largest public interest groups in the United States, Common Cause, focuses on the demographics, organization, and policies of the group.

Wolpe, Bruce C. *Lobbying Congress: How the System Works.* Washington, D.C.: Congressional Quarterly Press, 1990. This is a combination of a how-to manual and a case-study collection dealing with basic lobbying theory, lobbying dos and don'ts, and specific cases in which lobbying has been effective.

8
Political Parties

CHAPTER OUTLINE

WHAT IF . . .
Independent Voters Were the Majority?

Sometimes it seems as if the two American political parties—the Democrats and the Republicans—are as much a part of American democracy as the flag and the Statue of Liberty. Imagine how different our campaigns, elections, and government might be if the majority of voters in the United States were *independent* voters rather than partisans of one of the two traditional parties.

If the majority of voters were independents, it is likely that there would be many more independent candidates for office. Because of the success of H. Ross Perot in 1992, who ran as a presidential candidate without party affiliation, more individuals are now choosing to run as independents. Most states make it more difficult for minor-party and independent candidates to get on the ballot than candidates of the two major parties by requiring more voters' signatures on the petitions. With a majority of independent voters, such constraints likely would be dropped. The independent candidates would multiply, each running on a separate platform or wooing voters on the basis of experience.

Independent candidates have some advantages and disadvantages. The advantage of being an independent is that the candidate is not saddled with the mistakes of the party and can probably claim that he or she does not owe his or her job or decisions to any party elites. The independent can address issues that cross party lines or take new positions on social or economic policies that a party

candidate would find difficult to defend.

One disadvantage of being an independent candidate is that independent candidates have no other candidates with whom to share campaign costs and fund-raising efforts, as do party candidates. They may have to raise more funds for advertising and other forms of media, because voters will need to know more about them than they do about those with a party tag. Additionally, if too many independents crowd the field, they may split the vote, thus giving an advantage to party candidates.

If the majority of voters were independents, without even partial ties to parties, campaigns and political decisions would be even more complicated than they are now. Let's say, for example, that independents were running and won all twenty congressional seats from Illinois, a state with strong urban, rural, and suburban districts. Would each independent candidate attempt to represent only the strictly defined interests of his or her district? Would there be any basis on which Illinois representatives could initiate policies together? It might be that independent representatives would be more responsive to their districts, because there would be fewer other sources for taking a position. Or the independent officeholder might feel that the voters supported a completely unique viewpoint—say, a world government or ending the welfare sys-

tem altogether. Because no other representative held such views, it is unlikely that they would be adopted.

Independent voters would need to organize the information about candidates for themselves. There would be no party literature for them; each candidate would provide his or her own platform statements. This places on the voter the burden of determining what each candidate stands for. In some cases, independent candidates might be backed by one particular interest group, a fact that might not be known to the voters.

Finally, having a majority of independent voters who are choosing between multiple independent candidates might lead to an even greater emphasis on media campaigns and the politics of personalities. The more difficult it becomes for voters to sort out the campaign promises of different candidates, the more likely it is that people will rely on television reports and advertising, and the more likely it is that the charismatic personality will win votes because that person is memorable to voters. Thus, the advantages of independent voting—moving away from party influence—may be offset by the shallowness of personality-centered campaigns.

---

1. How would independent voters find out about the positions and experience of multiple independent candidates?
2. How do independent voters in a district or state decide what their common interests are and then ensure that they are represented?

WHAT IS A POLITICAL PARTY?

Almost every political survey completed in the United States includes the question, "Do you consider yourself to be a Democrat, a Republican, or an independent?" The question refers to the respondent's self-identification with a particular political party. Although a majority of Americans are willing to identify themselves with one of the two major parties, more than 30 percent of voters consciously identify themselves as **independents.** This group could become a majority, as discussed in the *What If . . .* that opens this chapter.

In the United States, being a member of a political party does not require paying dues, passing an examination, or swearing an oath of allegiance.[1] If nothing is really required to be a member of a political party, what, then, is a **political party?**

A political party might be formally defined as a group of political activists who organize to win elections, to operate the government, and to determine public policy. This definition explains the difference between an interest group and a political party. Interest groups do not want to operate government, and they do not put forth political candidates—even though they support candidates who will promote their interests if elected or reelected. Another important distinction is that interest groups tend to sharpen issues, whereas American political parties tend to blur their issue positions to attract voters.

A political party is not a **faction** (see Chapter 2). Factions, which historically preceded political parties, were simply groups of individuals who joined together to win a benefit for themselves, like the interest groups of today. They were limited to the period in our political history when there were relatively few elective offices and when only a small percentage of the population could meet the requirements for voting. Today, we still use the term *faction,* but only for a particular group within a political party. For example, we speak of the conservative faction within the Democratic party or the liberal faction within the Republican party. A faction is founded on a particular philosophy, personality, or even geographic region. Sometimes a faction can be based on a political issue. The main feature differentiating a faction from a political party is that the faction generally does not have a permanently organized structure.

FUNCTIONS OF POLITICAL PARTIES IN THE UNITED STATES

Political parties in the United States engage in a wide variety of activities, many of which are discussed in this chapter. Through these activities, parties perform a number of functions for the political system. These functions include the following:

1. *Recruiting candidates for public office.* Because it is the goal of parties to gain control of government, they must work to recruit candidates for all

INDEPENDENT
A voter or candidate who does not identify with a political party.

POLITICAL PARTY
A group of political activists who organize to win elections, to operate the government, and to determine public policy.

FACTION
A group or bloc in a legislature or a political party acting together in pursuit of some special interest or position.

Supporters of Bill Clinton lead the cheers for the candidate during the 1992 Democratic convention.

---

1. L. Sandy Maisel, *Political Parties and Elections in the United States: An Encyclopedia* (New York: Garland, 1991), p. 747.

That in 1824, the voters were offered the choice between "John Quincy Adams who can write and Andy Jackson who can fight"?

CADRE
The nucleus of political party activists carrying out the major functions of American political parties.

Thomas Jefferson, founder of the Democratic Republicans. His election to the presidency in 1800 was decided in the House of Representatives, because the Democratic Republican party did not carry enough electoral votes.

elective offices. Often this means recruiting candidates to run against powerful incumbents or for unpopular jobs. Yet if parties did not search out and encourage political hopefuls, far more offices would be uncontested, and voters would have limited choices.

2. *Organizing and running elections.* Although elections are a government activity, political parties actually organize the voter-registration drives, recruit the volunteers to work at the polls, provide most of the campaign activity to stimulate interest in the election, and work to increase participation.

3. *Presenting alternative policies to the electorate.* The difference between political parties and factions is that factions are often centered on individual politicians, whereas parties are focused on a set of political positions. The Democrats or Republicans in Congress who vote together do so because they represent constituencies that have similar expectations and demands.

4. *Accepting responsibility for operating the government.* When the party elects the president or governor and members of the legislature, it accepts the responsibility for running the government. This includes staffing the executive branch with managers from the party and developing linkages among the elected officials to gain support for policies and their implementation.

5. *Acting as the organized opposition to the party in power.* The "out" party, or the one that does not control the executive branch, is expected to articulate its own policies and oppose the winning party when appropriate. By organizing the opposition to the "in" party, the opposition party forces debate on the policy alternatives.

Students of political parties, such as Leon D. Epstein, point out that the major functions of American political parties are carried out by a small, relatively loose-knit **cadre**, or nucleus, of party activists.[2] This is quite a different arrangement from the more highly structured, mass-membership party organization typical of certain European working-class parties. American parties concentrate on winning elections rather than on signing up large numbers of deeply committed, dues-paying members who believe passionately in the party's program.

A SHORT HISTORY OF POLITICAL PARTIES IN THE UNITED STATES

Political parties in the United States have a long tradition dating back to the 1790s (see Figure 8–1). The function and character of these political parties, as well as the emergence of the two-party system itself, have much to do with the unique historical forces operating from this country's beginning as an independent nation.

Generally, we can divide the evolution of our nation's political parties into six periods:

1. The creation of parties, from 1789 to 1812.
2. The era of one-party rule, or personal politics, from 1816 to 1824.
3. The period from Andrew Jackson's presidency to the Civil War, from 1828 to 1860.
4. The post–Civil War period, from 1864 to 1892.
5. The progressive period, from 1896 to 1928.
6. The modern period, from 1932 to the present.

---

2. *Political Parties in Western Democracies* (New Brunswick, N.J.: Transaction, 1980).

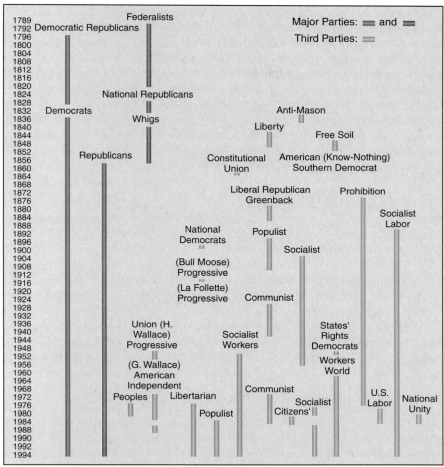

1789 1792	Federalists Democratic Republicans

Major Parties: ▬ and ▬
Third Parties: ▬

1789
1792
1796
1800
1804
1808
1812
1816
1820
1824
1828
1832
1836
1840
1844
1848
1852
1856
1860
1864
1868
1872
1876
1880
1884
1888
1892
1896
1900
1904
1908
1912
1916
1920
1924
1928
1932
1936
1940
1944
1948
1952
1956
1960
1964
1968
1972
1976
1980
1984
1988
1990
1992
1994

Federalists
Democratic Republicans
National Republicans
Democrats
Whigs
Republicans
National Democrats
(Bull Moose) Progressive
(La Follette) Progressive
Union (H. Wallace) Progressive
(G. Wallace) American Independent
Peoples
Libertarian
Populist

Anti-Mason
Liberty
Free Soil
Constitutional Union
American (Know-Nothing)
Southern Democrat
Liberal Republican
Greenback
Prohibition
Populist
Socialist
Socialist Labor
Communist
Socialist Workers
States' Rights Democrats
Workers World
Communist
Socialist
Citizens'
U.S. Labor
National Unity

SOURCE: Congressional Quarterly, *Congressional Quarterly's Guide to U.S. Elections*, 2d ed. (Washington, D.C.: Congressional Quarterly, 1985), p. 224; *Congressional Quarterly Weekly Report* (1988), p. 3184; and J. David Gillespie, *Politics at the Periphery* (Columbia, S.C.: University of South Carolina Press, 1993).

FIGURE 8-1 ▪

American Political Parties Since 1789

The chart indicates the years that parties either ran presidential candidates or held national conventions. The life span for many political parties can only be approximated, because parties existed at the state or local level before they ran candidates in presidential elections, and parties continued to exist at local levels long after they ceased running presidential candidates. Not every party fielding a presidential candidate is represented in the chart. For instance, in 1992, at least twelve other parties fielded a presidential candidate in at least one state.

The Formative Years: Federalists and Anti-Federalists

The first partisan political division in the United States occurred prior to the adoption of the Constitution. The **Federalists** proposed adoption of the Constitution, whereas the **Anti-Federalists** were against ratification.

In September 1796, George Washington, who had served as president for almost two full terms, decided not to run again. In his farewell address, he made a somber assessment of the nation's future. Washington felt that the country might be destroyed by the "baneful effects of the spirit of party." He viewed parties as a threat to both national unity and the concept of popular government. Early in his career, Thomas Jefferson did not like political parties either. In 1789, he stated, "If I could not go to heaven but with a party, I would not go there at all."[3]

What Americans found out during the first decade or so after the ratification of the Constitution was that even a patriot-king (as George

FEDERALISTS
The first American political party, led by Alexander Hamilton and John Adams. Many of its members had strongly supported the adoption of the new Constitution and the creation of the federal union.

ANTI-FEDERALISTS
Those who opposed the adoption of the Constitution because of its centralist tendencies and attacked the failure of the Constitution's framers to include a bill of rights.

3. Letter to Francis Hopkinson written from Paris while Jefferson was minister to France. In John P. Foley, ed., *The Jeffersonian Cyclopedia* (New York: Russell & Russell, 1967), p. 677.

Washington has been called) could not keep everyone happy. There is no such thing as a neutral political figure who is so fair minded that everyone agrees with him or her. During this period, it became obvious to many that something more permanent than a faction would be necessary to identify candidates for the growing number of citizens who would be participating in elections. Thus, according to many historians, the world's first democratic political parties were established in this country. Also, in 1800, when the Federalists lost the presidential election to the Jeffersonian Republicans (also known as Democratic Republicans), one of the first peaceful transfers of power from one party to another was achieved.

The Era of Personal Politics

ERA OF PERSONAL POLITICS
An era when attention centered on the character of individual candidates rather than on party identification.

ERA OF GOOD FEELING
The years from 1817 to 1825, when James Monroe was president and there was, in effect, no political opposition.

DEMOCRATIC PARTY
One of the two major American political parties evolving out of the Democratic (Jeffersonian) Republican group supporting Thomas Jefferson.

WHIG PARTY
One of the foremost political organizations in the United States during the first half of the nineteenth century, formally established in 1836. The Whig party was dominated by the same anti-Jackson elements that organized the National Republican faction within the Jeffersonian Republicans and represented a variety of regional interests. It fell apart as a national party in the early 1850s.

REPUBLICAN PARTY
One of the two major American political parties, which emerged in the 1850s as an antislavery party. It was created to fill the vacuum caused by the disintegration of the Whig party. The Republican party traces its name—but not its ideology—to Jefferson's Democratic Republican party.

From 1816 to 1828, the voters regularly elected Jeffersonian Republicans to the presidency and to Congress. Two-party competition did not really exist. This was the so-called **era of personal politics**, when attention centered on the character of individual candidates rather than on party identification. Although during elections the Jeffersonian Republicans opposed the Federalist call for a stronger, more active central government, they acquired the Louisiana Territory and Florida, established a national bank, enforced a higher tariff, and resisted European intrusion into the Western Hemisphere. Domestic tranquility was sufficiently in evidence that the administration of James Monroe (1817 to 1825) came to be known as the **era of good feeling**.

National Two-Party Rule: Democrats and Whigs

During the era of personal politics, one-party rule did not prevent the Jeffersonian Republican factions from competing against each other. Indeed, there was quite a bit of intraparty rivalry. Finally, in 1824 and 1828, Jeffersonian Republicans who belonged to the factions of Henry Clay and John Quincy Adams split with the rest of the party to oppose Andrew Jackson in those elections. Jackson's supporters and the Clay-Adams bloc formed separate parties, the **Democratic party** and the **Whig party**, respectively. That same Democratic party is now the oldest continuing political party in the Western world.

The Whigs were those Jeffersonian Republicans who were often called the "National Republicans." At the national level, the Whigs were able to elect two presidents—William Henry Harrison in 1840 and Zachary Taylor in 1848. The Whigs, however, were unable to maintain a common ideological base when the party became increasingly divided over the issue of slavery in the late 1840s. During the 1850s, the Whigs fell apart as a national party.

The Post–Civil War Period

The existing two-party system was disrupted by the election of 1860, in which there were four major candidates. Abraham Lincoln, the candidate of the newly formed **Republican party**, was the victor with a majority of the electoral vote, although with only 39.9 percent of the popular vote. This newly formed Republican party—not to be confused with the Jeffersonian Republicans—was created in the mid-1850s from the various groups that sought to fill the vacuum left by the disintegration of the Whigs. It took the label of Grand Old Party, or GOP. Its first national convention was held in 1856, but its presidential candidate, John C. Frémont, lost.

After the end of the Civil War, the South became heavily Democratic (the Solid South), and the North became heavily Republican. This era of Republican dominance was highlighted by the election of 1896, when the Republicans, emphasizing economic development and modernization under William McKinley, resoundingly defeated the Democratic and Populist candidate, William Jennings Bryan. The Republicans' control was solidified by winning over the urban working-class vote in northern cities. From the election of Abraham Lincoln until the election of Franklin D. Roosevelt in 1932, the Republicans won all but four presidential elections.

The Progressive Movement

In 1912, a major schism occurred in the Republican party when former Republican president Theodore Roosevelt ran for the presidency as a Progressive. Consequently, there were three significant contenders in that presidential contest. Woodrow Wilson was the Democratic candidate, William Howard Taft was the regular Republican candidate, and Roosevelt was the Progressive candidate. The Republican split allowed Wilson to be elected. The Wilson administration, although Democratic, ended up enacting much of the Progressive party's platform. Left without any reason for opposition, the Progressive party collapsed in 1921.

Republican Warren Harding's victory in 1920 reasserted Republican domination of national politics until the Republicans' defeat by Franklin D. Roosevelt in 1932 in the depths of the Great Depression.

Andrew Jackson earned the name "Old Hickory" for his exploits during the War of 1812. In 1828, Jackson was elected president as the candidate of the new Democratic party.

William McKinley campaigning in 1896 on a platform draped with the flag. The decorations are no different from those that candidates used almost a century later.

The Modern Era: From the New Deal to the Present

Franklin D. Roosevelt was elected in 1932 and reelected in 1936, 1940, and 1944. The impact of his successive Democratic administrations and the New Deal that he crafted is still with us today. Roosevelt used his enormous personal appeal to unify Democrats under his leadership, and he established direct communication between the president and the public through his radio "fireside chats." It wasn't until 1940 that the Republicans made even a small dent in the Democratic hegemony, when Wendell Willkie reduced Roosevelt's popular vote to 54.8 percent from the 60.5 percent and the 57.4 percent of the two previous elections.

In April 1945, Roosevelt died; Vice President Harry Truman became president through succession and, in 1948, through election. The New Deal coalition, under Truman's revised theme of the Fair Deal, continued. It was not until Republican Dwight Eisenhower won the 1952 election that the Democrats lost their control of the presidency. Eisenhower was reelected in 1956.

From 1960 through 1968, the Democrats, led first by John F. Kennedy and then by Lyndon B. Johnson, held national power. Republicans again came to power with Richard Nixon's victory in 1968 and retained it in 1972, but they lost prestige after the Watergate scandal forced Nixon's resignation on August 8, 1974. For this and other reasons, the Democrats were back in power after the presidential elections in 1976. But Democratic president Jimmy Carter was unable to win reelection against Ronald Reagan in 1980. The Republicans also gained control of the Senate in 1980 and retained it in the elections of 1982 and 1984. The 1984 reelection of Ronald Reagan appeared to some pollsters to signal the resurgence of the Republican party as a competitive force in American politics as more people declared themselves to be Republicans than they had in the previous several decades.

In 1988, George Bush won the White House for the Republicans without converting many voters to the party. Democrats gained seats in the House of Representatives and one seat in the Senate. The same phenomenon occurred, in reverse, in 1992: Bill Clinton won the presidency, but the Democrats lost nine seats in the House. The midterm election of 1994 was a stunning reversal for the Democrats. Republicans won majorities in both the House and the Senate as well as gaining a majority of governorships.

THE THREE FACES OF A PARTY

Although American parties are known by a single name and, in the public mind, have a common historical identity, each party is really composed of three major subunits. The first subunit is the **party-in-electorate.** This phrase refers to all those individuals who claim a linkage to the political party. They need not be members in the sense that they pay dues or even participate in election campaigns. Rather, the party-in-electorate is the large number of Americans who feel some loyalty to the party or who use partisanship as a cue to decide who will earn their vote. This is a rather fluid and unstable group, one that can become disenchanted with the candidates and policies offered by the Democrats or Republicans and that can freely switch parties or be drawn to independent or third-party candidates. Needless to

FIRESIDE CHAT
One of the warm, informal talks by Franklin D. Roosevelt to a few million of his intimate friends—via the radio. Roosevelt's fireside chats were so effective that succeeding presidents have been urged by their advisers to emulate him by giving more radio and television reports to the nation.

PARTY-IN-ELECTORATE
Those members of the general public who identify with a political party or who express a preference for one party over the other.

say, the party leaders pay close attention to the affiliation of their members in the electorate.

The second subunit, the **party organization**, provides the structural framework for the political party by recruiting volunteers to become party leaders; identifying potential candidates; and organizing caucuses, conventions, and election campaigns for its candidates. It is the party organization and its active workers that keep the party functioning between elections, as well as make sure that the party puts forth electable candidates and clear positions in the elections. When individuals accept paid employment for a political party, they are considered party professionals. Among that group are found campaign consultants; fund raisers; local, state, and national executives; and national staff members. If the party-in-electorate declines in numbers and loyalty, the party organization must try to find a strategy to rebuild the grass-roots following.

The **party-in-government** is the third subunit of American political parties. The party-in-government consists of those elected and appointed officials who identify with a political party. Generally, elected officials cannot also hold official party positions within the formal organization. Executives such as the president, governors, and mayors often have the informal power to appoint party executives, but their duties in office preclude them from active involvement in the party organization most of the time.

Ties to a political party are essential to the functioning of government and the operation of the political process in the United States. Republican representatives, senators, and governors expect to receive a hearing at a Republican-controlled White House if they request it. In return, Republican presidents call on party loyalty when they ask the legislators to support their programs. Finally, the electorate at the polls is asked to judge the party-in-government by its policies and candidates. American political parties, although not nearly as ideological as many European parties, do claim to present alternative positions to the voters. If the party organization and the party-in-government are in conflict, the party-in-electorate is likely to look for other party leadership to articulate its preferences.

PARTY ORGANIZATION

PARTY ORGANIZATION
The formal structure and leadership of a political party, including election committees; local, state, and national executives; and paid professional staff.

PARTY-IN-GOVERNMENT
All of the elected and appointed officials who identify with a political party.

PARTY ORGANIZATION

In theory, each of the American political parties has a standard, pyramid-shaped organization (see Figure 8–2). The pyramid, however, does not reflect accurately the relative power and strengths of the individual parts of the party organization. If it did, the national chairperson of the Democratic or Republican party, along with the national committee, could simply dictate how the organization was to be run, just as if it were Exxon Corporation or Ford Motor Company.

In reality, the formal structure of political parties resembles a layer cake with autonomous strata more than it does a pyramid. Malcolm E. Jewell and David M. Olson point out that "there is no command structure within political parties. Rather, each geographic unit of the party tends to be autonomous from the other units at its same geographic level."[4]

---

4. Malcolm E. Jewell and David M. Olson, *American State Political Parties and Elections,* rev. ed. (Homewood, Ill.: Dorsey Press, 1982), p. 73.

FIGURE 8–2   ■
A Theoretical Structure of the American Political Party

The relationship between state and local parties varies from state to state. Further, some state parties resist national party policies.

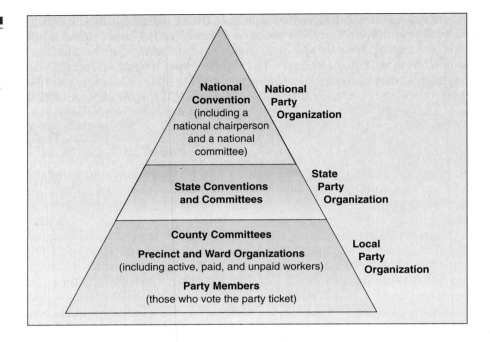

NATIONAL CONVENTION
The meeting held every four years by each major party to select presidential and vice presidential candidates, to write a platform, to choose a national committee, and to conduct party business. In theory, the national convention is at the top of a hierarchy of party conventions (the local and state conventions are below it) that consider candidates and issues.

PARTY PLATFORM
A document drawn up by the platform committee at each national convention, outlining the policies, positions, and principles of the party; it is then submitted to the entire convention for approval.

NATIONAL COMMITTEE
A standing committee of a national political party established to direct and coordinate party activities during the four-year period between national party conventions.

The National Party Organization

Each party has a national organization, the most clearly institutional part of which is the **national convention**, held every four years. The convention is used to nominate the presidential and vice presidential candidates. In addition, the **party platform** is written, ratified, and revised at the national convention. The platform sets forth the party's position on the issues and makes promises to initiate certain policies if the party wins the presidency. Often, platforms represent compromises among the various factions of a party, in an attempt to make peace before the campaign begins.

After the convention, the platform frequently is neglected or ignored by party candidates who disagree with it. Because candidates are trying to win votes from a wide spectrum of voters, it is counterproductive to emphasize the fairly narrow and sometimes controversial goals set forth in the platform. The work of Gerald M. Pomper has shown, however, that once elected, the parties do try to carry out platform promises and that roughly three-fourths of the promises eventually become law.[5] Of course, some general goals, such as economic prosperity, are included in the platforms of both parties.

Choosing the National Committee.   At the national convention, each of the parties formally chooses a national standing committee, elected by the individual state parties. This **national committee** is established to direct and coordinate party activities during the following four years. The Democrats include at least two members, a man and a woman, from each state, from the District of Columbia, and from the several territories. Gov-

5. Gerald M. Pomper and Susan S. Lederman, *Elections in America: Control and Influence in Democratic Politics,* 2d ed. (New York: Longman, 1980).

Senator Robert Dole, majority leader of the U.S. Senate, arrives at yet another campaign stop in his quest to be the Republican nominee for the presidency. Senator Dole ran for the vice presidency in 1976 and attempted to win the Republican nomination in 1980 and 1988. In 1994, he embarked on another primary campaign. At that time, he was serving his fifth term as the Republican senator from Kansas.

ernors, members of Congress, mayors, and other officials may be included as at-large members of the national committee. The Republicans, in addition, add state chairpersons from every state carried by the Republican party in the preceding presidential, gubernatorial, or congressional elections. The selections of national committee members are ratified by the delegations to the national convention.

One of the jobs of the national committee is to ratify the presidential nominee's choice of a national chairperson, who in principle acts as the spokesperson for the party. Even though we have placed the national committee at the top of the hierarchy of party organization (see Figure 8–2), it has very little direct influence. Basically, the national chairperson and the national committee simply plan the next campaign and the next convention, obtain financial contributions, and publicize the national party.

Picking a National Chairperson.   In general, the party's presidential candidate chooses the national chairperson.[6] The major responsibility of that person is the management of the national election campaign. In some cases, a strong national chairperson has considerable power over state and local party organizations. There is no formal mechanism with which to exercise direct control over subnational party structures, however. The national chairperson does such jobs as establish a national party headquarters, raise and distribute campaign funds, and appear in the media as a party spokesperson. The national chairperson, along with the national committee, also attempts basically to maintain some sort of liaison among the different levels of the party organization. The real strength and power of a national party, though, is at the state level.

---

6. If that candidate loses, however, the chairperson is often changed.

The State Party Organization

There are fifty states in the Union, plus the territories and the District of Columbia, and an equal number of party organizations for each major party. Therefore, there are more than a hundred state parties (and even more, if we include local parties and minor parties). Because every state party is unique, it is impossible to describe what an "average" state political party is like. Nonetheless, state parties have several organizational features in common.

This commonality can be described in one sentence: Each state party has a chairperson, a committee, and a number of local organizations. In principle, each **state central committee**—the principal organized structure of each political party within each state—has a similar role in the various states. The committee, usually composed of those members who represent congressional districts, state legislative districts, or counties, has responsibility for carrying out the policy decisions of the party's state convention, and in some states the state central committee will direct the state chairperson with respect to policymaking.

Also, like the national committee, the state central committee has control over the use of party campaign funds during political campaigns. Usually, the state central committee has little, if any, influence on party candidates once they are elected. In fact, state parties are fundamentally loose alliances of local interests and coalitions of often bitterly opposed factions.

State parties are also important in national politics because of the **unit rule**, which awards electoral votes in presidential elections as an indivisible bloc (except in Maine and Nebraska). Presidential candidates concentrate their efforts in states in which voter preferences seem to be evenly divided or in which large numbers of electoral votes are at stake.

Local Party Machinery: The Grass Roots

The lowest layer of party machinery is the local organization, supported by district leaders, precinct or ward captains, and party workers. Much of the work is coordinated by county committees and their chairpersons. In the past, the institution of **patronage**—rewarding the party faithful with government jobs or contracts—held the local organization together. For immigrants and the poor, the political machine often furnished important services and protections. The big-city machine was the archetypal example, and Tammany Hall, or the Tammany Society, which dominated New York City government for nearly two centuries, was perhaps the highest refinement of this political form. (See this chapter's *Politics and Ethics.*)

The last big-city local political machine to exercise a great deal of power was run by Chicago's Mayor Richard J. Daley, who was also an important figure in national Democratic politics. Daley, as mayor, ran the Chicago Democratic machine from 1955 until his death in 1976. The Daley organization, largely Irish in candidate origin and voter support, was split by the successful candidacy of African-American Democrat Harold Washington in the racially divisive 1983 mayoral election. (See also this chapter's *Politics: The Human Side.*)

City machines are now dead, mostly because their function of providing social services (and reaping the reward of votes) has been taken over by state

STATE CENTRAL COMMITTEE
The principal organized structure of each political party within each state. This committee is responsible for carrying out policy decisions of the party's state convention.

UNIT RULE
All of most states' electoral votes are cast for the presidential candidate receiving a plurality of the popular vote.

PATRONAGE
Rewarding faithful party workers and followers with government employment and contracts.

POLITICS AND ETHICS
Tammany Hall: The Quintessential Local Political Machine

The Tammany Society dominated New York City politics for nearly two centuries. Founded in 1786 with the express purpose of engaging in cultural, social, and patriotic activities, the society evolved into a major political force and became known as Tammany Hall. In the beginning, it organized and provided social services for the foreign born, who made up the bulk of the Democratic party in New York City.

One of its more notorious leaders was William Tweed, head of the so-called Tweed ring, whose scandals were unearthed by the *New York Times* in 1871. Readers were entertained and horrified by stories of millions of dollars in kickbacks received from giving out government contracts, of civil and criminal violations that were being overlooked, and of phony leases and padded bills that were paid to members of the Tweed ring. As a result of the exposé, Tweed was imprisoned; but the other members of the ring managed to flee the country (as very wealthy men and women). Richard Crocker took over the leadership of Tammany Hall in 1886 and kept it until 1901.

Tammany Hall's influence declined when its slate of candidates was defeated in a reform movement in 1901. It was not until Franklin D. Roosevelt's victory in 1932, how-

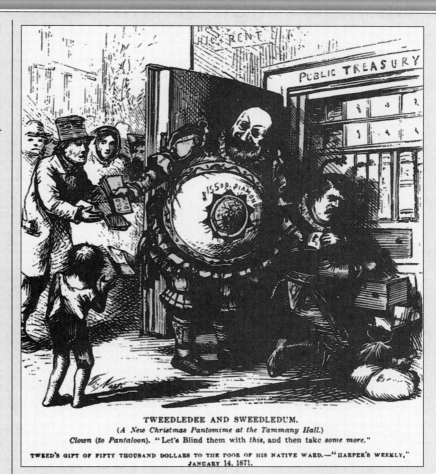

TWEEDLEDEE AND SWEEDLEDUM.
(*A New Christmas Pantomime at the Tammany Hall.*)
Clown (to Pantaloon). "Let's Blind them with *this*, and then take *some more.*"

TWEED'S GIFT OF FIFTY THOUSAND DOLLARS TO THE POOR OF HIS NATIVE WARD.—"HARPER'S WEEKLY,"
JANUARY 14, 1871.

ever, that Tammany lost its political clout almost completely—but only for a couple of decades. In the 1950s, there was a short-lived resur-gence in the influence of the Tammany Society. It has enjoyed no political influence in New York City politics since then.

and national government agencies. This trend began in the 1930s, when the social legislation of the New Deal established Social Security and unemployment insurance. The local party machine has little, if anything, to do with deciding who is eligible to receive these benefits.

Local political organizations, whether located in cities, townships, or at the county level, still can contribute a great deal to local election campaigns. These organizations provide the foot soldiers of politics—individuals who pass out literature and get out the vote on election day, which can be crucial in local elections. In many regions, local Democratic and Republican

POLITICS: THE HUMAN SIDE
Carol Moseley Braun, the First African-American Woman Senator

"If you call people to right, if you call them to the moral high ground, they can and will respond."

BIOGRAPHICAL NOTES

Carol Moseley Braun, the first African-American woman to be elected to the U.S. Senate, is one of the new generation of female politicians. Born in 1947, Carol Moseley was raised in a neighborhood of middle-class African-American families on Chicago's South Side. Her father was a police officer and her mother, a hospital worker. When pressed, Braun will tell a story of being refused service at a restaurant because of her race during her teen years. She attended public schools and graduated from the University of Illinois at Chicago. She then won a scholarship to the elite University of Chicago Law School, where she met and married her husband. Braun began a legal career in Chicago, living in one of its progressive neighborhoods, Hyde Park, the home of the University of Chicago.

In 1978, a neighbor persuaded her to run for the Illinois legislature as an independent Democrat. Braun won and continued her political career as the statehouse leader for Mayor Harold Washington of Chicago. She then ran for and won election as the Cook County recorder of deeds. At some point during the Anita Hill–Clarence Thomas hearings, Braun began receiving requests that she run for the Senate in opposition to the incumbent, Alan Dixon, who had voted for Thomas's confirmation.

In 1992, Braun upset Dixon in the primary and defeated a Republican millionaire to become the senior senator from Illinois and the first African-American woman in that chamber.

POLITICAL CONTRIBUTIONS

Carol Moseley Braun's campaign was only one of the surprising women's victories of 1992, but because she was an African American and had been given virtually no chance to win early in the campaign, she quickly became a rising star in the Democratic party, showcased at every opportunity.

Braun's record in her first years in the Senate was uneven. At times she was criticized for giving in to the publicity and media attention. Some would argue that she did not deal well with accusations of sexual harassment lodged against her campaign manager and close personal friend, Ksogie Mathews. On several occasions, however, Braun's passion and eloquence on the floor of the Senate changed votes. In a case involving the granting of a patent to a design including the Confederate flag, Braun's speech forced the Senate to reverse itself in a vote. Her charismatic personality and compelling oratory have earned her more attention on the floor of the Senate than most of the other new male or female members of the body.

organizations still exercise some patronage, such as awarding courthouse jobs, contracts for street repair, and other lucrative construction contracts. Local party organizations are also the most important vehicles for recruiting young adults into political work, because political involvement at the local level offers activists many opportunities to gain experience.

THE PARTY AND ITS MEMBERS

The two major American political parties are often characterized as being too much like Tweedledee and Tweedledum, the twins in Lewis Carroll's

Through the Looking Glass. When both parties nominate moderates for the presidency, the similarities between the parties seem to outweigh their differences. Yet the political parties do generate strong conflict for political offices throughout the United States, and there are significant differences between the parties, both in the characteristics of their members and in their platforms.

Although Democrats and Republicans are not divided along religious or class lines to the extent that some European parties are, certain social groups are more likely to identify with each. Since the New Deal of Franklin D. Roosevelt, the Democratic party has appealed to the more disadvantaged groups in society. African-American voters are far more likely to identify with the Democrats, as are members of union households, Jewish voters, and lower-income families. Republicans draw more of their support from upper-income families, professionals, and businesspersons. In recent years, more women than men have tended to identify themselves as Democrats than as Republicans.

The coalition of minorities, the working class, and various ethnic groups has been the core of Democratic party support since the presidency of Franklin D. Roosevelt. The social programs and increased government intervention in the economy that were the heart of Roosevelt's New Deal were intended to ease the strain of economic hard times on these groups. This goal remains important for many Democrats today. In general, Democratic identifiers are more likely to approve of social-welfare spending, to support government regulation of business, to approve of measures to improve the situation of minorities, and to support assistance to the elderly with their medical expenses. Republicans are more supportive of the private marketplace, and many Republicans feel that the federal government should be involved in fewer social programs.

Table 8–1 shows that the general public shares these views on which groups are served by each party. It would seem that a larger proportion of the population falls into those groups that most people think are better served by the Democratic party than by the Republican party, yet the Republican party has captured the presidency in five of the last seven

TABLE 8–1

Which Party Is Better?

QUESTION: *In the view of the public, which party serves the interests of groups in society better?*			
BETTER FOR	**REPUBLICAN**	**DEMOCRAT**	**SAME/ DON'T KNOW**
Business and professional people	65%	19%	16%
White-collar workers	56	25	19
Skilled workers	58	40	22
Small business people	36	45	19
Farmers	27	49	24
Retired people	28	51	21
Unemployed people	20	59	21
Women	26	45	29
Labor union members	22	55	23
African Americans	17	59	24

SOURCE: *Gallup Report,* 1992.

elections. Turning from the interests of specific groups to the interest of the nation as a whole, Table 8–2 shows the percentage of Americans who think that the Republican or Democratic party is better for preserving peace and promoting prosperity. Since 1984, a greater proportion of the public has felt that the Republican party was better able than the Democratic party to keep peace and to keep the country prosperous. If it is true, as some researchers suggest, that voters are more likely to consider the good of the whole nation than their individual interests in choosing a presidential candidate, then the success of the Republican party at the presidential level may be due to public perceptions of its effectiveness on the issues of peace and the economy.

The differences separating those who identify with the Democrats and those who identify with the Republicans are magnified greatly among the leadership of the Democrats and the Republicans. Generally, a much greater percentage of Democratic leaders consider themselves to be liberals than do their followers, and Republican elites are far more likely to identify their philosophy as conservative than are their followers. Polls of the national convention delegates demonstrate the wide gap in policy preferences between elites and general party identifiers. Such differences are reflected in the party platforms that are adopted at each party's convention. Democratic platforms recently have stressed equality of opportunity, the government's responsibility to help citizens, and ending tax loopholes for business. Recent Republican platforms have sought to ban abortions, opposed quotas to remedy discrimination, and supported prayer in public schools.

In 1994, the Republicans attempted to put forth a new kind of party platform—the "Contract with America." Although they won a great victory in that election, it seems unlikely that the contract was as great a factor on election day as was later claimed. See the *Politics and Public Opinion* in this chapter for a discussion of the Republican strategy.

THE PARTY-IN-GOVERNMENT

After the election is over and the winners are announced, the focus of party activity shifts from getting out the vote to organizing and controlling the government. As you will see in Chapter 10, party membership plays an im-

TABLE 8–2

Public Perceptions of the Parties on Peace and Prosperity

QUESTION: *Which party is better for keeping peace?*			QUESTION: *Which party is better for prosperity?*		
YEAR	REPUBLICAN	DEMOCRATIC	YEAR	REPUBLICAN	DEMOCRATIC
1980	25%	42%	1980	35%	36%
1982	29	38	1982	34	43
1984	38	38	1984	49	33
1986	34	29	1986	41	30
1988	43	33	1988	52	34
1991	42	33	1991	49	32
1993	36	40	1993	30	31
1994	42	38	1994	48	38

SOURCE: *Gallup Report,* 1995.

POLITICS AND PUBLIC OPINION
How Important Was the "Contract with America"?

After losing a number of legislative battles to President Clinton and the Democratic majorities in the House and the Senate, House Republicans tried a new strategy in the 1994 congressional campaigns—a strategy that was generally ridiculed before election day and admired afterwards. On September 27, 1994, the House Republicans unveiled the Contract with America, a set of ten proposals for new legislation that they promised they would bring to the floor of the House of Representatives within the first 100 days of the next Congress. The contract was signed by about 170 Republican incumbent members of the House and more than 100 Republican challengers.

While Republicans lauded the contract as a way to regain America's trust in Congress, the Democratic Congressional Campaign Committee described the plan as "snake oil," warning that the Republicans were pitching it as "a magic elixir for everything that ails us."* The White House played off the contract, attacking the Republicans for their proposals. The Republicans, in contrast, were trying once more to nationalize their party's

*Congressional Quarterly Weekly Report, September 24, 1995, p. 2711.

themes, in an attempt to broaden their appeal to voters across the country. In addition, some Republican leaders believed that the contract might attract the Perot voters of 1992 to their banner.

After the Republicans seized control of both houses of Congress in the 1994 election, the new leader of the party in the House, Newt Gingrich, quickly moved to make the Contract with America a reality. He produced drafts of all of the pieces of legislation in the contract and promised to live up to the pledge to bring them to the floor within the first 100 days. Yet the question remains: How well known was the contract to the voters? Did it really bring victory to the Republicans?

The data from most national polls show that the Contract with America was not well known by a great majority of voters. In fact, few pollsters even asked about it until close to election day. As shown in the table in November 1994, only 28 percent of the public had heard anything about it. Three months later, after the Republicans had been working on it for a month, only 45 percent of Americans were aware of the contract. Americans were aware that change had taken place in Congress, how-

ever. By February 1995, 54 percent of Americans believed that the new Congress would accomplish more than the preceding Congress, and 79 percent believed that the Republicans in Congress would have more influence over the direction of the country in the near future than would President Clinton.[†] Other polling data gathered in December 1994 showed that, while most Americans were not familiar with all of the specific details of the contract, most of the planks in the platform received support from more than 70 percent of those polled.[‡]

Awareness of the Contract with America

Question: Have you heard or read anything about the Republican Contract with America?

	Yes	No	Don't Know
Nov. 1994	28%	70%	2%
Dec. 1994	27	72	1
Feb. 1995	45	54	1

[†]*New York Times/CBS Newspolls,* February 1995.

[‡]Gallup Poll reported in *The Public Perspective,* February/March 1995, p. 29.

portant role in the day-to-day operations of Congress, with partisanship determining everything from office space to committee assignments and power on Capitol Hill. For the president, the political party furnishes the pool of qualified applicants for political appointments to run the government. Although it is uncommon to do so, presidents can and occasionally do appoint executive personnel, such as cabinet secretaries, from the opposition party. As we note in Chapter 11, there are not as many of these appointed positions as presidents might like, and presidential power is limited by the permanent bureaucracy. Judicial appointments, however, offer a great opportunity to the winning party. For the most part, presidents are likely to appoint federal judges from their own party.

All of these party appointments suggest that the winning political party, whether at the national, state, or local level, has a great deal of control in the American system. Because of the checks and balances and the relative lack of cohesion in American parties, however, such control is an illusion. In fact, many Americans, at least implicitly, prefer a "divided government," with the executive and legislative branches controlled by different parties. The trend of splitting votes between president and House members has increased sharply since 1944. Voters seem comfortable with a president affiliated with one party and a Congress controlled by the other. This practice may indicate a lack of trust in government or the relative weakness of party identification among many voters.

WHY DO WE HAVE A TWO-PARTY SYSTEM?

It would be difficult to imagine a political system in the United States in which there were four, five, six, or seven major political parties. The United States has a **two-party system**, and that system has been around from about 1800 to the present. Considering the range of political ideology among voters and the variety of local and state party machines, the fact that we still have just two major political parties is somewhat unusual.

Strong competition between the parties at the national level in general has not filtered down to the state level. From 1900 to 1992, the Republicans won thirteen presidential elections and the Democrats, eleven. In state and local elections, however, one-party dominance is the rule in many regions of the United States. The Solid South was almost totally Democratic at all levels of government from 1880 to 1944. The northeastern states and much of the Midwest were solidly Republican from approximately 1860 to 1930. Almost 60 percent of the states today are dominated by either the Republican or the Democratic party. (See this chapter's feature on *Politics and Political Parties*.)

There are several reasons why two major parties have dominated the political landscape in the United States for almost two centuries. These reasons

TWO-PARTY SYSTEM
A political system in which only two parties have a reasonable chance of winning.

Former speaker of the House Tom Foley discusses the 1992 Democratic party convention for a television show. Conventions can boost party loyalty through television coverage.

"The euonymus likes partial shade and does equally well under Republican and Democratic Administrations."

Drawing by Farris © 1994 The New Yorker Magazine, Inc.

have to do with (1) the historical foundations of the system, (2) the self-perpetuation of the parties, (3) the commonality of views among Americans, (4) the winner-take-all electoral system, and (5) state and federal laws favoring the two-party system.

The Historical Foundations of the Two-Party System

As we have seen, the first two opposing groups in U.S. politics were the Federalists and the Anti-Federalists. The Federalists, who remained in power and solidified their identity as a political party, represented those with commercial interests, including merchants, shipowners, and manufacturers. The Federalists supported the principle of a strong national government. The Anti-Federalists, who gradually became known as the Democratic Republicans, represented artisans and farmers. They strongly supported states' rights. These interests were also fairly well split along geographic lines, with the Federalists dominant in the North and the Democratic Republicans dominant in the South.

POLITICS AND POLITICAL PARTIES
The Republican Wave of 1994

Since the beginning of the American political party system, there have been cycles of party dominance with one party controlling Congress and the presidency for several decades. The periods when parties rapidly increase or decrease their following in the electorate are sometimes called periods of realignment.

From 1789 until the present, there have been four "critical realignments" of the nation's party system: in 1828, when the Democratic party became the majority party under the leadership of Andrew Jackson; in 1860, when Lincoln led the Republicans to victory; in 1896, when William McKinley and the eastern Republicans held power; and in 1932, when Franklin Delano Roosevelt and the Democrats took control of the government. All of those realignments took place at approximately forty-year intervals.

Since the 1970s, political scientists have wondered whether another realigning election would ever occur. Some analysts thought that Ronald Reagan's election was the beginning of a Republican era. The midterm elections of 1994, however, signaled a greater resurgence for the Republican party than the Reagan landslide of 1980.

The Republican victories in 1994 were impressive on several dimensions. First, the Republicans took control of the House and the Senate, a majority of governorships, and more state legislative seats than they had held for many decades. The scale of the victory can be measured by the fact that no Republican incumbent in Congress lost his or her seat. Democrats lost 52 seats in the House, a record midterm loss for that party.

The electoral surge for the Republicans was also remarkable for its sheer size. In 1994, Republicans won 36.6 million votes for the House of Representatives, all totaled. That was 9 million more votes than they had won in the last midterm election, in 1990. It was the largest increase in midterm election votes for one party in American history. It is true that between 1990 and 1994 the population increased and turnout increased from 33 percent of the eligible voters to 36 percent, but the Democratic House candidates won almost 1 million votes *less* than they had in 1990.

Even more impressive were the gains of the Republicans across the nation. Their wins were not confined to one or two regions of the country. As the table shows, Republicans gained almost 4 million votes over the Democrats in the South, more than 2 million votes in the midwestern states, 1.7 million votes in the West (although Democrats did maintain control of the House delegation from California), and 1.3 million in the East—long a Democratic stronghold.

Finally, the 1994 election signaled the permanent shift of parts of the South to the Republican column. Republicans not only gained 4 million votes in the South but they took control of most of the southern congressional delegations. Democrats lost 19 House seats in the South in 1994, most of them by large margins. The shift can be seen in the makeup of the Georgia delegation to the House: In 1990, it was 9–1 Democratic; after Representative Nathan Deal switched to the Republicans in April 1995, the delegation became 8–3 Republican. The only Democratic congresspersons from the South are African Americans who represent minority districts.

Was 1994 a realigning election? That will only be known some years in the future when we see whether the Republicans can keep their gains among the voters and keep control of Congress. Such a permanent realignment would be likely only if the nation really does accept the Republican view of a smaller government and an end to the period of social welfare programs begun by Roosevelt's New Deal.

The Republican Gains

	1994 HOUSE VOTE (IN MILLIONS)		VOTES GAINED OR LOST, (IN MILLIONS) 1990–1994	
	REPUBLICANS	DEMOCRATS	REPUBLICANS	DEMOCRATS
South	10.3	7.8	+3.8	− .8
Midwest	10.1	8.4	+2.2	−1.0
West	8.2	7.4	+1.7	+ .4
East	7.8	7.9	+1.3	+ .6
TOTAL	36.6	31.7	+8.9	− .8

SOURCE: *Congressional Quarterly Weekly Report*, April 15, 1995, p. 1077.

Two relatively distinct sets of interests continued to characterize the two different parties. During Andrew Jackson's time in power, eastern commercial interests were pitted against western and southern agricultural and frontier interests. Before the Civil War, the major split again became North versus South. The split was ideological (over the issue of slavery), as well as economic (the Northeast's industrial interests versus the agricultural interests of the South). After the Civil War and until the 1920s, the Republicans found most of their strength in the Northeast and the Democrats, in the Solid South. The West and the Midwest held the balance of power at that time. The period from the Civil War to the 1920s has been called one of **sectional politics.**

Sectional politics gave way to **national politics** as the cities became more dominant and as industry flowed to the South and to the West. Some political scientists classify the period from 1920 to today as one of **class politics,** with the Republicans generally finding support among groups of higher economic status and the Democrats appealing more to working-class constituencies. The modern parties also have reversed their traditional views on the issue of states' rights versus a strong central government. Now, it is the Democrats who advocate a stronger role for the national government, whereas the Republicans want the central government to play less of a role in the political and economic life of the nation.

This handbill was used in the election campaign of 1860. Handbills served the same purpose as today's direct-mail advertisements, appealing directly to the voters with the candidate's message.

SECTIONAL POLITICS
The pursuit of interests that are of special concern to a region or section of the country.

NATIONAL POLITICS
The pursuit of interests that are of concern to the nation as a whole.

CLASS POLITICS
Political preferences based on income level, social status, or both.

Self-Perpetuation of the Two-Party System

As we saw in Chapter 6, most children identify with the political party of their parents. Children learn at a young age to think of themselves as either Democrats or Republicans. Relatively few are taught to think of themselves as Libertarians or Socialists or even independents. This generates a built-in mechanism to perpetuate a two-party system. According to most studies of the process of political socialization, psychological attachment to party identity intensifies during adulthood.[7]

Also, many politically oriented people who aspire to work for social change consider that the only realistic way to capture political power in this country is to be either a Republican or a Democrat. Of course, the same argument holds for those who involve themselves in politics largely for personal gain. Thus, political parties offer avenues for the expression of the personal ambitions of politicians and supply government with men and women anxious to serve the public by satisfying their own goals.[8]

The Political Culture of the United States

Another determining factor in the perpetuation of our two-party system is the commonality of goals among Americans. Most Americans want continuing material prosperity. They also believe this goal should be achieved through individual, rather than collective, initiative. There has never been much support for establishing the government as the owner of the major means of production. Most Americans take a dim view of left-wing political

---

7. See, for example, Lester W. Milbrath, *Political Participation: How and Why Do People Get Involved in Politics?* (Chicago: Rand McNally, 1965), pp. 134–135.
8. This is the view of, among others, Joseph Schlesinger. See his *Ambition and Politics: Political Careers in the United States* (Chicago: Rand McNally, 1966).

ELECTORAL COLLEGE
A group of persons called electors who are selected by the voters in each state. This group officially elects the president and the vice president of the United States. The number of electors in each state is equal to the number of each state's representatives in both houses of Congress.

Republicans look to the future, using campaign buttons to identify their favorites for 1996.

movements that wish to limit the ownership of private property. Private property is considered a basic American value, and the ability to acquire and use it the way one wishes commonly is regarded as a basic American right.

Another reason we have had a basic consensus about our political system and the two major parties is that we have managed largely to separate religion from politics. Religion was an issue in 1928, when Governor Alfred Smith of New York became the first Roman Catholic to be nominated for the presidency (he was defeated by Republican Herbert Hoover), and again in 1960, when John F. Kennedy was running for president. But religion has never been a dividing force triggering splinter parties. There has never been a major Catholic party or a Protestant party or a Jewish party or a Moslem party.

The major division in American politics has been economic. As we mentioned earlier, the Democrats have been known—at least since the 1920s—as the party of the working class. They have been in favor of government intervention in the economy and more government redistribution of income from the wealthy to those with lower incomes. The Republican party has been known in modern times as the party of the middle and upper classes and commercial interests, in favor of fewer constraints on the market system and less redistribution of income.

Not only does the political culture support the two-party system, but also the parties themselves are adept at making the necessary shifts in their platforms or electoral appeal to gain new members. Because the general ideological structure of the parties is so broad, it has been relatively easy for them to change their respective platforms or to borrow popular policies from minor parties to attract voter support. Both parties perceive themselves as being broad enough to accommodate every group in society. The Republicans try to gain support from the African-American community, and the Democrats strive to make inroads among professional and business groups.

The Winner-Take-All Electoral System

At virtually every level of government in the United States, the outcome of elections is based on the plurality, winner-take-all principle. A plurality system is one in which the winner is the person who obtains the most votes, even if a majority is not obtained. Whoever gets the most votes gets everything. Because most legislators in the United States are elected from single-member districts in which only one person represents the constituency, the candidate who finishes second in such an election receives nothing for the effort.

The winner-take-all system also operates in the **electoral college** (see Chapter 9). Each state's electors are pledged to presidential candidates chosen by their respective national party conventions. During the popular vote in November, in each of the fifty states and in the District of Columbia, the voters choose one slate of electors from those on the state ballot. If the slate of electors wins a plurality in a state, then usually *all* the electors so chosen cast their ballots for the presidential and vice presidential candidates of the winning party. This means that if a particular candidate's slate of electors receives a plurality of, say, 40 percent of the votes in a state, that candidate will receive all the state's electoral votes. Minor parties have a difficult time competing under such a system, even though they may influence the final outcome of the election. Because voters know that minor parties cannot succeed, they often will not vote for minor-party candidates, even if the voters are ideologically in tune with them.

Not all countries, or even all states in the United States, use the plurality, winner-take-all electoral system. Some hold run-off elections until a candidate obtains at least one vote over 50 percent of the votes. Such a system also may be used in countries with multiple parties. Small parties hope to be able to obtain a sufficient number of votes at least to get into a run-off election. Then the small-party candidate can form an alliance with one or more of those parties that did not make the run-off. Such alliances also occur in the United States, but with the winner-take-all system these coalitions normally must be made before the first election, because usually there is no run-off.

State and Federal Laws Favoring the Two Parties

Many state and federal election laws offer a clear advantage to the two major parties. In some states, the established major parties need to gather only a few signatures to place their candidates on the ballot, whereas a minor party or an independent candidate must get many more signatures. The criterion for making such a distinction is often based on the total party vote in the last general election, penalizing a new political party that did not compete in the election.

At the national level, minor parties face different obstacles. All of the rules and procedures of both houses of Congress divide committee seats, staff members, and other privileges on the basis of party membership. A legislator who is elected on a minor-party ticket, such as the Liberal party of New York, must choose to be counted with one of the major parties to get a committee assignment. The Federal Election Commission (FEC) rules for campaign financing also place restrictions on minor-party candidates. Such candidates are not eligible for federal matching funds in either the primary or the general election. In the 1980 election, John Anderson, running for president as an independent, sued the FEC for campaign funds. The commission finally agreed to repay part of his campaign costs after the election in proportion to the votes he received.

THE ROLE OF MINOR PARTIES IN U.S. POLITICAL HISTORY

Minor parties find it difficult, if not impossible, to compete within the American two-party political system. Nonetheless, minor parties have played an important role in our political life. Frequently, dissatisfied groups have split from major parties and formed so-called **third parties**, which have acted as barometers of changes in the political mood.[9] Such barometric indicators have forced the major parties to recognize new issues or trends in the thinking of Americans. Political scientists also believe that third parties have acted

THIRD PARTY
A political party other than the two major political parties (Republican and Democratic). Usually, third parties are composed of dissatisfied groups that have split from the major parties. They act as indicators of political trends and as safety valves for dissident groups.

---

9. The term *third party* is erroneous, because sometimes there have been third, fourth, fifth, and even sixth parties. Because it has endured, however, we will use it here.

Eugene V. Debs was the founder of the Socialist party and a candidate for president on that ticket five times. Despite its longevity, the party has had little impact on the American political system.

as a safety valve for dissident political groups, perhaps preventing major confrontations and political unrest.

Historically Important Minor Parties

Most minor parties that have endured have had a strong ideological foundation that is typically at odds with the majority mindset. Ideology has at least two functions. First, the members of the minor party regard themselves as outsiders and look to one another for support; ideology provides tremendous psychological cohesiveness. Second, because the rewards of ideological commitment are partly psychological, these minor parties do not think in terms of immediate electoral success. A poor showing at the polls therefore does not dissuade either the leadership or the grass-roots participants from continuing their quest for change in American society. Some of the notable third parties include the following:

1. The Socialist Labor party, started in 1877.
2. The Socialist party, founded in 1901.
3. The Communist party, started in 1919 as the radical left wing that split from the Socialist party.
4. The Socialist Workers' party, formerly a Trotskyite group, started in 1938.
5. The Libertarian party, formed in 1972 and still an important minor party.

As we can see from their labels, several of these minor parties have been Marxist oriented. The most successful was Eugene Debs's Socialist party, which captured 6 percent of the popular vote for president in 1912 and elected more than a thousand candidates at the local level. About eighty mayors were affiliated with the Socialist party at one time or another. It owed much of its success to the corruption of big-city machines and to antiwar sentiment. Debs's Socialist party was vociferously opposed to American entry into World War I, a view shared by many Americans. The other, more militant parties of the left (the Socialist Labor, Socialist Workers', and Communist parties) have never enjoyed wide electoral success. At the other end of the ideological spectrum, the Libertarian party supports a *laissez-faire* capitalist economic program combined with a hands-off policy on regulating matters of moral conduct.

Spin-Off Minor Parties

SPIN-OFF PARTY
A new party formed by a dissident faction within a major political party. Usually, spin-off parties have emerged when a particular personality was at odds with the major party.

The most successful minor parties have been those that split from major parties. The impetus for these **spin-off parties,** or factions, has usually been a situation in which a particular personality was at odds with the major party. The most famous spin-off was the Bull Moose Progressive party, which split from the Republican party in 1912 over the candidate chosen to run for president. Theodore Roosevelt rallied his forces and announced the formation of the Bull Moose Progressive party, leaving the regular Republicans to support William Howard Taft. Although the party was not successful in winning the election for Roosevelt, it did succeed in splitting the Republican vote so that Democrat Woodrow Wilson won.

Among the Democrats, there have been three splinter third parties since the late 1940s: (1) the Dixiecrat (States Rights) party of 1948, (2) Henry Wallace's Progressive party of 1948, and (3) the American Independent party supporting George Wallace in 1968. The strategy employed by Wallace in the 1968 election was to deny Richard Nixon or Hubert Humphrey the necessary majority in the electoral college. Many political scientists believe that Humphrey still would have lost to Nixon in 1968 even if Wallace had not run, because most Wallace voters would probably have given their votes to Nixon. The American Independent party emphasized mostly racial issues, and to a lesser extent, foreign policy. Wallace received 9.9 million popular votes and 46 electoral votes.

Other Minor Parties

Numerous minor parties have coalesced around specific issues or aims. The goal of the Prohibition party, started in 1869, was to ban the sale of liquor. The Free Soil party, active from 1848 to 1852, was dedicated to preventing the spread of slavery.

Some minor parties have had specific economic interests as their reason for being. When those interests are either met or made irrelevant by changing economic conditions, these minor parties disappear. Such was the case with the Greenback party, which lasted from 1876 to 1884. It was one of the most prominent farmer-labor parties that favored government intervention

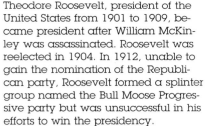

Theodore Roosevelt, president of the United States from 1901 to 1909, became president after William McKinley was assassinated. Roosevelt was reelected in 1904. In 1912, unable to gain the nomination of the Republican party, Roosevelt formed a splinter group named the Bull Moose Progressive party but was unsuccessful in his efforts to win the presidency.

in the economy. Similar to the Greenbacks, but with broader support, was the Populist party, which lasted from about 1892 to 1908. Farmers were the backbone of this party, and agrarian reform was its goal. In 1892, it ran a presidential candidate, James Weaver, who received 1 million popular votes and twenty-two electoral votes. The Populists, for the most part, joined with the Democrats in 1896, when both parties endorsed the Democratic presidential candidate, William Jennings Bryan.

The Impact of Minor Parties

Minor parties clearly have had an impact on American politics. What is more difficult to ascertain is how great that impact has been. Simply by showing that third-party issues were taken over some years later by a major party really does not prove that the third party instigated the major party's change. The case for the importance of minor parties may be strongest for the spin-off parties. These parties do indeed force a major party to reassess its ideology and organization. There is general agreement that Teddy Roosevelt's Progressive party in 1912 and Robert La Follette's Progressive party in 1924 caused the major parties to take up business regulation as one of their major issues.

Minor parties also can have a serious impact on the outcomes of an election. Although Bill Clinton may well have won the 1992 election in any case, the campaign of H. Ross Perot left its imprint on American politics.

In the fall of 1995, Ross Perot, the independent candidate of 1992, announced that he was starting a new political party, the Independence Party, to compete in the 1996 elections. He noted that the party would try to get on the ballots of all fifty states.

FIGURE 8–3 ■

Third-Party Impact on Elections

In eight presidential elections a non–major party's candidate received more than 10 percent of the popular vote—in six of those elections the incumbent party lost. As shown here, only in 1856 and 1924 did the incumbent party manage to hold onto the White House in the face of a significant third-party showing.

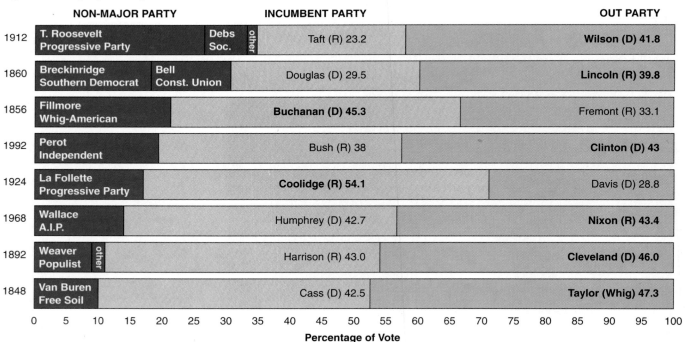

SOURCE: *Congressional Quarterly Weekly Report*, June 13, 1992, p. 1729.

Perot was not the candidate of a third party; rather, he was antiparty, attacking both major political parties for being ineffective and beholden to special interests. Perot had a very strong appeal to young voters, to independent voters, and to disaffected party identifiers.

Perot's share of the votes could have been divided unevenly between Bush and Clinton, thereby changing the outcome of the election. His success followed the pattern of other third parties that have polled enough votes to affect an election. As Figure 8–3 shows, when a third or minor party makes a strong showing, the incumbent party is likely to lose the White House. Counting 1992, this has happened in six out of the eight elections in which third parties were important.

Calling the U.S. system a two-party system is an oversimplification. The nature and names of the major parties have changed over time, and smaller parties almost always have enjoyed a moderate degree of success. Whether they are splinters from the major parties or expressions of social and economic issues not addressed adequately by factions within the major parties, the minor parties attest to the vitality and fluid nature of American politics.

POLITICAL PARTIES: UNFINISHED WORK

Figure 8–4 shows trends in **party identification,** as measured by standard polling techniques from 1937 to 1994. What is evident is the rise of the independent voter combined with a more recent surge of support for the Republican party, so that the traditional Democratic advantage in party identification is relatively small today.

DID YOU KNOW . . .
That New York sent two delegations to the 1848 Democratic convention—the Barnburners and the Hunkers?

PARTY IDENTIFICATION
Linking oneself to a particular political party.

FIGURE 8–4
Party Identification from 1937 to 1994.

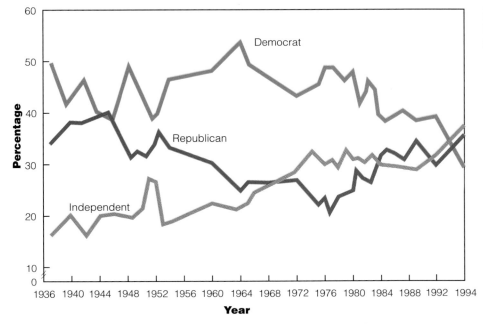

SOURCE: Gallup Organization, as reported in Everett C. Ladd, ed., America at the Polls, 1994 (The Roper Center, 1995), p. 21

TICKET SPLITTING
Voting for candidates of two or more parties for different offices. For example, a voter splits her ticket if she votes for a Republican presidential candidate and for a Democratic congressional candidate.

In the 1940s, only about 20 percent of voters classified themselves as independents. By 1975, this percentage had increased to about 33 percent, and more recent polls show it holding steady at about that level. At times, the Democrats have captured the loyalty of about half the electorate, and the Republicans, until 1960, had more than 30 percent support. By the 1990s, the Democrats could count on less than 40 percent of the electorate and the Republicans, on about 30 percent.

Not only have ties to the two major parties weakened in the last three decades, but voters also are less willing to vote a straight ticket—that is, to vote for all the candidates of one party. The percentage of voters who engage in **ticket splitting** has increased from 12 percent in 1952 to more than 36 percent in the presidential election of 1992. This trend, along with the increase in the number of voters who call themselves independents, suggests that parties have lost much of their hold on the loyalty of the voters.

There is considerable debate over the reasons for the upsurge in independent voters and split tickets. The increased importance of the media in American politics, the higher educational levels of Americans, and the mobility of American voters may all work to weaken party ties. The work of the political parties in the years to come is to reaffirm their importance to the nation and to the voters. To do this, they will need to move beyond slick media campaigns and money raising to answer the voters' true concerns.

GETTING INVOLVED
Electing Convention Delegates

The most exciting political party event, staged every four years, is the national convention. Surprising as it might seem, there are opportunities for you, as a voter, to become involved in nominating delegates to the national convention or to become such a delegate yourself. For both the Republican and Democratic parties, most delegates must be elected at the local level—either the congressional district or the state legislative district. These elections take place at the party primary election or at a neighborhood or precinct caucus level. If the delegates are elected in a primary, persons who want to run for these positions must file petitions with the board of elections in advance of the election. If you are interested in committing yourself to a particular presidential candidate and running for the delegate position, check with the local county committee or with the party's national committee about the rules you must follow.

It is even easier to get involved in the grass-roots politics of presidential caucuses. In some states—Iowa being the earliest and most famous one—delegates are first nominated at the local precinct caucus. According to the rules of the Iowa caucuses, anyone can participate in a caucus if he or she is eighteen years old, a resident of the precinct, and registered as a party member. These caucuses, in addition to being the focus of national media attention in January or February, select delegates to the county conventions who are pledged to specific presidential candidates. This is the first step toward going to the national convention.

At both the county caucus and the convention levels, both parties try to find younger members to fill some of the seats. Contact the state or county political party to find out when the caucuses or primaries will be held. Then gather local supporters and friends, and prepare to join in an occasion during which political persuasion and debate are practiced at their best.

For further information about these opportunities (some states hold caucuses and state conventions in every election year), contact the state party office or your local state legislator for specific dates and regulations. Or write to the national committee for their informational brochures on how to become a delegate.

Republican National Committee
Republican National Headquarters
310 1st St. S.E.
Washington, DC 20003
202-484-6500

Democratic National Committee
Democratic National Headquarters
1625 Massachusetts Ave. N.W.
Washington, DC 20036
202-797-5900

KEY TERMS

CHAPTER SUMMARY

1. A political party is a group of political activists who organize to win elections, operate the government, and determine public policy. Political parties perform a number of functions for the political system. These functions include recruiting candidates for public office, organizing and running elections, presenting alternative policies to the voters, assuming responsibility for operating the government, and acting as the opposition to the party in power.

2. The evolution of our nation's political parties can be divided into six periods: (1) the creation and formation of political parties from 1789 to 1812; (2) the era of one-party rule, or personal politics, from 1816 to 1824; (3) the period from Andrew Jackson's presidency to the Civil War, from 1828 to 1860; (4) the post–Civil War period, from 1864 to 1892, ending with solid control by the modern Republican party; (5) the progressive period, from 1896 to 1928; and (6) the modern period, from 1932 to the present.

3. A political party is composed of the party-in-electorate, the party organization, and the party-in-government. Each party element maintains linkages to the others to keep the party strong. In theory, each of the political parties has a pyramid-shaped organization with a hierarchical command structure. In reality, each level of the party—local, state, and national—has considerable autonomy. The national party organization is responsible for holding the national convention in presidential election years, writing the party platform, choosing the national committee, and conducting party business.

4. Although it may seem that the two major American political parties do not differ substantially on the issues, each has a different core group of supporters. The general shape of the parties' coalitions reflects the party divisions of Franklin Roosevelt's New Deal. It is clear, however, that party leaders are much further apart in their views than are the party followers.

5. The party-in-government comprises all of the elected and appointed officeholders of a party. The linkage of party is crucial to building support for programs among the branches and levels of government.

6. Two major parties have dominated the political landscape in the United States for almost two centuries. The reasons for this include (1) the historical foundations of the system, (2) the self-perpetuation of the parties, (3) the commonality of views among Americans, (4) the winner-take-all electoral system, and (5) state and federal laws favoring the two-party system. Minor parties have emerged from time to time, often as dissatisfied splinter groups from within major parties, and have acted as barometers of changes in political moods. Spin-off parties, or factions, usually have emerged when a particular personality was at odds with the major party, as when Teddy Roosevelt's differences with the Republican party resulted in formation of the Bull Moose Progressive party. Numerous other minor parties, such as the Prohibition party, have formed around single issues.

7. From 1937 until recently, independent voters have formed an increasing proportion of the electorate, with a consequent decline of strongly Democratic or strongly Republican voters. Minor parties have also had a serious impact on the outcome of elections. In 1992, for example, the candidacy of H. Ross Perot drew enough support to affect the outcome of the presidential election.

QUESTIONS FOR REVIEW AND DISCUSSION

1. What are the major incentives that keep the political parties alive? To what extent are these incentives shared by party officials and ordinary citizens who think of themselves as Democrats or Republicans?

2. Why would a third party appeal to today's voters? What would cause party identifiers to turn away from the traditional parties?

3. What are the major issues and concerns that divide voters today? To what extent are these similar to, or different from, the issues that divided parties in the Great Depression or after the Civil War? How should parties change to respond to the issues that face today's voters?

LOGGING ON: POLITICAL PARTIES

If you want to engage in Republican and conservative discussions
and receive messages about them, you can subscribe to

LISTSERV@PCCVM.EDU

and sign up by typing

SUBSCRIBE GOP-L

Another Republican group is

alt.politics.usa.republican

You can access this group through the Internet or by going down
the Michigan state **gopher** to

News & Weather;USENET News;alt;/politics/

to find it.

Discussions from a Democratic party perspective are at

alt.politics.democrats

Go down the Michigan state **gopher** to

News & Weather;USENET News;alt;/politics/

Libertarian perspectives are found at the following:

MAJORDOMO@DARTMOUTH.EDU

Sign up for the magazine LIBERNET by sending a message
that says

libernet-batch-lists

or

libernet-reflect-list

(*Batch* means that you get a message once a day, and *reflect* means
that you receive magazine articles as they are posted.)

 ## SELECTED REFERENCES

Ceaser, James, and Andrew Busch. *Upside Down and Inside Out: The 1992 Elections and American Politics.* Lanham, Md.: Rowman and Littlefeld, 1993. The authors address what they view as a major dimension of American politics that came to the forefront during the 1992 presidential campaign—political outsider versus political insider—and the historic rise of populist sentiment as a prelude to "outsiderism."

Gillespie, J. David. *Politics at the Periphery.* Columbia, S.C.: University of South Carolina Press, 1993. This work provides both a historical review of the roles played by third parties and minor parties in American politics and a look at the impact of H. Ross Perot on party voting in the 1992 election. The volume is a valuable source of data on third-party voting.

Goldman, Ralph M. *The National Party Chairmen and Committees: Factionalism at the Top.* Armonk, N.Y.: M. E. Sharpe, 1990. Goldman traces party leadership from the founding of the United States to the present time and focuses on the management and socialization of conflict.

Keith, Bruce E., *et al. The Myth of the Independent Voter.* Berkeley, Calif.: University of California Press, 1992. The result of extensive survey research, this study examines the implication of the growth of nonpartisanship. The authors contend that most self-declared independents exhibit some degree of partisanship—in fact, often more than do self-declared partisans.

McSweeney, Dean, and John Zvesper. *American Political Parties: The Formation, Decline, and Reform of the American*

Party System. New York: Routledge, 1991. This work discusses in detail the evolution of, and influences on, today's American political party system.

Milkis, Sidney M. *The President and the Parties: The Transformation of the American Party System since the New Deal.* New York: Oxford University Press, 1993. Milkis argues that the original party system worked against the creation of a modern state and that Franklin D. Roosevelt's shift from party to administrative politics displaced parties and precipitated their decline.

Reichley, A. James. *The Life of the Parties: A History of the American Political Parties.* New York: Free Press, 1992. The author presents a history of the political parties in the United States in the context of contemporary concerns about the parties and their functioning in the system. The book examines the differences among the parties and the current issues facing the parties.

Schramm, Peter W., and Bradford P. Wilson, eds. *American Political Parties and Constitutional Politics.* Lanham, Md.: Rowman and Littlefield, 1993. This collection of essays explores the role of political parties in American constitutional government and how the parties' movement away from a focus on the Constitution is contributing to party decline.

Sundquist, James L. *Dynamics of the Party System: Alignment and Realignment of Political Parties in the United States.* Washington, D.C.: Brookings Institute, 1973. Sundquist analyzes three major realignments in party strength, why they happened, and what they meant.

Wattenberg, Martin P. *The Decline of American Political Parties, 1952–1988.* Cambridge Mass.: Harvard University Press, 1989. Wattenberg examines the decline in party identification and the increase in split-ticket voting at the same time that campaigns are becoming more image oriented and media driven. All of these factors contribute to a decline in the strength of parties but not to their complete disappearance.

White, John Kenneth, and Jerome M. Mileur, eds. *Challenges to Party Government.* Carbondale, Ill.: Southern Illinois University Press, 1992. This collection of essays reviews American political parties of the early 1990s and contrasts them with the parties of the 1950s.

9
Campaigns, Elections, and the Media

CHAPTER OUTLINE

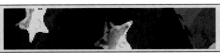

WHAT IF . . .
Voting Were Compulsory?

Casting a ballot is often seen as the prime symbol of a democracy. It is the way we choose our leaders, a source of legitimacy for our government, and a means by which citizens can influence public policy. For most Americans, voting is the only form of political participation they experience. Yet a large number of Americans do not vote. In 1994, only 36 percent of those old enough to vote actually showed up at the polls to elect their representatives and senators. In the 1992 presidential elections, only about half of those eligible actually voted. Voter participation in the United States appears to be much lower than in other democracies, in which 80 to 90 percent of the population goes to the polls on voting day.

In the United States, laws give Americans the right to vote, but they do not make voting a requirement. In some countries, voting is compulsory. What if we had a law making it compulsory for all eligible citizens to vote, perhaps by levying a fine on those who did not? What would the outcome be if *all* eligible U.S. citizens *had* to vote?

The immediate effects might not be that significant. Studies indicate that nonvoters' attitudes are simi-

lar to those of voters, so the results of elections would likely be very much the same. There would be about the same proportion of Democrats, about 4 percent fewer Republicans, and a similar proportion of independent voters. Because nonvoters are usually less interested in politics and lack firm positions on issues, the new voters from that pool probably would not change issue preferences in the electorate. Nonvoters are not distinctly liberal or conservative.

The longer-term consequences are harder to calculate, but they might be more significant. Those who stay away from the polls tend to be the poor, the young, minorities, southerners, and the unemployed. Parties and candidates do not have to make specific appeals to these groups because of their low voter turnout. But if these constituencies were compelled by law to vote, their interests might be given more attention. Perhaps the population would be better represented on the whole. The political influence of younger people—who most often are nonvoters—would likely be enhanced significantly. Younger candidates who are less partisan in appeal could win the younger voters. Policies favoring job opportunities, home ownership, and possibly child care would appeal to this group.

Some argue that the country would be worse off if its least-interested and least-informed citizens voted and that people who consider voting more trouble than it is worth are likely to make poor

choices. Further, it would be unhealthful for a democracy to compel people to vote.

Others say that voting is not only a right but an obligation in a country that claims to have a representative government. Through elections, the people express approval or disapproval of the government's actions, and there would be a stronger sense of the government's legitimacy and of the worthiness of its elected officials if everyone voted. Proponents of compulsory voting would argue that when almost half the population avoids the polls, democracy functions badly.

---

1. How would compulsory voting change the outcomes of national elections?
2. Which groups might be better represented by compulsory voting? Which interests might be poorly served?

THE PEOPLE WHO RUN FOR POLITICAL OFFICE

In the winter of 1992, a fairly unlikely cast of characters competed for the Democratic nomination for the presidency. Senator Tom Harkin of Iowa, Senator Bob Kerrey of Nebraska, Governor Douglas Wilder of Virginia, Governor Bill Clinton of Arkansas, Paul Tsongas (former senator from Massachusetts), and Jerry Brown (former governor of California) tramped the fields of New Hampshire to earn primary votes. Two of these contenders—Jerry Brown and Paul Tsongas—were semiretired politicians. Brown was governor more than a decade ago, and Tsongas had retired from the Senate to fight cancer six years earlier. None of the others had the national recognition or big-state backing to be likely candidates.

What they had, instead, were campaign strategies that sometimes appealed to different groups of voters. (See this chapter's *What If . . .* for a discussion of how such differences could affect the outcomes of elections if voting were compulsory.) Clinton had spent several years in fund raising, making friends throughout the Democratic party, and convincing the press that he was a bright, effective, moderate governor from the New South. Tsongas, the first to announce his candidacy, pursued a strategy of "speaking the truth" about economic issues, which attracted many educated voters. Brown attacked the system as an outsider and promised not to accept large campaign contributions. His constant reminder to voters to call an 800 number to give money to his campaign netted him great publicity, as well as cash. Harkin ran as a left-of-center populist, whereas Kerrey traded on his youth and Vietnam-veteran status. Wilder, a southerner, was the first African-American governor. He also made a moderate pitch.

Of all these campaigns, the most traditional strategy worked best: Clinton's years of making grass-roots contacts, of gaining support in big states, and of building a campaign-financing base in Arkansas, New York, and Washington, D.C., eventually eliminated all of the competitors but Brown, who lasted until the convention.

These volunteer workers are part of United We Stand, the political "non-organization" that supported H. Ross Perot's presidential candidacy in the 1992 elections. Every political candidate has to have an effective campaign organization in order to win. Because Perot was campaigning against the two major parties and "business as usual," he talked in terms of his campaign organization belonging to its workers rather than to him.

In the face of Clinton's winning primary strategy and George Bush's advantage as an incumbent, the real surprise of 1992 was the rise of H. Ross Perot, a Texas businessperson and billionaire, as an undeclared independent candidate. Until he bowed out of the race in July, Perot threatened to turn the presidential race into a three-way contest and amazed political pundits with his broad support. After a hiatus of two months, Perot reentered the presidential race in October 1992.

The question always remains: Why do they do it?

Why They Run

People who choose to run for office can be divided into two groups—those who are "self-starters" and those who are recruited. The volunteers, or self-starters, get involved in political activities to further their careers, to carry out specific political programs, or in response to certain issues or events. The campaign of Senator Eugene McCarthy in 1968 to deny Lyndon Johnson's renomination was rooted in McCarthy's opposition to the Vietnam War. H. Ross Perot's run for the presidency in 1992 was a response to public alienation and discontent with the major parties' candidates.

Issues are important, but self-interest and personal goals—status, career objectives, prestige, and income—are central in motivating some candidates to enter political life. Political scientist Joseph Schlesinger suggests that personal ambition is a major force in politics, as political office is often seen as the stepping stone to achieving certain career goals. A lawyer or an insurance agent may run for office only once or twice and then return to private life with enhanced status. Other politicians may aspire to long-term political office—for example, county offices such as commissioner or sheriff sometimes offer attractive opportunities for power, status, and income and are in themselves career goals. Finally, we think of ambition as the desire for ever-more-important offices and higher status. Politicians who run for lower office and then set their sights on Congress or a governorship may be said to have "progressive" ambitions.[1]

We tend to pay far more attention to the flamboyant politician or to the personal characteristics of those with presidential ambitions than to their "lesser" colleagues. But it is important to note that there are far more opportunities to run for office than there are citizens eager to take advantage of them. To fill the slate of candidates for election to such jobs as mosquito-abatement district commissioner, the political party must recruit individuals to run. The problem of finding candidates is compounded in states or cities where the majority party is so dominant that the minority candidates have virtually no chance of winning. In these situations, candidates are recruited by party leaders on the basis of loyalty to the organization and civic duty.

Who Runs?

There are few constitutional restrictions on who can become a candidate in the United States. As detailed in the Constitution, the formal requirements for a national office are as follows:

---

1. See the discussion in Linda Fowler, *Candidates, Congress, and the American Democracy* (Ann Arbor, Mich.: University of Michigan Press, 1993), pp. 56–59.

1. *President.* Must be a natural-born citizen, have attained the age of thirty-five years, and be a resident of the country for fourteen years by the time of inauguration.

2. *Vice president.* Must be a natural-born citizen, have attained the age of thirty-five years, and not be a resident of the same state as the candidate for president.

3. *Senator.* Must be a citizen for at least nine years, have attained the age of thirty by the time of taking office, and be a resident of the state from which elected.

4. *Representative.* Must be a citizen for at least seven years, have attained the age of twenty-five by the time of taking office, and be a resident of the state from which elected.

The qualifications for state legislators are set by the state constitutions and likewise relate to age, place of residence, and citizenship. (Usually, the requirements for the upper house are somewhat higher than those for the lower house.) The legal qualifications for running for governor or other state office are similar.

In spite of these minimal legal qualifications for office at both the national and state levels, a quick look at the slate of candidates in any election—or at the U.S. House of Representatives—will reveal that not all segments of the population take advantage of these opportunities. Holders of political office in the United States are overwhelmingly white and male. Until this century, politicians were also predominantly of northern European origin and predominantly Protestant. Laws enforcing segregation in the South and many border states, as well as laws that effectively denied voting rights, made it impossible to elect African-American public officials in many areas in which African Americans constituted a significant portion of the population. As a result of the passage of major civil rights legislation in the last several decades, the number of African-American public officials has increased throughout the United States.

Until recently, women generally were considered to be suited only for lower-level offices, such as state legislator or school board member. The last

Dwight D. Eisenhower campaigns for president in 1952. Few presidential candidates would take the time to ride in a parade today.

In 1984, Geraldine Ferraro became the first woman to be nominated for vice president by a major party.

ten years have seen a tremendous increase in the number of women who run for office, not only at the state level but for the U.S. Congress as well. Figure 9–1 shows the increase in female candidates. (In 1994, 170 women ran for Congress, and 52 were elected). Whereas African Americans were restricted from running for office by both law and custom, women generally were excluded by the agencies of recruitment—parties and interest groups—because they were thought to have no chance of winning or because they had not worked their way up through the party organization. Women also had a more difficult time raising campaign funds. Today, it is clear that women are increasingly participating in many political activities, and a majority of Americans say they would vote for a qualified woman or for an African American for president of the United States.

Not only are candidates for office likely to be male and white, but they are also likely to be professionals, particularly lawyers, businesspersons, and teachers. Political campaigning and officeholding are simply easier for some occupational and economic groups than for others, and political involvement can make a valuable contribution to certain careers. Lawyers, for example, have more flexible schedules than do other professionals, can take time off for campaigning, and can leave their jobs to hold public office full time. Furthermore, holding political office is good publicity for their professional practices, and they usually have partners or associates to keep their firms going while they are in office. Perhaps most important, many jobs that lawyers aspire to—federal or state judgeships, state attorney offices, or work in a federal agency—can be attained by political appointment. Such appointments most likely come to loyal partisans who have served their

FIGURE 9–1 ■
Women Running for Congress

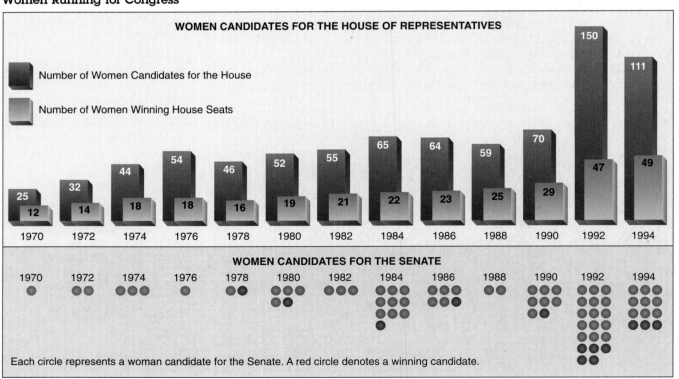

party by running for and holding office. Personal ambitions, then, are well served for certain groups by entering the political arena, whereas it could be a sacrifice for others whose careers demand full-time attention for many years.

THE MODERN CAMPAIGN MACHINE

American political campaigns are extravagant, year-long events that produce campaign buttons and posters for collectors, hours of film and sound to be relayed by the media, and eventually winning candidates who become the public officials of the nation. Political campaigns exhaust candidates, their staff members, and the journalists covering the campaign—to say nothing of the public's patience. Campaigns are also enormously expensive.

The Changing Campaign

Campaigns seem to be getting longer and more excessive each year. The goal of the frantic activity of campaigns is the same for all of them—to convince voters to choose a candidate or a slate of candidates for office. Part of the reason for the increased intensity of campaigns in the last decade is that they have changed from being party centered to being candidate centered. The candidate-centered campaign emerged in response to changes in the electoral system, to the importance of television in campaigns, and to technological innovations such as computers.

To run a successful and persuasive campaign, the candidate's organization must be able to raise funds for the effort, get coverage from the media, produce and pay for political commercials and advertising, schedule the candidate's time effectively with constituent groups and prospective supporters, convey the candidate's position on the issues, conduct research on the opposing candidate, and get the voters to go to the polls. When party identification was stronger among voters and before the advent of television campaigning, a strong party organization on the local, state, or national

These campaign workers have volunteered their time to support the candidate or the party of their choice. Political parties and candidates at all levels would have a difficult time conducting their campaigns without such volunteers. Volunteering for a campaign is one way to participate actively in the political process, to learn more about it, and to take advantage of one's rights as a citizen.

level could furnish most of the services and expertise that the candidate needed. Political parties provided the funds for campaigning until the 1970s. Parties used their precinct organizations to distribute literature, register voters, and get out the vote on election day. Less effort was spent on advertising for a single candidate's positions and character, because the party label communicated that information to many of the voters.

One of the reasons that campaigns no longer depend on parties is that fewer people identify with them (see Chapter 8), as is evident from the increased number of independent voters. In 1952, about 22 percent of the voters were independent voters, whereas in 1994, about 37 percent classified themselves this way. Independent voters include not only those voters who are well educated and issue oriented but also many voters who are not very interested in politics or well informed about candidates or issues. One campaign goal is to give such voters the most information about the political stance of each candidate.

The Professional Campaign

Whether the candidate is running for the state legislature, for the governor's office, for the U.S. Congress, or for the presidency, every campaign has some fundamental tasks to accomplish. What is most striking about today's campaigns is that most of these tasks are now put into the hands of paid professionals rather than volunteers or amateur politicians.

POLITICAL CONSULTANT
A paid professional hired to devise a campaign strategy and manage a campaign. Image building is the crucial task of the political consultant.

Political Consultants.   The most sought-after and possibly the most criticized expert is the **political consultant,** who, for a large fee, devises a campaign strategy, thinks up a campaign theme, and possibly chooses the campaign colors and candidate's portrait for all literature to be distributed. The paid consultant monitors the campaign's progress, plans all media appearances, and coaches the candidate for debates. The consultants and the firms they represent are not politically neutral; most will work only for candidates from one party or only for candidates of a particular ideological persuasion.

Political consultants began to displace volunteer campaign managers in the 1960s, about the same time that television became a force in campaigns. Some of the first "superfirms" of consultants operated in California; Ronald Reagan engaged one of these pioneer firms, Spencer-Roberts, to organize his first campaign for governor of California. Several new generations of political consultants have succeeded these early firms. Today's most sought-after firms include those of Roger Ailes (works for Republicans), Bob Squier (Democrats), Carville and Begala (Democrats), and Bob Teeter (Republicans). Following the 1992 campaign, a documentary film about the Clinton campaign, which featured the president's consultants (James Carville and Paul Begala) and campaign staff, was released under the title *The War Room,* a reference to the center of campaign planning.

Pitfalls with Professional Campaign Managers.   As more and more political campaigns are run exclusively by professional campaign managers, critics of the campaign system are becoming increasingly vociferous. Their worry is this: Professional campaign managers are concerned almost solely with personalities rather than with philosophies and issues. Bob

Squier notes that few candidates know much about the details of the campaign. "It is not to our advantage to explain to them. It is to our advantage to get them to do what we want—what's best for them—with the least amount of fuss."[2] A professional campaign manager is a public relations person. He or she looks at an upcoming election as a contest of personalities rather than as a contest between two opposing parties or opposing principles. According to critics, professional campaign managers are willing to do anything to get their candidate to win, even if this means reshaping the public image of the candidate so that it bears little relation to reality.

Image building is seen to be the crucial task of campaign consultants and is increasingly necessary to a successful campaign. Using public and private opinion polls as guidelines, consultants mold the candidate's image to meet the campaign's special needs. Image building is a far cry from the "ear to the ground" technique used by party leaders in the past to select candidates and platforms. Yet the alternative to such image building is almost certain failure—regardless of the candidate's stand on significant issues.

DID YOU KNOW . . .
That a candidate can buy lists of all the voters in a precinct, county, or state for only about 2 cents per name from a commercial firm?

IMAGE BUILDING
Using public and private opinion polls to mold the candidate's image to meet the particular needs of the campaign. Image building is done primarily through the media.

THE STRATEGY OF WINNING

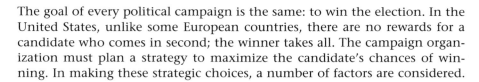

The goal of every political campaign is the same: to win the election. In the United States, unlike some European countries, there are no rewards for a candidate who comes in second; the winner takes all. The campaign organization must plan a strategy to maximize the candidate's chances of winning. In making these strategic choices, a number of factors are considered.

Candidate Visibility and Appeal

One of the most important concerns is how well known the candidate is. If he or she is a highly visible incumbent, there may be little need for campaigning except to remind the voters of the officeholder's good deeds. If, however, the candidate is an unknown challenger or a largely unfamiliar character attacking a well-known public figure, the campaign must devise a strategy to get the candidate before the public.

In the case of the **independent candidate** or the candidate representing a minor party, the problem of name recognition is serious. There are usually a number of **third-party candidates** in each presidential election. (See Chapter 8 for a figure showing the most successful third parties in American history.) Such candidates must present an overwhelming case for the voter to reject the major-party candidate. Both the Democratic and the Republican candidates use the strategic ploy of labeling third-party candidates as "not serious" and therefore not worth the voter's time.

Because neither of the major parties can claim a majority of voters in its camp, the task that faces them is threefold. Each party and its presidential candidate must reinforce the party loyalty of its followers, motivate the undecided or independents to vote for their candidate, and—the most difficult task—try to convince some followers of the other major party to cross party

INDEPENDENT CANDIDATE
A political candidate who is not affiliated with a political party.

THIRD-PARTY CANDIDATE
A political candidate running under the banner of a party other than the two major political parties.

2. As quoted in Frank I. Luntz, *Candidates, Consultants and Campaigns* (New York: B. Blackwell, 1988), p. 57.

Candidates Bill Clinton and Al Gore reuse an old campaign tactic. Instead of using a train to reach small towns, the Democratic team campaigned through small towns and rural areas on a bus. Part of the strategy was to create strong visual images for the rest of the nation to watch on television.

lines. The Republicans, who historically have had fewer adherents than the Democrats, spend more time and money trying to attract independents and Democrats, whereas the Democrats know that they can win normally if they can secure all of the votes of their party plus a significant share of the independents. To accomplish these tasks, the campaign organization, whether at the presidential level or otherwise, plans a mix of strategies—including televised campaign appearances, debates, and position papers—to sway the voters.

The Use of Opinion Polls

Because the decision-making power for presidential nominations has shifted from the elites to the masses, one of the major sources of information for both the media and the candidates is polls. Poll taking is widespread during the primaries. Often, presidential hopefuls will have private polls taken to make sure that there is at least some chance they could be nominated and, if nominated, elected. Also, because the party nominees depend on polls to fine-tune their campaigns, during the presidential campaign itself continual polls are taken. Polls are taken not only by the regular pollsters—Roper, Harris, Gallup, and others—but also privately by each candidate's campaign organization. These private polls, as opposed to the independent public polls conducted by Gallup and others, are for the exclusive and secret use of the candidate and his or her campaign organization.

By polling the potential voters in the state or nation, the candidate can find out his or her strengths and weaknesses and attempt to address problem areas through campaign advertising. As the election approaches, many candidates use **tracking polls**, which are polls taken almost every day, to find out how well they are competing for votes. Tracking polls, by indicating

TRACKING POLL
A poll taken for the candidate on a nearly daily basis as election day approaches.

The purpose of signs like these is to increase name recognition, yet it is doubtful that any one name will be recognized when signs proliferate in number and crowd together as they do here.

how well the campaign is going, enable consultants to fine-tune the advertising and the candidate's speeches in the last days of the campaign.

WHERE DOES THE MONEY COME FROM?

In a book published in 1932 entitled *Money in Elections*, Louise Overacker had the following to say about campaign financing:

> The financing of elections in a democracy is a problem which is arousing increasing concern. Many are beginning to wonder if present-day methods of raising and spending campaign funds do not clog the wheels of our elaborately constructed mechanism of popular control, and if democracies do not inevitably become plutocracies.[3]

Although writing more than sixty years ago, Overacker touched on a sensitive issue in American political campaigns: the connection between money and elections. It is estimated that over $1.75 billion was spent at all levels of campaigning in 1992. At the federal level, a total of more than $248 million is estimated to have been spent in races for the House of Representatives, $180 million in senatorial races, and $220 million in the presidential campaign. In the 1994 congressional races, candidates spent $724 million—breaking the record established in the 1992 election cycle. Except for the presidential campaign in the general election, all of the other money had to be provided by the candidates and their families, borrowed, or raised by other means. For the general presidential campaign, most of the money comes from the federal government.

---

3. Louise Overacker, *Money in Elections* (New York: Macmillan, 1932), p. vii.

Regulating Campaign Financing

CORRUPT PRACTICES ACTS
A series of acts passed by Congress in an attempt to limit and regulate the size and sources of contributions and expenditures in political campaigns.

HATCH ACT
An act passed in 1939 that prohibited a political committee from spending more than $3 million in any campaign and limited individual contributions to a committee to $5,000. The act was designed to control political influence buying.

There have been a variety of federal **corrupt practices acts** designed to regulate campaign financing. The first, passed in 1925, limited primary and general election expenses for congressional candidates. In addition, it required disclosure of election expenses and, in principle, put controls on contributions by corporations. Numerous loopholes were found in the restrictions on contributions, and the acts proved to be ineffective.

The **Hatch Act** (Political Activities Act) of 1939 was passed in another attempt to control political influence buying. That act forbade a political committee to spend more than $3 million in any campaign and limited individual contributions to a committee to $5,000. Of course, such restrictions were easily circumvented by creating additional committees.

The Federal Election Campaign Acts of 1972 and 1974

It was not until the 1970s that more effective regulation of campaign financing was undertaken. The Federal Election Campaign Act of 1972 essentially replaced all past laws and instituted a major reform. The act placed no limit on overall spending but restricted the amount that could be spent on mass-media advertising, including television. It limited the amount that candidates and their families could contribute to their own campaigns and required disclosure of all contributions and expenditures in excess of $100. In principle, the 1972 act limited the role of labor unions and corporations in political campaigns. It also provided for a voluntary $1 check-off on federal income tax returns for general campaign funds to be used by major-party presidential candidates (first applied in the 1976 campaign).

But the act still did not go far enough. In 1974, Congress passed another Federal Election Campaign Act. It did the following:

1. *Created the Federal Election Commission.* This commission consists of six nonpartisan administrators whose duties are to enforce compliance with the requirements of the act.
2. *Provided public financing for presidential primaries and general elections.* Any candidate running for president who is able to obtain sufficient contributions in at least twenty states can obtain a subsidy from the U.S. Treasury to help pay for primary campaigns. Each major party was given $11 million for the national convention in 1992. The major party candidates have federal support for almost all of their expenses, provided they are willing to accept campaign-spending limits.
3. *Limited presidential campaign spending.* Any candidate accepting federal support has to agree to limit campaign expenditures to the amount prescribed by federal law.
4. *Limited contributions.* Citizens can contribute up to $1,000 to each candidate in each federal election or primary; the total limit of all contributions from an individual is $25,000 per year. Groups can contribute up to a maximum of $5,000 to a candidate in any election.
5. *Required disclosure.* Periodic reports must be filed by each candidate with the Federal Election Commission, listing who contributed, how much was spent, and for what the money was spent.

The 1972 act limited the amount that each individual could spend on his or her own behalf. Senator Jim Buckley of New York challenged that aspect of the law, and the Supreme Court declared the provision unconstitutional in 1976.[4]

The 1974 act, as modified by certain amendments in 1976, allows corporations, labor unions, and special interest groups to set up PACs to raise money for candidates. For a PAC to be legitimate, the money must be raised from at least fifty volunteer donors and must be given to at least five candidates in the federal election. Each corporation or each union is limited to one PAC. As you might imagine, corporate PACs obtain funds from executives, employees, and stockholders in their firms, and unions obtain PAC funds from their members.[5] (See Chapter 7 for more details on PAC activities.)

On March 27, 1990, in the case of *Austin v. Michigan State Chamber of Commerce,* the United States Supreme Court ruled six to three that the federal and state governments have the power to restrict the involvement of business corporations in political campaigns.[6] The Court did so by barring corporations from spending general corporate funds on a candidate's behalf, such as newspaper advertisements. Corporations were left free to make political contributions through their PACs. At the time of the Court's action, both federal law and the laws of twenty-one states contained the limitation on corporate political spending.

RUNNING FOR PRESIDENT: THE LONGEST CAMPAIGN

The American presidential election is the culmination of two different campaigns linked by the parties' national conventions. The **presidential primary** campaign lasts officially from January until June of the election year, and the final presidential campaign heats up around Labor Day.

Primary elections were first mandated in 1903 in Wisconsin. The purpose of the primary was to open the nomination process to ordinary party members and to weaken the influence of party bosses in the nomination process. Until 1968, however, there were fewer than twenty primary elections for the presidency. They were generally **"beauty contests"** in which the contending candidates for the nomination competed for popular votes, but the results had little or no impact on the selection of delegates to the national convention. National conventions were meetings of the party elite—legislators, mayors, county chairpersons, and loyal party workers—who were mostly appointed to their delegations. These party faithfuls frequently voted as a bloc under the direction of their leaders. Chicago's Mayor Richard J. Daley was famous for the control he exercised over the Illinois delegation to the Democratic convention. National conventions saw numerous trades and bargains among competing candidates and the leaders of large blocs of delegate votes.

---

4. *Buckley v. Valeo,* 424 U.S. 1 (1976).
5. See Anthony Corrado, *Creative Campaigning: PACs and the Presidential Selection Process* (Boulder Colo.: Westview Press, 1992) for a discussion of how PACs influence early efforts in presidential campaigns.
6. 494 U.S. 652 (1990).

PRESIDENTIAL PRIMARY
A statewide primary election of delegates to a political party's national convention to help a party determine its presidential nominee. Such delegates are either pledged to a particular candidate or unpledged.

"BEAUTY CONTEST"
A presidential primary in which contending candidates compete for popular votes but the results have little or no impact on the selection of delegates to the national convention, which is made by the party elite.

Riots outside the 1968 Democratic convention in Chicago. The riots influenced the party to reform its delegate selection rules.

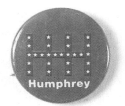

SUPERDELEGATE
A party leader or elected official who is given the right to vote at the party's national convention. Superdelegates are not elected at the state level.

Reforming the Primaries

In recent years, the character of the primary process and the make-up of the national convention have changed dramatically. The mass public, rather than party elites, now controls the nomination process, owing to extraordinary changes in the party rules. After the massive riots outside the doors of the 1968 Democratic convention in Chicago, many party leaders pushed for serious reforms of the convention process. They saw the general dissatisfaction with the convention, and the riots in particular, as stemming from the inability of the average party member to influence the nomination system.

The reforms instituted by the Democratic party, which were imitated in most states by the Republicans, revolutionized the nomination process for the presidency. The most important changes require that convention delegates not be nominated by the elites in either party; they must be elected by the voters in primary elections, in caucuses held by local parties, or at state conventions. Delegates are mostly pledged to a particular candidate, although the pledge is not formally binding at the convention. The delegation from each state must also include a proportion of women, younger party members, and representatives of the minority groups within the party. At first, virtually no special privileges were given to elected party officials, such as senators or governors. In 1984, however, many of these officials returned to the Democratic convention as **superdelegates.**

Primaries: Criticisms and Alternatives

Some political scientists believe presidential primaries perform several useful functions. First, it is through primaries that a relatively unknown candidate can get his or her "bandwagon" going. Primaries also provide an opportu-

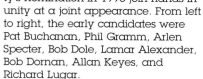

Republican candidates for their party's nomination in 1996 join hands in unity at a joint appearance. From left to right, the early candidates were Pat Buchanan, Phil Gramm, Arlen Specter, Bob Dole, Lamar Alexander, Bob Dornan, Allan Keyes, and Richard Lugar.

nity for candidates to organize their campaigns and to try out different issue positions before the public. The long primary season, stretching from February until mid-June, can even be regarded as an endurance test, in which the voters can see how candidates stand up under stress. Finally, the primaries may put pressure on an incumbent to change his or her policy. Lyndon B. Johnson decided not to run for the presidency again after the 1968 New Hampshire primary showed that he was losing party support.

Critics of the system argue that the primaries drag out the presidential elections to such a length that by the time they are over, the public is tired of the whole business. The result is that people may take less interest in the general election.

The states that do not have presidential primaries use the **caucus** to choose convention delegates. The caucus was originally a secret meeting of party leaders for the purpose of nominating the party's candidates. In the early years of this century, the caucus was frequently referred to as "the smoke-filled room." Caucuses are still used by local parties in many states and counties to determine which candidates will be endorsed by the party in primary elections. For the presidential nominating process, caucuses can be used to nominate the delegates to the national convention or to county and state conventions at which the official delegates will be chosen. In the latter case, the caucus must be open to all members of the political party who live within a specified geographic area—which may be a precinct, a legislative district, or a county. These neighbors gather, discuss presidential candidates, decide who the delegates will be, and determine whether the delegates will be pledged to one or more presidential candidates. Some critics of the primary system feel that the caucus is a better way of finding out how loyal party workers feel about the candidates and that its more widespread use would lead to stronger political parties.

CAUCUS
A closed meeting of party leaders to select party candidates or to decide on policy; also, a meeting of party members designed to select candidates and propose policies.

Types of Primaries

The two most common types of primaries are the *closed primary* and the *open primary*. In addition, there are the *blanket primary* and the *run-off primary*.

Closed Primary.   In a **closed primary**, the selection of a party's candidates in an election is limited to avowed or declared party members. In other words, voters must declare their party affiliation, either when they register or at the primary election. A closed-primary system makes sure that registered voters cannot cross over into the other party's primary in order to nominate the weakest candidate of the opposing party or to affect the ideological direction of that party.

Open Primary.   An **open primary** is a primary in which voters can vote in either party primary without disclosing their party affiliation. Basically, the voter makes the choice in the privacy of the voting booth. The voter must, however, choose one party's list from which to select candidates. Open primaries place no restrictions on independent voters. Few states use such a system.

Blanket Primary.   A **blanket primary** is one in which the voter may vote for candidates of more than one party. Alaska, Louisiana, and Washington all have blanket primaries.

Run-off Primary.   Some states have a two-primary system. If no candidate receives a majority of the votes in the first primary, the top two candidates must compete in another primary, called a **run-off primary.**

On to the National Convention

Presidential candidates have been nominated by the convention method in every election since 1832. The delegates are sent from each state and are apportioned on the basis of state representation. Extra delegates are allowed to attend from states that had voting majorities for the party in the preced-

CLOSED PRIMARY
The most widely used primary, in which voters may participate only in the primary of the party with which they are registered.

OPEN PRIMARY
A direct primary in which voters may cast ballots in the primary of either party without having to declare their party registration. Once voters choose which party primary they will vote in, they must select among only the candidates of that party.

BLANKET PRIMARY
A primary in which all candidates' names are printed on the same ballot, regardless of party affiliation. The voter may vote for candidates of more than one party.

RUN-OFF PRIMARY
An election that is held to nominate candidates within the party if no candidate receives a majority of the votes in the first primary election.

Party members hold a caucus in a firehouse to choose delegates. It takes considerable confidence to speak up for less popular candidates in a caucus situation.

ing elections. Parties also accept delegates from the District of Columbia, the territories, and certain overseas groups.

At the convention, each political party uses a **credentials committee** to determine which delegates may participate. The credentials committee usually prepares a roll of all delegates entitled to be seated. Controversy arises when rival groups claim to be the official party organization for a county, district, or state. At that point, the credentials committee will make a recommendation, which is usually approved by the convention without debate or even a roll call. On occasion, conventions have rejected recommendations of the credentials committee, and in some cases that decision has been a decisive factor in the selection of the presidential nominee.

The goal of any presidential hopeful at the national convention is to obtain a majority of votes on the earliest ballot. Because delegates generally arrive at the convention committed to presidential candidates, no convention since 1952 has required more than one ballot to choose a nominee. This surprising result is accomplished by a lengthy single ballot during which delegations shift and realign so that the appearance, if not the actuality, of unity may be conveyed to the TV audience. Since 1972, candidates have usually come into the convention with enough committed delegates to win.

There is no federal regulation of conventions. Each party makes its own rules and policies as it sees fit. The typical convention lasts only a few days. The first day consists of speech making, usually against the opposing party. During the second day, there are committee reports, and during the third day, there is presidential balloting. On the fourth day, a vice presidential candidate is usually nominated, and the presidential nominee gives the acceptance speech.

These citizens are voting in the New Hampshire primary, which has a strong influence on the presidential campaign because it is the first primary.

THE ELECTORAL COLLEGE

Most voters who vote for the president and vice president think that they are voting directly for a candidate. In actuality, they are voting for a slate of **electors** who will cast their ballots in the **electoral college**. Article II, Section 1, of the Constitution outlines in detail the number and choice of electors for president and vice president. The framers of the Constitution wanted to avoid the selection of president and vice president by the excitable masses. Rather, they wished the choice to be made by a few supposedly dispassionate, reasonable men (but not women).

The Choice of Electors

Each state's electors are selected during each presidential election year. The selection is governed by state laws and by the applicable party apparatus (see Table 9–1). After the national party convention, the electors are pledged to the candidates chosen. The total number of electors today is 538, equal to 100 senators, 435 members of the House, plus 3 electors for the District of Columbia (subsequent to the Twenty-third Amendment, ratified in 1961). Each state's number of electors equals that state's number of senators (two) plus its number of representatives.

CREDENTIALS COMMITTEE
A committee used by political parties at their national conventions to determine which delegates may participate. The committee inspects the claim of each prospective delegate to be seated as a legitimate representative of his or her state.

ELECTOR
A person on the partisan slate that is selected early in the presidential election year according to state laws and the applicable political party apparatus. Electors cast ballots for president and vice president. The number of electors in each state is equal to that state's number of representatives in both houses of Congress.

ELECTORAL COLLEGE
The constitutionally required method for the selection of the president and the vice president. To be elected president or vice president, a candidate must have a majority of the electoral votes (currently, 270 out of 538).

The Electors' Commitment

PLURALITY
The total votes cast for a candidate who receives more votes than any other candidate but not necessarily a majority. Most national, state, and local electoral laws provide for winning elections by a plurality vote.

If a **plurality** of voters in a state chooses one slate of electors, then those electors are pledged to cast their ballots on the first Monday after the second Wednesday in December in the state capital for the presidential and vice presidential candidates for the winning party.[7] The Constitution does not, however, require the electors to cast their ballots for the candidate of their party.

The ballots are counted and certified before a joint session of Congress early in January. The candidates who receive a majority of the electoral votes (270) are certified as president-elect and vice president–elect. According to

7. In Maine and Nebraska, electoral votes are based on congressional districts. Each district chooses one elector. The remaining two electors are chosen statewide.

TABLE 9–1

How Electors Are Selected

BY STATE POLITICAL PARTY CONVENTION	BY POLITICAL PARTY'S CENTRAL COMMITTEE	BY POLITICAL PARTY
Alabama	California	Arizona
Alaska	District of Columbia	Maryland
Arkansas	Florida	
Colorado	Louisiana	
Connecticut	Massachusetts	
Delaware	Missouri	
Georgia	Montana	
Hawaii	New Jersey	
Idaho	New York	
Illinois	Pennsylvania	
Indiana	South Carolina	
Iowa	Tennessee	
Kansas		
Kentucky		
Maine		
Michigan		
Minnesota		
Mississippi		
Nebraska		
Nevada		
New Hampshire		
New Mexico		
North Carolina		
North Dakota		
Ohio		
Oklahoma		
Oregon		
Rhode Island		
South Dakota		
Texas		
Utah		
Vermont		
Virginia		
Washington		
West Virginia		
Wisconsin		
Wyoming		

SOURCE: Michael J. Glennon, *When No Majority Rules: The Electoral College and Presidential Succession* (Washington, D.C.: Congressional Quarterly, 1992), p. 24.

the Constitution, in cases in which no candidate receives a majority of the electoral vote, the election of the president is decided in the House from among the three candidates with the highest number of votes (decided by a plurality of each state delegation, each state having one vote). The selection of the vice president is determined by the Senate in a choice between the two highest candidates, each senator having one vote. Congress was required to choose the president and vice president in 1801 (Thomas Jefferson and Aaron Burr), and the House chose the president in 1825 (John Quincy Adams). The entire process is outlined in Figure 9–2.

It is possible for a candidate to become president without obtaining a majority of the popular vote. There have been numerous minority presidents in our history, including Abraham Lincoln, Woodrow Wilson, Harry S Truman, John F. Kennedy, Richard Nixon (in 1968), and Bill Clinton. Such an event can always occur when there are third-party candidates.

Perhaps more distressing is the possibility of a candidate's being elected when the candidate's major opposition receives a larger popular vote. This occurred on three occasions—in the elections of John Quincy Adams in 1824, Rutherford B. Hayes in 1876, and Benjamin Harrison in 1888, all of whom won elections without obtaining a plurality of the popular vote.

FIGURE 9–2

How Presidents and Vice Presidents Are Chosen

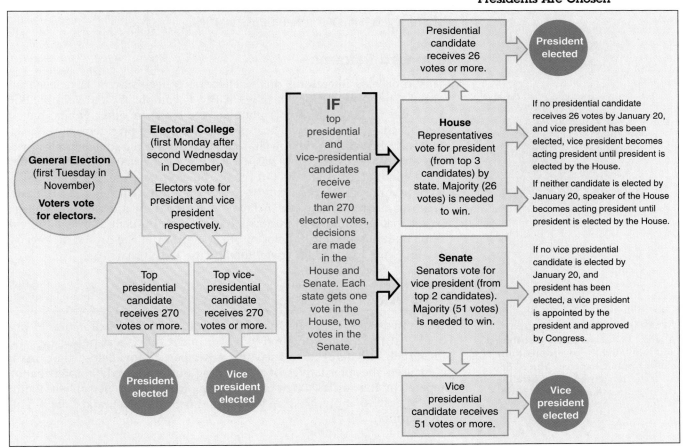

SOURCE: Adapted from Michael J. Glennon, *When No Majority Rules: The Electoral College and Presidential Succession* (Washington, D.C.: Congressional Quarterly, 1992), p. 20.

Criticisms of the Electoral College

Besides the possibility of a candidate's becoming president even though his or her major opponent obtains more popular votes, there are other complaints about the electoral college. The idea of the Constitution's framers was to have electors use their own discretion to decide who would make the best president. But electors no longer perform the selecting function envisioned by the founders, because they are committed to the candidate who has a plurality of popular votes in their state in the general election.[8]

One can also argue that the current system, which gives all of the electoral votes to the candidate who has a statewide plurality, is unfair to other candidates and their supporters. The unit system of voting also means that presidential campaigning will be concentrated in those states that have the largest number of electoral votes and in those states in which the outcome is likely to be close. All of the other states generally get second-class treatment during the presidential campaign.

It can also be argued that there is something of a less-populous-state bias in the electoral college, because including Senate seats in the electoral vote total partly offsets the edge of the more populous states in the House. A state such as Alaska (with two senators and one representative) gets an electoral vote for roughly each 183,000 people (based on the 1990 census), whereas Iowa gets one vote for each 397,000 people, and New York has a vote for every 545,000 inhabitants.

Proposed Reforms

Many proposals for reform of the electoral college system have been advanced. The most obvious is to get rid of it completely and simply allow candidates to be elected on a popular-vote basis; in other words, have a direct election, by the people, for president and vice president.

A less radical reform is a federal law that would require each elector to vote for the candidate who has a plurality in the state. Another system would eliminate the electors but retain the electoral vote, which would be given on a proportional basis rather than on a unit (winner-take-all) basis.

The major parties are not in favor of eliminating the electoral college, fearing that it would give minor parties a more influential role. Also, less populous states are not in favor of direct election of the president, because they feel they would be overwhelmed by the large urban vote.

AUSTRALIAN BALLOT
A secret ballot prepared, distributed, and tabulated by government officials at public expense. Since 1888, all states have used the Australian ballot rather than an open, public ballot.

HOW ARE ELECTIONS CONDUCTED?

The United States uses the **Australian ballot**—a secret ballot that is prepared, distributed, and counted by government officials at public expense. Since 1888, all states have used the Australian ballot. Before that, many states used the alternatives of oral voting and differently colored ballots prepared by the parties. Obviously, knowing which way a person was voting made it easy to apply pressure to change his or her vote, and vote buying was common.

---

8. Note, however, that there have been revolts by so-called *faithless electors*—in 1796, 1820, 1948, 1956, 1960, 1968, 1972, 1976, and 1988.

Office-Block and Party-Column Ballots

There are two types of ballots in use in the United States in general elections. The first, called an **office-block ballot,** or sometimes called a **Massachusetts ballot,** groups all the candidates for each elective office under the title of each office. Politicians dislike the office-block ballot, because it places more emphasis on the office than on the party; it discourages straight-ticket voting and encourages split-ticket voting.

A **party-column ballot** is a form of general election ballot in which the candidates are arranged in one column under their respective party labels and symbols. It is also called the **Indiana ballot.** In some states, it allows voters to vote for all of a party's candidates for local, state, and national offices by simply marking a single "X" or by pulling a single lever. Most states use this type of ballot. As it encourages straight-ticket voting, majority parties favor this form. When a party has an exceptionally strong presidential or gubernatorial candidate to head the ticket, the **coattail effect** is increased by the party-column ballot.

Counting the Votes and Avoiding Fraud

State and local election officials tabulate the results of each election after the polls are closed. Although most votes are tallied electronically, there is still the possibility of voting fraud. To minimize this possibility, the use of

OFFICE-BLOCK, OR MASSACHUSETTS, BALLOT
A form of general election ballot in which candidates for elective office are grouped together under the title of each office. It emphasizes voting for the office and the individual, rather than for the party.

PARTY-COLUMN, OR INDIANA, BALLOT
A form of general election ballot in which candidates for elective office are arranged in one column under their respective party labels and symbols. It emphasizes voting for the party, rather than for the office or individual.

COATTAIL EFFECT
The influence of a popular or unpopular candidate on the electoral success or failure of other candidates on the same party ticket. The effect is increased by the party-column ballot, which encourages straight-ticket voting.

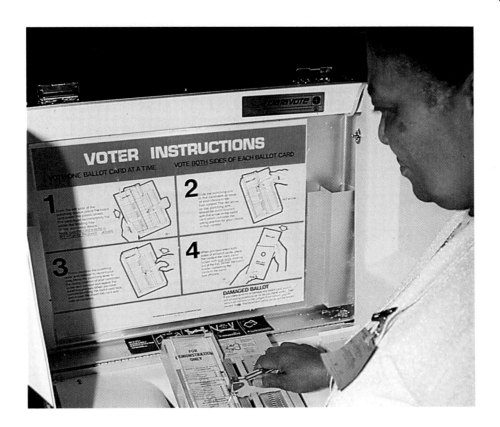

CANVASSING BOARD
An official group at the city, county, or state level that receives vote counts from every precinct in the area, tabulates the figures, and sends them to the state canvassing authority, which certifies the winners.

POLL WATCHER
An individual appointed by a political party to scrutinize the voting process on election day. Usually, there are two poll watchers at every voting place, representing the Democratic and the Republican parties, both attempting to ensure the honesty of the election.

CHALLENGE
An allegation by a poll watcher that a potential voter is unqualified to vote or that a vote is invalid; designed to prevent fraud in elections.

VOTER TURNOUT
The percentage of citizens taking part in the election process; the number of eligible voters that actually "turn out" on election day to cast their ballots.

canvassing boards is common. A **canvassing board** is an official body that tabulates and consolidates the returns and forwards them to the state canvassing authority. The authority will usually certify the election of the winners within a few days.

To avoid fraud at the polling places themselves, each party may appoint **poll watchers** to monitor elections. In virtually all polling places throughout the country during partisan elections, major parties have their own poll watchers. Poll watching is particularly important when there is a challenge to an entrenched, local political machine. At any time, a poll watcher may make a **challenge**, which is an allegation either that a potential voter is unqualified or that his or her vote is invalid. Once a challenge is made, a bipartisan group of election judges in each precinct will decide on the merits of the challenge.

VOTING IN NATIONAL, STATE, AND LOCAL ELECTIONS

In 1992, there were 189 million eligible voters. Of that number, 132 million, or 70 percent, actually registered to vote in the general presidential election. Of those who registered, 101 million actually went to the polls. The participation rate during the 1992 presidential election was only 76 percent of registered voters and 55 percent of eligible voters (see Table 9–2).

Figure 9–3 shows that the **voter turnout** in the United States compared with that of other countries places Americans in the bottom 20 percent. Figure 9–4 shows voter turnout for presidential and congressional elections from 1896 to 1994. The last "good" year of turnout for the presidential elections was 1960, when almost 65 percent of the eligible voters actually voted. Each of the peaks in the figure represents voter turnout in a presidential election. Thus, we can also see that voting for U.S. representativesis greatly influenced by whether there is a presidential election in thesame year.

The same is true at the state level. When there is a race for governor, more voters participate both in the general election for governor and in the elec-

Election judges check the registration of each voter before giving out the ballot. Most local election boards require judges from both political parties at each precinct.

That in 1962, Representative Clem Miller, a California Democrat, was reelected to his congressional seat over challenger Don Clausen despite the fact that Miller had died more than a month earlier in a plane crash?

TABLE 9–2

Elected by a Majority?

Most presidents have won a majority of the votes cast in the election. We generally judge the extent of their victory by whether they have won more than 51 percent of the votes. Some presidential elections have been proclaimed *landslides*, meaning that the candidates won by an extraordinary majority of votes cast. As indicated below, however, no modern president has been elected by more than 38 percent of the total voting-age electorate.

YEAR—WINNER (PARTY)	PERCENTAGE OF TOTAL POPULAR VOTE	PERCENTAGE OF VOTING-AGE POPULATION
1932—Roosevelt (D)	57.4	30.1
1936—Roosevelt (D)	60.8	34.6
1940—Roosevelt (D)	54.7	32.2
1944—Roosevelt (D)	53.4	29.9
1948—Truman (D)	49.6	25.3
1952—Eisenhower (R)	55.1	34.0
1956—Eisenhower (R)	57.4	34.1
1960—Kennedy (D)	49.7	31.2
1964—Johnson (D)	61.1	37.8
1968—Nixon (R)	43.4	26.4
1972—Nixon (R)	60.7	33.5
1976—Carter (D)	50.1	26.8
1980—Reagan (R)	50.7	26.7
1984—Reagan (R)	58.8	31.2
1988—Bush (R)	53.4	26.8
1992—Clinton (D)	43.3	23.1

SOURCE: *Congressional Quarterly Weekly Report*, January 31, 1989, p. 137; and *New York Times*, November 5, 1992.

tion for state representatives. Voter participation rates in gubernatorial elections are also greater in presidential election years. The average turnout in state elections is about 14 percentage points higher when a presidential election is held.

Now consider local elections. In races for mayor, city council, county auditor, and the like, it is fairly common for only 25 percent or less of the electorate to vote. Is something amiss here? It would seem obvious that

FIGURE 9–3

Voter Turnout in the United States Compared with Other Countries in Elections during the 1980s

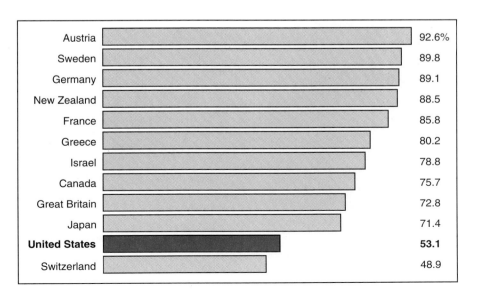

Austria	92.6%
Sweden	89.8
Germany	89.1
New Zealand	88.5
France	85.8
Greece	80.2
Israel	78.8
Canada	75.7
Great Britain	72.8
Japan	71.4
United States	**53.1**
Switzerland	48.9

people would be more likely to vote in elections that directly affect them. At the local level, each person's vote counts more (because there are fewer voters). Furthermore, the issues—crime control, school bonds, sewer bonds, and so on—touch on the immediate interests of the voters. The facts, however, do not fit the theory. Potential voters are most interested in national elections, when a presidential choice is involved. Otherwise, voter participation in our representative government is very low (and, as we have seen, it is not overwhelmingly great even at the presidential level).

The Effect of Low Voter Turnout

There are two schools of thought concerning low voter turnout. Some view the decline in voter participation as a clear threat to our representative democratic government. Fewer and fewer individuals are deciding who wields political power in our society. Also, low voter participation presumably signals apathy about our political system in general. It also may signal that potential voters simply do not want to take the time to learn about the issues. When only a handful of people do take the time, it will be easier, say the alarmists, for an authoritarian figure to take over our government.

Others are less concerned about low voter participation. They believe that a decline in voter participation simply indicates more satisfaction with the status quo. Also, they believe that representative democracy is a reality even if a very small percentage of eligible voters vote. If everyone who does not vote believes that the outcome of the election will accord with his or her own desires, then representative democracy is working. The nonvoters are obtaining the type of government—with the type of people running it—that they want to have anyway.

FIGURE 9–4

Voter Turnout for Presidential and Congressional Elections, 1896 to 1994

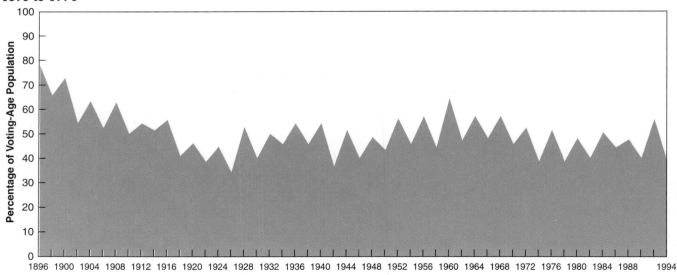

SOURCE: Historical Data Archive, Inter-university Consortium for political and social research: U.S. Department of Commerce, *Statistical Abstract of the United States: 1980,* 101st ed. (Washington, D.C.: U.S. Government Printing Office, 1980), p. 515; William H. Flanigan and Nancy H. Zingale, *Political Behavior of the American Electorate,* 5th ed. (Boston: Allyn and Bacon, 1983), p. 20; and *Congressional Quarterly,* various issues.

Factors Influencing Who Votes

A clear association exists between voter participation and the following characteristics: age, educational attainment, minority status, income level, and the existence of two-party competition.

1. *Age.* Look at Table 9–3, which shows the breakdown of voter participation by age group for the 1992 presidential election. It would appear from these figures that age is a strong factor in determining voter turnout on election day. The reported turnout increases with older age groups. Greater participation with age is very likely due to the fact that older voters are more settled in their lives, are already registered, and have had more time to experience voting as an expected activity.

2. *Educational attainment.* Education also influences voter turnout. In general, the more education you have, the more likely you are to vote. This pattern is clearly evident in the 1992 election results, as we can see in Table 9–4. Reported turnout was over 30 percentage points higher for those who had some college education than it was for people who had never been to high school.

3. *Minority status.* Race is important, too, in determining the level of voter turnout. Whites in 1992 voted at a 59 percent rate, whereas the African-American turnout rate was 51.5 percent.

4. *Income levels.* Differences in income can also lead to differences in voter turnout. Wealthier people tend to be overrepresented in the electorate. In 1992, turnout among whites varied from less than 40 percent of those with annual family incomes under $15,000 to about 70 percent for people with annual family incomes of $50,000 or more.

5. *Two-party competition.* Another factor in voter turnout is the extent to which elections are competitive within a state. More competitive states generally have higher turnout rates, although the highest average percentage turnout for the past two decades has been in states in which Republicans were elected to most state offices.

TABLE 9–3

Voting in the 1992 Presidential Election by Age Group (in Percentages)

AGE	REPORTED TURNOUT
18–20	38.5
21–24	45.7
25–34	53.2
35–44	63.6
45–64	70.0
65 and over	70.1

SOURCE: U.S. Department of Commerce, *Statistical Abstract of the United States: 1995* (Washington, D.C.: U.S. Government Printing Office, 1995).

TABLE 9–4

Voting in the 1992 Presidential Election by Education Level (in Percentages)

YEARS OF SCHOOL COMPLETED	REPORTED TURNOUT
8 years or less	35.1
9–11 years	42.2
12 years	57.5
1–3 years of college	68.7
4+ years of college	81.0

SOURCE: U.S. Department of Commerce, *Statistical Abstract of the United States: 1995* (Washington, D.C.: U.S. Government Printing Office, 1995).

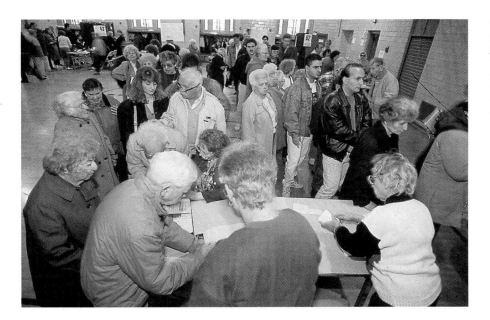

These residents of New York are voting in the 1992 presidential elections. The long lines seemed to indicate a high turnout. Indeed, voter turnout rates during presidential election years are consistently much higher than voter turnout rates during off years.

The foregoing statistics reinforce one another. White voters are likely to be wealthier than African-American voters, who are also less likely to have obtained a college education.

LEGAL RESTRICTIONS ON VOTING

Legal restrictions on voter registration have existed since the founding of the nation. Most groups in the United States have been concerned with the suffrage issue at one time or another.

Historical Restrictions

In colonial times, only white males who owned property with a certain minimum value were eligible to vote, leaving a far greater number of Americans ineligible than eligible to take part in the democratic process. Because many government functions are in the economic sphere and concern property rights and the distribution of income and wealth, some of the founders of our nation felt it was appropriate that only people who had an interest in property should vote on these issues. The idea of extending the vote to all citizens was, according to South Carolina delegate Charles Pinckney, merely "theoretical nonsense." Of paramount concern to the backers of the Constitution was that the government should be as insulated as possible from the shifting electoral will of the population. A restricted vote meant a more stable government. An unrestricted vote would result, as Elbridge Gerry of Massachusetts declared at the Constitutional Convention, in "the evils . . . [which] flow from the excess of democracy."

The logic behind this restriction of voting rights to property owners was questioned seriously by Thomas Paine in his pamphlet *Common Sense:*

Voter registration is an important part of our political process. This worker is helping a citizen register to vote in the next elections. The requirements for voter registration vary across states.

Here is a man who today owns a jackass, and the jackass is worth $60. Today the man is a voter and goes to the polls and deposits his vote. Tomorrow the jackass dies. The next day the man comes to vote without his jackass and cannot vote at all. Now tell me, which was the voter, the man or the jackass?[9]

The writers of the Constitution allowed the states to decide who should vote. Thus, women were allowed to vote in Wyoming in 1870 but not in the entire nation until the Nineteenth Amendment was ratified in 1920.

It was not until the Jacksonian era of the 1830s that the common man (but not woman) began to be heralded as the backbone of democracy. Men without property were first given the right to vote in the western states. By about 1850, most white adult males in virtually all the states could vote without any property qualification. North Carolina was the last state to eliminate its property test for voting—in 1856.

Extension of the franchise to black males occurred with the passage of the Fifteenth Amendment in 1870. This enfranchisement was short-lived, however, as the "redemption" of the South by white racists rolled back these gains by the end of the century. As discussed in Chapter 5, it was not until the 1960s that African Americans, both male and female, were able to participate in large numbers in the electoral process. Women received full national voting rights with the Nineteenth Amendment in 1920. The most recent extension of the franchise occurred when the voting age was reduced to eighteen by the Twenty-sixth Amendment in 1971.

Current Eligibility and Registration Requirements

Voting requires **registration**, and registration requires satisfying voter qualifications, or legal requirements. These requirements are the following: (1) citizenship, (2) age (eighteen or older), and (3) residency—the duration varying widely from state to state and with types of elections. In addition, most states disqualify people who are mentally incompetent, prison inmates, convicted felons, and election-law violators.

Each state has different qualifications for voting and registration. In every state except North Dakota, registration must take place before voting. In general, a person must register well in advance of an election, although voters in Maine, Minnesota, Oregon, and Wisconsin are allowed to register up to, and on, election day.

Until recently, many states required a personal appearance at an official building during normal working hours to order to register. In 1993, however, Congress passed the "motor voter" bill, which requires that states provide voter registration materials when people receive or renew driver's licenses, that all states allow voters to register by mail, and that voter registration forms be made available at a wider variety of public places and agencies.[10]

HOW DO VOTERS DECIDE?

Political scientists and survey researchers have collected much information about voting behavior. This information sheds some light on which people

---

9. Thomas Paine, *Common Sense* (London: H. D. Symonds, 1792), p. 28.
10. The law took effect in 1995.

REGISTRATION
The entry of a person's name onto the list of eligible voters for elections. Registration requires meeting certain legal requirements relating to age, citizenship, and residency.

Signs in English and Spanish encourage voters to register for the next election. The Supreme Court has ruled that registration and ballots must be available in other languages if a specified proportion of the citizens speak a language other than English.

vote and why people decide to vote for particular candidates. We have already discussed factors influencing voter turnout. Generally, the factors that influence voting decisions can be divided into two groups: (1) socioeconomic and demographic factors and (2) psychological factors.

Socioeconomic and Demographic Factors

SOCIOECONOMIC STATUS
The position held in society by virtue of one's level of income or type of occupation.

As Table 9–5 indicates, a number of socioeconomic and demographic factors appear to influence voting behavior, including (1) education, (2) income and **socioeconomic status**, (3) religion, (4) ethnic background, (5) gender,

TABLE 9–5

Vote by Groups in Presidential Elections Since 1960 (in Percentages)

	1960		1964		1968			1972		1976		
	JFK (DEM.)	NIXON (REP.)	LBJ (DEM.)	GOLDWATER (REP.)	HUMPHREY (DEM.)	NIXON (REP.)	WALLACE (IND.)	McGOVERN (DEM.)	NIXON (REP.)	CARTER (DEM.)	FORD (REP.)	McCARTHY (IND.)
NATIONAL	50.1	49.9	61.3	38.7	43.0	43.4	13.6	38	62	50	48	1
SEX												
Male	52	48	60	40	41	43	16	37	63	53	45	1
Female	49	51	62	38	45	43	12	38	62	48	51	*
RACE												
White	49	51	59	41	38	47	15	32	68	46	52	1
Nonwhite	68	32	94	6	85	12	3	87	13	85	15	*
EDUCATION												
College	39	61	52	48	37	54	9	37	63	42	55	2
High school	52	48	62	38	42	43	15	34	66	54	46	*
Grade school	55	45	66	34	52	33	15	49	51	58	41	1
OCCUPATION												
Professional	42	58	54	46	34	56	10	31	69	42	56	1
White collar	48	52	57	43	41	47	12	36	64	50	48	2
Manual	60	40	71	29	50	35	15	43	57	58	41	1
AGE (Years)												
Under 30	54	46	64	36	47	38	15	48	52	53	45	1
30–49	54	46	63	37	44	41	15	33	67	48	49	2
50 and older	46	54	59	41	41	47	12	36	64	52	48	*
RELIGION												
Protestants	38	62	55	45	35	49	16	30	70	46	53	*
Catholics	78	22	76	24	59	33	8	48	52	57	42	1
POLITICS												
Republicans	5	95	20	80	9	86	5	5	95	9	91	*
Democrats	84	16	87	13	74	12	14	67	33	82	18	*
Independents	43	57	56	44	31	44	25	31	69	38	57	4
REGION												
East	53	47	68	32	50	43	7	42	58	51	47	1
Midwest	48	52	61	39	44	47	9	40	60	48	50	1
South	51	49	52	48	31	36	33	29	71	54	45	*
West	49	51	60	40	44	49	7	41	59	46	51	1
MEMBERS OF LABOR UNION FAMILIES	65	35	73	27	56	29	15	46	54	63	36	1

*Less than 1 percent.
NOTE: 1976 and 1980 results do not include votes for minor-party candidates.

(6) age, and (7) geographic region. These influences all reflect the voter's personal background and place in society. Some factors have to do with the family into which a person is born: race, religion (for most people), and ethnic background. Others may be the result of choices made throughout an individual's life: place of residence, educational achievement, or profession. It is also clear that many of these factors are related. People who have more education are likely to have higher incomes and to hold professional jobs. Similarly, children born into wealthier families are far more likely to

TABLE 9–5 (Continued)

Vote by Groups in Presidential Elections Since 1960 (in Percentages)

	1980			1984		1988		1992		
	CARTER (DEM.)	REAGAN (REP.)	ANDERSON (IND.)	MONDALE (DEM.)	REAGAN (REP.)	DUKAKIS (DEM.)	BUSH (REP.)	CLINTON (DEM.)	BUSH (REP.)	PEROT (IND.)
NATIONAL	41	51	7	41	59	45	53	43	38	19
SEX										
Male	38	53	7	36	64	41	57	41	38	21
Female	44	49	6	45	55	49	50	46	37	17
RACE										
White	36	56	7	34	66	40	59	39	41	20
Nonwhite	86	10	2	87	13	86	12	NA	NA	NA
EDUCATION										
College	35	53	10	39	61	43	56	44	39	18
High school	43	51	5	43	57	49	50	43	36	20
Grade school	54	42	3	51	49	56	43	56	28	NA
OCCUPATION										
Professional	33	55	10	34	66	40	59	NA	NA	NA
White collar	40	51	9	47	53	42	57	NA	NA	NA
Manual	48	46	5	46	54	50	49	NA	NA	NA
AGE (Years)										
Under 30	47	41	11	40	60	47	52	44	34	22
30–49	38	52	8	40	60	45	54	42	38	20
50 and older	41	54	4	41	59	49	50	50	38	12
RELIGION										
Protestants	39	54	6	39	61	33	66	33	46	21
Catholics	46	47	6	39	61	47	52	44	36	20
POLITICS										
Republicans	8	86	5	4	96	8	91	10	73	17
Democrats	69	26	4	79	21	82	17	77	10	13
Independents	29	55	14	33	67	43	55	38	32	30
REGION										
East	43	47	9	46	54	49	50	47	35	NA
Midwest	41	51	7	42	58	47	52	42	37	NA
South	44	52	3	37	63	41	58	42	43	NA
West	35	54	9	40	60	46	52	44	34	NA
MEMBERS OF LABOR UNION FAMILIES	50	43	5	52	48	57	42	55	24	NA

*Less than 1 percent.
NOTE: 1976 and 1980 results do not include votes for minor-party candidates.
SOURCE: *Gallup Report*, November 1984, p. 32; *New York Times*, November 10, 1988, p. 18; *New York Times*, November 15, 1992, p. B9.

complete college than are children from poorer families. Furthermore, some of these demographic factors relate to psychological factors—as we shall see.

Education.   More education generally is correlated with voting Republican, although this was not the case in 1992. As can be seen in Table 9–5, 39 percent of college graduates voted for George Bush in the 1992 election, whereas 44 percent voted for Bill Clinton. Another exception to the rule that more educated voters vote Republican occurred in 1964, when college graduates voted 52 percent for Democrat Lyndon Johnson and 48 percent for Republican Barry Goldwater. Typically, those with less education are more inclined to vote for the Democratic nominee. In 1984, Democrat Walter Mondale received 43 percent and Republican Ronald Reagan, 57 percent of the vote from high school graduates, whereas those with only a grade school education voted 51 percent for Mondale and 49 percent for Reagan. The same pattern held in 1992, when 39 percent of the college graduates voted for Republican George Bush, compared with 28 percent of those who had not completed high school.

Income and Socioeconomic Status.   If we measure socioeconomic status by profession, then those of higher socioeconomic status—professionals and businesspersons, as well as white-collar workers—tend to vote Republican. Manual laborers, factory workers, and especially union members are more likely to vote Democratic. The effects of income are much the same. The higher the income, the more likely it is that a person will vote Republican. Conversely, a much larger percentage of low-income individuals vote Democratic. But there are no hard and fast rules. There are some very poor individuals who are devoted Republicans, just as there are some extremely wealthy supporters of the Democratic party. In some recent elections, the traditional pattern did not hold. In 1980, for example, many blue-collar Democrats voted for Ronald Reagan, although the 1992 election showed those votes going to Bill Clinton.

Religion.   In the United States, Protestants traditionally have voted Republican, and Catholics and Jews have voted Democratic. As with the other patterns discussed, however, this one is somewhat fluid. Republican Richard Nixon obtained 52 percent of the Catholic vote in 1972, and Democrat Lyndon Johnson won 55 percent of the Protestant vote in 1964. The Catholic vote was evenly split between Democrat Jimmy Carter and Republican Ronald Reagan in 1980 but went heavily for Reagan in 1984. In 1992, Republican candidate George Bush obtained fewer votes from Catholics than did Democratic candidate Bill Clinton.

Ethnic Background.   Traditionally, the Irish have voted for Democrats. So, too, have voters of Slavic, Polish, and Italian heritages. But Anglo-Saxon and northern European ethnic groups have voted for Republican presidential candidates. These patterns were disrupted in 1980, when Ronald Reagan obtained much of his support from several of the traditionally Democratic ethnic groups, with the help of fundamentalist religious groups.

African Americans voted principally for Republicans until Democrat Franklin D. Roosevelt's New Deal. Since then, they have identified largely with the Democratic party. Indeed, Democratic presidential candidates have received, on average, more than 80 percent of the African-American vote since 1956.

Gender. Until relatively recently, there seemed to have been no fixed pattern of voter preference by gender in presidential elections. One year, more women than men would vote for the Democratic candidate; another year, more men than women would do so. Some political analysts believe that a ''gender gap'' became a major determinant of voter decision making in the 1980 presidential election. Ronald Reagan obtained 15 percentage points more than Jimmy Carter among male voters, whereas women gave about an equal number of votes to each candidate. In 1984, the gender gap amounted to 9 percent nationally, with 64 percent of male voters casting their ballots for Ronald Reagan and 55 percent of female voters doing the same. The gender gap decreased in 1988 to about 7 percentage points and in 1992 to only 5 percentage points.

Age. Traditionally, younger voters have tended to vote Democratic; older voters have tended to vote Republican. It was only the voters under thirty who clearly favored Jimmy Carter during the Carter-Reagan election in 1980. This trend was reversed in 1984, however, when voters under thirty voted heavily for Ronald Reagan and again voted Republican in 1988. In 1992, Bill Clinton won back the young voters by 10 percentage points.

Geographic Region. As we noted earlier, the former Solid (Democratic) South has crumbled. In 1972, Republican Richard Nixon obtained 71 percent of the southern vote, whereas Democrat George McGovern obtained only 29 percent. Ronald Reagan drew 52 percent of the southern vote in 1980, and 63 percent in 1984.

Democrats still draw much of their strength from large northern and eastern cities. Rural areas tend to be Republican (and conservative) throughout the country except in the South, where the rural vote still tends to be heavily Democratic. On average, the West has voted Republican in presidential elections. Except for the 1964 election between Barry Goldwater and Lyndon Johnson, and again in the 1992 election, the Republicans have held the edge in western states in every presidential election since 1956.

Psychological Factors

In addition to socioeconomic and demographic explanations for the way people vote, at least three important psychological factors play a role in voter decision making. These factors, which are rooted in attitudes and beliefs held by voters, are (1) party identification, (2) perception of the candidates, and (3) issue preferences.

Party Identification. With the possible exception of race, party identification has been the most important determinant of voting behavior in national elections. As we pointed out in Chapter 6, party affiliation is influenced by family and peer groups, by age, and by psychological attachment. During the 1950s, independent voters constituted a little more than 20 percent of the eligible electorate. In the middle to late 1960s, however, party identification began to weaken, and by the 1970s, the number of independent voters had

increased to roughly 30 percent of all voters. In 1992, the estimated proportion of independent voters was 33 percent. Independent voting seems to be concentrated among new voters, particularly among new young voters. Thus, we can still say that party identification for established voters is an important determinant in voter choice.

Perception of the Candidates.   The image of the candidate also seems to be important in a voter's choice for president. We do not know as much about the effect of candidate image as we do about party identification, however, because it is difficult to make systematic comparisons of candidate appeal over time. The evidence is mixed. Data compiled by Warren E. Miller and others show some important differences in the strength of this factor on voter choice from one election to the next.[11] These researchers found that perceptions of *both* candidates were positive in 1952, 1960, and 1976, whereas in 1956 Dwight Eisenhower's image was highly favorable and Adlai Stevenson's was neutral. In 1964, very positive ratings for Lyndon Johnson contrasted with very negative perceptions of Barry Goldwater. Richard Nixon's positive 1968 and 1972 ratings allowed him to defeat his negatively evaluated opponents. In 1980, both Ronald Reagan and Jimmy Carter had negative images.

The researchers also determined that, except in 1964 and 1976, Republican candidates were evaluated more favorably by the voters than were the Democratic candidates. To some extent, voter attitudes toward candidates are based on emotions (such as trust) rather than on any judgment about experience or policy. In 1992, voters' decisions were largely guided by their

11. Warren E. Miller, Arthur H. Miller, and Edward J. Schneider, *American National Election Studies Data Sourcebook* (Cambridge, Mass.: Harvard University Press, 1980), pp. 127, 129.

Retired General Colin Powell, perhaps one of the most popular public figures in the nation, considers running for president in 1996. Powell, who has no formal links to either political party, could choose to run as a Republican or as an independent.

perceptions of who they could trust to run the economy. George Bush tried to reduce the voters' trust in Bill Clinton but failed to make an impact.

Issue Preferences.   Issues make a difference in presidential and congressional elections. Although personality or image factors may be very persuasive, most voters have some notion of how the candidates differ on basic issues or at least know that the candidates want a change in the direction of government policy.

Historically, economic issues have the strongest influence on voters' choices. When the economy is doing well, it is very difficult for a challenger, particularly at the presidential level, to defeat the incumbent. In contrast, increasing inflation, a rising rate of unemployment, or high interest rates are likely to work to the disadvantage of the incumbent. Studies of how economic conditions affect the vote differ in their conclusions. Some indicate that people vote on the basis of their personal economic well-being, whereas other studies seem to show that people vote on the basis of the nation's overall economic health.

Foreign policy issues become more prominent in a time of crisis. Although the parties and candidates have differed greatly over policy toward trade with China, for example, foreign policy issues are truly influential only when armed conflict is a possibility. Clearly, public dissension over the war in Vietnam had an effect on elections in 1968 and 1972. In 1980, the Reagan campaign capitalized on Soviet initiatives and the Iranian hostage crisis to persuade the voters that the United States was declining in power and respect.

Some of the most heated debates in American political campaigns take place over the social issues of abortion, the role of women, the rights of lesbians and gay males, and prayer in the public schools. In general, presidential candidates would prefer to avoid such issues, because voters who care about these questions are likely to be offended if a candidate does not share their views.

All candidates try to set themselves apart from their opposition on crucial issues in order to attract voters. What is difficult to ascertain is the extent to which issues overshadow partisan loyalty or personality factors in the voters' minds. It appears that some campaigns are much more issue oriented than others. Some research has shown that **issue voting** was most important in the presidential elections of 1964, 1968, and 1972, was moderately important in 1980, and was less important in 1992.

Reverend Jesse Jackson, civil rights leader and candidate for the Democratic nomination in 1992, considers a run for the presidency in 1996 as an independent candidate. Jackson's candidacy would force President Clinton to take more liberal positions on social issues.

THE MEDIA'S FUNCTIONS

The study of people and politics—of how people gain the information that they need to be able to choose between political candidates, to organize for their own interests, and to formulate opinions on the policies and decisions of the government—needs to take into account the role played by the media in the United States. Historically, the print medium played the most important role in informing public debate. It was this medium that developed, for the most part, our understanding of how news is to be reported. Today, however, more than 90 percent of all Americans use television news as their

ISSUE VOTING
Voting for a candidate based on how he or she stands on a particular issue.

primary source of information. In the future, the information superhighway may become the most important source of information and political debate for Americans. If that happens, control over the gathering and sharing of news and information will be changed greatly from a system in which the media have a primary role to one in which the individual citizen may play a greater role. With that future in mind, it is important to analyze the current relationship between the media and politics.

The mass media perform a number of different functions in any country. In the United States, we can list at least six. Almost all of them can have political implications, and some are essential to the democratic process. These functions are as follows: (1) entertainment, (2) reporting the news, (3) identifying public problems, (4) socializing new generations, (5) providing a political forum, and (6) making profits. Added up, these factors form the basis for a complex relationship among the media, the government, and the public.

Entertainment

By far the greatest number of radio and television hours are dedicated to entertaining the public. The battle for prime-time ratings indicates how important successful entertainment is to the survival of networks and individual stations.

There is no direct linkage between entertainment and politics; however, network dramas often introduce material that may be politically controversial and that may stimulate public discussion. For example, one controversial segment of *L.A. Law* discussed the "right to die" of a paralyzed woman. Made-for-TV movies have focused on many controversial topics, including AIDS, incest, and wife battering.

A view of the Republican convention floor from the platform illustrates the presence of the media. In 1992, only the public broadcasting network (PBS) and CNN provided close to complete coverage of the conventions. The major networks provided only a few hours of convention coverage each evening and emphasized commentary about the speeches rather than coverage of the events on the floor.

Reporting the News

The mass media in all their forms—newspapers, radio, television, cable, magazines—have as their primary goal the reporting of news. The media convey words and pictures about events, facts, personalities, and ideas. The protections of the First Amendment are intended to keep the flow of news as free as possible, because it is an essential part of the democratic process. If citizens cannot get unbiased information about the state of their community and their leaders' actions, how can they make voting decisions? Perhaps the most incisive comment about the importance of the media was made by James Madison, who said, "A people who mean to be their own governors must arm themselves with the power knowledge gives. A popular government without popular information or the means of acquiring it, is but a prologue to a farce or a tragedy or perhaps both."[12]

Identifying Public Problems

The power of information is important, not only in revealing what the government is doing but also in determining what the government ought to do—in other words, in setting the **public agenda.** The mass media identify public problems, such as the scandal of "missing children," and sometimes help to set up mechanisms to deal with them (in this example, the missing children hotline, "Childfind"). American journalists also work in a long tradition of uncovering public wrongdoing, corruption, and bribery and of bringing such wrongdoing to the public's attention. Closely related to this investigative function is that of presenting policy alternatives. Public policy is often complex and difficult to make entertaining, but programs devoted to public policy increasingly are being scheduled for prime-time television. Most networks produce "news magazine" format shows that sometimes include segments on foreign policy and other issues.

Socializing New Generations

The media are a major influence on the ideas and beliefs of all adults, but they influence particularly the younger generation and recent immigrants. Through the transmission of historical information (sometimes fictionalized), the presentation of American culture, and the portrayal of all the diverse regions and groups in the United States, the media teach young people and immigrants about what it means to be an American. The extensive coverage of elections is a socializing process for these groups.

Providing a Political Forum

As part of their news function, the media also provide a political forum for leaders and the public. Candidates for office use news reporting to sustain interest in their campaigns, whereas officeholders use the media to gain support for their policies or to present an image of leadership. Presidential trips abroad are an outstanding way for the chief executive to get colorful, positive, and exciting news coverage that makes the president look "presidential."

PUBLIC AGENDA
Issues that commonly are perceived by members of the political community as meriting public attention and governmental action. The media play an important role in setting the public agenda by focusing attention on certain topics.

12. As quoted in "Castro vs. (Some) Censorship," editorial in the *New York Times*, November 22, 1983, p. 24.

President Bill Clinton and Speaker Newt Gingrich shared a stage in New Hampshire in early summer, 1995, to discuss their views on Medicare reform and other topics. Since New Hampshire would be the first state to hold a presidential primary in 1996, the media touted this joint appearance as the possible beginning of a Gingrich campaign. Instead of angry debate, the two men engaged in respectful dialogue, surprising the media and their supporters.

The town meeting of yesterday gave way to the electronic town meeting of today. Here Bill Clinton answers a question asked by a citizen in another location but whose image and voice were transmitted through video conferencing telecommunications equipment. As telecommunications that include video and voice become better and cheaper, politicians will be able to use Clinton's electronic town-meeting concept more and more.

The media also offer a way for citizens to participate in public debate, through letters to the editor, for example, or talk shows (see the *Politics: The Human Side* on Rush Limbaugh, on page 322).

Making Profits

Most of the news media in the United States are private, for-profit corporate enterprises. One of their goals is to make profits—for employee salaries, for expansion, and for dividends to the stockholders who own the companies. Profits are made, in general, by charging for advertising. Advertising revenues usually are related directly to circulation or to listener/viewer ratings.

Several well-known outlets are publicly owned—public television stations in many communities and National Public Radio. These operate without extensive commercials and are locally supported and often subsidized by the government and corporations.

THE PRIMACY OF TELEVISION

Television is the most influential of the media. It also is big business. National news TV personalities like Dan Rather may earn in excess of $2 million per year from their TV news–reporting contracts alone. They are paid so much because they command large audiences, and large audiences command high prices for advertising on national news shows. Indeed, news *per se* has become a major factor in the profitability of TV stations. In 1963, the major networks—ABC, CBS, and NBC—devoted only eleven minutes daily to national news. By 1996, the amount of time on the networks devoted to news-type programming had increased to three hours. In addition, a twenty-four-hour-a-day news cable channel—CNN—started operating in 1980. With the addition of CNN—Headline News, CNBC, and other news-format cable channels and shows in the 1980s and 1990s, the amount of news-type programming continues to increase. News is obviously good business.

H. Ross Perot proved himself a master of using the media when he decided to run for president as an independent in 1992. Here he is shown with Larry King during one of King's radio programs. Perot was also a frequent guest on "Larry King Live," the CNN television show. In fact, Perot announced his candidacy on that show.

Television's influence on the political process today is recognized by all who engage in it. Its special characteristics are worthy of attention. Television news is often criticized for being superficial, particularly compared with the detailed coverage available in the *New York Times,* for example. In fact, television news is constrained by its peculiar technical characteristics, the most important being the limitations of time; stories must be reported in only a few minutes.

The most interesting aspect of television is, of course, the fact that it relies on pictures rather than words to attract the viewer's attention. Therefore, the videotapes or slides that are chosen for a particular political story have exaggerated importance. Viewers do not know what other photos may have been taken or events recorded—they note only those appearing on their screens. Television news can also be exploited for its drama by well-constructed stories. Some critics suggest that there is pressure to produce television news that has a "story line," like a novel or movie. The story should be short, with exciting pictures and a clear plot. In the extreme case, the news media are satisfied with a **sound bite**, a several-second comment selected or crafted for its immediate impact on the viewer.

SOUND BITE
A brief, memorable comment that can easily be fit into news broadcasts.

THE MEDIA AND POLITICAL CAMPAIGNS

All forms of the media—television, newspapers, radio, and magazines—have an enormous political impact on American society. Media influence is most obvious during political campaigns. Because television is the primary news source for the majority of Americans, candidates and their consultants spend much of their time devising strategies to use television to their benefit. Three types of TV coverage are generally used in campaigns for the presidency and other offices: paid-for political announcements, management of news coverage, and campaign debates.

POLITICS: THE HUMAN SIDE
Rush Limbaugh, Entertainer and Political Conservative

"Nothing in my heart is liberal."

BIOGRAPHICAL NOTES

In less than seven years, Rush Limbaugh has become one of the most widely listened-to radio and television talk show hosts in the nation. His "attack-style" journalism, quick wit, and outrageous conservatism both attract and repel listeners. Born in 1951, Rush Hudson Limbaugh III was the son and grandson of lawyers; his family had lived in Cape Girardeau, Missouri, for three generations. Rush, whose childhood nickname was "Rusty," was a rather insecure boy; he was teased about being overweight and was domi-nated by a powerful father who had strong opinions on all subjects. Limbaugh admits to having had difficulty in school and having preferred to listen to the radio. He admired the disk jockey: "He didn't have to go to school as far as I knew, and that's the first allure. The second allure was that I love music . . . I wanted to stand out. I've always had an ego that wants to be up front, not background."*

While still in high school, Limbaugh was able to try out being host of a local radio show. He defied his family by choosing to enroll in a radio broadcasting school rather than completing college. After an appearance on Ted Koppel's "Nightline," Limbaugh gained a national following. Today, his live call-in radio talk show is carried by more than five hundred radio stations, and his cable TV show airs in almost every major media market.

POLITICAL CONTRIBUTIONS

Rush Limbaugh has become an important political force in the United States, primarily through his ability to motivate his listeners to take political action. Although Limbaugh defines himself as an entertainer rather than a politician, he is an outspoken opponent of gay rights, attacks feminism regularly, and refers to environmentalists as "tree huggers" and "owl lovers."

*Paul D. Colford, "Rush Limbaugh Finds Calling after Uneasy Childhood," *Minneapolis Star Tribune*, September 26, 1993, p. 1E.

Limbaugh has become so immensely popular and well known because he was one of the first members of the media to understand the value of the 800 telephone number and satellite technology. His radio audience, on a given afternoon, numbers more than 4.5 million listeners, many of whom call him, call their senators and representatives about issues he raises, and send Internet messages to one another as well as to the White House. Limbaugh's shows have generated widespread opposition to some of the programs proposed by the Clinton administration. The shows and their audiences have even generated political rumors that, in regard to the Whitewater controversy, caused the stock market to decline steeply during the time the shows were broadcast.

Limbaugh not only profits from his roles on radio and television but also attacks his fellow journalists and the media in general. To criticisms that he is unduly negative, Limbaugh explains that he is not being original but only expressing what the listeners already believe: "I validate. I don't orchestrate, dictate or otherwise cause people to ponder. I simply validate."†

†David Rennick, "Day of the Dittohead: Rush Limbaugh Entertains. But His Mean, Conspiratorial Message Has a Serious Future," *Washington Post*, February 20, 1994, p. C1.

PAID-FOR POLITICAL ANNOUNCEMENT
A message about a political candidate conveyed through the media and designed to elicit positive public opinion.

Paid-for Political Announcements

Perhaps one of the most effective **paid-for political announcements** of all time was a short, thirty-second spot created by President Lyndon Johnson's media adviser. In this ad, a little girl stood in a field of daisies. As she held a daisy, she pulled the petals off and quietly counted to herself. Suddenly, when she reached number ten, a deep bass voice cut in and began a count-down: 10, 9, 8, 7, 6 . . . When the voice intoned "zero," the unmistakable mushroom cloud of an atom bomb began to fill the screen. Then President Johnson's voice was heard: "These are the stakes. To make a world in which all of God's children can live, or to go into the dark. We must either love each other or we must die." At the end of the commercial, the message read, "Vote for President Johnson on November 3."

To understand how effective this daisy girl commercial was, you must know that Johnson's opponent was Barry Goldwater, a Republican conservative candidate known for his expansive views on the role of the U.S. military. The ad's implication was that Goldwater would lead the United States into nuclear war. Although the ad was withdrawn within a few days, it has a place in political campaign history as the classic negative campaign announcement.

Since the daisy girl advertisement, negative advertising has come into its own. Candidates vie with one another to produce "attack" ads and then to counterattack when the opponent responds. The public claims not to like negative advertising, but as one consultant put it, "Negative advertising works." Any advertising "works" when viewers or listeners remember an ad. It is clear that negative ads are more memorable than ones that praise the candidate's virtues. The purpose of campaigns is to confirm the votes of the supporters and attract the votes of independents. Negative advertising, which supporters and independents remember longer than positive advertising, works well. For those members of the other party or supporters of the candidate under attack, no vote gain is expected anyway.

Management of News Coverage

Using paid-for political announcements to get a message across to the public is a very expensive tactic. Coverage by the news media is, however, free; it simply demands that the campaign ensure that coverage takes place. In recent years, campaign managers have shown increasing sophistication in creating newsworthy events for journalists to cover. As Doris Graber points out, "To keep a favorable image of their candidates in front of the public, campaign managers arrange newsworthy events to familiarize potential voters with their candidates' best aspects."[13]

To take advantage of the media's interest in campaign politics, whether at the presidential level or perhaps in a Senate race, the campaign staff tries to influence the quantity and type of coverage the campaign receives. First, it is important for the campaign staff to understand the technical aspects of media coverage—camera angles, necessary equipment, timing, and deadlines—and to plan their political events to accommodate the press. Second, the campaign organization learns that political reporters and their sponsors—networks or newspapers—are in competition for the best stories and can be manipulated through the granting of favors, such as a personal interview with the candidate. Third, an important task for the scheduler in the campaign is the planning of events that will be photogenic and interesting enough for the evening news.

---

13. Doris Graber, *Mass Media and American Policies,* 4th ed. (Washington, D.C.: Congressional Quarterly Press, 1993), p. 59.

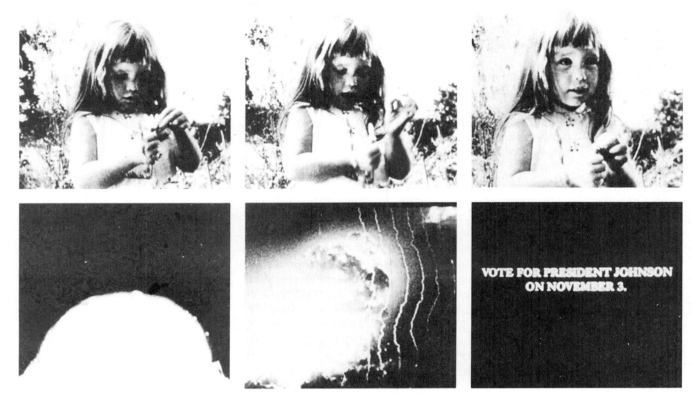

President Lyndon Johnson's "Daisy Girl" ad contrasted the innocence of childhood with the horror of an atomic attack.

SPIN
An interpretation of campaign events or election results that is most favorable to the candidate's campaign strategy.

SPIN DOCTOR
A political campaign adviser who tries to convince journalists of the truth of a particular interpretation of events.

A related goal, although one that is more difficult to attain, is to convince reporters that a particular interpretation of an event is correct. By the 1992 presidential campaign, the art of putting the appropriate **spin** on a story or event had become highly developed. Each presidential candidate's press advisers, known as **spin doctors**, tried to convince the journalists that their interpretations of the primary results were correct. For example, Bill Clinton's people tried to convince the press that he didn't really expect to win the New Hampshire primary anyway, while the Paul Tsongas camp insisted that winning the New England state was a great and unexpected victory. Journalists began to report on the different spins and how the candidates tried to manipulate campaign news coverage.

Going for the Knockout Punch—Presidential Debates

Perhaps of equal importance to paid-for political advertisements is the performance of the candidate in a televised presidential debate. After the first such debate, which took place in 1960, candidates became aware of the great potential of television for changing the momentum of a campaign. In that first meeting, John Kennedy, the young senator from Massachusetts, took on the vice president of the United States, Richard Nixon. Kennedy's fresh, energetic appearance on television gave him an advantage over the vice president, who looked tired, unshaven, and haggard. Polls taken by Gallup indicated that 43 percent of the respondents felt that Kennedy was the leader in the race after the first debate. By the end of the third debate, Nixon,

A family watches the 1960 Kennedy-Nixon debate on television. After the debate, TV viewers thought Kennedy had won, whereas radio listeners thought Nixon had won.

who had had a slight lead in September, was 3 percentage points behind.[14] What the Kennedy-Nixon debate emphasized was the importance to the campaign of the candidate's televised image.

The presidential debates of 1992 were distinguished by the addition of the independent candidate, H. Ross Perot, and by the use of two different formats. The first and third debates were more formal, with a panel of journalists asking questions of the three candidates. Perot constantly surprised the panel and the audience with his down-to-earth humor and common-sense responses. George Bush's performances in the first two debates were lackluster, but some of his fighting spirit appeared in the third one. The innovative format of the second debate certainly increased the interest of the viewing public. All three candidates fielded questions from members of the studio's nonpartisan audience. Bill Clinton seemed to be at home with this format, whereas Bush was more uncomfortable, and Perot had fewer opportunities to capitalize on the forum. Most observers of the three debates noted that the questions posed by the audience were as complex and probing as any raised by the media during the campaign.

The crucial fact about the practice of televising debates is that, although debates are justified publicly as an opportunity for the voters to find out how candidates differ on the issues, what the candidates want is to capitalize on the power of television to project an image. They view the debate as a strategic opportunity to improve their own images or to point out the failures of their opponents. Candidates are very aware not only that the actual performance is important but also that the morning-after interpretation of the debate by the news media may play a crucial role in what the public

14. Theodore H. White, *The Making of the President, 1960* (New York: Atheneum, 1961), pp. 294–295.

WHITE HOUSE PRESS CORPS
A group of reporters assigned full time to cover the presidency.

PRESS SECRETARY
The individual responsible for representing the White House before the media. The press secretary writes news releases, provides background information, sets up press conferences, and so on.

The format of the second presidential debate of the 1992 campaign proved to be especially well suited to Bill Clinton. His responses to ordinary citizens' questions were often deemed to be more effective than Ross Perot's or George Bush's.

thinks. Regardless of the risks of debating, the potential for gaining votes is so great that candidates undoubtedly will continue to seek televised debates.

THE MEDIA AND THE GOVERNMENT

The mass media not only wield considerable power when it comes to political campaigns, but they also, in one way or another, can wield power over the affairs of government and over government officials. Perhaps the most notable example in recent times concerns the activities of *Washington Post* reporters Bob Woodward and Carl Bernstein. These two reporters were assigned to cover the Watergate break-in, and they undertook an investigation that eventually led to the resignation of President Richard Nixon (and later to a best-selling book and a film, *All the President's Men*). More recent investigations have included the Iran-*contra* scandal, the savings and loan debacle, and the congressional check-kiting scandals. As discussed in the feature on *Politics and Privacy*, journalists also often delve into the private lives of politicians to investigate issues of ethics and morality.

The Media and the Presidency

A love-hate relationship clearly exists between the president and the media. During the administration of John F. Kennedy, the president was seen in numerous photos scanning the *New York Times,* the *Washington Post,* and other newspapers each morning to see how the press tallied his successes and failures. This led to frequent jocular comments about his speed-reading ability.

In the United States, the prominence of the president is cultivated by a **White House press corps** that is assigned full time to cover the presidency. These reporters even have a lounge in the White House where they spend their days, waiting for a story to break. Most of the time, they simply wait for the daily or twice-daily briefing by the president's **press secretary.** Because of the press corps's physical proximity to the president, the chief executive cannot even take a brief stroll around the presidential swimming pool without its becoming news. Perhaps no other nation allows the press such access to its highest government official. Consequently, no other nation has its airwaves and print media so filled with absolute trivia regarding the personal lives of the chief executive and the chief executive's family (again, see this chapter's feature on *Politics and Privacy*).

President Franklin D. Roosevelt brought new spirit to a demoralized country and led it through the Great Depression through his effective use of the media, particularly radio broadcasts. His radio "fireside chats" brought hope to millions. Roosevelt's speeches were masterly in their ability to forge a common emotional bond among his listeners. His decisive announcement in 1933 on the reorganization of the banks, for example, calmed a jittery nation and prevented the collapse of the banking industry, which was threatened by a run on banks, from which nervous depositors were withdrawing their assets. His famous Pearl Harbor speech, following the Japanese attack on the U.S. Pacific fleet on December 7, 1941 ("a day that will live in infamy"), mobilized the nation for the sacrifices and effort necessary to win World War II.

A relatively recent use of the media by presidents has been regularly scheduled press conferences. Here President Clinton addresses questions from the Washington press corps. Clinton has shown himself to be quick on his feet when asked even embarrassing questions. He and others before him have learned to memorize the names of virtually all of the members of the Washington press corps.

Perhaps no president exploited the electronic media more effectively than did Ronald Reagan. The "great communicator," as he was called, was never more dramatic than in his speech to the nation following the October 1983 U.S. invasion of Grenada. In this address, the president, in an almost flawless performance, appeared to many to have decisively laid to rest the uncertainty and confusion surrounding the event.

The relationship betweeen the media and the president took a new turn with the rise of radio talk shows. Liberal and conservative radio hosts take telephone calls and respond with political commentary. President Clinton frequently expressed his resentment at being a target for these media stars, especially conservative Rush Limbaugh (refer back to the *Politics: The Human Side* on page 322). In the aftermath of the bombing of the Oklahoma City federal building in 1995, Clinton and others wondered if the proliferation of radio talk shows encouraged feelings of hate among some Americans.

The relationship between the media and the president has thus been reciprocal. Both institutions have used each other, sometimes positively, sometimes negatively. The presidency and the news media are mutually dependent.

Setting the Public Agenda

Given that government officials have in front of them an array of problems with which they must deal, the process of setting the public agenda is constant. To be sure, what goes on the public agenda for discussion, debate, and, ultimately, policy action depends on many factors—not the least being each official's personal philosophy.

According to a number of studies, the media play an important part in setting the public agenda, as well as in helping government officials to better understand society's needs and desires. In recent years, television coverage has brought a number of issues to public attention and, consequently, to the attention of policymakers. Videotaped footage of the refugee camps in

POLITICS AND PRIVACY
The Private Lives of Public Figures

In the summer of 1987, Craig Whitney, Washington editor of the *New York Times,* sent a letter to all aspirants for the 1988 presidential nomination. In the letter, he asked them to provide the *Times* with personal information. He also asked that they waive their privacy rights and allow the *Times* to obtain files from the Federal Bureau of Investigation and from confidential records of House or Senate ethics committees.

This unprecedented intrusion by the media into candidates' private lives followed on the heels of the "Gary Hart affair," which broke in May 1987. Democratic presidential frontrunner Gary Hart, senator from Colorado, was rumored for many years to be having extramarital affairs. When asked about these allegations, Hart invited the media to follow him around to see for themselves that there was nothing to the rumors. Acting on a tip, *Miami Herald* reporters flew to Washington, D.C., staked out Hart's townhouse, and observed him in the company of an attractive woman, twenty-nine-year-old Donna Rice, a model and aspiring movie actress. When the story broke, Hart denied any wrongdoing. When it was revealed that

he had met her before, called her several times, and had gone on a weekend trip with her to the Bahamas, Hart withdrew from the race.

There were rumors about other candidates' infidelity. Jesse Jackson said he would refuse to answer questions about allegations regarding his personal sexual life. In 1992, the marriage of Bill and Hillary Rodham Clinton came under scrutiny, particularly after an Arkansas woman claimed to have had an affair with Governor Clinton.

The Clinton White House continued to come under fire when allegations about misdoings in the Whitewater real estate deal surfaced. The allegations and media speculation mixed together possible bank fraud, income tax evasion on a small scale, potential illegalities in funding Clinton's early gubernatorial campaigns, and the commodities trading of Hillary Rodham Clinton. Yet another element in the mix was the suicide of Vincent Foster, a White House adviser to President Clinton, an old friend of both Clintons, and a former law partner of Hillary Rodham Clinton. After early pressure from Republicans, Bill Clinton finally asked for the appointment of a special prosecutor to untangle the allegations. Even

then, Whitewater speculations, particularly about the personal behavior of the Clintons, continued to surface, often on talk shows.

All of these developments signaled increasing intrusion by the media into the private lives of public figures, setting off a lively debate on the rights of the media to explore such allegations. Some argued that this is an appropriate function of the media in a free society in which people have "the right to know" about character issues. Others feared that the lack of privacy would discourage many bright, experienced, and valuable persons from presenting themselves as candidates for public office. In fact, retired admiral Bobby Ray Inman withdrew as a nominee for secretary of defense, citing the media's attacks on his character as the reason for his withdrawal.

Whatever the pros and cons of media investigations, it appears that the precedent has been set for public figures to have, in the future, all aspects of their personality and behavior open to public scrutiny. Some commentators have called this process the *"People* magazining of politics."

Zaire was captured by journalists. The painful images of thousands of children starving while relief shipments were stopped by the clan wars aroused public concern around the globe. President Bill Clinton sent U.S. troops to operate water-purification equipment and improve camp conditions.

In another instance, radio reporter Nina Totenberg forced the Senate Judiciary Committee to reopen charges against Supreme Court nominee Clarence Thomas that he had sexually harassed an employee, Anita Hill. Totenberg's contributions are detailed in the *Politics: The Human Side* on page 330.

Interest groups understand well the power of the media. After campaigning unsuccessfully for years against the tuna industry's practice of using

President Franklin D. Roosevelt, the first president to fully exploit the airwaves for his benefit, reported to the nation through radio "fireside chats."

fishing nets that also captured dolphins, one group infiltrated a fishing crew and shot video film of the slaughter of hundreds of dolphins. The broadcast of this tape led to public outrage, congressional investigations of the industry, and a self-imposed ban on the practice by the major tuna-marketing firms in the United States.

CAMPAIGNS, ELECTIONS, AND THE MEDIA: UNFINISHED WORK

Few areas in American politics seem to be in such need of change and reform as campaigns, voting, and elections. Every four years, polls show that the majority of Americans are dissatisfied with the length of campaigns, with vicious campaign strategies, with the caliber of candidates, and with the influence of campaign contributions on the system. Yet very few serious reforms result, and after the campaign fury subsides, most citizens are willing to get on with their personal business and allow the officials elected in that campaign to take office and hold political authority.

Until a crisis or scandal of the magnitude of the Watergate affair of 1972 to 1974 occurs, it is unlikely that the political parties, officeholders, and other interested groups will seriously reform the electoral system. In the meantime, Congress will continue to consider and make minor changes in the rules governing the influence of PACs on elections. Until officials can see alternate means to raise funds for their own campaigns, however, some form of PACs will exist. Congress also will try to increase citizen interest in voting. It will try to improve the process of presidential campaigns, perhaps by shortening the primary season, simply because it is too long and too expensive.

The power of the media and its impact on American politics is also a controversial and important subject. The increasing dependence of campaigns and candidates on the media makes this an area of symbolic politics and weakened political attachments. At the same time, the greatly expanded

POLITICS: THE HUMAN SIDE
Nina Totenberg, Radio Journalist

"When I walk into the Capitol every morning, I'm walking into the smallest town in America. And I know that at least 300 of the key residents—the congressmen—have heard me fifteen minutes before I've arrived."

BIOGRAPHICAL NOTES

Known by other journalists as a tireless worker who never shies away from a controversial story, Nina Totenberg is now a force in radio journalism as a lead reporter for National Public Radio (NPR). Born in 1944, the daughter of an immigrant Polish violinist and a homemaker, Totenberg dropped out of Boston University to work on the women's page of the *Boston Record-American* and later the *Peabody Times*. She moved to Washington, D.C., in 1968 to cover the Supreme Court for the *Observer*. Gaining notice for her hard-hitting style and flare, she moved to *New Times* magazine, where she earned the notice of Congress for her article "The Ten Dumbest Members of Congress." She became a radio reporter for NPR in 1975, continuing to cover the Supreme Court. A few years later, she married Floyd Haskell, a former senator from Colorado.

POLITICAL CONTRIBUTIONS

Totenberg had already achieved some journalistic scoops, including the revelation that Supreme Court nominee Douglas Ginsburg had smoked marijuana while he was a faculty member at Harvard, when the Clarence Thomas hearings began in 1991. As it appeared clear that Thomas would be confirmed as a Supreme Court justice, Totenberg came into possession of a document prepared by Anita Hill, a former Thomas assistant, charging Thomas with sexual harassment when Thomas was Hill's supervisor. Totenberg began to seek corroboration for the story, finally receiving such confirmation from another judge. She interviewed Hill and confirmed her allegations. Totenberg then wrote up the story and went on the air, charging the Senate Judiciary Committee with ignoring Hill's charges.

A firestorm followed, during which senators attacked Totenberg for refusing to reveal her sources, attacked her professional reputation, and dragged out a twenty-year-old story that Totenberg had once been fired for plagiarizing quotes without giving the complete source. The Judiciary Committee reopened the hearings to deal with the allegations, mesmerizing most radio listeners and TV viewers in the United States. Totenberg and Senator Alan Simpson got into a nasty confrontation on ABC's "Nightline" about the ethics of Totenberg's reporting. Later, Totenberg admitted that the Anita Hill charges had been particularly interesting to her because she herself had suffered sexual harassment from a boss as a young journalist.

Totenberg's influence on the outcome of the Supreme Court appointment was slight—Clarence Thomas was confirmed as a Supreme Court justice. Her willingness to investigate and report Hill's charges, however, raised the discussion of sexual harassment—its extent, its effects on the workplace, and the sensitivity of the subject—to a totally new level in the United States. Nina Totenberg continues to report for NPR as one of the nation's leading female reporters.

number of media outlets, including cable television and on-line computer services, has offered Americans more freedom to choose what they watch and read. The number of partisan talk shows and cable TV channels is also increasing, so Americans can choose to listen only to media outlets that support their own positions. Obviously, how we harness the potential of mass media to allow for national debate about the good of the nation is an issue yet to be resolved.

GETTING INVOLVED
Registering and Voting

In nearly every state, before you are allowed to cast a vote in an election, you must first register. Registration laws vary considerably from state to state, and, depending on how difficult a state's laws make it to register, some states have much higher rates of registration and voting participation than do others.

What do you have to do to register and cast a vote? Most states require that you meet minimum residence requirements. In other words, you must have lived in the state in which you plan to be registered for a specified period of time. You may retain your previous registration, if any, in another state, and you can cast an absentee vote if your previous state permits that. The minimum-residency requirement is very short in some states, such as one day in Alabama or ten days in New Hampshire and Wisconsin. In other states, however, as many as fifty days (in Arizona or Tennessee) must elapse before you can vote. Other states with voter residency requirements have minimum-day requirements in between these extremes. Twenty states do not have any minimum-residency requirement at all.

Nearly every state also specifies a closing date by which you must be registered before an election. In other words, even if you have met a residency requirement, you still may not be able to vote if you register too close to the day of the election. The closing date is different in certain states (Connecticut, Delaware, and Louisiana) for primary elections than for other elections. The closing date for registration varies from election day itself (Maine, Minnesota, Oregon, and Wisconsin) to fifty days (Arizona). Delaware specifies the third Saturday in October as the closing date. In North Dakota, no registration is necessary.

In most states, your registration can be revoked if you do not vote within a certain number of years.

This process of automatically "purging" the voter registration lists of nonactive voters happens every two years in about a dozen states, every three years in Georgia, every four years in more than twenty other states, every five years in Maryland and Rhode Island, every eight years in North Carolina, and every ten years in Michigan. Ten states do not require this purging at all.

What you must do to register and remain registered to vote varies from state to state and even from county to county within a state. In general, you must be a citizen of the United States, at least eighteen years old on or before election day, and a resident of the state in which you intend to register.

Using Iowa as an example, you normally would register through the local county auditor. If you moved to a new address within the state, you would also have to change your registration to vote by contacting the auditor. Postcard registrations must be postmarked or delivered to the county auditor no later than the twenty-fifth day before an election. Party affiliation may be changed or declared when you register or reregister, or you may change or declare a party at the polls on election day. Postcard registration forms in Iowa are available at many public buildings, from labor unions, at political party headquarters, at the county auditors' offices, or from campus groups. Registrars who will accept registrations at other locations may be located by calling your party headquarters or your county auditor. Under recently enacted "motor voter" legislation, effective in 1995, many of these provisions have been implemented nationwide.

For more information on voting registration, contact your county or state officials, party headquarters, labor union, or local chapter of the League of Women Voters.

KEY TERMS

Australian ballot   304

"beauty contest"   297

blanket primary   300

canvassing board   306

caucus   299

challenge   306

closed primary   300

coattail effect   305

corrupt practices acts   296

credentials committee   301

elector   301

electoral college   301

Hatch Act   296

image building   293

independent candidate   293

issue voting   317

office-block, or Massachusetts, ballot   305

open primary   300

paid-for political announcement   322

party-column, or Indiana, ballot   305

plurality   302

political consultant   292

poll watcher   306

press secretary   326

presidential primary   297

public agenda   319

registration   311

run-off primary   300

socioeconomic status   312

sound bite   321

spin   324

spin doctor   324

superdelegate   298

third-party candidate   293

tracking poll   294

voter turnout   306

White House press corps   326

CHAPTER SUMMARY

1. People may choose to run for political office to further their careers, to carry out specific political programs, or in response to certain issues or events. The legal qualifications for holding political office are minimal at both the state and local levels, but holders of political office still are predominantly white and male and are likely to be from the professional class.

2. American political campaigns are lengthy and extremely expensive. In the last decade, they have become more candidate centered rather than party centered in response to technological innovations and decreasing party identification. Candidates have begun to rely less on the party and more on paid professional consultants to perform the various tasks necessary to wage a political campaign. The crucial task of professional political consultants is image building. The campaign organization devises a campaign strategy to maximize the candidate's chances of winning. Candidates use public opinion polls to gauge their popularity and to test the mood of the country.

3. The amount of money spent in financing campaigns is steadily increasing. A variety of corrupt practices acts have been passed to regulate campaign finance. The Federal Election Campaign Acts of 1972 and 1974 instituted major reforms by limiting spend-

ing and contributions; the acts allowed corporations, labor unions, and interest groups to set up political action committees (PACs) to raise money for candidates.

4. Following the Democratic convention of 1968 in Chicago and the attending riots, many party leaders pushed for reforms in the primary process. New rules were formulated, which were adopted by all Democrats and by Republicans in many states. These reforms opened up the nomination process for the presidency to all voters.

5. A presidential primary is a statewide election to help a political party determine its presidential nominee at the national convention. Some states use the caucus method of choosing convention delegates. Different types of presidential primaries include the closed primary, the open primary, the blanket primary, and the run-off primary.

6. In making a presidential choice on election day, the voter technically does not vote directly for a candidate but chooses between slates of presidential electors. The slate that wins the most popular votes throughout the state gets to cast all the electoral votes for the state. The candidate receiving a majority (270) of the electoral votes wins. The United States uses the Australian ballot, a secret ballot that is prepared, distributed, and counted by government officials. The office-block ballot groups candidates according to office. The party-column ballot groups candidates according to party labels and symbols.

7. Voter participation in the United States is low (and generally declining) compared with that in other countries. Current voter eligibility requires registration, citizenship, and specified age and residency requirements. Each state has different qualifications. Socioeconomic or demographic factors that influence voting decisions include (a) education, (b) income and socioeconomic status, (c) religion, (d) ethnic background, (e) gender, (f) age, and (g) geographic region. Psychological factors that influence voting decisions include (a) party identification, (b) perception of candidates, and (c) issue preferences.

8. The media are enormously important in American politics today. They perform a number of functions, in-cluding (a) entertainment, (b) news reporting, (c) identifying public problems, (d) socializing new generations, (e) providing a political forum, and (f) making profits.

9. The media wield enormous political power during political campaigns and over the affairs of government and government officials by focusing attention on their actions. Today's political campaigns use paid-for political announcements and expert management of news coverage. Of equal importance for presidential candidates is how they appear in presidential debates.

10. The relationship between the media and the president is close; each has used the other—sometimes positively, sometimes negatively. The media play an important role in investigating the government, in getting government officials to understand better the needs and desires of American society, and in setting the public agenda.

QUESTIONS FOR REVIEW AND DISCUSSION

1. Should we change the system of nomination for political office in order to encourage more control by political parties or interest groups? How would the behavior of members of Congress change, for example, if most members were nominated by their respective parties rather than being self-nominated?

2. How should political campaigns be financed? Should all campaigns be financed by the general public, with strict limits on expenditures? How would such regulations change the nature of campaign advertising and other strategies?

3. Compare the coverage of a major political event by the printed media, the network news, CNN, and talk shows. What can you learn from each type of presentation? In which format is the most information available? Are different aspects of the event emphasized by different presentations? How does editing change the theme of the story in each case?

4. What should be the role of mass media in a presidential campaign? How could the media become a vehicle for improving debate over the major issues of a campaign? To what extent should the media focus on the personality and character of the candidates? What impact does the focus on the "horse race" aspect of a campaign have on the voters?

LOGGING ON: CAMPAIGNS, ELECTIONS, AND THE MEDIA

You can get the political party platforms of the Democratic, Libertarian, and Green parties through **gopher** at

wiretap.spies.com

and then choose

government docs

Work your way down to

Political Platforms of the US

You can follow discussions of the 1996 Republican presidential campaigns at

us.politics.bob-dole

or at

us.politics.phil-gramm

Keep an eye out for the 1994 campaigns, and the 1996 races, too, at this address.

To view White House press releases and other general political information, you can access

alt.politics.usa.misc

on the Michigan State University **gopher.** Go to

News & Weather; USENET News; alt/; politics/

This is often a good source of information for what is going on in the executive branch of government. After all, 90 percent of all news concerning the government comes from prearranged events, such as those covered in White House press releases. This service gives you the opportunity to read those releases just as the media see them.

For information on current political affairs, you can subscribe to *The Electronic Newsstand* by accessing

gopher.internet.com2100

This service provides a wide range of information of a political nature.

For everything you ever wanted to know about Rush Limbaugh and more, try

cathouse.org

and use the path

/publ cathouse/rush limbaugh/*

Another source for Rush trivia and information is

alt.fan.rush-limbaugh

SELECTED REFERENCES

Corrado, Anthony. *Creative Campaigning: PACs and the Presidential Selection Process*. Boulder, Colo.: Westview Press, 1992. This book investigates and explains the use of political action committees for presidential campaigns. It shows how a candidate can raise early money to enter the campaign through what the author calls "shadow campaigns."

Felknor, Bruce L. *Political Mischief: Smear, Sabotage, and Reform in U.S. Elections*. New York: Praeger, 1992. Analyzing campaigns from that of George Washington to the present, the author discusses and classifies forms of political mischief. He concentrates on the two most serious types of political corruption: deceiving the voter and preventing citizens from voting.

Gilder, George. *Life after Television: The Coming Transformation of Media and American Life*. New York: Norton, 1993. The author predicts a future when the commu-nications networks that we currently have—telephones and televisions—are made obsolete by fiber-optic computer networks that link everyone in the United States. Gilder believes that such direct connections will enable people to take control of their own democracy and free themselves from the influence of the mass media.

Glennon, Michael J. *When No Majority Rules: The Electoral College and Presidential Succession*. Washington, D.C.: Congressional Quarterly Press, 1992. This clear explanation of how the electoral college functions discusses the possible options for the political system if no candidate obtains a majority of electoral votes.

Graber, Doris A. *Media Power in Politics,* 4th ed. Washington, D.C.: Congressional Quarterly Press, 1994. This book explores the profound impact of the mass media on the political system. It has both a historical and a topical focus.

MacArthur, John R. *Second Front: Censorship and Propaganda in the Gulf War*. New York: Hill and Wang, 1992. This book evaluates media coverage of the war against Iraq as having been overly susceptible to manipulation by the military and the Bush administration. The author advocates a more adversarial form of reporting.

Mitchell, Greg. *The Campaign of the Century: Upton Sinclair's Race for Governor of California and the Birth of Media Politics*. New York: Random House, 1992. The subject of this book is the 1934 campaign of muckraking novelist Upton Sinclair, who ran for governor of California on an antipoverty platform. Frightened by his "radical" politics, the Hollywood studios and the business community hired consultants and mounted against Sinclair the first major media campaign ever, inventing the idea of political consulting.

Nelson, Michael, ed. *The Elections of 1992*. Washington, D.C.: Congressional Quarterly Press, 1993. This collection of essays by prominent scholars discusses the issues and events of the 1992 presidential race and congressional campaigns.

Rosenstiel, Tom. *Strange Bedfellows: How Television and the Presidential Candidates Changed American Politics, 1992*. New York: Hyperion, 1993. The author, who is a correspondent for the *Los Angeles Times*, criticizes the press for its treatment of the campaign as a horse race, for searching for gossip rather than news, and for wanting to become pundits rather than journalists. This is an interesting account of the 1992 campaign.

Sorauf, Frank J. *Inside Campaign Finance: Myths and Realties*. New Haven, Conn.: Yale University Press, 1992. This leading scholar of political parties and elections provides an extensive and balanced treatment of current issues in campaign finance, including the power of political action committees, the ways in which candidates and parties avoid finance regulations, possible reforms of the system, and obstacles to reform.

Teixeira, Ruy A. *The Disappearing American Voter*. Washington, D.C.: Brookings Institution, 1992. This thoughtful study examines the historical causes for the decline in voter turnout in the United States and suggests that the reasons for this decline include the relatively high costs of registration and voting for the citizen and the perceived low benefits of voting to the average person.

Wriston, Walter. *The Twilight of Sovereignty: How the Information Revolution Is Transforming Our World*. New York: Scribner's, 1993. The author argues that the microchip and satellite technologies have created a world community, with political and economic ramifications far beyond our imagination. He believes that the new technology fosters democracy and can be used to improve economic conditions throughout the world.

PART FOUR

Political Institutions

10
The Congress

 CHAPTER OUTLINE

WHAT IF . . .
Congresspersons Were Limited to Two Terms?

We all know that members of the U.S. House of Representatives serve terms that last for two years, that members of the U.S. Senate serve terms that last for six years, and that both House and Senate members can be reelected indefinitely. In fact, some members of Congress have been able to achieve reelection so easily and so often that occasionally they have served for as long as half a century in the national legislature! Most members, of course, serve far less time in office than that, but once elected, representatives and senators are usually hard to dethrone. What might happen, though, if members of the U.S. Congress were limited to serving, say, only two terms (four years in the House or twelve years in the Senate)?

The most obvious impact of the two-term limit would come in the area of seniority. Seniority, or the length of continuous service on the record of a member of Congress in either chamber, is the single most important factor in determining who gets to be the chair of a committee, who becomes a party leader, who becomes speaker of the House or president pro tempore of the Senate, who is influential in floor debate, and who has an easier time getting his or her legislative measures adopted on the floor of Congress. With everyone limited to just two terms in office, distinctions of rank based on seniority would all but vanish. As was true in the early history of Congress, greater influence today would probably go to those who are the best natural leaders because of personal magnetism, spellbinding oratorical powers, or intricate knowledge of the rules of procedure. Power on committees would likely become even more diffuse than it is now.

Relationships between Congress and the White House would quite likely be affected, too, by a change to a two-term limit on membership in Congress. Presidents, assuming that their own terms were not changed, would know that they could easily last in office longer than most members of Congress. From the presidential viewpoint, then, the two-term limit would seem to even the odds of success when dealing with members of Congress. At the same time, however, the two-term limit might increase all the more the executive power that senators and representatives fear and that has grown so significantly since World War II.

From the voters' perspective, we would all have to get used to an entirely new set of people running for the House and Senate every few years. That would make it imperative that voters have "cues" about the personalities and issue positions taken by these new sets of candidates so they can determine how to vote. Voters would have to depend, as they do today, on political parties to furnish information about the candidates' positions and qualifications. Rich or well-funded candidates would have a great advantage in buying media exposure—as is also the case today.

Interest groups might not be very interested in backing candidates, however, because a two-term legislator probably could do little for them. In fact, these short-term representatives might ignore not only interest groups but also the voters, figuring that they might as well cast their congressional votes on the basis of their personal preferences.

After the 1994 elections, twenty-four states had approved congressional term limits. In 1995, the Supreme Court held the Arkansas term limits law to be unconstitutional. In a five-to-four decision, the Court held that neither the states nor Congress could limit congressional terms. Only a constitutional amendment can accomplish this. The movement to limit terms is strong, however, and a constitutional amendment remains a possibility.

---

1. Would two-term members of Congress be more in touch with the voters? Would they be less in touch with the voters?
2. In a Congress in which members could serve for only two terms, what would seniority mean?

Most Americans spend little time thinking about the Congress of the United States, and when they do, their opinions are frequently unflattering. In the early 1990s, the *New York Times* reported that only 23 percent of the American people approved of the job that Congress was doing. But 56 percent still approved of the performance of their own representatives. This is one of the paradoxes of the relationship between the people and Congress. Members of the public hold the institution in low regard while expressing satisfaction with their individual representatives. (For a discussion of how different Congress might be if each member's term was limited, see the *What If . . .* that opens this chapter.)

Part of the explanation for these seemingly contradictory appraisals is that members of Congress spend considerable time and effort serving their constituents. If the federal bureaucracy makes a mistake, the senator's or representative's office tries to resolve the issue. What most Americans see of Congress, therefore, is the work of their own representatives in their home states. Congress, however, was created to work not just for local constituents but also for the nation as a whole. Understanding the nature of the institution and the process of lawmaking is an important part of understanding how the policies that shape our lives are made.

WHY WAS CONGRESS CREATED?

The founders of the American republic believed that the bulk of the power that would be exercised by a national government should be in the hands of the legislature. As you will recall from Chapter 2, the authors of the Constitution were strongly influenced by their fear of tyrannical kings and powerful, unchecked rulers. They were also aware of how ineffective the confederal Congress had been during its brief existence under the Articles of Confederation.

John Lewis, former civil rights worker, was elected to Congress in 1986, representing a state in which he had been denied political participation twenty-five years earlier.

The leading role envisioned for Congress in the new government is apparent from its primacy in the Constitution. Article I deals with the structure, the powers, and the operation of Congress, beginning in Section 1 with an application of the basic principle of separation of powers: "All legislative Powers herein granted shall be vested in a Congress of the United States, which shall consist of a Senate and House of Representatives." These legislative powers are spelled out in detail in Article I and elsewhere.

BICAMERALISM
The division of a legislature into two separate assemblies.

The **bicameralism** of Congress—its division into two legislative houses—was in part an outgrowth of the Connecticut Compromise, which tried to balance the big-state population advantage, reflected in the House, and the small-state demand for equality in policymaking, which was satisfied in the Senate. Beyond that, the two chambers of Congress also reflected the social class biases of the founders. They wished to balance the interests and the numerical superiority of the common citizen with the property interests of the less numerous landowners, bankers, and merchants. This goal was achieved by providing in Sections 2 and 3 of Article I that members of the House of Representatives should be elected directly by "the People," whereas members of the Senate were to be chosen by the elected representatives sitting in state legislatures, who were more likely to be members of the elite. (The latter provision was changed by the Seventeenth Amendment in 1913 to provide that senators also be elected directly.)

The elected House, then, was to be the common person's chamber, and the nonelected Senate was to be the chamber of the elite, similar to the division between the House of Commons and the House of Lords in England. Also, the House was meant to represent the people, whereas the Senate was meant to represent the states, in accordance with the intent of the Connecticut Compromise. The issue of who counted as part of "the People" for electing members of the House was left up to the states. The logic of separate constituencies and separate interests underlying the bicameral Congress was reinforced by differences in length of tenure. Members of the House were required to face the electorate every two years, whereas senators could serve for a much more secure term of six years—even longer than the four-year term provided for the president. Furthermore, the senators' terms were staggered so that only one-third of the senators would face election with all of the House members.

THE POWERS OF CONGRESS

The Constitution is both highly specific and extremely vague about the powers that Congress may exercise. The first seventeen clauses of Article I, Section 8, specify most of the **enumerated powers** of Congress—that is, powers expressly given to that body.

Enumerated Powers

ENUMERATED POWER
A power specifically granted to the national government by the Constitution. The first seventeen clauses of Article I, Section 8, specify most of the enumerated powers of Congress.

The enumerated, or expressed, powers of Congress include the right to impose taxes and import tariffs; borrow money; regulate interstate commerce and international trade; establish procedures for naturalizing citizens; make laws regulating bankruptcies; coin (and print) money and regulate its value; establish standards of weights and measures; punish counterfeiters; establish post offices and postal routes; regulate copyrights and patents; establish lower federal courts; punish pirates and others committing illegal acts on the high seas; declare war; raise and regulate an army and a navy; call up and regulate the state militias to enforce laws, to suppress insurrections, and to repel invasions; and govern the District of Columbia.

The most important of the domestic powers of Congress, listed in Article I, Section 8, are the rights to collect taxes, to spend money, and to regulate commerce, whereas the most important foreign policy power is the power to declare war. Other sections of the Constitution give Congress a wide range of further powers. Generally, Congress is also able to establish rules for its own members, to regulate the electoral college, and to override a presidential veto.

Some functions are restricted to only one house. Under Article II, Section 2, the Senate must advise on, and consent to, the ratification of treaties and must accept or reject presidential nominations of ambassadors, Supreme Court justices, and "all other Officers of the United States." But the Senate may delegate to the president, the courts, or department heads the power to make lesser appointments. Congress may regulate the appellate jurisdiction of the Supreme Court, regulate relations between states, and propose amendments to the Constitution.

The amendments to the Constitution provide for other congressional powers. Congress must certify the election of a president and a vice president or itself choose these officers if no candidate has a majority of the electoral vote (Twelfth Amendment). It may levy an income tax (Sixteenth Amendment) and determine who will be acting president in case of the death or incapacity of the president or vice president (Twentieth Amendment, Sections 3 and 4, and Twenty-fifth Amendment, Sections 2, 3, and 4). In addition, Congress explicitly is given the power to enforce, by appropriate legislation, the provisions of several other amendments.

The president appoints Supreme Court justices only with the advice and consent of the Senate. On occasion, presidents have nominated individuals who were not confirmed by the Senate. Here, in contrast, President Clinton's successful first nominee, Ruth Bader Ginsburg, is being congratulated by Senator Dianne Feinstein (D., Cal.) and Carol Moseley Braun (D., Ill.).

The Necessary and Proper Clause

Beyond these numerous specific powers, Congress enjoys the right under Article I, Section 8 (the "elastic," or "necessary and proper," clause), "[t]o make all Laws which shall be necessary and proper for carrying into Execution the foregoing Powers [of Article I], and all other Powers vested by this Constitution in the Government of the United States, or in any Department or Officer thereof." This vague statement of congressional responsibilities has set the stage for a greatly expanded role for the national government relative to the states. It has also constituted, at least in theory, a check on the expansion of presidential powers. By continuing to delegate powers to the executive branch, however, over time Congress has reduced the role it otherwise might play in national and international affairs.

THE FUNCTIONS OF CONGRESS

Congress, as an institution of government, is expected by its members, by the public, and by other centers of political power to perform a number of functions. Our perceptions of how good a job Congress is doing overall are tied closely to evaluations of whether and how it fulfills certain specific tasks. These tasks include the following:

1. Lawmaking.
2. Service to constituents.
3. Representation.
4. Oversight.
5. Public education.
6. Conflict resolution.

The Lawmaking Function

LAWMAKING
The process of deciding the legal rules that govern our society. Such laws may regulate minor affairs or establish broad national policies.

The principal and most obvious function of any legislature is **lawmaking.** Congress is the highest elected body in the country charged with making binding rules for all Americans. Lawmaking requires decisions about such matters as the size of the federal budget, gun control, and the long-term prospects for war or peace. This does not mean, however, that Congress initiates most of the ideas for legislation that it eventually considers. Most of the bills that Congress acts on originate in the executive branch, and many other bills are traceable to interest groups and political party organizations. Through the processes of compromise and **logrolling** (offering to support a fellow member's bill in exchange for that member's promise to support your bill in the future), backers of legislation attempt to fashion a winning majority coalition.

LOGROLLING
An arrangement by which two or more members of Congress agree in advance to support each other's bills.

Service to Constituents

CASEWORK
Personal work for constituents by members of Congress.

Individual members of Congress are expected by their constituents to act as brokers between private citizens and the imposing, often faceless, federal government. **Casework** is the usual form taken by this function of providing service to constituents. The legislator and his or her staff spend a considerable portion of their time in casework activity, such as tracking down a missing Social Security check, explaining the meaning of particular bills to people who may be affected by them, promoting a local business interest, or interceding with a regulatory agency on behalf of constituents who disagree with proposed agency regulations.

Legislators and many analysts of congressional behavior regard this **ombudsman** role as an activity that strongly benefits the members of Congress. A government characterized by a large, confusing bureaucracy and complex public programs offers innumerable opportunities for legislators to come to the assistance of (usually) grateful constituents. Morris P. Fiorina suggests somewhat mischievously that senators and representatives prefer to maintain bureaucratic confusion in order to maximize their opportunities for performing good deeds on behalf of their constituents:

> Some poor, aggrieved constituent becomes enmeshed in the tentacles of an evil bureaucracy and calls upon Congressman St. George to do battle with the dragon. . . . In dealing with the bureaucracy, the congressman is not merely one vote of 435. Rather, he is a nonpartisan power, someone whose phone call snaps an office to attention. He is not kept on hold. The constituent who receives aid believes that his congressman and his congressman alone got results.[1]

The Representation Function

If constituency service carries with it nothing but benefits for most members of Congress, the function of **representation** is less certain and even carries with it some danger that the legislator will lose his or her bid for reelection. Generally, representation means that the many competing interests in society should be represented in Congress. It follows that Congress should be a body acting slowly and deliberately and that its foremost concern should be to maintain a carefully crafted balance of power among competing interests.

How is representation to be achieved? There are basically two points of view on this issue. The first approach to the question of how representation should be achieved is that legislators should act as **trustees** of the broad interests of the entire society and that they should vote against the narrow interests of their constituents as their conscience and their perception of national needs dictate. For example, some Democratic legislators voted for the North American Free Trade Agreement (NAFTA) in late 1993 in spite of strong opposition from unions in their districts.

Directly opposed to the trustee view of representation is the notion that the members of Congress should behave as **instructed delegates**. That is, they should mirror the views of the majority of the constituents who elected them to power in the first place. On the surface, this approach is plausible and rewarding. For it to work, however, we must assume that constituents actually have well-formed views on the issues that are decided in Congress and, further, that they have clear-cut preferences about these issues. Neither condition is likely to be satisfied very often. Most people generally do not have well-articulated views on major issues. Among those who do, there

OMBUDSMAN
An individual in the role of hearing and investigating complaints by private individuals against public officials or agencies.

REPRESENTATION
The function of members of Congress as elected officials to represent the views of their constituents.

TRUSTEE
In regard to a legislator, one who acts according to his or her conscience and the broad interests of the entire society.

INSTRUCTED DELEGATE
A legislator who is an agent of the voters who elected him or her and who votes according to the views of constituents regardless of personal assessments.

---

1. Morris P. Fiorina, *Congress: Keystone of the Washington Establishment,* 2d ed. (New Haven, Conn.: Yale University Press, 1989), pp. 44, 47.

POLITICO
The legislative role that combines the instructed-delegate and trustee concepts. The legislator varies the role according to the issue under consideration.

OVERSIGHT
The responsibility Congress has for following up on laws it has enacted to ensure that they are being enforced and administered in the way in which they were intended.

LEGISLATIVE VETO
A provision in a bill reserving to Congress or to a congressional committee the power to reject an act or regulation of a national agency by majority vote; declared unconstitutional by the Supreme Court in 1983.

AGENDA SETTING
Determining which public policy questions will be debated or considered by Congress.

frequently is no clear majority position but rather a range of often conflicting minority perspectives.

In a major study of the attitudes held by members of Congress about their proper role as representatives, Roger Davidson found that neither a pure trustee view nor a pure instructed-delegate view was held by most legislators. Davidson's sampling of members of Congress showed that about the same proportion endorsed the trustee approach (28 percent) and delegate approach (23 percent) to representation. The clear preference, however, was for the **politico** position—which combines both perspectives in a pragmatic mix.[2]

The Oversight Function

Oversight of the bureaucracy is essential if the decisions made by Congress are to have any force. **Oversight** is the process by which Congress follows up on the laws it has enacted to ensure that they are being enforced and administered in the way Congress intended. This is done by holding committee hearings and investigations, changing the size of an agency's budget, and cross-examining high-level presidential nominees to head major agencies. Also, until 1983, Congress could refuse to accede to proposed rules and regulations by resorting to the **legislative veto.** This allowed one, or sometimes both, chambers of Congress to disapprove of an executive rule within a specified period of time by a simple majority vote and thereby prevent its enforcement. In 1983, however, the Supreme Court ruled that such a veto violated the separation of powers mandated by the Constitution, because the president had no power to veto the legislative action. Thus, the legislative veto was declared unconstitutional.[3]

Senators and representatives increasingly see their oversight function as a critically important part of their legislative activities. In part, oversight is related to the concept of constituency service, particularly when Congress investigates alleged arbitrariness or wrongdoing by bureaucratic agencies.[4]

The Public-Education Function

Educating the public is a function that is exercised whenever Congress holds public hearings, exercises oversight over the bureaucracy, or engages in committee and floor debate on such major issues and topics as political assassinations, aging, illegal drugs, or the concerns of small businesses. In so doing, Congress presents a range of viewpoints on pressing national questions. Congress also decides what issues will come up for discussion and decision; **agenda setting** is a major facet of its public-education function.

The Conflict-Resolution Function

Congress is commonly seen as an institution for resolving conflicts within American society. Organized interest groups and representatives of different racial, religious, economic, and ideological interests look on Congress as an

---

2. Roger Davidson, *The Role of the Congressman* (New York: Pegasus, 1969), p. 117.
3. *Immigration and Naturalization Service v. Chadha,* 454 U.S. 812 (1983).
4. Mary W. Cohn, ed., *How Congress Works* (Washington, D.C.: Congressional Quarterly Press, 1991), p. 99.

access point for airing their grievances and possibly for stimulating government action on their behalf. A logical extension of the representation function, this focus on conflict resolution puts Congress in the role of trying to resolve the differences among competing points of view by passing laws to accommodate as many interested parties as possible. Clearly, this is not always achieved. Every legislative decision results in some winners and some losers. Congress commonly is regarded as the place to go in Washington to get a friendly hearing or a desired policy result. To the extent that Congress does accommodate competing interests, it tends to build support for the entire political process by all branches of government.

HOUSE-SENATE DIFFERENCES

The preceding functions of Congress describe how that body is expected to perform and what it does as a whole. To understand better what goes on in the national legislature, however, we need to examine the effects of bicameralism, for Congress is composed of two markedly different—although coequal—chambers. Although the Senate and the House of Representatives exist within the same legislative institution, each has developed certain distinctive features that clearly distinguish life on one end of Capitol Hill from conditions on the other (the Senate wing is on the north side of the Capitol building, and the House wing is on the south side). A summary of these differences is given in Table 10–1.

Size and Rules

The central difference between the House and the Senate is simply that the House is much larger than the Senate. The House has 435 representatives,

TABLE 10–1

Differences between the House and the Senate

HOUSE*	SENATE*
Members chosen from local districts	Members chosen from an entire state
Two-year term	Six-year term
Originally elected by voters	Originally (until 1913) elected by state legislatures
May impeach (indict) federal officials	May convict federal officials of impeachable offenses
Larger (435 voting members)	Smaller (100 members)
More formal rules	Fewer rules and restrictions
Debate limited	Debate extended
Floor action controlled	Unanimous consent rules
Less prestige and less individual notice	More prestige and more media attention
Originates bills for raising revenues	Has power to advise the president on, and to consent to, presidential appointments and treaties
Local or narrow leadership	National leadership

*Some of these differences, such as the term of office, are provided for in the Constitution. Others, such as debate rules, are not.

plus delegates from the District of Columbia, Puerto Rico, Guam, American Samoa, and the Virgin Islands, compared with just 100 senators. This size difference means that a greater number of formal rules are needed to govern activity in the House, whereas correspondingly looser procedures can be followed in the less crowded Senate. This difference is most obvious in the rules governing debate on the floors of the two chambers.

The Senate normally permits extended debate on all issues that arise before it. In contrast, the House operates with an elaborate system in which its **Rules Committee** normally proposes time limitations on debate for any bill, and a majority of the entire body accepts or modifies those suggested time limits. As a consequence of its stricter time limits on debate, and despite its greater size, the House often is able to act on legislation more quickly than the Senate.

Debate and Filibustering

According to historians, the Senate tradition of unlimited debate, which is known as **filibustering**, dates back to 1790, when a proposal to move the U.S. capital from New York to Philadelphia was stalled by such time-wasting tactics. This unlimited-debate tradition—which also existed in the House until 1811—is not absolute, however.

Under Senate Rule 22, debate may be ended by invoking **cloture**, or shutting off discussion on a bill. Amended in 1975 and 1979, Rule 22 states that debate may be closed off on a bill if sixteen senators sign a petition requesting it and if, after two days have elapsed, three-fifths of the entire membership (sixty votes, assuming no vacancies) vote for cloture.[5] After cloture is invoked, each senator may speak on a bill for a maximum of one hour before a vote is taken. A final vote must take place within one hundred hours of debate after cloture has been imposed. The rule also limits the use of multiple amendments to stall postcloture final action on a bill.

Prestige

As a consequence of the greater size of the House, representatives generally cannot achieve as much individual recognition and public prestige as can members of the Senate. Senators, especially those who openly express presidential ambitions, are better able to gain media exposure and to establish careers as spokespersons for large national constituencies. To obtain recognition for his or her activities, a member of the House generally must do one of two things. He or she might survive in office long enough to join the ranks of the leadership on committees or within the party. Alternatively, the representative could become an expert on some specialized aspect of legislative policy—such as tax laws, the environment, or education.

CONGRESSPERSONS AND THE CITIZENRY: A COMPARISON

Government institutions are given life by the people who work in them and shape them as political structures. Who, then, are the members of Congress, and how are they elected?

---

5. Edward V. Schneier and Bertram Gross, *Congress Today* (New York: St. Martin's Press, 1993), p. 221.

RULES COMMITTEE
A standing committee of the House of Representatives that provides special rules under which specific bills can be debated, amended, and considered by the House.

FILIBUSTERING
In the Senate, unlimited debate to halt action on a particular bill.

CLOTURE
A method to close off debate and to bring the matter under consideration to a vote in the Senate.

Senator Strom Thurmond leaves the chamber after completing a record-setting filibuster that lasted for twenty-four hours and eighteen minutes. The purpose of the filibuster was to thwart the passage of the 1957 Civil Rights Act.

Members of the U.S. Senate and the U.S. House of Representatives are not typical American citizens, as can be seen in Table 10–2. Members of Congress are, of course, older than most Americans, partly because of constitutional age requirements and partly because a good deal of political experience normally is an advantage in running for national office. Members of Congress are also disproportionately white, male, Protestant, and trained in higher-status occupations.

TABLE 10–2
Characteristics of the 104th Congress (1995 to 1997)

CHARACTERISTIC	U.S. POPULATION (1990)	HOUSE	SENATE
Age (median)	33.0	50.9	58.4
Percentage minority	28.0	14.2	4
Religion			
Percentage church members	61.0	98	99
Percentage Roman Catholic	39.0	29	20
Percentage Protestant	56.0	63	61
Percentage Jewish	4.0	5.5	9
Percentage female	51.9	11	8
Percentage with college degrees	21.4	98	99
Occupation			
Percentage lawyers	2.8	39	54
Percentage blue-collar workers	20.1	0	0
Family income			
Percentage of families earning over $50,000 annually	22.0	100	100
Personal wealth			
Percentage of population with assets over $1 million	0.7	16	33

Some recent trends in the social characteristics of Congress should be noted, however. The average age of members of the 104th Congress is 52.2 years—a slight decrease from an average age of 53 three decades ago. The Protestant domination of Congress has been loosened, with substantial increases being made in the representation of Jews and Roman Catholics. Some Protestant denominations, notably Episcopalians and Presbyterians, are overrepresented in Congress. Baptists and Lutherans are underrepresented, relative to their numbers among U.S. Protestants.

Lawyers are by far the largest occupational group among congresspersons: 54 senators and 170 representatives in the 104th Congress reported that they were trained in the legal profession. The proportion of lawyers in the House is lower now than at nearly any time in the last thirty years, however.

CONGRESSIONAL ELECTIONS

The process of electing members of Congress is decentralized. Congressional elections are operated by the individual state governments, which must conform to the rules established by the U.S. Constitution and by national statutes. The Constitution states that representatives are to be elected every second year by popular ballot, and the number of seats awarded to each state is to be determined by the results of the decennial census. Each state has at least one representative, with most congressional districts having about half a million residents. Senators are elected by popular vote (since the passage of the Seventeenth Amendment) every six years; approximately one-third of the seats are chosen every two years. Each state has two senators. Under Article I, Section 4, of the Constitution, state legislatures are given control over "[t]he Times, Places and Manner of holding Elections for

After African Americans gained the right to vote in 1870, several southern states elected African-American senators and representatives to Congress.

Senators and Representatives"; however, "the Congress may at any time by Law make or alter such Regulations."

Candidates for Congressional Elections

Reasons for Making the Race.   At least three major factors are important in determining who will run for congressional office and whether party leaders are willing to recruit someone for the race. As discussed by James David Barber, these are *motivation, resources,* and *opportunity.*[6] Motivation means that a candidate must be able to achieve a sense of self-satisfaction from participating in the contest. It also implies that a candidate must project a positive attitude toward electoral politics. Important resources for the campaign include money, the political skills of the candidate and of his or her supporters, the ability of the candidate and staff to take time off from their regular jobs and other commitments, and the candidate's access to the mass media. Opportunity relates to such questions as whether an incumbent is running for office, whether many candidates are contending for the same nomination, how strong the opposition party may be in November, and whether the local party activists form a positive image of the candidate.[7]

The Nomination Process.   Since the early part of the century, control over the process of nominating congressional candidates has been shifting from party conventions—which reformers charged with being corrupt and boss controlled—to **direct primaries,** in which **party identifiers** in the electorate select the candidate who will carry that party's endorsement into the actual election. All fifty states currently use the direct primary to select party nominees for senator or representative. In general, there are more candidates running and the competition is more intense when a party is strong and a November victory is likely.

The Congressional Campaign.   Most candidates win through the effectiveness of their personal organizations, although sometimes with assistance from the state party organization. Congressional candidates have only a loose affiliation to the party at the national and state level. Even the effect of presidential "coattails," in which a victorious president helps bring into office legislators who would not have won otherwise, is minimal. For example, Richard Nixon's smashing victory over George McGovern in 1972, with 61 percent of the popular vote and 520 out of 538 electoral votes, resulted in a gain of only twelve Republican seats in the House.

In midterm congressional elections—those held between presidential contests—voter turnout falls sharply. In these elections, party affiliation of the voters who turn out is a stronger force in deciding election outcomes, and the party controlling the White House normally loses seats in Congress. Additionally, voters in midterm elections often are responding to incumbency issues, because there is no presidential campaign. Table 10–3 shows

DIRECT PRIMARY
An intraparty election in which the voters select the candidates who will run on a party's ticket in the subsequent general election.

PARTY IDENTIFIER
A person who identifies himself or herself with a political party.

---

6. James David Barber, *The Lawmakers: Recruitment and Adaptation to Legislative Life* (New Haven, Conn.: Yale University Press, 1965), pp. 10–15.

7. See the work of Gary Jacobson, *The Politics of Congressional Elections,* 3d ed. (New York: Harper Collins, 1993).

TABLE 10–3

Midterm Losses by the Party of the President, 1942 to 1994

SEATS LOST BY THE PARTY OF THE PRESIDENT IN THE HOUSE OF REPRESENTATIVES	
1942	−45 (D.)
1946	−55 (D.)
1950	−29 (D.)
1954	−18 (R.)
1958	−47 (R.)
1962	− 4 (D.)
1966	−47 (D.)
1970	−12 (R.)
1974	−48 (R.)
1978	−15 (D.)
1982	−26 (R.)
1986	− 5 (R.)
1990	− 8 (R.)
1994	−52 (D.)

the pattern for midterm elections since 1942. The result is a fragmentation of party authority and a loosening of the ties between Congress and the president.

The Power of Incumbency

The power of incumbency in the outcome of congressional elections cannot be overemphasized. Table 10–4 shows that the overwhelming majority of representatives and a smaller proportion of senators who decide to run for reelection usually are successful. This conclusion holds for both presidential-year and midterm elections.

David R. Mayhew argues that the pursuit of reelection is the strongest motivation behind the activities of members of Congress.[8] The reelection goal is pursued in three major ways: by *advertising,* by *credit claiming,* and by *position taking.* Advertising includes using the mass media, making personal appearances with constituents, and sending newsletters—all to produce a favorable image and to make the incumbent's name a household word.

8. David R. Mayhew, *Congress: The Electoral Connection* (New Haven, Conn.: Yale University Press, 1974).

TABLE 10–4

The Power of Incumbency

	PRESIDENTIAL-YEAR ELECTIONS						MIDTERM ELECTIONS						
	1972	1976	1980	1984	1988	1992	1970	1974	1978	1982	1986	1990	1994
House													
Number of incumbent candidates	390	384	398	409	409	368	401	391	382	393	393	407	382
Reelected	365	368	361	390	402	325	379	343	358	352	385	391	347
Percentage of total	93.6	95.8	90.7	95.4	98.3	88.9	94.5	87.7	93.7	90.1	98.0	96.1	90.8
Defeated	25	16	37	19	7	43	22	48	24	39	8	16	35
In primary	12	3	6	3	1	19	10	8	5	10	2	1	1
In general election	13	13	31	16	6	24	12	40	19	29	6	15	34
Senate													
Number of incumbent candidates	27	25	29	29	27	28	31	27	25	30	28	32	26
Reelected	20	16	16	26	23	23	24	23	15	28	21	31	24
Percentage of total	74.1	64.0	55.2	89.6	85	82.1	77.4	85.2	60.0	93.3	75.0	96.9	92.3
Defeated	7	9	13	3	4	5	7	4	10	2	7	1	2
In primary	2	0	4	0	0	1	1	2	3	0	0	0	0
In general election	5	9	9	3	4	4	6	2	7	2	7	1	2

SOURCE: Norman Ornstein, Thomas E. Mann, and Michael J. Malbin, *Vital Statistics on Congress, 1993–1994* (Washington, D.C.: Congressional Quarterly Press, 1994), pp. 56–57; *Congressional Quarterly Weekly Report,* November 7, 1992, pp. 3551, 3576; and authors' update.

Members of Congress try to present themselves as informed, experienced, and responsive to people's needs. Credit claiming focuses on the things a legislator claims to have done to benefit his or her constituents—by fulfilling the congressional casework function or by supplying material goods in the form of, say, a new post office or a construction project, such as a dam or highway. Position taking occurs when an incumbent explains his or her voting record on key issues; makes public statements of general support for presidential decisions; or indicates that he or she specifically supports positions on key issues, such as gun control or anti-inflation policies. Position taking carries with it certain risks, as the incumbent may lose support by disagreeing with the attitudes of a large number of constituents.

The Shakeup of 1992

Because of the many scandals and the stalemate between President George Bush and Congress over many issues, 1992 was a year of change. Public disgust was reflected in the attempts by several states to impose term limits on congresspersons. A record number of the legislators who were up for reelection in 1992 decided to retire rather than face bitter campaigns. In some cases, the redistricting of congressional seats left two sitting members competing against each other, or district boundaries were redrawn in such a way as to make reelection of the incumbent impossible. When the polls closed, forty-eight incumbents had been defeated.

The 1992 congressional election changed the make-up of the legislature even more by the victories of historic numbers of minority and female legislators. In the 103d Congress, 15 percent of the members represented ethnic minorities. At the same time, the number of women elected to the House of Representatives doubled, with forty-eight women taking seats in that chamber in the 103d Congress. Four new female senators (Barbara Boxer and Dianne Feinstein of California, Carol Moseley Braun of Illinois, and Patty Murray of Washington) joined the two already in the chamber (Barbara Mikulski of Maryland and Nancy Landon Kassebaum of Kansas). All four of the new female senators were Democrats, with liberal positions on many issues. One, Moseley Braun, became the first female African American ever to join the upper chamber. A seventh female member joined the senatorial ranks when Kay Bailey Hutchison, a Republican, won a special election in Texas to fill the seat vacated when Lloyd Bentsen became Bill Clinton's secretary of the treasury. The 103d Congress also saw the first Native-American senator in more than sixty years, Ben Nighthorse Campbell of Colorado, take his seat (see this chapter's *Politics: The Human Side*).

The 1994 Elections

The 1994 midterm elections swept the Democratic majority in both houses of Congress out of power and brought in a Republican majority in a nationwide change of government that surprised and shocked the members of Congress and the parties themselves. According to exit polls taken on election day, Republican candidates for the Congress won the votes of their own party identifiers, of the majority of independents, and of those who had voted for Perot in 1992, but of very few Democratic voters. Republicans captured the votes of white males with a gender gap of about 8 percentage points.

POLITICS: THE HUMAN SIDE
Ben Nighthorse Campbell, Native-American Senator

"Sometimes I think there ought to be more Indians in Congress, or else no Indians, because its damn tough being the only Indian."

BIOGRAPHICAL NOTES

Senator Ben Nighthorse Campbell was born on April 13, 1933, in Auburn, California. The child of a troubled family—his father was an alcoholic and his mother had tuberculosis—he was sent to orphanages; committed some juvenile offenses; and finally learned a skill, the martial art of judo. Campbell left high school to join the Air Force and, during his tour of duty in Korea, studied judo seriously. He became a college judo champion after completing his military service and eventually became the captain of the U.S. Olympic judo team in 1964. Soon after, he married, settled in Colorado, and began a career ranching and making contemporary Navajo-inspired jewelry. Campbell entered politics as a Democratic representative to the Colorado House of Representatives in 1983; won a seat in the U.S. House of Representatives in 1986; and then won election to the U.S. Senate in 1992, the first Native American in sixty years to sit in that body. In 1995, Senator Campbell announced that he was switching to the Republican party, bringing their majority up to 54.

POLITICAL CONTRIBUTIONS

Senator Campbell can best be described as a moderate. Although his heritage as a Northern Cheyenne makes him a strong advocate for Native-American issues, he is fairly conservative on government issues, particularly when they pit the federal government against the small rancher or businessperson. Campbell usually opposes environmental groups, believing that their views ignore the economic needs of the western regions. He supports term limits for Congress and has stated that he will stay in the Senate only for two terms.

Campbell already has established several new traditions in Congress. Arriving for his first term in Congress in 1987, he sought permission to wear a string tie with a silver bolo rather than the standard neckware. He has not asked permission from either the House or the Senate to appear in jeans, leather jackets, and cowboy boots, his standard attire. The attire, Campbell notes, is more convenient for riding his motorcycle to work. He is also the only senator to sport a ponytail. As Campbell puts it, "I've never believed that to be part of America, we all have to look alike, dress alike, talk alike and ride around in black limousines."

One of Campbell's proudest moments was his successful passage of legislation that changed the name of the Custer National Monument to the Little Bighorn Monument. His legislation also provided for a memorial to be erected at that site to honor the Native Americans who died there, as well as the soldiers. Although the senator is seen as the representative of Native-American interests by many tribes besides his own, some Native-American groups criticize him for his unwillingness to oppose mining and ranching on public lands.

Such criticism means little to the senator. Still a practicing silversmith, he intends to accomplish some of his own goals and represent his state in the Senate and then retire to his ranch, where he expects to "make more money than I need and have more fun than ought to be legal."

Republicans won 19 more seats in the South, giving them a 73–64 seat majority in that region. In Washington, the speaker of the House, Tom Foley, was defeated, the first Speaker to be denied reelection since 1862. In total, the Democrats lost 52 seats, with 190 incumbents reelected and 35 defeated. All Republican incumbents in the house were reelected.

The Republican victory in the Senate was even stronger than expected, sweeping all nine open seats and defeating two incumbent Democrats, Jim

Sasser of Tennessee and Harris Wofford of Pennsylvania. The day after the election, Senator Richard Shelby of Alabama announced his switch to the Republican party, giving the Republicans a majority of 53 to 47. Following the Senate's failure to pass the Balanced Budget Amendment in 1995, Ben Nighthorse Campbell also switched to the Republican party. (See the feature entitled *Politics and Elections: The Winners and the Losers* for more details on the 1994 elections.)

Control of both houses of Congress gave the Republicans an unprecedented opportunity to put forward their agenda if they could agree on its principles. For the first time in more than four decades, Republicans assumed the chairs of all the committees in both Houses. With Bob Dole as the majority leader of the Senate and Newt Gingrich as speaker of the House, the Republicans began to act on their program of change: The agenda included reforming Congress itself, including the cutting of staff and the deletion of some committees; reforming the tax code; passing a constitutional amendment for balancing the budget; cutting federal programs and spending; and creating new programs to reform the welfare system and fight crime.

CONGRESSIONAL REAPPORTIONMENT

By far the most complicated aspects of the mechanics of congressional elections are the issues of **reapportionment** (the allocation of seats in the House to each state after each census) and **redistricting** (the redrawing of the boundaries of the districts within each state).[9] In a landmark six-to-two vote in 1962, the Supreme Court made reapportionment a **justiciable** (that is, a reviewable) **question** in the Tennessee case of *Baker v. Carr*[10] by invoking the Fourteenth Amendment principle that no state can deny to any person "the equal protection of the laws." This principle was applied directly in the 1964 ruling, *Reynolds v. Sims*,[11] when the Court held that *both* chambers of a state legislature must be apportioned with equal populations in each district. This "one person, one vote" principle was applied to congressional districts in the 1964 case of *Wesberry v. Sanders*,[12] based on Article I, Section 2, of the Constitution, which requires that congresspersons be chosen "by the People of the several States."

Severe malapportionment of congressional districts prior to *Wesberry* had resulted in some districts containing two or three times the populations of other districts in the same state, thereby diluting the effect of a vote cast in the larger districts. This system generally had benefited the conservative populations of rural areas and small towns and harmed the interests of the more heavily populated and liberal urban areas. In fact, suburban areas have benefited the most from the *Wesberry* ruling, as suburbs account for an increasingly larger proportion of the nation's population, and cities include a correspondingly smaller segment of the population.

REAPPORTIONMENT
The allocation of seats in the House to each state after each census.

REDISTRICTING
The redrawing of the boundaries of the districts within each state.

JUSTICIABLE QUESTION
A question that may be raised and reviewed in court.

---

9. For an excellent discussion of these issues, see *Congressional Districts in the 1990s* (Washington, D.C.: Congressional Quarterly Press, 1993).
10. 369 U.S. 186 (1962).
11. 377 U.S. 533 (1964).
12. 376 U.S. 1 (1964).

POLITICS AND ELECTIONS:
The Winner and the Losers

The 1994 elections signaled a stunning change in the American political landscape: For the first time in about four decades, the Republican party secured control of both houses of Congress. Additionally, thirty states now have Republican governors, and nearly half of the ninety-nine state legislative houses and senates are controlled by Republicans.

The 1994 Elections at a Glance

Senate	Old	New
Republicans	44	53
Democrats	56	47
House		
Republicans	178	230
Democrats	256	203
Independents	1	1

Some of the most expensive congressional campaigns ever waged occurred during 1994. In California, Representative **Michael Huffington** (R., Calif.) reportedly spent almost $30 million in his attempt to defeat his Democratic opponent, Senator **Dianne Feinstein. Oliver North** of Virginia broke all records, though, in spending per registered voter. Whereas Huffington spent about $1.20 per registered voter, North spent about $3.20 per registered voter, or over $17 million, in his campaign against Senator **Charles Robb,** the Democratic incumbent. Nonetheless, he did not succeed in defeating Robb.

Key Democratic governors not reelected were **Ann Richards** of Texas and **Mario Cuomo** of New York. George Bush's son, **G. W. Bush,** now governs Texas, and **George Pataki** governs New York, in spite of a last-minute endorsement of Cuomo by New York City Republican Mayor Rudolph W. Giuliani.

For the first time since 1860, a sitting speaker of the House lost his bid for reelection. **Tom Foley** lost in Washington state to a little-known Republican, **George Nethercutt.** Major losing congressional incumbents were Senator **Jim Sasser** of Tennessee (in spite of Vice President Al Gore's efforts to help him) and Representative **Dan Rostenkowski** of Illinois. The latter had served so many terms in the House that he had become practically a permanent fixture there.

Republican **Olympia Snowe** of Maine, who had served in the House for sixteen years, won the

THE DEMOCRATS
Key Losers:

Cuomo

Foley   Rostenkowski

Richards   Wofford   Sasser

Key Winners:

T. Kennedy   Moynihan   Robb

Chiles   Feinstein

POLITICS AND ELECTIONS:
The Winner and the Losers—Continued

THE REPUBLICANS
Key Winners:

Gingrich   G. W. Bush   Kassebaum   Wilson   Hutchinson

Snowe   Watts   Pataki

Key Losers:

North   J. Bush   Huffington

race for the Senate seat of retiring Senator **George Mitchell.** For the first time in over five decades, three women now chair standing committees in Congress. Senator **Nancy Kassebaum** (R., Kans.) chairs the Senate Labor and Human Resources Committee, Representative **Jan Meyers** (R., Kans.) chairs the Small Business Committee in the House, and Nancy L. Johnson of Connecticut chairs the House Standards of Official Conduct Committee.

The Republican majority meant that **Newt Gingrich** (R., Ga.) would take over control of the House. Gingrich, immediately upon learning of Foley's defeat, made it clear that he was unlikely to accommodate what he terms the "McGovernick" global thinking and programs of the Clinton administration. Gingrich said that he would "cooperate" but not "compromise." Senator **Jesse Helms** (R., N.C.) was even more forthright in his statements about not compromising. As the new head of the Senate Foreign Relations Committee, he vowed to strengthen the military and to try to undo some of the Clinton administration's previous foreign policies.

Senator **Robert Dole** of Kansas became the Senate majority leader. While not the outspoken critic of the Clinton administration that his counterpart in the House has been, Dole certainly was not expected to ignore Gingrich's "Contract with America." Nonetheless, Dole's critics in the Republican party claim that he has been too willing to make compromises with the Clinton administration. At least for the next couple of years, "sparks may fly" between the leaders of the two chambers of Congress.

GERRYMANDERING
The drawing of legislative district boundary lines for the purpose of obtaining partisan or factional advantage. A district is said to be gerrymandered when its shape is manipulated by the dominant party in the state legislature to maximize electoral strength at the expense of the minority party.

Gerrymandering

Although the general issue of reapportionment has been dealt with fairly successfully by the one person, one vote principle, the **gerrymandering** issue has not yet been resolved. This term refers to the legislative boundary-drawing tactics that were used by Elbridge Gerry, the governor of Massachusetts, in the 1812 elections (see Figure 10–1). A district is said to have been gerrymandered when its shape is altered substantially by the dominant party in a state legislature to maximize its electoral strength at the expense of the minority party. This can be achieved by either concentrating the opposition's voter support in as few districts as possible or by diffusing the minority party's strength by spreading it thinly across many districts.

In 1986, the Supreme Court heard a case that challenged gerrymandered congressional districts in Indiana. The Court ruled for the first time that redistricting for the political benefit of one group could be challenged on constitutional grounds. In this specific case, *Davis v. Bandemer*, the Court, however, did not agree that the districts were drawn unfairly, because it could not be proved that a group of voters would consistently be deprived of its influence at the polls as a result of the new districts.[13]

13. 478 U.S. 109 (1986).

FIGURE 10–1   ■
The Original Gerrymander

The practice of "gerrymandering"—the excessive manipulation of the shape of a legislative district to benefit a certain incumbent or party—is probably as old as the republic, but the name originated in 1812. In that year, the Massachusetts legislature carved out of Essex County a district that historian John Fiske said had a "dragonlike contour." When the painter Gilbert Stuart saw the misshapen district, he penciled in a head, wings, and claws and exclaimed, "That will do for a salamander!" Editor Benjamin Russell replied, "Better say a Gerrymander" (after Elbridge Gerry, then governor of Massachusetts).

SOURCE: *Congressional Quarterly's Guide to Congress,* 3d ed. (Washington, D.C.: Congressional Quarterly Press, 1982), p. 695.

"Majority Minority" Districts

In the early 1990s, the federal government encouraged another type of gerrymandering that made possible the election of a minority representative from a "majority minority" area. Under the mandate of the Voting Rights Act of 1965, the Justice Department issued directives to states after the 1990 census instructing them to create congressional districts that would maximize the voting power of minority groups—that is, create districts in which minority voters were the majority. One such district—the Fourth District in Illinois—took the shape of a pair of earmuffs, to maximize the number of Hispanic voters in the district. Another such district—the Twelfth District of North Carolina—is 165 miles long, following Interstate 85 for the most part (see Figure 10–2). According to a local joke, the district is so narrow that a car traveling down the interstate highway with both doors open would kill most of the voters in the district.

Many of these "majority minority" districts were challenged in court by citizens who claimed that to create districts based on race or ethnicity alone violates the equal protection clause of the Constitution. In a case challenging a Texas district, a federal judge agreed and held that three minority districts were unconstitutional. In a case challenging the North Carolina district, however, a federal judge found that the district was constitutional.

In June 1995, the Supreme Court issued a sweeping decision on the issue. The case before the Court involved the Georgia's Eleventh District, which was one of three new "majority minority" congressional districts in Georgia that had been created after the 1990 census to comply with the Justice Department's directive. The district stretched from Atlanta to the Atlantic, splitting eight counties and five municipalities along the way. In 1994, five white voters from the Eleventh District claimed that the district was a racial gerrymander that violated the equal protection clause. A federal district court agreed.

On appeal, the Supreme Court aggressively attacked congressional redistricting on the basis of race. The Court referred to the Eleventh District as a "monstrosity" linking "widely spaced urban centers that have absolutely nothing to do with each other." The Court went on to state that when a state assigns voters on the basis of race, "it engages in the offensive and demeaning assumption that voters of a particular race, because of their race, think alike, share the same political interests, and will prefer the same candidates at the polls." The Court also chastised the Justice Department for

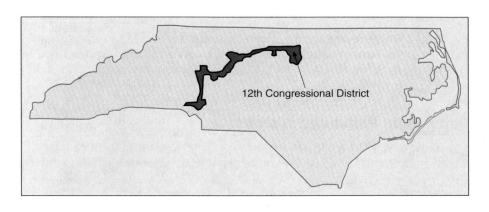

12th Congressional District

FIGURE 10–2

The Twelfth District of North Carolina

The Twelfth District was created to make possible the election of a minority representative. It snakes through North Carolina along Interstate 85.

POLITICS AND CONGRESS
It's a Tough Job, but It Has Great Benefits

Approval of Congress dropped to a new low in 1992. Only 23 percent of Americans approved of the legislature's performance. The discontent was fueled by the check-kiting scandal in the House bank, which cast a new light on the many perquisites of being a legislator. Ordinary Americans were angered by the seeming congressional indifference to the problem of bouncing checks and by the legislators' surprise that the public disapproved of congressional perks.

Not only did members of the House of Representatives have a private bank from which they could borrow against future paychecks, but they also received numerous other privileges not available to most Americans. Members of Congress now receive a salary of over $130,000, far above that of most managers in the private sector.

Among their perks are the following:

- The House sergeant-at-arms sees to it that D.C. parking tickets are dismissed if the legislator says that he or she was on official business.
- Stationery stores in the House and Senate sell gift items, as well as stationery, at cost.
- Airport parking is free for 147 members at a time. The spaces are available on a first-come, first-served basis.
- Haircuts are cheap—$5.00 on the House side and $4.50 on the Senate side. (These prices are for men. There are no comparable services for female members.)
- Free health care, including physical examinations and tests, is available.
- Members are able to reserve accommodations in five lodges run by the National Park Services in the Grand Tetons, Cape Hatteras, Shenandoah National Park, and the Virgin Islands, and on Catoctin Mountain. The lodges are not available to the public.

- Congressional members and staff receive free assistance from the Internal Revenue Service from February to April 15 each year.
- There are secret offices within the basement and corners of the Senate for seventy-seven of the one hundred senators. Many of these have been decorated with antique furniture from the collection of the sergeant-at-arms. No one has a key to these private hideaways except the senators and those to whom they choose to give keys.

Many legislators defend these perks as small benefits that make them more efficient as legislators. In fact, it does a constituent little good to have his or her representative spend hours looking for a parking space at the airport. But when legislators regard these benefits as routine and fail to show appreciation for them—or even abuse them—the legislators risk public hostility.

---

concluding that race-based districting was mandated under the Voting Rights Act of 1965: "When the Justice Department's interpretation of the Act compels race-based districting, it by definition raises a serious constitutional question."[14]

PAY, PERKS, AND PRIVILEGES

Compared with the average American citizen, members of Congress are well paid. In 1996, annual congressional salaries were $133,600. As described in this chapter's *Politics and Congress*, legislators have many benefits not available to most workers.

Permanent Professional Staffs

More than 38,660 people are employed in the Capitol Hill bureaucracy.[15] About half of this total consists of personal and committee staff members.

---

14. *Miller v. Johnson*, 115 S.Ct. 2475 (1995).
15. The Tax Foundation, *Tax Features*, March 1992, p. 6.

The personal staff includes office clerks and secretaries; professionals who deal with media relations, draft legislation, and satisfy constituency requests for service; and staffers who maintain local offices in the member's home district or state.

The average Senate office on Capitol Hill employs about thirty staff members, and twice that number work on the personal staff of senators from the most populous states. House office staffs typically are about half as large as those of the Senate. As Figure 10–3 shows, the number of staff members increased dramatically since 1960. One of the Republicans' first moves in 1995 was to cut one-third of the committee staff.

Individual staff members sometimes amass great power over certain government departments or policies. For example, Kevin Kelly, top staff member on the Senate Appropriation Subcommittee for Housing and Urban Development (HUD), was nicknamed "Mayor of HUD."[16] Kelly effectively blocked former HUD secretary Jack Kemp's attempts to gain more control over project grants by slipping legislators' favorite projects into a committee report that was not voted on. After George Bush's defeat, Kemp was out of office, but Kevin Kelly was not.

Privileges and Immunities under the Law

Members of Congress also benefit from a number of legal privileges and immunities. Under Article I, Section 6, of the Constitution, they "shall in

16. Eric Felten, "Little Princes: The Petty Despotism of Congressional Staff," *Policy Review*, Vol. 63 (Winter 1993), p. 55.

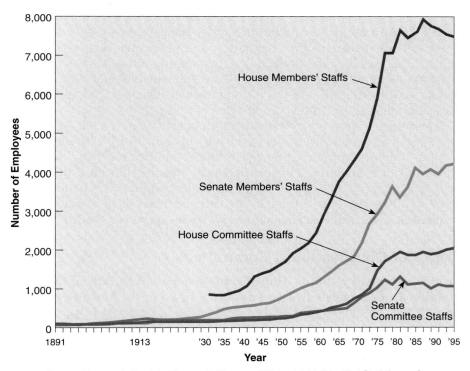

SOURCE: Norman J. Ornstein, Thomas E. Mann, and Michael J. Malbin, *Vital Statistics on Congress, 1993–1994* (Washington, D.C.: Congressional Quarterly Press, 1994), p. 129, and authors' update.

FIGURE 10–3

Growth in Congressional Staff, 1891 to 1995

As the graph indicates, staff increased dramatically from 1960 to 1980, most notably staff who serve in the members' offices.

all Cases, except Treason, Felony and Breach of the Peace, be privileged from Arrest during their Attendance at the Session of their respective Houses, and in going to and returning from the same; and for any Speech or Debate in either House, they shall not be questioned in any other Place." The arrest immunity clause is not really an important provision today. The "speech or debate" clause, however, means that a member may make any allegations or other statements he or she wishes in connection with official duties and normally not be sued for libel or slander or otherwise be subject to legal action.

THE COMMITTEE STRUCTURE

Most of the actual work of legislating is performed by the committees and subcommittees within Congress. Thousands of bills are introduced in every session of Congress, and no single member can possibly be adequately informed on all the issues that arise. The committee system is a way to provide for specialization, or a division of the legislative labor. Members of a committee can concentrate on just one area or topic—such as taxation or energy—and develop sufficient expertise to draft appropriate legislation when needed. The flow of legislation through both the House and the Senate is determined largely by the speed with which the members of these committees act on bills and resolutions.

The Power of Committees

Commonly known as "little legislatures," committees usually have the final say on pieces of legislation.[17] Committee actions may be overturned on the floor by the House or Senate, but this rarely happens. Legislators normally defer to the expertise of the chairperson and other members of the committee who speak on the floor in defense of a committee decision. Chairpersons of committees exercise control over the scheduling of hearings and formal action on a bill. They also decide which subcommittee will act on legislation falling within their committee's jurisdiction.

Committees only very rarely are deprived of control over a bill—although this kind of action is provided for in the rules of each chamber. In the House, if a bill has been considered by a standing committee for thirty days, the signatures of a majority (218) of the House membership on a **discharge petition** can pry a bill out of an uncooperative committee's hands. From 1909 to 1990, however, although 909 such petitions were made, only 26 resulted in successful discharge efforts. Of those, 20 passed the House.[18]

DISCHARGE PETITION
A procedure by which a bill in the House of Representatives may be forced out of a committee (discharged) that has refused to report it for consideration by the House. The discharge petition must be signed by an absolute majority (218) of representatives and is used only on rare occasions.

Types of Congressional Committees

Over the past two centuries, Congress has created several different types of committees, each of which serves particular needs of the institution.

---

17. The term *little legislatures* is from Woodrow Wilson, *Congressional Government* (New York: Meridian Books, 1956 [first published in 1885]).
18. *Congressional Quarterly's Guide to Congress*, 3d ed. (Washington, D.C.: Congressional Quarterly Press, 1982), p. 426; and authors' research.

Standing Committees.   By far the most important committees are the standing committees—permanent bodies established by the rules of each chamber of Congress and that continue from session to session. A list of the standing committees of the 104th Congress is presented in Table 10–5. In addition, most of the standing committees have created several subcommittees to carry out their work. In the 104th Congress, there were sixty-eight subcommittees in the Senate and eighty-five in the House, a decline of almost one-third in the number of subcommittees in the previous Congress.[19] The Republican-controlled Congress eliminated three full committees, consolidated subcommittees, and reduced the budget for committee staff.

Each standing committee is given a specific area of legislative policy jurisdiction, and almost all legislative measures are considered by the appropriate standing committees. Because of the importance of their work and the traditional influence of their members in Congress, certain committees are considered to be more prestigious than others. If a congressperson seeks to be influential, he or she will usually aspire to a seat on the Appropriations Committee in either chamber, on the Ways and Means Committee in the House, the House Education and Labor Committee, or the Senate Foreign Relations Committee.

Each member of the House serves generally on two standing committees, except when the member sits on the Appropriations, Rules, or Ways and Means Committee—in which case he or she serves on only that one standing committee. Each senator may serve on two major committees and one minor committee (only the Rules and Administration Committee and the Veterans' Affairs Committee are considered minor).

STANDING COMMITTEE
A permanent committee within the House or Senate that considers bills within a certain subject area.

---

19. "Players, Politics, and Turf of the 104th Congress," *Congressional Quarterly Weekly Report,* March 25, 1995, Supplement No. 12.

A committee hearing on a constitutional amendment to balance the budget. Starting from the chair of the committee in the center, Democratic senators sit on the left in order of seniority on the committee, while Republicans take the seats on the right in order of seniority.

TABLE 10–5

Standing Committees of the 104th Congress, 1995 to 1997

HOUSE COMMITTEE	CHAIR	SENATE COMMITTEE	CHAIR
Agriculture	Pat Roberts (R., Kans.)	Agriculture, Nutrition, and Forestry	Richard G. Lugar (R., Ind.)
Appropriations	Bob Livingston (R., La.)	Appropriations	Mark O. Hatfield (R., Ore.)
Armed Services	Floyd Spence (R., S.C.)	Armed Services	Strom Thurmond (R., S.C.)
Banking, Finance, and Urban Affairs	Jim Leach (R., Iowa)	Banking, Housing, and Urban Affairs	Alfonse M. D'Amato (R., N.Y.)
Budget	John Kasich (R., Ohio)	Budget	Pete V. Domenici (R., N.M.)
Education and Labor	Bill Goodling (R., Pa.)	Commerce, Science, and Transportation	Larry Pressler (R., S.D.)
Energy and Commerce	Thomas Bliley, Jr. (R., Pa.)	Energy and Natural Resources	Frank H. Murkowski (R., Alaska)
Foreign Affairs	Benjamin A. Gilman (R., N.Y.)	Environment and Public Works	John H. Chafee (R., R.I.)
Judiciary	Henry Hyde (R., Ill.)	Finance	William V. Roth, Jr. (R., Del.)
Natural Resources	Don Young (R., Alaska)	Foreign Relations	Jesse Helms (R., N.C.)
Public Works and Transportation	Bud Shuster (R., Pa.)	Governmental Affairs	Ted Stevens (R., Alaska)
Rules	Gerald B. H. Solomon (R., N.Y.)	Indian Affairs	John McCain (R., Ariz.)
Science and Technology	Robert S. Walker (R., Pa.)	Judiciary	Orrin Hatch (R., Utah)
Small Business	Jan Meyers (R., Kans.)	Labor and Human Resources	Nancy Landon Kassebaum (R., Kans.)
Standards of Official Conduct	Nancy L. Johnson (R., Conn.)	Rules and Administration	John W. Warner (R., Va.)
Veterans' Affairs	Bob Stump (R., Ariz.)	Small Business	Christopher Bond (R., Mo.)
Ways and Means	Bill Archer (R., Tex.)	Veterans' Affairs	Alan K. Simpson (R., Wyo.)

SELECT COMMITTEE
A temporary legislative committee established for a limited time period and for a special purpose.

Select Committees.   A **select committee** normally is created for a limited period of time and for a specific legislative purpose. For example, a select committee may be formed to investigate a public problem, such as nutrition or aging. Select committees are disbanded when they have reported to the chamber that created them. They rarely create original legislation.

JOINT COMMITTEE
A legislative committee composed of members from both chambers of Congress.

Joint Committees.   A **joint committee** is formed by the concurrent action of both chambers of Congress and consists of members from each chamber. Joint committees, which may be permanent or temporary, have dealt with the economy, taxation, and the Library of Congress.

CONFERENCE COMMITTEE
A special joint committee appointed to reconcile differences when bills pass the two chambers of Congress in different forms.

Conference Committees.   Special types of joint committees called **conference committees** are formed for the purpose of achieving agreement between the House and the Senate on the exact wording of legislative acts when the two chambers pass legislative proposals in different forms. No bill can be sent to the White House to be signed into law unless it first passes both chambers in identical form. Sometimes called the ''third house'' of Congress, conference committees are in a position to make significant alterations in legislation and frequently become the focal point of policy debates.

The House Rules Committee. Because of its special "gatekeeping" power over the terms on which legislation will reach the floor of the House of Representatives, the House Rules Committee holds a uniquely powerful position. A special committee rule sets the time limit on debate and determines whether and how a bill may be amended. This practice dates back to 1883. The Rules Committee has the unusual power to meet while the House is in session, to have its resolutions considered immediately on the floor, and to initiate legislation on its own.

The Selection of Committee Members

In the House, representatives are appointed to standing committees by the Steering and Policy Committee (for Democrats) and by the Committee on Committees (for Republicans). Committee chairpersons normally are appointed according to seniority.

The rule regarding seniority specifies that majority party members with longer terms of continuous service on the committee will be given preference when committee chairpersons—as well as holders of other significant posts in Congress—are selected. This is not a law but an informal, traditional process. The **seniority system**, although deliberately unequal, provides a predictable means of assigning positions of power within Congress.

The general pattern until the 1970s was that members of the House or Senate who represented **safe seats** would be reelected continually and eventually would accumulate enough years of continuous committee service to enable them to become the chairpersons of their committees—if their party gained control of the appropriate chamber of Congress. Traditionally, this avenue of access to power benefited southern Democrats and midwesterners within the Republican party, who seldom faced serious, organized opposition either in their own party's primaries or during the general election. This resulted in a predominance of committee chairpersons from the more conservative ranks of both political parties.

In the 1970s, a number of reforms in the chairperson selection process somewhat modified the seniority system. The reforms introduced the use of a secret ballot in electing House committee chairpersons and established rules for the selection of subcommittee chairpersons that resulted in a greater dispersal of authority within the committees themselves.

SENIORITY SYSTEM
A custom followed in both chambers of Congress specifying that members with longer terms of continuous service will be given preference when committee chairpersons and holders of other significant posts are selected.

SAFE SEAT
A district that returns the legislator with 55 percent of the vote or more.

THE FORMAL LEADERSHIP

The limited amount of centralized power that exists in Congress is exercised through party-based mechanisms. Congress is organized by party. When the Democratic party, for example, wins a majority of seats in either the House or the Senate, Democrats control the official positions of power in that chamber, and every important committee has a Democratic chairperson and a majority of Democratic members. The same process holds when Republicans are in the majority, as in 1995.

We consider the formal leadership positions in the House and Senate separately, but you will note some broad similarities in the way leaders are selected and in the ways they exercise power in the two chambers.

SPEAKER OF THE HOUSE
The presiding officer in the House of Representatives. The speaker is always a member of the majority party and is the most powerful and influential member of the House.

Leadership in the House

The House leadership is made up of the speaker, the majority and minority leaders, and the party whips.

The Speaker.   The foremost power holder in the House of Representatives is the **speaker of the House.** The speaker's position is technically a nonpartisan one, but in fact, for the better part of two centuries, the speaker has been the official leader of the majority party in the House. When a new Congress convenes in January of odd-numbered years, each party nominates a candidate for speaker. In one of the very rare instances of perfect party cohesion, all Democratic members of the House ordinarily vote for their party's nominee, and all Republicans support their alternative candidate.

The extent of the speaker's power has varied markedly over time. Throughout most of the nineteenth century, speakers had to share power with groups of powerful members or with key committee chairpersons. Beginning about 1890 and continuing through 1910, speakers gained dictatorial powers, including control over all committee appointments and the agenda. In the aftermath of a revolt in 1910 and 1911, however, these extensive powers of the speaker were reduced substantially.

The influence of modern-day speakers is based primarily on their personal prestige, persuasive ability, and knowledge of the legislative process—plus the acquiescence or active support of other representatives. The major formal powers of the speaker include the following:

1. Presiding over meetings of the House.
2. Appointing members of joint committees and conference committees.
3. Scheduling legislation for floor action.
4. Deciding points of order and interpreting the rules with the advice of the House parliamentarian.
5. Referring bills and resolutions to the appropriate standing committees of the House.

Within a few days of the bombing of the Oklahoma City Federal Building, this bipartisan group of leaders met to discuss the passage of a law increasing the power of the federal government to deal with domestic terrorism. In this picture, Speaker Newt Gingrich, Republican from Georgia, President Bill Clinton, Democrat, Majority Leader Bob Dole, Republican from Kansas, and Attorney General Janet Reno, Democrat, are waiting for the discussion of this measure to begin.

A speaker may take part in floor debate and vote, as can any other member of Congress, but recent speakers usually have voted only to break a tie.

In general, the powers of the speaker are related to his or her control over information and communications channels in the House. This is a significant power in a large, decentralized institution in which information is a very important resource. With this control, the speaker attempts to ensure the smooth operation of the chamber and to integrate presidential and congressional policies.

The Majority Leader.   The **majority leader of the House** has been a separate position since 1899, when a power that had usually been exercised by the chairperson of the Ways and Means Committee was transferred to a new office. The majority leader is elected by a caucus of party members to foster cohesion among party members and to act as a spokesperson for the party. The majority leader influences the scheduling of debate and generally acts as the chief supporter of the speaker. The majority leader cooperates with the speaker and other party leaders, both inside and outside Congress, to formulate the party's legislative program and to guide that program through the legislative process in the House. The majority leader's post is a very prestigious one because of the power and responsibility inherent in the office and also because, at least among Democrats, future speakers are recruited from that position.

The Minority Leader.   The **minority leader of the House** is the candidate nominated for speaker by a caucus of the minority party. Like the majority leader, the leader of the minority party has as his or her primary responsibility the maintaining of cohesion within the party's ranks. As the official spokesperson for the minority party, he or she consults with the ranking minority members of the House committees and encourages them to adhere to the party position. The minority leader also acts as a morale booster for the usually less successful minority and speaks on behalf of the president if the minority party controls the White House. In relations with the majority party, the minority leader consults with both the speaker and the majority leader on recognizing members who wish to speak on the floor, on House rules and procedures, and on the scheduling of legislation. Minority leaders have no actual power in these areas, however.

Whips.   The formal leadership of each party includes assistants to the majority and minority leaders, who are known as **whips.** These positions have existed throughout this century. Over the past fifty years, they have developed into a complex network of deputy and regional whips supervised by the chief party whip. The whips assist the party leader by passing information down from the leadership to party members and by ensuring that members show up for floor debate and cast their votes on important issues. Whips conduct polls among party members about the members' views on major pieces of legislation, inform the leaders about whose vote is doubtful and whose is certain, and may exert pressure on members to support the leader's position.

Leadership in the Senate

The two highest-ranking formal leadership positions in the Senate are essentially ceremonial in nature. Under the Constitution, the vice president

MAJORITY LEADER OF THE HOUSE
A legislative position held by an important party member in the House of Representatives. The majority leader is selected by the majority party in caucus or conference to foster cohesion among party members and to act as a spokesperson for the majority party in the House.

MINORITY LEADER OF THE HOUSE
The party leader elected by the minority party in the House.

WHIP
An assistant who aids the majority or minority leader of the House or the majority or minority floor leader of the Senate.

Representative Newt Gingrich (R., Ga.), speaker of the House.

PRESIDENT PRO TEMPORE
The temporary presiding officer of the Senate in the absence of the vice president.

MAJORITY FLOOR LEADER
The chief spokesperson of the major party in the Senate, who directs the legislative program and party strategy.

MINORITY FLOOR LEADER
The party officer in the Senate who commands the minority party's opposition to the policies of the majority party and directs the legislative program and strategy of his or her party.

Robert Dole (R., Kans.), Senate majority floor leader.

of the United States is the president (that is, the presiding officer) of the Senate and may vote to break a tie. The vice president, however, only rarely is present for a meeting of the Senate. The Senate elects instead a **president pro tempore** ("pro tem") to preside over the Senate in the vice president's absence. Ordinarily, the president pro tem is the member of the majority party with the longest continuous term of service in the Senate. The president pro tem is mostly a ceremonial position. Junior senators take turns actually presiding over the sessions of the Senate.

The real leadership power in the Senate rests in the hands of the **majority floor leader**, the **minority floor leader**, and their respective whips. The Senate majority and minority leaders have the right to be recognized first in debate on the floor and generally exercise the same powers available to the House majority and minority leaders. They control the scheduling of debate on the floor in conjunction with the majority party's Policy Committee, influence the allocation of committee assignments for new members or for senators attempting to transfer to a new committee, influence the selection of other party officials, and participate in selecting members of conference committees. The leaders are expected to mobilize support for partisan legislative initiatives or for the proposals of a president who belongs to the same party. The leaders act as liaisons with the White House when the president is of their party, try to get the cooperation of committee chairpersons, and seek to facilitate the smooth functioning of the Senate through the senators' unanimous consent. Floor leaders are elected by their respective party caucuses.

Senate party whips, like their House counterparts, maintain communication within the party on platform positions and try to ensure that party colleagues are present for floor debate and important votes. The Senate whip system is far less elaborate than its counterpart in the House, simply because there are fewer members to track.

A list of the formal party leaders of the 104th Congress is presented in Table 10–6. Party leaders are a major source of influence over the decisions about public issues that senators and representatives must make every day. We consider the nature of partisan and other pressures on congressional decision making in the next section.

HOW MEMBERS OF CONGRESS DECIDE

Why congresspersons vote as they do is difficult to know with any certainty. One popular perception of the legislative decision-making process is that legislators take cues from other trusted or more senior colleagues.[20] This model holds that because most members of Congress have neither the time nor the incentive to study the details of most pieces of legislation, they frequently arrive on the floor with no clear idea about what they are voting on or how they should vote. Their decision is simplified, according to the cue-taking model, by quickly checking how key colleagues have voted or intend to vote. More broadly, verbal and nonverbal cues can be taken from fellow committee members and chairpersons, party leaders, state delegation members, or the president.

---

20. Donald Matthews and James Stimson, *Yeas and Nays: Normal Decision Making in the U.S. House of Representatives* (New York: Wiley, 1975).

TABLE 10–6
Party Leaders in the 104th Congress, 1995 to 1997

POSITION	INCUMBENT	PARTY/ STATE	LEADER SINCE
House			
Speaker	Newt Gingrich	R., Ga.	Jan. 1995
Majority leader	Dick Armey	R., Tex.	Jan. 1995
Majority whip	Tom DeLay	R., Tex.	Jan. 1995
Chairperson of the Republican Conference	John Boehner	R., Ohio	Jan. 1995
Minority leader	Richard Gephardt	D., Mo.	Jan. 1995
Minority whip	David Bonior	D., Mich.	Jan. 1995
Chairperson of the Democratic Caucus	Vic Fazio	D., Calif.	Jan. 1995
Senate			
President pro tempore	Strom Thurmond	R., S.C.	Jan. 1995
Majority floor leader	Robert Dole	R., Kans.	Jan. 1995
Assistant majority leader	Trent Lott	R., Miss.	Jan. 1995
Chairperson of the Republican Conference	Thad Cochran	R., Miss.	Jan. 1995
Minority floor leader	Tom Daschle	D., S.D.	Jan. 1995
Assistant floor leader	Wendell Ford	D., Ky.	Jan. 1995
Chairperson of the Democratic Caucus	Tom Daschle	D., S.D.	Jan. 1995

A different theory of congressional decision making places the emphasis on the policy content of the issues being decided, on the desires of a congressperson's constituents, and on the pressures brought to bear by his or her supporters.[21] The degree of constituency influence on congressional voting patterns depends on the extent to which a state or district is urbanized, the region and state that a member represents, and the blue-collar proportion of the labor force.

Most people who study the decision-making process in Congress agree that the single best predictor for how a member will vote is the member's party membership.[22] Republicans tend to vote similarly on issues, as do Democrats. Of course, even though liberals generally predominate among the Democrats in Congress and conservatives predominate among the Republicans, the parties still may have internal disagreements about the proper direction that national policy should take. This was generally true for the civil rights legislation of the 1950s and 1960s, for example, when the greatest disagreement was between the conservative southern wing and the liberal northern wing of the Democratic party.

---

21. Aage R. Clausen, *How Congressmen Decide* (New York: St. Martin's Press, 1973).
22. David Mayhew, *Party Loyalty among Congressmen* (Cambridge, Mass.: Harvard University Press, 1966).

Roll-call votes posted in the House. Since electronic voting was instituted, attendance at roll calls has increased. Legislators were quite aware that their absences would also be recorded.

CONSERVATIVE COALITION
An alliance of Republicans and southern Democrats that can form in the House or the Senate to oppose liberal legislation and support conservative legislation.

TABLE 10–7 ■

Party Voting in Congress

This table lists the percentage of all roll calls in which a majority of Democratic legislators voted against a majority of Republican legislators.

YEAR	HOUSE	SENATE
1994	61.8	51.7
1993	65.0	67.0
1992	64.0	53.0
1991	55.0	49.0
1990	49.0	54.0
1989	55.0	35.0
1988	47.0	42.0
1987	64.0	41.0
1986	57.0	52.0
1985	61.0	50.0
1984	47.1	40.0
1983	55.6	43.6
1982	36.4	43.4
1981	37.4	47.8
1980	37.6	45.8
1979	47.3	46.7
1978	33.2	45.2
1977	42.2	42.4
1976	35.9	37.2
1975	48.4	47.8
1974	29.4	44.3
1973	41.8	39.9

SOURCE: *Congressional Weekly Report*, December 31, 1994, p. 3658.

One way to measure the degree of party unity in Congress is to look at how often a majority of one party votes against the majority of members from the other party. Table 10–7 displays the percentage of all votes in the House and the Senate when this type of party voting has occurred. Note that party voting increased in 1992, George Bush's last year in office, and stayed high in 1994, as President Bill Clinton pressed Democrats in Congress to vote for his programs.

Regional differences, especially between northern and southern Democrats, may overlap and reinforce basic ideological differences among members of the same party. One consequence of the North-South split among Democrats has been the **conservative coalition** policy alliance between southern Democrats and Republicans. This conservative, cross-party grouping formed regularly on votes that split liberals and conservatives. The coalition was active during the Reagan years, declined under Bush, and virtually disappeared during Clinton's first year.

HOW A BILL BECOMES LAW

Each year, Congress and the president propose and approve many laws. Some are budget and appropriation laws that require extensive bargaining but must be passed for the government to continue to function. Other laws are relatively free of controversy and are passed with little dissension between the branches of government. Still other proposed legislation is extremely controversial and reaches to the roots of differences between Democrats and Republicans and between the executive and legislative branches. Such a piece of legislation was the Brady Bill, or the Handgun Violence Prevention Act of 1993, a bill that had been debated by Congress for seven years. The Brady Bill illustrates the path a bill may take that, although involving relatively few committees, still generates an extraordinary amount of legislative action.

The Brady Bill

At the end of his first year in the presidency in 1981, Ronald Reagan was the target of an assassination attempt as he left a Washington hotel. Although the president was wounded, his injuries were not nearly as serious as those sustained by his press secretary, James Brady. Brady, hit by shots fired from a handgun that had been purchased by a former mental patient, had extremely serious head injuries that damaged his ability to speak and partially paralyzed him. From the time of his recovery until 1993, Brady and his wife, Sarah, headed a national campaign to institute a waiting period for purchasers of handguns. The waiting period would allow gun sellers to check the backgrounds of prospective purchasers.

The first version of the now-named Brady Bill was debated in 1987. The bill was opposed by Ronald Reagan, many western and southern members of Congress, and the National Rifle Association. In September 1988, the waiting-period proposal was defeated in the House by a vote of 228 to 182. After the election of George Bush, the bill was reintroduced even though Bush, a gun owner, was ambivalent about it. In 1991, the House of Representatives passed the bill, in a stunning victory for the Bradys. Although it was clear that the Senate would not pass the bill in 1991, it seemed likely that the Senate might be ready to approve some version of it in the future.

The Bradys and the House sponsors of gun control legislation reintroduced the bill in February 1993 after the election of Bill Clinton. The bill was referred to the House Judiciary Committee for hearings. The bill was then referred to a subcommittee for hearings—in this case, it was the House Subcommittee on Crime and Criminal Justice. After hearings in September, the bill was reported back to the full committee and then approved. The bill was sent to the House Rules Committee before it was sent to the House floor. (Figure 10–4 shows the typical path of proposed legislation.)

The bill came to the House floor on November 10, 1993, where it was debated and amended. Most of the amendments dealt with the date on

President Clinton signs the Brady gun control bill. James Brady, shown sitting next to the president, was seriously wounded in an attempt on President Reagan's life in 1981. At that time, Brady was Reagan's press secretary. For over ten years, James and Sarah Brady led the movement for handgun control. Some critics of the bill that finally passed claim that it does not go far enough and will have little effect. Others believe that there are so many handguns and rifles currently in existence in the United States (over 200 million) that such legislation will have little effect on the crime problem in America.

FIGURE 10-4

How a Bill Becomes Law

This illustration shows the most typical way in which proposed legislation is enacted into law. The process is illustrated with two hypothetical bills, House bill No. 100 (HR 100) and Senate bill No. 200 (S 200). Bills must be passed by both chambers in identical form before they can be sent to the president. The path of HR 100 is traced by a blue line, and that of S 200 by a red line. In practice, most bills begin as similar proposals in both chambers.

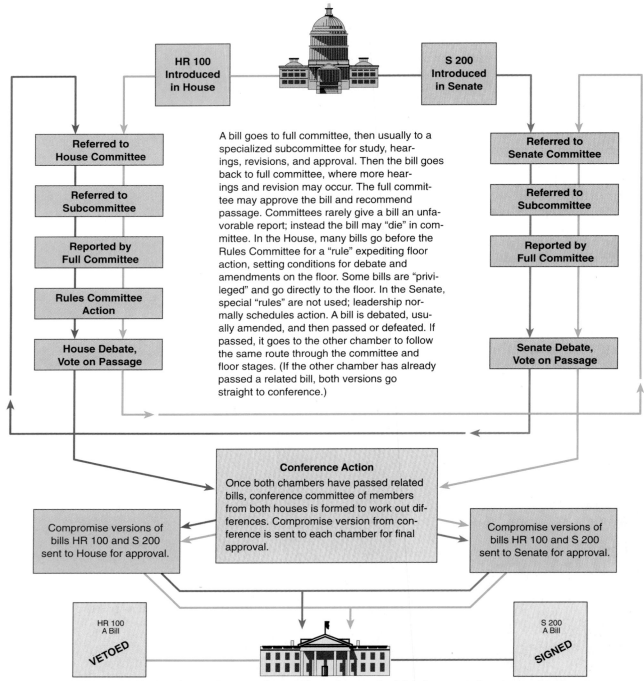

A compromise bill approved by both houses is sent to the president, who can sign it into law or veto it and return it to Congress. Congress may override veto by a two-thirds majority vote in both houses; the bill then becomes law without the president's signature.

which the law would expire, subject to the institution of a national "instant check" system to be in place at that time. Finally, the bill passed with a six-year limit to substitute the instant check system for the waiting period. The House then requested the "concurrence" of the Senate.

On November 13, 1993, the bill was read for the first time (that is, introduced) in the Senate. Because the bill was well known and had been debated several times before, the Senate went right to conference to request amendment of the bill. The chair of the Judiciary Committee and several of its members formed a conference committee with the House members. The Senate passed its own version of the bill and sent it to the House, which rejected it. Then the two chambers went to conference. The House passed the conference report, which was the result of intensive negotiations between House and Senate representatives on November 22.

As the Thanksgiving recess loomed, the Senate needed to take up the bill and make a decision. Republicans, claiming that the Senate Democrats had bargained away their own agreement to have a five-year period for the bill, began a filibuster. The first two cloture votes failed. Finally, Senators Robert Dole, Joseph Biden, and George Mitchell ironed out a compromise that the Republicans would support. They agreed to the five-year sunset period and to reconsider the legislation with some changes in the next session. The Senate then ended the filibuster and passed the Brady Bill by voice vote on November 24, 1993. It was signed into law by the president on November 30. As Jim Brady put it, "It's an awfully nice Thanksgiving present for the American people."[23]

The Republican One Hundred Days

In late September 1994, when the possibility of winning control of the House and the Senate seemed fairly remote, three hundred of the Republican incumbent House members and candidates signed the Contract with America, a list of legislative actions that they promised to bring to the floor of the House in the first one hundred days of the new Congress if they were elected. As discussed in Chapter 8, not many Americans knew about the "contract" when they went to the polls in November. Even after the first month of the new Congress, only half of the people knew about the contract. But the House Republicans, with their new speaker, Newt Gingrich of Georgia, proceeded with a speed and unity rarely seen in the Capitol.

As shown in Table 10–8, the Republicans managed to introduce bills addressing all of the planks of their platform, hold committee hearings, and bring all of the items to the floor of the House in the first one hundred days of the Congress. Several of the bills passed the Senate and were signed into law by the president during that period. The Balanced Budget Amendment to the Constitution, which passed the House overwhelmingly, failed in the Senate by one vote. Then the Senate majority leader, Robert Dole, also voted against it to preserve his right to recall the legislation later. The only item that failed to win a majority in the House was the constitutional amendment setting term limits for members of Congress.

How did the Republicans manage to complete so much business when Congress is usually so slow? The Brady Bill took six years, and Medicare took

23. "Brady Bill Goes to the Brink, but the Senate Finally Clears It," *Congressional Quarterly Weekly Report,* November 27, 1993, p. 3271.

Speaker Newt Gingrich, leader of the Republican majority in the House of Representatives, pushes his colleagues to pass legislation from the Contract with America, to cut the budget, and to maintain their majority position. Gingrich also became the center of controversy over his book deal with a major media corporation, which raised suspicions of conflict of interest.

TABLE 10–8

The Contract with America

The Republicans promised to bring these items to the floor of the House of Representatives in the first one hundred days of the 104th Congress.

	100 Days' Action
Preface: Put Congress under workplace laws	Law
Revise House rules	Passed House
1) Budget reform:	
Balanced Budget Amendment	Passed House
Line item veto	Law
2) Toughen crime bill	Passed House
3) Reform welfare programs	Passed House
4) Strengthen families:	Passed House
Tax credits for adoptions	
Penalties for sex crimes with children	
Enforce child support	
5) Middle class tax cut	Passed House
6) National security: keep U.S. troops from U.N. command	Passed House
7) Social Security: decrease taxes on retirees' income and benefits	Passed House
8) Capital gains and regulations:	
Curb new unfunded mandates on states	Law
Reduce federal paperwork	Law
Cut capital gains tax rate	Passed House
Require risk assessment on regulations	Passed House
9) Civil law and liability:	
Change product liability law	Passed House
Change lawsuit rules	Passed House
10) Term limits constitutional amendment	Failed in House

SOURCE: *Congressional Quarterly Weekly Report*, Aprill 8, 1995, pp. 996–997.

thirty years to pass. Because the Republicans controlled all of the committees and had a majority on the floor, they had the power to get the bills considered. Because they saw the 104th Congress as a unique political opportunity to make an impression on the voters and, perhaps, gain enough supporters to stay in power, the Republican representatives accepted the discipline of party leadership and voted for the bills.

Some pundits had predicted that the Republicans could not accomplish the promises made in the Contract with America. The House members had an advantage, however: They could vote for items that they might not totally support, knowing that the Senate would act slowly and deliberately on these bills. The Republican House members were assured that the Senate would amend, rewrite, and possibly defeat some of these bills, even though the Senate was also controlled by the Republicans. The Senate, after all, was, as Jefferson put it, "like the saucer that you pour tea into to cool." It was the intent of the founders that the Senate be the "cooling off" branch, in contrast to the House, which can quickly reflect election returns. The Republicans' first one hundred days provided the opportunity to watch this constitutional balance in action.

HOW MUCH WILL THE GOVERNMENT SPEND?

The Constitution is extremely clear about where the power of the purse lies in the national government: All money bills, whether for taxing or spending, must originate in the House of Representatives. Today, much of the business of Congress is concerned with approving government expenditures through the budget process and with raising the revenues to pay for government programs.

From 1922, when Congress required the president to prepare and present to the legislature an **executive budget**, until 1974, the congressional budget process was so disjointed that it was difficult to visualize the total picture of government finances. The president presented the executive budget to Congress in January. It was broken down into thirteen or more appropriations bills. Some time later, after all of the bills were debated, amended, and passed, it was more or less possible to estimate total government spending for the next year.

Frustrated by the president's ability to impound funds and dissatisfied with the entire budget process, Congress passed the Budget and Impoundment Control Act of 1974 to regain some control over the nation's spending. The act required the president to spend the funds that Congress had appropriated, frustrating the president's ability to kill programs of which the administration disapproved by withholding funds. The other major accomplishment of the act was to force Congress to examine total national taxing and spending at least twice in each budget cycle.

The budget cycle of the federal government is described in the following sections. (See Figure 10–5 for a graphic illustration of the budget cycle.)

EXECUTIVE BUDGET
The budget prepared and submitted by the president to Congress.

FIGURE 10–5 ■

The Budget Cycle

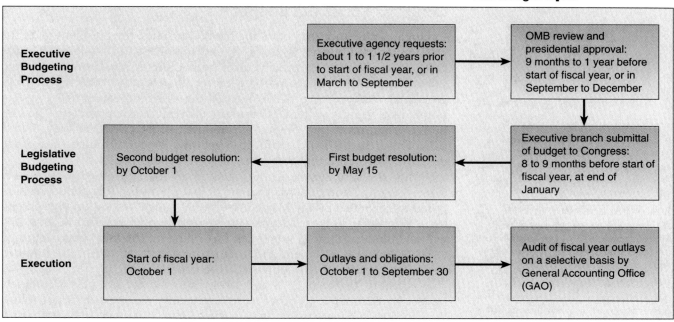

Preparing the Budget

FISCAL YEAR (FY)
The twelve-month period that is used for bookkeeping, or accounting, purposes. Usually, the fiscal year does not coincide with the calendar year. For example, the federal government's fiscal year runs from October 1 through September 30.

The federal government operates on a **fiscal year (FY)**. The fiscal year runs from October through September, so that fiscal 1997, or FY97, runs from October 1, 1996, through September 30, 1997. Eighteen months before a fiscal year starts, the executive branch begins preparing the budget. The Office of Management and Budget (OMB) receives advice from the Council of Economic Advisers (CEA) and the Treasury Department. The OMB outlines the budget and then sends it to the various departments and agencies. Bargaining follows, in which—to use only two of many examples—the Department of Health and Human Services argues for more welfare spending, and the armed forces argue for fewer defense spending cuts.

Even though the OMB has only six hundred employees, it is known as one of the most powerful agencies in Washington. It assembles the budget documents and monitors the agencies throughout each year. Every year, it begins the budget process with a **spring review**, in which it requires all of the agencies to review their programs, activities, and goals. At the beginning of each summer, the director of the OMB sends out a letter instructing agencies to submit their requests for funding for the next fiscal year. By the end of the summer, each agency must submit a formal request to the OMB.

SPRING REVIEW
The time every year when the Office of Management and Budget requires federal agencies to review their programs, activities, and goals and submit their requests for funding for the next year.

FALL REVIEW
The time every year when, after receiving formal federal agency requests for funding for the next fiscal year, the Office of Management and Budget reviews the requests, makes changes, and submits its recommendations to the president.

In actuality, the "budget season" begins with the **fall review**. At this time, the OMB looks at budget requests and, in almost all cases, routinely cuts them back. Although the OMB works within guidelines established by the president, specific decisions often are left to the director and the director's associates. By the beginning of November, the director's review begins. The director meets with cabinet secretaries and budget officers. Time becomes crucial. The budget must be completed by January so that it can go to the printer to be included in the *Economic Report of the President*.

Congress Faces the Budget

In January, nine months before the fiscal year starts, the president takes the OMB's proposed budget, approves it, and submits it to Congress. Then the congressional budgeting process takes over. Congressional committees and subcommittees look at the proposals from the executive branch. The Congressional Budget Office (CBO) advises the different committees on economic matters, just as the OMB and the CEA advise the president. The **first budget resolution** by Congress is supposed to be passed in May. It sets overall revenue goals and spending targets and, by definition, the size of the deficit (or surplus, if that were ever to occur again).

FIRST BUDGET RESOLUTION
A resolution passed by Congress in May that sets overall revenue and spending goals and hence, by definition, the size of the budget deficit for the following fiscal year.

SECOND BUDGET RESOLUTION
A resolution passed by Congress in September that sets "binding" limits on taxes and spending for the next fiscal year beginning October 1.

CONTINUING RESOLUTION
A temporary law that Congress passes when an appropriations bill has not been decided by the beginning of the new fiscal year on October 1.

During the summer, bargaining among all the concerned parties takes place. Spending and tax laws that are drawn up during this period are supposed to be guided by the May congressional budget resolution. By September, Congress is supposed to pass its **second budget resolution**, one that will set "binding" limits on taxes and spending for the fiscal year beginning October 1. Bills passed before that date that do not fit within the limits of the budget resolution are supposed to be changed.

In actuality, between 1978 and 1994, Congress did not pass a complete budget by October 1. In other words, generally, Congress does not follow its own rules. Budget resolutions are passed late, and when they are passed, they are not treated as binding. In each fiscal year that starts without a budget, every agency operates on the basis of **continuing resolutions**,

Republicans target the National Endowment for the Arts (NEA) for major funding cuts, ostensibly undertaken to balance the national budget. The NEA had long been in disfavor with conservatives for funding controversial work of artists. The NEA, however, also has provided major support for museums and for young artists.

which enable the agencies to keep on doing whatever they were doing the previous year with the same amount of funding. Even continuing resolutions have not always been passed on time.

Dealing with the budget is a recurring nightmare for Congress and the president. George Bush's 1990 budget battle, which forced him to raise taxes, may have cost him the presidency in 1992. President Bill Clinton won his first big budget fight in 1993 by a margin of one vote in the Senate, cast by Vice President Al Gore to break the tie, and by a single vote in the House. Clinton's budget deficit reduction package included large new taxes on the rich, on gasoline, and on tobacco. The Republicans challenged President Clinton early in the 104th Congress by bringing a Balanced Budget Amendment to the floor of the House in January 1995. The amendment cleared the House by a vote of 300 to 132. It ran into trouble in the Senate, however. The amendment won 66 votes in the upper house, one short of the 67 needed to send the amendment to the states for ratification.

When the Republicans approached the first budget resolution of 1995, they continued to show unity. They passed budget resolutions in both the House and the Senate that cut billions of dollars in federal programs. President Clinton could do little to influence the process in 1995, although he offered a ten-year plan to balance the budget as an alternative to the Republicans' seven-year plan.

THE QUESTION OF CONGRESSIONAL ETHICS

Ethics is the most serious public relations problem confronting Congress today. Perhaps nothing has so tarnished the public's perception of Congress as the revelations concerning the abuse of staff members, the misuse of public funds, and the personal indiscretions and corruption of members of that institution.

Congress's response to revelations of member misconduct has been mixed. The House Democratic caucus in June 1980 voted 160 to 0 to require

Senator Bob Packwood (R., Ore.) faced charges from the Senate Ethics Committee concerning his purported sexual harassment of female assistants over a period that lasted more than twenty years. The accusations against Packwood came at a time in the 1990s when the public's perception of Congress was at an all-time low. Packwood resigned in the fall of 1995 after the committee voted to expel him from the Senate.

that chairpersons of committees or subcommittees be stripped of their posts automatically if they have been censured or indicted on a felony charge carrying a prison sentence of at least two years. This rule can be waived, however, by the same caucus.

Public financing of congressional campaigns may offer a partial solution to recurring problems of financial misconduct. Nonetheless, Congress has refused to use tax money for, or to impose spending limits on, its members' campaigns, even though it adopted such provisions for presidential campaigns in 1974. Part of the campaign-funding problem is illustrated by the former member of Congress who used leftover campaign funds to make a down payment on a fifty-five-foot houseboat in Florida and to finance a limousine carrying the congressional seal. The practice of diverting unused campaign funds to personal use was outlawed in January 1980, but members of Congress were exempted from coverage by the law until 1992. By the early 1990s, the public's regard for Congress had reached an all-time low (see this chapter's *Politics and Ethics*).

THE U.S. CONGRESS: UNFINISHED WORK

The U.S. Congress, although respected by the public for its authority and history, has not inspired voter confidence for some time. Voters generally are likely to be supportive of their individual representatives but cynical about the institution itself. One of the results of this frustration and cynicism has been the popularity of term limits as a device to make the members more responsive to the public's will and less likely to see Congress as a lifelong career.

Another aspect of Congress's fall from grace is its inability to avoid ethical scandals. It is hard for the voter not to regard the members as willing to take advantage of perks and privileges, to work closely with interest groups, and to forget life back home. Add to the general impression of disregard for public values the actual events of recent years—sexual harassment scandals, checks bouncing, and legislators charged with corruption—and the public's approval rating for Congress continues to slide downhill.

POLITICS AND ETHICS
Congress Examines Its Own for Improprieties

Public approval of Congress as a body has continued to be very low, in part because of the succession of ethical problems and improprieties that have become public. Both the House and the Senate have attempted to deal with the ethical lapses of their respective members through internal processes, but the public perception continues to be that many members are involved in shady dealings that the ordinary citizen finds hard to justify.

Ethical problems for elected representatives fall into several categories. The most flamboyant involve sexual misconduct involving staff members or constituents. In recent years, Representative Gus Savage of Illinois was accused of making sexual advances to a Peace Corps volunteer while on an official trip, and Representative Donald "Buz" Lukens of Ohio was convicted of having sex with a sixteen-year-old girl. Both representatives were defeated in subsequent elections. Representative Barney Frank of Massachusetts, who has acknowledged his own homosexuality, was reprimanded by the House Ethics Committee for hiring a former lover as a staff assistant and allow-

ing that person the use of his office for personal business.

The Senate's most famous case recently has been that of Senator Robert Packwood of Oregon, who was accused of sexually harassing a number of women. Packwood admitted some of his guilt, citing abuse of alcohol as the reason for his misbehavior. Packwood's case put the Senate in the limelight, because some of its female members petitioned for the Senate to deny him his seat on the basis that he was elected fraudulently (that is, Packwood denied allegations of wrongdoing before the election and pressured the media to suppress them). Packwood resigned in September 1995, after the Senate Ethics Committee voted to expel him from the Senate.

Both the House and the Senate have also dealt with the ethical problems that arise when a member takes advantage of his or her office for personal benefit. Several House members—including Jim Wright, a former speaker, and Tony Coelho, a former Democratic whip—resigned from Congress after investigations of their personal finances. Five Senators, known as the Keating Five for their association with the convicted Arizona financier Charles Keating, were reprimanded for their attempts to limit the investigation of

Keating's failed savings and loans. None of the five was censured, (which is a stronger action). One did not seek reelection.

In a 1994 ethics incident, Representative Dan Rostenkowski, the one-time powerful chair of the House Ways and Means Committee, was indicted for violating House rules in the purchase of stamps and personal gifts from House stores and for misusing funds for staff and office expenses. The indictment of this powerful congressperson forced him, under House rules, to resign his chairmanship. (He lost his congressional seat in 1994, when the voters did not reelect him.) In 1995, Illinois Representative Melvin Reynolds resigned following his conviction for having had sexual relations with a sixteen-year-old girl.

The public perception of corruption and unethical behavior in Congress probably is increased by the media coverage of such incidents. Until the Congress can reestablish its overall standing in the public's view, however, cynicism about its members and their privileges will continue.

One of the areas that the members of Congress have struggled to reform is campaign financing. With expenditures in the 1994 congressional elections exceeding half a billion dollars and the average House race costing more than $600,000, members must spend a great deal of time raising funds while trying to avoid appearing to be completely dependent on political action committees (PACs). In fact, many members receive more than $100,000 per year in PAC money. The parties are deeply divided over the possibility of public financing for congressional elections. Many public interest groups support public financing, but the electorate is suspicious of how much money Congress would give its members to run for reelection.

GETTING INVOLVED
How to Be an Intern in Washington, D.C.

John Stuart Mill, the British political philosopher and economist, wrote in the last century, "There are many truths of which the full meaning cannot be realized until personal experience has brought it home." Hundreds of students each year flock to Washington, D.C., for a summer, a semester, or a full year to gain personal experience in one of the myriad institutions of the nation's capital. For those with "Potomac fever," an internship in Washington earning college credit while working is an extraordinary opportunity. If you are interested in a Washington experience, here are some things to keep in mind.

First, make sure that you discuss your internship plan with your faculty adviser. He or she will have useful tips. Some colleges have strict rules on who may obtain credit for internships, what preparation is necessary, in what year students are allowed to participate in internships, and other such matters. Internships are most useful if you are in your junior or senior year.

There are several ways to plan an internship. First, contact an existing program, such as the following:

The Washington Center
514 10th St. N.W., Suite 600
Washington, DC 20004
202-289-8680

Such an organization will assist you in finding a suitable internship in government, the private sector, foundations, and nonprofit or volunteer organizations, as well as in considering other opportunities. "Organized" internship programs will also find you housing and usually provide field trips, special seminars, internship advisers, and other support. Ask if your college or university is affiliated with a Washington program or has an internship program of its own.

Second, find your own internship. There are several avenues for identifying and pursuing opportunities. Contact the local office of your representative or senator, which is usually listed in the telephone directory under "United States Government." Many members of Congress have internship coordinators and large, well-supervised programs. Some even may be able to pay part of your expenses.

Yet another route to finding your own internship is to study carefully one of the many directories on internships, such as the *Directory of Washington Internships*, which can be obtained from the following organization:

Society for Internships and Experimental Education
122 St. Mary's St.
Raleigh, NC 27605

Always make sure that you explore in detail what a specific job offers. Think carefully about internships that are glorified secretarial jobs in which all you do is typing and filing. Good internships should give you an insider's view on how a profession works. It should furnish some real "hands-on" opportunities to do research, deal with the public, learn about legislation, and watch government officials in action.

Remember that most internships are nonpaying. Make sure that you understand all the costs involved. Arrange for financing through your college, a guaranteed student loan, personal savings, or family support.

Finally, keep in mind that there are also internships in most members' district offices close to home. Such jobs may not have the glamor of Washington, but they may offer excellent opportunities for political experience.

A very useful booklet with which you should start is *Storming Washington: An Intern's Guide to National Government,* by Stephen E. Frantzich. It is available from the following association:

American Political Science Association
1527 New Hampshire Ave. N.W.
Washington, DC 20036
202-483-2512

KEY TERMS

agenda setting 346	instructed delegate 345	president pro tempore 368
bicameralism 342	joint committee 364	reapportionment 355
casework 344	justiciable question 355	redistricting 355
cloture 348	lawmaking 344	representation 345
conference committee 364	legislative veto 346	Rules Committee 348
conservative coalition 370	logrolling 344	safe seat 365
continuing resolution 376	majority floor leader 368	second budget resolution 376
direct primary 351	majority leader of the House 367	select committee 364
discharge petition 362		seniority system 365
enumerated power 342	minority floor leader 368	speaker of the House 366
executive budget 375	minority leader of the House 367	spring review 376
fall review 376		standing committee 363
filibustering 348	ombudsman 345	trustee 345
first budget resolution 376	oversight 346	whip 367
fiscal year (FY) 376	party identifier 351	
gerrymandering 358	politico 346	

 # CHAPTER SUMMARY

1. The authors of the Constitution, believing that the bulk of national power should be in the legislature, set forth the structure, power, and operation of Congress. The Constitution states that Congress will consist of two chambers. Partly an outgrowth of the Connecticut Compromise, this bicameral structure established a balanced legislature, with the membership in the House of Representatives based on population and the membership in the Senate based on the equality of states.

2. The first seventeen clauses of Article I, Section 8, of the Constitution specify most of the enumerated, or expressed, powers of Congress, including the right to impose taxes, to borrow money, to regulate commerce, and to declare war. Besides its enumerated powers, Congress enjoys the right to "make all Laws which shall be necessary and proper for carrying into Execution the foregoing Powers, and all other Powers vested by this Constitution in the Government of the United States, or in any Department or Officer thereof." This is called the elastic, or necessary and proper, clause.

3. The functions of Congress include (a) lawmaking, (b) service to constituents, (c) representation, (d) oversight, (e) public education, and (f) conflict resolution.

4. There are 435 members in the House of Representatives and 100 members in the Senate. Owing to its larger size, the House has a greater number of formal rules. The Senate tradition of unlimited debate, or filibustering, dates back to 1790 and has been used over the years to frustrate the passage of bills. Under Senate Rule 22, cloture can be used to shut off debate on a bill.

5. Members of Congress are not typical American citizens. They are older than most Americans; disproportionately white, male, and Protestant; and trained in professional occupations.

6. Congressional elections are operated by the individual state governments, which must abide by rules established by the Constitution and national statutes. The process of nominating congressional candidates has shifted from party conventions to the direct primaries currently used in all states. The overwhelming majority of incumbent representatives and a smaller proportion of senators who run for reelection are successful. The most complicated aspect of the mechanics of congressional elections is reapportionment—the allocation of legislative seats to constituencies. The

Supreme Court's one person, one vote rule has been applied to equalize the populations of state legislative and congressional districts.

7. Members of Congress are well paid and enjoy other benefits. Members of Congress have personal and committee staff members available to them and also benefit from a number of legal privileges and immunities.

8. Most of the actual work of legislating is performed by committees and subcommittees within Congress. Legislation introduced into the House or Senate is assigned to the appropriate standing committees for review. Select committees are created for a limited period of time for a specific legislative purpose. Joint committees are formed by the concurrent action of both chambers and consist of members from each chamber. Conference committees are special joint committees set up to achieve agreement between the House and the Senate on the exact wording of legislative acts passed by both chambers in different forms. The seniority rule specifies that longer-serving members will be given preference when committee chairpersons and holders of other important posts are selected.

9. The foremost power holder in the House of Representatives is the speaker of the House. Other leaders are the House majority leader, the House minority leader, and the majority and minority whips. Formally, the vice president is the presiding officer of the Senate, with the majority party choosing a senior member as the president pro tempore to preside when the vice president is absent. Actual leadership in the Senate rests with the majority floor leader, the minority floor leader, and their respective whips.

10. A bill becomes law by progressing through both chambers of Congress (and their appropriate standing and joint committees) to the president.

11. The budget process for a fiscal year begins with the preparation of an executive budget by the president. This is reviewed by the Office of Management and Budget and then sent to Congress, which is supposed to pass a final budget by the end of September. Since 1978, Congress has not followed its own time rules.

12. Ethics is the most serious public relations problem facing Congress. Financial misconduct, sexual improprieties, and other unethical behavior on the part of several House and Senate members have resulted in a significant lowering of the public's regard for the institution of Congress.

 ## QUESTIONS FOR REVIEW AND DISCUSSION

1. What should be the balance of power between the president and Congress? Should Congress be a reactive body, waiting for presidential proposals and then debating them, or should Congress take the initiative? How does the Constitution constrain this relationship? Under what conditions would the Constitution favor congressional leadership in policymaking?

2. Think about your senator or representative. As a constituent, what are your expectations of him or her? To what extent do you expect your member of Congress to try to represent the constituents' views or to take a national perspective? What are the political risks to a member of being oriented more to national problems than to local ones?

3. Given the emphasis on media campaigning and the growth in campaign expenditures, how should congressional campaigning be reformed to reduce the amount of time and energy that candidates must spend on fund-raising? Should the public fund campaigns? Should campaign spending for the House and Senate be limited? How would limits change the process of campaigning?

4. Is it possible for an assembly of elected officials to make complex public policies, or is the task too difficult? What sources of information do members of Congress need in order to write and understand public policies? Which political actors and forces focus their concerns on certain interests or regional problems? Is that focus on constituent concerns important in drafting important legislation, such as health-care reform?

 ## LOGGING ON: THE CONGRESS

Internet users have access to tremendous amounts of raw information from the federal government. One particularly

useful source provides information on all federal legislation
introduced on Capitol Hill since the 93d Congress:

acc.wuacc.edu

To log on, type **lawnet** and follow **old menu/federal government
information/U.S. legislation menu/LOCIS.** This source allows
you to view in their entirety all pieces of legislation
submitted in both the House of Representatives and in the
Senate since the 93d Congress.

If you would like to know a little more about the members of
Congress or are looking for background and career information
on a particular legislator, the following service will be of
particular interest to you. To find information on all 535
members of the 104th Congress, you can access

riceinfo.rice.edu

and then go to **Congressional Directory 104th.** Or if you would
like to access congressional E-mail and send an electronic
mail message to a member of Congress, go to **Congressional
Electronic Mail Access.**

The House of Representatives plans to hold hearings on
the Internet in the near future, to allow for public
participation. This will allow the average person to ''listen
in'' on congressional hearings and even to give testimony! The
first of these hearings is scheduled to start soon and may be of
particular interest to you, because it concerns regulation of
the electronic superhighway. For information on this service,
send an E-mail message to

hearing-info@town.hall.org.

As yet, the U.S. Senate has not scheduled any committee
hearings on the Internet, although it is considering doing so.
You can still receive information on hearings held by the
Senate, however. To receive summaries of Senate hearings, try

dewey.lib.ncsu.edu

 ## SELECTED REFERENCES

Barone, Michael, and Grant Ujifusa. *The Almanac of American Politics, 1995.* Washington, D.C.: National Journal, 1994. This is a comprehensive summary of current political information on each member of Congress, his or her state or congressional district, recent congressional election results, key votes and ratings of roll-call votes by various organizations, sources of campaign contributions, and records of campaign expenditures.

Benjamin, Gerald, and Michael J. Malbin, eds. *Limiting Legislative Terms,* Washington, D.C.: Congressional Quarterly Press, 1992. This collection of essays looks at the history of term limit proposals and the campaigns for their passage, and suggests possible effects on the legislature if term limits are imposed.

Boller, Paul F. *Congressional Anecdotes.* New York: Oxford University Press, 1991. Boller's lively and informative history of Congress is filled with revealing stories about members of Congress and entertaining anecdotes made by, or about, congresspersons over the years.

Campbell, James E. *The Presidential Pulse of Congressional Elections.* Lexington, Ky.: University Press of Kentucky, 1993. The author examines and compares various theories of surge and decline in party strength in Congress relative to presidential elections.

Congress A to Z: A Ready Reference Encyclopedia. 2d ed. Washington, D.C.: Congressional Quarterly Press, 1993. The most recent edition of this reference work includes essays on aspects of Congress, historical treatment of many topics, and a wealth of tables and statistics about Congress.

Harris, Fred R. *Deadlock or Decision: The U.S. Senate and the Rise of National Politics*. New York: Oxford University Press, 1993. Harris, a former senator, presents an excellent overview of the forces that have affected the Senate over the years. He believes that those forces have weakened the Senate's ability to debate and write policy for the nation.

Hibbing, John, ed. *The Changing World of the U.S. Senate*. Berkeley, Calif.: Institute of Governmental Studies Press, 1990. This book on the Senate, which is one of the best available, provides an excellent history of the institution and its internal operations, as well as a thoughtful debate on the need for more theoretical exploration and analysis of this institution.

Kingdon, John W. *Congressmen's Voting Decisions*. 3d ed. Ann Arbor: University of Michigan Press, 1990. This is considered to be one of the best studies of the ways in which members of Congress vote. It includes the roles played in this process by constituents, colleagues, interest groups, the executive branch, and staff members.

Marini, John. *The Politics of Budget Control: Congress, the Presidency, and the Growth of the Administrative State*. Bristol, Pa.: Crane Russak, 1992. This text examines the management of the federal budget from the early 1900s to the early 1990s and stresses the centrality of the budget in defining the respective powers of the legislative and executive branches.

Ornstein, Norman J., Thomas E. Mann, and Michael J. Malbin. *Vital Statistics on Congress, 1993–1994*. Washington, D.C.: Congressional Quarterly Press, 1994. The authors bring together from various sources information on eight areas related to Congress, including data on the members themselves, elections, campaign finances, budgeting, committees, and so on.

Peabody, Robert L., and Nelson W. Polsby. *New Perspectives on the House of Representatives*. 4th ed. Baltimore, Md.: Johns Hopkins University Press, 1992. This is a comprehensive, behind-the-scenes look at practices and procedures in the House of Representatives.

Reeves, Andree E. *Congressional Committee Chairmen: Three Who Made an Evolution*. Lexington, Ky.: University Press of Kentucky, 1993. Reeves examines the careers of three very strong House committee chairpersons of the House Education and Labor Committee. Her work shows how committees develop and change under the direction of different chairpersons.

Rohde, David W. *Parties and Leaders in the Postreform House*. Chicago: University of Chicago Press, 1991. Rohde argues that the sectional divisions within the Democratic and Republican parties, particularly between the northern and southern Democrats, have been reduced due to a realignment of electoral forces and that there is an increased divergence between the parties on many significant issues brought before Congress.

Schneier, Edward V., and Bertram Gross. *Congress Today*. New York: St. Martin's Press, 1993. Two individuals with extensive experience on Capitol Hill provide an excellent overview of Congress and the changing context in which it works.

11
The Presidency

Chapter Outline

WHAT IF . . . The Vice President Served as the President's Chief of Staff?

Traditionally, vice presidents are chosen to "balance the ticket" by appealing to a regional, ethnic, religious, or philosophical perspective different from that of the presidential candidate. After the election, they perform the duties assigned by the Constitution—namely, presiding over the Senate occasionally and doing whatever the president asks them to do. In recent times, presidential candidates have frequently announced their intention to pick a skillful and talented vice president and then to give him or her very important duties.

The problem with this good intention is that it is more difficult to fulfill than it seems. Vice presidents usually cannot act as effective liaisons with Congress, because the legislators resent it. Vice presidents cannot run cabinet departments, because that would create a conflict of interest. When Vice President Al Gore acts as a leader on environmental issues, for example, senators appeal directly to the president when they disagree with Gore's views. Vice presidents can attend funerals of heads of states and perform other honorary duties, but they are *not* the president and are often regarded as unimportant substitutes by foreign nations.

It seems that the vice president's abilities are underused, whereas presidents continue to be overburdened by their official, ceremonial, and political duties. To cope with their responsibilities, modern presidents have tried numerous organizational schemes for the White House and have exhausted aides in the process. Why not

solve both problems by having the president pick an effective, closely allied politician for vice president who could then act as the president's chief of staff?

Giving the job of chief of staff to the vice president means that he or she would be responsible for running the White House, screening visitors to the president, keeping tabs on the president's popularity, and making sure that the president gets the kind of advice and assistance that he or she needs from advisers and federal executives. The job would demand excellent organizational and political skills. The vice president would have to be able to speak for the president on some matters and command the respect of other federal and state officials. In effect, the vice president would become the president's closest assistant and adviser.

To choose a vice president for this new responsibility would totally upset the traditional way of building a ticket. Instead of looking for a vice president whose political strengths make up for the presidential candidate's weaknesses, the ideal candidate would complement the president in ideology, partisanship, and policy positions. This might be seen as a

disadvantage to the national ticket, because people who did not like the presidential nominee's views would not like the vice presidential nominee's either. If both parties adopted this strategy, there might be a large number of Americans who could find no one on either ticket to support. Furthermore, some groups within each party would claim to have lost their representation and threaten to leave the political family.

More important, presidents would have to change their view of their next in command—their vice presidents. Although a presidential nominee always wants a running mate who will be an asset to the ticket, the chief executive does not want a vice president who is more popular with the people than the president. By making the vice president the White House chief of staff, the president would either have to limit the vice president's authority, thus making him or her less able to do the job, or be prepared to see a vice president grow in power and public reputation. Vice presidents often have moved on to compete for the top post. Being chief of staff might sharpen the number two executive's ambition and speed up his or her timetable to the White House.

---

1. What kind of running mate would a president need for that person to be an effective chief of staff?

2. Would the vice president as chief of staff gain or lose popularity with the public and Congress in taking on this difficult task?

It is ironic that the Founding Fathers, rejecting so emphatically the model of a king, created an office presently invested with authority far beyond that of any surviving king and only to be rivaled by the powers of absolute monarchs.[1]

The writers of the Constitution created the presidency of the United States without any models on which to draw. Nowhere else in the world was there a democratically selected chief executive. What the founders did not want was a king. In fact, given their previous experience with royal governors in the colonies, many of the delegates to the Constitutional Convention wanted to create a very weak executive who could not veto legislation. Other delegates, especially those who had witnessed the need for a strong leader in the revolutionary army, believed a strong executive to be necessary for the republic. The delegates, after much debate, created a chief executive who had enough powers granted in the Constitution to balance those of the Congress.[2]

The power exercised by each president who has held the office has been scrutinized and judged by historians, political scientists, the media, and the public. Indeed, it would seem that Americans are fascinated by presidential power. In this chapter, after looking at who can become president and at the process involved, we examine closely the nature and extent of the constitutional powers held by the president. (For a discussion of the power granted to the vice president, see the *What If . . .* that opens this chapter.)

WHO CAN BECOME PRESIDENT?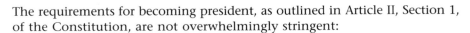

The requirements for becoming president, as outlined in Article II, Section 1, of the Constitution, are not overwhelmingly stringent:

> No person except a natural born Citizen, or a Citizen of the United States, at the time of the Adoption of this Constitution, shall be eligible to the Office of President; neither shall any Person be eligible to that Office who shall not have attained to the Age of thirty-five Years, and been fourteen Years a Resident within the United States.

The only question that arises about these qualifications relates to the term "natural born Citizen." Does that mean only citizens born in the United States and its territories? What about a child born to a U.S. citizen (or to a couple who are U.S. citizens) while visiting or living in another country? Although the question has not been dealt with directly by the Supreme Court, it is reasonable to expect that someone would be eligible if his or her parents were Americans. The first presidents, after all, were not even American citizens at birth, and others were born in areas that did not become part of the United States until later. These questions were debated when George Romney, who was born in Chihuahua, Mexico, made a serious bid for the Republican presidential nomination in the 1960s.[3]

---

1. Page Smith, *The Constitution: A Documentary and Narrative History* (New York: Morrow, 1978), p. 528.
2. Forrest McDonald, *The American Presidency: An Intellectual History* (Lawrence, Kans.: University Press of Kansas, 1994), p. 179.
3. George Romney was governor of Michigan from 1963 to 1969. Romney was not nominated, and the issue remains unresolved.

Abraham Lincoln is usually classified as one of the greatest presidents because of his dedication to preserving the Union.

From left to right, the first cabinet—Henry Knox, Thomas Jefferson, Edmund Randolph, Alexander Hamilton, and the first president—George Washington.

TWELFTH AMENDMENT
An amendment to the Constitution, adopted in 1804, that specifies the separate election of the president and vice president by the electoral college.

The great American dream is symbolized by the statement that "anybody can become president of this country." It is true that in modern times, presidents have included a haberdasher (Harry Truman—for a short period of time), a peanut farmer (Jimmy Carter), and an actor (Ronald Reagan). But if you examine Appendix C, you will see that the most common previous occupation of presidents in this country has been the legal profession. Out of forty-two presidents, twenty-five have been lawyers, and many have been wealthy.

Although the Constitution states that the minimum-age requirement for the presidency is thirty-five years, most presidents have been much older than that when they assumed office. John F. Kennedy, at the age of forty-three, was the youngest elected president, and the oldest was Ronald Reagan, at age sixty-nine. The average age at inauguration has been fifty-four. There has clearly been a demographic bias in the selection of presidents. All have been male, white, and Protestant, except for John F. Kennedy, a Roman Catholic. Presidents have been men of great stature—George Washington, for example—and men in whom leadership qualities were not so pronounced—such as Warren Harding. (See the *Politics: The Human Side* on the following page for a profile of George Washington.)

THE PROCESS OF BECOMING PRESIDENT

Major and minor political parties nominate candidates for president and vice president at national conventions every four years. As discussed in Chapter 9, the nation's voters do not elect a president and vice president directly but rather cast ballots for presidential electors, who then vote for president and vice president in the electoral college.

Because the election is decided by a majority in the electoral college, it is conceivable that someone could be elected to the office of the presidency without having a plurality of the popular vote cast. Indeed, as discussed previously, in three cases candidates won elections even though their major opponents received more popular votes. In cases in which there were more than two candidates running for office, many presidential candidates have won the election with less than 50 percent of the total popular votes cast for all candidates—including Abraham Lincoln, Woodrow Wilson, Harry S Truman, John F. Kennedy, and Richard Nixon. In the 1992 election, Bill Clinton, with only 43 percent of the vote, defeated incumbent George Bush. Independent candidate H. Ross Perot garnered a surprising 19 percent of the vote.

On occasion, the electoral college has failed to give any candidate a majority. At this point, the election is thrown into the House of Representatives. The president is then chosen from among the three candidates having the most electoral college votes. Only two times in our past has the House had to decide on a president. Thomas Jefferson and Aaron Burr tied in the electoral college in 1800. This happened because the Constitution had not been explicit in indicating which of the two electoral votes was for president and which was for vice president. In 1804, the **Twelfth Amendment** clarified the matter. In 1824 the House again had to make a choice, this time among William H. Crawford, Andrew Jackson, and John Quincy Adams. It chose Adams, even though Jackson had more electoral and popular votes.

POLITICS: THE HUMAN SIDE
George Washington, the First President

"The constitution which at any time exists, till changed by an explicit and authentic act of the whole people is sacredly obligatory upon all."

BIOGRAPHICAL NOTES

George Washington was born in colonial Virginia on February 22, 1732. The second son in the family, he was educated to be a surveyor, and, later in his life, he surveyed much of what became West Virginia and Kentucky for the British government. He inherited a plantation, Mount Vernon, from his brother, Lawrence, and began to acquire more land, becoming one of the largest landholders in the region. Washington spent some time under British command in the French and Indian War. Later, Washington became a supporter of the American Revolution. He was a delegate to the Continental Congress and was its unanimous choice to lead the Revolutionary army. After the war, he retired to his plantation. He later returned to public life to chair the Constitutional Convention and then to serve as the first president of the new nation. After

refusing a third term in 1796, he retired again to Mount Vernon, where he died in 1799.

POLITICAL CONTRIBUTIONS

Although he had spent most of his life as a surveyor and planter, Washington was revered by his colleagues for his integrity, his courage, and his strong talent for leadership. From the time he entered politics during colonial days through his long tenure as commander of the Revolutionary army, he never disappointed his supporters. When the Constitutional Convention finally agreed to create a single executive that was vested with some executive powers (although most were shared with Congress), only the thought that Washington was sure to win the presidency convinced delegates to accept the creation of this new and powerful office. Indeed, he won a unanimous election in the new electoral college.

Washington himself believed that public expectations were too high. He wrote, "I greatly apprehend that my Countrymen will expect too much from me."* Under his leadership, however, new cabinet departments were established, decisions were made to deal with the debts remaining from the war, and many other nations recognized the United States as a sovereign state.

George Washington was an aristocrat in his upbringing and tastes—he did not think of himself as a commoner. As the new president, he often insisted on certain rituals and was concerned over the title to

be given to the executive. (In his view, *Mr. President* was too humble.) He established a sense of formality and fairness in the White House. He invited government officials to dinner on Thursdays, for example, but only by rotation, so no favorites would be created. He visited the various states to build support for the government and tried to find out what the ordinary citizen was thinking from friends out in the more rural areas.

The first president's view of government was decidedly nonpartisan. He did not wish to see the new republic divided by factions or political parties. He had recruited some of the brightest members of the elite into his cabinet—Alexander Hamilton as secretary of the treasury, Thomas Jefferson as secretary of state, and Henry Knox as secretary of the War Department. As Hamilton put forth his plans for a national bank, Jefferson and James Madison opposed it strongly, saying that the Constitution did not allow for such an institution. Jefferson left the cabinet and, with Madison, began to organize a political party to oppose Hamilton and the other Federalists in the government.

Washington, in his farewell address to the nation, warned against the spirit of party. He also told Americans to avoid "entangl[ing] our peace and prosperity in the toils of European ambition, rivalship, interest, humor or caprice." The nation rejected his advice on parties but often has recalled it to guide foreign policy decisions.

*Forrest McDonald, *The American Presidency: An Intellectual History* (Lawrence, Kans.: University Press of Kansas, 1994), p. 211.

THE MANY ROLES OF THE PRESIDENT

The Constitution speaks briefly about the duties and obligations of the president. Based on a brief list of powers and the precedents of history, the presidency has grown into a very complicated job that requires balancing at least five constitutional roles. These are (1) chief of state, (2) chief executive, (3) commander in chief of the armed forces, (4) chief diplomat, and (5) chief legislator of the United States. Here we examine each of these significant presidential functions, or roles. It is worth noting that one person plays all these roles simultaneously and that the needs of these roles may at times be contradictory.

Chief of State

Every nation has at least one person who is the ceremonial head of state. In most democratic governments, the role of **chief of state** is given to someone other than the chief executive, who is the head of the executive branch of government. In Britain, for example, the chief of state is the queen. In France, where the prime minister is the chief executive, the chief of state is the president. But in the United States, the president is both chief executive and chief of state. According to William Howard Taft, as chief of state, the president symbolizes the "dignity and majesty" of the American people. In his capacity as chief of state, the president engages in a number of activities that are largely symbolic or ceremonial, such as the following:

- Decorating war heroes.
- Throwing out the first ball to open the baseball season.
- Dedicating parks and post offices.
- Launching charity drives.
- Receiving visiting chiefs of state at the White House.
- Going on official state visits to other countries.
- Making personal telephone calls to congratulate the country's heroes.

CHIEF OF STATE
The role of the president as ceremonial head of the government.

One of the traditional activities as chief of state requires the president to throw out the first ball that starts the baseball season. Here President Clinton is throwing the first pitch at the Cleveland Indians game. Some critics of the American presidency contend that one person should not be required to be both chief of state and chief executive, mainly because the duties of the chief of state take up too much time.

Many students of the American political system believe that having the president serve as both the chief executive and the chief of state drastically limits the time available to do "real" work. Not all presidents have agreed with this conclusion, however—particularly those presidents who have been able to blend skillfully these two roles with their role as politician. Being chief of state gives the president tremendous public exposure. When that exposure is positive, it helps the president deal with Congress over proposed legislation and increases the chances of being reelected—or getting the candidates of the president's party elected.

Chief Executive

According to the Constitution, "The executive Power shall be vested in a President of the United States of America. . . . [H]e may require the Opinion, in writing, of the principal Officer in each of the executive Departments, upon any Subject relating to the Duties of their respective Offices . . . and he shall nominate, and by and with the Advice and Consent of the Senate, shall appoint . . . Officers of the United States. . . . [H]e shall take Care that the Laws be faithfully executed."

As **chief executive** the president is constitutionally bound to enforce the acts of Congress, the judgments of federal courts, and treaties signed by the United States. To assist in the various tasks of the chief executive, the president has a federal bureaucracy (see Chapter 12), which currently consists of some three million civilian employees and which spends over $1.5 trillion per year.

CHIEF EXECUTIVE
The role of the president as head of the executive branch of the government.

The Powers of Appointment and Removal.   Because the president is head of the largest bureaucracy in the United States, you might think that the chief executive wields enormous power. The president, however, only nominally runs the executive bureaucracy, because most of its jobs are

One of the president's jobs is to act as chief of state, thereby representing the United States throughout the world. Here President Clinton gives a speech commemorating the fiftieth anniversary of D-Day, which began about 12:15 A.M. on June 6, 1944. This military campaign, which started on the beaches of Normandy, France, was credited with causing the German war effort on the Western front to collapse. Germany signed an unconditional surrender on May 7, 1945.

CIVIL SERVICE
A collective term for the body of employees working for the government. Generally, civil service is understood to apply to all those who gain government employment through a merit system.

APPOINTMENT POWER
The authority vested in the president to fill a government office or position. Positions filled by presidential appointment include those in the executive branch, the federal judiciary, commissioned officers in the armed forces, and members of the independent regulatory commissions.

protected by laws governing the **civil service**.[4] Therefore, even though the president has **appointment power**, it is not very extensive, being limited to cabinet and subcabinet jobs, federal judgeships, agency heads, and about two thousand lesser jobs. This means that most of the three million federal employees owe no political allegiance to the president. They are more likely to owe loyalty to congressional committees or to interest groups representing the sector of the society that they serve. Table 11–1 shows what percentage of the total employment in each executive department is available for political appointment by the president.

The president's power to remove from office officials who are not doing a good job or who do not agree with the president is not explicitly granted by the Constitution and has been limited. In 1926, however, a Supreme Court decision prevented Congress from interfering with the president's ability to fire those executive-branch officials whom the president had appointed with Senate approval.[5]

The ten agencies whose directors the president can remove at any time are as follows:

1. ACTION (coordinates volunteer programs).
2. Arms Control and Disarmament Agency.

4. See Chapter 12 for a discussion of the Civil Service Reform Act.
5. *Meyers v. United States*, 272 U.S. 52 (1926).

TABLE 11–1

Total Civilian Employment in Cabinet Departments Available for Political Appointment by the President

EXECUTIVE DEPARTMENT	TOTAL NUMBER OF EMPLOYEES	POLITICAL APPOINTMENTS AVAILABLE	PERCENTAGE
Agriculture	125,640	501	0.40
Commerce	38,087	399	1.00
Defense	1,012,216	853	0.08
Education	5,081	252	4.95
Energy	19,539	503	2.57
Health and Human Services	129,483	541	0.42
Housing and Urban Development	14,998	188	1.25
Interior	81,683	311	0.38
Justice	90,821	543	0.59
Labor	17,938	214	1.19
State	25,699	454	1.76
Transportation	69,831	429	0.61
Treasury	166,433	283	0.17
Veterans' Affairs	256,145	364	0.14
TOTAL	2,054,094	5,835	0.28

SOURCE: U.S. Department of Commerce, *Statistical Abstract of the United States, 1994* (Washington, D.C.: U.S. Government Printing Office, 1994).

3. Commission on Civil Rights.

4. Energy Research and Development Agency.

5. Environmental Protection Agency.

6. Federal Mediation and Conciliation Service.

7. General Services Administration.

8. National Aeronautics and Space Administration.

9. Postal Service.

10. Small Business Administration.

In addition, the president can remove all heads of cabinet departments, all individuals in the Executive Office of the President, and all of the political appointees listed in Table 11–1.

Harry Truman spoke candidly of the difficulties a president faces in trying to control the executive bureaucracy. Upon leaving office, he referred to the problems that Dwight Eisenhower, as a former general of the army, was going to have: "He'll sit here and he'll say do this! do that! and nothing will happen. Poor Ike—it won't be a bit like the Army. He'll find it very frustrating."[6]

The Power to Grant Reprieves and Pardons.   Section 2 of Article II of the Constitution gives the president the power to grant **reprieves** and **pardons** for offenses against the United States except in cases of impeachment. All pardons are administered by the Office of the Pardon Attorney in the Department of Justice. In principle, pardons are granted to remedy a mistake made in a conviction.

The Supreme Court upheld the president's right to reprieve in a 1925 case concerning the pardon granted by the president to an individual convicted of contempt of court. The judiciary had contended that only judges had the authority to convict individuals for contempt of court when court orders were violated and that the courts should be free from interference by the executive branch. The Supreme Court simply stated that the president could reprieve or pardon all offenses "either before trial, during trial, or after trial, by individuals, or by classes, conditionally or absolutely, and this without modification or regulation by Congress."[7] In a controversial decision, President Gerald Ford pardoned former president Richard Nixon for his role in the Watergate affair before any charges were brought in court. After his defeat in the 1992 presidential election, George Bush also exercised the right of executive pardon for six former members of the Reagan administration who had been charged with various offenses in regard to the Iran-*contra* investigation.

Commander in Chief

The president, according to the Constitution, "shall be Commander in Chief of the Army and Navy of the United States, and of the Militia of the several States, when called into the actual Service of the United States." In other words, the armed forces are under civilian, rather than military, control.

DID YOU KNOW . . .
That John F. Kennedy was the youngest elected president, taking office at the age of forty-three, but that Theodore Roosevelt assumed office at the age of forty-two after the assassination of President William McKinley?

REPRIEVE
The presidential power to postpone the execution of a sentence imposed by a court of law; usually done for humanitarian reasons or to await new evidence.

PARDON
The granting of a release from the punishment or legal consequences of crime; a pardon can be granted by the president before or after a conviction.

---

6. Quoted in Richard E. Neustadt, *Presidential Power: The Politics of Leadership* (New York: Wiley, 1960), p. 9.

7. *Ex parte Grossman*, 267 U.S. 87 (1925).

COMMANDER IN CHIEF
The role of the president as supreme commander of the military forces of the United States and of the state national guard units when they are called into federal service.

WAR POWERS ACT
A law passed in 1973 spelling out the conditions under which the president can commit troops without congressional approval.

President Clinton is shown here working in the Oval Office. This oval-shaped office in the White House, with its immense seal of the United States in the carpet, is often used to represent the power of the presidency and of the United States. Indeed, common references to "the Oval Office" mean specifically the president who is in power at that time.

Certainly those who wrote the Constitution had George Washington in mind when they made the president the **commander in chief.** Although we no longer expect our president to lead the troops to battle, presidents as commanders in chief have wielded dramatic power. Harry Truman made the awesome decision to drop atomic bombs on Hiroshima and Nagasaki in 1945 to force Japan to surrender and thus bring to an end World War II. Lyndon Johnson ordered bombing missions against North Vietnam in the 1960s, and he personally selected the targets. Richard Nixon decided to invade Cambodia in 1970. Ronald Reagan sent troops to Lebanon and Grenada in 1983 and ordered U.S. fighter planes to attack Libya in 1986. George Bush sent troops to Panama in 1989 and to the Middle East in 1990. Bill Clinton sent troops to Haiti in 1994. The president is the ultimate decision maker in military matters. Everywhere he goes, so too goes the "football"—a briefcase filled with all the codes necessary to order a nuclear attack. Only the president has the power to order the use of nuclear force.

As commander in chief, the president has probably exercised more authority than in any other role. Constitutionally, Congress has the sole power to declare war, but the president can send the armed forces into a country in situations that are certainly the equivalent of war. When President William McKinley ordered troops into Peking to help suppress the Boxer Rebellion in 1900, he was sending them into a combat situation. Harry Truman dispatched troops to Korea as part of a "police action" in 1950. Kennedy, Johnson, and Nixon waged an undeclared war in Southeast Asia, where over 58,000 Americans were killed and 300,000 were wounded. In none of these situations did Congress declare war.

In an attempt to gain more control over such military activities, in 1973 Congress passed a **War Powers Act**—over President Nixon's veto—requiring that the president consult with Congress before sending American forces into action. Once they are sent, the president must report to Congress within forty-eight hours. Unless Congress has passed a declaration of war within sixty days or has extended the sixty-day time limit, the forces must be withdrawn. The War Powers Act was tested in the fall of 1983, when

Reagan requested that troops be left in Lebanon. The resulting compromise was a congressional resolution allowing troops to remain there for eighteen months. Shortly after the resolution was passed, however, more than 240 sailors and marines were killed in the suicide bombing of a U.S. military housing compound in Beirut. That event provoked a furious congressional debate over the role American troops were playing in the Middle East, and all troops were withdrawn shortly afterward.

In spite of the War Powers Act, the powers of the president as commander in chief are more extensive today than they were in the past. These powers are linked closely to the president's powers as chief diplomat, or chief crafter of foreign policy.

Chief Diplomat

The Constitution gives the president the power to recognize foreign governments; to make treaties, with the **advice and consent** of the Senate; and to make special agreements with other heads of state that do not require congressional approval. In addition, the president nominates ambassadors. As **chief diplomat**, the president dominates American foreign policy.

Recognition Power.   An important power of the president as chief diplomat is **recognition power,** or the power to recognize—or refuse to recognize—foreign governments. In the role of ceremonial head of state, the president has always received foreign diplomats. In modern times, the simple act of receiving a foreign diplomat has been equivalent to accrediting the diplomat and officially recognizing his or her government. Such recognition of the legitimacy of another country's government is a prerequisite to diplomatic relations or negotiations between that country and the United States.

Deciding when to recognize a foreign power is not always simple. The United States, for example, did not recognize the Soviet Union until 1933— sixteen years after the Russian Revolution of 1917. It was only after all

ADVICE AND CONSENT
The power vested in the U.S. Senate by the Constitution (Article II, Section 2) to give its advice and consent to the president concerning treaties and presidential appointments.

CHIEF DIPLOMAT
The role of the president in recognizing foreign governments, making treaties, and making executive agreements.

RECOGNITION POWER
The president's power, as chief diplomat, to extend diplomatic recognition to foreign governments.

An international economic summit took place in Vancouver, British Columbia (Canada), in the summer of 1993. Two of the attendees were President Bill Clinton and President Boris Yeltsin of Russia. Periodically, leaders from major economic powers around the world meet to develop common goals and policies. Clinton used the Vancouver Summit to propose policies to increase employment worldwide. Yeltsin, in contrast, attempted to convince world leaders that he should be taken seriously and that Russia should be given billions of dollars of unrestricted aid. He partially succeeded in his goals.

attempts to reverse the effects of that revolution—including military invasion of Russia and diplomatic isolation—had proved futile that Franklin Roosevelt extended recognition to the Soviet government. U.S. presidents faced a similar problem with the Chinese communist revolution. In December 1978, long after the communist victory in China, Jimmy Carter granted official recognition to the People's Republic of China.[8]

When Lithuania declared its independence from the Soviet Union in 1990, President Bush was placed in a difficult position. The United States had never recognized the Soviet occupation of the Lithuanian republic after World War II. Should Bush have sent an ambassador as soon as Lithuania declared its freedom? Should Bush have gone himself? (For a discussion of the cost of traveling with the president, see this chapter's *Politics and Economics*.) Bush moved cautiously, giving Lithuania moral support but avoiding direct recognition so as to avoid disrupting newly cordial relations with the Soviet Union. Similarly, when Croatia and Slovenia declared independence from Yugoslavia, Bush again moved slowly, only recognizing these new nations after many other European nations had done so.

Proposal and Ratification of Treaties.   The president has the sole power to negotiate treaties with other nations. These treaties must be presented to the Senate, where they may be modified and must be approved by a two-thirds vote. After ratification, the president can approve the senatorial version of the treaty. Approval poses a problem when the Senate has tacked on substantive amendments or reservations to a treaty, particularly when such changes may require reopening negotiations with the other signatory governments. Sometimes a president may decide to withdraw a treaty if the senatorial changes are too extensive—as Woodrow Wilson did with the Versailles Treaty in 1919. Wilson felt that the senatorial reservations would weaken the treaty so much that it would be ineffective. His refusal

8. The Nixon administration first encouraged new relations with the People's Republic of China by allowing a cultural exchange of ping-pong teams.

U.S. President Jimmy Carter, Egyptian President Anwar el-Sadat, and Israeli Prime Minister Menachem Begin sign the Camp David accords, bringing peace between Egypt and Israel.

POLITICS AND ECONOMICS
Traveling with the President

Whenever the president travels in the United States or overseas, reporters for national newspapers and for television travel with him. Sometimes these correspondents are invited to travel on *Air Force One*, the president's plane. More often, a press plane is chartered. Early in the Clinton presidency, the staff members of the White House Travel Office were fired from their jobs, and the task of arranging presidential and press travel was turned over to a private travel agency. After some criticism, most of those workers were reinstated on a temporary basis.

One of the duties of the White House Travel Office is to arrange travel for the press and then to bill the press for those trips. The cost for a reporter to travel with the president is approximately three times the cost of a first-class ticket, with no discounts for Saturday night stayovers.

The president's airplane, the Boeing 747 *Air Force One*, was inaugurated in 1990. It costs $26,000 per hour to operate *Air Force One*.

The bill for one Associated Press reporter traveling with Bill Clinton to Brussels, Prague, Kiev, Moscow, Minsk, and Geneva in January 1994 totaled $6,658.18, exclusive of ground transportation and other expenses. The charges for travel within Russia were modest, but the return trip from Geneva to Washington, D.C., cost $2,904.93.

to accept the senatorial version of the treaty led to the eventual refusal of the United States to join the League of Nations.

President Bill Clinton won a major political and legislative victory in 1993 by persuading Congress to ratify the North American Free Trade Agreement (NAFTA). He succeeded in overcoming opposition from Democrats and most of organized labor, and in gaining Republican support for the treaty.

Executive Agreements. Presidential power in foreign affairs is enhanced greatly by the use of **executive agreements** made between the president and other heads of state. Such agreements do not require Senate approval, although the House and Senate may refuse to appropriate the funds necessary to implement them. Whereas treaties are binding on all succeeding administrations, executive agreements are not binding without each new president's consent.

Among the advantages of executive agreements are speed and secrecy. The former is essential during a crisis; the latter is important when the administration fears that open senatorial debate may be detrimental to the best interests of the United States or to the interests of the president. There have been far more executive agreements (about 9,000) than treaties (about

EXECUTIVE AGREEMENT
An international agreement made by the president, without senatorial ratification, with the head of a foreign state.

CHIEF LEGISLATOR
**The role of the president in influenc-
ing the making of laws.**

STATE OF THE UNION MESSAGE
**An annual message to Congress in
which the president proposes a legislative program. The message is addressed not only to Congress but also
to the American people and to the
world. It offers the opportunity to
dramatize policies and objectives and
to gain public support.**

Each year the president presents his
State of the Union message, which is
required by Article II, Section 3, of the
Constitution and is usually given in
late January, shortly after Congress
reconvenes. Because the floor of the
House of Representatives is so much
larger than that of the Senate, the
State of the Union speech is given
there. Attendees are, of course, all
members of Congress, plus usually
the justices of the U.S. Supreme Court,
the heads of the executive departments, and certain others, such as the
chairman of the Federal Reserve
Board of Governors. The press, of
course, is in attendance, too.

1,300). In 1905, Theodore Roosevelt implemented the Dillingham-Sanchez
Protocol, which permitted American control of customs houses in Santo
Domingo (now the Dominican Republic), as an executive agreement. In
1970, Richard Nixon concluded an executive agreement with the government of Spain to operate military bases. Franklin Roosevelt used executive
agreements to bypass congressional isolationists in trading American de-
stroyers for British Caribbean naval bases and in arranging diplomatic and
military affairs with Canada and Latin American nations. Many executive
agreements contain secret provisions calling for American military assistance
or other support.

Chief Legislator

Constitutionally, presidents must recommend to Congress legislation that
they judge necessary and expedient. Not all presidents have wielded their
powers as **chief legislator** in the same manner. President John Tyler was
almost completely unsuccessful in getting his legislative programs implemented by Congress. Presidents Theodore Roosevelt, Franklin Roosevelt, and
Lyndon Johnson, however, saw much of their proposed legislation put into
effect.

In modern times, the president has played a dominant role in creating
the congressional agenda. In the president's annual **State of the Union
message**, which is required by the Constitution (Article II, Section 3) and is
usually given in late January shortly after Congress reconvenes, the president as chief legislator presents the administration's program. The message
gives a broad, comprehensive view of what the president wishes the legislature to accomplish during its session. It is as much a message to the American people and to the world as it is to Congress. Its impact on public
opinion can determine the way in which Congress responds to the president's agenda.

Christine Whitman, the Republican governor of New Jersey, watches President Clinton give the State of the Union speech in January 1995. After the speech, Governor Whitman delivered the Republican reply. The choice of Governor Whitman was historic both because she is a woman and because Republicans selected a governor rather than a member of Congress for this address. It was suggested that they were showcasing Governor Whitman as a future national candidate and trying to emphasize the importance of state policies for the Republican-controlled Congress.

Getting Legislation Passed.   The president can propose legislation, but Congress is not required to pass any of the administration's bills. How, then, does the president get those proposals made into law? One way is the power of persuasion. The president writes to, telephones, and meets with various congressional leaders; makes public announcements to force the weight of public opinion onto Congress in favor of a legislative program; and, as head of the party, exercises legislative leadership through the congresspersons of the president's party.

To be sure, a president whose party represents a majority in both houses of Congress may have an easier time getting legislation passed than does a president who faces a hostile Congress. But one of the ways in which a president who faces a hostile Congress still can wield power is through the ability to veto legislation.

Saying No to Legislation.   The president has the power to say no to legislation through use of the veto, by which the White House returns a bill unsigned to the legislative body with a **veto message** attached.[9] Because the Constitution requires that every bill passed by the House and the Senate be sent to the president before it becomes law, the president must act on each bill:

VETO MESSAGE
The president's formal explanation of a veto when legislation is returned to the Congress.

1. If the bill is signed, it becomes law.
2. If the bill is not sent back to Congress after ten congressional working days, it becomes law without the president's signature.
3. The president can reject the bill and send it back to Congress with a veto message setting forth objections. Congress then can change the bill, hoping to secure presidential approval and repass it. Or it can simply reject the

_____
9. *Veto* in Latin means "I forbid."

POCKET VETO
A special veto power exercised by the
chief executive after a legislative
body has adjourned. Bills not signed
by the chief executive die after a
specified period of time. If Congress
wishes to reconsider such a bill, it
must be reintroduced in the following session of Congress.

president's objections by overriding the veto with a two-thirds roll-call vote
of the members present in each house.

4. If the president refuses to sign the bill and Congress adjourns within ten
working days after the bill has been submitted to the president, the bill is
killed for that session of Congress. If Congress wishes the bill to be reconsidered, the bill must be reintroduced during the following session. This is
called a **pocket veto.**

Presidents employed the veto power infrequently until the administration
of Andrew Johnson, but it has been used with increasing vigor since then
(see Table 11–2). The total number of vetoes from George Washington
through Bill Clinton's second year in office was 2,496, with about two-thirds
of those vetoes being exercised by Grover Cleveland, Franklin Roosevelt,
Harry Truman, and Dwight Eisenhower.

A veto is a clear-cut indication of the president's dissatisfaction with congressional legislation. It is a very effective tool as well, because it denies the
legislative power of the Congress. Nonetheless, Congress rarely overrides a
presidential veto. Consider that two-thirds of the members of each chamber
who are present must vote to override the president's veto in a roll-call vote.
This means that if only one-third plus one of the members voting in one of
the chambers of Congress do not agree to override the veto, the veto holds.
Table 11–2 tells us that it was not until the administration of John Tyler
that Congress overrode a presidential veto. In the first sixty-five years of
American federal government history, out of thirty-three regular vetoes,
Congress overrode only one, or less than 3 percent. Overall, only about 7
percent of all vetoes have been overridden.

**Measuring the Success or Failure of a President's Legislative
Program.**   One way of determining a president's strength is to evaluate
that president's success as chief legislator. A strong president is one who has
achieved much of the administration's legislative program; a weak president
is one who has achieved little. Using these definitions of strong and weak,
it is possible to rank presidents according to their legislative success.

Figure 11–1 shows the percentages of presidential victories measured by
congressional votes in situations in which the president took a clear-cut
position. Based on this information, Lyndon Johnson appears to have been
the most successful president in recent years until Clinton. Such data provide a statistical measure but do not indicate the importance of the legislation, the bills not introduced, or whether the president was perceived as
a successful national leader regardless of this measure. Clinton, for example,
was very successful in getting many laws passed but lost on his priority
issue—health-care reform. More seriously, he lost control of the Congress in
the 1994 elections. Some scholars suggest that the skill or popularity of a
president is less important than the partisan and ideological composition of
Congress at a given time in determining the president's success or failure at
achieving the desired legislative program.

Other Presidential Powers

CONSTITUTIONAL POWER
A power vested in the president by
Article II of the Constitution.

The powers of the president discussed in the preceding sections are called
constitutional powers, because their basis lies in the Constitution. In ad-

TABLE 11–2

Presidential Vetoes, 1789 to 1995

YEARS	PRESIDENT	REGULAR VETOES	VETOES OVERRIDDEN	POCKET VETOES	TOTAL VETOES
1789–1797	Washington	2	0	0	2
1797–1801	J. Adams	0	0	0	0
1801–1809	Jefferson	0	0	0	0
1809–1817	Madison	5	0	2	7
1817–1825	Monroe	1	0	0	1
1825–1829	J. Q. Adams	0	0	0	0
1829–1837	Jackson	5	0	7	12
1837–1841	Van Buren	0	0	1	1
1841–1841	Harrison	0	0	0	0
1841–1845	Tyler	6	1	4	10
1845–1849	Polk	2	0	1	3
1849–1850	Taylor	0	0	0	0
1850–1853	Fillmore	0	0	0	0
1853–1857	Pierce	9	5	0	9
1857–1861	Buchanan	4	0	3	7
1861–1865	Lincoln	2	0	5	7
1865–1869	A. Johnson	21	15	8	29
1869–1877	Grant	45	4	48	93
1877–1881	Hayes	12	1	1	13
1881–1881	Garfield	0	0	0	0
1881–1885	Arthur	4	1	8	12
1885–1889	Cleveland	304	2	110	414
1889–1893	Harrison	19	1	25	44
1893–1897	Cleveland	42	5	128	170
1897–1901	McKinley	6	0	36	42
1901–1909	T. Roosevelt	42	1	40	82
1909–1913	Taft	30	1	9	39
1913–1921	Wilson	33	6	11	44
1921–1923	Harding	5	0	1	6
1923–1929	Coolidge	20	4	30	50
1929–1933	Hoover	21	3	16	37
1933–1945	F. Roosevelt	372	9	263	635
1945–1953	Truman	180	12	70	250
1953–1961	Eisenhower	73	2	108	181
1961–1963	Kennedy	12	0	9	21
1963–1969	L. Johnson	16	0	14	30
1969–1974	Nixon	26*	7	17	43
1974–1977	Ford	48	12	18	66
1977–1981	Carter	13	2	18	31
1981–1989	Reagan	39	9	28	67
1989–1993	Bush	37	1	0	37
1993–1995	Clinton	1	0	0	1
TOTAL		1,457	104	1039	2,496

*Two pocket vetoes, overruled in the courts, are counted here as regular vetoes.
SOURCE: Louis Fisher, *The Politics of Shared Power: Congress and the Executive,* 2d ed. (Washington, D.C.: Congressional Quarterly Press, 1987), p. 30: *Congressional Quarter Weekly Report,* October 17, 1992, p. 3249; and authors' update.

dition, Congress has established by law, or statute, numerous other presidential powers—such as the ability to declare national emergencies. These are called **statutory powers.** Both constitutional and statutory powers have been labeled the **expressed powers** of the president, because they are expressly written into the Constitution or into law.

Presidents also have what have come to be known as **inherent powers.** These depend on the loosely worded statement in the Constitution that "the

STATUTORY POWER
A power created for the president through laws established by Congress.

EXPRESSED POWER
A constitutional or statutory power of the president, which is expressly written into the Constitution or into congressional law.

INHERENT POWER
A power of the president derived from the loosely worded statement in the Constitution that "the executive Power shall be vested in a President" and that the president should "take Care that the Laws be faithfully executed"; defined through practice rather than through constitutional or statutory law.

President Clinton fulfills his campaign promise to enlarge what he considered to be a successful government program—Head Start. This program targets "at risk" children before and after they enter kindergarten. Its goal has been to form strong educational and other positive values so that such children will continue to do well in school.

executive Power shall be vested in a President" and that the president should "take Care that the Laws be faithfully executed." The most common example of inherent powers are those emergency powers invoked by the president during wartime. Franklin Roosevelt used his inherent powers to relocate the Japanese living in the United States during World War II.

THE PRESIDENT AS PARTY CHIEF AND SUPERPOLITICIAN

Presidents are by no means above political partisanship, and one of their many roles is that of chief of party. Although the Constitution says nothing

FIGURE 11–1

Presidential Support on Congressional Votes, 1953 to 1994

Most presidents have had their greatest successes in the first years of their terms in office.

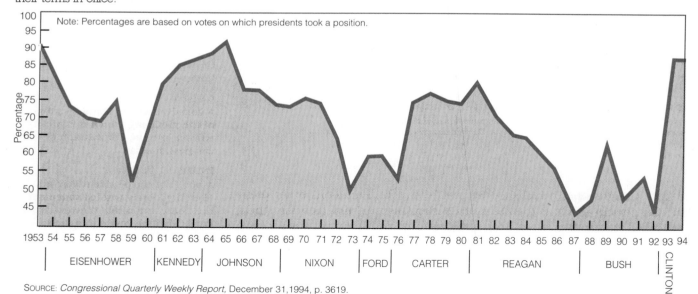

SOURCE: *Congressional Quarterly Weekly Report,* December 31,1994, p. 3619.

about the function of the president within a political party (the mere concept of political parties was abhorrent to most of the authors of the Constitution), today presidents are the actual leaders of their parties.

The President as Chief of Party

As party leader, the president chooses the national committee chairperson and can try to discipline party members who fail to support presidential policies. One way of exerting political power within the party is by the use of **patronage**—appointing individuals to government or public jobs. This power was more extensive in the past, before the establishment of the civil service in 1882 (see Chapter 12), but the president still retains impressive patronage power. As we noted earlier, the president can appoint several thousand individuals to jobs in the cabinet, the White House, and the federal regulatory agencies.

Presidents have a number of other ways of exerting influence as party chief. The president may make it known that a particular congressperson's choice for federal judge will not be appointed unless that member of Congress is supportive of the president's legislative program.[10] The president may agree to campaign for a particular program or for a particular candidate. Presidents also reward loyal supporters in Congress with funding for local projects, tax breaks for regional industries, and other forms of "pork."

Constituencies and Public Approval

All politicians worry about their constituencies, and presidents are no exception. Presidents, however, have numerous constituencies. In principle, they are beholden to the entire electorate—the public of the United States—even to those who did not vote. They are certainly beholden to their party constituency, because its members put them in office. The president's constituencies also include members of the opposing party whose cooperation the president needs. Finally, the president has to take into consideration a constituency that has come to be called the **Washington community**. This community consists of individuals who—whether in or out of political office—are intimately familiar with the workings of government, thrive on gossip, and daily measure the political power of the president.

All of these constituencies are impressed by presidents who maintain a high level of public approval, partly because this is very difficult to accomplish. Presidential popularity, as measured by national polls, gives the president an extra political resource to use in persuading legislators or bureaucrats to pass legislation. After all, refusing to do so might be going against public sentiment. President Reagan showed amazing strength in the public opinion polls for a second-term chief executive, as Figure 11–2 indicates, although there was a one-month drop of 20 points during the Iran-*contra* hearings. President Clinton began his term in office with a 58 percent approval rating and then saw it plummet to 38 percent six months later. By the end of his first year, his rating returned to 48 percent approving his performance. By 1995, it hovered in the 40 to 45 percent range.

DID YOU KNOW . . .
That the shortest inaugural address was George Washington's, at 135 words?

PATRONAGE
Rewarding faithful party workers and followers with government employment and contracts.

WASHINGTON COMMUNITY
Individuals regularly involved with politics in Washington, D.C.

---

10. "Senatorial courtesy" often puts the judicial appointment in the hands of the Senate, however.

DID YOU KNOW . . .
That our tenth president, John Tyler, had fifteen children?

The presidential preoccupation with public opinion has been criticized by at least one scholar as changing the balance of national politics. Samuel Kernell proposed that the style of presidential leadership since World War II has changed, owing partly to the influence of television.[11] Presidents frequently go over the heads of Congress and the political elites, taking their case directly to the people. This strategy, which Kernell dubbed "going public," gives the president additional power through the ability to persuade and manipulate public opinion. By identifying their own positions so clearly, presidents make compromises with Congress much more difficult and weaken the legislators' positions. Given the increasing importance of the media as the major source of political information for citizens and elites, presidents will continue to use public opinion as part of their arsenal of weapons to get support from Congress and to achieve their policy goals.

THE SPECIAL USES OF PRESIDENTIAL POWER

Presidents have at their disposal a variety of special powers and privileges not available in other branches of the U.S. government. These include (1) emergency powers, (2) executive orders, (3) executive privilege, and (4) impoundment of funds.

Emergency Powers

If you were to read the Constitution, you would find no mention of the additional powers that the executive office may exercise during national

11. Samuel Kernell, *Going Public: New Strategies of Presidential Leadership,* 2d ed. (Washington, D.C.: Congressional Quarterly Press, 1992).

FIGURE 11–2
Public Popularity of Bill Clinton and His Predecessors

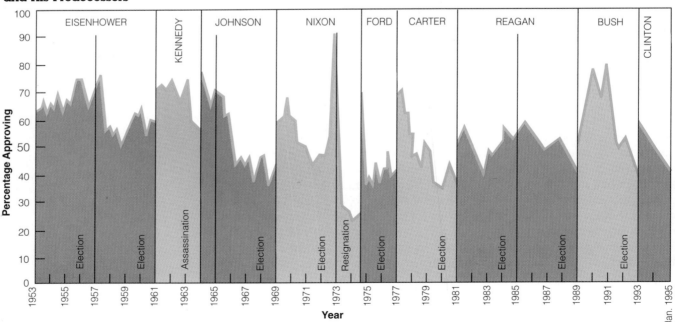

SOURCE: *Public Opinion,* February/March 1988, pp. 36–39; Gallup Polls, March 1992; and *Public Perspective,* April/May 1995, p. 50.

emergencies. Indeed, the Supreme Court has indicated that an "emergency does not create power."[12] But it is clear that presidents have used their inherent powers during times of emergency, particularly in the realm of foreign affairs. The **emergency powers** of the president were first enunciated in the Supreme Court's decision in *United States v. Curtiss-Wright Export Corporation.*[13] In that case, President Franklin Roosevelt, without authorization by Congress, ordered an embargo on the shipment of weapons to two warring South American countries. The Court recognized that the president may exercise inherent powers in foreign affairs and that the national government has primacy in foreign affairs.

Examples of emergency powers are abundant, coinciding with real or contrived crises in domestic and foreign affairs. Abraham Lincoln's suspension of civil liberties at the beginning of the Civil War, his calling of the state militias into national service, and his subsequent governance of conquered areas and even of areas of northern states were justified by claims that such actions were essential to preserve the Union. Franklin Roosevelt declared an "unlimited national emergency" following the fall of France in World War II and mobilized the federal budget and the economy for war.

A more recent example occurred when President Harry Truman authorized the federal seizure of steel plants and their operation by the national government in 1952 during the Korean War. Truman claimed that he was using his inherent emergency power as chief executive and commander in chief to safeguard the nation's security, as the ongoing steel mill strike threatened the supply of weapons to the armed forces. The Supreme Court did not agree, holding that the president had no authority under the Constitution to seize private property or to legislate such action.[14] According to legal scholars, this was the first time a limit was placed on the exercise of the president's emergency powers.

Executive Orders

Congress allows the president (as well as administrative agencies) to issue **executive orders** that have the force of law. (These are not the same as the executive agreements discussed earlier in this chapter.) Executive orders can do the following: (1) enforce legislative statutes, (2) enforce the Constitution or treaties with foreign nations, and (3) establish or modify practices of executive administrative agencies.

An executive order, then, represents the president's legislative power. The only apparent requirement is that under the Administrative Procedure Act of 1946, all executive orders must be published in the *Federal Register,* a daily publication of the U.S. government.

Executive orders have been used to establish some procedures for appointing noncareer administrators, to implement national affirmative action regulations, to restructure the White House bureaucracy, to ration consumer goods and to administer wage and price controls under emergency conditions, to classify government information as secret, and to regulate the export of restricted items. More than thirteen thousand executive orders have been promulgated in a numbered series officially compiled by the State Department, and many more have never been compiled.

EMERGENCY POWER
An inherent power exercised by the president during a period of national crisis, particularly in foreign affairs.

EXECUTIVE ORDER
A rule or regulation issued by the president that has the effect of law. Executive orders can implement and give administrative effect to provisions in the Constitution, to treaties, and to statutes.

FEDERAL REGISTER
A publication of the executive branch of the U.S. government that prints executive orders, rules, and regulations.

---

12. *Home Building and Loan Association v. Blaisdell,* 290 U.S. 398 (1934).
13. 229 U.S. 304 (1936).
14. *Youngstown Sheet and Tube Co. v. Sawyer,* 343 U.S. 579 (1952).

EXECUTIVE PRIVILEGE
The right of executive officials to refuse to appear before, or to withhold
information from, a legislative committee. Executive privilege is enjoyed
by the president and by those executive officials accorded that right by
the president.

Executive Privilege

Another inherent executive power that has been claimed by presidents concerns the ability of the president and the president's executive officials to
refuse to appear before, or to withhold information from, Congress or the
courts. This is called **executive privilege**, and it relies on the constitutional
separation of powers for its basis. Critics of executive privilege believe that
it can be used to shield from public scrutiny actions of the executive branch
that should be open to Congress and to the American public.

Limits to executive privilege went untested until the Watergate affair in
the early 1970s. The Supreme Court subpoenaed secret tapes containing
Richard Nixon's Oval Office conversations during his tenure at the White
House. Nixon refused to turn them over, claiming executive privilege. He
argued that "no president could function if the private papers of his office,
prepared by his personal staff, were open to public scrutiny." In 1974, in
one of the Court's most famous cases, *United States v. Nixon*, the justices
unanimously ruled that Nixon had to hand over the tapes to the Court.[15]
Executive privilege could not be used to prevent evidence from being heard
in criminal proceedings.

Impoundment of Funds

By law, the president proposes a budget, and Congress approves it. But there
is no clear-cut constitutional indication that the president, as chief executive, is required by law to *spend* all of the funds appropriated by Congress,
and many presidents have not done so. In 1803, Thomas Jefferson deferred
a $50,000 appropriation for gunboats. Ulysses Grant returned to the Treas-
ury unspent money for public works. In 1932, Herbert Hoover canceled projects funded by Congress. Franklin Roosevelt deferred spending on a number
of appropriations to later fiscal years. Harry Truman did not spend all of the
money that Congress had allocated for the military, nor did Lyndon Johnson spend the money allocated for highway construction. John Kennedy
did not spend all of the money allocated for weapons systems.

The question of whether the president is required to spend all appropriated funds came to a head during the Nixon administration after a number
of confrontations over this issue between the president and an antagonistic,
Democratic-controlled Congress. When Nixon vetoed appropriation bills,
Congress often overrode his veto. In retaliation, Nixon refused to spend the
appropriated funds, claiming that he wanted to reduce overall federal
spending.

As part of its Budget and Impoundment Control Act of 1974, Congress
required that the president spend all appropriated funds, although Congress
gave the president some leeway. A president who is not going to spend all
appropriated funds must tell Congress, and only if Congress agrees within
forty-five days can the president withhold spending. If the president simply
wishes to delay spending, this must be indicated to Congress. If Congress
does not agree, it can pass a resolution requiring the immediate spending
of the appropriated funds. While Congress was deliberating on the budget
bill, cities, states, and certain members of Congress sued President Nixon
over his refusal to spend appropriated funds. The Supreme Court in 1975

---

15. 318 U.S. 683 (1974).

unanimously ruled that the president had to spend money appropriated by Congress because of his obligation to "take care that the laws be faithfully executed."[16]

ABUSES OF EXECUTIVE POWER AND IMPEACHMENT

Presidents normally leave office either because their first term has expired and they do not seek (or win) reelection or because, having served two full terms, they are not allowed to seek reelection (owing to the Twenty-second Amendment, passed in 1951). Eight presidents have died in office. But there is still another way for a president to leave office—by **impeachment.** Articles I and II of the Constitution authorize the House and Senate to remove the president, the vice president, or other civil officers of the United States for crimes of "Treason, Bribery, or other high Crimes and Misdemeanors." No one has really defined "high Crimes and Misdemeanors," but at least twice Congress and the American public were pretty sure that a president had engaged in them.

The authority to impeach (that is, to accuse) is vested in the House of Representatives, and formal impeachment proceedings are initiated there. In the House, a representative must list the charges against the president, vice president, or other civil officer. The impeachment charges are referred either to the Judiciary Committee or to a special investigating committee. If a majority in the House votes for impeachment, then articles of impeachment are drawn up, which set forth the basis for the removal of the executive-branch officer. The actual trial of impeachment is conducted in the Senate, with all members sitting in judgment. The chief justice of the United States Supreme Court presides over the Senate. A two-thirds vote of the senators present is required for conviction. The only punishment that Congress can mete out is removal from office and disqualification from holding any other federal office. The convicted official, however, is subject to further punishment according to law.

In the history of the United States, no president has ever been impeached and also convicted. The only president who was actually impeached by the House was Andrew Johnson, but he was acquitted by the Senate by the margin of a single vote in 1868. Some argue that Johnson's impeachment was simply a case of partisan politics. Impeachment attempts also were made against John Tyler, Herbert Hoover, and Vice President Schuyler Colfax.

The case of Richard Nixon, however, was more serious and certainly less questionable in terms of its political motivation (see the feature entitled *Politics and the Law* in this chapter). In 1974, the House was ready to vote on Nixon's impeachment and to send the Articles of Impeachment to the Senate when Nixon resigned.

THE EXECUTIVE ORGANIZATION

Gone are the days when presidents answered their own mail, as George Washington did. It was not until 1857 that Congress authorized a private secretary for the president, to be paid by the federal government. Woodrow Wilson typed most of his correspondence, even though he did have several secretaries. At the beginning of Franklin Roosevelt's long tenure in the

IMPEACHMENT
As authorized by Article I of the Constitution, an action by the House of Representatives and the Senate to remove the president, vice president, or civil officers of the United States from office for crimes of "Treason, Bribery, or other high Crimes and Misdemeanors."

---

16. *Train v. City of New York,* 420 U.S. 35 (1975).

Richard Nixon (right) leaves the White House after his resignation on August 9, 1974. Next to him are his wife, Pat, Betty Ford, and Gerald Ford, the new president.

CABINET
An advisory group selected by the president to aid in making decisions. The cabinet presently numbers thirteen department secretaries and the attorney general. Depending on the president, the cabinet may be highly influential or relatively insignificant in its advisory role.

KITCHEN CABINET
The informal advisers to the president.

White House, the entire staff consisted of thirty-seven employees. It was not until the New Deal and World War II that the presidential staff became a sizable organization.

Today, the executive organization includes a White House Office staff of about 600, including some workers who are part-time employees and others who are detailed from their departments to the White House. Not all of these employees have equal access to the president, nor are all of them likely to be equally concerned about the administration's political success. The more than 350 employees who work in the White House Office itself are closest to the president. They often include many individuals who worked in the president's campaign. These assistants are most concerned with preserving the president's reputation (see the *Politics and Ethics* on page 411). Also included in the president's staff are a number of councils and advisory organizations, such as the National Security Council (NSC). Although the individuals who hold staff positions in these offices are appointed by the president, they are really more concerned with their own area than with the president's overall success. The group of appointees who perhaps are least helpful to the president is the cabinet, each member of which is the principal officer of a government department.

The Cabinet

Although the Constitution does not include the word *cabinet,* it does state that the president "may require the Opinion, in writing, of the principal Officer in each of the executive Departments." Since the time of our first president, there has always been an advisory group, or **cabinet,** to which the president turns for counsel. Originally, the cabinet consisted of only four officials—the secretaries of state, treasury, and war, and the attorney general. Today, the cabinet numbers thirteen secretaries and the attorney general. Table 11–3 lists the members of the Clinton cabinet.

The cabinet may consist of more than the secretaries of the various departments. The president at his or her discretion can, for example, ascribe cabinet rank to the National Security Council adviser, to the ambassador to the United Nations, or to others. Because neither the Constitution nor statutory law requires the president to consult with the cabinet, its use is purely discretionary. Some presidents have relied on the counsel of their cabinets more than others. Dwight Eisenhower frequently turned to his cabinet for advice on a wide range of governmental policies—perhaps because he was used to the team approach, from his experience in the U.S. Army, to solving problems. Other presidents solicited the opinions of their cabinets and then did what they wanted to do anyway. Lincoln supposedly said—after a cabinet meeting in which a vote was seven nays against his one aye—"Seven nays and one aye, the ayes have it."[17]

In general, few presidents have relied heavily on the advice of their cabinet members. Often, a president will use a **kitchen cabinet** to replace the formal cabinet as a major source of advice. The term *kitchen cabinet* originated during the presidency of Andrew Jackson, who relied on the counsel of close friends who often met with him in the kitchen of the White House.

17. Quoted in Thomas E. Cronin, *The State of the Presidency,* 2d ed. (Boston: Little, Brown, 1980), p. 11.

POLITICS AND THE LAW
Watergate: A Crime of Power?

On June 17, 1972, at 2:30 A.M., five men were arrested in the headquarters of the Democratic National Committee in the Watergate apartment complex in Washington, D.C. It was obvious from the outset that this was no ordinary burglary. The five men, dressed in business suits and wearing surgical gloves, were also found to have in their possession some extraordinary items: two cameras, forty rolls of film, lock picks, pen-sized tear-gas guns, bugging devices, a walkie-talkie, and nearly $2,300 in cash among them. In the following days and months, as investigations of the Watergate break-in continued, a story was pieced together that shocked the nation.

The five men had been searching for documents that would connect Senator George McGovern, the Democratic nominee for president, with Fidel Castro and thereby discredit McGovern in the eyes of the American public. They were also looking for any information the Democratic National Committee might have stumbled on that could prove embarrassing to the Nixon administration.

Six days after the break-in, President Richard Nixon and his White House chief of staff, H. R. (Bob) Haldeman, formulated a plan by which the Central Intelligence Agency would impede the investigation of the affair that was being undertaken by the Federal Bureau of Investigation.

By early 1973, however, a select Senate committee was established, under the chairmanship of Senator Sam Ervin of North Carolina, to investigate the Watergate affair. During the Senate investigation, information about the White

John Dean testifies at Richard Nixon's impeachment hearing.

House–sponsored criminal activities and subsequent cover-up began to leak out. John Dean III, President Nixon's legal counsel, eventually told the committee that the president himself was responsible for the cover-up. The committee also learned that the Oval Office conversations between Nixon and his advisers had been tape-recorded.

Archibald Cox, the Watergate special prosecutor in charge of legal investigations into the affair, subpoenaed several of the tapes, an action upheld by the federal district and appeals courts. The "Saturday Night Massacre" ensued, in which Nixon fired Cox, and the attorney general and deputy attorney general were both forced to resign because they refused to obey Nixon's order to fire Cox.

Many of Nixon's closest White House aides were indicted in the scandal, and Nixon himself was

named an unindicted (not formally charged) co-conspirator by the grand jury. A new special prosecutor and Congress subpoenaed a large number of tapes, which the president refused to make available—except in edited form—to Congress. On July 24, 1974, the Supreme Court ruled that Nixon had to give up the information requested by the special prosecutor. Three days later, the House Judiciary Committee passed the first of three Articles of Impeachment against President Nixon. On August 9, Nixon resigned, and his vice president, Gerald Ford, became president.

TABLE 11–3

The Clinton Cabinet

THE CLINTON CABINET

- **Bruce Babbitt,**
  Secretary of Interior
- **Robert E. Rubin,**
  Secretary of the Treasury
- **Jesse Brown,**
  Secretary of Veterans Affairs
- **Ronald H. Brown,**
  Secretary of Commerce
- **Warren M. Christopher,**
  Secretary of State
- **Henry G. Cisneros,**
  Secretary of Housing and
  Urban Development
- **Dan Glickman**
  Secretary of Agriculture
- **Hazel R. O'Leary,**
  Secretary of Energy
- **Federico Pena,**
  Secretary of Transportation
- **William Perry,**
  Secretary of Defense
- **Robert B. Reich,**
  Secretary of Labor
- **Janet Reno,**
  Attorney General
- **Richard W. Riley,**
  Secretary of Education
- **Donna E. Shalala,**
  Secretary of Health and
  Human Services

EXECUTIVE OFFICE OF THE PRESIDENT (EOP)
Established by President Franklin Roosevelt by executive order under the Reorganization Act of 1939, the EOP currently consists of ten staff agencies that assist the president in carrying out major duties.

WHITE HOUSE OFFICE
The personal office of the president, which tends to presidential political needs and manages the media.

CHIEF OF STAFF
The person who is named to direct the White House Office and advise the president.

A kitchen cabinet is a very informal group of advisers who may or may not otherwise be connected with the government.

Presidents meet with their cabinet heads only reluctantly. Often the departmental heads are more responsive to the wishes of their own staffs or to their own political ambitions than they are to the president. They may be more concerned with obtaining resources for their departments than with helping presidents achieve their goals. So there is often a strong conflict of interest between presidents and their cabinet members. It is likely that formal cabinet meetings are held more out of respect for the cabinet tradition than for their problem-solving value.

The Executive Office of the President

When President Franklin Roosevelt appointed a special committee on administrative management, he knew that the committee would conclude that the president needed help. Indeed, the committee proposed a major reorganization of the executive branch. Congress did not approve the entire reorganization, but it did create the **Executive Office of the President (EOP)** to provide staff assistance for the chief executive and to help coordinate the executive bureaucracy. Since that time, a number of agencies within the EOP have been created to supply the president with advice and staff help. These agencies are as follows:

- White House Office (1939).
- Council of Economic Advisers (1946).
- National Security Council (1947).
- Office of the United States Trade Representative (1963).
- Council on Environmental Quality (1969).
- Office of Management and Budget (1970).
- Office of Science and Technology Policy (1976).
- Office of Administration (1977).
- National Critical Materials Council (1984).
- Office of National Drug Control Policy (1988).

Several of the other offices within the EOP are especially important, including the White House Office, the Council of Economic Advisers, the Office of Management and Budget, and the National Security Council.

The White House Office. One of the most important of the agencies within the EOP is the **White House Office**, which includes the majority of the key personal and political advisers to the president. Among the jobs held by these aides are those of legal counsel to the president, secretary, press secretary, and appointments secretary. Often, the individuals who hold these positions are recruited from the president's campaign staff. Their duties—mainly protecting the president's political interests—are similar to campaign functions. In all recent administrations, one member of the White House Office is named **chief of staff**. This person, who is responsible for coordinating the office, is one of the president's chief advisers.

Employees of the White House Office have been both envied and criticized. The White House Office, according to most former staffers, grants its employees access and power. They are able to use the resources of the White

POLITICS AND ETHICS
The Whitewater Affair

During the 1980s, then Governor Bill Clinton and his wife, Hillary Rodham Clinton, a lawyer with a prominent Little Rock, Arkansas, law firm, invested in a real estate development called the Whitewater Development Company. Although the total amount of money that the Clintons invested and lost was only about $68,000, the irregularities surrounding that investment triggered a sequence of events in 1994 that raised a number of issues about the ethical decisions of White House staff and other political appointees.

The Whitewater investment had raised interest among Republicans and other opponents of the Clinton administration soon after the Clinton victory. Although the Clintons dismissed the investment as a bad family financial decision, their partner in the scheme, James McDougal, was also the owner of a failed savings and loan that was under investigation by the federal regulators in 1984.

The thrift's failure cost the American taxpayers about $68 million to repay depositors. Furthermore, McDougal was a close political friend of the Clintons and had arranged political fund raisers for the governor's campaigns. He had also lent money to Clinton's presidential campaign in its early months. After much delay, in January 1994, Attorney General Reno named a special prosecutor, Robert Fiske, to investigate the matter.

Media attention, the prosecutor's interviews, and Republican investigations brought forward a number of ethical lapses among White House staff and other political appointees:

—Jean Hansen, an attorney at the Treasury Department, had briefed White House officials about an impending investigation of Madison Guaranty Savings with a possible criminal charge against the Clintons as early as September 29, 1993.

—In February, after the special prosecutor had begun his investigation, Roger Altman, the Deputy Treasury Secretary, continued to contact the White House to let the Clintons know the status of the investigation of the savings and loan institution.

—Vince Foster's papers were removed from his office in the White House after his suicide and stored by Mrs. Clinton's aide.

—Congressional hearings in the summer of 1994 brought to light a number of denials, lies, and contradictions by staff and Treasury appointees.

After the hearings, a number of officials in the Treasury Department and in the White House resigned. Although no charges of wrongdoing have been lodged by the prosecutor (Fiske or his successor, Kenneth Starr) and a government ethics office found no breaches of ethical conduct among those involved, the case made clear the conflict of interest between presidential appointees and any investigation involving a sitting president. The investigation continued during 1995 and into 1996.

House to contact virtually anyone in the world by telephone, cable, or fax, as well as to use the influence of the White House to persuade legislators and citizens. Because of this influence, staffers are often criticized for overstepping the bounds of the office (see the *Politics and Ethics* on page 413). It is the appointments secretary who is able to grant or deny senators, representatives, and cabinet secretaries access to the president. It is the press secretary who grants to the press and television journalists access to any information about the president. White House staff members are closest to the president and may have considerable influence over the administration's decisions. Often, when presidents are under fire for their decisions, the staff is accused of keeping the chief executive too isolated from criticism or help. Presidents insist that they will not allow the staff to become too powerful, but given the difficulty of the office, each president eventually turns to staff members for loyal assistance and protection.

The Council of Economic Advisers.   The Employment Act of 1946 created a three-member **Council of Economic Advisers (CEA)** to advise the

COUNCIL OF ECONOMIC
ADVISERS (CEA)
A staff agency in the Executive Office of the President that advises the president on measures to maintain stability in the nation's economy; established in 1946.

OFFICE OF MANAGEMENT
AND BUDGET (OMB)
A division of the Executive Office of the President created by executive order in 1970 to replace the Bureau of the Budget. The OMB's main functions are to assist the president in preparing the annual budget, to clear and coordinate all departmental agency budgets, to help set fiscal policy, and to supervise the administration of the federal budget.

NATIONAL SECURITY
COUNCIL (NSC)
A staff agency in the Executive Office of the President established by the National Security Act of 1947. The NSC advises the president on domestic and foreign matters involving national security.

After several attempts by individuals to scale the White House fence, one assault on the White House by a man with an automatic weapon, and several other incidents, President Clinton reluctantly agreed to prohibit automobile traffic on Pennsylvania Avenue in front of the building. The president had not been in danger from any of the incidents and preferred not to limit access to the White House, but officials charged with protecting the president and his family convinced him that barriers would make their job easier.

president on economic matters. Their advice serves as the basis for the president's annual economic report to Congress. Each of the three members is appointed by the president and can be removed at will. In principle, the CEA was also created to advise the president on economic policy, but for the most part the function of the CEA has been to prepare the annual report.

Office of Management and Budget.   The Office of Management and Budget (OMB) was originally the Bureau of the Budget, which was created in 1921 within the Department of the Treasury. Recognizing the importance of this agency, Franklin Roosevelt moved it into the White House Office in 1939. Richard Nixon reorganized the Bureau of the Budget in 1970 and changed its name to reflect its new managerial function. It is headed by a director, who must make up the annual federal budget that the president presents to Congress each January for approval. In principle, the director of the OMB has broad fiscal powers in planning and estimating various parts of the federal budget, because all agencies must submit their proposed budget to the OMB for approval. In reality, it is not so clear that the OMB truly can affect the greater scope of the federal budget. The OMB may be more important as a clearinghouse for legislative proposals initiated in the executive agencies.

National Security Council.   The National Security Council (NSC) is a link between the president's key foreign and military advisers and the president. Its members consist of the president, the vice president, and the secretaries of state and defense, plus other informal members. The NSC has the resources of the National Security Agency (NSA) at its disposal in giving counsel to the president. (The NSA protects U.S. government communications and produces foreign intelligence information.) Included in the NSC is the president's special assistant for national security affairs. Richard Nixon had Henry Kissinger in this post; Jimmy Carter had the equally visible Zbigniew Brzezinksi. In the Reagan years, staff members of the NSC, including Lieutenant Colonel Oliver North and Admiral John Poindexter, became involved in an illegal plan to aid the *contras* in Nicaragua (again, see the *Politics and Ethics* on page 413).

THE VICE PRESIDENCY

Vice presidents usually have not been overly ecstatic about their position. Franklin Roosevelt's vice president for his first two terms, John Nance Garner, said, in effect, that "the vice presidency isn't worth a pitcher of warm spit." Walter Mondale, Carter's hard-working vice president and one of the few who truly took an active role in the executive branch, said, "They know who Amy is, but they don't know me." (He was referring to Carter's grammar school–aged daughter.)

The Vice President's Job

The Constitution does not give much power to the vice president. The only formal duty is to preside over the Senate—which is rarely necessary. This obligation is fulfilled when the Senate organizes and adopts its rules and

POLITICS AND ETHICS
The Iran-*Contra* Investigations and the Abuse of Power

The risks created by unchecked presidential advisers were made clear in the Iran-*contra* affair. The Reagan administration was shaken by the revelation that government officials had sold weapons to Iran in return for Iranian promises to help negotiate the release of American and other hostages held by pro-Iranian terrorist groups in the Middle East. Profits from these arms sales had then been used to finance operations of the *contras* in Nicaragua, who were attempting to overthrow the Sandinista government there.

These efforts began to unravel after an American C123K cargo plane carrying guns and other weapons to the *contras* was shot down over Nicaragua on October 5, 1986. The Justice Department launched a full-scale investigation by the Federal Bureau of Investigation into the Iran weapons shipments. President Ronald Reagan announced on the same day the appointment of the President's Special Review Board, chaired by former Republican Texas senator John G. Tower. This became known as the Tower Commission and was charged with studying the role of the National Security Council in the scandal.

In early March 1987, the Tower Commission released its report. The report concluded that Reagan had let his emotional commitment to obtain release of the hostages overrule his better judgment, faulted him for failing to conduct a forceful review of the programs once they were under way, and determined that the president's aides had manipulated him and had made their own private foreign policy through a process of lying, surreptitiously diverting arms-deal profits, and trying to cover up the scandal.

Through congressional testimony, it became clearer that control over the general policy in this regard and control over operational details had rested with National Security Adviser John Poindexter and his aide, Marine Lieutenant Colonel Oliver North, rather than with the Central Intelligence Agency. North, who testified under a congressional grant of immunity, argued that Congress did not have a right to oversee the activities in which he was engaged and did not even have the right to know what he was up to.

North, Poindexter, former Air Force general Richard Secord, and an arms dealer were all indicted on charges that included conspiracy to divert government funds to buy arms for the *contras*. North was convicted on three counts but found innocent on five charges by a jury that reportedly felt he was the "fall guy" for those higher up. A federal court overturned one of North's convictions in July 1990, because he had been granted immunity for his congressional testimony. Poindexter was convicted and sentenced to six months in prison, but his conviction was overturned in late 1991 on the same grounds as North's had been. After his election defeat in 1992, President George Bush pardoned all of the higher administration officials who could have been charged.

What remains unresolved is how to control the activities of presidential aides and how presidents can be held responsible for what their aides do.

when the vice president is needed to decide a tie vote. In all other cases, the president pro tempore manages parliamentary procedures in the Senate. The vice president is expected to participate only informally in senatorial deliberations, if at all.

As mentioned in the *What If . . .* feature at the beginning of this chapter, vice presidents traditionally have been chosen by presidential nominees to balance the ticket or to reward or appease party factions. If a presidential nominee is from the North, it is not a bad idea to have a vice presidential nominee who is from the South or the West. If the presidential nominee is from a rural state, perhaps someone with an urban background would be most suitable as a running mate. Presidential nominees who are strongly conservative or strongly liberal would do well to have vice presidential nominees who are more in the middle of the political road.

Presidential nominee Bill Clinton ignored almost all of the conventional wisdom when he selected Senator Al Gore of Tennessee as his running mate in 1992. Not only was Gore close in age and ideology to Clinton, but he also came from the mid-South. The advantage gained from choosing Gore was his experience in the Senate, his strong position on issues such as the environment, and his compatibility with Clinton. Clinton and Gore and their families became a very successful campaign team whose friendship continued after the inauguration. Although Clinton's position as president has not been challenged by Gore's activity, the vice president continues to lead the administration on most environmental issues. He maintains a close relationship with the president, meeting with him as regularly, as he does with members of the White House staff. (For a more in-depth look at Vice President Gore, see the *Politics: The Human Side* on page 415.)

Vice presidents infrequently have become elected presidents in their own right. John Adams and Thomas Jefferson were the first to do so. Then Martin Van Buren was elected president in 1836 after he had served as Andrew Jackson's vice president for the previous eight years. In 1988, George Bush was elected to the presidency after eight years as Ronald Reagan's vice president.

The job of vice president is not extremely demanding, even when the president gives some specific task to the vice president. Typically, vice presidents spend their time supporting the president's activities. All of this changes, of course, if the president becomes disabled or dies in office.

Presidential Succession

Eight vice presidents have become president because of the death of the president. John Tyler, the first to do so, took over William Henry Harrison's position after Harrison's death. No one knew whether Tyler should simply be a caretaker until a new president could be elected three and a half years later or whether he actually should be president. Tyler assumed that he was supposed to be the chief executive and he acted as such—although he was commonly referred to as "His Accidency." On all occasions since then, vice presidents taking over the position of the presidency because of the incumbent's death have assumed all of the presidential powers.

But what should a vice president do if a president becomes incapable of carrying out necessary duties while in office? When James Garfield was shot in 1881, he stayed alive for two and a half months. What was Vice President Chester Arthur's role?

This question was not addressed in the original Constitution. Article II, Section 1, says only that "in Case of the Removal of the President from Office, or of his Death, Resignation, or Inability to discharge the Powers and Duties of the said Office, the same shall devolve on the Vice President." There have been many instances of presidential disability. When Dwight Eisenhower became ill a second time in 1958, he entered into a pact with Richard Nixon that provided that the vice president could determine whether the president was incapable of carrying out his duties if the president could not communicate. John Kennedy and Lyndon Johnson entered into similar agreements with their vice presidents. Finally, in 1967, the **Twenty-fifth Amendment** was passed, establishing procedures in case of presidential incapacity.

TWENTY-FIFTH AMENDMENT
An amendment to the Constitution, adopted in 1967, that establishes procedures for filling vacancies in the two top executive offices and that makes provisions for situations involving presidential disability.

Presidential Incapacity

According to the Twenty-fifth Amendment, a president who feels incapable of performing the duties of office must inform the Congress in writing. Then

POLITICS: THE HUMAN SIDE
Albert Arnold Gore, Jr., Vice President and Environmentalist

"For generations, we have believed that we could abuse the Earth because we were somehow not really connected to it. But now we must face the truth."

BIOGRAPHICAL NOTES

Vice President Albert Arnold Gore, Jr., is the second child of Albert A. Gore, congressperson and senator from Tennessee. Al Gore, Jr., was born on March 31, 1949, in a hospital in the nation's capital. He spent much of his youth in Washington, D.C., graduating from St. Alban's, an exclusive D.C. school and then attending Harvard University. During the Vietnam War, Gore opposed U.S. involvement but chose to enter the army rather than leave the country. He served as a re-

porter for an army newspaper in Saigon and never engaged in combat.

Gore returned from Vietnam to begin life as a reporter and farmer in Tennessee. In 1974, he ran for and won a seat in Congress. Ten years later, in 1984, he became the junior senator from Tennessee. By 1988, the senator decided to run for the presidency. After a disastrous campaign in which he ran up a debt of $2.3 million, he dropped out of that race, however. Soon after this, his young son was injured critically in an automobile accident. The senator gave up thoughts of the presidency to stay with his family, announcing in 1991 that he would not seek the office.

In 1992, Democratic nominee Bill Clinton tapped Gore to be his vice presidential candidate. Gore, who shared Clinton's southern origins and moderate philosophy, turned out to be an excellent running mate.

POLITICAL CONTRIBUTIONS

Al Gore, Jr., has played a more important role as vice president than any other in many decades. He comes well qualified: He has extensive Washington experience, an impeccable manner and personal integrity, and good political instincts. Before the election, Gore's book, *Earth in the Balance,* had reached the nonfiction best-seller list, and his expertise in environmental issues surpasses that of most other politicians. Gore, like Clinton, is a "policy wonk," enjoying the details of policy formation and implementation. In addition, Gore and Clinton have become friends.

Clinton sends Gore to speak for the administration in Congress and in international arenas. Clinton has also sent Gore to negotiate for the United States in difficult situations. It was Gore who convinced leaders in the Ukraine to surrender their nuclear warheads. He was also the president's representative in the debate with H. Ross Perot over the approval of the North American Free Trade Agreement (NAFTA) held on CNN's "Larry King Live." Gore outperformed Perot and gave an excellent defense of the treaty, defusing Perot's attacks.

In yet another demonstration of his trust in Gore, Clinton asked the vice president to recommend ways to make the federal government more efficient. Gore and a team of experts studied the issues and made a series of recommendations for downsizing government and eliminating bureaucracy in a report that was called "From Red Tape to Results: Creating a Government that Works Better and Costs Less." Most of the proposed reforms were recommended to Congress for study, although attention has been deflected by other major policy debates.

Al Gore, Jr., is still relatively young. With his credentials and performance as vice president, he has not only created a new model of achievement for that office but may also have built a base to support a bid for the presidency in the future.

An attempted assassination of Ronald Reagan occurred on March 31, 1981. In the foreground, press secretary James Brady lies seriously wounded. In the background, two men bend over President Reagan.

the vice president serves as acting president until the president can resume his normal duties. When the president is unable to communicate, a majority of the cabinet, including the vice president, can declare that fact to Congress. Then the vice president serves as acting president until the president resumes his normal duties. If a dispute arises over the return of the president's ability to discharge his normal functions, a two-thirds vote of Congress is required to decide whether the vice president shall remain acting president or whether the president shall resume his duties.

Although President Reagan did not formally invoke the Twenty-fifth Amendment during his surgery for the removal of a cancerous growth in his colon on July 13, 1985, he followed its provisions in temporarily transferring power to the vice president, George Bush. At 10:32 A.M., before the operation began, Reagan signed letters to the speaker of the House and the president pro tempore of the Senate directing that the vice president "shall discharge those powers and duties in my stead commencing with the administration of anesthesia to me." In the early evening of that same day, Reagan transmitted another letter to both officials announcing that he was again in charge. During this period, Vice President Bush signed no bills and took no actions as acting president. Although the Reagan administration claimed that the president's action set no precedents, most legal experts saw Reagan's acts as the first official use of the Twenty-fifth Amendment.

When the Vice Presidency Becomes Vacant

The Twenty-fifth Amendment also addresses the issue of how the president should fill a vacant vice presidency. Section 2 of the amendment simply states, "Whenever there is a vacancy in the office of the Vice President, the President shall nominate a Vice President who shall take office upon confirmation by a majority vote of both Houses of Congress." This is exactly what occurred when Richard Nixon's vice president, Spiro Agnew, resigned in 1973 because of his alleged receipt of construction contract kickbacks during his tenure as governor of Maryland. Nixon turned to Gerald Ford as his choice for vice president. After extensive hearings, both houses confirmed the appointment. Then, when Nixon resigned on August 9, 1974, Ford automatically became president and nominated as his vice president Nelson Rockefeller. Congress confirmed Ford's choice. For the first time in the history of the country, both the president and the vice president were individuals who were not elected to their positions.

The question of who shall be president if both the president and vice president die is answered by the Succession Act of 1947. If the president and vice president die, resign, or are disabled, the speaker of the House will act as president, after resigning from Congress. Next in line is the president pro tempore of the Senate, followed by the cabinet officers in the order of the creation of their department (see Table 11–4).

Spiro Agnew was Richard Nixon's vice president from 1969 to 1973. Agnew resigned amid allegations of income tax evasion in connection with money he received when he was governor of Maryland.

THE PRESIDENCY: UNFINISHED WORK

In the twentieth century, the responsibilities of world leadership and the growth of government have led to enormous changes in the American presidency. The office has changed from being that of "chief clerk" to being leader of the most powerful military in the Western world and the chief operating officer of a huge organization that affects the lives of everyone in the nation. At the same time, the relationship between the president and the electorate has changed, most notably through the growth of television as the most often used source of news. The presidency is now defined in large part by the electronic media.

Because the presidency has undergone such enormous evolution and is so influenced by societal changes, a number of unresolved issues surround the chief executive. One of the most troublesome is the role of the president in engaging the nation in military action. To what extent does the War Powers Act limit presidential action? How can Congress play a role in critical war-related decisions? Combined with that concern is the uncertainty about what role the United States should play in a world without superpower competition.

In recent years, the power of the White House and its occupants, including its staff, has raised a number of issues about the abuse of executive power. Can executive branch employees thwart the will of Congress or use the privileges of the White House to protect themselves? What principles exist to guide White House behavior so that the presidency can retain the respect of the voters?

Finally, to what extent is the presidency dependent on television and other visual media to gain public approval and favor so that the chief executive can be successful? It may be that our nation's fixation on image and popularity keeps us from considering the substance of public policy and tackling the work of making real policy choices. Perhaps the media stardom of presidents eventually undermines the public's trust of the president, because so much attention is paid to image rather than to accomplishments. All of these and many other issues surrounding the American president will attract discussion in years to come.

TABLE 11–4

Line of Succession to the Presidency of the United States

1. Vice President.
2. Speaker of the House of Representatives.
3. Senate President Pro Tempore.
4. Secretary of State.
5. Secretary of the Treasury.
6. Secretary of Defense.
7. Attorney General.
8. Secretary of the Interior.
9. Secretary of Agriculture.
10. Secretary of Commerce.
11. Secretary of Labor.
12. Secretary of Health and Human Services.
13. Secretary of Housing and Urban Development.
14. Secretary of Transportation.
15. Secretary of Energy.
16. Secretary of Education.
17. Secretary of Veterans' Affairs.

GETTING INVOLVED
Influencing the Presidency

On June 14, 1990, James Baker, the secretary of state, rebuked Israel for not responding to the U.S. peace plan to resolve the Israel-Palestinian conflict, saying, "When you're serious about peace, call us. The phone number is 202-456-1414." In the next twenty-four hours, the White House switchboard received about eight thousand calls.

If you wish to contact the president, that switchboard is open twenty-four hours a day. If you ask for the president, you will be directed to the appropriate department or to the comment line. If you call the comment line (202-456-1111), an operator will take down your comment or question and forward it to the president's office. You can also contact the White House through the Internet (see this chapter's *Logging On*).

Expressions of public support or opposition are important either to legitimize the administration's actions or to voice disapproval. Although you will probably not have the opportunity to express your personal opinions directly to the president, your views and those of others who think the same way can be brought to the president's attention. If you

strongly agree with, or oppose, certain actions taken by the president, call the White House or write a letter to the president. Address your letter as follows:

The President of the United States
The White House
1600 Pennsylvania Ave. N.W.
Washington, DC 20500

If you wish to call or write to the first lady, her address and telephone number are as follows:

First Lady Hillary Rodham Clinton
1600 Pennsylvania Ave. N.W.
Washington, DC 20500
202-456-2957

Another way to communicate your views to the executive branch is to write a letter to the editor of a major newspaper. The White House clips letters from newspapers across the country to provide a digest of public opinion for the president and the presidential staff.

 KEY TERMS

CHAPTER SUMMARY

1. The office of the presidency in the United States, combining as it does the functions of chief of state and chief executive, is unique. The framers of the Constitution were divided over whether the president should be a weak executive controlled by the legislature or a strong executive.

2. The requirements for the office of the presidency are outlined in Article II, Section 1, of the Constitution. The president's roles include both formal and informal duties. The president is chief of state, chief executive, commander in chief, chief diplomat, chief legislator, and party chief.

3. As chief of state, the president is ceremonial head of the government. As chief executive, the president is bound to enforce the acts of Congress, the judgments of the federal courts, and treaties. The chief executive has the power of appointment and the power to grant reprieves and pardons.

4. As commander in chief, the president is the ultimate decision maker in military matters. As chief diplomat, the president recognizes foreign governments, negotiates treaties, signs agreements, and nominates and receives ambassadors.

5. The role of chief legislator includes recommending legislation to Congress, lobbying for the legislation, ap-

proving laws, and exercising the veto power. The president also has statutory powers written into law by Congress. The president is also leader of his or her political party. Presidents use their power to persuade and their access to the media to fulfill this function.

6. Presidents have a variety of special powers not available to other branches of the government. These include emergency power, executive power, executive privilege, and impoundment of funds.

7. Abuses of executive power are dealt with by Articles I and II of the Constitution, which authorize the House and Senate to impeach and remove the president, vice president, or other officers of the government for crimes of "Treason, Bribery or other high Crimes and Misdemeanors."

8. The president gets assistance from the cabinet and from the Executive Office of the President (including the White House Office).

9. The vice president is the constitutional officer assigned to preside over the Senate and to assume the presidency in case of the death, resignation, removal, or disability of the president. The Twenty-fifth Amendment, passed in 1967, established procedures to be followed in case of presidential incapacity and when filling a vacant vice presidency.

 ## QUESTIONS FOR REVIEW AND DISCUSSION

1. What talents and skills must an individual have to be successful in the job of the president? To what extent should a candidate's experience, personality, and organizational skills be relevant to voting for a president?

2. How do the president and Congress share power in policymaking and legislation? What resources does each bring to this joint lawmaking process? Should the president play a leading role in most major legislation?

3. What factors make the presidency seem to be powerful? To what extent does the president's command of the media and access to the news enhance the public's expectations of the president and contribute to a powerful image? How does that presidential image of power contribute to the president's ability to persuade members of Congress or other national leaders to take a particular position?

 ## LOGGING ON: THE PRESIDENCY

Numerous sources exist for information on the presidency. White House press releases, presidential performance ratings, discussions of executive politics, and other sources are available on nearly every **gopher** system. One major source that you might find interesting is

alt.politics.clinton

This can be accessed through Michigan State University's **gopher** through **News & Weather; USENET News; alt/; politics/.** This service provides a discussion on White House political issues and debate on the performance of the president.

A great way to find out what is going on in the executive branch is to read White House daily press releases. After all, 90 percent of the news comes from prearranged events, such as those contained in these documents. For White House press releases and position papers, as well as a daily summary of press conferences, one good source is

wh-summary@almanac@esusda.gov

You can now also send your praise or complaints directly to the White House via the electronic superhighway rather than through the mail. To send E-mail messages to President Bill Clinton and Vice President Al Gore, the address is

president@whitehouse.gov

vice-president@whitehouse.gov

To get information on the activities and special projects of members of the White House staff, access

riceinfo.rice.edu

and go to **Information from the White House.**

If you need a good joke about the first family (Socks included), this service has a joke for every occasion:

cco.caltech.edu

Follow the path **/pub/humor/political**.

If you are looking for discussions on past U.S. presidents, you may look into various USENET News discussion groups. Fans of Ronald Reagan might try

alt.fan.ronald.reagan

For some good (and bad) conspiracy theories about the November 1963 assassination of President John Kennedy, look into

alt.conspiracy.jfk

 ## SELECTED READINGS

Bond, Jon R., and Richard Fleisher. *The President in the Legislative Arena.* Chicago: University of Chicago Press, 1990. Bond and Fleisher examine the concept of presidential success in legislation to try to determine the factors that make some presidents more successful legislators than others. Their intensive analysis suggests that the partisan make-up and ideology of Congress has more to do with success than any specific presidential skills.

Brace, Paul, and Barbara Hinckley. *Follow the Leader: Opinion Polls and the Modern Presidents.* New York: Basic Books, 1992. This study examines the nature, conduct, and interpretation of public opinion polls that generate presidential approval ratings. The authors identify factors, including events, that influence these ratings and question the use of such data.

Burke, John P. *The Institutional Presidency.* Baltimore: Johns Hopkins University Press, 1992. Burke gives a detailed examination of the interplay between the White House staff system and the style and management abilities of particular presidents, from Franklin Roosevelt to George Bush.

Hinkley, Barbara. *The Symbolic Presidency: How Presidents Portray Themselves.* New York: Routledge, 1990. This excellent book looks at how presidents, in their speeches and other actions, reinforce the symbolism surrounding the presidential office.

Kernell, Samuel. *Going Public: New Strategies of Presidential Leadership.* 2d ed. Washington, D.C.: Congressional Quarterly Press, 1992. This fascinating book explores how presidents increasingly have bypassed the traditional process of bargaining with Congress and have "gone public" with presidential priorities in an effort to bring direct public pressure on Congress.

Langston, Thomas S. *Ideologies and Presidents: From the New Deal to the Reagan Revolution.* Baltimore, Md.: Johns Hopkins University Press, 1992. In this study of the influence of ideologues ("people of ideas") on the American presidency and presidential administrations, the author concludes that U.S. presidents are increasingly dependent on unelected ideologues who are not accountable to the electorate.

McDonald, Forrest. *The American Presidency: An Intellectual History.* Lawrence, Kans.: University Press of Kansas, 1994. This intellectual history traces the development of the presidency and its powers from the early colonial governors through the American Revolution, the Constitutional Convention, and the early presidents.

Mezey, Michael L. *Congress, the President, and Public Policy.* 2d ed. Boulder, Colo.: Westview Press, 1993. This book studies the relationship between the executive branch and Congress that makes it possible to pass legislation, particularly on major public policy issues. The tendency to stalemate, according to this author, is rooted in our institutions and Constitution rather than in a particular president.

Milkis, Sydney M., and Michael Nelson. *The American Presidency: Origins and Development, 1776–1990.* Washington, D.C.: Congressional Quarterly Press, 1990. This is a comprehensive overview of the American presidential office, how it has changed over time, and the factors influencing that change.

Rourke, John T. *Presidential Wars and American Democracy: Rally 'Round the Chief.* New York: Paragon House, 1993. The author traces the recent history of presidents who have chosen military action, including the Persian Gulf War, and raises a number of constitutional and theoretical issues about how a democracy should decide to use military force.

Thomas, Norman C., Joseph A. Pika, and Richard A. Watson. *The Politics of the Presidency.* 3d ed. Washington, D.C.: Congressional Quarterly Press, 1994. This excellent, up-to-date book covers the changing presidency and the relationship between the president and the other branches of government.

Thompson, Kenneth W., ed. *Papers on Presidential Disability and the Twenty-fifth Amendment by Six Medical, Legal, and Political Authorities.* Vol. 2. Lanham, Md.: University Press of America, 1991. An in-depth study of presidential disability and the transfer of presidential powers in accordance with the Twenty-fifth Amendment.

12
The Bureaucracy

 CHAPTER OUTLINE

WHAT IF . . .
Independent Agencies Had to Be Profitable?

The federal government is huge. It employs millions of individuals. It provides innumerable services to Americans every day. As you will read in this chapter, the federal bureaucracy consists of the fourteen departments in the executive branch, independent regulatory agencies, government corporations, and independent executive agencies. The last two categories include the National Science Foundation, the Federal Communications Commission, and the U.S. Postal Service.

Currently, there is no legal requirement that independent agencies or government corporations make a profit. Indeed, one might suspect that the legal requirement is the reverse—that they must lose money, because they almost always do. The U.S. Postal Service, for example, routinely loses a billion dollars or more a year.

What if independent agencies and government corporations had to make a profit each year? What if a law were passed that required such agencies to charge enough money for their services to cover all of their costs? Now to make this scenario somewhat more realistic, we will assume that each government agency and corporation is given, say, five years until it has to be profitable.

The first thing that would happen is that certain government agencies and corporations would have to start charging user fees for the services they render to the public. Those agencies that are already charging user fees would have to raise them significantly. For example, the Tennessee Valley Authority—if forced to take account of the true costs of all its operations—would have to raise the price of electricity to its customers. The U.S. Postal Service would have to raise its rates probably more than it already has done. The Small Business Administration would have to charge small businesses for any services rendered. The National Mediation Board would have to bill unions and businesses for its mediation services in labor-management disputes.

But what about those agencies that were not put into existence with the idea of charging for their services? They would have to rethink their charters. The National Aeronautics and Space Administration would basically have to become a commercial satellite-launching operation. It might even advertise throughout the world. It would have to refocus its efforts away from big, bold plans, such as plans for a manned space station, to more mundane operations, such as communication satellites.

Something else might have to happen on the cost side with all government independent agencies and corporations. They might actually have to be run like private businesses. Managers would be required under law to contain costs to enable such agencies to make a profit. The U.S. Postal Service, for example, would be run more like Federal Express and United Parcel Service. U.S. postal workers, who are now part of a very strong union, would find postal management much less willing to accept union demands for higher wages. After all, the profit requirement means keeping costs down, and labor accounts for about 80 percent of the U.S. Postal Service's budget.

Nationwide, the requirement that independent agencies and corporations make a profit would certainly lead to the elimination of a large number of them. Many publicly offered services in the areas of medical care, welfare, the arts, science, and technology would disappear. Other services, now being furnished at bargain rates, would become much more expensive and would reflect more accurately the true cost to the nation of providing those services.

Some groups would undoubtedly be hurt. The American public would see smaller federal budget deficits and less federal government spending, however. The net effect would be that those who pay most of the tax dollars to the government (the middle class and the wealthy) would be better off, and those who receive the greater share of many government services (generally, the "working poor," the unemployed, single mothers and their children, and persons with disabilities, to name a few) would lose.

---

1. What government agencies and corporations would be good candidates for the requirement that they turn a profit?
2. Why should some government agencies never be required to make a profit?

In the fall of 1993, flashbulbs popped as President Bill Clinton and Vice President Al Gore stood on the White House lawn in front of a forklift loaded with paper on which federal regulations were printed. President Clinton proclaimed that "the government is broken, and we intend to fix it." He followed in the footsteps of a long line of presidents of both parties who have declared that they will end government inefficiency and wastefulness (see Table 12–1). Of course, none has come out in favor of making independent agencies earn a profit, as this chapter's opening *What If . . .* suggested.

Presidents have been virtually powerless to affect significantly the structure and operation of the federal bureaucracy. It has been called the "fourth branch of government," even though you will find no reference to the bureaucracy in the original Constitution or in the twenty-seven amendments that have been passed since 1787. But Article II, Section 2, of the Constitution gives the president the power to appoint "all other Officers of the United States, whose Appointments are not herein otherwise provided for." Article II, Section 3, states that the president "shall take Care that the Laws be faithfully executed, and shall Commission all the Officers of the United States." Constitutional scholars believe that the legal basis for the bureaucracy rests on these two sections in Article II.

One of Vice President Gore's first tasks was to help President Clinton "change government as we know it." Gore was responsible for managing a project that became known as "reinventing government." Here Clinton and Gore announce the publication of their program on how to reinvent government. The book and manuals surrounding them represent existing government regulations, many of which they suggested should be eliminated.

THE NATURE OF BUREAUCRACY

A **bureaucracy** is the name given to a large organization that is structured hierarchically to carry out specific functions. Generally, most bureaucracies are characterized by an organization chart. The units of the organization are divided according to the specialization and expertise of the employees.

Public and Private Bureaucracies

We should not think of bureaucracy as unique to government. Any large corporation or university can be considered a bureaucratic organization. The fact is that the handling of complex problems requires a division of labor.

BUREAUCRACY
A large organization that is structured hierarchically to carry out specific functions.

TABLE 12–1

Selected Presidential Plans to End Government Inefficiency

PRESIDENT	NAME OF PLAN
Lyndon Johnson (1963–1969)	Programming, Planning, and Budgeting Systems
Richard Nixon (1969–1974)	Management by Objectives
Jimmy Carter (1977–1981)	Zero-Based Budgeting
Ronald Reagan (1981–1989)	President's Private Sector Survey on Cost Control (the Grace Commission)
George Bush (1989–1993)	Right-Sizing Government
Bill Clinton (1993–)	"From Red Tape to Results: Creating a Government that Works Better and Costs Less"

Workers must concentrate their skills on specific, well-defined aspects of a problem and depend on others to solve the rest of it.

But public or government bureaucracies differ from private organizations in some important ways. A private corporation, such as Microsoft, has a single set of leaders, its board of directors. Public bureaucracies, in contrast, do not have a single set of leaders. Although the president is the chief administrator of the federal system, all bureaucratic agencies are subject to the desires of Congress for their funding, staffing, and indeed, for their continued existence. Furthermore, public bureaucracies supposedly serve the citizen rather than the stockholder.

One other important difference between private corporations and government bureaucracies is that government bureaucracies are not organized to make a profit. Rather, they are supposed to perform their functions as efficiently as possible to conserve the taxpayers' dollars. Perhaps it is this aspect of government organization that makes citizens hostile toward government employees when citizens experience inefficiency and red tape.

These characteristics, together with the prevalence and size of the government bureaucracies, make them an important factor in American life.

THEORIES OF BUREAUCRACY

Several theories have been offered to help us better understand the ways in which bureaucracies function. Each of these theories focuses on specific features of bureaucracies.

The Weberian Model

The classic model, or **Weberian model**, of the modern bureaucracy was proposed by Max Weber.[1] He argued that the increasingly complex nature

1. Max Weber, *Theory of Social and Economic Organization*, ed. by Talcott Parsons (New York: Oxford University Press, 1974).

WEBERIAN MODEL
A model of bureaucracy developed by the German sociologist Max Weber, who viewed bureaucracies as rational, hierarchical organizations in which power flows from the top downward and decisions are based on logical reasoning and data analysis.

The Department of Agriculture inspects meat-packing facilities throughout the United States, certifying the quality and condition of the meat to be sold.

of modern life, coupled with the steadily growing demands placed on governments by their citizens, made the formation of bureaucracies inevitable. According to Weber, most bureaucracies—whether in the public or private sector—are organized hierarchically and governed by formal procedures. The power in a bureaucracy flows from the top downward. Decision-making processes in bureaucracies are shaped by detailed technical rules that promote similar decisions in similar situations. Bureaucrats are specialists who attempt to resolve problems through logical reasoning and data analysis instead of "gut feelings" and guesswork. Individual advancement in bureaucracies is supposed to be based on merit rather than political connections. Indeed, the modern bureaucracy, according to Weber, should be an apolitical organization.

The Acquisitive Model

Other theorists do not view bureaucracies in terms as benign as Weber's. Some believe that bureaucracies are acquisitive in nature. Proponents of the **acquisitive model** argue that top-level bureaucrats will always try to expand, or at least to avoid any reductions in, the size of their budgets. Although government bureaucracies are not-for-profit enterprises, bureaucrats want to maximize the size of their budgets and staffs, because these things are the most visible trappings of power in the public sector. These efforts are also prompted by the desire of bureaucrats to "sell" their product—national defense, public housing, agricultural subsidies, and so on—to both Congress and the public.

ACQUISITIVE MODEL
A model of bureaucracy that views top-level bureaucrats as seeking constantly to expand the size of their budgets and the staffs of their departments or agencies so as to gain greater power and influence in the public sector.

The Monopolistic Model

Because government bureaucracies seldom have competitors, some theorists have suggested that bureaucratic organizations may be explained best by using a **monopolistic model**. The analysis is similar to that used by economists to examine the behavior of monopolistic firms. Monopolistic bureaucracies—like monopolistic firms—are less efficient and more costly to operate because they have no competitors. Because monopolistic bureaucracies are not usually penalized for chronic inefficiency, they have little reason to adopt cost-saving measures or to make more productive uses of their resources. Some economists have argued that such problems can be cured only by privatizing certain bureaucratic functions.

MONOPOLISTIC MODEL
A model of bureaucracy that compares bureaucracies to monopolistic business firms. Lack of competition within a bureaucracy leads to inefficient and costly operations, just as it does within monopolistic firms. Because bureaucracies are not penalized for inefficiency, there is no incentive to save costs or use resources more productively.

The Garbage Can Model

The image of a bumbling, rudderless organization is offered by proponents of the **garbage can model** of bureaucracy. This theory presupposes that bureaucracies rarely act in any purposeful or coherent manner but instead bumble along aimlessly in search of solutions to particular problems. This model views bureaucracies as having relatively little formal organization. The solutions to problems are obtained not by the smooth implementation of well-planned policies but instead by trial and error. Choosing the right policy is tricky, because usually it is not possible to determine in advance which solution is best. Thus, bureaucrats may have to try one, two, three, or even more policies before they obtain a satisfactory result.

GARBAGE CAN MODEL
A model of bureaucracy that characterizes bureaucracies as rudderless entities with little formal organization in which solutions to problems are based on trial and error rather than rational policy planning.

THE SIZE OF THE BUREAUCRACY

In 1789, the new government's bureaucracy was minuscule. There were three departments—State (with nine employees), War (with two employees), and Treasury (with thirty-nine employees). This bureaucracy was still small in 1798. At that time, the secretary of state had seven clerks and spent a total of $500 (about $5,390 in 1996 dollars) on stationery and printing. In that same year, the Appropriations Act allocated $1.4 million to the War Department (or $14.9 million in 1996 dollars).[2]

Times have changed, as we can see in Figure 12–1, which lists the various federal agencies and the number of civilian employees in each. Excluding the military, approximately three million government employees constitute the federal bureaucracy. That number has remained relatively stable for the last several decades. It is somewhat deceiving, however, because there are many others working directly or indirectly for the federal government as subcontractors or consultants and in other capacities.

The figures for federal government employment are only part of the story. Figure 12–2 shows the growth in government employment at the federal, state, and local levels. Since 1950, this growth has been mainly at the state and local levels. If all government employees are counted, then, 15.2 percent of the entire civilian labor force works directly for the government.

The costs of the bureaucracy are commensurately high and growing. The share of the gross national product taken up by total government spending was only 8.5 percent in 1929, but today it exceeds 40 percent.

---

2. Leonard D. White *The Federalists: A Study in Administrative History, 1789–1801* (New York: Free Press, 1948).

FIGURE 12–1 ■

Federal Agencies and Their Respective Numbers of Civilian Employees

EXECUTIVE OFFICE OF THE PRESIDENT 1,758

JUDICIAL BRANCH 25,805

LEGISLATIVE BRANCH 38,504

EXECUTIVE DEPARTMENTS 2,054,094

- Agriculture 125,640
- Commerce 38,087
- Defense 1,012,716
- Education 5,081
- Energy 19,539
- Health and Human Services 129,483
- Housing and Urban Development 14,998
- Interior 81,683
- Justice 90,821
- Labor 17,938
- State 25,699
- Transportation 69,831
- Treasury 166,433
- Veterans' Affairs 256,145

INDEPENDENT AGENCIES (including Postal Service) 991,751

SOURCE: U.S. Department of Commerce, *Statistical Abstract of the United States* (Washinton, D.C.: U.S. Government Printing Office, 1994).

THE ORGANIZATION OF THE FEDERAL BUREAUCRACY

Within the federal bureaucracy are a number of different types of government agencies and organizations. Figure 12–3 on the next page outlines the several bureaucracies within the executive branch, as well as the separate organizations that provide services to Congress, to the courts, and directly to the president. In Chapter 11, we discussed those agencies that are considered to be part of the Executive Office of the President.

The executive branch, which employs most of the bureaucrats, has four major types of bureaucratic structures. They are (1) cabinet departments, (2) independent executive agencies, (3) independent regulatory agencies, and (4) government corporations. Each has a distinctive relationship to the president, and some have unusual internal structures, overall goals, and grants of power.

Cabinet Departments

The fourteen **cabinet departments** are the major service organizations of the federal government. They can also be described in management terms as **line organizations.** This means that they are directly accountable to the president and are responsible for performing government functions, such as printing money or training troops. These departments were created by Congress when the need for each department arose. The first department to be created was State, and the most recent one was Veterans Affairs, established in 1988. A president might ask that a new department be created or an old one abolished, but the president has no power to do so without legislative approval from Congress.

Each department is headed by a secretary (except for the Justice Department, which is headed by the attorney general) and has several levels of undersecretaries, assistant secretaries, and so on. (For information on the current secretary of defense, William J. Perry, see this chapter's *Politics: The Human Side.*)

Presidents theoretically have considerable control over the cabinet departments, because presidents are able to appoint or fire all of the top officials. Even cabinet departments do not always respond to the president's wishes, though. One reason for the frequent unhappiness of presidents with their departments is that the entire bureaucratic structure below the top political levels is staffed by permanent employees, many of whom are committed to established programs or procedures and who resist change. As we can see from Table 12–2 on pages 432 and 433, each cabinet department employs thousands of individuals, only a handful of whom are under the control of the president. The table also describes the functions of each of the cabinet departments.

Independent Executive Agencies

Independent executive agencies are bureaucratic organizations that are not located within a department and report directly to the president, who appoints their chief officials. When a new federal agency is created—such as the Environmental Protection Agency—a decision is made by Congress about where it will be located in the bureaucracy. In this century, presidents

FIGURE 12–2 ■

Growth in Government Employment at Federal, State, and Local Levels

There are more local government employees than federal and state employees combined.

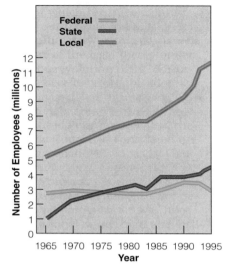

SOURCE: U.S. Department of Labor, Bureau of Labor Statistics, *Monthly Labor Review*, October 1994. 1995 data are estimates.

CABINET DEPARTMENT
One of the fourteen departments of the executive branch (State, Treasury, Defense, Justice, Interior, Agriculture, Commerce, Labor, Health and Human Services, Housing and Urban Development, Education, Energy, Transportation, and Veterans Affairs).

LINE ORGANIZATION
Government or corporate units that provide direct services or products for the public.

INDEPENDENT EXECUTIVE AGENCY
A federal agency that is not part of a cabinet department but reports directly to the president.

often have asked that a new organization be kept separate or independent rather than added to an existing department, particularly if a department may in fact be hostile to the agency's creation. Table 12–3 on page 434 describes the functions of several selected independent executive agencies.

INDEPENDENT REGULATORY AGENCY
An agency outside the major executive departments charged with making and implementing rules and regulations to protect the public interest.

Independent Regulatory Agencies

The **independent regulatory agencies** are typically responsible for a specific type of public policy. Their function is to make and implement rules and regulations in a particular sector of the economy to protect the public interest. The earliest such agency was the Interstate Commerce Commission (ICC), which was established in 1887 when Americans began to seek some form of government control over the rapidly growing business and industrial sector. This new form of organization, the independent regulatory

FIGURE 12–3 ■
Organization Chart of the Federal Government

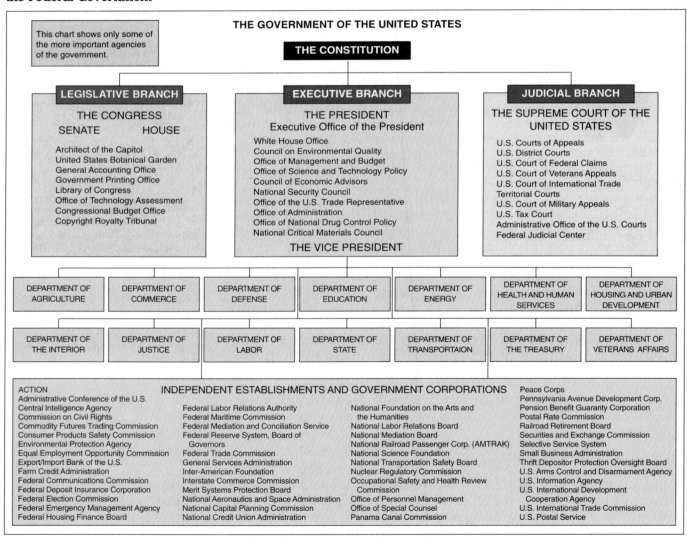

THE GOVERNMENT OF THE UNITED STATES

This chart shows only some of the more important agencies of the government.

THE CONSTITUTION

LEGISLATIVE BRANCH

THE CONGRESS
SENATE HOUSE

Architect of the Capitol
United States Botanical Garden
General Accounting Office
Government Printing Office
Library of Congress
Office of Technology Assessment
Congressional Budget Office
Copyright Royalty Tribunal

EXECUTIVE BRANCH

THE PRESIDENT
Executive Office of the President

White House Office
Council on Environmental Quality
Office of Management and Budget
Office of Science and Technology Policy
Council of Economic Advisors
National Security Council
Office of the U.S. Trade Representative
Office of Administration
Office of National Drug Control Policy
National Critical Materials Council

THE VICE PRESIDENT

JUDICIAL BRANCH

THE SUPREME COURT OF THE UNITED STATES

U.S. Courts of Appeals
U.S. District Courts
U.S. Court of Federal Claims
U.S. Court of Veterans Appeals
U.S. Court of International Trade
Territorial Courts
U.S. Court of Military Appeals
U.S. Tax Court
Administrative Office of the U.S. Courts
Federal Judicial Center

DEPARTMENT OF AGRICULTURE | DEPARTMENT OF COMMERCE | DEPARTMENT OF DEFENSE | DEPARTMENT OF EDUCATION | DEPARTMENT OF ENERGY | DEPARTMENT OF HEALTH AND HUMAN SERVICES | DEPARTMENT OF HOUSING AND URBAN DEVELOPMENT

DEPARTMENT OF THE INTERIOR | DEPARTMENT OF JUSTICE | DEPARTMENT OF LABOR | DEPARTMENT OF STATE | DEPARTMENT OF TRANSPORTAION | DEPARTMENT OF THE TREASURY | DEPARTMENT OF VETERANS AFFAIRS

INDEPENDENT ESTABLISHMENTS AND GOVERNMENT CORPORATIONS

ACTION
Administrative Conference of the U.S.
Central Intelligence Agency
Commission on Civil Rights
Commodity Futures Trading Commission
Consumer Products Safety Commission
Environmental Protection Agency
Equal Employment Opportunity Commission
Export/Import Bank of the U.S.
Farm Credit Administration
Federal Communications Commission
Federal Deposit Insurance Corporation
Federal Election Commission
Federal Emergency Management Agency
Federal Housing Finance Board

Federal Labor Relations Authority
Federal Maritime Commission
Federal Mediation and Conciliation Service
Federal Reserve System, Board of Governors
Federal Trade Commission
General Services Administration
Inter-American Foundation
Interstate Commerce Commission
Merit Systems Protection Board
National Aeronautics and Space Administration
National Capital Planning Commission
National Credit Union Administration

National Foundation on the Arts and the Humanities
National Labor Relations Board
National Mediation Board
National Railroad Passenger Corp. (AMTRAK)
National Science Foundation
National Transportation Safety Board
Nuclear Regulatory Commission
Occupational Safety and Health Review Commission
Office of Personnel Management
Office of Special Counsel
Panama Canal Commission

Peace Corps
Pennsylvania Avenue Development Corp.
Pension Benefit Guaranty Corporation
Postal Rate Commission
Railroad Retirement Board
Securities and Exchange Commission
Selective Service System
Small Business Administration
Thrift Depositor Protection Oversight Board
U.S. Arms Control and Disarmament Agency
U.S. Information Agency
U.S. International Development Cooperation Agency
U.S. International Trade Commission
U.S. Postal Service

SOURCE: *U.S. Government Manual, 1993–1994.*

POLITICS: THE HUMAN SIDE
William J. Perry, Secretary of Defense

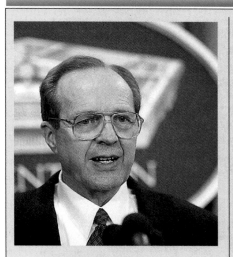

"The British novelist Graham Greene once wrote, 'There always comes a moment in time when a door opens and lets the future in.' The ending of the Cold War opened such a door. The summit agreements will help us guide the future as it comes in."

BIOGRAPHICAL NOTES

William J. Perry was born in 1927 in Vandergrift, Pennsylvania. He served in the U.S. Army in 1946 and 1947 and attended Stanford University and Pennsylvania State University, obtaining degrees in 1949, 1950, and 1957.

In the early 1950s, Perry was a math instructor at Penn State and senior mathematician with the HRB-Singer Company. Between 1954 and 1964, he was the director of the electronic defense laboratories at the GTE Sylvania Company. In the late 1960s and early 1970s, Perry was president of ESL, Inc., which he co-founded, and a technical consultant to the Department of Defense.

In the late 1970s, Perry was the undersecretary of defense for research and engineering in President Jimmy Carter's administration. When Carter lost his bid for reelection, Perry left the Department of Defense to become managing director of Hambrecht and Quist, Inc. In the late 1980s and early 1990s, he was simultaneously the chairman of Technology Strategies & Alliances and, at Stanford University, a professor of engineering and a co-director of the Center for International Security and Arms Control.

In 1993, the Senate approved President Bill Clinton's appointment of Perry to the post of deputy secretary of defense. Less than a year later, Clinton appointed Perry secretary of defense. The Senate approved Perry's appointment unanimously.

POLITICAL CONTRIBUTIONS

In the 1970s, Perry's work as undersecretary of defense included responsibility for weapon-systems procurement, research, and development. He was the principal advisor to the secretary of defense on technology, communications, intelligence, and atomic energy. His work involved the development of "stealth" technology, which enables aircraft to elude radar.

In the 1980s and 1990s, Perry's political contributions included redesigning the procedures through which the Department of Defense purchases weapons. He revealed that the Department of Defense spends on overhead as much as 33 percent of its budget for weapons purchases.

Perry also has served as a trustee of the Carnegie Endowment for International Peace and on a number of federal government advisory boards, including the President's Foreign Intelligence Advisory Board and the Technical Review Panel of the U.S. Senate's Select Committee on Intelligence. He is a member of the Carnegie Commission on Science, Technology, and Government and the Committee on International Security and Arms Control of the National Academy of Science.

agency, was supposed to make technical, nonpolitical decisions about rates, profits, and rules that would be for the benefit of all and that did not require congressional legislation. In the years that followed the creation of the ICC, other agencies were formed to regulate aviation (the Civil Aeronautics Board), communication (the Federal Communications Commission), nuclear power (the Nuclear Regulatory Commission), and so on. (See the *Politics and the Bureaucracy* on page 434 for a discussion of what has happened to the ICC.)

TABLE 12–2

Executive Departments

Department and Year Established	Principal Duties	Most Important Subagencies
State (1789) (25,699 employees)	Negotiates treaties; develops foreign policy; protects citizens abroad.	Passport Agency; Bureau of Diplomatic Security; Foreign Service; Bureau of Human Rights and Humanitarian Affairs; Bureau of Consular Affairs.
Treasury (1789) (166,433 employees)	Pays all federal bills; borrows money; collects federal taxes; mints coins and prints paper currency; operates the Secret Service; supervises national banks.	Internal Revenue Service (IRS); Bureau of Alcohol, Tobacco, and Firearms; U.S. Secret Service; U.S. Mint; Customs Service.
Interior (1849) (81,683 employees)	Supervises federally owned lands and parks; operates federal hydroelectric power facilities; supervises Native-American affairs.	U.S. Fish and Wildlife Service; National Park Service; Bureau of Indian Affairs; Bureau of Land Management.
Justice (1870)* (90,821 employees)	Furnishes legal advice to the president; enforces federal criminal laws; supervises the federal corrections system (prisons).	Federal Bureau of Investigation (FBI); Drug Enforcement Administration (DEA); Bureau of Prisons (BOP); Immigration and Naturalization Service (INS).
Agriculture (1889) (125,640 employees)	Provides assistance to farmers and ranchers; conducts research to improve agricultural activity and to prevent plant disease; works to protect forests from fires and disease.	Soil Conservation Service; Agricultural Research Service; Food and Safety Inspection Service; Federal Crop Insurance Corporation; Farmers Home Administration.
Commerce (1913)† (38,087 employees)	Grants patents and trademarks; conducts a national census; monitors the weather; protects the interests of businesses.	Bureau of the Census; Bureau of Economic Analysis; Minority Business Development Agency; Patent and Trademark Office; National Oceanic and Atmospheric Administration; U.S. Travel and Tourism Administration.
Labor (1913)† (17,938 employees)	Administers federal labor laws; promotes the interests of workers.	Occupational Safety and Health Administration (OSHA); Bureau of Labor Statistics; Employment Standards Administration; Office of Labor-Management Standards.

*Formed from the Office of the Attorney General (created in 1789).
†Formed from the Department of Commerce and Labor (created in 1903).

The Purpose and Nature of Regulatory Agencies. The regulatory agencies are administered independently of all three branches of government. They were set up because Congress felt it was unable to handle the complexities and technicalities required to carry out specific laws in the public interest. The regulatory commissions in fact combine some functions of all three branches of government—executive, legislative, and judicial. They are legislative in that they make rules that have the force of law. They are executive in that they provide for the enforcement of those rules. They are judicial in that they decide disputes involving the rules they have made.

Regulatory agency members are appointed by the president with the consent of the Senate, although they do not report to the president. By law, the members of regulatory agencies cannot all be from the same political party. Presidents can influence regulatory agency behavior by appointing people of their own parties or people who share their political views when vacancies occur, in particular when the chair is vacant. Members may be removed by the president only for causes specified in the law creating the agency. Table 12–4 on page 435 describes the functions of several selected independent regulatory agencies.

433

TABLE 12–2, Continued
Executive Departments

DEPARTMENT AND YEAR ESTABLISHED	PRINCIPAL DUTIES	MOST IMPORTANT SUBAGENCIES
Defense (1947)‡ (1,012,716 employees)	Manages the armed forces (army, navy, air force, and marines); operates military bases; is responsible for civil defense.	National Guard; National Security Agency; Joint Chiefs of Staff; Departments of the Air Force, Navy, Army.
Housing and Urban Development (1965) (14,998 employees)	Deals with the nation's housing needs; develops and rehabilitates urban communities; promotes improvement in city streets and parks.	Assistant Secretary for Community Planning and Development; Government National Mortgage Association; Assistant Secretary for Housing—Federal Housing Commissioner; Assistant Secretary for Fair Housing and Equal Opportunity.
Transportation (1967) (69,831 employees)	Finances improvements in mass transit; develops and administers programs for highways, railroads, and aviation; is involved with offshore maritime safety.	Federal Aviation Administration (FAA); Federal Highway Administration; National Highway Traffic Safety Administration; U.S. Coast Guard; Federal Transit Administration.
Energy (1977) (19,539 employees)	Is involved in the conservation of energy and resources; analyzes energy data; conducts research and development.	Office of Civilian Radioactive Waste Management; Bonneville Power Administration; Office of Nuclear Energy; Energy Information Administration; Office of Conservation and Renewable Energy.
Health and Human Services (1979)§ (129,483 employees)	Administers the Social Security and Medicare programs; promotes public health; enforces pure food and drug laws; is involved in health-related research.	Social Security Administration; Administration for Children and Families; Health Care Financing Administration; Public Health Service.
Education (1979)§ (5,081 employees)	Coordinates federal programs and policies for education; administers aid to education; promotes educational research.	Office of Special Education and Rehabilitation Services; Office of Elementary and Secondary Education; Office of Postsecondary Education; Office of Vocational and Adult Education.
Veterans Affairs (1988) (256,145 employees)	Promotes the welfare of veterans of the U.S. armed forces.	Veterans Health Administration; Veterans Benefits Administration; National Cemetery System.

‡Formed from the Department of War (created in 1789) and the Department of Navy (created in 1798).
§Formed from the Department of Health, Education, and Welfare (created in 1953).

Over the last several decades, some observers have concluded that these agencies, although nominally independent of the three branches of the federal government, may in fact not always be so. They also contend that many independent regulatory agencies have been **captured** by the very industries and firms that they were supposed to regulate. The results have been less competition rather than more competition, higher prices rather than lower prices, and less choice rather than more choice for consumers.

CAPTURE
The act of gaining direct or indirect control over agency personnel and decision makers by the industry that is being regulated.

Deregulation and Reregulation. During the presidency of Ronald Reagan in the 1980s, some significant deregulation (the removal of regulatory restraints—the opposite of regulation) occurred, much of which started under President Jimmy Carter. For example, Carter appointed a chairperson of the Civil Aeronautics Board (CAB) who gradually eliminated regulation of airline fares and routes. Then, under Reagan, the CAB was eliminated on January 1, 1985. During the Bush administration, calls for *re*regulation of many businesses increased. Indeed, under President Bush, the Americans with Disabilities Act of 1990, the Civil Rights Act of 1991, and the Clean Air Act Amendments of 1991, all of which increased or changed the

POLITICS AND THE BUREAUCRACY
The ICC Just Keeps Going and Going

In 1980, the trucking industry was deregulated. Prior to that time, all rates and routes had to be approved by the Interstate Commerce Commission (ICC). But a decade and a half after the purported demise of the ICC, 630 employees try to make their jobs relevant. Every day, five days a week, sixteen thousand pages of rates are brought in from the nation's trucking companies. ICC examiners then inspect every line of each new filing. The question, of course, is why? The ICC no longer has any power to regulate shipping rates that are listed in these sixteen thousand pages a day. It is all part of the game, insiders say, to keep the agency alive even after it was attacked viciously by both Ralph Nader and Ronald Reagan.

The ICC's five commissioners are paid $115,000 a year each (plus benefits). In any one year, they meet as many as eleven times. An equal number of commission sessions are canceled for lack of anything to talk about. One thorny issue the ICC commissioners have been grappling with involves candy canes. Should candy canes have a classification that is different from candy with respect to the shipping rates charged? Also, the commissioners have worked for fourteen years on a dispute over whether the rates for shipping corn syrup from Texas to California are "appropriate." (All such rates are now determined by supply and demand in an unregulated market.)

So the question remains: Why is the ICC still in business if it may seem that it has nothing to do? The fact is that the Interstate Commerce Act of 1887, which created the ICC, has not yet been repealed. The stature of members of Congress depends partly on how many agencies their committees oversee. In both the House and the Senate, therefore, the committees with jurisdiction over the ICC have stonewalled proposals to eliminate that agency. When Congressman Norman Mineta (D., Calif.), then chairman of the House Public Works and Transportation Committee, attended a celebration for the ICC, he told the agency that he would not let anybody cut off "the funding [the ICC] needs, so all of you can do your very, very important jobs."

TABLE 12–3

Selected Independent Executive Agencies

NAME	DATE FORMED	PRINCIPAL DUTIES
Central Intelligence Agency (CIA)*	1947	Gathers and analyzes political and military information about foreign countries so that the United States can improve its own political and military status; conducts activities outside the United States, with the goal of countering the work of intelligence services operated by other nations whose political philosophies are inconsistent with our own.
General Services Administration (GSA) (21,122 employees)	1949	Purchases and manages all property of the federal government; acts as the business arm of the federal government in overseeing federal government spending projects; discovers overcharges in government programs.
National Science Foundation (NSF) (1,200 employees)	1950	Promotes scientific research; provides grants to all levels of schools for instructional programs in the sciences.
Small Business Administration (SBA) (4,867 employees)	1953	Protects the interests of small businesses; provides low-cost loans and management information to small businesses.
National Aeronautics and Space Administration (NASA) (25,737 employees)	1958	Is responsible for the U.S. space program, including the building, testing, and operating of space vehicles.
Environmental Protection Agency (EPA) (18,218 employees)	1970	Undertakes programs aimed at reducing air and water pollution; works with state and local agencies to help fight environmental hazards.

* The CIA will not release information on the number of employees who work for this agency (because it is "classified information").

TABLE 12–4

Selected Independent Regulatory Agencies

NAME	DATE FORMED	PRINCIPAL DUTIES
Federal Reserve System Board of Governors (Fed) (1,640 employees)	1913	Determines policy with respect to interest rates, credit availability, and the money supply.
Federal Trade Commission (FTC) (1,000 employees)	1914	Prevents businesses from engaging in unfair trade practices; stops the formation of monopolies in the business sector; protects consumer rights.
Securities and Exchange Commission (SEC) (2,500 employees)	1934	Regulates the nation's stock exchanges, in which shares of stocks are bought and sold; requires full disclosure of the financial profiles of companies that wish to sell stocks and bonds to the public.
Federal Communications Commission (FCC) (1,900 employees)	1934	Regulates all communications by telegraph, cable, telephone, radio, and television.
National Labor Relations Board (NLRB) (2,100 employees)	1935	Protects employees' rights to join unions and bargain collectively with employers; attempts to prevent unfair labor practices by both employers and unions.
Equal Employment Opportunity Commission (EEOC) (2,889 employees)	1964	Works to eliminate discrimination based on religion, sex, race, color, national origin, age, or disability; examines claims of discrimination.
Federal Election Commission (FEC) (300 employees)	1974	Ensures that candidates and states follow the rules established by the Federal Election Campaign Act.
Nuclear Regulatory Commission (NRC) (3,534 employees)	1974	Ensures that electricity-generating nuclear reactors in the United States are built and operated safely; regularly inspects the operations of such reactors.

regulation of many businesses, were passed. Additionally, there was the passage of the Cable Reregulation Act of 1992. Under President Clinton, there has been increased environmental regulation and regulation of the banking industry.

Government Corporations

The newest form of bureaucratic organization to be adopted in the United States is the **government corporation.** Although the concept is borrowed from the world of business, distinct differences exist between public and private corporations.

A private corporation has shareholders (stockholders) who elect a board of directors, who in turn choose the corporate officers, such as president and vice president. When a private corporation makes a profit, it must pay taxes (unless it avoids them through various legal loopholes). It either distributes part or all of the after-tax profits to shareholders as dividends or plows the profits back into the corporation to make new investments.

A government corporation has a board of directors and managers, but it does not have any stockholders. We cannot buy shares of stock in a government corporation. If the government corporation makes a profit, it does not distribute the profit as dividends. Also, if it makes a profit, it does not have to pay taxes; the profits remain in the corporation. Table 12–5 describes the functions of selected government corporations.

GOVERNMENT CORPORATION
An agency of government that administers a quasi-business enterprise. These corporations are used when an activity is primarily commercial. They produce revenue for their continued existence, and they require greater flexibility than is permitted for departments and agencies.

U.S. Postal Service employees sort the mail during the night shift at a New York post office.

STAFFING THE BUREAUCRACY

There are two categories of bureaucrats: political appointees and civil servants. As noted earlier, the president is able to make political appointments to most of the top jobs in the federal bureaucracy. The president also can appoint ambassadors to the most important foreign posts. All of the jobs that are considered "political plums" and that usually go to the politically well connected are listed in *Policy and Supporting Positions*, published by the

TABLE 12–5
Selected Government Corporations

NAME	DATE FORMED	PRINCIPAL DUTIES
Tennessee Valley Authority (TVA) (18,944 employees)	1933	Operates a Tennessee River control system and generates power for a seven-state region and for the U.S. aeronautics and space programs; promotes the economic development of the Tennessee Valley region; controls floods and promotes the navigability of the Tennessee River.
Federal Deposit Insurance Corporation (FDIC) (19,400 employees)	1933	Insures individuals' bank deposits up to $100,000; oversees the business activities of banks.
Commodity Credit Corporation (CCC) (3,543 employees)	1933	Attempts to stabilize farm prices and protect farmers' income by purchasing designated farm products at prices above what farmers would get in the marketplace.
Export/Import Bank of the United States (Ex/Im Bank) (400 employees)	1933	Promotes American-made goods abroad; grants loans to foreign purchasers of American products.
National Railroad Passenger Corporation (AMTRAK) (25,000 employees)	1970	Provides a balanced national and inter-city rail passenger service network; controls 23,000 miles of track with 505 stations.
U.S. Postal Service* (847,764 employees)	1970	Delivers mail throughout the United States and its territories; is the largest government corporation.

*Formed from the Office of the Postmaster General in the Department of the Treasury (created in 1789).

Government Printing Office after each presidential election. This has been informally (and correctly) called "The Plum Book." The rest of the individuals who work for the national government belong to the civil service and obtain their jobs through a much more formal process.

Political Appointees

To fill the positions listed in "The Plum Book," the president and the president's advisers solicit suggestions from politicians, businesspersons, and other prominent individuals. Appointments to these positions offer the president a way to pay off outstanding political debts. But the president must also take into consideration such things as the candidate's work experience, intelligence, political affiliations, and personal characteristics. Presidents have differed over the importance they attach to appointing women and minorities to plum positions. Presidents often use ambassadorships, however, to reward selected individuals for their campaign contributions.

Political appointees are in some sense the aristocracy of the federal government. But their powers, although appearing formidable on paper, are often exaggerated. Like the president, a political appointee will occupy his or her position for a comparatively brief time. Political appointees often leave office before the president's term actually ends. The average term of service for political appointees is less than two years. As a result, the professional civil servants who make up the permanent civil service but serve under a normally temporary political appointee may not feel compelled to carry out their current boss's directives quickly, because they know that he or she will not be around for very long.

This inertia is compounded by the fact that it is extremely difficult to discharge civil servants. In recent years, less than one-tenth of 1 percent of federal employees have been fired for incompetence. Because discharged employees may appeal their dismissals, many months or even years may pass before the issue is resolved conclusively. This occupational rigidity helps to ensure that most political appointees, no matter how competent or driven, will not be able to exert much meaningful influence over their subordinates, let alone implement dramatic changes in the bureaucracy itself.

History of the Federal Civil Service

When the federal government was formed in 1789, it had no career public servants but rather consisted of amateurs who were almost all Federalists. When Thomas Jefferson took over as president, he found that few in his party were holding federal administrative jobs, so he fired more than one hundred officials and replaced them with members of the so-called **natural aristocracy**—that is, with his own Jeffersonian Republicans. For the next twenty-five years, a growing body of federal administrators gained experience and expertise, becoming in the process professional public servants. These administrators stayed in office regardless of who was elected president. The bureaucracy had become a self-maintaining, long-term element within government.

To the Victor Belong the Spoils.   When Andrew Jackson took over the White House in 1828, he could not believe how many appointed

NATURAL ARISTOCRACY
A small ruling clique of the state's "best" citizens, whose membership is based on birth, wealth, and ability. The Jeffersonian era emphasized government rule by such a group.

officials (appointed before he became president, that is) were overtly hostile toward him and his Democratic party. The bureaucracy—indeed an aristocracy—considered itself the only group fit to rule. But Jackson was a man of the people, and his policies were populist in nature. As the bureaucracy was reluctant to carry out his programs, Jackson did the obvious: He fired federal officials—more than had all his predecessors combined. The **spoils system**— an application of the principle that to the victor belong the spoils—reigned. The aristocrats were out, and the common folk were in. The spoils system was not, of course, a Jacksonian invention. Thomas Jefferson, too, had used this system of patronage in which the boss, or patron, rewards his or her workers for the job they did in winning the election.

The Civil Service Reform Act of 1883.   Jackson's spoils system survived for a number of years, but it became increasingly corrupt. Also, the size of the bureaucracy increased by 300 percent between 1851 and 1881. Reformers began to examine the professional civil service that was established in several European countries, which operated under a **merit system** in which job appointments were based on competitive examinations. The cry for civil service reform began to be heard more loudly.

The ruling Lincoln-Grant Republican party was divided in its attitude toward reform, with the "stalwart" faction's opposing reform of any sort. When President James A. Garfield, a moderate reformer, was assassinated in 1881 by a disappointed office seeker, Charles J. Guiteau, the latter was heard to shout, "I am a stalwart, and Arthur is president now!" He was correct: Chester A. Arthur, a stalwart vice president, became president. Ironically, it was under the stalwart Arthur that civil service reform actually occurred— partly as a result of public outrage over Garfield's assassination. The movement to replace the spoils system with a permanent career civil service had the cause that would carry it to victory.

In 1883, the **Pendleton Act**—or **Civil Service Reform Act**—was passed, bringing to a close the period of Jacksonian spoils. The act established the principle of employment on the basis of open, competitive examinations

SPOILS SYSTEM
The awarding of government jobs to political supporters and friends; generally associated with President Andrew Jackson.

MERIT SYSTEM
The selection, retention, and promotion of government employees on the basis of competitive examinations.

PENDLETON ACT
(CIVIL SERVICE REFORM ACT)
The law, as amended over the years, that remains the basic statute regulating federal employment personnel policies. It established the principle of employment on the basis of merit and created the Civil Service Commission to administer the personnel service.

The assassination of President James A. Garfield on September 19, 1881, was by a disappointed office seeker, Charles J. Guiteau. The long-term effect of this event was to replace the spoils system with a permanent career civil service, with the passage of the Pendleton Act in 1883, which established the Civil Service Commission.

and created the **Civil Service Commission** to administer the personnel service. Only 10 percent of federal employees were covered initially by the merit system. Later laws, amendments, and executive orders, however, increased the coverage to more than 90 percent of the federal civil service.

The Supreme Court put an even heavier lid on the spoils system in *Elrod v. Burns*[3] in 1976 and *Branti v. Finkel*[4] in 1980. In those two cases, the Court used the First Amendment to forbid government officials from discharging or threatening to discharge public employees solely for not being supporters of the political party in power unless party affiliation is an appropriate requirement for the position. Additional curbs on political patronage were added in *Rutan v. Republican Party of Illinois* in 1990.[5] The Court's ruling effectively prevented the use of partisan political considerations as the basis for hiring, promoting, or transferring most public employees. An exception was permitted, however, for senior policymaking positions, which usually go to officials who will support the programs of the elected leaders.

The Hatch Act of 1939.   The growing size of the federal bureaucracy created the potential for political manipulation. In principle, a civil servant is politically neutral. But civil servants certainly know that it is politicians who pay the bills through their appropriations and that it is politicians who decide about the growth of agencies. In 1933, when President Franklin D. Roosevelt set up his New Deal, a virtual army of civil servants was hired to staff the numerous new agencies that were created. Because the individuals who worked in these agencies owed their jobs to the Democratic party, it seemed natural for them to campaign for Democratic candidates. The Democrats controlling Congress in the mid-1930s did not object. But in 1938, a coalition of conservative Democrats and Republicans took control of Congress and forced through the **Hatch Act**—or the **Political Activities Act**—of 1939.

The main provision of this act is that civil service employees cannot take an active part in the political management of campaigns. It also prohibits the use of federal authority to influence nominations and elections and outlaws the use of bureaucratic rank to pressure federal employees to make political contributions.

In 1972, a federal district court declared the Hatch Act prohibition against political activity to be unconstitutional. The United States Supreme Court, however, reaffirmed the challenged portion of the act in 1973, stating that the government's interest in preserving a nonpartisan civil service was so great that the prohibitions should remain.[6]

CURRENT ATTEMPTS AT BUREAUCRATIC REFORM

As long as the federal bureaucracy exists, there will continue to be attempts to make it more open, efficient, and responsive to the needs of U.S. citizens. The most important actual and proposed reforms in the last few years

---

CIVIL SERVICE COMMISSION
The initial central personnel agency of the national government; created in 1883.

**HATCH ACT
(POLITICAL ACTIVITIES ACT)**
The act that prohibits the use of federal authority to influence nominations and elections or the use of rank to pressure federal employees to make political contributions. It also prohibits civil service employees from active involvement in political campaigns.

---

3. 427 U.S. 347 (1976).
4. 445 U.S. 507 (1980).
5. 497 U.S. 62 (1990).
6. *United States Civil Service Commission v. National Association of Letter Carriers*, 413 U.S. 548 (1973).

include sunshine and sunset laws, privatization, and more protection for so-called whistleblowers.

Sunshine Laws

In 1976, Congress enacted the **Government in the Sunshine Act**. It required for the first time that all multiheaded federal agencies—about fifty of them—hold their meetings regularly in public session. The bill defined *meetings* as almost any gathering, formal or informal, of agency members, including conference telephone calls. The only exceptions to this rule of openness are discussions of matters such as court proceedings or personnel problems, and these exceptions are listed specifically in the bill.

Sunset Laws

A potential type of control on the size and scope of the federal bureaucracy is **sunset legislation**, which would place government programs on a definite schedule for congressional consideration. Unless Congress specifically reauthorized a particular federally operated program at the end of a designated period, it would be terminated automatically; that is, its sun would set.

The idea of sunset legislation—the first hint at the role of the bureaucracy in the legislative process—was initially suggested by Franklin D. Roosevelt when he created the plethora of New Deal agencies. His assistant, William O. Douglas, recommended that each agency's charter should include a provision allowing for its termination in ten years. Only an act of Congress could revitalize it. Obviously, the proposal was never adopted. It was not until 1976 that a state legislature—Colorado's—adopted sunset legislation for state regulatory commissions, giving them a life of six years before their suns would set. Today most states have some type of sunset law.

Privatization

One approach to bureaucratic reform is **privatization**, or **contracting out**. Privatization occurs when government services are replaced by services from the private sector. For example, the government might contract with private firms to operate prisons. Supporters of privatization argue that some services could be provided more efficiently by the private sector. Another privatization scheme is to furnish vouchers to clients in lieu of services. For example, it has been proposed that instead of federally supported housing assistance, the government should offer vouchers that recipients could use to "pay" for housing in privately owned buildings. Privatization also includes selling government assets.

Incentives for Efficiency and Productivity

An increasing number of state governments are beginning to experiment with a variety of schemes to run their operations more efficiently and capably. They focus on maximizing the efficiency and productivity of government workers by providing incentives for improved performance.[7]

---

7. These views are expressed by David Osborne and Ted Gaebler, *Reinventing Government: How the Entrepreneurial Spirit Is Transforming the Public Sector* (Reading, Mass.: Addison-Wesley, 1992).

Tough economic times have forced many governors, mayors, and city administrators to consider ways in which government can be made more entrepreneurial. Some of the more promising measures have included such tactics as permitting agencies that do not spend their entire budgets to keep some of the difference and rewarding employees with performance-based bonuses.

These measures are supported by the assertion that although society and industry have changed enormously in the past century, the form of government used in Washington, D.C., and in most states has remained the same. Some observers believe that the nation's diverse economic base cannot be administered competently by traditional bureaucratic organizations. Consequently, government must become more responsive to cope with the increasing number of demands placed on it.

Helping Out the Whistleblowers

The term **whistleblower** as applied to the federal bureaucracy has a special meaning: It is someone who blows the whistle on a gross governmental inefficiency or illegal action. Whistleblowers may be clerical workers, managers, or even specialists, such as scientists. Dr. Aldric Saucier is an army research scientist who had claimed since 1987 that the Strategic Defense Initiative, known as "Star Wars," was plagued by mismanagement. Saucier asserted that the army tried to dismiss him for reporting his criticisms about the program to his superiors. In particular, Saucier charged that the program had been beset by wasteful and flawed research and that his dismissal was ordered after he submitted detailed reports documenting those criticisms to the military. Representative John Conyers (D., Mich.) intervened on Saucier's behalf and obtained the assistance of the federal Office of Special Counsel. The office conducted a preliminary examination and concluded in March 1992 that some of Saucier's claims might have merit. Shortly thereafter, the army agreed to suspend Saucier's dismissal until his claims could be investigated fully.

The 1978 Civil Service Reform Act prohibits reprisals against whistleblowers by their superiors, and it set up the Merit Systems Protection Board as part of this protection. There is little evidence, though, that potential whistleblowers truly have received more protection as a result.

Many federal agencies also have toll-free hotlines that employees can use anonymously to report bureaucratic waste and inappropriate behavior. About 35 percent of all calls result in agency action or follow-up. Some calls lead to dramatic savings for the government. The General Accounting Office (GAO) hotline was reported to have generated $36 million in savings in 1994 alone. Excluding crank calls, the GAO hotline received more than eleven thousand calls during that period, which resulted in the conviction or reprimand of 240 federal employees.

WHISTLEBLOWER
Someone who brings to public attention gross governmental inefficiency or an illegal action.

BUREAUCRATS AS POLITICIANS AND POLICYMAKERS

Agencies in the federal bureaucracy are created by Congress to implement legislation. Because Congress is unable to oversee the day-to-day administration of its programs, it must delegate certain powers to administrative

Members of a Federal Aviation Administration investigation team try to find the cause of a crash at the Los Angeles airport. The federal government essentially controls all air traffic in the United States and sets the regulations for commercial and private aircraft.

agencies. In theory, the agencies should put into effect laws passed by Congress. Laws are often drafted in such vague and general terms, however, that they provide little guidance to administrators as to how they should be put into effect. This means that the agencies themselves must decide how best to carry out the wishes of Congress.

The discretion given to administrative agencies is not accidental. Congress has long realized that it lacks the technical expertise and the resources to monitor the implementation of its laws. Hence, the administrative agency is created to fill the gaps. This gap-filling role requires the agency to formulate administrative rules (regulations) to put flesh on the bones of the law. But it also forces the agency itself to assume the role of an unelected policymaker.

The Rule-Making Environment

Rule making does not occur in a vacuum. Suppose that Congress passes a new air-pollution law. The Environmental Protection Agency (EPA) might decide to implement the new law by a technical regulation relating to factory emissions. This proposed regulation would be published in the *Federal Register* so that interested parties would have an opportunity to comment on it. Individuals and companies that opposed parts or all of the rule might then try to convince the EPA to revise or redraft the regulation. Some parties might try to persuade the agency to withdraw the proposed regulation altogether. In any event, the EPA would consider these comments in drafting the final version of the regulation following the expiration of the comment period.

Once the final regulation has been published, it might be vetoed by Congress, in line with any provisions for such a legislative veto. (See the discussion on legislative vetoes later in the chapter.) Or the regulation might be challenged in court by a party having a direct interest in the rule, such as a company that could expect to incur significant costs in complying with it.

The company could argue that the rule misinterprets the applicable law or goes beyond the agency's statutory purview. An allegation by the company that the EPA made a mistake in judgment probably would not be enough to convince the court to throw out the rule. The company instead would have to demonstrate that the rule itself was "arbitary and capricious." To meet this standard, the company would have to show that the rule reflected a serious flaw in the EPA's judgment—such as a steadfast refusal by the agency to consider reasonable alternatives to its rule.

Negotiated Settlements

Since the end of World War II, companies have filed lawsuits regularly to block the implementation of agency regulations. Environmentalists and other special interest groups have also challenged government regulations. In the 1980s and 1990s, however, the sheer wastefulness of attempting to regulate through litigation has become more and more apparent, particularly in an era when the government is besieged by high budget deficits. A growing number of federal agencies have begun encouraging businesses and public interest groups to become directly involved in the drafting of regulations. Agencies hope that such participation might help to prevent later courtroom battles over the meaning, applicability, and legal effect of the regulations.

One example of this trend was the EPA's decision to seek an agreement with business interests and environmental groups about implementing certain provisions of the Clean Air Act of 1990. The only condition was that the participants—which included such perennial targets of environmentalists as the National Petroleum Refiners Association (NPRA)—promise not to challenge in court the outcome of any agreement to which they were a party and to support the agreement if one of the other participating companies filed suit to have the agreement overturned. Representatives of the NPRA and other business organizations have hailed this process as being more productive than the past practice of simply challenging agency regulations in court. This new approach has also been supported by environmental groups, such as the Environmental Defense Fund, which view such agreements as a way to conserve their own limited resources and to deal with potential pollution problems before they arise.

Bureaucrats Are Policymakers

Theories of public administration once assumed that bureaucrats do not make policy but only implement the laws and policies promulgated by the president and legislative bodies. A more realistic view of the role of the bureaucracy in policymaking, which is now held by most bureaucrats and elected officials, is that the agencies and departments of government play important roles in policymaking. As we have seen, many government rules, regulations, and programs are in fact initiated by the bureaucracy, based on its expertise and scientific studies. How a law passed by Congress eventually is translated into concrete action—from the forms to be filled out to decisions about who gets the benefits—usually is determined within each agency or department. Even the evaluation of whether a policy has achieved its purpose usually is based on studies that are commissioned and interpreted

Agents of the Treasury Department's Bureau of Alcohol, Tobacco, and Firearms (BATF) are photographed as they begin their raid on the Branch Davidian compound in Waco, Texas. News of the raid had leaked to the sect's leader, David Koresh, who ordered return fire. Several agents were killed or wounded. Some weeks later, BATF agents again tried to force Koresh and his followers out using tear gas. The compound exploded in flames and more than eighty sect members were killed. Congressional hearings in 1995 explored the decision making process that led to both unsuccessful BATF attempts.

IRON TRIANGLE
The three-way alliance among legislators, bureaucrats, and interest groups to make or preserve policies that benefit their respective interests.

by the agency administering the program. As discussed in the feature entitled *Politics and People: Attacking the Federal Government,* the functions carried out by bureaucrats have also made them targets for disaffected Americans.

Policy is made by several groups. The bureaucracy's policymaking role can be better understood by examining what has been called the **iron triangle.**

The Iron Triangle

Consider the bureaucracy within the Department of Agriculture. It consists of 125,640 individuals working directly for the federal government and thousands of others who, directly or indirectly, work as contractors, subcontractors, or consultants to the department. Now consider that there are various interest, or client, groups that are concerned with what the federal government does for farmers. These include the American Farm Bureau Federation, the National Cattleman's Association, the National Milk Producers Association, the Corn Growers Association, and the Citrus Growers Association. Finally, go directly to Congress, and you will see that there are two major congressional committees concerned with agriculture—the House Committee on Agriculture and the Senate Committee on Agriculture, Nutrition, and Forestry—each of which has several subcommittees.

Figure 12–4 is a schematic view of the iron triangle. This triangle, or subgovernment, is an alliance of mutual benefit among some unit within the bureaucracy, its interest or client group, and committees or subcommittees of Congress and their staff members. The workings of iron triangles are complicated, but they are well established in almost every subgovernment.

Consider again the Department of Agriculture. The secretary of agriculture is nominated by the president (and confirmed by the Senate) and is nominally the head of the Department of Agriculture. But that secretary cannot even buy a desk lamp if Congress does not approve the appropriations for the Department of Agriculture's budget. Within Congress, the responsibility

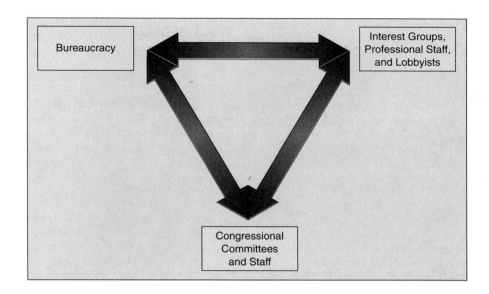

FIGURE 12–4   ■

The Iron Triangle

The players in the triangle include the congressional committees and staff, the bureaucrats, and the interest groups that share a common viewpont.

for considering the Department of Agriculture's request for funding belongs to the House and Senate appropriations committees and to the agriculture subcommittees under them. The members of those committees, most of whom represent agricultural states, have been around a long time. They have their own ideas about what amount of funds is appropriate for the Agriculture Department's budget. They have their own program concepts. They carefully scrutinize the ideas of the president and the secretary of agriculture.

Finally, the various interest groups—including producers of farm chemicals and farm machinery, consumer groups, agricultural cooperatives, grain dealers, and exporters—have vested interests in whatever the Department of Agriculture does and in whatever Congress lets the Department of Agriculture do. Those interests are well represented by the lobbyists who crowd the halls of Congress. Many lobbyists have been working for agricultural pressure groups for decades. They know the congressional committee members and Agriculture Department staff members extremely well and meet with them routinely. Industry representatives may be named to administrative positions in the Department of Agriculture, or they may be former bureaucrats. When the president proposes policies that benefit or harm the interests or constituents of groups of the triangle, they present a united front either to pass or to oppose such legislation.

Such iron triangles—of which there are many, not only on Capitol Hill, but also in state capitals—at times have completely thwarted efforts by the president to get the administration's programs enacted or to reform government.

CONGRESSIONAL CONTROL OF THE BUREAUCRACY

Although Congress is the ultimate repository of political power under the Constitution, many political pundits doubt whether Congress can

POLITICS AND PEOPLE
Attacking the Federal Government

On April 19, 1995, a homemade bomb concocted of fertilizer chemicals and fuel oil exploded in front of the lobby of the Oklahoma City federal office building. Delivered by a Ryder truck, the explosion caused the nine floors to pancake to the ground, totally destroying the building. By the time the search for victims was called off two weeks later, more than 160 persons were declared dead and hundreds were treated for injuries. Perhaps the most shocking scenes from the disaster were those of the children in the day-care center who were killed or injured by the blast.

Most of us think of the federal government as located in Washington, D.C. The bombing of the Alfred P. Murrah Federal Building reminded the nation that the majority of federal bureaucrats work in their home towns, located in almost every major city in the country. These employees of the national government issue Social

meaningfully control the burgeoning federal bureaucracy. These commentators forget that Congress has the power of the purse and could, theoretically, refuse to authorize or appropriate money for a particular agency. Whether Congress would actually take such a drastic measure in exercising its responsibility of legislative oversight would depend on the circumstances. It is clear, however, that Congress does have the legal authority to decide whether to fund or not to fund administrative agencies.

POLITICS AND PEOPLE
Attacking the Federal Government—continued

Security numbers and determine benefits for retirees, work with veterans, recruit members of the armed forces, investigate drug and tax violations, and enforce agricultural regulations. Offices in the Oklahoma City Federal Building included branch offices of the Social Security Administration, the General Accounting Office, the Department of Housing and Urban Development, the Small Business Administration, the Drug Enforcement Agency, and the Department of Agriculture, among others. Perhaps the target of the bombing was the office of the Bureau of Alcohol, Tobacco, and Firearms, where the investigators who were involved in the Waco, Texas, incident worked. Perhaps the target was the federal bureaucracy itself.

The primary suspect in the bombing, Timothy McVeigh, was arrested on a minor traffic offense, in a town north of Oklahoma City a few hours after the explosion. After he was identified with the bombing, investigators learned that McVeigh was a man who violently objected to many of the actions of the federal government and who had been enraged by the federal officers' raid on the Waco, Texas, compound of the Branch Davidians. That raid,

which resulted in the fiery death of members of the sect, also had taken place on April 19th—two years earlier. Although none of the private militia groups or antigovernment sects claimed McVeigh as a member, it seemed clear that he shared some of their views.

Why do groups form based on hatred for the federal government? To the ordinary citizen who disagrees with some national laws or regulations, their hatred seems extreme. Most of the militia groups are made up of men and women who enjoy using high-powered weapons and participating in semi-military maneuvers as a hobby. They are all dedicated to the right to keep arms and oppose any legislation to control guns. Some of the militia and other "patriot" groups are genuinely convinced that the federal government intends to take away citizens' basic liberties. They may be fundamentalist Christians or neo-Nazis, or they may favor local control of public lands. Some of their members believe in an elaborate conspiracy theory of contemporary events. The United States, in their view, is going to surrender its sovereignty to the United Nations as part of a one-world government. The Bureau of Alcohol, Tobacco,

and Firearms will take away all weapons from citizens and kill those who resist.

The anger of individuals who share Timothy McVeigh's views increased after the federal raid on the Branch Davidian compound in Waco, Texas. They also saw the attack by federal agents on Idaho white separatist Randy Weaver, in which Weaver's wife and child were killed, as an unwarranted use of federal power. The passage of the Brady bill under the Clinton administration seemed to confirm this view.

The president and many members of Congress responded to the Oklahoma City bombing by proposing new legislation that would give more power to federal agencies to infiltrate and investigate such antigovernment groups. While such legislation may make it easier to prevent such tragedies as the Oklahoma City bombing, many liberals remember that the federal agencies used such powers to investigate protesters against the Vietnam War and civil rights groups in the 1960s and 1970s. Such legislation illustrates the constant tension between liberty and security within our society.

Creating Administrative Agencies

Nearly every administrative agency is created through an act of Congress. The legislation that results in the creation of an agency is usually proposed to address a pressing national problem. The Occupational Safety and Health Act of 1970, for example, was created to address the problem of workplace hazards. But the act itself would have been rendered nearly useless had it not included provisions for the creation of a regulatory agency, the

AUTHORIZATION
A formal declaration by a legislative committee that a certain amount of funding may be available to an agency. Some authorizations terminate in a year; others are renewable automatically without further congressional authorization.

APPROPRIATION
The passage, by Congress, of a spending bill, specifying the amount of authorized funds that actually will be allocated for an agency's use.

Occupational Safety and Health Administration (OSHA), to create and enforce safety standards. Although Congress delegated significant powers to OSHA in the enabling legislation, Congress did define the parameters within which the agency could operate.

Authorizing Funds

Once an agency is created, Congress must authorize funds for it. The **authorization** is a formal declaration by the appropriate legislative committee that a certain amount of funding may be available to the agency. The authorization itself may terminate in a year, or it may be renewed automatically without further action by Congress. The National Aeronautics and Space Administration (NASA) is one agency in which authorizations must be periodically renewed; Social Security, in contrast, is funded through a permanent authorization. Periodic authorizations enable Congress to exercise greater control over the spending programs of an agency, whereas permanent authorizations free Congress from the task of having to review the authorization each year. The drawback of permanent authorizations is that they can become almost impossible to control politically.

Appropriating Funds

After the funds are authorized, they must be appropriated by Congress. The appropriations committees of both the House and the Senate forward spending bills to their respective bodies. The **appropriation** of funds occurs when the final bill is passed. Congress is not required to appropriate the entire authorized amount. It may appropriate less if it so chooses. If the appropriated funds are substantially less than the authorized amount, however, it may signal that the agency's agenda soon may be revamped by Congress.

The space shuttle Discovery landing in the California desert. While the National Aeronautics and Space Administration works to build support for its programs in the future, many members of the public question the need for this expensive public program.

The Legislative Veto

The appropriations process is not the only way in which Congress can assert control over federal agencies. Congress also may try to limit the power of executive agencies through the use of a **legislative veto,** a procedural device by which Congress requires that actions by the executive branch be placed before Congress for a specified period of time before becoming effective. During that time, Congress may disapprove the action by a vote of the House, the Senate, or both. In general, the legislative veto has been used by Congress as a way to assert greater control over the president's conduct of foreign policy.

In 1983, the United States Supreme Court declared legislative vetoes to be unconstitutional in the case of *Immigration and Naturalization Service v. Chadha.*[8] The Court's decision was apparently not the last word on the subject, however, because Congress has since passed laws that contain provisions for legislative vetoes. How this particular legislative device will fare if it is challenged legally in the future remains to be seen. But the precedent set by the *Chadha* case indicates that Congress should not rely too heavily on legislative vetoes to control the federal bureaucracy.

Investigations and Hearings

Congressional committees conduct investigations and hold hearings to oversee an agency's actions, reviewing them to ensure compliance with congressional intentions. The agency's officers and employees can be ordered to testify before a committee about the details of an action. Through these oversight activities, especially in the questioning and commenting by members of the House or Senate during the hearings, Congress indicates its positions on specific programs and issues. Congress can also ask the General Accounting Office (GAO) to investigate particular agency actions. The Congressional Budget Office (CBO) also conducts oversight studies. The results of a GAO or CBO study may encourage Congress to hold further hearings or make changes in the law. Even if a law is not changed explicitly by Congress, however, the views expressed in any investigations and hearings are taken seriously by agency officials, who often act on those views.

THE BUREAUCRACY: UNFINISHED WORK

Given the swelling of the national debt and controversies over government regulations, reforming the bureaucracy will be serious unfinished business as long as we have a representative democratic form of government. The way members of the House and Senate get reelected and the way in which lobbyists fit into that process practically guarantee that the bureaucracy will never be reformed completely.

This does not mean that we will not see improvements. Indeed, competition in the private marketplace is forcing changes on some federal government institutions. For example, the efficiency of private overnight delivery

8. 462 U.S. 919 (1983).

LEGISLATIVE VETO
A procedural device that allows Congress to veto executive actions before they become effective and thus control, to some extent, the bureaucracy.

services, such as Federal Express, Airborne, and United Parcel Service (UPS), has forced many changes on the U.S. Postal Service. Increasingly, the use of fax machines and high-speed modems also has put more pressure on the U.S. Postal Service to become more efficient. Such changes are bound to continue as communications technology improves.

The actual job of the federal bureaucracy, of course, will never disappear. Federal agencies are the primary means by which the laws of Congress are put into practice. This "gap-filling" power gives federal agencies significant discretion to make policy. Such policymaking has certain advantages: Bureaucrats are often specialists in their fields and are more knowledgeable than members of Congress about specific issues relating to the legislation passed by Congress.

GETTING INVOLVED
What the Government Knows about You

The federal government collects billions of pieces of information on tens of millions of Americans each year. These are stored in files and gigantic computers and often are exchanged among agencies. You probably have at least several federal records (for example, those in the Social Security Administration; the Internal Revenue Service; and, if you are a male, the Selective Service).

The 1966 Freedom of Information Act requires that the federal government release, at your request, any identifiable information it has in the administrative agencies of the executive branch. This information can be about you or about any other subject. Ten categories of material are exempted, however (classified material, confidential material dealing with trade secrets, internal personnel rules, personal medical files, and the like). To request material, you must write the Freedom of Information Act officer directly at the agency in question (say, the Department of Education). You must also have a relatively specific idea about the document or information you wish to obtain.

A second law, the Privacy Act of 1974, gives you access specifically to information the government may have collected about you. This is a very impor-

tant law, because it allows you to review your records on file with federal agencies (for example, with the Federal Bureau of Investigation) and to check those records for possible inaccuracies. Cases do exist in which two people with similar or the same names have had their records confused. In some cases, innocent persons have had the criminal records of another person erroneously inserted into their files.

If you wish to look at any records or find out if an agency has a record on you, write to the agency head or Privacy Act officer, and address your letter to the specific agency. State that "under the provisions of the Privacy Act of 1974, 5 U.S.C. 522a, I hereby request a copy of (or access to) _____ ." Then describe the record that you wish to investigate.

If you have trouble finding out about your records or wish to locate an attorney in Washington, D.C., to help you with this matter, you can contact the following:

Lawyer Referral Service
Washington Bar Association
1819 H St. N.W., Suite 300
Washington, DC 20036
202-223-1484

KEY TERMS

acquisitive model   427

appropriation   448

authorization   448

bureaucracy   425

cabinet department   429

capture   433

Civil Service Commission   439

garbage can model   427

government corporation   435

Government in the Sunshine
  Act   440

Hatch Act (Political Activities
  Act)   439

independent executive
  agency   429

independent regulatory
  agency   430

iron triangle   444

legislative veto   449

line organization   429

merit system   438

monopolistic model   427

natural aristocracy   437

Pendleton Act (Civil Service
  Reform Act)   438

privatization, or contracting
  out   440

spoils system   438

sunset legislation   440

Weberian model   426

whistleblower   441

 CHAPTER SUMMARY

1. Presidents have long complained about their inability to control the federal bureaucracy. There is no reference to the bureaucracy itself in the Constitution, but Article II gives the president the power to appoint officials to execute the laws of the United States. Most scholars cite Article II as the constitutional basis for the federal bureaucracy.

2. Bureaucracies are rigid hierarchical organizations in which the tasks and powers of lower-level employees are defined clearly. Job specialties and extensive procedural rules set the standards for behavior. Bureaucracies are the primary form of organization of most major corporations and universities.

3. Several theories have been offered to explain bureaucracies. The Weberian model posits that bureaucracies have developed into centralized hierarchical structures in response to the increasing demands placed on governments by their citizens. The acquisitive model views top-level bureaucrats as pressing for ever greater funding, staffs, and privileges to augment their own sense of power and security. The monopolistic model focuses on the environment in which most government bureaucracies operate, stating that bureaucracies are inefficient and excessively costly to operate because they often have no competitors. Finally, the garbage can model posits that bureaucracies are rudderless organizations that flounder about in search of solutions to problems.

4. Since the founding of the United States, the federal bureaucracy has grown from 50 to approximately three million employees (excluding the military). Federal, state, and local employees together make up some 14 percent of the nation's civilian labor force. The federal bureaucracy consists of fourteen cabinet departments, as well as numerous independent executive agencies, independent regulatory agencies, and government corporations. These entities enjoy varying degrees of autonomy, visibility, and political support.

5. A self-sustaining federal bureaucracy of career civil servants was formed during Thomas Jefferson's presidency. Andrew Jackson implemented a spoils system through which he appointed his own political supporters. A civil service based on professionalism and merit was the goal of the Civil Service Reform Act of 1883. Concerns that the civil service be freed from the pressures of politics prompted the passage of the Hatch Act in 1939.

6. There have been many attempts to make the federal bureaucracy more open, efficient, and responsive to the needs of U.S. citizens. The most important attempts have included sunshine and sunset laws, privatization, schemes to provide incentives for increased productivity and efficiency, and protection for whistleblowers.

7. Congress delegates much of its authority to federal agencies when it creates new laws. The bureaucrats who run these agencies may become important policymakers, because Congress has neither the time nor the technical expertise to oversee the administration of its laws. In the agency rule-making process, a proposed regulation is published. A comment period follows, during which interested parties may offer suggestions for changes. Because companies have challenged many regulations in court, federal agencies are now trying to engage such interested parties in the drafting of certain regulations.

8. Congress exerts ultimate control over all federal agencies, because it controls the federal government's purse strings. It also establishes the general guidelines by which regulatory agencies must abide. The appropriations process may also provide a way to send messages of approval or disapproval to particular agencies, as do congressional hearings and investigations relating to agency actions.

 ## QUESTIONS FOR REVIEW AND DISCUSSION

1. The size of the federal bureaucracy has been declining in recent years. Yet the total size of the government at all levels has risen. Does it matter to individuals which part of the government bureaucracy is growing and which part is not? If so, why? If not, why not?
2. How do the interests of private businesses and individuals help create inefficiency in government?
3. What might some of the conflicts be between different bureaucracies within the federal government? [Hint: Do the Central Intelligence Agency (CIA) and the Federal Bureau of Investigation (FBI) cooperate smoothly?]

4. "Congress purposely creates vague laws that the federal bureaucracy must interpret. In this way, members of Congress make sure that they always have areas in the economy in which they can intervene to help voters in their jurisdictions." Do you agree or disagree with this quote? Why would Congress purposely make vague laws?
5. The U.S. Postal Service is a government corporation. How does this corporation differ from a private, non-government corporation?

 ## LOGGING ON: THE BUREAUCRACY

Vice President Al Gore's report on reinventing government has the potential to alter the structure of the bureaucracy and to have a huge impact on the way our federal government does business. For information on the proposal to reinvent government, access

rego-1@pandora.sf.ca.us

The Library of Congress is an excellent source for information on the federal government. To use this source, access

riceinfo.rice.edu

and go to **Federal Government Information from Library of Congress.** To find information about the numerous agencies of the federal government, go to **United States Federal Register.**

Every year, the government publishes thousands of reports on virtually every topic imaginable. To look up government information researched and produced by government agencies and departments, use the University of Minnesota **gopher** at

gopher.micro.umn.edu

and choose **Libraries/Information from US Federal Government.**
The information is categorized by source.

A good source for other information on just about anything in
the federal government is provided by the National Science
Foundation; access

stis.nsf.gov

and, by choosing **Other U.S. Government Gopher Servers,** you can
log on to a vast number of government-sponsored **gophers** and find
endless amounts of information.

If you want to find out what is going on in our government
agencies, you may want to look into the following service:

clari.news.gov.agency

You can find information there on education reform from the
Department of Education or housing news from the Department of
Housing and Urban Development (HUD).

Maybe you are involved in student government and would like
to know what student leaders from across the country think
about the current hot topics for students. If so, access

bit.listserv.sganet

 ## SELECTED REFERENCES

Burnham, David. *A Law unto Itself: The IRS and the Abuse of Power*. New York: Random House, 1990. This is a very critical study of the role of the Internal Revenue Service, the most powerful and least accountable enforcement agency in the federal government.

Downs, Anthony. *Inside Bureaucracy*. Boston: Little, Brown, 1967. In this classic work, Downs provides an economist's explanation of why the bureaucracy is what it is and why bureaucrats and their agencies conduct themselves as they do.

Dunleavy, Patrick. *Democracy, Bureaucracy, and Public Choice: Economic Approaches in Political Science*. Englewood Cliffs, N.J.: Prentice-Hall, 1994. The author examines the public choice theory of bureaucracy and shows how the public choice model can help predict governmental actions.

Eisner, Marc Allen. *Regulatory Politics in Transition*. Baltimore, Md.: Johns Hopkins University Press, 1993. The author argues that the only way to understand the importance of regulatory policy fully is to understand the policy shifts that have occurred during the Progressive period (1890–1920), during the New Deal (1932–1945), and today. He argues that the 1960s and 1970s brought about a new social structure in which policies addressed the social consequences of economic activities in the areas of occupational health and safety, as well as environmental protection. He then claims that there was

an efficiency regime that occurred after the 1970s, when the competence of the government and its processes to perform its tasks were under scrutiny.

Mieczkowski, Bogdan. *Dysfunctional Bureaucracy*. Lanham, Md.: University Press of America, 1991. This book looks at the history of bureaucracy through the ages, its present forms both in America and abroad, and the conditions under which a functional bureaucracy becomes dysfunctional.

Robinson, Glen. *American Bureaucracy*. Ann Arbor, Mich.: University of Michigan Press, 1991. Robinson states that all public power must at some point rest on a justification—a legitimacy that goes beyond the collection of voting preferences. He discusses the methods by which the "administrative state" has become a dominant political and legal force in the life of all Americans.

Schoenbrod, David. *Power without Responsibility*. New Haven, Conn.: Yale University Press, 1993. The author claims that the president and Congress do not make laws that govern us but rather give bureaucrats the power to make laws through agency regulations. He argues that delegation then allows the president and Congress to wield power by pressuring agency lawmakers in private and at the same time, to shed responsibility by avoiding the need personally to support or oppose these "laws."

13
The Judiciary

CHAPTER OUTLINE

WHAT IF . . .
Federal Judges Were Elected?

It is commonly argued that the federal judiciary is, and many say ought to be, insulated from the fierce winds of politics. The notion of a Supreme Court justice's having to go out to the populace to attempt to save his or her job on the Court every few years would be unseemly to many Americans. Although there certainly is a lot to be said for having the federal courts act without regard to politics, it must be kept in mind that judges in most state court systems have long been elected.

Many state judicial officers would not be in power except by the will of the voters. Even appointed judges, such as the justices on the United States Supreme Court, are nominated to office through the highly political apparatus of presidential appointment, followed by either the confirmation or rejection of that nomination by the U.S. Senate. Moreover, judges on the federal courts are not necessarily out of tune with changing political attitudes.

There is the general sense among judicial experts, as expressed pointedly by the humorist Finley Peter Dunne, that "th' Supreme Court follows th' iliction returns." In fact, the surest way to get a federal judiciary that is to your liking politically is to vote for presidents and U.S. senators who have taken campaign positions in support of hiring judges with certain specific views on major issues. The federal courts, in this sense, have always been part of the electoral process.

What might happen if we did elect federal judges, up to and including the Supreme Court justices? One possibility is that the public's wishes—as measured, for example, in public opinion polls or in national referenda on key issues—could be put into effect more rapidly and more certainly. If strong majorities of the public were to favor, say, a federal flag-burning law or an end to legalized abortion, that is the way the courts might be expected to rule. The uneven track record of our Congress and presidents in translating popular will into public policy, however, suggests that success through this process is not at all assured.

Another real possibility is that the federal judiciary would become as thoroughly influenced by special interest groups (such as large corporations, labor unions, or ideologically motivated political action committees) as the Congress and the presidency are. That would undoubtedly increase the cost of the electoral process overall, as judicial candidates would be added to those running for legislative and executive office who seek millions of dollars from organized interests. Judges might even run on "tickets" with candidates for the presidency or for other offices, so that when you voted for a new team in the White House, you also would be voting for a set of judges.

Think, too, about what might happen if your judicial candidates lost and you, as, say, a registered Republican, were in court against a Democrat and had to have your case argued before a panel of Democratic judges. The federal judicial system as it is currently constituted is, of course, not always fair or free of bias. Nonetheless, the chances that overt partisanship might enter into the administration of justice might increase the likelihood of decisions that were arbitrary and capricious or vindictive against the losing party.

Would the political affiliation of an elected judge make any difference in how he or she decided cases? After all, judges are supposed to rule on issues of law—not advance their own personal political agenda. But judges are human, and their court rulings are colored to varying degrees by their political and ideological convictions. Many people would not be surprised to find that Republican judges have been more conservative than their Democratic counterparts, particularly on issues relating to the rights of criminal defendants and to abortion.

Keep in mind, though, that many of the decisions that are made by judges are about obscure clauses in tax laws, bureaucratic regulations, or other complicated points regarding statutes and rules that even expert lawyers cannot disentangle. Voters would not pay attention to these arcane arguments and would probably vote much as they do for congressional representatives or U.S. senators. In other words, the candidate's party label (if the elections were partisan), personality, and name recognition would probably decide most elections.

---

1. Who might benefit if federal judges were popularly elected?
2. Is it possible for any judiciary to be free of political motivation?

This chapter's opening *What If . . .* examined a hypothetical federal judiciary in which judges and justices are elected rather than appointed. Of course, the federal judiciary is 100 percent appointed in the United States, but that does not mean the judicial branch of the federal government is apolitical. Indeed, our courts play a larger role in making public policy than do courts in any other country in the world today. This quasi-legislative role was not envisioned by the framers of the Constitution, who were concerned primarily with abuses of power by the national government. Rather, the role evolved over time, particularly after Chief Justice John Marshall used the doctrine of judicial review to resolve the impasse in *Marbury v. Madison* (see the *Politics and the Law* on pages 460 and 461 for a discussion of this famous case).

As Alexis de Tocqueville, a nineteenth-century French commentator on American society, noted, "scarcely any political question arises in the United States that is not resolved, sooner or later, into a judicial question."[1] Our judiciary forms part of our political process. The instant that judges interpret the law, they become actors in the political arena—policymakers working within a political institution. As such, the most important political force within our judiciary is the United States Supreme Court. Because of its preeminence, we devote the major portion of this chapter to it. The remainder of the chapter deals with the lower federal courts and the state court systems.

THE FOUNDATION OF AMERICAN LAW: THE COURTS AND *STARE DECISIS*

Because of our colonial heritage, most of American law is based on the English legal system. In 1066, the Normans conquered England, and William the Conqueror and his successors began the process of unifying the country under their rule. One of the ways they did this was to establish the king's courts, or *curia regis*. Before the conquest, disputes had been settled according to local custom. The king's courts sought to establish a common or uniform set of rules for the whole country. As the number of courts and cases increased, portions of the more important decisions of each year were gathered together and recorded in *Year Books*. Judges settling disputes similar to ones that had been decided before used the *Year Books* as the basis for their decisions. If a case was unique, judges had to create new laws, but they based their decisions on the general principles suggested by earlier cases. The body of judge-made law that developed under this system is still used today and is known as the **common law**.

The practice of deciding new cases with reference to former decisions— that is, according to **precedent**—became a cornerstone of the English and American judicial systems and is embodied in the doctrine of *stare decisis* ("to stand on decided cases"). The rule of *stare decisis* performs many useful functions. First, it helps the courts to be more efficient. It would be time consuming if each judge had to establish reasons for deciding what the law should be for each case brought before the court. If other courts have confronted the same issue and reasoned through the case carefully, their

COMMON LAW
Judge-made law that originated in England from decisions shaped according to prevailing custom. Decisions were applied to similar situations and gradually became common to the nation. Common law forms the basis of legal procedures in the fifty states.

PRECEDENT
A court rule bearing on subsequent legal decisions in similar cases. Judges rely on precedents in deciding cases.

STARE DECISIS
To stand on decided cases; the policy of courts to follow precedents established by past decisions.

---

1. Alexis de Tocqueville, *Democracy in America* (New York: Harper & Row, 1966), p. 248.

opinions can serve as guides. Second, *stare decisis* creates a more uniform system. All courts try to follow precedent, and thus different courts often use the same rule of law. (Some variations occur, however, because different states and regions follow different precedents.) Also, the rule of precedent tends to neutralize the personal prejudices of individual judges to the degree that they feel obliged to use precedent as the basis for their decision. Finally, the rule makes the law more stable and predictable than it otherwise would be. If the law on a subject is relatively well settled, someone bringing a case to court usually can rely on the court to make a decision based on what the law has been.

MORE RECENT SOURCES OF LAW

Today, courts have sources other than precedents to consider when making their decisions. These sources are described below.

Constitutions

The constitutions of the federal government and the states set forth the general organization, powers, and limits of government. The U.S. Constitution is the supreme law of the land. A law in violation of the Constitution, no matter what its source, may be declared unconstitutional and thereafter cannot be enforced. Similarly, the state constitutions are supreme within their respective borders (unless they conflict with the U.S. Constitution or laws and treaties made in accordance with it). The Constitution thus defines the political playing field on which state and federal powers are reconciled. The idea that the Constitution should be supreme in certain matters stemmed from widespread dissatisfaction with the weak federal government that had existed previously under the Articles of Confederation adopted in 1781 (see Chapter 2).

Statutes and Administrative Regulations

ADMINISTRATIVE AGENCY
An agency that forms part of the executive branch, an independent regulatory agency, or an independent agency (for example, the Federal Trade Commission, the Securities and Exchange Commission, and the Federal Communications Commission). State and local governments also have administrative agencies.

Although the English common law provides the basis for both our civil and criminal legal systems, statutes (laws enacted by legislatures) increasingly have become important in defining the rights and obligations of individuals. Federal statutes may relate to any subject that is a concern of the federal government and may cover areas ranging from hazardous wastes to federal taxation. Statutes are often extremely detailed and complex on both the federal and state levels. State statutes include criminal codes, commercial laws, and laws relating to a variety of other matters. Cities, counties, and other local political bodies also pass statutes, which are called ordinances. These ordinances may deal with such things as zoning schemes and public safety. Rules and regulations issued by **administrative agencies** are another source of law.

Legislative bodies and administrative agencies have assumed an ever-increasing share of lawmaking. Today, much of the work of courts consists of interpreting these laws and regulations and applying them to circumstances in cases before the courts.

A jury is being sworn in. Most jury trials have between six and twelve jurors. Some trials are held without juries.

Judicial Review

The process for deciding whether a law is contrary to the mandates of the Constitution is known as **judicial review**. The power of judicial review is mentioned nowhere in the U.S. Constitution. As *The Federalist Papers* indicate, however, those in attendance at the Constitutional Convention probably expected that the courts would have some authority to review the legality of acts by the executive and legislative branches. Otherwise, there would be no one to decide whether Congress or the executive branch was overstepping its bounds. But it fell to the Supreme Court itself and its chief justice, John Marshall, to claim this power. The doctrine of judicial review was first established in the famous case of *Marbury v. Madison*, which determined that the Supreme Court had the power to decide that a law passed by Congress violated the Constitution:

> It is emphatically the province and duty of the Judicial Department to say what the law is. Those who apply the rule to a particular case, must of necessity expound and interpret that rule. If two laws conflict with each other, the courts must decide on the operation of each.[2]

The Supreme Court has ruled parts or all of acts of Congress to be unconstitutional only about 150 times in its history. State laws, however, have

JUDICIAL REVIEW
The power of the courts to declare acts of the executive and legislative branches unconstitutional; first established in *Marbury v. Madison*.

---

2. 1 Cranch 137 (1803).

POLITICS AND THE LAW
Judicial Review—*Marbury v. Madison* (1803)

In the edifice of American public law, the *Marbury v. Madison* decision in 1803 can be viewed as the keystone of the constitutional arch. The story is often told, and for a reason—it shows how seemingly insignificant cases can have important and enduring results.

Consider the facts behind *Marbury v. Madison*. John Adams had lost his bid for reelection to Thomas Jefferson in 1800. Adams, a Federalist, thought the Jeffersonian Republicans (Anti-Federalists) would weaken the power of the national government by asserting states' rights. He also feared the Anti-Federalists' antipathy toward business. During the final hours of Adams's presidency, he worked feverishly to "pack" the judiciary with loyal Federalists by giving what came to be called "midnight appointments," just before Jefferson took office.

All of the judicial appointments had to be certified and delivered. The task of delivery fell on Adams's secretary of state, John Marshall. Out of the fifty-nine midnight ap-

John Marshall

James Madison

pointments, Marshall delivered only forty-two. He assumed that the remaining seventeen would be sent out by Jefferson's new secretary of state, James Madison. Of course, the new administration refused to cooperate in packing the judiciary: Jefferson refused to deliver the remaining commissions. William Marbury, along with three other Federalists to whom the commissions had not been delivered, de-

cided to sue. The suit was brought directly to the Supreme Court, seeking a writ of *mandamus* (an order issued by a court to compel the performance of an act), authorized by the Judiciary Act of 1789.

As fate would have it, the man responsible for the lawsuit, John Marshall, had stepped down as Adams's secretary of state only to become chief justice. He was now in a position to decide the case for

been declared unconstitutional by the Court much more often—about 1,000 times. Most of these rulings date from the period after the Civil War, before which time only two acts of Congress were declared unconstitutional. There have been two periods of relatively extensive use of the process of judicial negation—from 1921 to 1940, when a conservative Court upheld private interests over public statutes, and in the 1960s and 1970s, when more liberal justices upheld individual and group rights to racial and political equality.

A significant modern example of judicial review was the Supreme Court's ruling in *Term Limits v. Arkansas*,[3] a case decided in 1995. The Court held that an Arkansas state constitutional amendment limiting the terms of congresspersons was unconstitutional. As a consequence of this decision, laws establishing term limits in twenty-three other states were also invalidated.

---

3. *115 S.Ct. 1842 (1995).*

Politics and the Law
Judicial Review—*Marbury v. Madison* (1803)—Continued

which he was responsible.* Marshall was faced with a dilemma: If he ordered the commissions delivered, the new secretary of state could simply refuse. The Court had no way to compel action, because it has no police force. Also, Congress was controlled by the Jeffersonian Republicans. It might impeach Marshall for such an action.† But if Marshall simply allowed Secretary of State Madison to do as he wished, the Court's power would be eroded severely.

Marshall stated for the unanimous Court that Jefferson and Madison had acted incorrectly in refusing to deliver Marbury's commission. Marshall also stated, however, that the highest court did not have the power to act as a court of original jurisdiction (the authority

*Today, any justice who has been involved in an issue before the Court would probably disqualify himself or herself because of a conflict of interest.
†In fact, in 1805, Congress did impeach Supreme Court Justice Samuel Chase, a Federalist, though he was not convicted. The charge was abusive behavior under the Sedition Act.

of a court to hear a case in the first instance) in this particular case, because the section of the law that gave it original jurisdiction was unconstitutional. The Judiciary Act of 1789 specified that the Supreme Court could issue writs of *mandamus* as part of its original jurisdiction, but Marshall pointed out that Article III of the Constitution, which spelled out the Supreme Court's original jurisdiction, did not mention writs of *mandamus*. In other words, Congress did not have the right to expand the Court's jurisdiction, so this section of the Judiciary Act of 1789 was unconstitutional and hence void.

The decision avoided a showdown between the Federalists and the Jeffersonian Republicans. The power of the Supreme Court was enlarged.

Was the Marshall Court's assumption of judicial review power justified by the Constitution? Whether it was or not, *Marbury v. Madison* confirmed a doctrine that was part of the legal tradition of the time.

Indeed, judicial review was a major premise (although an unarticulated one) on which the movement to draft constitutions and bills of rights ultimately was based, as well as a part of the legal theory underlying the revolution of 1776. During the decade before the adoption of the federal Constitution, cases in at least eight states involved the power of judicial review. Also, the Supreme Court had considered the constitutionality of an act of Congress in *Hylton v. United States,* in which Congress's power to levy certain taxes was challenged.‡ But because that particular act was ruled constitutional rather than unconstitutional, this first federal exercise of true judicial review was not clearly recognized as such.

In any event, because Marshall masterfully fashioned a decision that did not require anyone to do anything, there was no practical legal point to challenge. It still stands today as a judicial and political masterpiece.

‡3 Dallas 171 (1796).

Other Judicial Powers

Besides the power of judicial review, the courts have other powers, including the power to issue a warrant, a writ of *habeas corpus,* a writ of *mandamus,* or an injunction. A court also has the power to hold a party in contempt.

A warrant is a court order authorizing or commanding certain action. A court uses a warrant to bring a defendant within the court's **jurisdiction** and initiate proceedings involving him or her. For example, a judge issues an arrest warrant to order a police officer to arrest a person and bring him or her into court.

With a writ of *habeas corpus,* a judge can review the legality of any form of loss of personal liberty (such as imprisonment in a jail or detention in a police station). The writ orders the person responsible for the detention (such as the prison warden) to bring to court the person being held. A court

JURISDICTION
The authority of a court to decide certain cases. Not all courts have the authority to decide all cases. Where a case arises and what its subject matter is are two jurisdictional factors.

WRIT OF *MANDAMUS*
An order issued by a court to compel the performance of an act.

issues a **writ of *mandamus*** to a lower court or a government official to require the performance of a duty prescribed by law and not subject to discretion. Only ministerial acts (simple duties allowing for no exercise of discretion) are subject to control by this writ.

An injunction is a court's order to a party to do something or to stop doing something. Injunctions are used to enforce the law. For example, in the 1950s, the Supreme Court ordered the lower federal courts to eliminate segregated school systems. The courts were told to issue injunctions, if necessary, to close the schools and redraw school district lines.

When a party does not follow a court's order, the court can cite him or her for contempt. A party who commits *civil* contempt (failing to comply with a court's order for the benefit of another party to the proceeding) can be taken into custody, fined, or both, until the party complies with the court's order. A party who commits *criminal* contempt (obstructing the administration of justice or bringing the court into disrepect) can also be taken into custody and fined but cannot avoid the punishment by complying with a previous order.

OUR COURT SYSTEM TODAY

TRIAL COURT
The court in which most cases usually begin and in which questions of fact are examined.

The United States has a dual court system. There are state courts and federal courts. Each of the fifty states, as well as the District of Columbia, has its own fully developed, independent system of courts. The federal court system derives its power from the U.S. Constitution, Article III, Section 1.

Both the federal and state court systems have several tiers of authority. Figure 13–1 shows the components of the federal judiciary. There are ninety-six federal district courts, which are the basic **trial courts** in the federal system. The majority of cases that are appropriately within the jurisdiction of the federal courts start here.[4]

There are other federal trial courts. These have special, or limited, jurisdiction. They include the tax courts, which decide cases involving taxpayers' challenges to tax assessments, and the bankruptcy courts, which interpret and apply the federal bankruptcy laws. The U.S. Court of Federal Claims hears lawsuits against the government based on the Constitution, and federal laws and contracts. The U.S. Court of Federal Claims also decides cases concerning salaries of public officials, the payment of money to persons unjustly imprisoned for federal crimes, and some Native-American claims. The U.S. Court of International Trade hears cases involving taxes on imported merchandise.

When cases that have been decided in a federal trial court are appealed, they usually go to one of the judicial circuit courts of appeals (including the federal circuit court of appeals), the boundaries of which are outlined in Figure 13–2. Under normal circumstances, the decisions of the courts of appeals are final, but appeal to the United States Supreme Court is possible. At the top of the federal judiciary is the Supreme Court of the United States. According to the language of Article III of the U.S. Constitution, there can only be one Supreme Court, with all other courts in the federal system "inferior" to it. (See this chapter's *Politics and the Law: The Office of the Special*

---

4. The jurisdiction of the federal courts is limited by Article III, Section 2, of the U.S. Constitution.

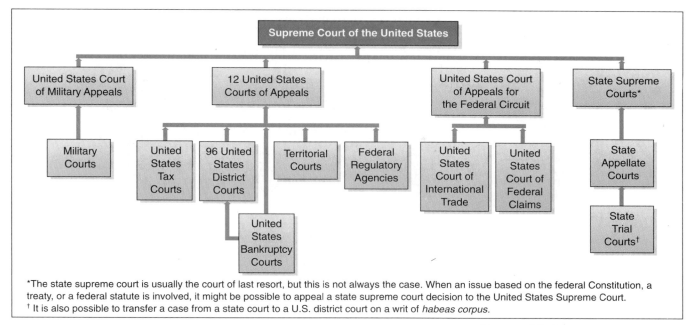

Supreme Court of the United States

- United States Court of Military Appeals
  - Military Courts
- 12 United States Courts of Appeals
  - United States Tax Courts
  - 96 United States District Courts
    - United States Bankruptcy Courts
  - Territorial Courts
  - Federal Regulatory Agencies
- United States Court of Appeals for the Federal Circuit
  - United States Court of International Trade
  - United States Court of Federal Claims
- State Supreme Courts*
  - State Appellate Courts
    - State Trial Courts†

*The state supreme court is usually the court of last resort, but this is not always the case. When an issue based on the federal Constitution, a treaty, or a federal statute is involved, it might be possible to appeal a state supreme court decision to the United States Supreme Court.

† It is also possible to transfer a case from a state court to a U.S. district court on a writ of *habeas corpus.*

FIGURE 13-1 ■

The Federal Court System

Prosecutor for information on a part of the judiciary that does not fit in with the regular system.)

State court systems are similar to the federal court system, except that only twenty-three states have intermediate courts of appeals, or **appellate courts,** between the trial courts (in which the majority of cases originate) and the highest reviewing courts of the states. Many cases that appear before trial courts require juries. A trial jury normally consists of six or twelve jurors, who determine the innocence or guilt of the defendant in criminal and civil trials. A **grand jury**, in contrast, is called for a *pretrial* proceeding. The grand jury consists of from six to twenty-three persons who are called to hear

APPELLATE COURT
A court having jurisdiction to review cases and issues that were originally tried in lower courts.

GRAND JURY
A jury called to hear evidence and determine whether indictments should be issued against persons suspected of having committed crimes.

Football superstar O. J. Simpson with two of his "dream team" lawyers. The public followed with great interest the pretrial and trial proceedings in Simpson's double-murder case during 1994 and 1995. He was acquitted in October of 1995.

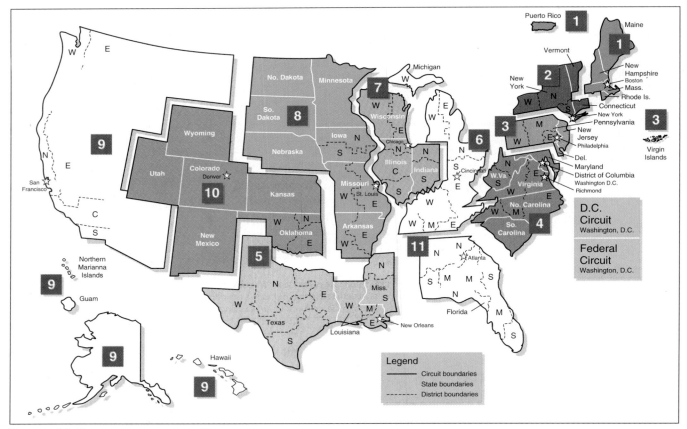

FIGURE 13-2

Geographic Boundaries of Federal Circuit Courts of Appeals

SOURCE: Administrative Office of the United States Courts, January 1983.

evidence and determine whether indictments should be issued against persons suspected of having committed a crime. Grand juries decide whether there is enough evidence to warrant a formal accusation by the state of wrongdoing; they do not determine guilt.

The decisions of each state's highest court on questions of state law are final. Only when issues relating to the U.S. Constitution or other federal laws are involved can the United States Supreme Court overrule a state court's decision. The United States Supreme Court has no power to hear appeals from a state supreme court concerning issues of purely state law. Recall that the Constitution reserves all powers to the states that are not expressly granted to the federal government. The federal courts, which derive their power from the Constitution, thus have no authority to rule on issues relating solely to state law.

THE SUPREME COURT—CHOOSING, HEARING, AND DECIDING CASES

Alexander Hamilton, writing in *Federalist Paper* No. 78, believed that the Supreme Court would be the "least dangerous branch" of the federal government, because it had no enforcement powers, nor could it raise money.

POLITICS AND THE LAW
The Office of the Special Prosecutor

A special part of our judicial system involves the special prosecutor, or independent counsel. During the 1970s, the most well-known use of a special prosecutor was during the Watergate affair, during which Richard Nixon first named Archibald Cox to the position, then refused to release tapes to him. Nixon fired Cox and named Leon Jaworski as special prosecutor. Since then, special prosecutors have been appointed to investigate Jimmy Carter's White House chief of staff (1979) and national campaign manager (1980), Secretary of Labor Ray Donovan (1981), presidential counselor Ed Meese (1984), White House aide Michael Deaver (1986),

and others. The lengthiest investigation conducted by a special prosecutor involved the Iran-*contra* affair (discussed in Chapter 11), which ultimately cost the American taxpayers over $40 million.

When serious allegations against President Clinton and his wife were raised concerning their dealings with certain real estate transactions, named in general the Whitewater affair, a special investigator was again appointed. Attorney General Janet Reno named Robert Fiske as Whitewater independent counsel. He conducted an investigation over many months and was heavily

criticized by Republicans, who claimed that he was not "hard enough."

When the new Independent Counsel Act (the act creating the Office of the Special Prosecutor) became law in 1994, Janet Reno asked a three-judge panel to ratify Robert Fiske as Whitewater independent prosecutor. They refused and named instead Kenneth Starr, a high-ranking Bush-administration lawyer. Amid calls of partisanship—two of the three-member judicial panel were Republicans—Starr undertook a new investigation. It is still going on.

The other two branches had to cooperate with it, and the public had to accept its decisions, or the Supreme Court would be superfluous.

In the Court's earliest years, it appeared that Hamilton's prediction would come true. The first Supreme Court chief justice, John Jay, resigned to become governor of New York because he thought the Court would never play an important role in American society. The next chief justice, Oliver Ellsworth, quit to become envoy to France. In 1801, when the federal capital was moved to Washington, somebody forgot to include the Supreme Court in the plans. It met in the office of the clerk of the Senate until 1935.

Of the total number of cases that are decided each year, those reviewed by the Supreme Court represent less than one-half of 1 percent. Included in these, however, are decisions that profoundly affect our lives—even issues of life and death. In recent years, the United States Supreme Court has decided numerous issues, including issues involving capital punishment, affirmative action programs, abortion, busing, term limits for congresspersons, sexual harassment, and pornography. Because the Supreme Court exercises a great deal of discretion over the types of cases it hears, it can influence the nation's policies by issuing decisions in some types of cases and refusing to hear appeals in others, thereby allowing lower court decisions to stand.

Which Cases Reach the Supreme Court?

Many people are surprised to learn that in a typical case, there is no absolute right of appeal to the United States Supreme Court. The Supreme Court is given original, or trial court, jurisdiction in a small number of situations. Under Article III, Section 2, Paragraph 2, the Supreme Court has original jurisdiction in all cases affecting foreign diplomats and in all cases in which a state is a party. The Eleventh Amendment, passed in 1798, removed from the judicial power of the United States suits commenced by, or prosecuted against, citizens of another state or by citizens or subjects of any foreign nation. Therefore, the Supreme Court today rarely acts as a court of original jurisdiction except in cases involving suits by one state against another, such as suits relating to territorial disputes or cross-border pollution. In all other cases, its jurisdiction is appellate "with such Exceptions, and under such Regulations as the Congress shall make." Appellate jurisdiction means the authority of the Court to review decisions of a lower court. With the Judicial Improvements and Access to Justice Act of 1988, Congress made the Court's appellate jurisdiction almost entirely discretionary—the court can choose which cases it will decide.

WRIT OF *CERTIORARI*
An order issued by a higher court to a lower court to send up the record of a case for review. It is the principal vehicle for United States Supreme Court review.

Writ of *Certiorari*.   With a **writ of *certiorari*** (pronounced sur-shee-uh-*rah*-ree), the Supreme Court orders a lower court to send it the record of a case for review. A party can petition the Supreme Court to issue a writ of *certiorari*. Typically, however, only petitions that raise the possibility of important constitutional questions or problems of statutory interpretation are granted. Within these limits, the granting of *certiorari* (or "cert," as it is popularly called) is done entirely at the discretion of the Court and seems to depend on such factors as who the petitioners are, the kinds of issues involved, and the ideologies of the individual justices of the Court.

The following situations indicate when the Court will issue a writ, although they are not a limit on the Court's discretion:

1. When a state court has decided a substantial federal question that has not been determined by the Supreme Court before, or the state court has decided it in a way that is probably in disagreement with the trend of the Supreme Court's decisions.
2. When two federal courts of appeals are in disagreement with each other.
3. When a federal court of appeals has decided an important state question in conflict with state law, has decided an important federal question not yet addressed by the Supreme Court but that should be decided by the Court, has decided a federal question in conflict with applicable decisions of the Court, or has departed from the accepted and usual course of judicial proceedings.
4. When a federal court of appeals holds a state statute to be invalid because it violates federal law.
5. When the state's highest court holds a federal law invalid or upholds a state law that has been challenged as violating a federal law.
6. When a federal court holds an act of Congress unconstitutional and the federal government or one of its employees is a party.

More than 90 percent of the petitions for writs of *certiorari* are denied. A denial is not a decision on the merits of a case, nor does it indicate agreement with the lower court's opinion. (The judgment of the lower court remains in force, however.) Therefore, denial of the writ has no value as a precedent.[5] The Court will not issue a writ unless at least four justices approve of it. This is called the **rule of four.**[6]

RULE OF FOUR
A United States Supreme Court procedure requiring four affirmative votes to hear the case before the full Court.

---

5. *Singleton v. Commissioner of Internal Revenue*, 439 U.S. 940 (1978).
6. The "rule of four" is modified when seven or fewer justices participate, which occurs from time to time. When that happens, as few as three justices can grant *certiorari*.

Group-Sponsored Litigation.   In Chapter 7, we discussed the role of interest groups in the United States. Interest groups play an important role in our judicial system, because they **litigate**—bring to trial—or assist in litigating most cases of race or sex discrimination, virtually all civil liberties cases, and more than one-third of cases involving business matters. In 1928, for example, interest groups filed ***amicus curiae*** briefs in fewer than 2 percent of the cases decided by the Supreme Court, but more than 50 percent of these cases are accompanied by such briefs today.

Interest groups see litigation as a political strategy complementing other activities, such as helping individuals favorable to the groups' causes to be elected to Congress or to the presidency. There are numerous litigating organizations today, such as the Washington Legal Foundation, the Capital Legal Foundation, and the Pacific Legal Foundation (all of which normally seek pro-business judicial outcomes), and the Center for the Study of Responsive Law and the Public Interest Research Group (both of which normally seek pro-consumer and pro-environment judicial outcomes). The interest group (or the litigating organization it supports) will directly challenge a law or administrative ruling and take it to court. Alternatively, such a group may have an individual test a law in court, while the interest group lends financial and legal support to the case.

Sometimes interest groups will start a **class-action suit,** in which whatever the court decides will affect all members of a class similarly situated. Significant class-action suits were brought on behalf of individuals suffering injuries associated with the use of the Dalkon Shield; individuals suffering from asbestos-related injuries; and individuals claiming injuries associated with automobiles, tampons, and chemicals such as formaldehyde, diethylstilbestrol (DES), and Agent Orange—a chemical used during the Vietnam War (1964–1975). More recently, those suffering from alleged illnesses caused by breast implants won a class-action suit in 1994. The $4.25 billion class settlement was the largest in U.S. history.

The strategy of class-action lawsuits was pioneered by such groups as the National Association for the Advancement of Colored People (NAACP), the Legal Defense Fund, and the Sierra Club, whose members believed that the courts—rather than Congress—would offer the most sympathetic forum for their views.

Political Questions.   The Supreme Court (and other courts, too) will hear only what are called **justiciable disputes,** which are disputes that arise out of actual cases and that can be settled by legal methods. When the Court deems a dispute to be a **political question,** it will refuse to rule under the doctrine of political questions. Basically, any dispute deemed a political question by the Supreme Court is one that it declares should be decided by the executive branch, the legislative branch, or those two branches together. For many years, for example, the Supreme Court refused to rule on the constitutionality of laws concerning legislative apportionment (the shaping of electoral districts), even when these laws resulted in grossly obvious gerrymandering (reshaping a district to enhance the political support of one political party—see Chapter 10). It was not until 1962, in *Baker v. Carr,* that the doctrine of political questions was put aside.[7] No political scientist or

LITIGATE
To engage in a legal proceeding or seek relief in a court of law; to carry on a lawsuit.

AMICUS CURIAE BRIEF
Latin for "friend of the court"; refers here to a brief filed by a third party (a party not directly involved in the litigation) who has an interest in the outcome of the case. These briefs are documents filed with the court that contain legal arguments supporting a particular desired outcome in a case.

CLASS-ACTION SUIT
A lawsuit filed by an individual seeking damages for "all persons similarly situated."

JUSTICIABLE DISPUTE
A dispute that raises questions about the law and that is appropriate for resolution before a court of law.

POLITICAL QUESTION
An issue that a court believes should be decided by the executive or legislative branches.

---

7. 369 U.S. 186 (1962).

DID YOU KNOW . . .
That the chief justice of the United States Supreme Court has the same salary as the vice president of the United States?

ORAL ARGUMENTS
The verbal arguments presented in person by attorneys to an appellate court. Each attorney presents reasons to the court why the court should rule in his or her client's favor.

legal expert has been able to develop a consistent definition of *political questions* that applies to all of the reasoning of the Court. The doctrine of political questions represents a conscious decision by the federal courts *not* to become involved in disputes that are more properly left to the executive and legislative branches to resolve.

The Supreme Court at Work

The Supreme Court, by law, begins its regular annual term on the first Monday in October and usually adjourns in late June or early July of the next year. Special sessions may be held after the regular term is over, but only a few cases are decided in this way. More commonly, cases are carried over until the next regular session.

The United States Supreme Court normally does not hear any evidence, as is true with all appeals courts. The Court's consideration of a case is based on the abstracts, the record, and the briefs. The attorneys can present **oral arguments.** The Court hears oral arguments on Monday, Tuesday, Wednesday, and sometimes Thursday, usually for seven two-week sessions scattered from the first week in October to the end of April or the first week in May. Recesses are held between periods of oral argument to allow the justices to consider the cases and handle other Court business. Oral arguments run from 10 A.M. to noon and again from 1 to 3 P.M., with thirty minutes for each side unless a special exception is granted. All statements and the justices' questions are tape-recorded during these sessions. Unlike the practice in most courts, lawyers addressing the Supreme Court can be (and often are) questioned by the justices at any time during oral argument.

Deciding a Case: Private Research.   All of the crucial work on accepted cases is done through private research and reflection. Each justice is entitled to four law clerks, recent graduates of law schools, who undertake much of the research and preliminary drafting necessary for the justice to form an opinion. It is sometimes suspected that because of their extensive assistance, the law clerks form a kind of junior court in themselves, deciding the fate of appeals and petitions to the Court. Some disgruntled lawyers have even suggested that the Senate should no longer confirm the appointment of justices but rather the appointment of law clerks. Such criticism is probably too harsh. Clerks do help in screening the large volume of petitions and in the preliminary research work for cases under review, but the justices make the decisions.

Deciding a Case: The Friday Conference.   Each Friday during the annual Court term, the justices meet in conference to discuss cases then under consideration and to decide which new appeals and petitions the Court will accept. These conferences take place in the oak-paneled chamber and are strictly private—no stenographers, tape recorders, or video cameras are allowed. There used to be two pages in attendance who waited on the justices while they were in conference, but fear of information leaks caused the Court to stop this practice.[8]

8. Even though it turned out that one supposed information leak came from lawyers making educated guesses.

In the justices' conference, certain procedures traditionally are observed. On entering the room, each justice shakes hands with all present. The justices then sit by order of seniority around a large, rectangular table. Each case is discussed by each justice in that order, with the chief justice starting the discussion. The chief justice determines the order in which the cases are called, guides the discussion generally, and in most cases, sets the tone for the proceedings.

Starting with the Court of John Marshall, after each discussion, a vote was taken in reverse order of seniority. Today, the justices seldom vote formally. Since 1965, decisions have been announced on any day that they are ready to be released. They are usually presented orally, in summary form, in open session by the author of the decision. Other views may be stated by members who have written concurring or dissenting opinions. After the necessary editing and the publication of preliminary prints, the official Court decision is placed in the *United States Reports,* the official record of the Court's decisions, which is available in most college libraries. (See this chapter's *Logging On* to learn how you can access Supreme Court opinions via the Internet almost immediately after the decisions are announced.)

Cases that are brought on petition (or appeal) to the Court are scheduled for an oral argument or denied a hearing in a written "orders list" released on Mondays.

Decisions and Opinions.   When the Court has reached a decision, its opinion is written. The **opinion** contains the Court's reasons for its decision, the rules of law that apply, and the judgment. In general, the Court will not **reverse** findings of fact unless the findings are unsupported or contradicted by the evidence. Rather, it will review the record for errors of law. If the Supreme Court feels that a reversible error was committed during the trial or that the jury was instructed improperly, the judgment will be reversed. Sometimes the case will be **remanded** (sent back to the court that originally heard the case) for a new trial or other proceeding. In many cases, the decision of the lower court is **affirmed**, resulting in the enforcement of that court's judgment or decree.

The Court's written opinion sometimes is brief and unsigned; this is called a *per curiam* opinion. Often, it is long and is signed by all the justices who agree with it. Usually, when in the majority, the chief justice will write the opinion. Whenever the chief justice is in the minority, the senior justice on the majority side decides who writes the opinion.

There are four types of written opinions for any particular case decided by the Supreme Court. When all justices unanimously agree on an opinion, the opinion is written for the entire Court (all the justices) and can be deemed a **unanimous opinion.** When there is not a unanimous opinion, a **majority opinion** is written, outlining the views of the majority of the justices involved in the particular case. Often, one or more justices who feel strongly about making or emphasizing a particular point that is not made or emphasized in the unanimous or majority written opinion will write a **concurring opinion.** That means the justice writing the concurring opinion agrees (concurs) with the conclusion given in the unanimous or majority written opinion, but for different reasons. Finally, in other than unanimous

OPINION
The statement by a judge or a court of the decision reached in a case tried or argued before it. The opinion sets forth the law that applies to the case and details the legal reasoning on which the judgment was based.

REVERSE
To annul or make void a judgment on account of some error or irregularity.

REMAND
To send a case back to the court that originally heard it.

AFFIRM
To declare that a judgment is valid and must stand.

UNANIMOUS OPINION
An opinion or determination on which all judges agree.

MAJORITY OPINION
The views of the majority of the judges.

CONCURRING OPINION
A separate opinion, prepared by a judge who supports the decision of the majority of the court but who wants to make or clarify a particular point or to voice disapproval of the grounds on which the decision was made.

DISSENTING OPINION
A separate opinion in which a judge dissents from the conclusion reached by the majority of the court and expounds his or her own views about the case.

JUDICIAL IMPLEMENTATION
The way in which court decisions are translated into policy.

opinions, one or more dissenting opinions are usually written by those justices who do not agree with the majority. The **dissenting opinion** is important because it often forms the basis of the arguments used years later that cause the Court to reverse the previous decision and establish a new precedent.

After a Decision Is Reached

President Andrew Jackson was once supposed to have said, after Chief Justice John Marshall made an unpopular decision, that "John Marshall has made his decision; now let him enforce it."[9] This purported quote goes to the heart of **judicial implementation**, or the way in which court decisions are actually translated into policy and thereby affect the behavior of individuals, businesspersons, police personnel, and the like. The Court does not have the executive power to implement its decisions, nor does it have control of the budget to pay for such implementation when government funds are required. Other units of government have to carry out the Court's decisions.

That means that the process of judicial implementation may take time, or it may never occur at all. Prayers were banned in public schools in 1962, yet it was widely known that the ban was (and is still) ignored in many southern districts. After the Court ordered schools to desegregate "with all deliberate speed" in 1955,[10] the inflammatory rhetoric against desegregation expounded by the governor and state legislators in Little Rock, Arkansas, encouraged citizens to take the law into their own hands. A riot broke out in 1957, and the president finally decided to act. President Dwight Eisenhower federalized (subjected to federal authority) the state's national guard, which quelled the riot.

Initially, the media reporting on Supreme Court decisions provide the most widespread information about what the Court has decided. (Often, though, such paraphrased information may be inaccurate.) Those persons affected by Supreme Court decisions somehow have to become aware of their new-found rights (or of the stripping of their existing rights). For example, the Supreme Court, in *Miranda v. Arizona* in 1966, set guidelines for police questioning of suspects (see Chapter 4).[11] It has been estimated that it took seventeen months before all of the police departments around the country were aware of the decision, and it certainly took even longer for suspected criminals to be aware that they should be "read their *Miranda* rights."

THE SELECTION OF FEDERAL JUDGES

All federal judges are appointed. The Constitution, in Article II, Section 2, states that the president appoints the justices of the Supreme Court with the advice and consent of the Senate.[12] Congress has provided the same

9. The decision referred to was *Cherokee Nation v. Georgia,* 5 Pet. [a nineteenth-century reporter of Supreme Court cases] 1 (1831).
10. *Brown v. Board of Education,* 349 U.S. 294 (1955), the second *Brown* decision.
11. 384 U.S. 436 (1966).
12. The terms *justice* and *judge* are two designations given to judges in various courts. All members of the United States Supreme Court are referred to as *justices*. In most states' highest appellate courts, the formal title given to the judge is *justice* also, although the converse is true in the state of New York.

procedure for staffing other federal courts. This means that the Senate and the president jointly decide who shall be a federal judge, no matter what the level.

There are over eight hundred federal judgeships in the United States. Once appointed to such a judgeship, a person holds that job for life. Judges serve until they resign, retire voluntarily, or die.

Federal judges may be removed through impeachment, although such action is extremely rare. Moreover, the conduct must be blatantly illegal, as was illustrated by the impeachment proceedings against federal judges Alcee Hastings and Walter Nixon. Hastings was impeached by the U.S. House of Representatives on a charge of conspiracy to obtain a $150,000 bribe and lying about his actions to a jury. Nixon was impeached for lying to a grand jury about a case in which he had discussed charges brought against the son of a wealthy friend with a district county attorney in Mississippi. Both Hastings and Nixon were removed from office.

Nominating Judicial Candidates

Judicial candidates for federal judgeships are suggested to the president by the Department of Justice, senators, other judges, the candidates themselves, and bar associations and other interest groups.

Since the Truman administration, the American Bar Association, through its Committee on the Federal Judiciary, furnishes the president with evaluations of those individuals being considered. No president is required to refer any nominees to the committee, but most presidents have done so.

The nomination process—no matter how the nominees are obtained—always works the same way. The president does the actual nomination, transmitting the name to the Senate. The Senate then either confirms or rejects the nomination. To reach a conclusion, the Senate Judiciary Committee (operating through subcommittees) invites testimony, both written and oral, at its various hearings. In the case of federal district court judgeship nominations, a practice used in the Senate, called **senatorial courtesy**, is a constraint on the president's freedom to appoint whomever the administration chooses. Senatorial courtesy allows a senator of the president's political party to veto a judicial appointment in his or her state.

Federal District Court Judgeship Nominations. Although the president nominates federal judges, the nomination of federal district court judges typically originates with a senator or senators of the president's party from the state in which there is a vacancy. If the Committee on the Federal Judiciary of the American Bar Association deems the nominee unqualified, as a matter of political courtesy the president will discuss with the senator or senators who originated the nomination whether the nomination should be withdrawn. Also, when a nomination is unacceptable politically to the president, the president will consult with the appropriate senator or senators, indicate that the nomination is unacceptable, and work with the senator or senators to seek an alternative candidate.

Federal Courts of Appeals Appointments. Although there are many fewer federal courts of appeals appointments than federal district court appointments, they are more important. This is because federal

SENATORIAL COURTESY
In regard to federal district court judgeship nominations, a Senate tradition allowing a senator of the president's political party to veto a judgeship appointment in his or her state simply by indicating that the appointment is personally not acceptable. At that point, the Senate may reject the nomination, or the president may withdraw consideration of the nominee.

appellate judges handle more important matters, at least from the point of view of the president, and therefore presidents take a keener interest in the nomination process for such judgeships. Also, appointments to the U.S. courts of appeals have become "stepping stones" to the Supreme Court. Typically, the president culls the Circuit Judge Nominating Commission's list of nominees for potential candidates. The president may also use this list to oppose senators' recommendations that may be unacceptable politically to the president.

SUPREME COURT APPOINTMENTS AND IDEOLOGY

The nomination of Supreme Court justices belongs solely to the president, as we have described. That is not to say that the president's nominations are always confirmed, however. In fact, almost 20 percent of presidential nominations for the Supreme Court have been either rejected or not acted on by the Senate. Numerous acrimonious battles over Supreme Court appointments have ensued when the Senate and the president have not seen eye to eye about political matters.

The Senate's Role

The U.S. Senate had a long record of refusing to confirm the president's judicial nominations from the beginning of Andrew Jackson's presidency in 1829 to the end of Ulysses Grant's presidency in 1877. During a fairly long period of relative acquiescence on the part of the Senate to presidential nominations, from 1894 until 1968, only three nominees were not confirmed. From 1968 through 1986, however, there were two rejections of presidential nominees to the highest court. Both were Nixon appointees, rejected because of questions about their racial attitudes. In 1987, two of President Ronald Reagan's nominees failed to be confirmed—Robert Bork was rejected

Demonstrators protest the possible confirmation of Judge Clarence Thomas in 1991, after Professor Anita Hill charged him with sexually harassing her while she was his employee. After long and difficult hearings on the subject, the Senate voted to confirm Judge Thomas.

for his views on the Constitution, and Douglas Ginsburg withdrew his nomination when it was reported that he had used marijuana in the 1970s.

President George Bush decided to use a different strategy when Justice William J. Brennan announced his retirement from the bench in 1989. Bush chose David H. Souter, a recent appointee to a federal court of appeals with extensive experience as a justice on the New Hampshire Supreme Court. Souter was dubbed a "stealth" candidate, because he had not written extensively on controversial social issues, such as abortion or racial equality. During the Senate Judiciary Committee hearings, various members attempted to elicit Souter's views on these subjects, but he refused to speculate as to how he would rule in any particular hypothetical case.

The same tactic was followed by Bush's second nominee, Clarence Thomas, who underwent an extremely volatile confirmation hearing replete with charges of sexual harassment. Were it not for the dramatic and televised allegations by his former aide, Anita Hill, Thomas's confirmation hearings might have been more similar in tone to those of Souter. Both men were confirmed, however, although members of the Senate Judiciary Committee complained about the lack of information concerning the nominees' views.

In 1993, President Clinton had little trouble gaining approval for his nominee to take the seat left vacant by Justice Byron White. Ruth Bader Ginsburg became the second female Supreme Court Justice. In 1994, Clinton nominated Stephen Breyer, a federal court of appeals judge, to fill the seat of retiring Supreme Court Justice Harry Blackmun. Seen by many as a consensus builder who might effectively pull together justices with divergent views, Breyer was confirmed without significant opposition.

Partisanship and Supreme Court Appointments

Ideology plays an important role in the president's choices for the Supreme Court (and for nominations to the lower federal courts, too). Ideology also plays a large role in the Senate's confirmation hearings. There has been an extremely partisan distribution of presidential appointments to the federal judiciary. In the over two hundred years of the Supreme Court's history, fewer than 13 percent of the justices nominated by a president have been from an opposing political party. Presidents see their federal judiciary appointments as the one sure way to institutionalize their political views long after they have left office. By 1993, for example, Presidents Reagan and Bush together had appointed nearly three-quarters of all federal court judges.[13] This preponderance of Republican-appointed federal judges strengthened the legal moorings of the conservative social agenda on a variety of issues, ranging from abortion to civil rights.

Nevertheless, President Bill Clinton had the opportunity to appoint more than 150 federal judges, marking a different shift in the ideological makeup of the federal judiciary. Also, Clinton's appointees matched more closely the actual U.S. demographics—nearly 38 percent of Clinton's nominees were women, for example, compared to Bush's 17 percent and Reagan's 8 percent.

---

13. Sheldon Goldman, "The Bush Imprint on the Judiciary: Carrying on a Tradition," *Judicature,* Vol. 74 (1991), p. 306.

WHO BECOMES A SUPREME COURT JUSTICE?

The make-up of the federal judiciary is far from typical of the American public. (See this chapter's *Politics and Cultural Diversity*.) Table 13–1 summarizes the background of all of the 108 Supreme Court justices to 1995.

TABLE 13–1

Background of Supreme Court Justices to 1995

	NUMBER OF JUSTICES (108 = TOTAL)
Occupational Position before Appointment	
Private legal practice	25
State judgeship	21
Federal judgeship	28
U.S. attorney general	7
Deputy or assistant U.S. attorney general	2
U.S. solicitor general	2
U.S. senator	6
U.S. representative	2
State governor	3
Federal executive post	9
Other	3
Religious Background	
Protestant	84
Roman Catholic	10
Jewish	6
Unitarian	7
No religious affiliation	1
Age on Appointment	
Under 40	5
41–50	31
51–60	58
61–70	14
Political Party Affiliation	
Federalist (to 1835)	13
Democratic Republican (to 1828)	7
Whig (to 1861)	1
Democrat	44
Republican	42
Independent	1
Educational Background	
College graduate	92
Not a college graduate	16
Sex	
Male	106
Female	2
Race	
Caucasian	106
Other	2

SOURCE: Congressional Quarterly, *Congressional Quarterly's Guide to the U.S. Supreme Court* (Washington, D.C.: Congressional Quarterly Press, 1995).

POLITICS AND CULTURAL DIVERSITY
Does Our Legal System Reflect Our Diversity?

Obviously, we are living in a culturally diverse society. Nonwhite minorities account for an increasing percentage of the U.S. population, and the traditional "white" complexion of many of our social institutions is changing to reflect this fact. But one very significant institution—the legal system—seems to be an exception to this rule.

Of the more than 350 judges who sit on the states' highest courts, less than 50 are women, less than 20 are African American, and only a couple are Hispanic. The situation is somewhat—but not much—brighter in the federal court system.

Of the 715 judges now sitting on the federal district courts and federal courts of appeal, only 103 are women, 42 are African American, 28 are Hispanic, 5 are Asian American, and 1 is Native American. In other words, women account for 14 percent of the judges; African Americans, for 6 percent; Hispanics, for 4 percent; and Asian Americans and Native Americans, for less than 1 percent.

What do these statistics mean for women and members of minority groups who enter the nation's courtrooms? Initially, it should be noted that the persons who sit on the lower federal courts are just as important as those who sit on the Supreme Court. Without some of those who sat on the lower federal courts in the 1960s, for example, many of the gains on such issues as civil rights never would have occurred.

Can justice be meted out impartially in a justice system composed largely of white males? Many African Americans maintain, for example, that although more than 40 percent of all prison inmates are African American, it is not because they committed a share of crimes that is disproportionate relative to the number of African Americans in the general population. Instead, it is because African Americans receive proportionately longer sentences within the predominantly white-operated criminal justice system.

After twelve years in which Presidents Reagan and Bush appointed mostly white male conservatives to the federal bench, President Clinton has begun appointing more women, as well as more minority-group members, to the federal courts. More than a third of Clinton's nominees have been women, and nearly 30 percent are either African American or Hispanic. In contrast, more than 70 percent of Bush's appointees were white males, as were more than 85 percent of Reagan's choices. In other words, there is a much higher degree of diversity among Clinton's nominees.

Another element in the judicial system, however, increasingly reflects the cultural and racial diversity of America: the jury. In many states, African Americans and Hispanics are now heavily represented in juries. In large part, this more proportionate representation is due to laws passed since the mid-1960s that prohibit courts from keeping African Americans and other minorities off juries through such requirements as property ownership, qualification examinations, and so on. Also, in 1986, the Supreme Court ruled that attorneys could not bar persons from jury participation on the basis of race. In 1994, the Supreme Court ruled that the same prohibition applies to gender.

The justices' partisan attachments have been mostly the same as those of the president who appointed them. There have been some exceptions, however. Nine nominal Democrats have been appointed by Republican presidents, three Republicans by Democratic presidents, and one Democrat by Whig president John Tyler.[14]

As you will note, the most common occupational background of the justices at the time of their appointments has been private legal practice or state or federal judgeships. Those nine justices who were in federal executive posts at the time of their appointments held the high offices of secretary of

---

14. Actually, Tyler was a member of the Democratic party who ran with William H. Harrison on the Whig ticket. When Harrison died, much to the surprise of the Whigs, Tyler—a Democrat—became president, although they tried to call him "acting president." Thus, there are historians who quibble over the statement that Tyler was a Whig.

state, comptroller of the treasury, secretary of the navy, postmaster general, secretary of the interior, chairman of the Securities and Exchange Commission, and secretary of labor. In the "Other" category under "Occupational Position before Appointment" in Table 13–1 are two justices who were professors of law (including William H. Taft, a former president) and one justice who was a North Carolina state employee with responsibility for organizing and revising the state's statutes.

Most justices were in their fifties when they assumed office, although two were as young as thirty-two and one as old as sixty-six. The average age of newly sworn justices is about fifty-three.

The great majority of justices have had a college education. By and large, those who did not attend college or receive a degree lived in the late eighteenth and early nineteenth centuries, when a college education was much less common than it is today. In recent years, degrees from such schools as Yale, Harvard, Columbia, and other prestigious institutions have been typical. Note that many of the earlier college-educated justices did not hold their degrees in law. In fact, it was not until 1957 that all of the sitting members of the Supreme Court were graduates of law schools.

The religious background of Supreme Court justices is clearly not typical of that of the American population as a whole, even making allowances for changes over time in the religious composition of the nation. Catholics (and certain Protestant denominations, notably Baptists and Lutherans) have been underrepresented, whereas Protestants in general (Episcopalians, Presbyterians, Methodists, and others), as well as Unitarians, have been overrepresented among the justices. Typically, there has been a "Catholic seat" on the Court, with interruptions, and a "Jewish seat" existed without a break from 1916 until 1969, when Abe Fortas resigned.

THE REHNQUIST COURT

William H. Rehnquist (see this chapter's *Politics: The Human Side*) became the sixteenth chief justice of the Supreme Court in 1986 after fifteen years as an associate justice. He was known as a strong anchor of the Court's conservative wing. With Rehnquist's appointment as chief justice, it seemed to observers that the Court necessarily would become more conservative. Proponents of civil liberties feared that the Rehnquist Court would eventually erode many of those liberties that the previous Courts under Earl Warren (1953 to 1969) and Warren Burger (1969 to 1986) had established or maintained.

In the late 1980s, the Rehnquist Court ruled on several extremely important matters that raised the question of the direction in which the Court was moving ideologically. These rulings also caused renewed speculation about the impact on the Court if one or more of the aging "liberal" justices should die or resign and be replaced with appointees of President George Bush. That is precisely what did happen following the resignations of William Brennan and Thurgood Marshall in 1990 and 1991, respectively, and the subsequent appointments by President Bush of conservative justices David Souter and Clarence Thomas.

The perception that the Rehnquist Court would take a rightward shift in the late 1980s and first half of the 1990s appeared to be borne out by its

The Supreme Court in 1995, shown here with President Clinton, who was the first Democratic president to make appointments to the Supreme Court since Lyndon Johnson.

conservative rulings in cases involving criminal confessions, racial dispari-ties in death-penalty sentencing, the burden of proof placed on litigants in civil rights cases, and the availability of abortion. Indeed, a primary impetus behind Congress's passage of the 1991 Civil Rights Act was its desire to overrule a group Supreme Court cases that had greatly restricted the ease with which discrimination suits could be brought by increasing the burden of proof on plaintiffs. The conservative shift of the Rehnquist Court also forced many special interest groups, including the American Civil Liberties Union and the National Association for the Advancement of Colored People, to view the Court as a brake on, rather than an accelerator of, the engine of social process. Consequently, these groups began petitioning Congress to enact laws to overturn Court rulings they considered to be undesirable. Con-gress was now viewed as the primary guarantor of civil liberties by these groups. This marked a stunning reversal of the situation that had existed in the late 1950s and early 1960s, at which time the Court was vehemently attacked by many members of Congress and by other prominent politicians for its expansive civil rights rulings.

A series of rulings in the mid-1990s again raised concerns that a conser-vative Supreme Court may be placing in jeopardy many of the gains in civil rights made during the last three decades. Supporters of progressive policies could no longer look to Congress for help, though. When Congress and most state governorships and legislatures fell under Republican control after the 1994 elections, conservative control over virtually all aspects of political and legal power left civil rights proponents with little recourse.

JUDICIAL ACTIVISM AND JUDICIAL RESTRAINT

Judicial scholars like to characterize different Supreme Courts and different Supreme Court justices as being either activist or restraintist. Those

POLITICS: THE HUMAN SIDE
William H. Rehnquist, Chief Justice of the Supreme Court

"It is basically unhealthy to have so much authority concentrated in a small group of lawyers who have been appointed to the Supreme Court and enjoy virtual life tenure."

BIOGRAPHICAL NOTES

Born in Milwaukee in 1924, William H. Rehnquist obtained a B.A. degree from Stanford University, two master's degrees in political science (one from Stanford in 1949 and one from Harvard University in 1950), and a J.D. from Stanford Law School, where he graduated first in his class in 1951. He clerked for Supreme Court Justice Robert Jackson in 1952 and 1953, before entering the practice of law in Arizona.

In 1969, Rehnquist became assistant attorney general and later head of the Justice Department's Office of Legal Counsel. He was appointed to the Supreme Court in 1971, after he was nominated by President Richard Nixon. Rehnquist was often identified as the justice with the most impressive intellectual ability. It has been suggested that federalism is the concept most central to Rehnquist's decision making.

President Ronald Reagan named Rehnquist to replace Warren Burger as chief justice when Burger retired in 1986. He faced a hard confirmation fight in the Senate because of his conservative views. The Senate ultimately approved of his nomination by the smallest margin in history.

POLITICAL CONTRIBUTIONS

As a practicing attorney, Rehnquist was an outspoken conservative. He participated in a variety of local activities, including a program of challenging voters at the polls. In 1964, Rehnquist campaigned for conservative Republican presidential candidate Barry Goldwater.

As head of the Justice Department's Office of Legal Counsel, Rehnquist successfully defended the government's program of secret surveillance of anti–Vietnam War groups in the United States. He supported the use of executive authority to order wiretapping without a court order, no-knock entry by the police, preventive detention of suspects, and abolishing the exclusionary rule.

During his fifteen years of service as an associate justice on the Supreme Court, Rehnquist led the Court conservatives' efforts to narrow the interpretation of defendants' rights in criminal cases. He urged his colleagues to limit Congress's power under the commerce clause, to restrain the power of the federal courts, and to shift power from the federal government to the states. He also dissented forcefully when the Court reaffirmed women's rights to abortion and wrote a strong decision upholding Missouri's restrictions on abortion rights.

His tenure as chief justice, however, has not seen dramatic erosions in the liberal precedents bequeathed by the Warren and Burger Courts. Instead, the increasingly conservative Court in the Reagan and Bush administrations gradually chipped away at some of the earlier Courts' decisions in areas ranging from racial discrimination to freedom of speech.

JUDICIAL ACTIVISM
A doctrine advocating an active role for the Supreme Court in enforcing the Constitution and in using judicial review.

JUDICIAL RESTRAINT
A doctrine holding that the Court should rarely use its power of judicial review or otherwise intervene in the political process.

advocating the doctrine of **judicial activism**, such as former justices William Brennan and Thurgood Marshall, believe that the Court should use its power to alter the direction of the activities of Congress, state legislatures, and administrative agencies to expand individual freedoms. Those advocating the doctrine of **judicial restraint**, such as Justice Antonin Scalia, believe that the Court should use its powers of judicial review only rarely. In other words, whatever elected legislatures decide should not be thwarted by the Supreme Court so long as such decisions are not unconstitutional.

The Role of Constitutional Interpretation

The basic difference between the two doctrines is in the way in which the justice believes the Constitution should be interpreted. Should the Court confine itself to interpreting the law, or should it, in effect, create new laws? In general, most justices who consider themselves to be conservatives would argue that the Constitution should be interpreted based on the intention of the framers who drafted it. According to Robert Bork, this approach does not require the Court to delve into the subjective intentions of the framers, but instead to interpret the law based on the ordinary meaning given to the words being examined.[15] Liberal jurists, such as former Justice William Brennan, have argued that any attempts to divine the original meanings of the Constitution from its text are inappropriate, because the social mores and values of society have changed considerably in the past two centuries. Brennan believed that any interpretation given to the Constitution itself must take into account current ideas regarding such concepts as "due process" and "equal protection." Even though all courts will consider what the authors of a particular law meant by examining its **legislative history** (such as statements by the bill's sponsors) prior to enactment, Brennan and other legal experts seem to have decided that such analyses are not appropriate when the Constitution itself is involved.

LEGISLATIVE HISTORY
The background and events leading up to the enactment of a law. This may include legislative committee reports, hearings, and floor debates.

Political Ideology and Judicial Approaches

The difference between activist judges and those who exercise restraint is not the same as the difference between political liberals and conservatives. In the early 1930s, for example, the Supreme Court was activist and conservative, ruling that much regulation of business was unconstitutional. In the later 1930s, however, the Court became restrained and liberal, ruling that similar business regulation was constitutional.

In the 1950s and 1960s, the Court was activist and liberal. Many of the Court's critics believed it should have exercised more restraint. They criticized the first *Brown* decision in 1954, which prohibited racial segregation in public schools (see Chapter 5), on the ground that the highest court settled a problem that should have been resolved by Congress or been left to the states. Critics of the activist tendencies of the courts call them "mini-legislatures." They argue, for example, that in *Baker v. Carr*,[16] the federal courts wrongly exercised jurisdiction over the issue of state legislative districting plans and that the Supreme Court had no right to intervene in such a state matter.

Another activist decision in the 1970s was *Roe v. Wade*, in which the Supreme Court gave women the right to an abortion during the first and second trimesters of pregnancy, thereby striking down state statutes permitting abortions only in special cases.[17] Recent Supreme Court decisions have indicated an unmistakably conservative change in the Court's attitude toward civil rights (see Chapter 5). Some critics fear that the current Court, with its conservative majority, is becoming increasingly activist in this and other areas in the 1990s.

---

15. See Robert H. Bork, *The Tempting of America* (New York: Free Press, 1990), pp. 143–146.
16. 369 U.S. 186 (1962).
17. 410 U.S. 113, rehearing denied 410 U.S. 959 (1973).

The fact that all presidents attempt to strengthen their legacy through the appointment of federal judges with similar political and ideological philosophies has been noted already. But the fact that a president appoints a justice who has supported the president's policies in the past is no guarantee that the newly appointed justice will continue to do so in the future. President Dwight Eisenhower, a conservative Republican, appointed Earl Warren, the former governor of California, to be chief justice of the Supreme Court in 1953. Warren's past moderate-to-conservative policies gave no indication that he would lead the Court in an unprecedented revision of the nation's existing laws, greatly expanding the protections afforded to minorities and criminal defendants. Indeed, Eisenhower later characterized his appointment of Warren as the biggest single mistake of his presidency.

Similarly, Richard Nixon appointed Warren Burger as chief justice in 1969 to replace Earl Warren. Nixon believed that Burger's conservative views would ensure that the court would minimize its involvement in controversial issues, such as school desegregation. But within two years, Burger authored the opinion of the Court in *Swann v. Charlotte-Mecklenburg Board of Education,* in which school authorities were directed to desegregate dual school systems.[18] Perhaps the ultimate irony of Nixon's appointment was that Burger wrote the Court's opinion in *United States v. Nixon,* in which the Court unanimously rejected the president's claims of executive privilege.[19]

The question of judicial activism is closely linked to the actual constraints on our judicial system. We examine these next.

WHAT CHECKS OUR COURTS?

Our judicial system is probably the most independent in the world. But the courts do not have absolute independence, for they are part of the political process. Political checks limit the extent to which courts can exercise judicial review and engage in an activist policy. These checks are exercised by the legislature, the executive, other courts, and the public.

Legislative Checks

Courts may make rulings, but often the legislatures at local, state, and federal levels are required to appropriate funds to carry out the courts' rulings. When such funds are not appropriated, the court that made the ruling, in effect, has been checked. A court, for example, may decide that prison conditions must be improved. Then a legislature has to find the funds to carry out such a ruling.

Courts' rulings can be overturned by constitutional amendments at both the federal and state levels. Many of the amendments to the U.S. Constitution (such as the Eleventh, Fourteenth, Sixteenth, and Twenty-sixth Amendments) check the state courts' ability to allow discrimination, for example. Proposed constitutional amendments that were created by a desire to reverse courts' decisions on school prayer and abortion have failed.

Finally, legislatures can pass new laws to overturn courts' rulings. This may happen particularly when a court interprets a statute in a way that

18. 402 U.S. 1 (1971).
19. 418 U.S. 683 (1974).

Congress had not intended or when a court finds no relevant statute to apply in certain cases. The legislature can then pass a new statute to negate the court's ruling, as was the case with the Civil Rights Act of 1991.

Executive Checks

Presidents have the power to change the direction of the Supreme Court and the federal judiciary. The president can appoint new judges who, in principle, have philosophies more in line with that of the administration. Also, a president, governor, or mayor can refuse to enforce courts' rulings. The possibility that a president might refuse to enforce an order is not merely theoretical. Several presidents, including Abraham Lincoln and Andrew Jackson, have refused to obey orders issued by the Supreme Court.[20] Such conduct does not appear to constitute an explicit violation of the Constitution, because there is no language in that document expressly authorizing the federal courts to review the actions of the executive and legislative branches.

Despite its lack of tangible enforcement mechanisms, the Supreme Court is widely perceived by the general public to be the final arbiter of national laws. Moreover, its decisions are regarded as the least partisan of all of the three branches of government. Had Richard Nixon refused to hand over the materials for which he claimed executive privilege after the Court's unanimous ruling in *United States v. Nixon,* for example, the Nixon presidency would have seen what little public support it still had further eroded and the chances of a conviction from an impeachment trial increased to a near certainty. In the absence of any threat of impeachment by Congress, however, the main weapon at the Court's disposal would appear to be public pressure. Whether a politician would be able to withstand the public firestorm that would likely result from a deliberate refusal to obey an order from the Supreme Court would depend, in large part, on the factual circumstances of the case and whether the Court's order otherwise appeared to be legally justified.

The Rest of the Judiciary

Higher courts can reverse the decisions of lower courts. Lower courts can put a check on higher courts, too. The United States Supreme Court, for example, cannot possibly hear all the cases that go through the lower courts. Lower courts can ignore and have ignored, directly or indirectly, Supreme Court decisions by deciding in the other direction in particular cases. Only if a case goes to the Supreme Court can the Court correct the situation.

The Public Has a Say

History has shown members of the Supreme Court that if the Court's decisions are noticeably at odds with a national consensus, it will lose its support and some of its power. (For a discussion of the effect media coverage could

---

20. Lincoln refused to obey a direct order by the Court in *Ex parte Merryman,* 17 F.Cas. [Federal Cases—an eighteenth- and nineteenth-century reporter of cases decided in the federal courts of appeals that was abolished in 1912] 144 (C.C.D.Md. 1861), whereas Jackson challenged the Court to enforce its order in *Cherokee Nation v. Georgia,* 5 Pet. 1 (1831).

POLITICS AND THE MEDIA
Trial by Television

During the 1980s, many state courts and some federal courts allowed broadcast journalists to bring their cameras into the courtroom for the first time. This increasing willingness of the courts to allow televised trials stimulated plans by Time Warner and NBC to launch a twenty-four-hour cable channel known as the Courtroom Television Network in 1991. All that was needed was a trial that would capture the interest of the new channel's viewers.

Enter William Kennedy Smith, a nephew of Senator Edward Kennedy of Massachusetts. The allegations by a young woman that Smith had raped her on the beach in front of the Kennedy estate in Palm Beach, Florida, in the summer of 1991 provided the perfect grist for the new network's mill.

In 1994, viewers considered Lorena Bobbitt's claim that she was raped immediately before she maimed her husband. The same winter, viewers watched the trial of Erik and Lyle Menendez, who sought to show that sexual molestation and fear provoked them to kill their parents. Viewers also saw the plea and sentencing of Olympic skater Tonya Harding, who was accused of obstructing justice in the investigation of an attack on Olympic skater Nancy Kerrigan. Starting in the summer of 1994 and continuing in 1995, millions watched on television virtually every phase of the capture, arraignment, hearings, and murder trial of O. J. Simpson.

Even within the courtroom, changes are being wrought by television. There is an increasing reliance on video testimony. Young children who allege physical or sexual abuse, for example, sometimes may give video testimony outside of a courtroom to be shown during trial proceedings. Lawyers who represent accident victims often commission videos to show the court visually the impact of accident-related injuries on the daily lives of their clients. In criminal trials, judges have allowed juries to see filmed reenactments of crimes.

Such approaches raise significant issues. There is a question about how the videos are edited. There is also the problem that for some people, a made-for-court movie—complete with actors and simulated explosions—may seem more real than live testimony.

Further blurring the line between simulation and reality is the increasing number of cameras that videotape the commission of alleged crimes and other wrongs. The most familiar example of an amateur's use of a camcorder is the videotape of the beating of motorist Rodney King, whose assault by Los Angeles police officers led to riots in the summer of 1992. There are other, more professional efforts to videotape misconduct, including the mounting of cameras in nearly every bank, grocery store, and automatic teller machine; on some police cars; and even on some stoplights.

What effect will these uses of television have on the judicial system? Will jurors someday be allowed to watch trials on their televisions at home and reach a verdict by interactive cable? Will a widespread familiarity with trials foster contempt or respect for the courts? Will jurors come to expect more excitement than is generated in the usual courtroom proceeding? Will lawyers argue their cases to appeal to home audiences? And what effect will all of the televising have on the American judicial system's avowed goal—impartiality and fairness?

have on the public's views, see this chapter's *Politics and the Media*.) Perhaps the best example was the *Dred Scott* decision of 1857, in which the Supreme Court held that slaves were not citizens of the United States and were not entitled to the rights and privileges of citizenship.[21] The Court ruled, in addition, that the Missouri Compromise banning slavery in the lands of the Louisiana Territory north of latitude 36°30′ north, except for Missouri, was unconstitutional. Most observers contend that the *Dred Scott* ruling contributed to making the Civil War inevitable.

---

21. *Dred Scott v. Sanford,* 19 Howard [a nineteenth-century reporter of Supreme Court cases] 393 (1857).

Observers of the court system believe that because of the judges' sense of self-preservation, they do act with restraint. Some argue that this self-restraint is the most important check of all.

THE JUDICIARY: UNFINISHED WORK

The judiciary remains one of the most active and important institutions in American political life. Particularly at the federal level, judicial activism through the years has affected the way all of us live and work.

During the Reagan-Bush years (1981 to 1993), there appeared to be a trend toward a less activist and noticeably more conservative federal judiciary. Some argued that this "conservative" legacy would remain effective for years to come. The election of Bill Clinton, however, may have changed that. When he took office, over one hundred judicial openings in the lower federal courts existed. And by 1996 he had already been able to appoint two Supreme Court justices. Consequently, some argue that if Clinton fills all of the vacancies in the federal courts, the direction of the federal judiciary will not continue necessarily to be in a conservative direction.

A number of key constitutional issues will continue to be brought before the federal judiciary. These issues include civil rights, the right to privacy, and many others. The work of the judiciary in this sense will always remain unfinished. Even when an issue seems to be "resolved," it may come up again many years later. After all, the Supreme Court decision in *Roe v. Wade* appeared to have put an end to discussion about restrictions on abortion. Yet in the 1990s, the issue continues to come back to the courts and is currently being settled there, as well as through decisions and movements in public opinion. In a dynamic nation with a changing population, we can never expect issues to be resolved once and for all.

GETTING INVOLVED
Changing the Legal System

Although impressed by the power of judges in American government, Alexis de Tocqueville stated:

> The power is enormous, but it is clothed in the authority of public opinion. They are the all-powered guardians of a people which respects law; but they would be impotent against public neglect or popular contempt.*

The U.S. court system may seem all powerful and too complex to be influenced by one individual, but its power nonetheless depends on our support. A hostile public has many ways of resisting, modifying, or overturning rulings of the courts. Sooner or later a determined majority will prevail. Even a determined minority can make a difference. As Alexander Hamilton suggested in *The Federalist Papers*, the people will always hold the scales of justice in their hands, and ultimately all constitutional government depends on their firmness and wisdom.

One example of the kind of pressure that can be exerted on the court system began with a tragedy. On a spring afternoon in 1980, thirteen-year-old Cari Lightner was hit from behind and killed by a drunk driver while walking in a bicycle lane. The driver turned out to be a forty-seven-year-old man with two prior drunk-driving convictions. He was at that time out on bail for a third arrest. Cari's mother, Candy, quit her job as a real estate agent to form Mothers Against Drunk Driving (MADD) and launched a personal campaign to stiffen penalties for drunk-driving convictions.

The organization grew to 20,000 members, with 91 regional offices and a staff of 160. Outraged by the estimated 23,000 lives lost every year because of drunk driving, the group not only seeks stiff penalties against drunk drivers but also urges police, prosecutors, and judges to crack down on such violators. MADD, by becoming involved, has gotten results. Owing to its efforts and the efforts of other citizen-

activist groups, many states have responded with stronger penalties and deterrents. If you feel strongly about this issue and want to get involved, contact the following:

MADD
5330 Primrose, Suite 146
Fair Oaks, CA 95628
916-966-6233

Several other organizations have been formed by people who want to change or influence the judicial system. A few of them follow:

Children's Legal Rights Information and Training
Program
2008 Hillyer Pl.
Washington, DC 20009
202-332-6575

Legal Defense Research Institute
733 N. Van Buren
Milwaukee, WI 53202
414-272-5995

HALT—An Organization of Americans for Legal
Reform
201 Massachusetts Ave. N.E., Suite 319
Washington, DC 2002
205-546-4258

National Legal Center for the Public Interest
1101 17th St. N.W.
Washington DC 20036
202-296-1683

If you want information about the Supreme Court, contact the following by telephone or letter:

Clerk of the Court
The Supreme Court of the United States
1 First St. N.E.
Washington, DC
202-393-1640

*Alexis de Tocqueville, *Democracy in America*, Vol. 1 (New York: Schocken Books, 1961), p. 166.

KEY TERMS

 CHAPTER SUMMARY

1. Courts often look to the precedents provided by earlier court decisions in deciding how to resolve a dispute. Although courts take into consideration the merits of past decisions, they will not hesitate to break with earlier cases when justice or changing attitudes in society so require. Courts must weigh any applicable state or federal statutes in deciding cases. As one of the three coequal branches of the government, the courts may pass on the constitutionality of actions taken by either the legislative or executive branches. This power of judicial review permits the courts to act as a check on the actions of the other two branches of government in the United States.

2. The federal court system and most state court systems have several tiers. All trials are conducted in the trial, or district, courts. The outcome of a trial may then be appealed to an intermediate court, or court of appeals. Whether a litigant can further appeal a claim to the state or federal supreme court will depend on the nature of the claim and the access afforded to litigants by the particular court. The United States Supreme Court, for example, exercises almost total discretion over the types of cases it chooses to hear.

3. The United States Supreme Court will issue a writ of *certiorari* to a lower court when it wishes to review the record of a particular case—for example, if a case involves a federal question or a conflict between a state law and a federal law, the Court may issue the writ. Some cases may involve political questions, such as cases relating to the policy decisions of the executive or legislative branches. Courts generally refrain from hearing cases concerning political questions, believing that such issues should be decided by the other branches of government.

4. There is no absolute right of appeal to the United States Supreme Court. Parties can petition the Court for a writ of *certiorari,* but the Court has almost complete discretion as to whether or not to take any particular case.

5. Because of the influence wielded by the United States Supreme Court and the members of the federal judiciary, the confirmation process for federal judges, particularly those who will sit on the Supreme Court, is often extremely politicized. Democrats and Republicans alike realize that most justices will occupy a seat on the Court for decades and naturally want to have persons appointed who share their basic views. Nearly one-fifth of all United States Supreme Court appointments have been either rejected or not acted on by the Senate—often for ideological reasons. The overwhelming majority of persons appointed to the Supreme Court have been white male Protestants. Of the 108 persons who have sat on the Court so far, only two have been African American, and only two have been women. The Court is perhaps the least representative government institution in the United States.

6. The Rehnquist Court seemed to have become a bastion of conservatism, so much so that liberals looked to Congress to overturn Court decisions that they disliked. There is no longer a liberal voting bloc to prevent more conservative rulings in areas ranging from civil rights to abortion.

7. Conservatives often argue that judges should exercise judicial restraint and confine themselves to interpreting the law instead of making new laws by issuing decisions having extensive social and political ramifications. Liberals are likely to believe that judges should

exercise judicial activism and fashion remedies that reflect today's social, political, and cultural values and needs and not concern themselves with attempts at divining the original meaning of the Constitution.

8. Presidents may influence the federal courts through the use of their appointment power. Legislatures that fail to appropriate funds to carry out courts' rulings effectively check those rulings. Legislatures can also pass new laws to overturn courts' rulings.

QUESTIONS FOR REVIEW AND DISCUSSION

1. The United States Supreme Court has no police force and a relatively small budget. How, then, can it be sure that its decisions are enforced?

2. What are some of the reasons why cases are not heard by the Supreme Court?

3. Why has the nomination of Supreme Court justices become so politicized?

4. "Judges are just making too much legislation."

What does this quotation mean? How can a judge "make legislation"?

5. The Supreme Court has never allowed television cameras in its chambers, but other courts have. What would be some of the arguments against videotaping the Supreme Court at work? What are some of the arguments in favor of doing so?

LOGGING ON: THE JUDICIARY

The members of the United States Supreme Court often have the last say on public policies and pieces of legislation. Their decisions are often very difficult to find, however. The Supreme Court now makes available its rulings in an electronic format within minutes of their release. By using this service, you can read the majority opinion, as well as any concurring or dissenting opinions, on cases that interest you. This is a great way to find out how individual justices interpret the U.S. Constitution as it applies to various laws. To view Supreme Court rulings, go to the University of Maryland **gopher** at

info.umd.edu

and choose **Educational Resources/United States/Supreme Court.**

   For legal discussions and reference material for U.S., foreign, and international law, use the Cleveland State University **gopher** at

gopher.law.csuohio.edu

   For a general listing of law-related **gophers** throughout the world, select

riceinfo.rice.edu

and choose **law-gophers.** This will provide you with a list of worldwide **gophers** that provide law-related information, and it allows you to access them. This is a great way to find out about laws in any of the fifty states or in foreign countries. It also allows you to access **gophers** set up by law schools around the world.

SELECTED REFERENCES

Abraham, Henry J. *The Judiciary: The Supreme Court in the Governmental Process.* 9th ed. Madison, Wis.: Brown & Benchmark, 1994. This classic textbook treats in much more detail virtually every topic in the chapter you have just read.

————. *Justices and Presidents: A Political History of Appointments to the Supreme Court.* New York: Oxford University Press, 1992. This classic history of judicial appointments to the Supreme Court since 1789 provides a readable and engaging account of the nomination and selection of each justice who has sat on the Supreme Court up to 1992; the presidential expectations attending each nomination; and the extent to which each justice's actual conduct on the Court fulfilled, or failed to fulfill, those expectations.

Barnum, David G. *The Supreme Court and American Democracy.* New York: St. Martin's Press, 1993. The author attempts to describe the unique status of the Supreme Court as a special type of democratic institution. He points out that the justices theoretically are accountable only to their own consciences for their decisions, even when such decisions may affect the most sensitive of personal affairs for the rest of the nation.

Barth, Alan. *Prophets with Honor: Great Dissents and Great Dissenters in the Supreme Court.* New York: Knopf, 1974. Six cases are described in which dissenting justices had their views vindicated years later when the Court reversed itself.

Goldstein, Joseph. *The Intelligible Constitution: The Supreme Court's Obligation to Maintain the Constitution as Something We the People Can Understand.* New York: Oxford University Press, 1992. Goldstein criticizes the Supreme Court for its failure to present its opinions concerning constitutional matters in a clear and comprehensible manner. The author argues that the Supreme Court has an obligation not only to decide cases but also to explicate, with candor and integrity, the principles embedded in the Constitution and to make the Constitution understandable for today's citizens.

Hall, Kermit L., ed., with James W. Ely, Jr., Joel B. Grossman, and William M. Wiecek. *The Oxford Companion to the Supreme Court of the United States.* New York: Oxford University Press, 1992. This volume contains more than a thousand entries on every aspect of the United States Supreme Court, biographies of all the justices who ever sat on the Court through 1992, the details concerning more than four hundred major decisions of the Court, and articles on important legal and constitutional debates.

Hazard, Geoffrey C., Jr., and Michele Taruffo. *American Civil Procedure: An Introduction.* New Haven, Conn.: Yale University Press, 1993. The authors describe and analyze civil litigation in the United States. They discuss specific details and broad themes, explaining the jury trial, the adversary system, the power of the courts to make law as well as declare it, and the role of civil justice in the government and in the resolution of controversial social issues.

Levine, James P. *Juries and Politics.* Pacific Grove, Calif.: Brooks/Cole, 1992. This engaging book discusses the role of jury verdicts in shaping American justice.

McGuigan, Patrick B., and Dawn M. Weyrich. *Ninth Justice: The Fight for Bork.* Lanham, Md.: University Press of America, 1990. Through a detailed description of what the parties involved in the Robert Bork Supreme Court nomination did and did not do, the authors give their recommendations and advice on what the conservatives should have done to win the nomination.

Schwartz, Bernard. *A History of the Supreme Court.* New Haven, Conn.: Yale University Press, 1993. In a comprehensive, one-volume work, Schwartz explains complex legal issues, tells the story of the Supreme Court justices and their jurisprudence, and describes the impact of the justices' decisions on American politics and society.

Snowiss, Sylvia. *Judicial Review and the Law of the Constitution.* New Haven, Conn.: Yale University Press, 1990. Using both the opinions of the framers of the Constitution and modern court cases through the 1980s, Snowiss examines the origin and development of judicial review.

Wolfe, Christopher. *Judicial Activism: Bulwark of Freedom or Precarious Security?* Pacific Grove, Calif.: Brooks/Cole, 1991. The author examines the merits of judicial activism by presenting the "building blocks" on which the various theories of judicial review are built.

PART FIVE
Public Policy

14
The Politics of Economic and Domestic Policymaking

CHAPTER OUTLINE

WHAT IF . . . The Federal Income Tax Became a Consumption Tax?

Americans in the 1960s saved nearly 10 cents for every dollar they earned. In the 1990s they save less than 5 cents for every dollar earned. Our country saves and invests less than do most other industrialized countries. Because saving and investment are important for future economic growth, many have argued that something needs to be done to encourage more saving by Americans. Currently, we have a federal income tax system that taxes income no matter what individuals do with that income—whether they spend (consume) it or save it. Why not, therefore, only tax what people spend, in order to encourage more saving? This idea has been called a spending tax, a consumed-income tax, or simply a consumption tax. Here is how it would work.

Each individual or family would add up all income, including wages, interest, dividends, capital gains, and gifts. Then the individual or family would subtract from this total income the amount of income saved or invested that year. Only the remainder—that is, the income that was spent (consumed)—would be taxed. We could still have a system in which higher taxes were applied to people who spent more income. There might be three brackets—for example, 18 percent, 28 percent, and 32 percent—applied to all income spent each year that exceeded, by specified amounts, a minimum threshold, such as $20,000, below which no taxes would have to be applied to spent income.

The idea for this system was first brought forward by the Treasury Department in its *Blueprints for Tax Reform,* published in 1977. Ever since then, the idea has appeared periodically as an alternative to our increasingly complicated federal income tax system.

What would happen if such a consumption tax replaced our current income tax system? Certainly, such a system would encourage saving and investment. After all, if you made $50,000 in income but knew you would not be taxed on any income you saved, you would have an incentive to save more than you do today.

Additionally, a switch to a consumption tax system probably would eliminate the work of a large number of tax lawyers and tax accountants. Under the current system, such professionals are hired to help individual and corporate taxpayers figure out our very complicated system. Also, such professionals help wealthier individual and corporate taxpayers seek out loopholes in the tax

code to reduce taxes owed. Presumably, with a simplified consumption tax system, there would be less need to figure out complicated forms, because they would not be so complicated. Additionally, there would be less incentive to try to figure out how to get around the tax code. In principle, then, the approximately $50 billion or $60 billion in time and money spent annually on filling out tax returns would be reduced.

Of course, no policy is without problems. It would be difficult to determine exactly what qualifies as saving and investment. Should the purchase of a home be considered saving? Should expenditures on higher education be considered saving, or spending? What about vocational training? Should interest on mortgages on second homes or boats be considered saving? And what about contributions to charities? Guidelines would have to be developed for determining which kinds of expenditures truly represent saving.

---

1. Who would benefit most from a switch to a consumption tax from our current federal income tax system?

2. What groups would fight politically to prevent such a switch?

3. Would the elderly fare better under a consumption tax system compared with the current income tax system? (*Hint:* Do the elderly save more or less than younger Americans do?)

As this point, we turn to an analysis of public policy, or the substance of what government does. In particular, we examine national economic policy-making, such as the switch to a consumption tax discussed in this chapter's opening *What If . . .* feature, as well as **domestic policies.** In Chapter 15, we look at foreign and national security policies. We begin by looking at how policies are made.

THE POLICYMAKING PROCESS

How does a problem, such as the need to address the high rate of crime in this country, get solved? The first thing that has to happen, of course, is for people to become aware of the problem. Policymakers can obtain information on such problems as crime from nationally published statistics. Some-times, policymakers only have to open their local newspapers—or letters from their constituents—to find out that a problem is brewing. Like most people, however, policymakers receive much of their information from the media. People who themselves are victimized by crime certainly will be con-cerned about their condition and about the availability of ways to combat criminal activity. Others who have not been affected directly by crime will be made aware of the problem by newspapers and television reports or by the plight of their afflicted friends or neighbors.

The Place for Debate in the Policymaking Process

As mentioned above, the first step in the policymaking process is the public's acknowledgment of a problem that needs a solution. Problems and possible solutions often emerge through public debate. For example, for centuries, social scientists, politicians, and concerned citizens have debated the appro-priate response to crime in the community. At one end of the spectrum are

DOMESTIC POLICY
Those public plans or courses of ac-tion that concern issues of national importance, such as poverty, crime, and the environment, in contrast to economic policies that normally re-late only to issues of inflation, inter-est rates, and unemployment.

Tobacco executives were asked to testify before Congress during 1994. Their companies were being investi-gated for having purportedly covered up information about the ill effects of nicotine. These congressional hear-ings followed an intense Food and Drug Administration (FDA) campaign against nicotine and the tobacco companies. Critics of both the FDA and the congressional hearings claimed that neither was necessary. After all, these critics pointed out, young kids fifty years ago referred to cigarettes as "coffin nails." So, many decades ago Americans knew that cigarette smoking was not good for your health. Also, the addictive quali-ties of nicotine have been known for hundreds of years.

those who believe that crime cannot be stopped without eliminating its root causes. Hence, they argue for reestablishing stronger family values, reforming the educational system to improve job opportunities, and improving the economic outlook to offer more of those job opportunities to individuals who might otherwise seek a life of crime. At the other end of the spectrum are those who simply want to "get tough" with criminals by locking them up forever. But, of course, that means more prisons and more state and federal revenues to pay for those prisons. Indeed, one of the major stumbling blocks in any crime legislation involves how to pay for increased law-enforcement activity, as well as tougher and longer prison sentences for convicted criminals.

Steps in the Policymaking Process

The problem, the reaction to the problem, and the solution to the problem all form part of the public policymaking process in the United States. No matter how simple or how complex the problem, those who make policy follow a number of steps. Based on observation, we can divide the process of policymaking into at least five steps:

1. Agenda building: *The issue must get on the agenda.* This occurs through crises, technological changes, or mass media campaigns, as well as through the efforts of strong political personalities.
2. Agenda formulation: *The proposals are discussed among government officials and the public.* Such discussions may appear in the press, on television, in the halls of Congress, and in scholarly journals. Congress holds hearings, the president voices the administration's views, and the topic may become a campaign issue.
3. Agenda adoption: *A specific strategy is chosen from among the proposals discussed.* That is, Congress must enact legislation, executive departments must write new regulations, or courts must interpret past policies differently.
4. Agenda implementation: *Government action must be implemented by bureaucrats, the courts, police, and individual citizens.*
5. Agenda evaluation: *More and more often, after a policy is implemented, groups undertake policy evaluation.* Groups both inside and outside government perform studies to show what actually happens after a policy has been instituted. Such policy evaluations do not always lead anywhere, though, because proponents of the program tend to exaggerate the positive benefits, whereas critics tend to exaggerate the lack of benefits or any negative side effects. Nonetheless, the test of the success of any program increasingly is its outcome rather than its content. Presidential commissions are often appointed after an obvious failure or crisis in a program.

Although the flow of the policy process is well understood, there are competing models of how and for whose benefit that process works. Table 14–1 lists a number of competing models of the policymaking process and gives a brief summary of each.

Policymaking in Action: The 1994 Crime Bill

Early in the summer of 1994, the House of Representatives passed a crime bill. The bill was backed by a substantial number of Republicans in Congress.

TABLE 14–1

Selected Models of the Policymaking Process

1. **The Bureaucratic Politics Model.** In the bureaucratic politics model, the relative power of the large bureaucracies in Washington determines which policy becomes part of the national agenda and which is implemented. This theory of American politics is based on the struggle among competing interest groups.

2. **The Power Elite, or Elitism, Model.** Powerful economic interests determine the outcome of policy struggles, according to the power elite, or elitism, model. The rich and those who know the rich determine what gets done. More important, the power elite decides what items do *not* get on the public agenda and which items get removed if they are already on it.

3. **The Marxist Model.** Closely aligned with the power elite model is the Marxist model of public policymaking, in which the ruling class institutes public policy at the expense of the working class.

4. **The Incrementalist Model.** Public policy evolves through small changes or adjustments, according to the incrementalist model. Consequently, policymakers examine only a few alternatives in trying to solve national problems. A good public policy decision is made when there is agreement among contesting interests, and agreement is obtained most easily when changes are minimal.

5. **The Rationalist Model.** The rationalist model, sometimes thought of as a pure textbook abstraction, hypothesizes a rational policymaker who sets out to maximize his or her own self-interest, rather than determining what the public, or collective, interest might be. Rational policymakers will rank goals and objectives according to their benefit to the policymaker. Such a model is often viewed as an alternative to the incrementalist model. This model is sometimes known as the theory of public choice.

6. **The Systems Model.** The most general, and perhaps the most ambitious, approach to modeling public policymaking is a systems approach, in which policy is a product of the relationships between the institutions of government and the socioeconomic-political environment. Such a model has (a) inputs from public opinion and crises; (b) a political process including legislative hearings, debates, court deliberations, party conventions, and so on; (c) a set of policy outputs consisting of legislation, appropriations, and regulations; and (d) policy outcomes, which may provide, for example, more job security, less unemployment, or more research on AIDS.

A revised version of the bill, however, coming back from a conference committee with changes proposed by the Senate, failed to pass the House on August 11, 1994. The House voted, by a margin of 225–210, to support a procedural motion that prevented the bill from reaching the floor of the House.

The August 11 vote saw 167 Republicans join with 58 Democrats in what appeared to many to be a revival of the "conservative coalition" that had dominated legislative decision making throughout earlier decades. What made this particular outcome different from the usual cross-party alliance of members of Congress opposed to progressive legislation, however, was the fact that the crime bill's provisions to extend the death penalty were opposed by enough Democrats, particularly members of the Black Caucus, to kill the bill's chances of immediate passage. Of the 65 Republicans who had supported the previous House version of the crime bill, 55 switched their votes and opposed the bill when it was presented in its conference-committee version.

The President Appeals for Action.   On August 14, 1994, President Clinton appealed for action on the crime bill, which was threatening to block all his other legislative initiatives in Congress. Speaking from the pulpit of a local Washington church, Clinton said that he was worried over the future of the crime bill "not because it's the answer to all life's problems, but because this country's literally coming apart at the seams." Clinton went on to say that because of the social problems associated with violent crime, there are "too many streets where old folks are afraid to sit and talk, and children are afraid to play." Clinton took aim at what he referred to as the "petty politics" that were holding up the crime package. Through television appearances, he and his aides attacked congressional Republicans for being in league with the National Rifle Association (NRA) and interest groups opposed to gun control. The Republican response was that Clinton's bill was not really a serious effort to fight crime. Rather, they said, it was a pork-barrel effort to expand government spending to compensate for his programs to stimulate the economy that had not been approved in previous legislative efforts.

The House Passes the Crime Bill. On Sunday evening, August 21, the House reversed itself and passed the crime bill. The passage of the bill followed protracted lobbying by the White House in support of the crime bill and equally vigorous activity—by Republican leaders and interest groups, such as the National Rifle Association—against it. President Clinton and the Democratic leadership in Congress wanted to force a straight up-or-down Senate vote on the merits of the bill. The Senate, however, immediately became bogged down in procedural and substantive debates designed by Republicans and some conservative Democrats to frustrate the wishes of Clinton and the Democratic leadership.

The Senate Passes the Crime Bill. On August 25, the Senate followed suit on the House's action, thwarting by a vote of 61–39 a procedural move by the Republican leadership to postpone action. The procedural move involved a provision of the Budget and Impoundment Control Act of 1974 that allows a point of order to kill a bill whose spending is not authorized in that year's joint budget resolution. To waive the objection requires approval of sixty senators, rather than a simple majority. If the point of order had been sustained with 40 votes or more, the Republicans had planned to introduce a series of amendments to cut spending in the bill and to toughen some of its criminal provisions. The vote was won only because six Republican senators voted to waive the point of order, going against their party's leaders and against the wishes of many Republican supporters in the electorate opposed to gun control or social betterment programs designed to prevent crime. One Democrat, Richard Shelby of Alabama, voted against his party's position. When that vote failed to uphold the Republican position, minority leader Bob Dole of Kansas decided that he also did not have the necessary forty votes to sustain a filibuster on the crime legislation, and a vote on final passage occurred quickly.

CRIME: THE COLD WAR OF THE 1990S

Public policy, like the 1994 crime bill, is not created in a vacuum. For an issue to get to the national agenda, typically the media have to get involved. This has been easy with crime. Look at Figure 14–1. Here you see that for the last several years, crime, violence, and guns have become America's most important problem, according to those polled. Virtually all polls taken in the United States today show that crime is the number-one concern of the public. Although there is some evidence that certain crime rates have fallen, on average the public's concern is not misplaced.

Crime in American History

In every period in the history of this nation, people have voiced their apprehension about crime. Some criminologists argue that crime was probably as frequent around the time of the American Revolution as it is currently. During the Civil War, mob violence and riots erupted in numerous cities. After the Civil War, people in San Francisco were told that "no decent man is in safety to walk the streets after dark; while at all hours, both night and day, his property is jeopardized by incendiarism and burglary."[1] In 1910, one author stated that "crime, especially in its more violent forms and among the young, is increasing steadily and is threatening to bankrupt the Nation."[2]

From 1900 to the 1930s, social violence and crime increased dramatically. Labor union battles and racial violence were common. Only during the three-decade period from the mid-1930s to the early 1960s did the United States experience, for the first time in its history, stable or slightly declining crime rates.

What most Americans are worried about is violent crime. Since the mid-1980s, its rate has been rising relentlessly. Look at Figure 14–2, where you see the changes in violent crime rates from 1970 to 1994. Going back even further, the murder rate per 100,000 people in 1964 was 4.9, whereas in 1994 it was estimated at 9.3, an almost 100 percent increase. These nationwide numbers, however, do not tell the full story. Murder rates in some major U.S. cities are between 50 and 100 per 100,000 people. These cities include Washington, D.C.; Detroit; New Orleans; St. Louis; and Birmingham.

---

1. President's Commission on Law Enforcement and Administration of Justice, *Challenge of Crime in a Free Society* (Washington, D.C.: Government Printing Office, 1967), p. 19.
2. President's Commission, *Challenge of Crime*, p. 19.

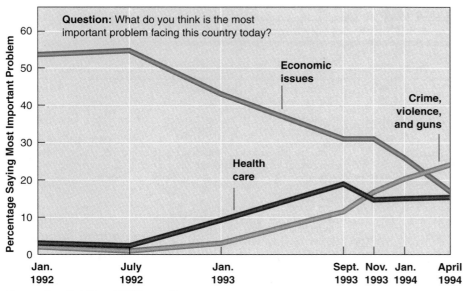

Question: What do you think is the most important problem facing this country today?

Economic issues

Crime, violence, and guns

Health care

Percentage Saying Most Important Problem

Jan. 1992   July 1992   Jan. 1993   Sept. 1993   Nov. 1993   Jan. 1994   April 1994

SOURCE: *New York Times*/CBS News poll.

FIGURE 14–1

Public Opinion Response to Rising Crime Rates

FIGURE 14–2

Changes in Violent Crime Rates from 1970 to 1994

Violent crime in the United States rose from 1970 to the beginning of the 1980s. Then crime rates dropped relatively dramatically until about 1986, when they again started to climb. Currently, rape and assault rates are at their highest recorded levels.

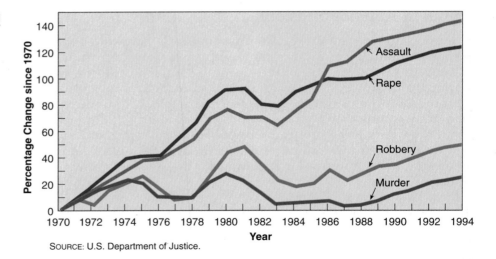

SOURCE: U.S. Department of Justice.

The Total Cost of Crime to American Society

For the perpetrator, crime may pay in certain circumstances—a successful robbery or embezzlement, for example—but crime certainly costs the American public. Consider one typical new home in Pico Rivera, a small city southeast of Los Angeles. The new two-story frame house has motion-sensitive floodlights, infrared alarms, video monitors, and a spiked fence topped with razor wire. The patio is surrounded by a metal cage, and bars are over every window. In the yard are two Doberman pinschers. Private security guards patrol the community. The additional costs of building that new house in terms of crime protection are part of the nationwide cost of crime. Table 14–2 summarizes what crime is costing us every year.

TABLE 14–2

The Total Yearly Cost of Crime in America

EXPENDITURE	EXPLANATION	TOTAL COST (PER YEAR)
Criminal justice	All the spending on police, courts, and prisons at the federal, state, and local levels	$ 90 billion
Private protection	Spending on private guards, security systems, alarms, etc.	$ 65 billion
Urban decay	The cost of lost jobs and fleeing residents because of excessive crime in inner cities	$ 50 billion
Property loss	The value of stolen goods and vandalized buildings	$ 45 billion
Destroyed lives	The economic value of lost lives (death) and broken lives as a result of robberies, rapes, loss of loved ones, etc.	$170 billion
Medical care	The cost of treating victims	$ 5 billion
TOTAL		**$425 billion**

SOURCE: Federal Bureau of Investigation; and *Business Week*, various issues.

The Prison Population Bomb

Virtually the instant a new prison is built, it is filled, and complaints arise about overcrowding. For example, the federal prison system was designed to hold about 40,000 prisoners. At last count, there were well over 100,000 inmates held in federal prisons. The total state prison population now exceeds 900,000, up more than 130 percent since 1980, and more than 300,000 above the capacity of existing prisons. Virtually all states have record numbers of inmates filling their prison systems. At the county and city levels across the nation, there are an estimated 445,000 inmates, far more than those facilities were designed to hold. By the mid-1990s, well over one million Americans were incarcerated in some form of prison or jail. (For a comparison of U.S. incarceration rates with those of other countries, see this chapter's feature entitled *Politics and Comparative Systems: Incarceration Worldwide.*)

As the number of arrests and incarcerations in the United States increases, so does the cost of building and operating prisons. An additional 1,500 new prison beds are needed each week. When operational costs are included and construction costs are amortized over the life of a facility, the cost of sentencing one person to one year in jail averages between $25,000 and $40,000. Thus, the annual nationwide cost of building, maintaining, and operating prisons is about $35 billion today.

When imprisonment keeps truly violent felons behind bars longer, it prevents them from committing more crimes. The average predatory street criminal commits fifteen or more crimes each year when not behind bars. But most prisoners are in for a relatively short time and released on parole early, often because of prison overcrowding. Then many find themselves back in prison because they have violated parole, typically by using illegal drugs. Indeed, of the over one million people who are arrested each year, the majority are arrested for drug offenses. Given that from twenty to forty million Americans violate one or more drug laws each year, the potential

To help ease the overcrowding, inmates at the New York State Prison at Watertown are incarcerated in barrack-style prison blocks.

POLITICS AND COMPARATIVE SYSTEMS
Incarceration Worldwide

The United States is known as "the home of the free and the land of the brave." It therefore may surprise many Americans to discover that the United States has the highest incarceration rate of any country in the world today. Just look at the figure in this feature. These data, relatively speaking, would have looked about the same ten years ago, when the Gulag prison camps still existed in the former Soviet Union and when repression in South Africa was at its peak. Some ask, then, why the U.S. prison population continues to rise while at the same time the number of violent crimes does, too.

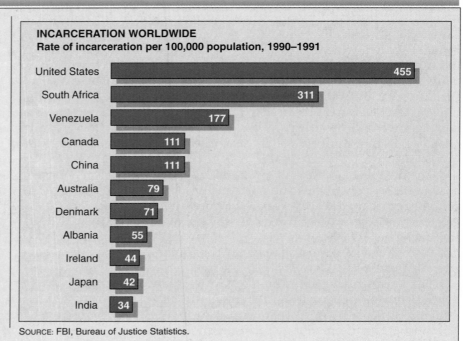

INCARCERATION WORLDWIDE
Rate of incarceration per 100,000 population, 1990–1991

United States	455
South Africa	311
Venezuela	177
Canada	111
China	111
Australia	79
Denmark	71
Albania	55
Ireland	44
Japan	42
India	34

SOURCE: FBI, Bureau of Justice Statistics.

"supply" of prisoners seems virtually without limit. Consequently, it may not matter how many prisons are built; there will still be overcrowding as long as we maintain the same legislation with respect to psychoactive drugs.

Three Strikes and You're Out

Many states are passing "three-strikes-and-you're-out" legislation. Typically, this legislation states that any "career" criminal who already has two violent felony convictions on his or her record will go to jail for life (without parole) if convicted of a third similar felony. Washington state adopted such a law by public referendum in 1990, and California has a similar law. The federal crime bill enacted in 1994 adopted this provision, too.

There are several problems with the three-strikes-and-you're-out plan. One of the most important relates to what we have already talked about: overcrowded prisons. A nationwide adoption of the plan definitely would increase the number of prisoners. Those convicted under such a law would be in prison for life. Thus, we would have a large population of aging prisoners who would require more health-care expenditures—all paid for by the state (or federal) government.

Additionally, in states that do not have capital punishment, the three-strikes-and-you're-out legislation actually reduces the potential cost of crime to those already convicted of two felonies. Consider an individual who already has spent time in prison for two felonies. While he is robbing a store, the police pull up. The robber knows that if he gets caught and convicted, he will stay in prison forever with no chance of parole. He therefore has an increased incentive to kill the police and all witnesses: It will make no difference to his fate. If he ends up being caught anyway, the most he can get is life imprisonment, which he was going to receive anyway.

Although such reasoning may not affect all criminals who find themselves in similar situations, it may affect enough of them to actually increase the murder rate. If it did, this would be the result of the law of unintended consequences—legislation sometimes leads to what is not desired, because it changes the incentives facing individuals.

Politics and Crime: The New Iron Triangle

In Chapter 12, you discovered the iron triangle at work within the federal government. The example used was the U.S. Department of Agriculture. The three points of the iron triangle were (1) the members of Congress who deal with agriculture; (2) the bureaucrats in Congress who administer the programs; and (3) interest groups, their professional staffs, and lobbyists paid for by agribusiness.

A similar type of iron triangle is now developing in the area of crime. A new version of the old military-industrial complex has been born. It is an infrastructure dependent on political rhetoric and federal, state, and local dollars. The politicians are trying to outdo each other as they stand up to the common enemy—crime. During the Eisenhower era in the 1950s, politicians did the same thing when the common enemy was communism. Instead of looking to military bases, communities today look to new prison sites to create jobs and improve their economies. Large and small businesses scramble to get contracts for developing prisons, new anticrime weapons, and so on.

As illustrated in Figure 14–3, the iron triangle in today's cold war against crime involves, on the legislative side, the appropriate congressional

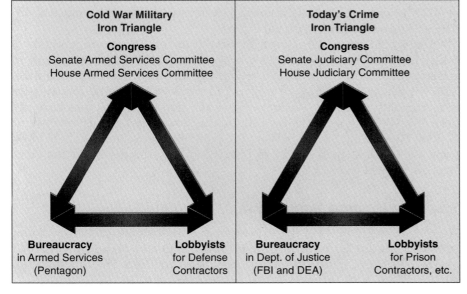

Cold War Military Iron Triangle	Today's Crime Iron Triangle
Congress Senate Armed Services Committee House Armed Services Committee	**Congress** Senate Judiciary Committee House Judiciary Committee
Bureaucracy in Armed Services (Pentagon) — **Lobbyists** for Defense Contractors	**Bureaucracy** in Dept. of Justice (FBI and DEA) — **Lobbyists** for Prison Contractors, etc.

FIGURE 14–3

Comparing the Iron Triangle for the Old Cold War with the Iron Triangle for the New Cold War against Crime

A narcotics officer arrests a cocaine dealer in New York. The war against drugs seemed to make little headway during the 1980s and 1990s, although government expenditures on the effort continued to rise.

INCOME TRANSFER
A transfer of income from some individuals in the economy to others. This is generally done by way of the government. It is a transfer in the sense that no current services are rendered by the recipients.

committees, such as the Senate Judiciary Committee and the House Judiciary Committee, as well as related subcommittees. Additionally, there are the lobbyists for prison contractors and those making sophisticated anticrime weapons. Finally, the bureaucracy in the Department of Justice—particularly in the Federal Bureau of Investigation, the Drug Enforcement Administration, and the Office of National Drug Control Policy—completes the triangle.

One good example of the lobbyists is Corrections Corporation of America, a publicly traded prison company whose annual revenues exceed $100 million. This corporation has learned how to play all sides of the new iron triangle. Its founders and officers include a former chairman of the Tennessee Republican party (who gave $8,000 to the Tennessee Republican party in 1993 and thousands more to congressional candidates), individuals who give large amounts of money to the national Democratic party, a former commissioner of corrections for Arkansas and Virginia, and a former director of the Federal Bureau of Prisons. The company uses the well-known Washington lobbying firm of Covington & Burling.

Communities seeking job growth via crime-related activities are numerous. According to Keith Cunningham of Business Executives for National Security, "There's a food fight among communities that want these prisons." When Senator Edward Kennedy (D., Mass.) announced that Fort Devons, which was supposed to be closed, would be converted to a federal prison, businesspersons in the audience stood up and cheered.

POVERTY, HOMELESSNESS, AND WELFARE

Throughout the world, historically poverty has been accepted as inevitable. The United States and other industrialized nations, however, have sustained enough economic growth in the past several hundred years to eliminate *mass* poverty. In fact, considering the wealth and high standard of living in the United States, the persistence of poverty here appears bizarre and anomalous. How can there still be so much poverty in a nation of so much abundance? And what can be done about it?

A traditional solution has been **income transfers**. There are methods of transferring income from relatively well-to-do to relatively poor groups in society, and as a nation, we have been using such methods for a long time. Today, we have a vast array of welfare programs set up for the sole purpose of redistributing income. We know, however, that these programs have not been entirely successful. Are there alternatives to our current welfare system? Is there a better method of helping the poor? Before we answer these questions, let's look at the concept of poverty in more detail and at the characteristics of the poor.

The Low-Income Population

We can see in Figure 14–4 that the number of individuals classified as poor fell rather steadily from 1959 through 1969. For about a decade, the number of poor leveled off, until the recession of 1981 to 1982. The number then fell somewhat until the early 1990s, when it began to increase slightly.

FIGURE 14–4

The Official Number of Poor in the United States

The number of individuals classified as poor fell steadily from 1959 through 1969. From 1970 to 1981, the number stayed about the same. It then increased during the 1981–1982 recession. The number of poor then fell somewhat, until the early 1990s.

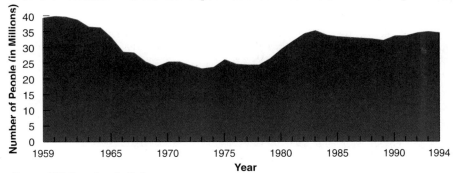

SOURCE: U.S. Department of Labor.

Defining Poverty. The threshold income level, which is used to determine who falls into the poverty category, was originally based on the cost of a nutritionally adequate food plan designed by the U.S. Department of Agriculture for emergency or temporary use. The threshold was determined by multiplying the food-plan cost times three, on the assumption that food expenses constitute approximately one-third of a poor family's expenditures. In 1969, a federal interagency committee examined the calculations of the threshold and decided to set new standards. Until then, annual revisions of the threshold level had been based only on price changes in the food budget. After 1969, the adjustments were made on the basis of changes in the consumer price index (CPI). The CPI is based on the average prices of a specified set of goods and services bought by wage earners in urban areas.

The low-income poverty threshold thus represents an absolute measure of income needed to maintain a specified standard of living as of 1963, with the constant-dollar value, or purchasing-power value, increased year by year in relation to the general increase in prices. For 1994, for example, the official poverty level for a family of four was $15,141. It has gone up since then by the amount of the change in the CPI during the intervening period. (The poverty level varies with family size and location.)

Transfer Payments as Income. The official poverty level is based on pre-tax income, including cash but not **in-kind subsidies**—food stamps, housing vouchers, and the like. If we correct poverty levels for such benefits, the percentage of the population that is below the poverty line drops dramatically, as can be seen in Figure 14–5. Some economists argue that the way in which the official poverty level is calculated makes no sense in a nation that redistributed over $800 billion in cash and noncash transfers in 1995.

IN-KIND SUBSIDY
A good or service—such as food stamps, housing, or medical care—provided by the government to lower-income groups.

The Homeless

The last fifteen years have brought a new awareness of the plight of the homeless, and this awareness has fostered a debate about how many homeless

FIGURE 14–5

Three Measures of Poverty

The percentage of the U.S. population living in poverty depends on what one includes in the definition of income. If one looks at private money income only, the
percentage of the population in poverty during the 1980s and 1990s was well above
20 percent. If one adds cash benefits paid to individuals by the government during
most of the 1980s and 1990s, less than 14 percent of the U.S. population was living in
poverty. Finally, if one takes account of cash benefits, in-kind benefits, and the under-
reporting of income, the share of the U.S. population in poverty was estimated to be
about 7.9 percent in 1994.

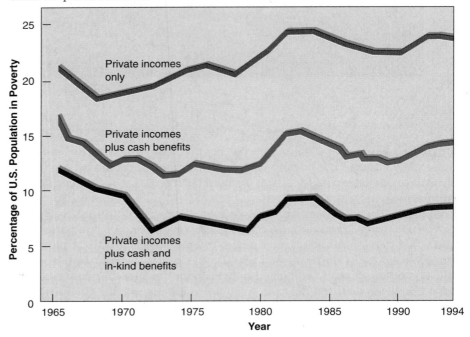

SOURCE: U.S. Congress, Office of the Budget.

persons there are and how they should be helped. Lack of information about
the homeless has led to conflicting claims. Although some observers maintain that the homeless are mostly mentally ill and few in number, people
who work to help the homeless claim that they number from two to three
million. New research has helped to resolve the differences in claims. A
survey by the Urban Institute, a nonpartisan research group, estimated that
there are about 600,000 homeless people in the United States; of those,
about one-third are mentally ill. We do know, in addition, that about two-
thirds of the homeless have serious personal problems that contribute to
their predicament. For example, recent studies show that over one-third are
alcoholics and that about one-fourth are either drug abusers or have previously been convicted of a serious crime.

A growing segment of the homeless population consists of entire families.
About one-fifth of today's homeless are families, most of them young single
women with children, who are housed in temporary shelters throughout
the country. In response to the plight of the homeless, shelters have been
established around the nation to provide short-term emergency needs, such
as hot meals and a bed for the night.

A homeless man lies in his sleeping bag with his belongings on the street of a major American city. Some of the homeless are alcohol or drug dependent, but many are simply men and women who have lost their jobs and all other resources.

Some major cities that have provided permanent shelters for the homeless and given them priority in obtaining public housing have had serious problems with their programs. For example, New York City's shelter system for homeless families has, according to city officials, attracted thousands of families that could live elsewhere, such as with relatives. Families that are certifiably homeless obtain priority in city-run public housing projects. The waiting list for such housing is about 200,000 names long, but the city sets aside only 2,000 of each year's 8,000 apartment vacancies for homeless families. To be certified as a homeless person, an individual has to be in a city homeless shelter. This system thus encourages families to move to the homeless shelters so that they can be put at the head of the list for subsidized public housing. New York's homeless program also faces a growing fiscal problem. From 1984 to the beginning of 1993, New York City spent $700 million to create 28,000 permanent apartments for homeless families. But because the demand for homeless housing continues to grow, the city is anticipating additional expenses for a program that its officials claim it can no longer afford. For the homeless to be helped permanently, they need the transitional services offered by the shelters, plus rehabilitative help (mental health services and substance-abuse counseling), classes in parenting, and assistance in finding employment or obtaining disability benefits.

Attacks on Poverty: Major Income-Maintenance Programs

A variety of income-maintenance programs have been designed to help the poor. A few are discussed here.

Social Security.   For the retired and the unemployed, certain social-insurance programs provide income payments in prescribed situations. The best known is **Social Security**, which includes Old Age, Survivors, and Disability Insurance (OASDI). Social Security is essentially a program of

SOCIAL SECURITY
A federal program that provides monthly payments to millions of people who are retired or unable to work.

The city of Santa Barbara, California, provides food to the homeless and indigent. In many cities, volunteer groups operate food pantries and provide meals to the poor. Such efforts, however, provide only temporary relief and do little to bring the recipients back into the productive economy.

obligatory taxation via payroll taxes imposed on both employers and employees. Workers pay for Social Security while they are employed and receive the benefits after retirement. When insured workers die before retirement, benefits go to the survivors, including spouses and children. Special benefits provide for disabled workers. Over 90 percent of all employed persons in the United States are covered by OASDI.

Social Security originally was designed, during the Great Depression of the 1930s, to transfer income only to poor elderly persons. It was intended to be a program that workers paid for themselves through their contributions. Today, it is merely an income transfer between generations that is only roughly related to past earnings. In other words, Social Security is a system in which income is transferred from Americans who work (young through middle-aged persons) to those who do not work (retired persons). In this way, the relatively young subsidize the relatively old. We pay in when we are younger and receive payments when we are older.

SUPPLEMENTAL
SECURITY INCOME (SSI)
A federal program established to provide assistance to elderly persons and persons with disabilities.

AID TO FAMILIES WITH
DEPENDENT CHILDREN (AFDC)
A state-administered program that furnishes assistance for families in which dependent children do not have the financial support of the father, owing to the father's desertion, disability, or death. The program is financed partially by federal grants.

FOOD STAMPS
Coupons issued by the federal government to low-income individuals to be used for the purchase of food.

Supplemental Security Income (SSI) and Aid to Families with Dependent Children (AFDC). Many people who are poor do not qualify for Social Security benefits. They are assisted through other programs. Starting in 1974, a federally financed and administered **Supplemental Security Income (SSI)** program was instituted. The purpose of SSI was to establish a nationwide minimum income for elderly persons and disabled persons.

Aid to Families with Dependent Children (AFDC) has been a program administered by the states but partially financed by federal grants. This program furnishes aid to families in which dependent children do not have the financial support of the father because of desertion, disability, or death. In 1995, Republicans proposed welfare reform measures that would effectively end AFDC and turn over all responsibility to the states.

Food Stamps. The government issues **food stamps**, coupons that can be used to purchase food. Food stamps are available for low-income individ-

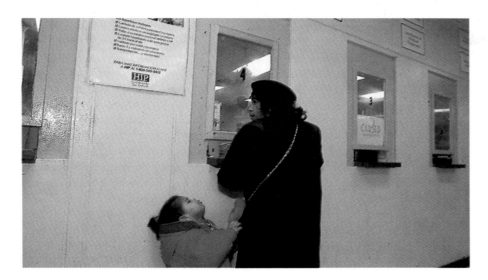

One of the major targets of the Republican majority is welfare reform. While most Republican and Democratic Legislators, as well as the president, agreed that the current system needs reform, there is widespread disagreement over the reform needed. Not even the state governors who seek reform agree on the best structure.

uals and families. Recipients must prove that they qualify by showing that they do not make very much money (or no money at all). In 1964, about 367,000 Americans were receiving food stamps. In 1995, the estimated number of those receiving food stamps was over 26,000,000. The annual cost of funding food stamps jumped from $860,000 in 1964 to more than $22 billion in 1995. Workers who find themselves on strike, and even some college students, are eligible to receive food stamps.

The food-stamp program has become a major part of the welfare system in the United States. Although it was started in 1964 mainly to shore up the nation's agricultural sector by distributing surplus food through retail channels, the program has become a method of preventing malnutrition among the poor.

Welfare Policy Problems

Today, over $800 billion is spent annually on various welfare programs. Many individuals have been helped, but others clearly have been left behind. Poverty rates reached their lowest in 1973. Despite massive government subsidies (and, of course, taxes), the distribution of income is as unequal today as it was in 1960.

Current programs attack income inequalities by transferring income to the poor to help them obtain the basic essentials of life. These programs, however, do not attack the problem of unequal employment *opportunities*. Moreover, the manner in which aid is currently delivered to those who need it generates unintended consequences, such as reduced work effort and changes in family structure.

Recipients of aid may reduce their work effort as a result of the easier-to-obtain income provided by welfare. The fact that the level of benefits is inversely related to income from other sources creates an even more powerful disincentive to work. That is, the more a recipient earns, the fewer benefits he or she receives. In the AFDC program, for example, a one-dollar increase in income earned by the recipient family reduces the benefits by one dollar—a 100 percent marginal tax rate. Recipients feel it is not worthwhile to work when their earned income is taxed so heavily.

As we have discussed, welfare payments are inversely related to the income of the family. Because the father's income is usually the highest in a family, the inclusion of his income may be enough to disqualify the family for welfare even though they are barely subsisting. This may force the father to move out, creating single-parent families headed by women.

Single-parent families headed by women constitute a growing portion of today's poor. Indeed, births to unmarried women as a percentage of all births is now over 30 percent. In some groups, such as those in America's inner cities, it is almost 80 percent. Food-stamp benefits, Medicaid, and AFDC payments to single mothers have risen dramatically since the 1960s.

As part of the Contract with America, House Republicans passed a welfare reform bill in 1995. The legislation returned control over AFDC and several other programs to the states. Funding for the programs would be transferred in a block grant, and the states could set many of the regulations governing the programs. Many Republicans wished to add a provision that would limit assistance to unwed mothers.

Is There an Optimal Welfare Policy?

Income inequality will exist as long as individuals differ in their abilities, family situations, and age and as long as society requires sharp differences in income and social status to stimulate competition. The more important question is, of course, the following: Can we ever eliminate poverty? In a relative sense, the answer is no, if we keep raising the poverty level as all incomes rise in the United States. In an absolute sense, income transfers through various welfare programs can eliminate some poverty but obviously not all. Moreover, as we have seen, certain welfare policies have negative side effects, such as increased disincentives to work and undesirable changes in family structure.

ENVIRONMENTAL POLICY

Human actions may create unwanted side effects—including the destruction of the environment and the ecology (the total pattern of environmental relationships). Every day, humans, through their actions, emit pollutants into the air and the water. Each year, the world atmosphere receives twenty million metric tons of sulfur dioxide, eighteen million metric tons of ozone pollutants, and sixty million metric tons of carbon monoxide.

The Government's Response to Air and Water Pollution

The government has been responding to pollution problems since before the American Revolution, when the Massachusetts Bay Colony issued regulations to try to stop the pollution of Boston Harbor. In the nineteenth century, states passed laws controlling water pollution after scientists and medical researchers convinced most policymakers that dumping sewage into drinking and bathing water caused disease. At the national level, the Federal Water Pollution Control Act of 1948 provided research and assistance to the

A number of urban locations have a landfill problem. The price of landfill has been going up in many of the major cities for many years. Nationwide, in contrast, the average per-ton price of landfill has gone down. In other words, cities in many regions of the United States pay less today to dump their garbage into landfills than they did ten years ago.

states for pollution control efforts, but little was done. In 1952, the first state air-pollution law was passed in Oregon. The federal Air Pollution Control Act of 1955 gave some assistance to states and cities. Table 14–3 describes the major environmental legislation in the United States.

The National Environmental Policy Act. The year 1969 marked the start of the most concerted national government involvement in solving pollution problems. In that year, the conflict between oil exploration interests and environmental interests literally erupted when a Union Oil Company's oil well six miles off the coast of Santa Barbara, California, exploded, releasing 235,000 gallons of crude oil. The result was an oil slick, covering an area of eight hundred square miles, that washed up on the city's beaches and killed plant life, birds, and fish. Hearings in Congress revealed that the Interior Department did not know which way to go in the energy-environment trade-off. Congress did know, however, and passed the National Environmental Policy Act in 1969. This landmark legislation established, among other things, the Council for Environmental Quality. Also, it mandated that an **environmental impact statement (EIS)** be prepared for every recommendation or report on legislation or major federal actions that significantly affected the quality of the environment. The act gave citizens and public interest groups concerned with the environment a weapon against the unnecessary and inappropriate use of natural resources by the government.

ENVIRONMENTAL IMPACT STATEMENT (EIS)
As a requirement mandated by the National Environmental Policy Act, a report that must show the costs and benefits of major federal actions that could significantly affect the quality of the environment.

TABLE 14–3

Major Federal Environmental Legislation

1899 Refuse Act. Made it unlawful to dump refuse into navigable waters without a permit. A 1966 court decision made all industrial wastes subject to this act.

1948 Federal Water Pollution Control Act. Set standards for the treatment of municipal water waste before discharge. Revisions to this act were passed in 1965 and 1967.

1955 Air Pollution Control Act. Authorized federal research programs for air-pollution control.

1963 Clean Air Act. Assisted local and state governments in establishing control programs and coordinated research.

1965 Clean Air Act Amendments. Authorized the establishment of federal standards for automobile exhaust emissions, beginning with 1968 models.

1965 Solid Waste Disposal Act. Provided assistance to local and state governments for control programs and authorized research in this area.

1965 Water Quality Act. Authorized the setting of standards for discharges into waters.

1967 Air Quality Act. Established air quality regions, with acceptable regional pollution levels. Required local and state governments to implement approved control programs or be subject to federal controls.

1969 National Environmental Policy Act. Established the Council for Environmental Quality (CEQ) for the purpose of coordinating all federal pollution control programs. Authorized the establishment of the Environmental Protection Agency (EPA) to implement CEQ policies on a case-by-case basis.

1970 Clean Air Act Amendments. Authorized the Environmental Protection Agency to set national air-pollution standards and restricted the discharge of six major pollutants into the lower atmosphere. Automobile manufacturers were required to reduce nitrogen oxide, hydrocarbon, and carbon monoxide emissions by 90 percent (in addition to the 1965 requirements) during the 1970s.

1972 Federal Water Pollution Control Act Amendments. Set national water quality goal of restoring polluted waters to swimmable, fishable waters by 1983.

1972 Federal Environmental Pesticide Control Act. Required that all pesticides used in interstate commerce be approved and certified as effective for their stated purpose. Required certification that they were harmless to humans, animal life, animal feed, and crops.

1974 Clean Water Act. Originally called the Safe Water Drinking Act, this law set (for the first time) federal standards for water suppliers serving more than twenty-five people, having more than fifteen service connections, or operating more than sixty days a year.

1976 Resource Conservation and Recovery Act. Encouraged the conservation and recovery of resources. Put hazardous waste under government control. Prohibited the opening of new dumping sites. Required that all existing open dumps be closed or upgraded to sanitary landfills by 1983. Set standards for providing technical, financial, and marketing assistance to encourage solid waste management.

1977 Clean Air Act Amendments. Postponed the deadline for automobile emission requirements.

1980 Comprehensive Environmental Response, Compensation, and Liability Act. Established a "Superfund" to clean up toxic waste dumps.

1990 Clean Air Act Amendments. Provided for precise formulas for new gasoline to be burned in the smoggiest cities, further reduction in carbon monoxide and other exhaust emissions in certain areas that still have dangerous ozone levels in the year 2003, and a cap on total emissions of sulfur dioxide from electricity plants. Placed new restrictions on toxic pollutants.

ACID RAIN
Rain that has picked up pollutants, usually sulfur dioxides, from industrial areas of the earth that are often hundreds of miles distant from where the rain falls.

The Clean Air Act of 1990. The most comprehensive government attempt at cleaning up our environment occurred in 1990. After years of lobbying by environmentalists and counterlobbying by industry, the Clean Air Act of 1990 was passed. This act amended the 1970 Clean Air Act, which, among other things, had required a reduction of 90 percent of the amount of carbon monoxide and other pollutants emitted by automobiles. In spite of the fact that an automobile purchased today emits only 4 percent of the pollutants that a 1970 model did, there is more overall air pollution. This is because so many more automobiles are being driven today. Currently, the urban ground-level ozone is as great as it was before any clean-air legislation. The 1990 Clean Air Act requires automobile manufacturers to cut new automobiles' exhaust emissions of nitrogen oxide by 60 percent and the emission of other pollutants by 35 percent. These requirements must be met by 1998.

Stationary sources of air pollution are also subject to more regulation. To reduce **acid rain**, 110 of the oldest coal-burning power plants in the United States must cut their emissions by 40 percent by the year 2001. Controls on

POLITICS: THE HUMAN SIDE
Carol Browner, Administrator of the EPA

"I want my son to be able to grow up and enjoy the natural wonders of the United States in the same way that I have."

BIOGRAPHICAL NOTES

Born in 1955, Carol Browner is a native of South Miami, Florida. She was the first in her family to grow up outside Ireland. Her father, an English professor, had come to the United States in the 1950s. Her mother teaches political science.

After obtaining a law degree from the University of Florida, Browner worked as a lawyer for the Govern-ment Operations Committee in the Florida House of Representatives. In 1983, she worked for Citizen Action, a public-interest lobbying group in Washington, D.C. Three years later, she joined the staff of Senator Lawton Chiles (D., Fla.). Chiles resigned from the Senate in 1988, and Browner went to work as a lawyer for the Senate's Committee on Energy and Natural Resources. Between 1989 and 1991, Browner worked as legislative director on the staff of Al Gore, then a Democratic senator from Tennessee.

In January 1991, Browner was re-cruited away from Washington by Chiles, who had been elected Florida's governor. He wanted Browner to serve as secretary of Florida's Department of Environ-mental Regulation. President Bill Clinton then appointed Browner to head the Environmental Protection Agency (EPA), and she assumed the post, with the approval of the Sen-ate, in 1993.

POLITICAL CONTRIBUTIONS

In her work with Senator Gore, Browner helped draft the Clean Air Act Amendments of 1990. As the secretary of Florida's Department of Environmental Regulation, Browner was credited with effecting tough enforcement of state regulations. To protect the Everglades—Florida's "River of Grass"—Browner negoti-ated a settlement in a federal pollu-tion lawsuit and also lobbied hard for the enactment of a state clean-up law. She arranged that Walt Dis-ney World, near Orlando, Florida, could develop its property in exchange for spending about $40 million to convert 8,500 acres of endangered wetlands into a wildlife refuge. Browner also helped to ban oil and gas drilling off virtually all of the Florida keys.

As head of the EPA, Browner de-clared pollution prevention to be her top priority and vowed to speed up the agency's decision-making procedures. Under Browner, the EPA announced a policy to protect children from the harmful pesticide residues on food, tightened controls on hazardous waste incinerators, and improved the administration of the Superfund law in cleaning up toxic sites. Under Browner, the agency has also enforced the envi-ronmental laws against a number of polluters and expanded the Toxic Release Inventory (requiring indus-try to inform the public of toxic emissions).

other factories and businesses are intended to reduce ground-level ozone pollution in ninety-six cities to healthful levels by 2005 (except in Los Angeles, which has until 2010 to meet the standards). The act also requires that the production of chlorofluorocarbons (CFCs) be stopped completely by the year 2002. CFCs are thought to deplete the ozone layer and increase global warming. CFCs are used in air conditioning and other refrigeration units.

The Costs of Clean Air.   Before the mid-1980s, environmental politics seemed to be couched in terms of "them against us." "Them" was everyone involved in businesses that cut down rain forests, poisoned rivers, and

FIGURE 14–6

Decreasing Annual Toxic Emissions (in billions of pounds)

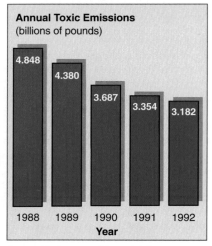

Annual Toxic Emissions (billions of pounds)

Year	
1988	4.848
1989	4.380
1990	3.687
1991	3.354
1992	3.182

SOURCE: Environmental Protection Agency.

FIGURE 14–7

The Ten-Most-Wanted List of Toxic Chemical Polluters

These ten states released the most toxic chemicals in 1992, according to the EPA. (The figures are in millions of pounds.)

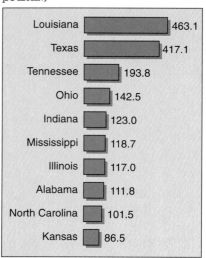

State	Millions of pounds
Louisiana	463.1
Texas	417.1
Tennessee	193.8
Ohio	142.5
Indiana	123.0
Mississippi	118.7
Illinois	117.0
Alabama	111.8
North Carolina	101.5
Kansas	86.5

SOURCE: Environmental Protection Agency.

created oil spills. "Us" was the government, and it was the government's job to stop "them." Today, particularly in the United States, more people are aware that the battle lines are blurred. According to the Environmental Protection Agency (EPA), we are already spending well over $100 billion annually to comply with federal environmental rules. (See this chapter's feature entitled *Politics: The Human Side* on Carol Browner for information on the current head of the EPA.) When the 1990 Clean Air Act is fully implemented, that amount may be as much as 50 percent higher. The government, particularly in Washington, D.C., has become interested in how to solve the nation's environmental problems at the lowest cost. Moreover, U.S. corporations are becoming increasingly engaged in producing recyclable and biodegradable products, as well as pitching in to solve some environmental problems.

Cost concerns clearly were in the minds of the drafters of the Clean Air Act of 1990 when they tackled, for example, the problem of sulfur emissions from electric power plants. Rather than tightening the existing standards, the new law simply limits total sulfur emissions. Companies have a choice of either rebuilding old plants or buying the right to pollute. The result is that polluters have an incentive to not even attempt to deal with exceptionally dirty plants. When closing down such plants, they can sell their pollution rights to those who value them more. The law is straightforward: An electric utility power plant is allowed to emit up to one ton of sulfur dioxide into the air in a given year. If the plant emits one ton of sulfur dioxide, the allowance disappears. If a plant switches to a low-sulfur-dioxide fuel, for example, or installs scrubbing equipment that reduces sulfur dioxide, it may end up emitting less than one ton. In this case, it can sell or otherwise trade its unused pollution allowance, or it can bank it for later use.

These rights to pollution allowances have already started to trade in the marketplace. Indeed, there is a well-established market in "smog futures" offered on the Chicago Board of Trade and the New York Mercantile Exchange.

There Have Been Improvements. The United States is making fairly significant progress in the war on toxic emissions. From 1988 to 1992, the latest years for which we have data, the Environmental Protection Agency showed that the volume of chemicals released into the environment declined 34 percent. In 1988, annual toxic emissions totaled 4.848 billion pounds, and in 1992, they totaled only 3.182 billion pounds, as you can see in Figure 14–6.

These data do not indicate, however, that the war against toxic emissions has been won. Figure 14–7 lists the states that generate the most toxic emissions.

Regulating Hazardous Waste: Superfund

In 1980, Congress passed the Comprehensive Environmental Response, Compensation, and Liability Act (CERCLA), commonly known as Superfund. The basic purpose of Superfund, which was amended in 1986 by the Superfund Amendments and Reauthorization Act, is to regulate the clean-up of leaking hazardous waste disposal sites. A special federal fund was created for that purpose. Superfund provides that when a release or a threatened release from a site occurs, the EPA can clean up the site and recover the cost of the clean-up from (1) the person who generated the wastes disposed of at the site, (2) the person who transported the wastes to the site, (3) the person who owned or operated the site at the time of the disposal, or (4) the current owner or operator. Liability is usually assessed on anyone who might have been responsible—for example, a person who generated only a fraction of the hazardous waste disposed of at the site may nevertheless be liable for all of the clean-up costs.

By the early 1990s, only 84 of the 1,245 designated sites on Superfund's high-priority list had been cleaned up. The cost has been $11.1 billion. Critics of the Superfund program point out that only 10 percent of the money spent by insurance companies to settle Superfund claims is used to clean up hazardous materials. According to the Rand Corporation, in Santa Monica, California, the remaining 90 percent goes to legal fees and related costs. Other critics point out that the potential benefits of such expensive toxic waste clean-ups are not worth the cost.

The EPA believes that one thousand cancer cases result each year from exposure to hazardous waste sites (although some sources estimate the number of cancer cases to be much higher). Through Superfund, the EPA is allocating $1.75 billion for clean-up. That comes out to $1.75 million per predicted cancer case—under the assumption, of course, that a significant number of the hazardous waste sites actually are cleaned up. In contrast, the National Cancer Institute's budget for breast cancer research is about $133 million, when there are an estimated 176,000 breast cancer cases diagnosed each year (that is, a cost of $755 per diagnosed case). Furthermore, new EPA studies suggest that other environmental problems pose a greater cancer risk than do hazardous wastes, in terms of the number of people who get cancer. For example, indoor air pollution may cause more cancer deaths per year than do uncleaned Superfund sites.

RECYCLING
The reuse of raw materials derived from already manufactured products.

Typical recycling laws in different cities and counties require that recyclable materials be separated by each household. In this photo, the household has carefully separated newspapers from glass and plastic bottles.

Recycling and Precycling

The current ecology movement includes intensive efforts to save scarce resources via recycling. **Recycling** involves reusing paper products, plastics, glass, and metals rather than putting them into solid waste dumps. Many cities have instituted mandatory recycling programs.

The benefits of recycling are straightforward: fewer *natural* resources are used. But some commentators argue that recycling does not necessarily save *total* resources. For example, recycling paper products may not necessarily save trees in the long run, according to A. Clark Wiseman, an economist for Resources for the Future, in Washington, D.C. He argues that an increase in paper recycling eventually will lead to a reduction in the demand for virgin paper and, thus, in the demand for trees. Because most trees are planted specifically to produce paper, a reduction in the demand for trees will mean that certain land now used to grow trees will be put to other uses. The end result may be smaller, rather than larger, forests. Nonetheless, every ton of recycled paper does save seventeen trees and three cubic yards of landfill space in the short run.

Recycling's Invisible Costs.   The recycling of paper can also pollute. Used paper has ink on it that has to be removed during the recycling process. According to the National Wildlife Federation, one hundred tons of de-inked fiber generates forty tons of sludge. This sludge has to be disposed of, usually in a landfill. Many paper companies, however, are beginning to produce nondyed, nonbleached paper, but its recycling still creates waste that has to be disposed of.

Recycling also requires human effort. The labor resources involved in recycling are often many times more costly than the potential savings in scarce natural resources. This means that net resource use—counting all sources—may sometimes be greater with recycling than without it.

Is Precycling the Answer?   One way to reduce the amount of our waste is to precycle. Although this term does not have a strict definition, it usually is used to mean making products in such a way that they are not overpackaged, can be refilled, or both. Detergent companies, for example, have found it beneficial for themselves, consumers, and the environment to package and sell concentrated forms of detergent. The packages are smaller, the resources used in packaging are fewer, and there is less waste to get rid of than is the case with the nonconcentrated forms of detergent. In principle, concentrated juices also represent a form of precycling. In short, the packaging of products in a more concentrated form represents precycling and may help the environment.

THE POLITICS OF ECONOMIC DECISION MAKING

Nowhere are the principles of public policymaking more obvious than in the area of economic decisions undertaken by the federal government. The president and Congress (and to a growing extent, the judiciary) are faced constantly with questions concerning economic policy. Consider some of these questions:

1. Should federal income taxes be raised on high-income-earning individuals in order to reduce the federal budget deficit?
2. Should Congress pass laws that restrict the ability of foreigners to buy U.S. companies and real estate?
3. Should interest rates be raised by the Federal Reserve System in order to quell potential overheating of the economy?

There are no clear-cut answers to such questions. Each policy action carries with it costs and benefits, known as **policy trade-offs.** The costs are typically borne by one group and the benefits enjoyed by another group.

THE POLITICS OF TAXES AND SUBSIDIES

Taxes are not just given to us from above. Rather, they are voted on by members of Congress. Members of Congress also vote on **subsidies,** which are a type of negative taxes or gifts to certain businesses and individuals.

We begin our analysis with the premise that in the world of taxes and subsidies, the following is always true: *For every action on the part of the*

POLICY TRADE-OFFS
The cost to the nation of undertaking any one policy in terms of all of the other policies that could have been undertaken. For example, an increase in the expenditures on one federal program means either a reduction in expenditures on another program or an increase in federal taxes (or the deficit).

SUBSIDY
A negative tax; usually a payment to a producer given on a per-unit basis according to the amount of production of a particular commodity.

government, there will be a reaction on the part of the public. Eventually, the government will react with another action, followed by the public's further reaction. The **action-reaction syndrome** is a reality that has plagued government policymakers since the beginning of this nation.

The Tax Code, Tax Rates, and Tax Loopholes

An examination of the Internal Revenue Code, encompassing thousands of pages, thousands of sections, and thousands of subsections, gives some indication that our tax system is not very simple. The 1986 Tax Reform Act was supposed to simplify it somewhat, but once you understand the action-reaction principle of taxation, you can predict that whatever simplification occurred in 1986 will be undone over time.

People are not assessed a lump-sum tax each year; each family does not just pay $1,000 or $10,000 or $20,000. Rather, individuals and businesses pay taxes based on tax rates. (Table 14–4 shows the 1995 tax rates for individuals and married couples.) The higher the tax rate—the action on the part of the government—the greater the public's reaction to that tax rate. Again, it is all a matter of costs and benefits. If the tax rate on all the income you make is 15 percent, that means that any method you can use to reduce your taxable income by one dollar saves you fifteen cents in tax liabilities that you owe the federal government. Therefore, those individuals paying a 15 percent rate have a relatively small incentive to reduce their taxable incomes. But consider individuals who were faced with a tax rate of 91 percent in the early 1960s They had a tremendous incentive to find legal ways to reduce their taxable incomes. For every dollar of income that was somehow deemed nontaxable, these taxpayers would reduce tax liabilities by 91 cents.

So, individuals and corporations facing high tax rates will always react by making concerted attempts to get Congress to add **loopholes** in the tax law that allow them to reduce their taxable incomes. Loopholes are defined as legal methods of avoiding taxes. When the Internal Revenue Code imposed very high tax rates on high incomes, it also provided for more loopholes. There were special provisions that enabled investors in oil and gas wells to reduce their taxable income. There were loopholes that allowed people to shift income from one year to the next. There were loopholes that allowed individuals to form corporations outside the United States in order to avoid some taxes completely. The same principles apply to other interest groups. As long as one group of taxpayers sees a specific benefit from getting the law changed and that benefit means a lot of money per individual, the

ACTION-REACTION SYNDROME
For every action on the part of government, there is a reaction on the part of the affected public. Then the government attempts to counter the reaction with another action, which starts the cycle all over again.

LOOPHOLE
A legal method by which individuals and businesses are allowed to reduce the tax liabilities owed to the government.

TABLE 14–4

1995 Tax Rates for Individuals and Married Couples

SINGLE PERSONS		MARRIED COUPLES	
MARGINAL TAX BRACKET	MARGINAL TAX RATE	MARGINAL TAX BRACKET	MARGINAL TAX RATE
$0–$23,350	15 %	$0–$39,000	15 %
$23,351–$56,550	28	$39,001–$94,250	28
$56,551–$117,950	31	$94,251–$143,600	31
$117,951–$256,500	36	$143,601–$256,500	36
$256,501 and up	39.6	$256,501 and up	39.6

President Clinton signs the budget package into law in 1993. He had campaigned on a platform that included tax cuts for the middle class and significant "jobs programs." The compromise budget package that he was forced to accept included neither but did include significant increases in the marginal tax rate for America's high-earning citizens.

interest group will aggressively support lobbying activities and the election and reelection of members of Congress who will push for special tax loopholes. In other words, if there is enough of a benefit to be derived from influencing tax legislation, such influence will be exerted by the affected parties.

Why We Will Never Have a Simple Tax System

After 1986, the federal tax code was simplified for most people. But astute policymakers then predicted that it would not stay simple for long. The federal government was running large deficits in the late 1980s, and these have continued into the 1990s. When faced with the proposition of having to cut the growth of federal government spending, Congress has balked. Instead, it has raised tax rates. This occurred under the Bush administration in 1990 and under the Clinton administration in 1993. Indeed, at the upper end of income earners, the tax rate paid on each extra dollar earned went up from 28 percent, based on the 1986 tax reform act, to 39.6 percent after the 1993 tax bill passed. That is an increase in the effective tax rate of 41.4 percent.

In response, the action-reaction syndrome is certainly going into effect as you read this text. As tax rates go up, those who are affected will spend more time and effort to get Congress to legislate special exceptions, exemptions, loopholes, and the like, so that the *full* impact of such tax-rate increases will not be felt by richer Americans. The U.S. tax code quickly will become as complex as, or more complicated than, it was before the Tax Reform Act of 1986. The average U.S. tax burden still may be lower than that in other countries, however.

The Underground Economy

UNDERGROUND ECONOMY
The part of the economy that does not pay taxes and so is not directly measured by government statisticians; also called the *subterranean economy* or *unreported economy*.

The other reaction by those who face a higher federal income tax rate is to seek relief in the underground economy. The **underground economy** consists of individuals who work for cash payments without paying any taxes. (It also consists of individuals who engage in illegal activities, such as prostitution, gambling, and drug trafficking.) As tax rates increase, individuals find a greater incentive to work "off the books."

The question, of course, is how big the underground economy is. If it is small, it is not a serious problem. Various researchers have come up with different estimates as to the size of the U.S. underground economy. These estimates range from 5 to 15 percent of total national income each year. This means that the underground economy in the United States represents anywhere from $325 billion to $1 trillion a year. The extent of the underground economy is estimated to be even greater in some other countries.

A particularly thorny aspect of the underground economy came under intense public scrutiny during the first year of President Bill Clinton's administration. Several of his appointees were discovered to have avoided paying the "nanny tax" for household help. In effect, the Clinton nominees in question had paid their nannies and housekeepers in cash, thus avoiding any payment of federal taxes owed. Those nannies and other household helpers were, in effect, part of the underground economy. (In 1994, Congress took action to eliminate the "nanny tax" problem.)

THE POLITICS OF FISCAL AND MONETARY POLICY

Changes in the tax code sometimes form part of an overall fiscal policy change. **Fiscal policy** is defined as the use of changes in government expenditures and taxes to alter national economic variables, such as the rate of inflation, the rate of unemployment, the level of interest rates, and the rate of economic growth. The federal government also has under its control **monetary policy**, defined as the use of changes in the amount of money in circulation so as to affect interest rates, credit markets, the rate of inflation, and employment. Fiscal policy is the domain of Congress and the president. Monetary policy, as we shall see, is much less under the control of Congress and the president, because the monetary authority in the United States, the Federal Reserve System, or the Fed, is an independent agency not directly controlled by either Congress or the president.

FISCAL POLICY
The use of changes in government spending or taxes to alter national economic variables, such as the rate of unemployment.

MONETARY POLICY
The use of changes in the amount of money in circulation to alter credit markets, employment, and the rate of inflation.

Fiscal Policy: Theory and Reality

The theory behind fiscal policy changes is relatively straightforward: When the economy is going into a recession (a period of rising unemployment), the federal government should stimulate economic activity by increasing government expenditures, by decreasing taxes, or both. When the economy is becoming overheated with rapid increases in employment and rising prices (a condition of inflation), fiscal policy should become contractionary, reducing government expenditures and increasing taxes. That particular view of fiscal policy was first implemented in the 1930s and again became popular during the 1960s. It was an outgrowth of the economic theories of the English economist John Maynard Keynes (pronounced *kains*). Keynes's ideas, published during the Great Depression of the 1930s, influenced the economic policymakers guiding President Franklin D. Roosevelt's New Deal.

Wall Street during the stock market crash of 1929.

KEYNESIAN ECONOMICS
An economic theory, named after English economist John Maynard Keynes, that gained prominence during the Great Depression of the 1930s. It is typically associated with the use of fiscal policy to alter national economic variables—for example, increased government spending during times of economic downturns.

Keynes believed that the forces of supply and demand operated too slowly in a serious recession and that government should step in to stimulate the economy. Such actions on the part of government thus are guided by **Keynesian economics.** Keynesian economists believe, for example, that the Great Depression resulted from a serious imbalance in the economy. The public was saving more than usual, and businesses were investing less than usual. According to Keynesian theory, at the beginning of the depression, government should have filled the gap that was created when businesses began limiting their investments. The government could have done so by increasing government spending or cutting taxes.

Since the Great Depression, many public officials and labor leaders have suggested starting "jobs programs" to reduce unemployment and stimulate the economy. Several suggestions for forming new government-sponsored jobs programs to bring down unemployment rates were made in the early 1980s and again in the 1990s.

Fiscal policy faces serious practical issues, however. These issues involve, at a minimum, proper timing, as well as the actual fiscal policymaking process within government.

Monetary Policy: Politics and Reality

The theory behind monetary policy, like that behind fiscal policy, is relatively straightforward. In periods of recession and high unemployment, we should stimulate the economy by expanding the rate of growth of the money supply. An easy-money policy is supposed to lower interest rates and induce consumers to spend more and producers to invest more. With rising inflation, we should do the reverse: reduce the rate of growth of the amount of money in circulation. Interest rates should rise, choking off some consumer spending and some business investment. But the world is never so simple as the theory we use to explain it. If the nation experiences stagflation—rising inflation *and* rising unemployment—expansionary monetary policy (expanding the rate of growth of the money supply) will lead to even more inflation. Ultimately, the more money there is in circulation, the higher prices will be—there will be inflation.

The Monetary Authority—The Federal Reserve System.   Congress established the nation's modern central bank, the Federal Reserve System, in 1913. It is governed by a board of governors consisting of seven individuals, including the very powerful chairperson. All of the governors, including the chairperson, are nominated by the president and approved by the Senate. Their appointments are for fourteen years.

Through the Federal Reserve System, or Fed, and its **Federal Open Market Committee (FOMC)**, decisions about monetary policy are made eight times a year. The Board of Governors of the Federal Reserve System is independent. The president can attempt to convince the board, and Congress can threaten to merge the Fed with the Treasury, but as long as the Fed retains its independence, its chairperson and governors can do what they please. Hence, talking about "the president's monetary policy" or "Congress's monetary policy" is inaccurate. To be sure, the Fed has, on occasion, yielded to presidential pressure, and for a while the Fed's chairperson felt constrained to follow a congressional resolution requiring him to report monetary targets over each six-month period. But now, more than ever before, the Fed remains one of the truly independent sources of economic power in the government. (See this chapter's feature entitled *Politics and Diversity*.)

FEDERAL OPEN MARKET COMMITTEE (FOMC)
The most important body within the Federal Reserve System. The FOMC decides how monetary policy should be carried out by the Federal Reserve.

Monetary Policy and Lags.   Monetary policy does not suffer from the same lengthy time lags as fiscal policy does, because the Fed can, within a very short period, put its policy into effect. Nonetheless, researchers have estimated that it takes almost fourteen months for a change in monetary policy to become effective, measured from the time the economy either slows down or speeds up too much to the time the economy feels the policy change.[3] This means that by the time monetary policy goes into effect, a different policy might be appropriate.

The Fed's Record.   Federal Reserve monetary policy, in principle, is supposed to be countercyclical. The economy goes through so-called business cycles, made up of recessions (and sometimes depressions) when unemployment is high, and boom times when unemployment is low and businesses are straining capacity. For the Fed to "ride against the wind," it must create policies that go counter to business activity. Researchers examining the evidence since 1914 have uniformly concluded that, on average, the Fed's policy has turned out to be pro-cyclical. That is, by the time the Fed started pumping money into the economy, it was time to do the opposite; by the time the Fed started reducing the rate of growth of the money supply, it was time for it to start increasing it. Perhaps the Fed's biggest pro-cyclical blunder occurred during the Great Depression. Many economists believe that what would have been a severe recession turned into the Great Depression in the 1930s because the Fed's action resulted in almost a one-third decrease in the amount of money in circulation. It has also been argued that the

---

3. Robert Gordon, *Macroeconomics*, 6th ed. (New York: HarperCollins, 1993), p. 431.

The Board of Governors of the Federal Reserve System meets in Washington, D.C.

rapid inflation experienced in the 1970s was in part the result of the Fed's increasing the rate of growth of the money supply too much.

In addition, some observers of Federal Reserve policy claim that former head of the Fed Paul Volker created one of the worst recessions since the Great Depression in 1981–1982, when he caused the Fed to engage in an extremely restrictive monetary policy. Others argue that he needed to do so to "break inflation's back." In fact, inflation did slow down to almost zero during the middle of the 1980s. It averaged about 4 percent in the early 1990s.

While inflation actually fell somewhat below 4 percent in certain years, Alan Greenspan, chairman of the Fed, seemed to be worried about a resurgence of inflation in 1994. He came under criticism from Treasury Secretary Lloyd M. Bentsen, Henry B. Gonzalez (head of the House Banking Committee), and others when he caused the Fed to increase interest rates several times. Each small increase in the interest rate that the Fed charges depository institutions when they borrow money from the Fed has far-reaching effects. On at least some of the occasions when Greenspan raised such interest rates, the stock market responded negatively.

REFLECTIONS ON THE PUBLIC DEBT AND BIG DEFICITS

U.S. TREASURY BOND
Evidence of debt issued by the federal government; similar to corporate bonds but issued by the U.S. Treasury.

PUBLIC DEBT, OR NATIONAL DEBT
The total amount of debt carried by the federal government.

The federal government has run a budget deficit—spent more than it received—in every year except two since 1960. Every time a budget deficit occurs, the federal government issues debt instruments in the form of **U.S. Treasury bonds.** The sale of these bonds to corporations, private individuals, pension plans, foreign governments, foreign businesses, and foreign individuals adds to the **public debt,** or **national debt,** defined as the total amount owed by the federal government. Thus, the relationship between the annual federal government budget deficit and the public debt is clear:

POLITICS AND DIVERSITY
The Fed Has a Cultural Diversity Problem

While President Clinton has pursued actively his goal of creating an administration that "looks like America," the Federal Reserve System continues its reign as one of the most male and least diverse groups in the federal government. For most of its history, its seven-member board of governors has been all white and has included almost no women. Of the top thirty jobs at the Fed, all are held by white males except for the director of maintenance services, who is an African-American male. As of 1994, at the regional Federal Reserve banks, all twelve presidents and ninety-eight of the 111 vice presidents were white men.

The chairman of the Board of Governors of the Federal Reserve System, Alan Greenspan, wrote to the chairman of the House Banking Committee, Henry B. Gonzalez (D., Tex.), that "we are working diligently to improve opportunities for women and minorities throughout the System." But Greenspan's efforts to change the Fed will not have rapid success. The Fed is an institution that has little turnover, and almost all promotions are from within. Those who are high-level staffers have been with the Fed for most of their professional lives. The reason is fairly clear: Working conditions are good, and the pay is great—top staff get $162,000 plus many perks, which is more than members of Congress or the cabinet earn.

There is some sign of change, though. At the Fed's Washington headquarters, almost 30 percent of second-tier staff jobs are held by women, and 14 percent are held by minorities. Currently, three women are first vice presidents at three of the twelve regional banks. They will be next in line to become presidents.

If the public debt is, say, $3 trillion this year and the federal budget deficit is $400 billion during the year, then at the end of the year the public debt will be $3.4 trillion. Table 14–5 shows what has happened to the net public debt over time.

It would seem that the nation increasingly is mortgaging its future. But this table does not take into account two important variables: inflation and increases in population. In Figure 14–8, we correct the public debt for inflation and increases in population. The per capita public debt in so-called **constant dollars** (dollars corrected for inflation) reached its peak, as you might expect, during World War II and fell steadily thereafter until the mid-1970s. Since then, except for a reduction in 1980, it has continued to rise. If we are not careful, it will exceed (in per capita constant-dollar terms) what it was during World War II. Politicians and the public alike are concerned.

Is the Public Debt a Burden?

We often hear about the burden of the public debt. Some argue that the government eventually is going to go bankrupt, but that, of course, cannot happen. As long as the government has the ability to pay for interest payments on the public debt through taxation, it will never go bankrupt. What happens is that when Treasury bonds come due, they are simply "rolled over." That is, if a $1 million Treasury bond comes due today, the U.S. Treasury pays it off and sells another $1 million bond.

What about the interest payments? Interest payments are paid by taxes, so what we are really talking about is taxing some people to pay interest to others who loaned money to the government. This cannot really be called a burden to all of society. There is one hitch, however. Not all of the interest payments are paid to Americans. A significant amount is paid to foreigners,

CONSTANT DOLLARS
Dollars corrected for inflation; dollars expressed in terms of purchasing power for a given year.

TABLE 14–5 ▪
Net Public Debt of the Federal Government

YEAR	TOTAL (BILLIONS OF CURRENT DOLLARS)
1940	$ 42.7
1945	235.2
1950	219.0
1960	237.2
1970	284.9
1980	709.3
1985	1,499.5
1990	2,410.1
1992	2,998.6
1993	3,247.2
1994	3,472.4
1996*	3,721.4

*Estimate.
SOURCE: U.S. Office of Management and Budget.

because foreigners own almost 15 percent of the public debt. This raises the fear of too much foreign control of U.S. assets. So it is no longer the case that we "owe it all to ourselves."

Another factor is also important. Even though we are paying interest to ourselves for the most part, the more the federal government borrows, the greater the percentage of the federal budget that is committed to interest payments. The ever-increasing portion of the budget committed to interest payments reduces the federal government's ability to purchase public goods, such as more national parks, in the future. In 1976, interest costs to the government were less than 9 percent of total federal outlays. The estimate for 1996 is over 15 percent. Indeed, if you wish to do a simple projection of current trends, some time in the next century the federal government will be spending almost 100 percent of its budget on interest payments! This, of course, will not occur, but it highlights the problem of running larger and larger deficits and borrowing more and more money to cover them.

The Problem of "Crowding Out"

Although it may be true that we owe the public debt to ourselves (except for what is owed to foreigners), another issue is involved. A large public debt is made up of a series of annual federal government budget deficits. Each time the federal government runs a deficit, we know that it must go into the financial marketplace to borrow the money. This process, in which the U.S. Treasury sells U.S. Treasury bonds, is called **public debt financing.** Public debt financing, in effect, "crowds out" private borrowing. Consider that to borrow, say, $100 billion, the federal government must bid for loanable funds in the marketplace, just as any business does. It bids for those loanable funds by offering to pay higher interest rates. Consequently, interest rates are increased when the federal government runs large deficits and borrows money to cover them. Higher interest rates can stifle or slow business investment, which reduces the rate of economic growth. Some critics of the large budget deficits during the Bush administration claim that the deficits were responsible, in part, for the 1990–1992 recession. (To see how the U.S. public debt compares with that of other nations, see this chapter's *Politics and Comparative Public Debts*.)

FIGURE 14–8

Per Capita Public Debt of the United States in Constant 1982 Dollars

If we correct the public debt for inter-governmental borrowing, the growth in the population, and changes in the price level (inflation), we obtain a graph that shows the per capita net public debt in the United States expressed in constant 1982 dollars. The public debt reached its peak during World War II and then dropped consistently until about 1975. In the last twenty years, except for a dip in 1980, it has risen steadily and is starting to approach World War II levels.

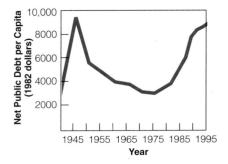

PUBLIC DEBT FINANCING
The government's spending more than it receives in taxes and paying for the difference by issuing U.S. Treasury bonds, thereby adding to the public debt.

BALANCING THE BUDGET: A CONSTITUTIONAL AMENDMENT?

Some argue that the way not to have deficits is to have a constitutional convention to draft a balanced budget amendment to the U.S. Constitution. Two-thirds of the state legislatures need to petition the Congress for a convention to be called. To date, the required number of legislative petitions has not been filed.

A Congress-Generated Amendment

Congress also has the option of passing a constitutional amendment, which it could then submit to the states for ratification. In 1986, the Senate voted on such an amendment. In 1992, Texas Democrat Charles Stenholm put

POLITICS AND COMPARATIVE PUBLIC DEBTS
How the U.S. Public Debt Compares with That of Other Nations

The net U.S. federal debt held by the public is estimated to be a little over $3.7 trillion in 1996, but that number alone does not tell us much. We need to compare the federal debt with a year's annual output in this country (gross domestic product, or GDP). The estimated U.S. GDP for 1996 is about $7.35 trillion. Therefore, the public debt expressed as a percentage of annual U.S. output is about 50 percent.

To know whether that is comparatively a low or high percentage, we need to compare the U.S. debt as a percentage of annual GDP with that of other industrialized countries.

Look at the accompanying table. You will see that relative to the public debt of the twelve countries in the European Union (EU), the U.S. public debt is relatively low.

The United States may, however, catch up with Ireland, Belgium, Italy, and Greece fairly soon. After all, at the beginning of the 1980s, the debt held by the public amounted to only 25 percent of annual U.S. output. By 1986, the percentage had risen to 40 percent, and it is now about 50 percent.

COUNTRY	FEDERAL DEBT AS A PERCENTAGE OF 1996 GDP
Belgium	141
Italy	124
Greece	116
Ireland	81
The Netherlands	77
Denmark	75
Portugal	71
Spain	65
Germany	58
France	53
Great Britain	52
United States	50
Luxembourg	8

SOURCE: European Union forecasts.

forth an amendment bill in the House with 268 co-sponsors. Simultaneously in the Senate, Democrat Paul Simon of Illinois introduced his own amendment.

In 1994, Congress got another chance to pass a balanced budget amendment. Again, Senator Paul Simon and Representative Charles Stenholm offered their balanced budget amendments. When it was under debate, White House Budget Director Leon Panetta predicted that economic "chaos," plus higher taxes and slashed federal programs, would result if the amendment succeeded. President Clinton wrote a letter to George Mitchell (D., Maine), then Senate majority leader, stating that the Simon-Stenholm amendment was "bad economics" and a "budget gimmick" that "would not reduce the deficit by a single penny."

In 1995, the Republican-controlled House of Representatives passed a balanced budget amendment with the support of many Democratic legislators. The amendment failed to receive the necessary two-thirds majority in the Senate, however.

Alternatives to a Balanced Budget Amendment

Critics of the balanced budget amendment concept argue that even if such an amendment were passed, Congress simply would figure out ways to put excessive spending "off budget." In 1985, Congress passed the Gramm-Rudman-Hollings Deficit Reduction Act in an effort to require that Congress reduce the size of its budget deficits. The deficit was required to drop from $171.9 billion in 1986 to zero in 1991. After the first two years of failure to comply with the target deficit reductions, Congress passed a revised act requiring that the 1988 deficit be $144 billion and that it drop to zero by

1993. The first three years of the Revised Deficit Reduction Act saw Congress again fail to meet deficit reductions. In 1990, another revised set of Gramm-Rudman targets was proposed, allowing for a 1991 deficit of over $200 billion, excluding the cost of the savings and loan bailout. In fact, the true deficit in 1991 turned out to be closer to $270 billion and was almost $300 billion in 1992.

Some observers believe that Congress's inability to comply with its own law indicates that our governing body can no longer be fiscally responsible, although the Republicans of the 104th Congress decided to try yet again to plan a balanced budget for the future.

HOW LARGE DEFICITS AND AN INCREASING PUBLIC DEBT AFFECT THE AVERAGE AMERICAN

Large federal deficits make headlines, and so does the increasing public debt. But the average American has seen such headlines for at least a decade now. The initial predictions in the mid-1980s that the United States was facing bankruptcy because of large federal government deficits did not prove to be true. How, then, has the average American been affected? How will that average American be affected in the future if, as predicted, federal budget deficits continue at record rates?

As with all issues in politics and economics, the answer is not simple. We already have discussed the crowding-out effect of government spending financed by deficits. The more that federal budget deficits crowd out investment, the poorer our children and our grandchildren will be. Why? Because we will have invested less today in machines, equipment, research and development, and the like.

Another way in which the average American has been affected by such large deficits is that the deficits have caused lawmakers in Washington to mandate many rules and regulations that the states and municipalities must now carry out on their own. We discussed this important issue in Chapter 3 when we talked about federal mandates. Congress, presumably embarrassed by the continuing large federal budget deficits, would rather see its programs carried out by the states with state money so that federal deficits will not be any larger.

Some observers argue, however, that the size of the deficit is irrelevant. Currently, federal, state, and local governments together spend anywhere from 33 to 42 percent of annual national economic output.[4] The figures are high because governments are large. The public policy question, according to these observers, is "What is the optimal size of government?" rather than "How should we finance government spending?"

DOMESTIC AND ECONOMIC POLICY: UNFINISHED WORK

At least in the public's eyes, the most important unfinished work with respect to domestic policy involves violence and crime in the United States. There is little indication that this problem will be solved in the foreseeable future. The latest FBI data indicate that homicide by handguns reached its

---

4. The estimates vary widely depending on who is doing the measuring.

Every president is responsible for formulating the administration's budget message to Congress. Here President Clinton is shown with his budget advisors, including Secretary of Labor Robert Reich. Note that although the president can suggest a budget, it is Congress that passes the budget. Every single budget submitted by the last five presidents has been exceeded by what Congress has actually budgeted.

highest level ever in 1992. Crime experts predict that we will continue to see similar headlines for several years to come. Those in favor of gun control and an outright ban on all handguns argue that if we implement such policies, crime rates will fall. (The 1994 crime bill included a ban on several types of automatic weapons. Whether this will help to reduce gun-related assaults, murders, and other crimes, of course, remains to be seen.)

It seems strange that poverty, homelessness, and welfare are still on the domestic policy agenda. After all, the federal government started its "war on poverty" back in the early 1960s. By some estimates, we have transferred well over a trillion dollars to eliminate poverty since then. Yet poverty remains a blight on the record of one of the world's richest countries—the United States. President Bill Clinton claimed he would eliminate welfare "as we know it." In 1995, the Republicans took up the challenge of returning control over welfare programs to the states.

Congress probably will never remove environmental policy from its domestic policy agenda. Even if the United States miraculously solved many of its environmental problems, there still would be the rest of the world to worry about. If we do, indeed, live on "spaceship earth," then as voyagers on this spaceship, Americans need to worry about how the rest of the world is treating the environment. There will also continue to be debates about the costs of cleaning up the environment. As we approach a cleaner environment, will the costs of additional clean-up be outweighed by the benefits?

Economic policymaking will always consist of unfinished work. The very nature of the federal government seems to be to engage in economic policymaking. Certainly, the federal government will never really get its house in order until it grapples successfully with continuing federal budget deficits and the consequent growing national debt. Thus, we expect to see a balanced budget proposal to pop up regularly in Congress.

If federal income tax rates continue to rise, another debate will become more strident. It will involve questioning whether high federal income tax rates reduce the incentives of individuals and businesses to work, save, and invest.

GETTING INVOLVED
The Importance of Government in Your Life

The federal budgetary process is a complex system that has many players. The ultimate test of the effectiveness of the federal budgetary process is how it affects each individual American. One way for you to take stock of how the federal government affects your life is as follows: (1) List what you have as assets (everything that you own). (2) List what you do during the day as activities. Then note the extent to which government is involved in your life—and at what cost. The emphasis should always be on the services that must be paid for, either directly or indirectly.

Consider the following example:

1. Rode bicycle to class—highway usage. How are the highways paid for? Who pays for them?

2. Checked out book from public library. Who paid for that library? Who owns it?
3. Received student loan—a subsidy from the government. Who ultimately paid for it?
4. Went to class. On average, in the United States, taxpayers pay approximately 70 percent of the cost of higher education, and students and their families directly pay only 30 percent.
5. Got groceries. How much of the meat was government inspected?

Where else did government intervene?

KEY TERMS

acid rain   510

action-reaction syndrome   515

Aid to Families with Dependent Children (AFDC)   506

constant dollars   521

domestic policy   493

environmental impact statement (EIS)   509

Federal Open Market Committee (FOMC)   519

fiscal policy   517

food stamps   506

in-kind subsidy   503

income transfer   502

Keynesian economics   518

loophole   515

monetary policy   517

policy trade-offs   514

public debt, or national debt   520

public debt financing   522

recycling   513

Social Security   505

subsidy   514

Supplemental Security Income (SSI)   506

underground economy   516

U.S. Treasury bond   520

CHAPTER SUMMARY

1. Domestic policy consists of all of the laws, government planning, and government actions that affect the lives of American citizens. Policies are created in response to public problems or public demand for government action. Four major policy problems now facing this nation are crime, health care, poverty and homelessness, and the environment.

2. The policymaking process is initiated when policymakers become aware—through the media or from their constituents—of a problem that needs to be addressed by the legislature and the president. The process of policymaking includes five steps: agenda building, agenda formulation, agenda adoption, agenda implementation, and agenda evaluation. All policy actions necessarily result in both costs and benefits for society.

3. American citizens are becoming increasingly alarmed over the rise in violent crime in the United States. Rape and assault rates are now at their highest recorded levels. Drug dealing and drug abusers have contributed significantly not only to escalating crime rates but also to overcrowded prisons. The prison "population bomb" presents a major challenge to today's policymakers.

4. In spite of the wealth of the United States, a significant number of Americans live in poverty or are homeless. The low-income poverty threshold represents an absolute measure of income needed to maintain a specified standard of living as of 1963, with the constant-dollar, or purchasing-power, value increased year by year in relation to the general increase in prices. The official poverty level is based on pretax income, including cash, and does not take into consideration in-kind subsidies (food stamps, housing vouchers, and so on).

5. A variety of income-maintenance programs have been designed to help the poor, including Social Security, Supplemental Security Income (SSI), and Aid to Families with Dependent Children (AFDC). The United States spends over $800 billion annually on various welfare programs. The welfare system has been criticized because it does not attack the problem of unequal employment opportunities and it creates disincentives for recipients to increase their work effort and for low-income families to live together.

6. Since the nineteenth century, at least fifteen significant federal acts have been passed in an attempt to curb the pollution of our environment. The National Environmental Policy Act of 1969 established the Council for Environmental Quality. That act also mandated that environmental impact statements be prepared for all legislation or major federal actions that might significantly affect the quality of the environment. In 1980, Congress passed the Comprehensive Environmental Response, Compensation and Liability Act, commonly known as Superfund, to regulate the clean-up of leaking hazardous waste disposal sites. Efforts to save resources include recycling and precycling (packaging products in more concentrated forms, for example).

7. In the area of taxes and subsidies (negative taxes), policymakers have long had to contend with what is

known as the action-reaction syndrome. For every action on the part of the government, there will be a reaction on the part of the public, to which the government will react with another action, to which the public will again react, and so on. In regard to taxes, as a general rule, individuals and corporations that pay the highest tax rates will react to those rates by pressuring Congress into creating exceptions and tax loopholes (loopholes allow high-income earners to reduce their taxable incomes). This action on the part of Congress results in a reaction from another interest group—consisting of those who want the rich to pay more taxes. In response, higher tax rates will be imposed on the rich, and so the cycle continues.

8. Fiscal policy is the use of changes in government expenditures and taxes to alter national economic variables, such as the rate of inflation or unemployment. Monetary policy is defined as the use of changes in the amount of money in circulation so as to affect interest rates, credit markets, the rate of inflation, and employment. The problem with fiscal policy and monetary policy is the lag between the time a problem occurs in the economy and the time when policy changes are actually felt in the economy.

9. Whenever the federal government spends more than it receives, it runs a deficit. The deficit is met by U.S. Treasury borrowing. This adds to the public debt of the federal government. Although the public debt has grown dramatically, when corrected for increases in population and inflation, it fell from the end of World War II to the middle of the 1970s. Since then, it has increased almost to its previous level at the height of the World War II. Those who oppose large increases in government spending argue that one effect of the federal deficit is the crowding out of private investment.

10. One congressional option for balancing the federal budget is passing a constitutional amendment. Such an amendment would require that whenever the federal government ran a deficit, Congress and the president would have to eliminate it by either lowering spending or raising taxes. Perhaps as an alternative to a constitutional amendment, Congress passed the Gramm-Rudman-Hollings Deficit Reduction Act in 1985. Its goal was to force the federal government to balance its budget. So far, Congress has been unable to meet the goals established by this act and later revisions of the act.

QUESTIONS FOR REVIEW AND DISCUSSION

1. In some major cities, crime rates have either stayed constant or fallen slightly over the last three or four years. Nonetheless, opinion polls still show that crime is considered the most serious problem by citizens in those same cities. How can you explain this anomaly?

2. If you had to come up with an agenda for solving the crime problem in the United States, what would be the four most important policy decisions you would implement?

3. "You can never eliminate poverty if you define it in relative terms." Is this statement correct or incorrect? Why?

4. Does the existence of the action-reaction syndrome imply that it is impossible to "soak the rich" through higher tax rates? Explain your answer.

5. Is there truly such a thing as fiscal policy in the United States? Why or why not? Explain your answer.

6. If most of the national debt is owned by Americans, how can it ever be a burden on Americans?

LOGGING ON: THE POLITICS OF ECONOMIC AND DOMESTIC POLICYMAKING

For discussion of all aspects of U.S. federal domestic policies, use the Michigan State University **gopher** at

alt.politics.usa.misc.

and choose

News & Weather; USENET News; alt/;politics/

This service will provide you with information on crime policy; environmental policy; welfare, housing, education reform; and other policy issues.

The federal budget-making process often involves substantial controversy and discussion. Information on past federal budgets and proposed budgets for the upcoming fiscal year can be obtained through the University of North Carolina **gopher** at

sunsite.und.edu

Choose **Sunsite Archives/US and World Politics/Sunsite Political Archives/US-Budget** . . . This service allows you to gather information on the federal budget in its final form. It also gives you information on the president's budget, as well as various other alternative budgets.

The federal budget has a very complicated framework. It would be impossible for most of us to understand the budget if we sat down and read it in its entirety. There is, however, a source that will provide you with the general details of the president's budget as proposed to Congress. To receive details of the president's economic plan, access

wiretap.spies.com

and go to **Government Docs/Clinton's Economic Plan.**

For discussion and information on political economy, access

pol-econ@shsu.edu

You may be interested in how the government makes its economic decisions. If so, you may want to look into a service

that will provide you with various viewpoints on how the
government should choose to collect and spend your tax
dollars. For a discussion on fiscal policy, access

fipefs-l@uicvm.bitnet

Do you like economic discussion? If so, the USENET newsgroup
for you is

alt.politics.economy

This service allows you to discuss economic performance and
provides you with a forum for debate on economic policy. For
news on the federal budget, economic performance, the budget
deficit, and other aspects of federal economic policy, try

clari.news.gov.budget

 ## SELECTED REFERENCES

Benjamin, Daniel K., and Roger LeRoy Miller. *Undoing Drugs: Beyond Legalization.* New York: Basic Books, 1993. This is a complete analysis of past and present U.S. drug policies, plus a new solution—the "constitutional alternative"—to the drug problem.

Blau, Joel. *The Visible Poor: Homelessness in the United States.* New York: Oxford University Press, 1992. Blau examines the sociopolitical causes of homelessness and calls for broad-based policies to remedy the problem.

Davis, Charles E. *The Politics of Hazardous Waste.* Englewood Cliffs, N.J.: Prentice-Hall, 1993. The author argues that state and local political institutions must be viewed as critical actors in the implementation of any hazardous waste program.

Friedman, Milton, and Walter Heller. *Monetary versus Fiscal Policy.* New York: Norton, 1969. This is a classic presentation of the pros and cons of monetary and fiscal policy given by a noninterventionist (Friedman) and an advocate of federal government intervention in the economy (Heller).

Fuchs, Victor R. *The Future of Health Policy.* Cambridge, Mass.: Harvard University Press, 1993. This health economist explains why any health-care reform that benefits society as a whole will burden certain individuals and groups. He looks at cost containment, managed competition, national health insurance, and the Canadian health-care system.

Guertin, Donald L., *et al.*, eds. *U.S. Energy Imperatives for the 1990s: Leadership, Efficiency, Environmental Responsibility, and Sustained Economic Growth.* Lanham, Md.: University Press of America, 1992. This book, which contains policy recommendations by some fifty experts on the need for an effective and responsible energy policy, also emphasizes the crucial leadership role that must be played by the United States in working toward environmentally sound economic development.

Kettel, Donald. *Deficit Politics: Public Budgeting in Its Institutional and Historical Context.* New York: Macmillan, 1992. The author provides a detailed overview of the federal government's budgeting process. He then examines the problems of deficit spending.

Kollman, Jeoffrey. *Social Security: The Relationship of Taxes and Benefits.* Congressional Research Service Report No. 92-956EPW, December 16, 1992. The author looks at the fact that current and past retirees have paid in far less Social Security taxes than they currently receive in benefits. He also looks at the future of the relationship between taxes and benefits.

Kuenne, Robert E. *Economic Justice in American Society.* Princeton, N.J.: Princeton University Press, 1993. The author argues for a distributive justice system that will meet the needs of the elderly, the impoverished, and those with disabilities.

The President's Council of Economic Advisers. *Economic Report of the President.* Washington, D.C.: U.S. Government Printing Office, published annually. This volume contains a wealth of details concerning current monetary and fiscal policy and what is happening to the economy.

Reich, Robert B. *The Work of Nations: Preparing Ourselves for 21st Century Capitalism.* New York: Random House, 1992. This much-talked-about book offers an analysis of the trends leading to greater globalization, a reduced significance of the nation-state, advances and prosperity for the well prepared and well trained, and alienation and poverty for Americans who fall behind.

Shuman, Howard E. *Politics and the Budget: The Struggle between the President and the Congress.* 3d ed. Englewood Cliffs, N.J.: Prentice-Hall, 1992. The author examines the continuing battle between Congress and the president in making up the annual federal budget.

15

Foreign and Defense Policy

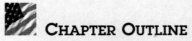 **CHAPTER OUTLINE**

WHAT IF . . .
The UN Enforced Human Rights Worldwide?

The goal of the United Nations (UN) is to engage the cooperative efforts of many nations to make the world a better place by reducing the threat of war, improving human conditions, and encouraging multilateral efforts to solve problems. Until the end of the 1980s, the effectiveness of the United Nations at maintaining world peace was limited by the conflict between the two superpowers, the United States and the former Soviet Union. Thus, the United States and the Soviet Union carried on the Cold War; engaged each other through surrogates in Vietnam, Central America, and the Middle East; and continued the nuclear arms race. Such actions produced a stalemate in the United Nations. With the end of the Cold War and the breakup of the Soviet Union, however, cooperation under UN auspices has partially resolved conflicts in several parts of the world.

Early in the history of the United Nations, the General Assembly passed the Universal Declaration of Human Rights, outlining the fundamental rights of all people on earth. Not all nations, including the United States, have signed the declaration, but it remains a UN goal. What if, in this new world of cooperation among former Cold War enemies, the United Nations turned its attention from peacekeeping to enforcing human rights throughout the world?

First, some agency or commission of the United Nations would have to be empowered either to survey the worldwide situation or, more likely, to receive complaints from aggrieved individuals or groups. Once the investigating

body was set up and processes agreed upon, the United Nations would be in the human rights business.

Next, priorities would have to be established. The Universal Declaration of Human Rights begins with the basic rights of survival—the need for food, shelter, and safety from violence. Would these basic rights be the first priority for the United Nations? If so, then the starvation of millions in various countries around the world would be the first problem to be confronted. But starvation problems are not always simply problems of scarcity. Sometimes, they are essentially political in nature. Groups in control may try to starve out rebel or opposing groups and resist UN intervention. Although the United Nations did intervene in Somalia in 1992, such interventions are attended by political risks. UN efforts to prevent the slaughter of hundreds of thousands of Rwandans in 1994 were futile—only France would send troops to help in this situation.

Another set of widely agreed-on rights includes freedom of speech, political freedoms (including the right to vote), and freedom of assembly. Would the UN be willing, for example, to use force or more severe economic sanctions to ensure that Haiti's democratically elected leader remains in power? Would the UN take on the destiny of the Kurds in Iraq? The gypsies in Eastern Europe? The Palestinians in Israel? The Native Americans in the United States?

Each of these situations involves not only the basic human rights of groups but also internal political problems. Although the UN advocates democracy and individual freedom, it has rarely been willing to engage in what might be defined as domestic political issues. Indeed, a nation's internal politics traditionally has been off limits to direct intervention.

Finally, who would organize and pay for investigations concerning human rights? Which nations would be willing to send investigators into other countries or armed police—or even military forces—to enforce human rights in those countries? To date, assembling and paying for peacekeeping operations has been difficult. By 1996, the annual cost of peacekeeping operations in thirteen nations was estimated to be over $3 billion. Not only are many nations spending money, but many nations are also contributing troops to support these efforts. How many nations would be willing to send troops into military conflicts to preserve human rights in a faraway land? It seems more likely that UN authority on these issues will remain mainly moral.

---

1. Would Americans be willing to send troops to enforce human rights in another country?
2. Why would some nations be unwilling to become concerned about human rights violations in other countries?
3. Should certain human rights take priority over political considerations?

When President Bill Clinton took office in January 1993, he was the first president to have been born after World War II and the only one since that war who had not served in the military. He was also the first post–Cold War president. Thus, he came into office during a period when the United States was attempting to assist the states of the former Soviet Union, including Russia, to achieve pro-Western economic and political changes. The issue facing the Clinton administration and the American people was to define the role that the United States, clearly the most powerful nation in the world, would play in international affairs in the coming decades.

No longer did the United States need to continue building up its nuclear arsenal to compete with that of the Soviet Union. Rather, the United States was disarming and downsizing its military forces while other nations were still trying to develop nuclear weapons.

Instead of confronting the communist regimes of the Soviet Union and Eastern Europe, the United States was encouraging the development of Western-style political practices and capitalist economic systems in that region. Relationships with the remaining communist nations were developing unique aspects: The United States remained antagonistic to North Korea and Cuba but was expanding trade with China and Vietnam.

Without a guiding theme to foreign policy—confrontation with the communist states—the creation and implementation of foreign policy and a national security strategy have become much more complex. The United States, faced with pressing domestic needs, could lower defense spending. Without the need to compete with the Soviet Union in different regions of the world, the United States could decide not to become engaged in regional conflicts. It could allow the United Nations to monitor human rights, as suggested in this chapter's *What If . . .* feature.

The Clinton administration, which had focused on domestic policies, including health-care reform, was criticized for not developing an equally clearly focused foreign policy. Yet it was certainly not clear what the right policy should be toward Bosnia, Rwanda, Haiti, Cuba, or North Korea, to name just a few trouble spots. It was clear, however, that in times of crisis, the nation still needed guiding principles for action.

WHAT IS FOREIGN POLICY?

As the cultural, military, and economic interdependence of the nations of the world has increased, it has become even more important for the United States to establish and carry out foreign policies to deal with external situations and to carry out its own national goals. By **foreign policy**, we mean both the goals the government wants to achieve in the world and the techniques and strategies to achieve them. For example, if one national goal is to achieve stability in Eastern Europe and to encourage the formation of pro-American governments there, U.S. foreign policy in that area may be carried out with the techniques of **diplomacy**, **economic aid**, **technical assistance**, or military intervention. Sometimes foreign policies are restricted to statements of goals or ideas, such as helping to end world poverty, whereas at other times foreign policies are comprehensive efforts to achieve particular objectives.

FOREIGN POLICY
A nation's external goals and the techniques and strategies used to achieve them.

DIPLOMACY
The total process by which states carry on political relations with each other; settling conflicts among nations by peaceful means.

ECONOMIC AID
Assistance to other nations in the form of grants, loans, or credits to buy the assisting nation's products.

TECHNICAL ASSISTANCE
The sending of experts with technical skills in agriculture, engineering, or business to aid other nations.

FOREIGN POLICY PROCESS
The steps by which external goals are decided and acted on.

NATIONAL SECURITY POLICY
Foreign and domestic policy designed to protect the independence and political and economic integrity of the United States; policy that is concerned with the safety and defense of the nation.

NATIONAL SECURITY COUNCIL (NSC)
A board created by the 1947 National Security Act to advise the president on matters of national security.

Foreign policy in the United States is established through the **foreign policy process**, which usually originates with the president and those agencies that provide advice on foreign policy matters. Foreign policy formulation often is affected by congressional action and national public debate.

National Security Policy

As one aspect of overall foreign policy, **national security policy** is designed primarily to protect the independence and the political integrity of the United States. It concerns itself with the defense of the United States against actual or potential (real or imagined) enemies, domestic or foreign.

U.S. national security policy is based on determinations made by the Department of Defense, the Department of State, and a number of other federal agencies, including the **National Security Council (NSC)**. The NSC acts as an advisory body to the president, but it has increasingly become a rival to the State Department in influencing the foreign policy process. This was particularly evident when it was revealed, in November 1986, that the Reagan administration had largely bypassed the Department of State (and Congress) in using the NSC to direct sales of U.S. military equipment to Iran.

Diplomacy

Diplomacy is another aspect of foreign policy. Diplomacy includes all of a nation's external relationships, from routine diplomatic communications to summit meetings among heads of state. More specifically, diplomacy refers to the settling of disputes and conflicts among nations by peaceful methods. Diplomacy is the set of negotiating techniques by which a nation attempts to carry out its foreign policy.

MORALITY VERSUS REALITY IN FOREIGN POLICY

From the earliest years of the republic, Americans have felt that their nation had a special destiny. The American experiment in democratic government and capitalism, it was thought, would provide the best possible life for men and women and be a model for other nations. As the United States assumed greater status as a power in world politics, Americans came to believe that the nation's actions on the world stage should be guided by American political and moral principles. As Harry Truman stated, "The United States should take the lead in running the world in the way that it ought to be run."

MORAL IDEALISM
A philosophy that sees all nations as willing to cooperate and agree on moral standards for conduct.

This view of America's mission has led to the adoption of many foreign policy initiatives that are rooted in **moral idealism**, a philosophy that sees the world as fundamentally benign and other nations as willing to cooperate for the good of all.[1] In this perspective, nations should come together and agree to keep the peace, as President Woodrow Wilson proposed for the League of Nations following World War I. Nations should see the wrong in violating the human rights of ethnic or religious minorities and should work

---

1. Charles W. Kegley, Jr., and Eugene Wittkopf, *American Foreign Policy, Pattern and Process,* 3d ed. (New York: St. Martin's Press, 1987), p. 73.

to end such injustice. Many of the foreign policy initiatives taken by the United States have been based on this idealistic view of the world, but few of these actions have been very successful.

The Peace Corps, however, which was created by President John Kennedy in 1961, is one example of an effort to spread American goodwill and technology that has achieved some of its goals. The Clinton administration's actions to return the democratically elected president of Haiti to power were rooted partly in moral conviction, although elements within the U.S. government regarded President Jean-Bertrand Aristide as unstable or left-leaning. Foreign policy based on moral imperatives often is unsuccessful because it assumes that other nations agree with American views of morality and politics.

In opposition to the moral perspective is what we might call **political realism.** Realists see the world as a dangerous place in which each nation strives for its own survival and interests. Foreign policy decisions must be based on a cold calculation of what is best for the United States without regard for morality. Realists believe that the United States must be prepared militarily to defend itself, because all other nations are, by definition, out to improve their own situations. A strong defense will show the world that the United States is willing to protect its interests. The practice of political realism in foreign policy allows the United States to sell weapons to military dictators who will support its policies, to support American business around the globe, and to repel terrorism through the use of force. Political realism leads, for example, to a policy of never negotiating with terrorists who take hostages, because such negotiations simply will lead to the taking of more hostages.

It is important to note that the United States never has been guided by only one of these principles. Instead, both moral idealism and political realism affect foreign policymaking. President Clinton wrestled with the situation in Bosnia to try to find a way for the United States to practice a pragmatic policy based on moral principles. Strongly opposed to using U.S. troops to establish peace in Bosnia, the president tried to convince the warring parties—the Bosnian Serbs and the Bosnian Muslims—to negotiate and accept a cease-fire. No policy that seemed realistic, however, really addressed the moral issues in that nation. Bombings of Serb positions by North Atlantic Treaty Organization (NATO) aircraft and confiscation of weapons by U. N. peacekeepers had little effect until heavy NATO bombing combined with a Croat-Muslim offensive forced the Serbs to retreat.

POLITICAL REALISM
A philosophy that sees each nation acting principally in its own interest.

WHO MAKES FOREIGN POLICY?

Is foreign policy made by the president, by the Congress, or by joint executive and congressional action? There is no easy answer to this question, because, as constitutional authority Edwin S. Corwin once observed, the Constitution created an "invitation to struggle" between the president and Congress for control over the foreign policy process. Let us look first at powers given to the president by the Constitution.

Constitutional Powers of the President

The Constitution confers on the president broad powers that are either explicit or implied in key constitutional provisions. Article II vests the

EXECUTIVE AGREEMENT
A binding international obligation made between chiefs of state without legislative sanction.

President Franklin D. Roosevelt signs the declaration of war against Japan on December 8, 1941.

executive power of the government in the president. The presidential oath of office given in Article II, Section 1, requires that the president "solemnly swear" to "preserve, protect and defend the Constitution of the United States."

In addition, and perhaps more important, Article II, Section 2, designates the president as "Commander in Chief of the Army and Navy of the United States." Starting with Abraham Lincoln, all presidents have interpreted this authority dynamically and broadly. Indeed, since the Washington administration, the United States has been involved in at least 125 undeclared wars that were conducted under presidential authority. For example, Harry Truman ordered U.S. armed forces in the Pacific to enter into North Korea's conflict with South Korea. Dwight Eisenhower threatened China and North Korea with nuclear weapons if the Korean peace talks were not successfully concluded. Bill Clinton sent troops to Haiti.

Article II, Section 2, of the Constitution also gives the president the power to make treaties, provided that two-thirds of the senators present concur. Presidents usually have been successful in getting treaties through the Senate. In addition to this formal treaty-making power, the president makes use of **executive agreements** (discussed in Chapter 11). Since World War II, executive agreements have accounted for almost 95 percent of the understandings reached between the United States and other nations.

Executive agreements have a long and important history. Significant in their long-term effects were the several agreements Franklin Roosevelt reached with the Soviet Union and other countries during World War II. The government of South Vietnam and the government of the United States, particularly under Dwight Eisenhower, John Kennedy, and Lyndon Johnson, made a series of executive agreements in which the United States promised support. All in all, between 1946 and 1996, over eight thousand executive agreements with foreign countries were made. There is no way to get an accurate count, because perhaps several hundred of these agreements have been secret.

An additional power conferred on the president in Article II, Section 2, is the right to appoint ambassadors, other public ministers, and consuls. In Section 3 of that article, the president is given the power to recognize foreign governments through receiving their ambassadors.

Informal Techniques of Presidential Leadership

Other broad sources of presidential power in the U.S. foreign policy process are tradition, precedent, and the president's personality. The president can employ a host of informal techniques that give the White House overwhelming superiority within the government in foreign policy leadership.

First, the president has access to information. More information is available to the president from the Central Intelligence Agency (CIA), the State Department, and the Defense Department than to any other governmental official. This information carries with it the ability to make quick decisions—and that ability is used often.

Second, the president is a legislative leader who can influence the amount of funds that are allocated for different programs. For example, with a huge budget deficit and the end of the Cold War, President Clinton proposed large cuts in defense spending.

Third, the president can influence public opinion. President Theodore Roosevelt once made the following statement:

> People used to say to me that I was an astonishingly good politician and divined what the people are going to think. . . . I did not "divine" how the people were going to think; I simply made up my mind what they ought to think and then did my best to get them to think it.[2]

Presidents are without equal in this regard, partly because of their ability to command the media. Depending on their skill in appealing to patriotic sentiment (and sometimes fear), they can make people think that their course in foreign affairs is right and necessary. Public opinion often seems to be impressed by the president's decision to make a national commitment abroad. Presidents normally, although certainly not always, receive the immediate support of the American people when reacting to (or creating) a foreign policy crisis.

Finally, the president can commit the nation morally to a course of action in foreign affairs. Because the president is the head of state and the leader of one of the most powerful nations on earth, once the president has made a commitment for the United States, it is difficult for Congress or anyone else to back down on that commitment.

Other Sources of Foreign Policymaking

There are at least four foreign policymaking sources within the executive branch, in addition to the president. These are (1) the Department of State, (2) the National Security Council, (3) the intelligence community and informational programs, and (4) the Department of Defense.

The Department of State. In principle, the State Department is the executive agency that is most directly concerned with foreign affairs. It supervises U.S. relations with the nearly two hundred independent nations around the world and with the United Nations and other multinational groups, such as the Organization of American States. It staffs embassies and consulates throughout the world. It has about 25,000 employees. This may sound impressive, but it is small compared with, say, the Department of Health and Human Services with its more than 129,000 employees. Also, the State Department had an annual operating budget of only $4.9 billion in fiscal year 1995—the smallest budget of the cabinet departments.

Newly elected presidents usually tell the American public that the new secretary of state is the nation's chief foreign policy adviser. Nonetheless, the State Department's preeminence in foreign policy has declined dramatically since World War II. The State Department's image within the White House Executive Office and Congress (and even foreign governments) is quite poor—a slow, plodding, bureaucratic maze of inefficient, indecisive individuals. There is even a story about how Premier Nikita Khrushchev of the Soviet Union urged President John Kennedy to formulate his own views rather than to rely on State Department officials who, according to Khrushchev, "specialized in why something had not worked forty years ago."[3] In any event, since the days of Franklin Roosevelt, the State

---

2. Sidney Warren, *The President as World Leader* (New York: McGraw-Hill, 1964), p. 23.
3. Theodore C. Sorensen, *Kennedy* (New York: Harper & Row, 1965), pp. 554–555.

Department sometimes has been bypassed and often has been ignored when crucial decisions are made.

It is not surprising that the State Department has been overshadowed in foreign policy. It has no natural domestic constituency as does, for example, the Department of Defense, which can call on defense contractors for support. Instead, the State Department has what might be called **negative constituents**—U.S. citizens who openly oppose American foreign policy. Also, within Congress, the State Department is often looked on as an advocate of unpopular and costly foreign involvement. It is often called "the Department of Bad News."

The National Security Council. The job of the National Security Council (NSC), created by the National Security Act of 1947, is to advise the president on the integration of "domestic, foreign, and military policies relating to the national security." Its larger purpose is to provide policy continuity from one administration to the next. As it has turned out, the NSC— consisting of the president, the vice president, the secretaries of state and defense, the director of emergency planning, and often the chairperson of the joint chiefs of staff and the director of the CIA—is used in just about any way the president wants to use it.

The role of national security adviser to the president seems to change to fit the player. Some advisers have come into conflict with heads of the State Department. Henry A. Kissinger, Nixon's flamboyant and aggressive national security adviser, rapidly gained ascendancy over William Rogers, the secretary of state, in foreign policy. When Carter became president he appointed Zbigniew Brzezinski as national security adviser. Brzezinski competed openly with Secretary of State Cyrus Vance (who apparently had little power). In the Clinton administration, neither National Security Adviser Anthony Lake nor Secretary of State Warren Christopher dominated the policy process. (See this chapter's *Politics: The Human Side* for a profile of Christopher.)

The Intelligence Community. No discussion of foreign policy would be complete without some mention of what is known generally as the **intelligence community.** This consists of the forty or more government agencies or bureaus that are involved in intelligence activities, informational and otherwise. On January 24, 1978, President Carter issued Executive Order 12036, in which he formally defined the official major members of the intelligence community. They are as follows:

1. Central Intelligence Agency (CIA).
2. National Security Agency (NSA).
3. Defense Intelligence Agency (DIA).
4. Offices within the Department of Defense.
5. Bureau of Intelligence and Research in the Department of State.
6. Federal Bureau of Investigation (FBI).
7. Army intelligence.
8. Air Force intelligence.
9. Department of the Treasury.
10. Drug Enforcement Administration (DEA).
11. Department of Energy.

The CIA was created as part of the National Security Act of 1947. The National Security Agency and the Defense Intelligence Agency were created

NEGATIVE CONSTITUENTS
Citizens who openly oppose government foreign policies.

INTELLIGENCE COMMUNITY
The government agencies involved in gathering information about the capabilities and intentions of foreign governments and that engages in covert activities to further U.S. foreign policy aims.

POLITICS: THE HUMAN SIDE
Warren Christopher, Secretary of State

"A wise nation, however powerful, understands the peril it invites in confronting the will of another people."

BIOGRAPHICAL NOTES

Although Warren Christopher may appear to be as much a member of the establishment as any other high-ranking official at the State Department, his origins were humble. Born on October 27, 1925, in Scranton, North Dakota, Christopher was the son of a small-town bank officer. After the bank collapsed during the Great Depression, Christopher's father suffered a stroke and died when Warren was only thirteen. The family moved to Los Angeles, where Warren attended Hollywood High and deliv-

ered newspapers to earn some money. He entered Redlands University on a scholarship and then completed his education at the University of Southern California. After a tour in the navy, Christopher entered Stanford Law School, graduating at the top of his class. As a successful corporate lawyer, Christopher was asked to perform some public services. In 1976, Cyrus Vance, nominated to be secretary of state in the Carter administration, asked Christopher to be his deputy. Then, in 1993, Bill Clinton nominated him for the top position at the Department of State.

POLITICAL CONTRIBUTIONS

Warren Christopher's career has included a number of posts and a share of successes as well as failures. The McCone Commission that Christopher chaired in 1966 put the blame for the Watts (Los Angeles) riots on "riff raff" and excused police behavior. Most recently, however, Christopher was asked to chair a group investigating the behavior of the Los Angeles police after the Rodney King beating in the summer of 1992. In that case, Christopher's report underscored the racism within the police force and essentially forced Chief Daryl Gates to resign.

In his years at the State Department during the Carter administration (1977–1981), Christopher developed a reputation for quiet ne-

gotiation and a passion for legal detail. He was credited with persuading the Senate to pass the Panama Canal treaties without adding too many damaging reservations and with convincing the Panamanian government to accept the Senate's version of the treaties. He also achieved successes in regard to relationships with Taiwan and the sale of arms to Saudi Arabia and Egypt. The entire Carter administration, however, suffered a foreign policy disaster when Islamic militants in Tehran, Iran, took hostages from the American embassy and held them until after Carter's electoral defeat in 1980.

In the Clinton administration, Christopher is the primary spokesperson for foreign policy. Unlike in former administrations, he is not overshadowed by the national security adviser (Anthony Lake) or the secretary of defense (William Perry). Christopher, however, with his diplomatic style, his emphasis on the importance of negotiations, and his reserved manner, has been unable to focus the president's efforts on developing a foreign policy perspective broader then the immediate problem. Clinton, who campaigned on the need to turn to domestic problems, does not have as much enthusiasm for foreign policy issues as many other presidents have had, so his foreign policy advisers do not get the energetic support that his domestic advisers enjoy.

by executive order. Until recently, Congress voted billions of dollars for intelligence activities with little knowledge of how the funds were being used. Intelligence activities consist mostly of overt information gathering, but covert actions also are undertaken. Covert actions, as the name implies, are done secretly, and rarely does the American public find out about them. In the late 1940s and early 1950s, the CIA covertly subsidized anticommunist labor unions in Western Europe. The CIA covertly aided in the overthrow of the Mossadegh regime in Iran, which allowed the restoration of the shah in 1953. The CIA helped to overthrow the Arbenz government of Guatemala in 1954 and was instrumental in destabilizing the Allende government in Chile from 1970 to 1973.

During the mid-1970s, the "dark side" of the CIA was at least partly uncovered when the Senate undertook an investigation of its activities. One of the major findings of the Senate Select Committee on Intelligence was that the CIA had spied routinely on American citizens domestically—a supposedly strictly prohibited activity. Consequently, the CIA came under the scrutiny of six, and later eight, oversight committees within Congress, which restricted the scope of its activity. By 1980, however, the CIA had regained much of its lost power to engage in covert activities. In the early 1990s, as the relationships with the states of the former Soviet Union eased, the attention of the CIA and other agencies began to turn from military to economic intelligence.

In addition to intelligence activities, U.S. foreign policy also makes use of propaganda and information programs. The United States Information Agency (which for a while was called the United States International Communication Agency) is part of an attempt to spread information and propaganda throughout the world on behalf of the American government.

The Department of Defense.   The Department of Defense (DOD) was created in 1947 to bring all of the various activities of the American military establishment under the jurisdiction of a single department headed by a civilian secretary of defense. At the same time, the joint chiefs of staff, consisting of the commanders of each of the military branches and a chairperson, was created to formulate a unified military strategy. The DOD is huge. It has more than one million civilian employees and more than two million military personnel. The fiscal year 1995 budget for defense was about $270 billion, a decrease of $27 billion from three years before. This budget cut was necessitated by the end of the Cold War and by the budget deficit.

Congress often does not agree with the plans of the DOD, particularly if the plans call for closing a military base or ending a contract in a powerful

The Pentagon—a five-sided building—has become the symbol of the Department of Defense. It has six million square feet of floor space and over seventeen miles of corridors.

legislator's state or district. Also, the branches of the military often differ in their points of view, thus weakening the department's political influence.

LIMITING THE PRESIDENT'S POWER

A new interest in the balance of power between Congress and the president on foreign policy questions developed during the Vietnam War. Sensitive to public frustration over the long and costly war and angry at Richard Nixon for some of his other actions as president, Congress attempted to establish some limits on the power of the president in setting foreign and defense policy. In 1973, Congress passed the War Powers Act over President Nixon's veto. The act limited the president's use of troops in military action without congressional approval (see Chapter 11). Most presidents, however, have not interpreted the "consultation" provisions of the act as meaning that Congress should be consulted before military action is taken. Instead, Presidents Ford, Carter, Reagan, and Bush ordered troop movements and then informed congressional leaders. Critics note that it is quite possible for a president to commit troops to a situation from which the nation could not withdraw without incurring heavy losses, regardless of whether Congress is consulted.

In recent years, Congress also has exerted its authority to limit or deny the president's requests for military assistance to Angolan rebels and to the government of El Salvador; requests for new weapons, such as the B-1 bomber; and requests for weapons sales through a legislative veto over sales greater than $50 million (although recent court decisions have left the veto technique in doubt). In general, Congress has been far more cautious in supporting the president in situations in which military involvement of American troops is possible.

At times, Congress can take the initiative in foreign policy. In 1986, Congress initiated and passed a bill instituting economic sanctions against South Africa to pressure that nation into ending apartheid. President Reagan vetoed the bill, but the veto was overridden by large majorities in both the House and the Senate.

DOMESTIC SOURCES OF FOREIGN POLICY

The making of foreign policy is often viewed as a presidential prerogative because of the president's constitutional power in that area and the resources of the executive branch that the president controls. Foreign policy-making is also influenced by a number of other sources, however, including elite and mass opinion and the military-industrial complex.

Elite and Mass Opinion

Public opinion influences the making of U.S. foreign policy through a number of channels. Elites in American business, education, communications, labor, and religion try to influence presidential decision making through several strategies. Some individuals, such as former secretary of state Henry Kissinger and the late president Richard Nixon, had a long-standing interest

ATTENTIVE PUBLIC
That portion of the general public that pays attention to foreign policy issues.

in foreign policy and were asked to advise the president privately. Several elite organizations, such as the Council on Foreign Relations and the Trilateral Commission, work to increase international cooperation and to influence foreign policy through conferences, publications, and research.

The members of the American elite establishment also exert influence on foreign policy through the general public by encouraging debate over foreign policy positions, by publicizing the issues, and by use of the media. Generally, the efforts of the president and the elites are most successful with the segment of the population called the **attentive public.** This sector of the mass public, which probably constitutes 10 to 20 percent of all citizens, is more interested in foreign affairs than most Americans. These Americans are also likely to transmit their opinions to the less interested members of the public through conversation and local leadership.

The Military-Industrial Complex

MILITARY-INDUSTRIAL COMPLEX
The mutually beneficial relationship between the armed forces and defense contractors.

A fear is often expressed that the military influences the making of U.S. foreign policy. Civilian fear of the relationship between the defense establishment and arms manufacturers (the **military-industrial complex**) dates back many years. In the 1930s, Franklin Roosevelt raised the specter of mammoth improper military influence in the domestic economy. On the eve of a Senate investigation of the munitions industry, he said that the arms race was a "grave menace . . . due in no small measure to the uncontrolled activities of the manufacturers and the merchants of the engines of destruction and it must be met by the concerted actions of the people of all nations."

During President Eisenhower's eight years in office, the former five-star general of the army experienced firsthand the kind of pressure that could be brought against him and other policymakers by arms manufacturers. Eisenhower decided to give the country a solemn and, as he saw it, necessary warning of the consequences of this influence. On January 17, 1961, in his last official speech, he said,

> In the councils of government, we must guard against the acquisition of unwarranted influence, whether sought or unsought, by the military-industrial complex. The potential for the disastrous rise of misplaced power exists and will persist. . . . Only an alert and knowledgeable citizenry can compel the proper meshing of the huge industrial and military machinery of defense with our peaceful methods and goals, so that security and liberty may prosper together.[4]

The Pentagon has supported a large sector of our economy through defense contracts. It also has supplied retired army officers as key executives to large defense-contracting firms. Perhaps the Pentagon's strongest allies have been members of Congress whose districts or states benefited from the economic power of military bases or contracts. As Russia and the United States worked to conclude treaties reducing their armaments, however, the Pentagon and defense contractors began to reassess their roles. They looked for new directions and programs to avoid substantial cutbacks in military spending.

---

4. *Congressional Almanac* (Washington, D.C.: Congressional Quarterly Press, 1961), pp. 938–939.

THE MAJOR FOREIGN POLICY THEMES

Although some observers might suggest that U.S. foreign policy is inconsistent and changes with the current occupant of the White House, the long view of American diplomatic ventures reveals some major themes underlying foreign policy. In the early years of the nation, presidents and the people generally agreed that the United States should avoid foreign entanglements and concentrate instead on its own development. From the beginning of the twentieth century until today, one major theme has been increasing global involvement, with the United States taking an active role in assisting the development of other nations, dominating the world economy, and in some cases acting as a peacemaker. The other major theme of the post–World War II years was the containment of communism. In the following brief review of American diplomatic history, these three themes predominate. The theme for the next century has not yet emerged.

The Formative Years: Avoiding Entanglements

U.S. foreign policy dates back to the colonial uprising against the British Crown. The Declaration of Independence formalized the colonists' desired break from Britain. Then, on September 3, 1783, the signing of the Treaty of Paris not only ended the War of Independence but also recognized the United States as an independent nation. In addition, the Treaty of Paris probably helped to reshape the world, for the American colonies were the first to secure independence against a "superpower."

Foreign policy was largely negative during the formative years. Remember that the new nation was operating under the Articles of Confederation. The national government had no right to levy and collect taxes, no control over commerce, no right to make commercial treaties, and no power to raise an army (the army was disbanded in 1783). The government's lack of international power was made clear when the United States was unable to recover American hostages who had been seized in the Mediterranean by Barbary pirates but ignominiously had to purchase the hostages in a treaty with Morocco.

The founders of this nation had a basic mistrust of corrupt European governments. George Washington said it was the U.S. policy "to steer clear of permanent alliances," and Thomas Jefferson echoed this sentiment when he said America wanted peace with all nations but "entangling alliances with none." This was also a logical position at a time when the United States was so weak militarily that it could not influence European development directly. Moreover, being protected by oceans that took weeks to traverse certainly allowed the nation to avoid entangling alliances. During the 1700s and 1800s, the United States generally stayed out of European conflicts and politics.

The Monroe Doctrine and the Americas

President James Monroe, in his message to Congress on December 2, 1823, stated that this country would not accept foreign intervention in the Western Hemisphere. In return, the United States would not meddle in European

MONROE DOCTRINE
The policy statement included in President James Monroe's 1823 annual message to Congress, which set out three principles: (1) European nations should not establish new colonies in the Western Hemisphere, (2) European nations should not intervene in the affairs of independent nations of the Western Hemisphere, and (3) the United States would not interfere in the affairs of European nations.

ISOLATIONIST FOREIGN POLICY
Abstaining from an active role in international affairs or alliances, which characterized U.S. foreign policy toward Europe during most of the nineteenth century.

affairs. The **Monroe Doctrine** was the underpinning of the U.S. **isolationist foreign policy** toward Europe, which continued throughout the nineteenth century.

In contrast to its isolationist policy toward Europe, the United States pursued an actively expansionist policy in the Americas and the Pacific area during the nineteenth century. The nation purchased Louisiana in 1803, annexed Texas in 1845, gained half of Mexico's territory in the 1840s, purchased Alaska in 1867, and annexed Hawaii in 1898. By first becoming a power in the Western Hemisphere, the United States laid the groundwork for becoming a world power in the twentieth century.

The Spanish-American War and World War I

The end of the isolationist policy started with the Spanish-American War in 1898. Winning that war gave the United States possession of Guam, Puerto Rico, and the Philippines (which gained independence in 1946). On the heels of that war came World War I (1914 to 1918). In his reelection campaign of 1916, President Woodrow Wilson ran on the slogan "He kept us out of war." Nonetheless, on April 6, 1917, the United States declared war on Germany. It was evident to Wilson that without help, the Allies would be defeated, and American property and lives, already under attack, increasingly would be endangered. Wilson also sought to promote American democratic ideals in Europe and to end international aggression by having the United States enter into the war.

In the 1920s, the United States did indeed go "back to normalcy," as President Warren G. Harding urged it to do. U.S. military forces were largely disbanded, defense spending dropped to about 1 percent of total national income, and the nation entered a period of isolationism.

A 1912 painting shows President James Monroe explaining the Monroe Doctrine to a group of government officials. Essentially, the Monroe Doctrine made the Western Hemisphere the concern of the United States.

The Era of Internationalism

Isolationism was permanently shattered and relegated to its place in history by the bombing of the U.S. naval base at Pearl Harbor, Hawaii, on December 7, 1941. The surprise attack by the Japanese resulted in the deaths of 2,403 American servicemen and the wounding of 1,143 others. Eighteen warships were sunk or seriously damaged, and 188 planes were destroyed at the airfields. Tales of the horrors experienced by the wounded survivors quickly reached the mainland. The American public was outraged. President Franklin Roosevelt asked Congress to declare war on Japan immediately, and the United States entered World War II.

This unequivocal response was certainly due to the nature of the provocation. American soil had not been attacked by a foreign power since the burning of Washington, D.C., by the British in 1814. World War II marked a lasting change in American foreign policy. It also produced a permanent change in defense spending. Except for brief periods during the Civil War and World War I, defense spending had been a fairly trivial part of total national income. By the end of World War II, in 1945, however, defense spending had increased to almost 40 percent of total national income. The number of U.S. military bases overseas increased from three at the beginning of 1940 to almost 450 by the end of World War II. National security had become a priority item on the federal government's agenda.

The United States was the only major participating country to emerge from World War II with its economy intact, and even strengthened. The Soviet Union, Japan, Italy, France, Germany, Britain, and a number of minor participants in the war were all economically devastated. The United States

The atomic bomb explodes over Nagasaki, Japan, on August 9, 1945.

Joseph Stalin, Franklin Roosevelt, and Winston Churchill met at Yalta in February 1945 to resolve their differences over the shape that the international community would take after World War II.

SOVIET BLOC
The Eastern European countries that installed communist regimes after World War II.

COLD WAR
The ideological, political, and economic impasse that existed between the United States and the Soviet Union following World War II.

IRON CURTAIN
The term used to describe the division of Europe between the Soviet Union and the West; popularized by Winston Churchill in a speech portraying Europe as being divided by an iron curtain, with the nations of Eastern Europe behind the curtain and increasingly under Soviet control.

CONTAINMENT
A U.S. diplomatic policy adopted by the Truman administration to "build situations of strength" around the globe to contain communist power within its existing boundaries.

TRUMAN DOCTRINE
The policy adopted by President Harry Truman in 1947 to halt communist expansion in southeastern Europe.

was also the only country to have control over operational nuclear weapons. President Harry S Truman had personally made the decision to use two atomic bombs, on August 6 and August 9, 1945, to end the war with Japan. (Historians still dispute the necessity of this action, which ultimately killed more than 100,000 Japanese civilians and left an equal number permanently injured.) The United States truly had become the world's superpower.

The Cold War

The United States had become an uncomfortable ally of the Soviet Union after Adolf Hitler's invasion. Soon after the war ended, relations between the Soviet Union and the West deteriorated. The Soviet Union wanted a weakened Germany, and to achieve this it insisted that the country be divided in two, with East Germany becoming a buffer. Little by little, the Soviet Union helped to install communist governments in Eastern European countries, which collectively became known as the **Soviet bloc.** In response, the United States encouraged the rearming of Western Europe. The "**Cold War**" had begun.[5]

In Fulton, Missouri, on March 5, 1946, Winston Churchill, in a striking metaphor, declared that from the Baltic to the Adriatic seas "an iron curtain has descended across the [European] continent." The term **iron curtain** became even more appropriate when the Soviet Union built a wall separating East Berlin from West Berlin on August 17 and 18, 1961.

Tests of Strength

In 1947, a remarkable article was published in *Foreign Affairs*. The article was signed by "X." The actual author was George F. Kennan, chief of the policy-planning staff for the Department of State. The doctrine of **containment** set forth in the article became—according to many—the Bible of Western foreign policy. "X" argued that whenever and wherever the Soviet Union could successfully challenge Western institutions, it would do so. He recommended that our policy toward the Soviet Union be "firm and vigilant containment of Russian expansive tendencies."[6]

The containment theory was expressed clearly in the **Truman Doctrine**, which was enunciated by President Harry S Truman in his historic address to Congress on March 12, 1947. In that address, he announced that the United States must help countries in which a communist takeover seemed likely, and he proposed the Greek-Turkish aid program specifically to counter Soviet influence in the eastern Mediterranean area. Greece was involved in a civil war that included communist forces, and Turkey was being pressured by the Soviet Union for political concessions. Truman proposed $400 million in aid to those two countries. He put the choice squarely before Congress—it either must support those measures required to preserve peace and security abroad or risk widespread global instability and perhaps World War III.[7]

---

5. See John Lewis Gaddis, *The United Nations and the Origins of the Cold War* (New York: Columbia University Press, 1972).
6. X, "The Sources of Soviet Conduct," *Foreign Affairs,* July 1947, p. 575.
7. *Public Papers of the Presidents of the United States: Harry S Truman, 1947* (Washington, D.C.: U.S. Government Printing Office, 1963), pp. 176–180.

During the Cold War, there was never any direct military confrontation between the United States and the Soviet Union. Rather, confrontations among "client" nations were used to carry out the policies of the superpowers. Only on occasion did the United States directly enter into a conflict in a significant way. Two such occasions were in Korea and Vietnam.

In 1950, North Korean troops were embroiled in a war with South Korea. President Truman asked for and received a Security Council order from the United Nations for the North Koreans to withdraw their troops. The Soviet Union was absent from the council on that day, protesting the exclusion of the People's Republic of China from the UN, and did not participate in the discussion. Truman then authorized the use of American forces in support of the South Koreans. For the next three years, American troops were engaged in a land war in Asia, a war that became a stalemate and a political liability to President Truman. One of Dwight Eisenhower's major 1952 campaign promises was to end the Korean war—which he did. An armistice was signed on July 27, 1953. (American troops have been stationed in South Korea ever since, however.)

U.S. involvement in Vietnam began to expand shortly after the end of the Korean conflict. When the French army in Indochina was defeated by the communist forces of Ho Chi Minh and the two Vietnams were created in 1954, the United States assumed the role of supporting the South Vietnamese government against North Vietnam. President John Kennedy sent 16,000 "advisers" to help South Vietnam, and after Kennedy's death, President Lyndon Johnson greatly increased the scope of that support. American forces in Vietnam at the height of the U.S. involvement totaled more than 500,000 troops. In excess of 58,000 Americans were killed and 300,000 wounded in the conflict. The debate over U.S. involvement in Vietnam divided the American electorate and spurred congressional efforts to limit the ability of the president to commit forces to armed combat.

The Cuban Missile Crisis

Nuclear power spread throughout the world. The two superpowers had enough nuclear bombs to destroy everyone at least twice and maybe three times. Obviously, confrontation between the United States and the Soviet Union could have taken on world-destroying proportions. Perhaps the closest we came to such a confrontation was the Cuban missile crisis in 1962. The Soviets had decided to place offensive missiles ninety miles off the U.S. coast, in Cuba, to help prevent an American-sponsored invasion like the Bay of Pigs. President Kennedy and his advisers rejected the possibility of armed intervention, setting up a naval blockade around the island instead. When Soviet vessels, apparently carrying nuclear warheads, appeared near Cuban waters, the tension reached its height. After intense negotiations between Washington and Moscow, the Soviet ships turned around on October 25, and on October 28 the Soviet Union announced the withdrawal of its missile operations from Cuba. In exchange, the United States agreed not to invade Cuba and to remove some of its own missiles that were located near the Soviet border.

A Period of Détente

The French word **détente** means a relaxation of tensions between nations. By the end of the 1960s, it was clear that some efforts had to be made to

DÉTENTE
A French word meaning the relaxation of tension. The term characterizes U.S.–Soviet policy as it developed under President Richard Nixon and Secretary of State Henry Kissinger. Détente stresses direct cooperative dealings with Cold War rivals but avoids ideological accommodation.

reduce the threat of nuclear war between the United States and the Soviet Union. The Soviet Union gradually had begun to catch up in the building of strategic nuclear delivery vehicles in the form of bombers and missiles, thus balancing the nuclear scales. Each nation acquired the military capacity to destroy the other with nuclear weapons.

As the result of protracted negotiations, in May 1972, the United States and the Soviet Union signed the **Strategic Arms Limitation Treaty (SALT I)**. That treaty "permanently" limited the development and deployment of anti-ballistic missiles (ABMs), and it limited for five years the number of offensive missiles each country could deploy. To further reduce tensions, under the policy of Secretary of State Henry Kissinger and President Nixon, new scientific and cultural exchanges were arranged with the Soviets, as well as new opportunities for Jewish emigration out of the Soviet Union.

The policy of détente was not limited to U.S. relationships with the Soviet Union. Seeing an opportunity to capitalize on increasing friction between the Soviet Union and the People's Republic of China, Kissinger secretly began negotiations to establish a new relationship with that nation. President Nixon eventually visited the People's Republic of China and set the stage for the formal diplomatic recognition of that country during the Carter administration (1977–1981).

The late 1970s saw increased tension between the United States and the Soviet Union. The Soviet Union intervened militarily in Afghanistan and suppressed the Polish Solidarity movement, which it saw as a threat to its political control throughout Eastern Europe.

STRATEGIC ARMS LIMITATION TREATY (SALT I)
A treaty between the United States and the Soviet Union to stabilize the nuclear arms competition between the two countries. SALT I talks began in 1969, and agreements were signed on May 26, 1972.

President Richard Nixon signs SALT I, a Cold War agreement with the Soviet Union, in 1972.

President Ronald Reagan took a hard line against the Soviet Union during his first term, proposing the strategic defense initiative (SDI), or "Star Wars," in 1983. The SDI was designed to serve as a space-stationed defense against enemy missiles. Reagan and others in his administration argued that the program would deter nuclear war by shifting the emphasis of defense strategy from offensive to defensive weapons systems.

In November 1985, President Reagan and Mikhail Gorbachev, the Soviet leader, held summit talks in Geneva. The two men agreed to reestablish cultural and scientific exchanges and to continue the arms control negotiations. Progress toward an agreement was slow, however.

In 1987, representatives of the United States and the Soviet Union continued work on an arms reduction agreement. Although there were setbacks throughout the year, the negotiations resulted in a historic agreement signed by Reagan and Gorbachev in Washington, D.C., on December 8, 1987. The terms of the Intermediate-Range Nuclear Force (INF) Treaty required the superpowers to dismantle a total of four thousand intermediate-range missiles within the first three years of the agreement. The verification procedures allowed each nation to keep a team of inspectors on the other nation's soil and to conduct up to twenty short-notice inspections of the disassembly sites each year. The Senate ratified the treaty in a vote of ninety-three to five on May 27, 1988, and the agreement was formally signed by Reagan and Gorbachev at the Moscow summit in 1988.

George Bush continued the negotiations with the Soviet Union after he became president. The goal of both nations was to reduce the number of nuclear weapons and the number of armed troops in Europe. The developments in Eastern Europe, the drive by the Baltic republics for independence, the unification of Germany, and the dissolution of the Soviet Union (in December 1991) made the process much more complex, however. American strategists worried as much about who now controlled the Soviet nuclear arsenal as about completing the treaty process. In 1992, the United States signed the Strategic Arms Reduction Treaty (START) with four former Soviet republics—Russia, Ukraine, Belarus, and Kazakhstan—to reduce the number of long-range nuclear weapons.

CHALLENGES IN WORLD POLITICS

The end of the Cold War, the dissolution of the Soviet Union, the economic unification of Europe, and the political changes in Eastern Europe have challenged U.S. foreign policy in ways that were unimaginable a few years ago. The United States had no contingency plans for these events. Also, predicting the consequences of any of these changes for world politics is all but impossible. Furthermore, such sweeping changes mean not only that the United States must adjust its foreign policy to deal with new realities but also that it must consider adjustments in the American military and intelligence establishments.

The Dissolution of the Soviet Union

After the fall of the Berlin Wall in 1989, it was clear that the Soviet Union had relinquished much of its political and military control over the states of Eastern Europe that formerly had been part of the Soviet bloc. Sweeping changes within the Soviet Union had been proposed by Gorbachev, and talks to reduce nuclear armaments were proceeding. No one expected the Soviet Union to dissolve into separate states as quickly as it did, however. While Gorbachev tried to adjust the Soviet constitution and political system to allow greater autonomy for the republics within the union, demands for political, ethnic, and religious autonomy grew. In August 1991, Soviet radio announced that Gorbachev was ill and would be taking a leave of absence from his office. It soon became clear that Gorbachev had been arrested and that military officers were attempting to take control through a coup.

When Soviet troops tried to surround the Soviet president, as well as Boris Yeltsin and the Russian government in its offices, many Soviet citizens rallied to their support in Moscow and other cities. Some units of the military refused to follow the coup leaders' orders. Yeltsin kept in contact with the media and the West, demanding to see and talk with Gorbachev. In three days, the coup leaders were under arrest, Gorbachev returned to Moscow, and Yeltsin was acclaimed as the new leader.

Following the aborted effort to preserve the Soviet Union, momentum for the states within the Soviet Union to pursue independent status grew rapidly, and after Christmas day, 1991, the Soviet Union no longer existed. American military and intelligence officials increasingly grew concerned about the placement and control of the former Soviet Union's nuclear weapons arsenal. Diplomats from Europe, the United States, and the new states met to discuss the future of the former superpower. Within a period of months, the new Commonwealth of Independent States was created, with Russia as its preeminent member. Some states, namely Georgia and the Baltic republics, declined to join. Georgia joined the Commonwealth later, however.

An uprising, this time by anti-Yeltsin members of the new parliament and their supporters, who wanted to restore the Soviet Union immediately, failed in 1993. Although Yeltsin stayed in office, the first national elections under the new constitution produced a parliament in which a majority opposed Yeltsin and most of his economic and political programs.

Russian soldiers arrest the guerrilla fighters in the breakaway republic of Chechnya. The small region, which is ethnically homogeneous, declared its autonomy as a Muslim state. President Boris Yeltsin of Russia reacted to the declaration by sending in thousands of Russian troops to quell the rebellion. The civil war lasted for months, costing many Russian lives and severely weakening Yeltsin's own political position. After Chechens captured a hospital in Russia and held hostages, Yeltsin agreed to negotiate with the rebel leaders.

Nuclear Proliferation

The dissolution of the Soviet Union by Boris Yeltsin and his supporters brought a true lowering of tensions between the major powers in the world. The United States and Russia agreed to continue negotiating the dismantling of nuclear warheads and delivery systems. The problems of nuclear proliferation were far from solved, however. The breakup of the Soviet Union left more than 1,600 warheads in the possession of the Ukrainian government, along with some in other new nations; the desire of other nations to have nuclear weapons also was not reduced. In 1994, North Korea resisted the efforts of the International Atomic Energy Commission to inspect parts of its nuclear power plant, particularly at a time when fuel rods were to be changed. The international inspectors suspected that spent fuel would be reprocessed to make a nuclear bomb or warhead. When North Korea continued to resist international pressure to comply with inspection, the United States sought approval for sanctions on Korea from the United Nations. As shown in Table 15–1, the number of warheads known to be in stock worldwide is more than twenty thousand; other nations do not report the extent of their nuclear stockpiles.

The Global Economy

Although the United States derives less than 20 percent of its total national income from world trade, it is deeply dependent on the world economy. A serious stock market crash of 1987 showed how closely other markets watch

Russian President Boris Yeltsin celebrated his August 1991 success against forces fighting to preserve the Soviet Union by waving the Russian flag. By 1993, Yeltsin was under severe criticism by the Russian Congress because of the failure of his economic reforms and his bloody suppression of an uprising intended to support the legislators whom Yeltsin forcibly disbanded.

The threat of nuclear destruction was perhaps reduced when President Clinton signed a nuclear accord with Russia, represented by President Boris Yeltsin, and the Ukraine, then represented by Leonid Kravchuk. Russia and the Ukraine currently own the majority of nuclear warheads from the former Soviet Union. One continuing problem today is that weapons-grade enriched uranium is being sold on the black market to certain countries that are working secretly on the development of their own nuclear bombs.

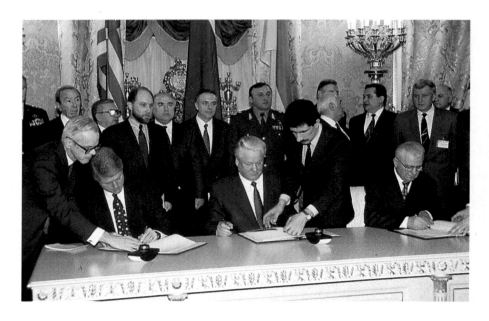

the economic situation of the United States and, conversely, how U.S. markets follow those of London and Japan. Furthermore, since the 1980s, the United States has become a debtor nation, meaning that we owe more to foreigners than foreigners owe to us. The reason for this is a huge trade deficit and the willingness of foreign individuals and nations to finance part of the U.S. national debt by purchasing U.S. government securities.

TABLE 15–1

The Nuclear Club

LOCATION	KNOWN AND SUSPECTED NUMBER OF WARHEADS	
Officially reported:		
United States	9,862 (to be reduced to 3,500 by 2003)	
Former Soviet Union	10,909 (to be reduced to 3,500 by 2003) In possession of:	
	Russia	7,762
	Ukraine	1,656
	Kazakhstan	1,410
	Belarus	81
France	525	
China	415	
Britain	200	
Not officially reported:		
Israel	50 to 200	
India	Suspected to have missiles	
Pakistan	Has capacity to build	
Nations that are capable of building weapons and/or suspected of having a nuclear program:		
Algeria, Argentina, Brazil, Iran, Iraq, Libya, North Korea, South Africa, and Syria.		

SOURCE: *New York Times*, January 10, 1993, p. E3.

One of the continuing "hot spots" in the world has been Korea. This country was divided into South and North Korea after World War II. After the Korean War (1950–1953), a demilitarized zone (DMZ) was established between the North and the South. Here President Clinton is shown with American soldiers at the DMZ. Such soldiers have been there since the end of the Korean War. Tension mounted between North and South Korea when North Korea prohibited international inspectors from attempting to ascertain whether North Korea was developing nuclear bombs. Tension also increased when North Korean leader Kim Il Sung died in 1994. He had stayed in power since the official formation of his country on May 1, 1948.

Because the United States imports more goods and services than it exports, it has a net trade deficit. These imports include BMWs, Sonys, Toshibas, and Guccis, as well as cheaper products such as shoes manufactured in Brazil and clothes from Taiwan. As Figure 15–1 shows, the biggest trade deficit is with Japan.

On December 31, 1992, the twelve countries of the former European Community became one consumer market—the European Union (EU). No one can predict how a unified Europe will affect world trade, but some expect Europe to gradually close some markets to outside economic powers. In view of its net trade deficit and the emergence of the EU, a priority goal for U.S. policymakers in the 1990s has been to develop a strategy for increasing U.S. competitiveness in foreign markets. Two important treaties will have an impact on this goal: the North American Free Trade Agreement and the final round of the General Agreement on Tariffs and Trade.

NAFTA.   The North American Free Trade Agreement (NAFTA), which was passed in 1993 and became effective on January 1, 1994, created a regional trading unit consisting of Mexico, Canada, and the United States. The primary goal of NAFTA is to eliminate tariffs among the three countries on substantially all goods over a period of fifteen to twenty years. NAFTA gives the three nations a competitive advantage by retaining tariffs on goods imported from countries outside the NAFTA trading unit. Additionally, NAFTA provides for the elimination of barriers that traditionally have prevented the cross-border movement of services, such as financial or transportation services.

GATT and the WTO.   Whereas the EU and NAFTA are regional agreements, the General Agreement on Tariffs and Trade (GATT) is a worldwide trade agreement. The original agreement was signed in 1947 and took effect

FIGURE 15–1

U.S. Exports and Imports, 1994

In 1994, the U.S. trade deficit continued to grow, reaching $166 billion. It is important to note, however, that Canada is the most important market for U.S. products and that Canada and Mexico together account for about 30 percent of all U.S. exports and imports.

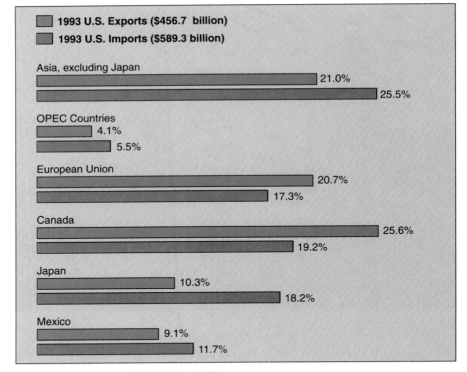

☐ **1993 U.S. Exports ($456.7 billion)**
☐ **1993 U.S. Imports ($589.3 billion)**

Asia, excluding Japan — 21.0% / 25.5%
OPEC Countries — 4.1% / 5.5%
European Union — 20.7% / 17.3%
Canada — 25.6% / 19.2%
Japan — 10.3% / 18.2%
Mexico — 9.1% / 11.7%

SOURCE: *Survey of Current Business*, March 1994.

January 1, 1948. Under GATT, countries have met periodically to negotiate tariff reductions that are mutually advantageous to all members. The 117 member nations of GATT account for between 85 and 90 percent of all world trade. The latest round of negotiations was called the Uruguay Round, because that was where the meetings were held. The final act of the Uruguay Round was signed in Marrakesh, Morocco, by over one hundred representatives in 1994.

The Uruguay Round provided for the reduction of tariffs on manufactured goods by an average of 37 percent and the complete elimination of tariffs in certain industries, such as drugs, medical equipment, and construction equipment. It also ordered member nations to cut their farm subsidies by an average of 21 percent and barred member countries from restricting competition by foreigners in most service industries, such as computer software and advertising. Finally, it provided for the protection of patents, trademarks, and copyrights for movies, computer programs, books, and music.

As of 1995, GATT no longer existed as an organization. In its place is the new World Trade Organization (WTO). The WTO has a permanent trade and environment committee, as well as arbitration boards that decide whether a country's domestic laws violate any of the terms of the GATT trade pact. No country has the power to veto the WTO's decisions, however, and the extent to which the WTO can compel member nations to comply with GATT provisions remains to be seen.

Part of America's foreign policy involves deciding how to deal with political and economic refugees. As the situation under the military rule in Haiti worsened in 1994, the Coast Guard picked up an increasing number of fleeing Haitians who wished to reestablish themselves in the United States. They were virtually all sent to Guantanamo Naval Base in Cuba. By the middle of the summer of 1994, there were 15,000 Haitians living there under U.S. protection. They were then joined by tens of thousands of Cuban refugees.

Regional Conflicts

The United States has played a role—sometimes alone, sometimes in conjunction with other powers—in many regional conflicts. Over the last ten years, the United States has been involved in conflicts in Latin America, the Middle East, Eastern Europe, and other regions around the globe.

Latin America and the Caribbean.   One region that traditionally has been of great interest to the United States is Central America. In 1823, President James Monroe declared a special U.S. interest in the region, and in the twentieth century, the Caribbean was known as an "American lake." In an attempt to restore order and to protect American property and lives, the United States has intervened militarily in Central America on many occasions. This interventionist policy did not generate much affection for the United States among Central American nations. In the 1980s, the United States began a serious involvement in at least three Central American states: in El Salvador, where the right-wing government was under attack from leftist opposition groups; in Nicaragua, where the United States backed the *contras* in their attempt to overthrow the pro-Soviet Sandinista government; and in Panama, where the military leader, general Manuel Noriega, an indicted drug trafficker, refused to leave office.

In 1989, when Noriega refused to resign from the presidency under pressure of economic sanctions on Panama, President Bush ordered military forces into that nation to capture and arrest Noriega for drug dealing. Although Noriega surrendered and was returned to the United States for trial, the invasion killed probably thousands of Panamanian civilians and leveled many blocks of the capital, Panama City.

In El Salvador, five Jesuit faculty members at a leading Salvadoran university and their housekeeper were massacred in 1989, possibly by a squad detailed by the rightist military. The United States continued to support the regime, although the administration expressed outrage at the murders and demanded, to no avail, that the perpetrators be found and brought to trial. Nicaragua successfully ended its civil war, held elections, and installed an anti-Sandinista and generally pro-American regime. Most of the *contras* surrendered their arms, at least temporarily.

The Caribbean nation of Haiti became a focal point of U.S. policy in the 1990s. The repressive military regime there ousted the democratically elected president Jean-Bertrand Aristide in 1992. The Clinton administration announced that it would support sanctions and other measures to reinstate Aristide in office. At the same time, the administration tried to stem the tide of refugees who tried to reach Florida by sea from the island nation. Although Clinton had promised in his campaign to admit the Haitian "boat people," he maintained the Bush policy of returning them to their native land. By 1994, he announced that the United States would at least listen to pleas for political asylum if refugees could reach Jamaica or other Caribbean islands. The Clinton administration also increased the sanctions on Haiti in 1994, and then sent troops to Haiti to assist in the reinstatement of President Aristide.

The United States continued to face problems with Cuba. In the last days of the summer of 1994, Castro threatened to "swamp" the United States with Cuban refugees. True to his word, he allowed thousands to leave the

U.S. troops arrive in Port-au-Prince, Haiti, in September 1994.

island on anything that would float. President Clinton was forced to rescind the U.S. open-door policy for Cuban refugees. He ordered the Coast Guard to return all refugees picked up at sea to the U.S. Naval Base at Guantanamo in Cuba. Then U.S. and Cuban authorities reached an agreement under which the United States would accept 20,000 legal Cuban immigrants a year. In exchange, Castro agreed to police Cuba's shores to prevent an exodus of Cuban refugees.

The Middle East.   The United States has also played a role in the Middle East. As a long-time supporter of Israel, the United States has undertaken to persuade the Israelis to agree to negotiations with the Palestinians who live as refugees within the occupied territories of the state of Israel. The conflict, which began in 1948, has been extremely hard to resolve. One reason is that it requires all the Arab states in the region to recognize Israel's right to exist. Another reason is that resolution of the conflict would require Israel to make some settlement with the Palestine Liberation Organization (PLO), which has launched attacks on Israel from within and outside its borders and which Israel has regarded as a terrorist organization. In December 1988, the U.S. began talking directly to the PLO, and in 1991, under great pressure from the United States, the Israelis opened talks with representatives of the Palestinians and other Arab states.

In 1993, the Israeli-Palestinian peace talks reached a breakthrough, with both parties agreeing to set up Palestinian territories in the West Bank and Gaza. The historic agreement, signed in Cairo on May 4, 1994, put in place a process by which the Palestinians would assume self-rule in the Gaza Strip and in the town of Jericho. They would elect their own officials and set up a Palestinian police force. The Israelis would withdraw their officials from the area within three weeks. Israel agreed to release five thousand prisoners

American tanks carry out maneuvers in Saudi Arabia during Operation Desert Shield. Subsequently, the United States, together with a coalition of other nations, instituted Operation Desert Storm—the Persian Gulf "hot war" that lasted for only one hundred hours. Such maneuvers again were undertaken in Kuwait in the fall of 1994, when Saddam Hussein moved troops close to the Kuwaiti border.

from their camps, and both sides agreed to consider further issues for peace. The United States had applied pressure to both sides to reach the agreement, with Secretary of State Warren Christopher acting as one of several mediators for the talks. With the success of this negotiation, it appeared that the entire region might be moving toward a more peaceful future. Jordan has already recognized Israel. For the United States, this should mean less need for foreign assistance to Israel and Egypt, as well as more stability in a vital region.

U.S. Response to Iraq's Invasion of Kuwait.   On August 2, 1990, the Middle East became the setting for a major challenge to the authority of the United States and its ability to buy oil from its allies there. President Saddam Hussein of Iraq initially sent more than 100,000 troops into the neighboring oil sheikdom of Kuwait, occupying the entire nation. Within less than two days, President George Bush took the position that the annexation of Kuwait must not be tolerated by the Western world and that the oil fields of Saudi Arabia must be protected. At the formal request of the king of Saudi Arabia, American troops were dispatched to set up a defensive line at the Kuwaiti border. In addition, the president announced an economic boycott of Iraq (supported by the United Nations) and sent American aircraft carrier groups to seal off the Iraqi ports, cutting off shipments of oil.

Bush continued to send troops—including reserve units called up from the United States—to Saudi Arabia. By the end of 1990, more than half a million troops were in place. After the United Nations approved a resolution authorizing the use of force if Saddam Hussein did not respond to sanctions, the U.S. Congress reluctantly also approved such an authorization. On January 17, 1991, two days after the deadline for President Hussein to withdraw, the coalition forces launched a massive air attack on Iraq. After several weeks of almost unopposed aerial bombardment, the ground offensive began. Iraqi troops retreated from Kuwait a few days later, and the Persian Gulf War ended within another week.

A United Nations (UN) convoy travels the rugged terrain of Bosnia as the peacekeeping force attempts to protect the Muslim "safe havens." In the summer of 1995, the Bosnian Serbs launched major offensives on a number of these locations, driving Muslim women and children to refugee camps while holding the men and boys as prisoners of war. UN efforts seemed fruitless in the face of these offensives. Counteroffensives by Croat and Muslim forces, combined with heavy NATO bombing, forced a major Serb withdrawal.

After the end of the armed conflict, many Americans criticized the Bush administration for not sending troops to Baghdad, where they might have deposed Saddam Hussein. Others faulted the effort for raising the expectations of the Kurdish people that the United States would eliminate President Hussein if they revolted. When no one helped their uprising, the entire community risked retaliation by the Iraqi dictator. Belatedly, American troops were sent to preserve peace. The war also created an enormous environmental disaster owing to the destruction of the oil fields by the Iraqis when they retreated from Kuwait. Saddam Hussein remains a force in the region today.

Eastern Europe.   Eastern Europe, a region that had been extremely stable while under Soviet domination, suddenly became an unknown quantity in U.S. policy. With the decision of the Soviet Union to allow elections and non-Marxist governments in Eastern Europe, these nations took separate paths to becoming democratic states with mixed or market-oriented economies. Some nations moved immediately to democratic elections; others struggled first to repair damaged economies; and still others attempted to deal with ethnic tensions within their populations.

It is difficult to overestimate the potential for civil disorder in these nations, particularly with regard to ethnic differences. (See this chapter's *Politics and Ethics.*) The world watched in 1991 as Yugoslavia split into a number of independent states. As former provinces of Yugoslavia—Slovenia, Croatia, and Bosnia and Herzegovina—tried to declare independence, Serbian military and government leaders launched attacks on their neighbors. The fighting was caused by historic conflicts and by strong ethnic and religious differences.

The fighting has been fiercest in the former province of Bosnia, where Serbs and Muslims launched attacks on each other's villages and cities. News reports suggested that many women were raped, and that the men were sent to camps to force their families to leave their homes. The city of Sarajevo had been under attack since early in the civil war, sustaining heavy artillery and small-arms attacks, while the United States and European nations tried to force the parties to negotiate. Efforts by U.N. peacekeepers to deliver humanitarian aid were only partially successful.

Africa.   The continent of Africa witnessed both great strides for freedom and savage civil strife during 1994. In South Africa, the first all-race elections were held—mostly in an orderly and peaceful manner—and Nelson Mandela was elected as the first president under a new constitution. Most South African constituencies took part in the election and seemed ready to support the new black-majority regime. The economic sanctions applied by the United States had helped bring the white South African government to a position of economic hardship and led, in part, to its negotiations with Mandela and his African National Congress party.

In central Africa, another situation arose that seemed to be totally beyond the influence of the United States, France, or the United Nations. After a plane crash that killed the presidents of Rwanda and of neighboring Burundi, civil war erupted in Rwanda. The political war between the government and the rebel forces was complicated by a terrible ethnic struggle between the Hutu and Tutsi tribes. Observers estimated that more than half a million people were killed within a few weeks, with many bodies dumped in the rivers. About 250,000 refugees arrived in Uganda, setting up a small city in less than a week. Over a million others fled into neighboring Zaire. The United Nations called for troops to assist in relief efforts, but only France responded (and pulled out shortly thereafter). The United States played virtually no part in this situation until small military and civilian contingents were sent to assist with the refugee crisis.

FOREIGN AND DEFENSE POLICY: UNFINISHED WORK

No president or secretary of state can predict the future of world politics. There is simply no way of knowing whether the states of the former Soviet

Here Nelson Mandela votes in 1994 in the first virtually unrestricted South African elections in that country's history. Among the various parties that participated, Mandela's party was triumphant, as expected. He is now head of a mixed white and black government in South Africa.

POLITICS AND ETHICS
The Demands of Ethnic Nationalism

The slaughter of civilians in Rwanda in 1994 and the continued fighting between Serbian and Moslem Bosnians is but a prelude to things to come. As new states are created from the wreckage of the Soviet Union and as postcolonial states mature, more and more people identifying with ethnic subnationalities will be claiming the right to sovereignty as new states or, at a minimum, the right to international protection for their culture and identity. According to one commentator, the first wave of twentieth-century nationalism followed World War II, when colonial powers like Great Britain and France allowed their former colonies to become independent states. At that time, the new states, including India, Pakistan, Vietnam, and others, fought to establish national unity against the colonial powers.*

*Joane Nagel, "Ethnic Nationalism: Politics, Ideology, and the World Order," *International Journal of Comparative Sociology*, Vol. 34 (1993), p. 107.

Since that time, several more waves of ethnic nationalism have followed, as people of ethnic nationalities within these new nations (and within old nations) claim independence or the need for greater rights within the nation. The response of the world's international organizations has also changed in this century; they now support human rights in every case.

The result has been an explosion of ethnic conflicts in developing nations, in the states of the former Soviet Union, and even in the industrialized nations. In June 1993, the *Los Angeles Times* listed fifty-three separate ethnic conflicts in the world. Although Rwanda was mentioned, at that time, the mass killings of more than 500,000 people had not yet occurred. In India, at least twenty thousand people have been killed in violence between the Sikhs and the Hindu government. In Azerbaijan, three thousand deaths have occurred since 1988. In Sri Lanka, twenty thousand Tamils have died in their

revolt against the Buddhist Sinhalese. In Iraq, persecution of the Kurds and the "marsh Arabs" continues.

The international community faces an ethical dilemma in these situations. Should all peoples who claim an ethnic identity be protected, either by outside forces or through the creation of a separate political entity? If that is the case, what is the right of a nation as a whole to protect its sovereignty and its borders for the good of all the citizens? It cannot be correct morally to allow the oppression of one group by another, but can outsiders intervene in the domestic affairs of a nation? Finally, the solution cannot be separate states for each people. Such a solution would produce a world of nations too small to survive and would require large-scale migrations of peoples back to their homelands. What the United States and other members of the world community will do about the increasing ethnic violence remains to be seen.

Union will be a source of future conflicts, whether ethnic tensions will erupt in more nations, or whether the United Nations will be able to assemble an effective peacekeeping force. Nonetheless, it is necessary for U.S. leaders to try to plan for the future. The United States needs to plan a strategy for self-defense rather than a strategy for confronting Russia. Among the foreign policy issues to be confronted, it is vitally important for the United States to plan an economic strategy that will increase U.S. exports and hold imports steady—in order to reduce the trade deficit. The passage of NAFTA was intended to be a part of that strategy, as the North American nations become one trading zone. It is also hoped that the new World Trade Organization will ultimately create a more level playing field in the global marketplace.

Other issues that need to be resolved include the role that the United States sees for the United Nations, the degree to which the United States must keep a vital intelligence service, the strategies for supporting American interests in the Western Hemisphere and throughout the world, and the degree to which the United States will play an active role in the world. Without the structure of the Cold War, it is likely that foreign policy for the United States, as well as for other leading nations, will need to be much more flexible than it has been in the past to deal with changing conditions and complex situations.

As the world moves toward the twenty-first century, the international experiences of the 1990s—and of the whole twentieth century—may be seen as a time of transition. The events of this century created the economic and social basis for the United States to change from a nation interested primarily in domestic policy to a major player on the world stage. The next century is likely to see that role grow, perhaps making possible a new variety of world politics.

GETTING INVOLVED
Working for Human Rights

In many countries throughout the world, human rights are not protected to the extent that they are in the United States. In some nations, people are imprisoned, tortured, or killed because they oppose the current regime. In other nations, certain ethnic or racial groups are oppressed by the majority population. In nations such as Somalia, in which civil war has caused starvation among millions of people, international efforts to send food relief to the refugee camps were hampered by the fighting among rival factions that raged within that country.

What can you do to work for the improvement of human rights in other nations? One way is to join one of the national and international organizations listed in the next column that attempt to keep watch over human rights violations. By publicizing human rights violations, these organizations try to pressure nations into changing their tactics. Sometimes, such organizations are able to apply enough pressure and cause enough embarrassment that selected individuals may be freed from prison or allowed to emigrate.

Another way to work for human rights is to keep informed about the state of affairs in other nations and to write personally to those governments or to their embassies, asking them to cease these violations. Again, the organizations listed here have newsletters or other publications to keep you aware of developments in other nations.

If you want to receive general information about the position of the United States on human rights violations, you could begin by writing to the State Department at the following address:

U.S. Department of State
Bureau of Human Rights and Humanitarian Affairs
U.S. Department of State, Room 7802
Washington, DC 20520

The following organizations are best known for their watchdog efforts in countries that violate human rights for political reasons. These include both leftist and rightist regimes.

Amnesty International U.S.A.
304 W. 58th St.
New York, NY 10017

American Friends Service Committee
1501 Cherry St.
Philadelphia, PA 19102

Clergy and Laity Concerned
198 Broadway
New York, NY 10038

KEY TERMS

attentive public   542

Cold War   546

containment   546

détente   547

diplomacy   533

economic aid   533

executive agreement   536

foreign policy   533

foreign policy process   534

intelligence community   538

iron curtain   546

isolationist foreign policy   544

military-industrial
  complex   542

Monroe Doctrine   544

moral idealism   534

National Security Council
  (NSC)   534

national security policy   534

negative constituents   538

political realism   535

Soviet bloc   546

Strategic Arms Limitation
  Treaty (SALT I)   548

technical assistance   533

Truman Doctrine   546

CHAPTER SUMMARY

1. Foreign policy includes national goals and the techniques used to achieve them. National security policy, which is one aspect of foreign policy, is designed to protect the independence and the political and economic integrity of the United States. Diplomacy involves the nation's external relationships and is an attempt to resolve conflict without resort to arms. Sometimes U.S. foreign policy is based on moral idealism. At other times, U.S. policies stem from political realism.

2. The formal power of the president to make foreign policy derives from the U.S. Constitution, which makes the president responsible for the preservation of national security and designates the president as commander in chief of the army and navy. Presidents have interpreted this authority broadly. They also have the power to make treaties and executive agreements. In principle, the State Department is the executive agency most directly involved with foreign affairs. The National Security Council (NSC) advises the president on the integration of "domestic, foreign, and military policies relating to the national security." The intelligence community consists of forty or more government agencies engaged in intelligence activities varying from information gathering to covert actions. In response to presidential actions in the Vietnam War, Congress attempted to establish some limits on the power of the president in foreign policy by passing the War Powers Act in 1973.

3. Three major themes have guided U.S. foreign policy. In the early years of the nation, isolationism was

the primary focus. With the start of the twentieth century, this view gave way to global involvement. From the end of World War II through the 1980s, the major goal was to contain communism and the influence of the Soviet Union.

4. During the 1700s and 1800s, the United States had little international power and generally stayed out of European conflicts and politics. The nineteenth century has been called the period of isolationism. The Monroe Doctrine of 1823 stated that the United States would not accept foreign intervention in the Western Hemisphere and would not meddle in European affairs. The United States pursued an actively expansionist policy in the Americas and the Pacific area during the nineteenth century, however.

5. The end of the policy of isolationism toward Europe started with the Spanish-American War of 1898. U.S. entanglement in European politics became more extensive when the United States entered World War I on April 6, 1917. World War II marked a lasting change in American foreign policy. The United States was the only major country to emerge from the war with its economy intact and the only country with operating nuclear weapons.

6. Soon after the close of World War II, the uncomfortable alliance between the United States and the Soviet Union ended, and the Cold War began. A policy of containment, which assumed an expansionist Soviet Union, was enunciated in the Truman Doctrine. Following the frustrations of the Vietnam War and the apparent arms equality of the United States and the

Soviet Union, the United States was ready for détente. As the arms race escalated, arms control became a major foreign policy issue. Although President Ronald Reagan established a tough stance toward the Soviet Union in the first term of his administration, the second term saw serious negotiations toward arms reduction, culminating with the signing of the Intermediate-Range Nuclear Force Treaty at the Moscow summit in 1988. Negotiations toward further arms reduction continued in the Bush administration. The Strategic Arms Reduction Treaty, which limited long-range nuclear missiles, was signed in 1992 with Russia and several other states of the former Soviet Union.

7. Nuclear proliferation continues to be an issue due to the breakup of the Soviet Union and the loss of control over its nuclear arsenal, along with the continued efforts of other nations to gain nuclear warheads. The number of warheads is known to be more than twenty thousand.

8. Ethnic tensions and political instability in many regions of the world provide challenges to the United States. The nations of Central America and the Caribbean, including Haiti, require American attention because of their proximity. Negotiations have brought agreement in the Middle East and South Africa, whereas civil wars have torn apart Rwanda and Yugoslavia.

9. The United States is dependent on the world economy, as shown by the vulnerability of its stock market to world forces, its status as a debtor nation, and its significant trade deficit. The effects of a united Europe on world trade are yet to be fully realized.

 ## QUESTIONS FOR REVIEW AND DISCUSSION

1. Without a clear enemy to confront, should the United States play an active role in the world? What advantages and disadvantages might accompany a return to isolationism?

2. Traditionally, the State Department has focused on diplomacy and on representing U.S. interests abroad, whereas the Defense Department has planned strategy for war. Should the State Department play a larger role in a post–Cold War world? Should the Treasury and Commerce Departments be more important in foreign policy decisions than they have been in recent decades?

3. As one of the founders of the United Nations and a permanent member of the Security Council, should the United States welcome the United Nations' expanded efforts in peacekeeping? Can you think of instances in which UN efforts might contradict the interests of the United States? To what extent should the United States support UN peace-keepers?

4. What are the interests of the United States today in world affairs? Identify three or four goals that you believe should be pursued by American diplomats and leaders. Why are those goals important to ordinary citizens? Which institutions of government must work to achieve those goals?

 ## LOGGING ON: FOREIGN AND DEFENSE POLICY

For information on foreign policy, including information on the conflicts in Bosnia, Haiti, Somalia, and Rwanda and information on human rights abuses in the People's Republic of China, look into

pofp-j@uga.cc.uga.edu

The United Nations is going on-line with its own ''Home Page'' on the Internet World Wide Web. It is a user-friendly gateway to a wealth of information about the organization and its activities. With just a click on an icon, a Home Page user can take an electronic tour of U.N. headquarters in New York, get basic information about U.N. activities, or access

Daily Highlights, a pictorial history of the organization with over 100 downloadable photographs. Anyone with an Internet connection and a Webb browsing program can access the Home Page. The address is

http://www.un.org

For information on military personnel, practices, and policies, use

gopher.well.sf.ca.us

and choose **The Military, Its People, Policies, and Practices.**

If you are looking for information on various aspects of the federal government's international trade policy, such as NAFTA or GATT, there is a good source to check out. For information on international trade policy, try

trade@csf.colorado.edu

 ## SELECTED REFERENCES

Allison, Graham, and Gregory F. Treverton, eds. *Rethinking America's Security: Beyond the Cold War to New World Order*. New York: Norton, 1992. This book, which was sponsored by the American Assembly and the Council on Foreign Relations, brings together the insights of leading experts on foreign policy and provides in-depth scrutiny of national security in the post–Cold War period.

Clinton, W. David. *The Two Faces of National Interest.* Baton Rouge: Louisiana State University Press, 1994. The concept of national interest is examined in this volume in the context of four major crisis points in the twentieth century. The author finds that this concept can be helpful in choosing foreign policy directions.

Durch, William J., ed. *The Evolution of UN Peacekeeping.* New York: St. Martin's Press, 1993. A collection of essays that discuss UN peacekeeping operations on different continents.

Feshbach, Murray, and Alfred Friendly, Jr. *Ecocide in the USSR: Health and Nature under Seige.* New York: Basic Books, 1992. The authors chronicle the ecological problems caused by the Soviet model of industrialization. They conclude that a major refocus of economic priorities in the post-Soviet era is essential to improve this situation and that the problems confronting the successor states of the Soviet Union serve as a warning to other countries of the dangers of ecological mismanagement.

Fuller, Graham E. *The Democracy Trap: The Perils of the Post–Cold War World.* New York: Dutton, 1992. The author, a former Foreign Service official and currently a senior political analyst at the RAND Corporation, argues that Americans may be unable to cope with the prob-

lems confronting the world following the end of the Cold War, because they are trapped in the democratic politics of immediate gratification, interest-group parochialism, positive-news propaganda, and the dominance of individualism over communal effort.

Gottlieb, Gideon. *Nation against State: A New Approach to Ethnic Conflicts and the Decline of Sovereignty.* New York: Council on Foreign Relations, 1993. Gottlieb explores the conflicts that arise when ethnic groups or nationalities demand physical territory to support their community. He reminds the reader that it is possible to have an ethnic identity or even a nation—for example, the Palestinian nation or the Jewish nation—without having the boundaries of a legally sovereign state.

Harding, Harry. *A Fragile Relationship: The United States and China, Since 1972.* Washington, D.C.: Brookings Institution, 1992. This book reviews and analyzes U.S.–China relations since President Richard Nixon's visit to Beijing. The author envisions better relationships in the future based on mutual economic interests. These relationships, he predicts, will replace the previous tacit strategic alliance against the former Soviet Union.

Kissinger, Henry. *Diplomacy.* New York: Simon and Schuster, 1994. Kissinger reviews much of the diplomatic history of the nineteenth century to provide a foundation for understanding America's twentieth-century foreign policy dilemmas. He remains committed to the national interest and to using national power in politics to create a more stable world.

Moynihan, Daniel Patrick. *Pandaemonium: Ethnicity in International Politics.* New York: Oxford University Press, 1993. The senior senator from New York discusses the rise of ethnicity in world politics and the difficulty of both encouraging ethnic groups to retain their separate identities and cultures and discouraging ethnic violence.

Nincic, Miroslav. *Democracy and Foreign Policy: The Fallacy of Political Realism.* New York: Columbia University Press, 1992. The author explores the tension between democratic decision making and the need for strong, effective foreign policy and finds that the two are compatible.

Volcker, Paul A., and Toyoo Gyohten. *Changing Fortunes: The World's Money and the Threat to American Leadership.* New York: Times Books/Random House, 1992. This book emphasizes the decline of American economic supremacy in international finance and focuses on the incompatibility of the government's desires for stable foreign exchange rates, highly mobile private capital, and autonomous national economic policy.

In Congress, July 4, 1776

A Declaration by the Representatives of the United States of America, in General Congress assembled. When in the Course of human Events, it becomes necessary for one People to dissolve the Political Bands which have connected them with another, and to assume among the Powers of the Earth, the separate and equal Station to which the Laws of Nature and of Nature's God entitle them, a decent Respect to the Opinions of Mankind requires that they should declare the causes which impel them to the Separation.

We hold these Truths to be self-evident, that all Men are created equal, that they are endowed by their Creator with certain unalienable Rights, that among these are Life, Liberty, and the Pursuit of Happiness—That to secure these Rights, Governments are instituted among Men, deriving their just Powers from the Consent of the Governed, that whenever any Form of Government becomes destructive of these Ends, it is the Right of the People to alter or to abolish it, and to institute new Government, laying its Foundation on such Principles, and organizing its Powers in such Forms, as to them shall seem most likely to effect their Safety and Happiness. Prudence, indeed, will dictate that Governments long established should not be changed for light and transient Causes; and accordingly all Experience hath shewn, that Mankind are more disposed to suffer, while Evils are sufferable, than to right themselves by abolishing the Forms to which they are accustomed. But when a long Train of Abuses and Usurpations, pursuing invariably the same Object, evinces a Design to reduce them under absolute Despotism, it is their Right, it is their Duty, to throw off such Government, and to provide new Guards for their future Security. Such has been the patient Sufferance of these Colonies; and such is now the Necessity which constrains them to alter their former Systems of Government. The History of the present King of Great-Britain is a History of repeated Injuries and Usurpations, all having in direct Object the Establishment of an absolute Tyranny over these States. To prove this, let Facts be submitted to a candid World.

He has refused his Assent to Laws, the most wholesome and necessary for the public Good.

He has forbidden his Governors to pass Laws of immediate and pressing Importance, unless suspended in their Operation till his Assent should be obtained; and when so suspended, he has utterly neglected to attend to them.

He has refused to pass other Laws for the Accommodation of large Districts of People, unless those People would relinquish the Right of Representation in the Legislature, a Right inestimable to them, and formidable to Tyrants only.

He has called together Legislative Bodies at Places unusual, uncomfortable, and distant from the Depository of their Public Records, for the sole Purpose of fatiguing them into Compliance with his Measures.

He has dissolved Representative Houses repeatedly, for opposing with manly Firmness his Invasions on the Rights of the People.

He has refused for a long Time, after such Dissolutions, to cause others to be elected; whereby the Legislative Powers, incapable of Annihilation, have returned to the People at large for their exercise; the State remaining in the mean time exposed to all the Dangers of Invasion from without, and Convulsions within.

He has endeavoured to prevent the Population of these States; for that Purpose obstructing the Laws for Naturalization of Foreigners; refusing to pass others to encourage their Migrations hither, and raising the Conditions of new Appropriations of Lands.

He has obstructed the Administration of Justice, by refusing his Assent to Laws for establishing Judiciary Powers.

He has made Judges dependent on his Will alone, for the Tenure of their offices, and the Amount and payment of their Salaries.

He has erected a Multitude of new Offices, and sent hither Swarms of Officers to harrass our People, and eat out their Substance.

He has kept among us, in Times of Peace, Standing Armies, without the consent of our Legislatures.

He has affected to render the Military independent of, and superior to the Civil Power.

He has combined with others to subject us to a Jurisdiction foreign to our Constitution, and unacknowledged by our Laws; giving his Assent to their Acts of pretended Legislation:

For quartering large Bodies of Armed Troops among us:

For protecting them, by a mock Trial, from Punishment for any Murders which they should commit on the Inhabitants of these States:

For cutting off our Trade with all Parts of the World:

For imposing Taxes on us without our Consent:

For depriving us, in many cases, of the Benefits of Trial by Jury:

For transporting us beyond Seas to be tried for pretended Offences:

For abolishing the free System of English Laws in a neighbouring Province, establishing therein an arbitrary Government, and enlarging its Boundaries, so as to render it at once an Example and fit Instrument for introducing the same absolute Rule into these Colonies:

For taking away our Charters, abolishing our most valuable Laws, and altering fundamentally the Forms of our Governments:

For suspending our own Legislatures, and declaring themselves invested with Power to legislate for us in all Cases whatsoever.

He has abdicated Government here, by declaring us out of his Protection and waging War against us.

He has plundered our Seas, ravaged our Coasts, burnt our towns, and destroyed the Lives of our People.

He is, at this Time, transporting large Armies of foreign Mercenaries to compleat the works of Death, Desolation, and Tyranny, already begun with circumstances of Cruelty and Perfidy, scarcely paralleled in the most barbarous Ages, and totally unworthy the Head of a civilized Nation.

He has constrained our fellow Citizens taken Captive on the high Seas to bear Arms against their Country, to become the Executioners of their Friends and Brethren, or to fall themselves by their Hands.

He has excited domestic Insurrections amongst us, and has endeavoured to bring on the Inhabitants of our Frontiers, the merciless Indian Savages, whose known Rule of Warfare, is an undistinguished Destruction, of all Ages, Sexes and Conditions.

In every state of these Oppressions we have Petitioned for Redress in the most humble Terms: Our repeated Petitions have been answered only by repeated Injury. A Prince, whose Character is thus marked by every act which may define a Tyrant, is unfit to be the Ruler of a free People.

Nor have we been wanting in Attentions to our British Brethren. We have warned them from Time to Time of Attempts by their Legislature to extend an unwarrantable Jurisdiction over us. We have reminded them of the Circumstances of our Emigration and Settlement here. We have appealed to their native Justice and Magnanimity, and we have conjured them by the Ties of our common Kindred to disavow these Usurpations, which, would inevitably interrupt our Connections and Correspondence. They too have been deaf to the Voice of Justice and of Consanguinity. We must, therefore, acquiesce in the Necessity, which denounces our Separation, and hold them, as we hold the rest of Mankind, Enemies in War, in Peace, Friends.

We, therefore, the Representatives of the UNITED STATES OF AMERICA, in General Congress Assembled, appealing to the Supreme Judge of the World for the Rectitude of our Intentions, do, in the Name, and by the Authority of the good People of these Colonies, solemnly Publish and Declare, That these United Colonies are, and of Right ought to be, Free and Independent States; that they are absolved from all Allegiance to the British Crown, and that all political Connection between them and the State of Great-Britain, is and ought to be totally dissolved; and that as Free and Independent States, they have full Power to levy War, conclude Peace, contract Alliances, establish Commerce, and to do all other Acts and Things which Independent States may of right do. And for the support of this declaration, with a firm Reliance on the Protection of divine Providence, we mutually pledge to each other our lives, our Fortunes, and our sacred Honor.

The Preamble

We the People of the United States, in Order to form a more perfect Union, establish Justice, insure domestic Tranquility, provide for the common defence, promote the general Welfare, and secure the Blessings of Liberty to ourselves and our Posterity, do ordain and establish this Constitution for the United States of America.

The Preamble declares that "We the People" are the authority for the Constitution (unlike the Articles of Confederation, which derived their authority from the states). The Preamble also sets out the purposes of the Constitution.

Article I. (Legislative Branch)

The first part of the Constitution is called Article 1; it deals with the organization and powers of the lawmaking branch of the national government, the Congress.

Section 1. Legislative Powers

All legislative Powers herein granted shall be vested in a Congress of the United States, which shall consist of a Senate and House of Representatives.

Section 2. House of Representatives

Clause 1: Composition and Election of Members. The House of Representatives shall be composed of Members chosen every second Year by the People of the several States, and the Electors in each State shall have the Qualifications requisite for Electors of the most numerous Branch of the State Legislature.

Each state has the power to decide who may vote for members of Congress. Within each state, those who may vote for state legislators may also vote for members of the House of Representatives (and, under the Seventeenth Amendment, for U.S. senators). When the Constitution was written, nearly all states limited voting rights to white male property owners or taxpayers at least twenty-one years old. Subsequent amendments granted voting power to African-American men, all women, and eighteen-year-olds.

Clause 2: Qualifications. No Person shall be a Representative who shall not have attained to the Age of twenty five Years, and been seven Years a Citizen of the United States, and who shall not, when elected, be an Inhabitant of that State in which he shall be chosen.

Each member of the House must (1) be at least twenty-five years old, (2) have been a U.S. citizen for at least seven years, and (3) be a resident of the state in which she or he is elected.

Clause 3: Apportionment of Representatives and Direct Taxes. Representatives [and direct Taxes][1] shall be apportioned among the several States which may be included within this Union, according to their respective Numbers [which shall be determined by adding to the whole Number of free Persons, including those bound to Service for a Term of Years, and excluding Indians not taxed, three fifths of all other Persons].[2] The actual Enumeration shall be made within three Years after the first Meeting of the Congress of the United States, and within every subsequent Term of ten Years, in such Manner as they shall by Law direct. The Number of Representatives shall not exceed one for every thirty Thousand, but each State shall have at Least one Representative; and until such enumeration shall be made, the State of New Hampshire shall be entitled to chuse three, Massachusetts eight, Rhode Island and Providence Plantations one, Connecticut five, New York six, New Jersey four, Pennsylvania eight, Delaware one, Maryland six, Virginia ten, North Carolina five, South Carolina five, and Georgia three.

A state's representation in the House is based on the size of its population. Population is counted in each decade's census, after which Congress reapportions House seats. Since early in this century, the number of seats has been limited to 435.

Clause 4: Vacancies. When vacancies happen in the Representation from any State, the Executive Authority thereof shall issue Writs of Election to fill such Vacancies.

---

*The spelling, capitalization, and punctuation of the original have been retained here. Brackets indicate passages that have been altered by amendments to the Constitution.

---

[1]Modified by the Sixteenth Amendment.
[2]Modified by the Fourteenth Amendment.

The "Executive Authority" is the state's governor. When a vacancy occurs in the House, the governor calls a special election to fill it.

Clause 5: Officers and Impeachment.   The House of Representatives shall chuse their Speaker and other Officers; and shall have the sole Power of Impeachment.

The power to impeach is the power to accuse. In this case, it is the power to accuse members of the executive or judicial branch of wrongdoing or abuse of power. Once a bill of impeachment is issued, the Senate holds the trial.

Section 3. The Senate
Clause 1: Term and Number of Members.   The Senate of the United States shall be composed of two Senators from each State [chosen by the Legislature thereof],[3] for six Years; and each Senator shall have one Vote.

tate has two senators, each of whom serves for six years and has one vote in the upper chamber. Since the Seventeenth Amendment in 1913, all senators are elected directly by voters of the state during the regular election.

Clause 2: Classification of Senators.   Immediately after they shall be assembled in Consequence of the first Election, they shall be divided as equally as may be into three Classes. The Seats of the Senators of the first Class shall be vacated at the Expiration of the second Year, of the second Class at the Expiration of the fourth Year, and of the third Class at the Expiration of the sixth Year, so that one third may be chosen every second Year; [and if Vacancies happen by Resignation, or otherwise, during the Recess of the Legislature of any State, the Executive thereof may make temporary Appointments until the next Meeting of the Legislature, which shall then fill such Vacancies].[4]

One-third of the Senate's seats are open to election every two years (unlike the House, all of whose members are elected simultaneously).

Clause 3: Qualifications.   No Person shall be a Senator who shall not have attained to the Age of thirty Years, and been nine Years a Citizen of the United States, and who shall not, when elected, be an Inhabitant of that State for which he shall be chosen.

Every senator must be at least thirty years old, a citizen of the United States for a minimum of nine years, and a resident of the state in which he or she is elected.

Clause 4: The Role of the Vice President.   The Vice President of the United States shall be President of the Senate, but shall have no Vote, unless they be equally divided.

The vice president presides over meetings of the Senate but cannot vote unless there is a tie. The Constitution gives no other official duties to the vice president.

Clause 5: Other Officers.   The Senate shall chuse their other Officers, and also a President pro tempore, in the Absence of the Vice President, or when he shall exercise the Office of President of the United States.

The Senate votes for one of its members to preside when the vice president is absent. This person is usually called the president pro tempore because of the temporary situation of the position.

Clause 6: Impeachment Trials.   The Senate shall have the sole Power to try all Impeachments. When sitting for that Purpose, they shall be on Oath or Affirmation. When the President of the United States is tried, the Chief Justice shall preside: And no Person shall be convicted without the Concurrence of two thirds of the Members present.

The Senate conducts trials of officials that the House impeaches. The Senate sits as a jury, with the vice president presiding if the president is not on trial.

Clause 7: Penalties for Conviction.   Judgment in Cases of Impeachment shall not extend further than to removal from Office, and disqualification to hold and enjoy any Office of honor, Trust, or Profit under the United States: but the Party convicted shall nevertheless be liable and subject to Indictment, Trial, Judgment, and Punishment, according to Law.

On conviction on impeachment charges, the Senate can only force an official to leave office and prevent him or her from holding another office in the federal government. The individual, however, can still be tried in a regular court.

Section 4. Congressional Elections: Times, Manner, and Places
Clause 1: Elections.   The Times, Places and Manner of holding Elections for Senators and Representatives, shall be prescribed in each State by the Legislature thereof; but the Congress may at any time by Law make or alter such Regulations, except as to the Places of chusing Senators.

Congress set the Tuesday after the first Monday in November in even-numbered years as the date for congressional elections. In states with more than one seat in the House, Congress requires that representatives be elected from districts within each state. Under the Seventeenth Amendment, senators are elected at the same places as other officials.

[3]Repealed by the Seventeenth Amendment.
[4]Modified by the Seventeenth Amendment.

Clause 2: Sessions of Congress. [The Congress shall assemble at least once in every Year, and such Meeting shall be on the first Monday in December, unless they shall by Law appoint a different Day.][5]

Congress has to meet every year at least once. The regular session now begins at noon on January 3 of each year, subsequent to the Twentieth Amendment, unless Congress passes a law to fix a different date. Congress stays in session until its members vote to adjourn. Additionally, the president may call a special session.

Section 5. Powers and Duties of the Houses
Clause 1: Admitting Members and Quorum. Each House shall be the Judge of the Elections, Returns, and Qualifications of its own Members, and a Majority of each shall constitute a Quorum to do Business; but a smaller Number may adjourn from day to day, and may be authorized to compel the Attendance of absent Members, in such Manner, and under such Penalties as each House may provide.

Each chamber may exclude or refuse to seat a member-elect.
The quorum rule requires that 218 members of the House and 51 members of the Senate be present in order to conduct business. This rule is normally not enforced in the handling of routine matters.

Clause 2: Rules and Discipline of Members. Each House may determine the Rules of its Proceedings, punish its Members for disorderly Behaviour, and, with the Concurrence of two thirds, expel a Member.

The House and the Senate may adopt their own rules to guide their proceedings. Each may also discipline its members for conduct that is deemed unacceptable. No member may be expelled without a two-thirds majority vote in favor of expulsion.

Clause 3: Keeping a Record. Each House shall keep a Journal of its Proceedings, and from time to time publish the same, excepting such Parts as may in their Judgment require Secrecy; and the Yeas and Nays of the Members of either House on any question shall, at the Desire of one fifth of those Present, be entered on the Journal.

The journals of the two houses are published at the end of each session of Congress.

Clause 4: Adjournment. Neither House, during the Session of Congress, shall, without the Consent of the other, adjourn for more than three days, nor to any other Place than that in which the two Houses shall be sitting.

---

[5]Changed by the Twentieth Amendment.

Congress has the power to determine when and where to meet, provided, however, that both houses meet in the same city. Neither house may recess in excess of three days without the consent of the other.

Section 6. Rights of Members
Clause 1: Compensation and Privileges. The Senators and Representatives shall receive a Compensation for their services, to be ascertained by Law, and paid out of the Treasury of the United States. They shall in all Cases, except Treason, Felony and Breach of the Peace, be privileged from Arrest during their Attendance at the Session of their respective Houses, and in going to and returning from the same; and for any Speech or Debate in either House, they shall not be questioned in any other Place.

Congressional salaries are to be paid by the U.S. Treasury rather than by the members' respective states. The original salaries were $6 per day; in 1857 they were $3,000 per year. Both representatives and senators currently are paid $133,600 each year.

Members cannot be arrested for things they say during speeches and debates in Congress. This immunity applies to the Capitol Building itself and not to their private lives.
Treason is defined in Article III, Section 3. A felony is any serious crime. A breach of the peace is any indictable offense less than treason or a felony. Members cannot be arrested for anything they say in speeches or debates in Congress.

Clause 2: Restrictions. No Senator or Representative shall, during the Time for which he was elected, be appointed to any civil Office under the Authority of the United States, which shall have been created, or the Emoluments whereof shall have been encreased during such time; and no Person holding any Office under the United States, shall be a Member of either House during his Continuance in Office.

During the term for which a member was elected, he or she cannot concurrently accept another federal government position.

Section 7. Legislative Powers: Bills and Resolutions
Clause 1: Revenue Bills. All Bills for raising Revenue shall originate in the House of Representatives; but the Senate may propose or concur with Amendments as on other Bills.

All tax and appropriation bills for raising money have to originate in the House of Representatives. The Senate, though, often amends such bills and may even substitute an entirely different bill.

Clause 2: The Presidential Veto. Every Bill which shall have passed the House of Representatives and the Senate, shall, before it becomes a Law, be presented to the President of the United States; If he approve he shall sign it, but if not he shall return it, with his Objections to the House in which it shall have originated, who shall enter the Objections at large on their Journal, and proceed to reconsider it. If after such Reconsideration two thirds of that House shall agree to pass the Bill, it shall be sent together with the Objections, to the other House, by which it shall likewise be reconsidered, and if approved by two thirds of that House, it shall become a Law. But in all such Cases the Votes of both Houses shall be determined by Yeas and Nays, and the Names of the Persons voting for and against the Bill shall be entered on the Journal of each House respectively. If any Bill shall not be returned by the President within ten Days (Sundays excepted) after it shall have been presented to him, the Same shall be a Law, in like Manner as if he had signed it, unless the Congress by their Adjournment prevent its Return in which Case it shall not be a Law.

When Congress sends the president a bill, he or she can sign it (in which case it becomes law) or send it back to the house in which it originated. If it is sent back, a two-thirds majority of each house must pass it again for it to become law. If the president neither signs it nor sends it back within ten days, it becomes law anyway, unless Congress adjourns in the meantime.

Clause 3: Actions on Other Matters. Every Order, Resolution, or Vote to which the Concurrence of the Senate and House of Representatives may be necessary (except on a question of Adjournment) shall be presented to the President of the United States; and before the Same shall take Effect, shall be approved by him, or being disapproved by him, shall be repassed by two thirds of the Senate and House of Representatives, according to the Rules and Limitations prescribed in the Case of a Bill.

The president must either sign or veto everything that Congress passes, except votes to adjourn and resolutions not having the force of law.

Section 8. The Powers of Congress

Clause 1: Taxing. The Congress shall have Power To lay and collect Taxes, Duties, Imposts and Excises, to pay the Debts and provide for the common Defence and general Welfare of the United States; but all Duties, Imposts and Excises shall be uniform throughout the United States;

Duties are taxes on imports and exports. Impost is a generic term for tax. Excises are taxes on the manufacture, sale, or use of goods.

Clause 2: Borrowing. To borrow Money on the credit of the United States;

Congress has the power to borrow money, which is normally carried out through the sale of U.S. treasury bonds on which interest is paid. Note that the Constitution places no limit on the amount of government borrowing.

Clause 3: Regulation of Commerce. To regulate Commerce with foreign Nations, and among the several States, and with the Indian Tribes;

This is the commerce clause, which gives to the Congress the power to regulate interstate and foreign trade. Much of the activity of Congress is based on this clause.

Clause 4: Naturalization and Bankruptcy. To establish a uniform Rule of Naturalization, and uniform Laws on the subject of Bankruptcies throughout the United States;

Only Congress may determine how aliens can become citizens of the United States. Congress may make laws with respect to bankruptcy.

Clause 5: Money and Standards. To coin Money, regulate the Value thereof, and of foreign Coin, and fix the Standard of Weights and Measures;

Congress mints coins and prints and circulates paper money. Congress can establish uniform measures of time, distance, weight, etc. In 1838, Congress adopted the English system of weights and measurements as our national standard.

Clause 6: Punishing Counterfeiters. To provide for the Punishment of counterfeiting the Securities and current Coin of the United States;

Congress has the power to punish those who copy American money and pass it off as real. Currently, the fine is up to $5,000 and/or imprisonment for up to fifteen years.

Clause 7: Roads and Post Offices. To establish Post Offices and post Roads;

Post roads include all routes over which mail is carried—highways, railways, waterways, and airways.

Clause 8: Patents and Copyrights. To promote the Progress of Science and useful Arts, by securing for limited Times to Authors and Inventors the exclusive Right to their respective Writings and Discoveries;

Authors' and composers' works are protected by copyrights established by copyright law, which currently is the 1978 Copyright Act. Copyrights are valid for the life of the author or composer plus fifty years. Inventors' works are protected by patents, which vary in length of protection from three and a half to seventeen years. A patent gives a person the exclusive right to control the manufacture or sale of her or his invention.

Clause 9: Lower Courts. To constitute Tribunals inferior to the supreme Court;

Congress has the authority to set up all federal courts, except the Supreme Court, and to decide what cases those courts will hear.

Clause 10: Punishment for Piracy. To define and punish Piracies and Felonies committed on the high Seas, and Offences against the Law of Nations;

Congress has the authority to prohibit the commission of certain acts outside U.S. territory and to punish certain violations of international law.

Clause 11: Declaration of War. To declare War, grant Letters of Marque and Reprisal, and make Rules concerning Captures on Land and Water;

Only Congress can declare war, although the president, as commander in chief, can make war without Congress's formal declaration. Letters of marque and reprisal authorized private parties to capture and destroy enemy ships in wartime. Since the middle of the nineteenth century, international law has prohibited letters of marque and reprisal, and the United States has honored the ban.

Clause 12: The Army. To raise and support Armies, but no Appropriation of Money to that Use shall be for a longer Term than two Years;

Congress has the power to create an army; the money used to pay for it must be appropriated for no more than two-year intervals. This latter restriction gives ultimate control of the army to civilians.

Clause 13: Creation of a Navy. To provide and maintain a Navy;

This clause allows for the maintenance of a navy. In 1947, Congress created the air force.

Clause 14: Regulation of the Armed Forces. To make Rules for the Government and Regulation of the land and naval Forces;

Congress sets the rules for the military mainly by way of the Uniform Code of Military Justice, which was enacted in 1950 by Congress.

Clause 15: The Militia. To provide for calling forth the Militia to execute the Laws of the Union, suppress Insurrections and repel Invasions;

The militia is known today as the National Guard. Both Congress and the president have the authority to call the National Guard into federal service.

Clause 16: How the Militia Is Organized. To provide for organizing, arming, and disciplining the Militia, and for governing such Part of them as may be employed in the Service of the United States, reserving to the States respectively, the Appointment of the Officers, and the Authority of training the Militia according to the discipline prescribed by Congress;

This clause gives Congress the power to "federalize" state militia (National Guard). When called into such service, the National Guard is subject to the same rules that Congress has set forth for the regular armed services.

Clause 17: Creation of the District of Columbia. To exercise exclusive Legislation in all Cases whatsoever, over such District (not exceeding ten Miles square) as may, by Cession of particular States, and the Acceptance of Congress, become the Seat of the Government of the United States, and to exercise like Authority over all Places purchased by the Consent of the Legislature of the State in which the Same shall be, for the Erection of Forts, Magazines, Arsenals, dock-Yards, and other needful Buildings;—And

Congress established the District of Columbia as the national capital in 1791. Virginia and Maryland had granted land for the District, but Virginia's grant was returned because it was believed it would not be needed. Today, the District covers sixty-nine square miles.

Clause 18: The Elastic Clause. To make all Laws which shall be necessary and proper for carrying into Execution the foregoing Powers, and all other Powers vested by this Constitution in the Government of the United States, or in any Department or Officer thereof.

This clause—the necessary and proper clause, or the elastic clause—grants no specific powers, and thus it can be stretched to fit different circumstances. It has allowed Congress to adapt the government to changing needs and times.

Section 9. The Powers Denied to Congress
Clause 1: Question of Slavery. The Migration or Importation of such Persons as any of the States now existing shall think proper to admit, shall not be prohibited by the Congress prior to the Year one thousand eight hundred and eight, but a Tax or duty may be imposed on such Importation, not exceeding ten dollars for each Person.

"Persons" referred to slaves. Congress outlawed the slave trade in 1808.

Clause 2: Habeas Corpus. The privilege of the Writ of Habeas Corpus shall not be suspended, unless when in Cases of Rebellion or Invasion the public Safety may require it.

A writ of habeas corpus *is a court order directing a sheriff or other public officer who is detaining another person to "produce the body" of the detainee so the court can assess the legality of the detention.*

Clause 3: Special Bills.   No Bill of Attainder or ex post facto Law shall be passed.

A bill of attainder is a law that inflicts punishment without a trial. An ex post facto *law is a law that inflicts punishment for an act that was not illegal when it was committed.*

Clause 4: Direct Taxes.   [No Capitation, or other direct, Tax shall be laid, unless in Proportion to the Census or Enumeration herein before directed to be taken.][6]

A capitation is a tax on a person. A direct tax is a tax paid directly to the government, such as a property tax. This clause was intended to prevent Congress from levying a tax on slaves per person and thereby taxing slavery out of existence.

Clause 5: Export Taxes.   No Tax or Duty shall be laid on Articles exported from any State.

Congress may not tax any goods sold from one state to another or from one state to a foreign country. (Congress does have the power to tax goods that are bought from other countries, however.)

Clause 6: Interstate Commerce.   No Preference shall be given by any Regulation of Commerce or Revenue to the Ports of one State over those of another: nor shall Vessels bound to, or from, one State, be obliged to enter, clear, or pay Duties in another.

Congress may not treat different ports within the United States differently in terms of taxing and commerce powers. Congress may not tax goods sent from one state to another. Finally, Congress may not give one state's port a legal advantage over those of another state.

Clause 7: Treasury Withdrawals.   No Money shall be drawn from the Treasury, but in Consequence of Appropriations made by Law; and a regular Statement and Account of the Receipts and Expenditures of all public Money shall be published from time to time.

Federal funds can be spent only as Congress authorizes. This is a significant check on the president's power.

---

[6]Modified by the Sixteenth Amendment.

Clause 8: Titles of Nobility.   No Title of Nobility shall be granted by the United States: And no Person holding any Office of Profit or Trust under them, shall, without the Consent of the Congress, accept of any present, Emolument, Office, or Title, of any kind whatever, from any King, Prince, or foreign State.

On no person in the United States may be bestowed a title of nobility, such as a duke or duchess. This clause also discourages bribery of American officials by foreign governments.

Section 10. Those Powers Denied to the States

Clause 1: Treaties and Coinage.   No State shall enter into any Treaty, Alliance, or Confederation; grant Letters of Marque and Reprisal; coin Money; emit Bills of Credit; make any Thing but gold and silver Coin a Tender in Payment of Debts; pass any Bill of Attainder, ex post facto Law, or Law impairing the Obligation of Contracts, or grant any Title of Nobility.

Prohibiting state laws "impairing the Obligation of Contracts" was intended to protect creditors. (Shays' Rebellion—an attempt to prevent courts from giving effect to creditors' legal actions against debtors—occurred only one year before the Constitution was written.)

Clause 2: Duties and Imposts.   No State shall, without the Consent of the Congress, lay any Imports or Duties on Imports or Exports, except what may be absolutely necessary for executing its inspection Laws; and the net Produce of all Duties and Imposts, laid by any State on Imports or Exports, shall be for the Use of the Treasury of the United States; and all such Laws shall be subject to the Revision and Controul of the Congress.

Only Congress can tax imports. Further, the states cannot tax exports.

Clause 3: War.   No State shall, without the Consent of Congress, lay any Duty of Tonnage, keep Troops, or Ships of War in time of Peace, enter into any Agreement or Compact with another State, or with a foreign Power or engage in War, unless actually invaded, or in such imminent Danger as will not admit of delay.

A duty of tonnage is a tax on ships according to their cargo capacity. No states may effectively tax ships according to their cargo unless Congress agrees. Additionally, this clause forbids any state to keep troops or warships during peacetime or to make a compact with another state or foreign nation unless Congress so agrees. States can, in contrast, maintain a militia, but its use has to be limited to internal disorders that occur within a state—unless, of course, the militia is called into federal service.

Article II. (Executive Branch)

Section 1. The Nature and Scope of Presidential Power

Clause 1: Four-Year Term. The executive Power shall be vested in a President of the United States of America. He shall hold his Office during the Term of four Years, and, together with the Vice President, chosen for the same Term, be elected, as follows.

The president has the power to carry out laws made by Congress, called the executive power. He or she serves in office for a four-year term after election. The Twenty-second Amendment limits the number of times a person may be elected president.

Clause 2: Choosing Electors from Each State. Each State shall appoint, in such Manner as the Legislature thereof may direct, a Number of Electors, equal to the whole Number of Senators and Representatives to which the State may be entitled in the Congress; but no Senator or Representative, or Person holding an Office of Trust or Profit under the United States, shall be appointed an Elector.

The "Electors" are more commonly known as the "electoral college." The president is elected by electors—that is, representatives chosen by the people—rather than by the people directly.

Clause 3: The Former System of Elections. [The Electors shall meet in their respective States, and vote by Ballot for two Persons, of whom one at least shall not be an Inhabitant of the same State with themselves. And they shall make a List of all the Persons voted for, and of the Number of Votes for each; which List they shall sign and certify, and transmit sealed to the Seat of the Government of the United States, directed to the President of the Senate. The President of the Senate shall, in the Presence of the Senate and House of Representatives, open all the Certificates, and the Votes shall then be counted. The Person having the greatest Number of Votes shall be the President, if such Number be a Majority of the whole Number of Electors appointed; and if there be more than one who have such Majority, and have an equal Number of Votes, then the House of Representatives shall immediately chuse by Ballot one of them for President; and if no Person have a Majority, then from the five highest on the List the said House shall in like Manner chuse the President. But in chusing the President, the Votes shall be taken by States, the Representation from each State having one Vote; A quorum for this Purpose shall consist of a Member or Members from two thirds of the States, and a Majority of all the States shall be necessary to a Choice. In every Case, after the Choice of the President, the Person having the greater Number of Votes of the Electors shall be the Vice President. But if there should remain two or more who have equal

Votes, the Senate shall chuse from them by Ballot the Vice President.][7]

The original method of selecting the president and vice-president was replaced by the Twelfth Amendment. Apparently, the framers did not anticipate the rise of political parties and the development of primaries and conventions.

Clause 4: The Time of Elections. The Congress may determine the Time of chusing the Electors, and the Day on which they shall give their Votes; which Day shall be the same throughout the United States.

Congress set the Tuesday after the first Monday in November every fourth year as the date for choosing electors. The electors cast their votes on the Monday after the second Wednesday in December of that year.

Clause 5: Qualifications for President. No person except a natural born Citizen, or a Citizen of the United States, at the time of the Adoption of this Constitution, shall be eligible to the Office of President; neither shall any Person be eligible to that Office who shall not have attained to the Age of thirty five Years, and been fourteen Years a Resident within the United States.

The president must be a natural-born citizen, be at least thirty-five years of age when taking office, and have been a resident within the United States for at least fourteen years.

Clause 6: Succession of the Vice President. [In Case of the Removal of the President from Office, or of his Death, Resignation or Inability to discharge the Powers and Duties of the said Office, the same shall devolve on the Vice President, and the Congress may by Law provide for the Case of Removal, Death, Resignation or Inability, both of the President and Vice President, declaring what Officer shall then act as President, and such Officer shall act accordingly, until the Disability be removed, or a President shall be elected.][8]

This former section provided for the method by which the vice president was to succeed to the presidency, but its wording is ambiguous. It was replaced by the Twenty-fifth Amendment.

Clause 7: The President's Salary. The President shall, at stated Times, receive for his Services, a Compensation, which shall neither be encreased nor diminished during the Period for which he shall have been elected, and he shall not receive within that Period any other Emolument from the United States, or any of them.

---

[7]Changed by the Twelfth Amendment.
[8]Modified by the Twenty-fifth Amendment.

The president maintains the same salary during each four-year term. Moreover, she or he may not receive additional cash payments from the government. Originally set at $25,000 per year, it is currently $200,000 a year plus a $50,000 taxable expense account.

Clause 8: The Oath of Office.

Before he enter on the Execution of his Office, he shall take the following Oath or Affirmation: "I do solemnly swear (or affirm) that I will faithfully execute the Office of President of the United States, and will to the best of my Ability, preserve, protect and defend the Constitution of the United States."

The president is "sworn in" prior to beginning the duties of the office. Currently, the taking of the oath of office occurs on January 20, following the November election. The ceremony is called the inauguration. The oath of office is administered by the chief justice of the United States Supreme Court.

Section 2. Powers of the President

Clause 1: Commander in Chief.

The President shall be Commander in Chief of the Army and Navy of the United States, and of the Militia of the several States, when called into the actual Service of the United States; he may require the Opinion, in writing, of the principal Officer in each of the executive Departments, upon any Subject relating to the Duties of their respective Offices, and he shall have Power to grant Reprieves and Pardons for Offences against the United States, except in Cases of Impeachment.

The armed forces are placed under civilian control because the president is a civilian, but still commander in chief of the military. The president may ask for the help of the heads of each of the executive departments (thereby creating the cabinet). The cabinet members are chosen by the president with the consent of the Senate, but they can be removed without Senate approval.

The president's clemency powers extend only to federal cases. In those cases, he or she may grant a full or conditional pardon, or reduce a prison term or fine.

Clause 2: Treaties and Appointment.

He shall have Power, by and with the Advice and Consent of the Senate, to make Treaties, provided two thirds of the Senators present concur; and he shall nominate, and by and with the Advice and Consent of the Senate, shall appoint Ambassadors, other public Ministers and Consuls, Judges of the supreme Court, and all other Officers of the United States, whose Appointments are not herein otherwise provided for, and which shall be established by Law; but the Congress may by Law vest the Appointment of such inferior Officers, as they think proper, in the President alone, in the Courts of Law, or in the Heads of Departments.

Many of the major powers of the president are identified in this clause, including the power to make treaties with foreign governments (with the approval of the Senate by a two-thirds vote) and the power to appoint ambassadors, Supreme Court justices, and other government officials. Most such appointments require Senate approval.

Clause 3: Vacancies.

The President shall have Power to fill up all Vacancies that may happen during the Recess of the Senate, by granting Commissions which shall expire at the end of their next Session.

The president has the power to appoint temporary officials to fill vacant federal offices without Senate approval if the Congress is not in session. Such appointments expire automatically at the end of Congress's next term.

Section 3. Duties of the President

He shall from time to time give to the Congress Information of the State of the Union, and recommend to their Consideration such Measures as he shall judge necessary and expedient; he may, on extraordinary Occasions, convene both Houses, or either of them, and in Case of Disagreement between them, with Respect to the Time of Adjournment, he may adjourn them to such Time as he shall think proper; he shall receive Ambassadors and other public Ministers; he shall take Care that the Laws be faithfully executed, and shall Commission all the Officers of the United States.

Annually, the president reports on the state of the union to Congress, recommends legislative measures, and proposes a federal budget. The State of the Union speech is a statement not only to Congress but also to the American people. After it is given, the president proposes a federal budget and presents an economic report. At any time he or she so chooses, the president may send special messages to Congress while it is in session. The president has the power to call special sessions, to adjourn Congress when its two houses do not agree for that purpose, to receive diplomatic representatives of other governments, and to ensure the proper execution of all federal laws. The president further has the ability to empower federal officers to hold their positions and to perform their duties.

Section 4. Impeachment

The President, Vice President and all civil Officers of the United States, shall be removed from Office on Impeachment for, and Conviction of, Treason, Bribery, or other high Crimes and Misdemeanors.

Treason denotes giving aid to the nation's enemies. The definition of high crimes and misdemeanors is usually given as serious abuses of political power. In either case, the president or vice president may be accused by the House (called an impeachment) and then removed from office if convicted by the Senate. (Note that impeachment *does not mean removal, but rather the state of being accused of treason or high crimes and misdemeanors.)*

Article III. (Judicial Branch)

Section 1. Judicial Powers, Courts, and Judges

The judicial Power of the United States, shall be vested in one supreme Court, and in such inferior Courts as the Congress may from time to time ordain and establish. The Judges, both of the supreme and inferior Courts, shall hold their Offices during good Behaviour, and shall, at stated Times, receive for their Services a Compensation, which shall not be diminished during their Continuance in Office.

The Supreme Court is vested with judicial power, as are the lower federal courts that Congress creates. Federal judges serve in their offices for life unless they are impeached and convicted by Congress. The payment of federal judges may not be reduced during their time in office.

Section 2. Jurisdiction

Clause 1: Cases Under Federal Jurisdiction. The judicial Power shall extend to all Cases, in Law and Equity, arising under this Constitution, the Laws of the United States, and Treaties made, or which shall be made, under their Authority;—to all Cases affecting Ambassadors, other public Ministers and Consuls;—to all Cases of admiralty and maritime Jurisdiction;—to Controversies to which the United States shall be a Party;—to Controversies between two or more States; [—between a State and Citizens of another State;—][9] between Citizens of different States;—between Citizens of the same State claiming Lands under Grants of different States, [and between a State, or the Citizens thereof, and foreign States, Citizens or Subjects.][10]

The federal courts take on cases that concern the meaning of the U.S. Constitution, all federal laws, and treaties. They also can take on cases involving citizens of different states and citizens of foreign nations.

Clause 2: Cases for the Supreme Court. In all Cases affecting Ambassadors, other public Ministers and Consuls, and those in which a State.shall be a Party, the supreme Court shall have original Jurisdiction. In all the other Cases before mentioned, the supreme Court shall have

---

[9]Modified by the Eleventh Amendment.
[10]Modified by the Eleventh Amendment.

appellate Jurisdiction, both as to Law and Fact, with such Exceptions, and under such Regulations as the Congress shall make.

In a limited number of situations, the Supreme Court acts as a trial court and has original jurisdiction. These cases involve a representative from another country or involve a state. In all other situations, the cases must first be tried in the lower courts and then can be appealed to the Supreme Court. Congress may, however, make exceptions. Today the Supreme Court acts as a trial court of first instance on rare occasions.

Clause 3: The Conduct of Trials. The Trial of all Crimes, except in Cases of Impeachment, shall be by Jury; and such Trial shall be held in the State where the said Crimes shall have been committed; but when not committed within any State, the Trial shall be at such Place or Places as the Congress may by Law have directed.

Any person accused of a federal crime is granted the right to a trial by jury in a federal court in that state in which the crime was committed. Trials of impeachment are an exception.

Section 3. Treason

Clause 1: The Definition of Treason. Treason against the United States, shall consist only in levying War against them, or, in adhering to their Enemies, giving them Aid and Comfort. No Person shall be convicted of Treason unless on the Testimony of two Witnesses to the same overt Act, or on Confession in open Court.

Treason is the making of war against the United States or giving aid to its enemies.

Clause 2: Punishment. The Congress shall have Power to declare the Punishment of Treason, but no Attainder of Treason shall work Corruption of Blood, or Forfeiture except during the Life of the Person attainted.

Congress has provided that the punishment for treason ranges from a minimum of five years in prison and/or a $10,000 fine to a maximum of death. "No Attainder of Treason shall work Corruption of Blood" prohibits punishment of the traitor's heirs.

Article IV. (Relations Among the States)

Section 1. Full Faith and Credit

Full Faith and Credit shall be given in each State to the public Acts, Records, and judicial Proceedings of every other State. And the Congress may by general Laws prescribe the Manner in which such Acts, Records and Proceedings shall be proved, and the Effect thereof.

All states are required to respect one another's laws, records, and lawful decisions. There are exceptions, however. A state does not have to enforce another state's criminal code. Nor does it have to recognize another state's grant of a divorce if the person obtaining the divorce did not establish legal residence in the state in which it was given.

Section 2. Treatment of Citizens
Clause 1: Privileges and Immunities. The Citizens of each State shall be entitled to all Privileges and Immunities of Citizens in the several States.

A citizen of a state has the same rights and privileges as the citizens of another state in which he or she happens to be.

Clause 2: Extradition. A Person charged in any State with Treason, Felony, or other Crime, who shall flee from Justice, and be found in another State, shall on Demand of the executive Authority of the State from which he fled, be delivered up, to be removed to the State having Jurisdiction of the Crime.

Any person accused of a crime who flees to another state must be returned to the state in which the crime occurred.

Clause 3: Fugitive Slaves. [No Person held to Service or Labour in one State, under the Laws thereof, escaping into another, shall, in Consequence of any Law or Regulation therein, be discharged from such Service or Labour, but shall be delivered up on Claim of the Party to whom such Service or Labour may be due.][11]

This clause was struck down by the Thirteenth Amendment, which abolished slavery in 1865.

Section 3. Admission of States
Clause 1: The Process. New States may be admitted by the Congress into this Union; but no new State shall be formed or erected within the Jurisdiction of any other State; nor any State be formed by the Junction of two or more States, or Parts of States, without the Consent of the Legislatures of the States concerned as well as of the Congress.

Only Congress has the power to admit new states to the union. No state may be created by taking territory from an existing state unless the state's legislature so consents.

Clause 2: Public Land. The Congress shall have Power to dispose of and make all needful Rules and Regulations respecting the Territory or other Property belonging to the United States; and nothing in this Constitution shall be so construed as to Prejudice any Claims of the United States, or of any particular State.

The federal government has the exclusive right to administer federal government public lands.

Section 4. Republican Form of Government
The United States shall guarantee to every State in this Union a Republican Form of Government, and shall protect each of them against Invasion; and on Application of the Legislature, or of the Executive (when the Legislature cannot be convened) against domestic Violence.

Each state is promised a form of government in which the people elect their representatives, called a republican form. The federal government is bound to protect states against any attack by foreigners or during times of trouble within a state.

Article V. (Methods of Amendment)
The Congress, whenever two thirds of both Houses shall deem it necessary, shall propose Amendments to this Constitution, or on the Application of the Legislatures of two thirds of the several States, shall call a Convention for proposing Amendments, which, in either Case, shall be valid to all Intents and Purposes, as Part of this Constitution, when ratified by the Legislatures of three fourths of the several States, or by Conventions in three fourths thereof, as the one or the other Mode of Ratification may be proposed by the Congress; Provided that no Amendment which may be made prior to the Year One thousand eight hundred and eight shall in any Manner affect the first and fourth Clauses in the Ninth Section of the First Article; and that no State, without its Consent, shall be deprived of its equal Suffrage in the Senate.

Amendments may be proposed in either of two ways: a two-thirds vote of each house (Congress) or at the request of two-thirds of the states. Ratification of amendments may be carried out in two ways: by the legislatures of three-fourths of the states or by the voters in three-fourths of the states. No state may be denied equal representation in the Senate.

Article VI. (National Supremacy)

Clause 1: Existing Obligations. All Debts contracted and Engagements entered into, before the Adoption of this Constitution shall be as valid against the United States under this Constitution, as under the Confederation.

During the Revolutionary War and the years of the Confederation, Congress borrowed large sums. This clause pledged that the new federal government would assume those financial obligations.

---

[11]Repealed by the Thirteenth Amendment.

Clause 2: Supreme Law of the Land. This Constitution, and the Laws of the United States which shall be made in Pursuance thereof; and all Treaties made, or which shall be made, under the Authority of the United States, shall be the supreme Law of the Land; and the Judges in every State shall be bound thereby, any Thing in the Constitution or Laws of any State to the Contrary notwithstanding.

This is typically called the supremacy clause; it declares that federal law takes precedence over all forms of state law. No government, at the local or state level, may make or enforce any law that conflicts with any provision of the Constitution, acts of Congress, treaties, or other rules and regulations issued by the president and his or her subordinates in the executive branch of the federal government.

Clause 3: Oath of Office. The Senators and Representatives before mentioned, and the Members of the several State Legislatures, and all executive and judicial Officers, both of the United States and of the several States, shall be bound by Oath or Affirmation, to support this Constitution; but no religious Test shall ever be required as a Qualification to any Office or public Trust under the United States.

Every federal and state official must take an oath of office promising to support the U.S. Constitution. Religion may not be used as a qualification to serve in any federal office.

Article VII. (Ratification)

The Ratification of the Conventions of nine States shall be sufficient for the Establishment of this Constitution between the States so ratifying the Same.

Nine states were required to ratify the Constitution. Delaware was the first and New Hampshire the ninth.

Done in Convention by the Unanimous Consent of the States present the Seventeenth Day of September in the Year of our Lord one thousand seven hundred and Eighty seven and of the Independence of the United States of America the Twelfth. In witness whereof we have hereunto subscribed our Names,

Go. WASHINGTON
Presid't. and deputy from Virginia

Attest
WILLIAM JACKSON
Secretary

DELAWARE
Geo. Read
Gunning Bedfordjun
John Dickinson
Richard Basset
Jaco. Broom

MASSACHUSETTS
Nathaniel Gorham
Rufus King

CONNECTICUT
Wm. Saml. Johnson
Roger Sherman

NEW YORK
Alexander Hamilton

NEW JERSEY
Wh. Livingston
David Brearley.
Wm. Paterson.
Jona. Dayton

PENNSYLVANIA
B. Franklin
Thomas Mifflin
Robt. Morris
Geo. Clymer
Thos. FitzSimons
Jared Ingersoll
James Wilson.
Gouv. Morris

NEW HAMPSHIRE
John Langdon
Nicholas Gilman

MARYLAND
James McHenry
Dan of St. Thos. Jenifer
Danl. Carroll.

VIRGINIA
John Blair
James Madison Jr.

NORTH CAROLINA
Wm. Blount
Richd. Dobbs Spaight.
Hu. Williamson

SOUTH CAROLINA
J. Rutledge
Charles Cotesworth
   Pinckney
Charles Pinckney
Pierce Butler.

GEORGIA
William Few
Abr. Baldwin

Articles in addition to, and amendment of the Constitution of the United States of America, proposed by Congress and ratified by the Legislatures of the several states, pursuant to the Fifth Article of the original Constitution.

Amendments to the Constitution of the United States

The Bill of Rights[12]

Amendment I.
Religion, Speech, Assembly, and Politics

Congress shall make no law respecting an establishment of religion, or prohibiting the free exercise thereof; or abridg-

---

[12]On September 25, 1789, Congress transmitted to the state legislatures twelve proposed amendments, two of which, having to do with congressional representation and congressional pay, were not adopted. The remaining ten amendments became the Bill of Rights. In 1992, the amendment concerning congressional pay was adopted as the Twenty-seventh Amendment.

ing the freedom of speech, or of the press; or the right of the people peaceably to assembly, and to petition the Government for a redress of grievances.

Congress may not create an official church or enact laws limiting the freedom of religion, speech, the press, assembly, and petition. These guarantees, like the others in the Bill of Rights (the first ten amendments), are not absolute—each may be exercised only with regard to the rights of other persons.

Amendment II.
Militia and the Right to Bear Arms

A well regulated Militia, being necessary to the security of a free State, the right of the people to keep and bear Arms, shall not be infringed.

To protect itself, each state has the right to maintain a volunteer armed force. States and the federal government regulate the possession and use of firearms by individuals.

Amendment III.
The Quartering of Soldiers

No Soldier shall, in time of peace be quartered in any house, without the consent of the Owner, nor in time of war, but in a manner to be prescribed by law.

Before the Revolutionary War, it had been common British practice to quarter soldiers in colonists' homes. Military troops do not have the power to take over private houses during peacetime.

Amendment IV.
Searches and Seizures

The right of the people to be secure in their persons, houses, papers, and effects, against unreasonable searches and seizures, shall not be violated, and no Warrants shall issue, but upon probable cause, supported by Oath or affirmation, and particularly describing the place to be searched, and the persons or things to be seized.

Here the word warrant *means "justification" and refers to a document issued by a magistrate or judge indicating the name, address, and possible offense committed. Anyone asking for the warrant, such as a police officer, must be able to convince the magistrate or judge that an offense probably has been committed.*

Amendment V.
Grand Juries, Self-incrimination, Double Jeopardy, Due Process, and Eminent Domain

No person shall be held to answer for a capital, or otherwise infamous crime, unless on a presentment or indictment of a Grand Jury, except in cases arising in the land or naval forces, or in the Militia, when in actual service in time of War or public danger; nor shall any person be subject for the same offence to be twice put in jeopardy of life or limb; nor shall be compelled in any criminal case

to be a witness against himself, nor be deprived of life, liberty, or property, without due process of law; nor shall private property be taken for public use, without just compensation.

There are two types of juries. A grand jury considers physical evidence and the testimony of witnesses, and decides whether there is sufficient reason to bring a case to trial. A petit jury hears the case at trial and decides it. "For the same offence to be twice put in jeopardy of life or limb" means to be tried twice for the same crime. A person may not be tried for the same crime twice or forced to give evidence against herself or himself. No person's right to life, liberty, or property may be taken away except by lawful means, called the due process of law. Private property taken for use in public purposes must be paid for by the government.

Amendment VI.
Criminal Court Procedures

In all criminal prosecutions, the accused shall enjoy the right to a speedy and public trial, by an impartial jury of the State and district wherein the crime shall have been committed, which district shall have been previously ascertained by law, and to be informed of the nature and cause of the accusation; to be confronted with the witnesses against him; to have compulsory process for obtaining witnesses in his favor, and to have the assistance of counsel for his defence.

Any person accused of a crime has the right to a fair and public trial by a jury in the state in which the crime took place. The charges against that person must be so indicated. Any accused person has the right to a lawyer to defend him or her and to question those who testify against him or her, as well as the right to call people to speak in his or her favor at trial.

Amendment VII.
Trial by Jury in Civil Cases

In Suits at common law, where the value in controversy shall exceed twenty dollars, the right of trial by jury shall be preserved, and no fact tried by jury, shall be otherwise re-examined in any Court of the United States, than according to the rules of the common law.

A jury trial may be requested by either party in a dispute in any case involving more than $20. If both parties agree to a trial by a judge without a jury, the right to a jury trial may be put aside.

Amendment VIII.
Bail, Cruel and Unusual Punishment

Excessive bail shall not be required, nor excessive fines imposed, nor cruel and unusual punishments inflicted.

Bail is that amount of money that a person accused of a crime may be required to deposit with the court as a guarantee that she or he will appear in court when requested. The amount of bail required or the fine imposed as punishment for a crime must be reasonable compared with the seriousness of the crime involved. Any punishment judged to be too harsh or too severe for a crime shall be prohibited.

Amendment IX.
The Rights Retained by the People

The enumeration in the Constitution, of certain rights, shall not be construed to deny or disparage others retained by the people.

Many civil rights that are not explicitly enumerated in the Constitution are still held by the people.

Amendment X.
Reserved Powers of the States

The powers not delegated to the United States by the Constitution, nor prohibited by it to the States, are reserved to the States respectively, or to the people.

Those powers not delegated by the Constitution to the federal government or expressly denied to the states belong to the states and to the people. This clause in essence allows the states to pass laws under its "police powers."

Amendment XI
(Ratified on February 7, 1795).
Suits Against States

The Judicial power of the United States shall not be construed to extend to any suit in law or equity, commenced or prosecuted against one of the United States by Citizens of another State, or by Citizens or Subjects of any Foreign State.

This amendment has been interpreted to mean that a state cannot be sued in federal court by one of its citizens, by a citizen of another state, or by a foreign country.

Amendment XII
(Ratified on June 15, 1804).
Election of the President

The Electors shall meet in their respective states, and vote by ballot for President and Vice-President, one of whom, at least, shall not be an inhabitant of the same State with themselves; they shall name in their ballots the person voted for as President, and in distinct ballots the person voted for as Vice-President, and they shall make distinct lists of all persons voted for as President, and of all persons voted for as Vice-President, and of the number of votes for each, which lists they shall sign and certify, and transmit sealed to the seat of the government of the United States, directed to the President of the Senate;—The President of the Senate shall, in the presence of the Senate and House of Representatives, open all the certificates and the votes shall then be counted;—The person having the greatest number of votes for President, shall be the President, if such number be a majority of the whole number of Elec-

tors appointed; and if no person have such majority, then from the persons having the highest numbers not exceeding three on the list of those voted for as President, the House of Representatives shall choose immediately, by ballot, the President. But in choosing the President, the votes shall be taken by States, the representation from each State having one vote; a quorum for this purpose shall consist of a member or members from two-thirds of the States, and a majority of all States shall be necessary to a choice. [And if the House of Representatives shall not choose a President whenever the right of choice shall devolve upon them, before the fourth day of March next following, then the Vice-President shall act as President, as in the case of the death or other constitutional disability of the President.][13]—The person having the greatest number of votes as Vice-President, shall be the Vice-President, if such number be a majority of the whole number of Electors appointed, and if no person have a majority, then from the two highest numbers on the list, the Senate shall choose the Vice President; a quorum for the purpose shall consist of two-thirds of the whole number of Senators, and a majority of the whole number shall be necessary to a choice. But no person constitutionally ineligible to the office of President shall be eligible to that of Vice-President of the United States.

The original procedure set out for the election of president and vice-president in Article II, Section 1, resulted in a tie in 1800 between Thomas Jefferson and Aaron Burr. It was not until the next year that the House of Representatives chose Jefferson to be president. This amendment changed the procedure by providing for separate ballots for president and vice president.

Amendment XIII
(Ratified on December 6, 1865).
Prohibition of Slavery

Section 1.
Neither slavery nor involuntary servitude, except as a punishment for crime whereof the party shall have been duly convicted, shall exist within the United States, or any place subject to their jurisdiction.

Some slaves had been freed during the Civil War. This amendment freed the others and abolished slavery.

Section 2.
Congress shall have power to enforce this article by appropriate legislation.

---

[13]Changed by the Twentieth Amendment.

Amendment XIV
(Ratified on July 9, 1868).
Citizenship, Due Process, and Equal Protection of the Laws

Section 1.
All persons born or naturalized in the United States, and subject to the jurisdiction thereof, are citizens of the United States and of the State wherein they reside. No State shall make or enforce any law which shall abridge the privileges or immunities of citizens of the United States; nor shall any State deprive any person of life, liberty, or property, without due process of law; nor deny to any person within its jurisdiction the equal protection of the laws.

Under this provision, states cannot make or enforce laws that take away rights given to all citizens by the federal government. States cannot act unfairly or arbitrarily toward, or discriminate against, any person.

Section 2.
Representatives shall be apportioned among the several States according to their respective numbers, counting the whole number of persons in each State, excluding Indians not taxed. But when the right to vote at any election for the choice of electors for President and Vice President of the United States, Representatives in Congress, the Executive and Judicial officers of a State, or the members of the Legislature thereof, is denied to any of the male inhabitants of such State, being [twenty-one][14] years of age, and citizens of the United States, or in any way abridged, except for participation in rebellion, or other crime, the basis of representation therein shall be reduced in the proportion which the number of such male citizens shall bear to the whole number of male citizens twenty-one years of age in such State.

Section 3.
No person shall be a Senator or Representative in Congress, or elector of President and Vice President, or hold any office, civil or military, under the United States, or under any State, who having previously taken an oath, as a member of Congress, or as an officer of the United States, or as a member of any State legislature, or as an executive or judicial officer of any State, to support the Constitution of the United States, shall have engaged in insurrection or rebellion against the same, or given aid or comfort to the enemies thereof. But Congress may by a vote of two-thirds of each House, remove such disability.

This provision forbade former state or federal government officials who had acted in support of the Confederacy during the Civil War to hold office again. It limited the president's power to pardon those persons. Congress removed this "disability" in 1898.

---

[14]Changed by the Twenty-sixth Amendment.

Section 4.
The validity of the public debt of the United States, authorized by law, including debts incurred for payment of pensions and bounties for services in suppressing insurrection or rebellion, shall not be questioned. But neither the United States nor any State shall assume or pay any debt or obligation incurred in aid of insurrection or rebellion against the United States, or any claim for the loss or emancipation of any slave, but all such debts, obligations and claims shall be held illegal and void.

Section 5.
The Congress shall have power to enforce, by appropriate legislation, the provisions of this article.

Amendment XV
(Ratified on February 3, 1870).
The Right to Vote

Section 1.
The right of citizens of the United States to vote shall not be denied or abridged by the United States or by any State on account of race, color, or previous condition of servitude.

No citizen can be refused the right to vote simply because of race or color or because that person was once a slave.

Section 2.
The Congress shall have power to enforce this article by appropriate legislation.

Amendment XVI
(Ratified on February 3, 1913).
Income Taxes
The Congress shall have power to lay and collect taxes on incomes, from whatever source derived, without apportionment among the several States, and without regard to any census or enumeration.

This amendment allows Congress to tax income without sharing the revenue so obtained with the states according to their population.

Amendment XVII
(Ratified on April 8, 1913).
The Popular Election of Senators
The Senate of the United States shall be composed of two Senators from each State, elected by the people thereof, for six years; and each Senator shall have one vote. The electors in each State shall have the qualifications requisite for electors of the most numerous branch of the State legislatures.

When vacancies happen in the representation of any State in the Senate, the executive authority of such State shall issue writs of election to fill such vacancies: *Provided,* That the legislature of any State may empower the executive thereof to make temporary appointments until the people fill the vacancies by election as the legislature may direct.

This amendment shall not be so construed as to affect the election or term of any Senator chosen before it becomes valid as part of the Constitution.

This amendment modified portions of Article I, Section 3, that related to election of senators. Senators are now elected by the voters in each state directly. When a vacancy occurs, either the state may fill the vacancy by a special election, or the governor of the state involved may appoint someone to fill the seat until the next election.

Amendment XVIII
(Ratified on January 16, 1919).
Prohibition.

Section 1.
After one year from the ratification of this article the manufacture, sale, or transportation of intoxicating liquors within, the importation thereof into, or the exportation thereof from the United States and all territory subject to the jurisdiction thereof for beverage purposes is hereby prohibited.

Section 2.
The Congress and the several States shall have concurrent power to enforce this article by appropriate legislation.

Section 3.
This article shall be inoperative unless it shall have been ratified as an amendment to the Constitution by the legislatures of the several States, as provided in the Constitution, within seven years from the date of the submission hereof to the States by the Congress.[15]

This amendment made it illegal to manufacture, sell, and transport alcoholic beverages in the United States. It was repealed by the Twenty-first Amendment.

A
mendment XIX
(Ratified on August 18, 1920).
Women's Right to Vote.
The right of citizens of the United States to vote shall not be denied or abridged by the United States or by any State on account of sex.

Congress shall have power to enforce this article by appropriate legislation.

Women were given the right to vote by this amendment, and Congress was given the power to enforce this right.

---

[15]The Eighteenth Amendment was repealed by the Twenty-first Amendment.

Amendment XX
(Ratified on January 23, 1933).
The Lame Duck Amendment

Section 1.
The terms of the President and Vice President shall end at noon on the 20th day of January, and the terms of Senators and Representatives at noon on the 3d day of January, of the years in which such terms would have ended if this article had not been ratified; and the terms of their successors shall then begin.

This amendment modified Article I, Section 4, Clause 2, and other provisions relating to the president in the Twelfth Amendment. The taking of the Oath of Office was moved from March 4 to January 20.

Section 2.
The Congress shall assemble at least once in every year, and such meeting shall begin at noon on the 3d day of January, unless they shall by law appoint a different day.

Congress changed the beginning of its term to January 3. The reason the Twentieth Amendment is called the Lame Duck Amendment is because it shortens the time between when a member of Congress is defeated for reelection and when he or she leaves office.

Section 3.
If, at the time fixed for the beginning of the term of the President, the President elect shall have died, the Vice President elect shall become President. If a President shall not have been chosen before the time fixed for the beginning of his term, or if the President elect shall have failed to qualify, then the Vice President elect shall act as President until a President shall have qualified; and the Congress may by law provide for the case wherein neither a President elect nor a Vice President elect shall have qualified, declaring who shall then act as President, or the manner in which one who is to act shall be selected, and such person shall act accordingly until a President or Vice President shall have qualified.

This part of the amendment deals with problem areas left ambiguous by Article II and the Twelfth Amendment. If the president dies before January 20 or fails to qualify for office, the presidency is to be filled in the order given in this section.

Section 4.
The Congress may by law provide for the case of the death of any of the persons from whom the House of Representatives may choose a President whenever the rights of choice shall have devolved upon them, and for the case of the death of any of the persons from whom the Senate may choose a Vice President whenever the right of choice shall have devolved upon them.

Congress has never created legislation subsequent to this section.

Section 5.
Sections 1 and 2 shall take effect on the 15th day of October following the ratification of this article.

Section 6.
This article shall be inoperative unless it shall have been ratified as an amendment to the Constitution by the legislatures of three-fourths of the several States within seven years from the date of its submission.

Amendment XXI
(Ratified on December 5, 1933).
The Repeal of Prohibition.

Section 1.
The eighteenth article of amendment to the Constitution of the United States is hereby repealed.

Section 2.
The transportation or importation into any State, Territory, or possession of the United States for delivery or use therein of intoxicating liquors, in violation of the laws thereof, is hereby prohibited.

Section 3.
This article shall be inoperative unless it shall have been ratified as an amendment to the Constitution by conventions in the several States, as provided in the Constitution, within seven years from the date of the submission hereof to the States by the Congress.

The amendment repealed the Eighteenth Amendment but did not make alcoholic beverages legal everywhere. Rather, they remained illegal in any state that so designated them. Many such "dry" states existed for a number of years after 1933. Today, there are still "dry" counties within the United States, in which alcoholic beverages are illegal.

Amendment XXII
(Ratified on February 27, 1951).
Limitation of Presidential Terms.

Section 1.
No person shall be elected to the office of the President more than twice, and no person who has held the office of President, or acted as President, for more than two years of a term to which some other person was elected President shall be elected to the office of President more than once. But this Article shall not apply to any person holding the office of President when this Article was proposed by the Congress, and shall not prevent any person who may be holding the office of President, or acting as President, during the term within which this Article becomes operative from holding the office of President or acting as President during the remainder of such term.

Section 2.
This article shall be inoperative unless it shall have been ratified as an amendment to the Constitution by the legislatures of three-fourths of the several States within seven years from the date of its submission to the States by the Congress.

No president may serve more than two elected terms. If, however, a president has succeeded to the office after the halfway point of a term in which another president was originally elected, then that president may serve for more than eight years, but not to exceed ten years.

Amendment XXIII
(Ratified on March 29, 1961).
Presidential Electors for
the District of Columbia.

Section 1.
The District constituting the seat of Government of the United States shall appoint in such manner as the Congress may direct:

    A number of electors of President and Vice President equal to the whole number of Senators and Representatives in Congress to which the District would be entitled if it were a State, but in no event more than the least populous State; they shall be in addition to those appointed by the States, but they shall be considered, for the purposes of the election of President and Vice President, to be electors appointed by a State; and they shall meet in the District and perform such duties as provided by the twelfth article of amendment.

Section 2.
The Congress shall have power to enforce this article by appropriate legislation.

Citizens living in the District of Columbia have the right to vote in elections for president and vice president. The District of Columbia has three presidential electors, whereas before this amendment it had none.

Amendment XXIV
(Ratified on January 23, 1964).
The Anti-Poll Tax Amendment.

Section 1.
The right of citizens of the United States to vote in any primary or other election for President or Vice President, for electors for President or Vice President, or for Senator or Representative in Congress, shall not be denied or abridged by the United States, or any State by reason of failure to pay any poll tax or other tax.

Section 2.
The Congress shall have power to enforce this article by appropriate legislation.

No government shall require a person to pay a poll tax in order to vote in any federal election.

Amendment XXV
(Ratified on February 10, 1967).
Presidential Disability and Vice Presidential Vacancies.

Section 1.
In case of the removal of the President from office or of his death or resignation, the Vice President shall become President.

Whenever a president dies or resigns from office, the vice president becomes president.

Section 2.
Whenever there is a vacancy in the office of the Vice President, the President shall nominate a Vice President who shall take office upon confirmation by a majority vote of both Houses of Congress.

Whenever the office of the vice presidency becomes vacant, the president may appoint someone to fill this office, provided Congress consents.

Section 3.
Whenever the President transmits to the President pro tempore of the Senate and the Speaker of the House of Representatives his written declaration that he is unable to discharge the powers and duties of his office, and until he transmits to them a written declaration to the contrary, such powers and duties shall be discharged by the Vice President as Acting President.

Whenever the president believes she or he is unable to carry out the duties of the office, she or he shall so indicate to Congress in writing. The vice president then acts as president until the president declares that she or he is again able to properly carry out the duties of the office.

Section 4.
Whenever the Vice President and a majority of either the principal officers of the executive departments or of such other body as Congress may by law provide, transmit to the President pro tempore of the Senate and the Speaker of the House of Representatives their written declaration that the President is unable to discharge the powers and duties of his office, the Vice President shall immediately assume the powers and duties of the office as Acting President.

Thereafter, when the President transmits to the President pro tempore of the Senate and the Speaker of the House of Representatives his written declaration that no inability exists, he shall resume the powers and duties of his office unless the Vice President and a majority of either the principal officers of the executive department or of such other body as Congress may by law provide, transmit within four days to the President pro tempore of the Senate and the Speaker of the House of Representatives their writ-

ten declaration that the President is unable to discharge the powers and duties of his office. Thereupon Congress shall decide the issue, assembling within forty-eight hours for that purpose if not in session. If the Congress, within twenty-one days after receipt of the latter written declaration, or, if Congress is not in session, within twenty-one days after Congress is required to assemble, determines by two-thirds vote of both Houses that the President is unable to discharge the powers and duties of his office, the Vice President shall continue to discharge the same as Acting President; otherwise, the President shall resume the powers and duties of his office.

Whenever the vice president and a majority of the members of the cabinet believe that the president cannot carry out his or her duties, they shall so indicate in writing to Congress. The vice president shall then act as president. When the president believes that she or he is able to carry out her or his duties again, she or he shall so indicate to the Congress. If, though, the vice president and a majority of the Cabinet do not agree, Congress must decide by a two-thirds vote within three weeks who shall act as president.

Amendment XXVI
(Ratified on July 1, 1971).
The Eighteen-Year-Old Vote.

Section 1.
The right of citizens of the United States, who are eighteen years of age or older, to vote shall not be denied or abridged by the United States or by any State on account of age.

No one over eighteen years of age can be denied the right to vote in federal or state elections by virtue of age.

Section 2.
The Congress shall have power to enforce this article by appropriate legislation.

Amendment XXVII
(Ratified on May 7, 1992).
Congressional Pay.
No law varying the compensation for the services of the Senators and Representatives shall take effect, until an election of representatives shall have intervened.

This amendment allows the voters to have some control over increases in salaries for congressional members. Originally submitted to the states for ratification in 1789, it was not ratified until 203 years later, in 1992.

APPENDIX C
The Presidents of the United States

	Term of Service	Age at Inauguration	Political Party	College or University	Occupation or Profession
1. George Washington	1789–1797	57	None		Planter
2. John Adams	1797–1801	61	Federalist	Harvard	Lawyer
3. Thomas Jefferson	1801–1809	57	Democratic-Republican	William and Mary	Planter, Lawyer
4. James Madison	1809–1817	57	Democratic-Republican	Princeton	Lawyer
5. James Monroe	1817–1825	58	Democratic-Republican	William and Mary	Lawyer
6. John Quincy Adams	1825–1829	57	Democratic-Republican	Harvard	Lawyer
7. Andrew Jackson	1829–1837	61	Democrat		Lawyer
8. Martin Van Buren	1837–1841	54	Democrat		Lawyer
9. William H. Harrison	1841	68	Whig	Hampden-Sydney	Soldier
10. John Tyler	1841–1845	51	Whig	William and Mary	Lawyer
11. James K. Polk	1845–1849	49	Democrat	U. of N. Carolina	Lawyer
12. Zachary Taylor	1849–1850	64	Whig		Soldier
13. Millard Fillmore	1850–1853	50	Whig		Lawyer
14. Franklin Pierce	1853–1857	48	Democrat	Bowdoin	Lawyer
15. James Buchanan	1857–1861	65	Democrat	Dickinson	Lawyer
16. Abraham Lincoln	1861–1865	52	Republican		Lawyer
17. Andrew Johnson	1865–1869	56	National Union†		Tailor
18. Ulysses S. Grant	1869–1877	46	Republican	U.S. Mil. Academy	Soldier
19. Rutherford B. Hayes	1877–1881	54	Republican	Kenyon	Lawyer
20. James A. Garfield	1881	49	Republican	Williams	Lawyer
21. Chester A. Arthur	1881–1885	51	Republican	Union	Lawyer
22. Grover Cleveland	1885–1889	47	Democrat		Lawyer
23. Benjamin Harrison	1889–1893	55	Republican	Miami	Lawyer
24. Grover Cleveland	1893–1897	55	Democrat		Lawyer
25. William McKinley	1897–1901	54	Republican	Allegheny College	Lawyer
26. Theodore Roosevelt	1901–1909	42	Republican	Harvard	Author
27. William H. Taft	1909–1913	51	Republican	Yale	Lawyer
28. Woodrow Wilson	1913–1921	56	Democrat	Princeton	Educator
29. Warren G. Harding	1921–1923	55	Republican		Editor
30. Calvin Coolidge	1923–1929	51	Republican	Amherst	Lawyer
31. Herbert C. Hoover	1929–1933	54	Republican	Stanford	Engineer
32. Franklin D. Roosevelt	1933–1945	51	Democrat	Harvard	Lawyer
33. Harry S Truman	1945–1953	60	Democrat		Businessman
34. Dwight D. Eisenhower	1953–1961	62	Republican	U.S. Mil. Academy	Soldier
35. John F. Kennedy	1961–1963	43	Democrat	Harvard	Author
36. Lyndon B. Johnson	1963–1969	55	Democrat	Southwest Texas State	Teacher
37. Richard M. Nixon	1969–1974	56	Republican	Whittier	Lawyer
38. Gerald R. Ford‡	1974–1977	61	Republican	Michigan	Lawyer
39. James E. Carter, Jr.	1977–1981	52	Democrat	U.S. Naval Academy	Businessman
40. Ronald W. Reagan	1981–1989	69	Republican	Eureka College	Actor
41. George H. W. Bush	1989–1993	64	Republican	Yale	Businessman
42. Bill Clinton	1993–	46	Democrat	Georgetown	Lawyer

*Church preference; never joined any church.
†The National Union Party consisted of Republicans and War Democrats. Johnson was a Democrat.
**Inaugurated Dec. 6, 1973, to replace Agnew, who resigned Oct. 10, 1973.
‡Inaugurated Aug. 9, 1974, to replace Nixon, who resigned that same day.
§Inaugurated Dec. 19, 1974, to replace Ford, who became president Aug. 9, 1974.

Religion	Born	Died	Age at Death	Vice President	
1. Episcopalian	Feb. 22, 1732	Dec. 14, 1799	67	John Adams	(1789–1797)
2. Unitarian	Oct. 30, 1735	July 4, 1826	90	Thomas Jefferson	(1797–1801)
3. Unitarian*	Apr. 13, 1743	July 4, 1826	83	Aaron Burr	(1801–1805)
				George Clinton	(1805–1809)
4. Episcopalian	Mar. 16, 1751	June 28, 1836	85	George Clinton	(1809–1812)
				Elbridge Gerry	(1813–1814)
5. Episcopalian	Apr. 28, 1758	July 4, 1831	73	Daniel D. Tompkins	(1817–1825)
6. Unitarian	July 11, 1767	Feb. 23, 1848	80	John C. Calhoun	(1825–1829)
7. Presbyterian	Mar. 15, 1767	June 8, 1845	78	John C. Calhoun	(1829–1832)
				Martin Van Buren	(1833–1837)
8. Dutch Reformed	Dec. 5, 1782	July 24, 1862	79	Richard M. Johnson	(1837–1841)
9. Episcopalian	Feb. 9, 1773	Apr. 4, 1841	68	John Tyler	(1841)
10. Episcopalian	Mar. 29, 1790	Jan. 18, 1862	71		
11. Methodist	Nov. 2, 1795	June 15, 1849	53	George M. Dallas	(1845–1849)
12. Episcopalian	Nov. 24, 1784	July 9, 1850	65	Millard Fillmore	(1849–1850)
13. Unitarian	Jan. 7, 1800	Mar. 8, 1874	74		
14. Episcopalian	Nov. 23, 1804	Oct. 8, 1869	64	William R. King	(1853)
15. Presbyterian	Apr. 23, 1791	June 1, 1868	77	John C. Breckinridge	(1857–1861)
16. Presbyterian*	Feb. 12, 1809	Apr. 15, 1865	56	Hannibal Hamlin	(1861–1865)
				Andrew Johnson	(1865)
17. Methodist*	Dec. 29, 1808	July 31, 1875	66		
18. Methodist	Apr. 27, 1822	July 23, 1885	63	Schuyler Colfax	(1869–1873)
				Henry Wilson	(1873–1875)
19. Methodist*	Oct. 4, 1822	Jan. 17, 1893	70	William A. Wheeler	(1877–1881)
20. Disciples of Christ	Nov. 19, 1831	Sept. 19, 1881	49	Chester A. Arthur	(1881)
21. Episcopalian	Oct. 5, 1829	Nov. 18, 1886	57		
22. Presbyterian	Mar. 18, 1837	June 24, 1908	71	Thomas A. Hendricks	(1885)
23. Presbyterian	Aug. 20, 1833	Mar. 13, 1901	67	Levi P. Morton	(1889–1893)
24. Presbyterian	Mar. 18, 1837	June 24, 1908	71	Adlai E. Stevenson	(1893–1897)
25. Methodist	Jan. 29, 1843	Sept. 14, 1901	58	Garret A. Hobart	(1897–1899)
				Theodore Roosevelt	(1901)
26. Dutch Reformed	Oct. 27, 1858	Jan. 6, 1919	60	Charles W. Fairbanks	(1905–1909)
27. Unitarian	Sept. 15, 1857	Mar. 8, 1930	72	James S. Sherman	(1909–1912)
28. Presbyterian	Dec. 29, 1856	Feb. 3, 1924	67	Thomas R. Marshall	(1913–1921)
29. Baptist	Nov. 2, 1865	Aug. 2, 1923	57	Calvin Coolidge	(1921–1923)
30. Congregationalist	July 4, 1872	Jan. 5, 1933	60	Charles G. Dawes	(1925–1929)
31. Friend (Quaker)	Aug. 10, 1874	Oct. 20, 1964	90	Charles Curtis	(1929–1933)
32. Episcopalian	Jan. 30, 1882	Apr. 12, 1945	63	John N. Garner	(1933–1941)
				Henry A. Wallace	(1941–1945)
				Harry S Truman	(1945)
33. Baptist	May 8, 1884	Dec. 26, 1972	88	Alben W. Barkley	(1949–1953)
34. Presbyterian	Oct. 14, 1890	Mar. 28, 1969	78	Richard M. Nixon	(1953–1961)
35. Roman Catholic	May 29, 1917	Nov. 22, 1963	46	Lyndon B. Johnson	(1961–1963)
36. Disciples of Christ	Aug. 27, 1908	Jan. 22, 1973	64	Hubert H. Humphrey	(1965–1969)
37. Friend (Quaker)	Jan. 9, 1913	Apr. 22, 1994	81	Spiro T. Agnew	(1969–1973)
				Gerald R. Ford**	(1973–1974)
38. Episcopalian	July 14, 1913			Nelson A. Rockefeller§	(1974–1977)
39. Baptist	Oct. 1, 1924			Walter F. Mondale	(1977–1981)
40. Disciples of Christ	Feb. 6, 1911			George H. W. Bush	(1981–1989)
41. Episcopalian	June 12, 1924			J. Danforth Quayle	(1989–1993)
42. Baptist	Aug. 19, 1946			Albert A. Gore	(1993–)

#10

Among the numerous advantages promised by a well-constructed Union, none deserves to be more accurately developed than its tendency to break and control the violence of faction. The friend of popular governments never finds himself so much alarmed for their character and fate as when he contemplates their propensity to this dangerous vice. He will not fail, therefore, to set a due value on any plan which, without violating the principles to which he is attached, provides a proper cure for it. The instability, injustice, and confusion introduced into the public councils have, in truth, been the mortal diseases under which popular governments have everywhere perished, as they continue to be the favorite and fruitful topics from which the adversaries to liberty derive their most specious declamations. The valuable improvements made by the American constitutions on the popular models, both ancient and modern, cannot certainly be too much admired; but it would be an unwarrantable partiality to contend that they have as effectually obviated the danger on this side, as was wished and expected. Complaints are everywhere heard from our most considerate and virtuous citizens, equally the friends of public and private faith and of public and personal liberty, that our governments are too unstable, that the public good is disregarded in the conflicts of rival parties, and that measures are too often decided, not according to the rules of justice and the rights of the minor party, but by the superior force of an interested and overbearing majority. However anxiously we may wish that these complaints had no foundation, the evidence of known facts will not permit us to deny that they are in some degree true. It will be found, indeed, on a candid review of our situation, that some of the distresses under which we labor have been erroneously charged on the operation of our governments; but it will be found, at the same time, that other causes will not alone account for many of our heaviest misfortunes; and, particularly, for that prevailing and increasing distrust of public engagements and alarm for private rights which are echoed from one end of the continent to the other. These must be chiefly, if not wholly, effects of the unsteadiness and injustice with which a factious spirit has tainted our public administration.

By a faction I understand a number of citizens, whether amounting to a majority or minority of the whole, who are united and actuated by some common impulse of passion, or of interest, adverse to the rights of other citizens, or the permanent and aggregate interests of the community.

There are two methods of curing the mischiefs of faction: the one, by removing its causes; the other, by controlling its effects.

There are again two methods of removing the causes of faction: the one, by destroying the liberty which is essential to its existence; the other, by giving to every citizen the same opinions, the same passions, and the same interests.

It could never be more truly said than of the first remedy that it was worse than the disease. Liberty is to faction what air is to fire, an aliment without which it instantly expires. But it could not be a less folly to abolish liberty, which is essential to political life, because it nourishes faction than it would be to wish the annihilation of air, which is essential to animal life, because it imparts to fire its destructive agency.

The second expedient is as impracticable as the first would be unwise. As long as the reason of man continues fallible, and his is at liberty to exercise it, different opinions will be formed. As long as the connection subsists between his reason and his self-love, his opinions and his passions will have a reciprocal influence on each other; and the former will be objects to which the latter will attach themselves. The diversity in the faculties of men, from which the rights of property originate, is not less an insuperable obstacle to a uniformity of interests. The protection of these faculties is the first object of government. From the protection of different and unequal faculties of acquiring property, the possession of different degrees and kinds of property immediately results; and from the influence of these on the sentiments and views of the respective proprietors ensues a division of the society into different interests and parties.

The latent causes of faction are thus sown in the nature of man; and we see them everywhere brought into different degrees of activity, according to the different circumstances of civil society. A zeal for different opinions concerning religion, concerning government, and many other points, as well of speculation as of practice; an attachment to different leaders ambitiously contending for pre-eminence and power; or to persons of other descriptions whose fortunes have been interesting to the human passions, have, in turn, divided mankind into parties, inflamed them with mutual animosity, and rendered them much more disposed to vex and oppress each other than to co-operate for their common good. So strong is this propensity of mankind to fall into mutual animosities that where no substantial occasion presents itself the most frivolous and fanciful distinctions have been sufficient to kindle their unfriendly passions and excite their most violent conflicts. But the most common and durable source of factions has been the various and unequal distribution of property. Those who hold and those who are without property have ever formed distinct interests in society. Those who are creditors, and those who are debtors, fall under a like discrimination. A landed interest, a manufacturing interest, a mercantile interest, a moneyed interest, with many lesser interests, grow up of necessity in civilized nations, and divide them into different classes, actuated by different sentiments and views. The regulation of these various and interfering interests forms the principal task of modern legislation and involves the spirit of party and faction in the necessary and ordinary operations of government.

No man is allowed to be a judge in his own cause, because his interest would certainly bias his judgment, and, not improbably, corrupt his integrity. With equal, nay with greater reason, a body of men are unfit to be both judges and parties at the same time; yet what are many of the most important acts of legislation but so many judicial determinations, not indeed concerning the rights of single persons, but concerning the rights of large bodies of citizens? And what are the different classes of legislators but advocates and parties to the causes which they determine? Is a law proposed concerning private debts? It is a question to which the creditors are parties on one side and the debtors on the other. Justice ought to hold the balance between them. Yet the parties are, and must be, themselves the judges; and the most numerous party, or in other words, the most powerful faction must be expected to prevail. Shall domestic manufacturers be encouraged, and in what degree, by restrictions on foreign manufacturers? Are questions which would be differently decided by the landed and the manufacturing classes, and probably by neither with a sole regard to justice and the public good. The apportionment of taxes on the various descriptions of property is an act which seems to require the most exact impartiality; yet there is, perhaps, no legislative act in which greater opportunity and temptation are given to a predominant party to trample on the rules of justice. Every shilling with which they overburden the inferior number is a shilling saved to their own pockets.

It is in vain to say that enlightened statesmen will be able to adjust these clashing interests and render them all subservient to the public good. Enlightened statesmen will not always be at the helm. Nor, in many cases, can such an adjustment be made at all without taking into view indirect and remote considerations, which will rarely prevail over the immediate interest which one party may find in disregarding the rights of another or the good of the whole.

The inference to which we are brought is that the *causes* of faction cannot be removed and that relief is only to be sought in the means of controlling its *effects*.

If a faction consists of less than a majority, relief is supplied by the republican principle, which enables the majority to defeat its sinister views by regular vote. It may clog the administration, it may convulse the society; but it will be unable to execute and mask its violence under the forms of the Constitution. When a majority is included in a faction, the form of popular government, on the other hand, enables it to sacrifice to its ruling passion or interest both the public good and the rights of other citizens. To secure the public good and private rights against the danger of such a faction, and at the same time to preserve the spirit and the form of popular government, is then the great object to which our inquiries are directed. Let me add that it is the great desideratum by which alone this form of government can be rescued from the opprobrium under which it has so long labored and be recommended to the esteem and adoption of mankind.

By what means is this object attainable? Evidently by one of two only. Either the existence of the same passion or interest in a majority at the same time must be prevented, or the majority, having such coexistent passion or interest, must be rendered, by their number and local situation, unable to concert and carry into effect schemes of oppression. If the impulse and the opportunity be suffered to coincide, we well know that neither moral nor religious motives can be relied on as an adequate control. They are not found to be such on the injustice and violence of individuals, and lose their efficacy in proportion to the number combined together, that is, in proportion as their efficacy becomes needful.

From this view of the subject it may be concluded that a pure democracy, by which I mean a society consisting of a small number of citizens, who assemble and administer the government in person, can admit of no cure for the mischiefs of faction. A common passion or interest will, in almost every case, be felt by a majority of the whole; a communication and concert results from the form of government itself; and there is nothing to check the inducements to sacrifice the weaker party or an obnoxious individual. Hence it is that such democracies have ever been spectacles of turbulence and contention; have ever been found incompatible with personal security or the rights of property; and have in general been as short in their lives as they have been violent in their deaths. Theoretic politicians, who have patronized this species of government, have erroneously supposed that by reducing mankind to a perfect equality in their political rights, they would at the same time be perfectly equalized and assimilated in their possessions, their opinions, and their passions.

A republic, by which I mean a government in which the scheme of representation takes place, opens a different prospect and promises the cure for which we are seeking. Let us examine the points in which it varies from pure democracy, and we shall comprehend both the nature of the cure and the efficacy which it must derive from the Union.

The two great points of difference between a democracy and a republic are: first, the delegation of the government, in the latter, to a small number of citizens elected by the rest; secondly, the greater number of citizens and greater sphere of country over which the latter may be extended.

The effect of the first difference is, on the one hand, to refine and enlarge the public views by passing them through the medium of a chosen body of citizens, whose wisdom may best discern the true interest of their country and whose patriotism and love of justice will be least likely to sacrifice it to temporary or partial considerations. Under such a regulation it may well happen that the public voice, pronounced by the representatives of the people, will be more consonant to the public good than if pronounced by the people themselves, convened for the purpose. On the other hand, the effect may be inverted. Men of factious tempers, of local prejudices, or of sinister designs, may, by intrigue, by corruption, or by other means, first obtain the suffrages, and then betray the interests of the people. The question resulting is, whether small or extensive republics are most favorable to the election of proper guardians of the public weal; and it is clearly decided in favor of the latter by two obvious considerations.

In the first place it is to be remarked that however small the republic may be the representatives must be raised to a certain number in order to guard against the cabals of a few; and that however large it may be they must be limited to a certain number in order to guard against the confusion of a multitude. Hence, the number of representatives in the two cases not being in proportion to that of the constituents, and being proportionally greatest in the small republic, it follows that if the proportion of fit characters be not less in the large than in the small republic, the former will present a greater option, and consequently a greater probability of a fit choice.

In the next place, as each representative will be chosen by a greater number of citizens in the large than in the small republic, it will be more difficult for unworthy candidates to practise with success the vicious arts by which elections are too often carried; and the suffrages of the people being more free, will be more likely to center on men who possess the most attractive merit and the most diffusive and established characters.

It must be confessed that in this, as in most other cases, there is a mean, on both sides of which inconveniencies will be found to lie. By enlarging too much the number of electors, you render the representative too little acquainted with all their local circumstances and lesser interests; as by reducing it too much, you render him unduly attached to these, and too little fit to comprehend and pursue great and national objects. The federal Constitution forms a happy combination in this respect; the great and aggregate interests being referred to the national, the local and particular to the State legislatures.

The other point of difference is the greater number of citizens and extent of territory which may be brought within the compass of republican than of democratic government; and it is this circumstance principally which renders factious combinations less to be dreaded in the former than in the latter. The smaller the society, the fewer probably will be the distinct parties and interests composing it; the fewer the distinct parties and interests, the more frequently will a majority be found of the same party; and the smaller the number of individuals composing a majority, and the smaller the compass within which they are placed, the more easily will they concert and execute their plans of oppression. Extend the sphere and you take in a greater variety of parties and interests; you make it less probable that a majority of the whole will have a common motive to invade the rights of other citizens; or if such a common motive exists, it will be more difficult for all who feel it to discover their own strength and to act in unison with each other. Besides other impediments, it may be remarked that, where there is a consciousness of unjust or dishonorable purposes, communication is always checked by distrust in proportion to the number whose concurrence is necessary.

Hence, it clearly appears that the same advantage which a republic has over a democracy in controlling the effects of faction is enjoyed by a large over a small republic—is enjoyed by the Union over the States composing it. Does this advantage consist in the substitution of representatives whose enlightened views and virtuous sentiments render them superior to local prejudices and to schemes of injustice? It will not be denied that the representation of the Union will be most likely to possess these requisite endowments. Does it consist in the greater security afforded by a greater variety of parties, against the event of any one party being able to outnumber and oppress the rest? In an equal degree does the increased variety of parties comprised within the Union increase this security. Does it, in fine, consist in the greater obstacles opposed to the concert and accomplishment of the secret wishes of an unjust and interested majority? Here again the extent of the Union gives it the most palpable advantage.

The influence of factious leaders may kindle a flame within their particular States but will be unable to spread a general conflagration through the other States. A religious sect may degenerate into a political faction in a part of the Confederacy; but the variety of sects dispersed over the entire face of it must secure the national councils against any danger from that source. A rage for paper money, for an abolition of debts, for an equal division of property, or for any other improper or wicked project, will be less apt to pervade the whole body of the Union than a particular member of it, in the same proportion as such a malady is more likely to taint a particular county or district than an entire State.

In the extent and proper structure of the Union, therefore, we behold a republican remedy for the diseases most

#51

To what expedient, then, shall we finally resort, for maintaining in practice the necessary partition of power among the several departments as laid down in the Constitution? The only answer that can be given is that as all these exterior provisions are found to be inadequate the defect must be supplied, by so contriving the interior structure of the government as that its several constituent parts may, by their mutual relations, be the means of keeping each other in their proper places. Without presuming to undertake a full development of this important idea I will hazard a few general observations which may perhaps place it in a clearer light, and enable us to form a more correct judgment of the principles and structure of the government planned by the convention.

In order to lay a due foundation for that separate and distinct exercise of the different powers of government, which to a certain extent is admitted on all hands to be essential to the preservation of liberty, it is evident that each department should have a will of its own; and consequently should be so constituted that the members of each should have as little agency as possible in the appointment of the members of the others. Were this principle rigorously adhered to, it would require that all the appointments for the supreme executive, legislative, and judiciary magistracies should be drawn from the same fountain of authority, the people, through channels having no communication whatever with one another. Perhaps such a plan of constructing the several departments would be less difficult in practice than it may in contemplation appear. Some difficulties, however, and some additional expense would attend the execution of it. Some deviations, therefore, from the principle must be admitted. In the constitution of the judiciary department in particular, it might be inexpedient to insist rigorously on the principle: first, because peculiar qualifications being essential in the members, the primary consideration ought to be to select that mode of choice which best secures these qualifications; second, because the permanent tenure by which the appointments are held in that department must soon destroy all sense of dependence on the authority conferring them.

It is equally evident that the members of each department should be as little dependent as possible on those of the others for the emoluments annexed to their offices. Were the executive magistrate, or the judges, not independent of the legislature in this particular, their independence in every other would be merely nominal.

incident to republican government. And according to the degree of pleasure and pride we feel in being republicans ought to be our zeal in cherishing the spirit and supporting the character of federalists.

But the great security against a gradual concentration of the several powers in the same department consists in giving to those who administer each department the necessary constitutional means and personal motives to resist encroachments of the others. The provision for defense must in this, as in all other cases, be made commensurate to the danger of attack. Ambition must be made to counteract ambition. The interest of the man must be connected with the constitutional rights of the place. It may be a reflection on human nature that such devices should be necessary to control the abuses of government. But what is government itself but the greatest of all reflections on human nature? If men were angels, no government would be necessary. If angels were to govern men, neither external nor internal controls on government would be necessary. In framing a government which is to be administered by men over men, the great difficulty lies in this: you must first enable the government to control the governed; and in the next place oblige it to control itself. A dependence on the people is, no doubt, the primary control on the government; but experience has taught mankind the necessity of auxiliary precautions.

This policy of supplying, by opposite and rival interests, the defect of better motives, might be traced through the whole system of human affairs, private as well as public. We see it particularly displayed in all the subordinate distributions of power, where the constant aim is to divide and arrange the several offices in such a manner as that each may be a check on the other—that the private interest of every individual may be a sentinel over the public rights. These inventions of prudence cannot be less requisite in the distribution of the supreme powers of the State.

But it is not possible to give to each department an equal power of self-defense. In republican government, the legislative authority necessarily predominates. The remedy for this inconveniency is to divide the legislature into different branches; and to render them, by different modes of election and different principles of action, as little connected with each other as the nature of their common functions and their common dependence on the society will admit. It may even be necessary to guard against dangerous encroachments by still further precautions. As the weight of the legislative authority requires that it should be thus divided, the weakness of the executive may require, on the other hand, that it should be fortified. An absolute negative on the legislature appears, at first view, to be the natural defense with which the executive magistrate should be armed. But perhaps it would be neither altogether safe nor alone sufficient. On ordinary occasions it might not be exerted with the requisite firmness, and on extraordinary occasions it might be perfidiously abused. May not this defect of an absolute negative be supplied by some qualified connection between this weaker department and the weaker branch of the stronger department, by which the latter may be led to support the constitutional rights of the former, without being too much detached from the rights of its own department?

If the principles on which these observations are founded be just, as I persuade myself they are, and they be applied as a criterion to the several State constitutions, and to the federal Constitution, it will be found that if the latter does not perfectly correspond with them, the former are infinitely less able to bear such a test.

There are, moreover, two considerations particularly applicable to the federal system of America, which place that system in a very interesting point of view.

First. In a single republic, all the power surrendered by the people is submitted to the administration of a single government; and the usurpations are guarded against by a division of the government into distinct and separate departments. In the compound republic of America, the power surrendered by the people is first divided between two distinct governments, and then the portion allotted to each subdivided among distinct and separate departments. Hence a double security arises to the rights of the people. The different governments will control each other, at the same time that each will be controlled by itself.

Second. It is of great importance in a republic not only to guard the society against the oppression of its rulers, but to guard one part of the society against the injustice of the other part. Different interests necessarily exist in different classes of citizens. If a majority be united by a common interest, the rights of the minority will be insecure. There are but two methods of providing against this evil: the one by creating a will in the community independent of the majority—that is, of the society itself; the other, by comprehending in the society so many separate descriptions of citizens as will render an unjust combination of a majority of the whole very improbable, if not impracticable. The first method prevails in all governments possessing an hereditary or self-appointed authority. This, at best, is but a precarious security; because a power independent of the society may as well espouse the unjust views of the major as the rightful interests of the minor party, and may possibly be turned against both parties. The second method will be exemplified in the federal republic of the United States. Whilst all authority in it will be derived from and dependent on the society, the society itself will be broken into so many parts, interests and classes of citizens, that the rights of individuals, or of the minority, will be in little danger from interested combinations of the majority. In a free government the security for civil rights must be the same as that for religious rights. It consists in the one case in the multiplicity of interests, and in the other in the multiplicity of sects. The degree of security in both cases will depend on the number of interests and sects; and this may be presumed to depend on the extent of country and number of people comprehended under the same government. This view of the subject must particularly recommend a proper federal system to all the sincere and considerate friends of republican government, since it shows that in exact proportion as the territory of the Union may be formed into more circumscribed Confederacies, or States, oppressive combinations of a majority will be facilitated; the best security, under the republican forms, for the rights of every class of citizen, will be diminished; and consequently the stability and independence of some member of the government, the only other security, must be proportionally increased. Justice is the end of government. It is the end of civil society. It ever has been and ever will be pursued until it be obtained, or until liberty be lost in the pursuit. In a society under the forms of which the stronger faction can readily unite and oppress the weaker, anarchy may as truly be said to reign as in a state of nature, where the weaker individual is not secured against the violence of the stronger; and as, in the latter state, even the stronger individuals are prompted, by the uncertainty of their condition, to submit to a government which may protect the weak as well as themselves; so, in the former state, will the more powerful factions or parties be gradually induced, by a like motive, to wish for a government which will protect all parties, the weaker as well as the more powerful. It can be little doubted that if the State of Rhode Island was separated from the Confederacy and left to itself, the insecurity of rights under the popular form of government within such narrow limits would be displayed by such reiterated oppressions of factious majorities that some power altogether independent of the people would soon be called for by the voice of the very factions whose misrule had proved the necessity of it. In the extended republic of the United States, and among the great variety of interests, parties, and sects which it embraces, a coalition of a majority of the whole society could seldom take place on any other principles than those of justice and the general good; whilst there being thus less danger to a minor from the will of a major party, there must be less pretext, also, to provide for the security of the former, by introducing into the government a will not dependent on the latter, or, in other words, a will independent of the society itself. It is no less certain than it is important, notwithstanding the contrary opinions which have been entertained, that the larger the society, provided it lie within a practicable sphere, the more duly capable it will be of self-government. And happily for the *republican cause*, the practicable sphere may be carried to a very great extent by a judicious modification and mixture of the *federal principle*.

Publius
(James Madison)

You are expected to complete a political science research project for your class and present the results in a paper. Research, you have learned, is a tool of science. At first you may ask, what is there about politics that is "scientific"? You can't study people the way you do rats in a maze, nor can you conduct experiments in the same manner as in the biology lab. Yet much of what we know today about how political processes work, and especially about how people act in political situations, is the result of scientific research. For the modern political scientist, the acts of voters, the decisions of presidents and Supreme Court justices, and the policy decisions of state and municipal governments are data to be analyzed according to the methods of science.

I. The Scientific Approach to Politics

When you conduct a research project, it is essential to adhere to certain rules of *epistemology*. Epistemology has to do with *how* we know what we think is true, and the answer to this question lies in whether our work is valid and reliable. A research result is *valid* if it tells you something that actually is true, and it is *reliable* if you or other researchers could reproduce the same results (or at least get approximately the same findings). Validity and reliability are the two hallmarks of the scientific method, which is applied to political science research as much as it is to other scientific research.

How do you know when your results are valid and reliable? The validity of your findings is difficult to establish, but your results are more likely to be valid if you follow these steps in the research process:

1. Formulate a fairly narrow problem to research in such a way that you can make a conclusion based on empirical evidence, that is, evidence based on observation or experience.
2. Set up one or more concrete research hypotheses, which are statements about what you expect to find from your observations.
3. Put together a research design, or a strategy for getting your observations (which might involve doing a sample survey, observing a city council meeting, or gathering information from an almanac or a computer file.)
4. Find an appropriate way to measure the key pieces of information, or data, that you need in order to determine whether your research hypotheses are supported by the factual evidence of your observations.
5. Go out and collect the data.
6. Conduct a careful analysis of the data that you have gathered (usually with appropriate statistical procedures).
7. Make some general conclusions about whether the data tend to support your research hypotheses.

This list of procedures makes empirical research in political science look very mechanical. In part, it is. However it takes intuition and clear thinking to decide how to study political phenomena. There are certain pitfalls to be avoided in analyzing data.

Pitfalls to Avoid. For one thing, you must show that there is some meaningful relationship, or covariation, between or among the variables on which you have collected information. For example, before you claim that Republicans tend to be in higher-income brackets, you must be able to show that the percentage of people who are Republicans is greater among those who have incomes over, say, $50,000 a year than the percentage of Republicans you find among those with incomes under $50,000 a year. The simple fact that you find this pattern of covariation, by itself, though, doesn't necessarily mean that income is what really causes people to choose political sides. It turns out that people's income level is closely related to how much education they have, what kind of job they hold (medical doctors make more money than secretaries), and even how old they are and whether they are married. In other words, you must attempt to eliminate possibly spurious relationships, that is, explanations that don't take into account the complex relationships among variables.

Sometimes empirical covariation can be completely misleading. You probably remember the old story about how storks bring babies. Well, it really is true that birthrates in Europe are higher when storks are busy with their own nesting activities. This empirical fact, however, doesn't mean that the storks bring human babies with them; it just means that there is a similar pattern of human and stork behavior. As another example, you can easily find that the more fire trucks that go to fight a fire, the greater is the amount of damage from the fire. Does sending more fire trucks actually cause the fire to be worse? Of course not. Rather, the correct conclusion would be that a bigger fire requires that more trucks be called in to help fight it, and the bigger fire also produces more property damage. The covariation between the number of fire trucks and the amount of damage is spurious, because both of those variables are affected by the severity of the fire.

The fire truck example also brings us to another point of caution—deciding what "causes" what. You might be led astray in your conclusions if you aren't careful about the order of causal patterns. The fact that you took an examination in your American government course before you went to the polls and voted a straight Democratic ticket doesn't mean that your course (or the exam) caused you to vote that way. Such an incorrect conclusion would be an example of the *post hoc ergo propter hoc* (after, and therefore because of) fallacy. As another example, consider the relationship between your decision to protest ROTC on your campus and your parents' views on whether it is legitimate for people to engage in protest behavior. What "causes" what here? Assume your parents in general support public protests. Does your parents' general approval of protesting tend to determine whether you participate in the protest, or does your protesting gradually intensify your parents' view? Or could your behavior and their attitudes be mutually "causal"? Probably, the fact that you grew up under your parents' influence (not that you listened to or did everything they said) meant that you absorbed their tolerance for protest behavior. They had a much better chance to influence your behavior than you had a chance to influence their attitudes. In other words, it is important to take into consideration the *time ordering* of the variables that you might measure. In general, a later event logically is not able to "cause" an earlier event. Still, there likely is some tendency for parents to modify their previous views if they can be persuaded that your way of doing things politically is legitimate.

How to Increase Reliability. For your results to be valid, they must first be reliable. Whether your conclusions are reliable depends on how carefully you designed the study to take into account random variation from what otherwise might be observed. There are four different ways to test for reliability in your work.

1. Measure everything a second time. This is called the **test–retest method.**
2. Measure the same phenomenon in more than one way. This is the **parallel forms method** for assessing reliability.
3. Split your sample of observations into two groups and see if the results correspond closely. This is the **split-half method.**
4. Conduct an **item analysis,** which entails looking at the degree to which any one item that you have measured relates to the entire set of results. Any variable that doesn't fit closely with the overall pattern may need to be thrown out, or at least be remeasured. (Incidentally, this is precisely what many university instructors do when they prepare computer analyses for the results of a multiple-answer examination).

II. Choosing a Topic

Choosing a topic is the most important decision you'll make. Avoid being too broad ("Civil Rights in the U.S."). Avoid being too current (you will find almost nothing published and little analysis on the subject). Your freedom to choose will depend on the instructions you have received. In any case, make sure the topic fits the course. Be specific and focused. Consider the data or variables you will need to complete your project, keeping in mind the need to present valid and reliable facts. Also pick a subject that interests and even excites you. Your research will be more fun and your written report more lively if your heart is really in the project.

III. Writing the Paper

After you have read the pamphlet that accompanies your text entitled, *Handbook on Critical Thinking and Writing in American Politics,* you are ready to start.

Begin with an outline. It is your road map, so, for most research papers, make sure you cover at least the following:

Title page (title, your name, class, date.)

1. Introduction (what you plan to do).
2. Problem statement or thesis (what you plan to prove; why this is an important topic).
3. Body of project (logically arranged discussion of facts; interpretation/analysis of the information).
4. Conclusion (what generalizations or overall insights you have gained from the study. Make sure these relate back to 2).
5. Endnotes or footnotes.
6. Appendix (put tables, charts, and other material here that are important to the paper but are not directly relevant in the body of the study).
7. Sources (bibliography).

Other Tips. Take notes on index cards or a yellow pad. Write down the complete citation, including page numbers of material. You may think it will be easy to do that later but it won't! The book or magazine may be gone, checked out, or missing. You may forget where it was. Label cards or pages so you can sort and organize them to fit the structure of your project.

Try to Be Objective. Let the facts lead you to conclusions. DON'T start with a conclusion (or bias) and then look for facts to prove you are right!

Type Your Paper. Make sure you number all pages. Cite sources, especially quotations or close paraphrasing. DON'T PLAGIARIZE (in other words, don't use ideas, analyses, or conclusions from other sources and pretend they are your own).

IV. Where to Find Information

Knowing where to find information quickly and efficiently is every researcher's goal. The following are excellent places to start:

We assume that you are familiar with the card catalog in your library and know how to search for books and other items indexed there. However, you will want to go beyond books (perhaps the subject is too recent for books or no one has quite focused on the subject the way you plan to approach it). You should also be familiar with the *Reader's Guide to Periodical Literature,* which cites material in popular periodicals such as *Time* and *People* magazines.

The Public Affairs Information Service (PAIS) publishes the *PAIS Bulletin,* which is an index (cumulated each year) with diverse citations on public affairs including books, journals, government documents, periodicals, fliers, and pamphlets.

Facts on File may be helpful in pinpointing and succinctly informing you about an event or person in the news. Its index is very complete and cross referenced. The *New York Times Index* is an annotated reference to the articles and stories that have appeared in the nation's complete newspaper, the *New York Times.*

The periodicals section of your library should have what we call *scholarly journals.* These are research-oriented publications in which political scientists report the results of their studies. Look for articles on your topic in *ABC POL SCI A Bibliography of Contents; Political Science and Government, Santa Barbara, CA: American Bibliographical Center, Clio Press.* This index is published five times a year and leads you to nearly 300 periodicals.

Familiarize yourself with some of the following scholarly journals: *The American Political Science Review, The Journal of Politics, Comparative Politics, Political Science Quarterly, The Western Political Quarterly, The American Journal of Political Science, Polity, Foreign Affairs, Presidential Studies Quarterly, Public Administration Review.*

For public opinion one of the most widely used sources is the *Gallup Opinion Index.*

The *Congressional Quarterly Weekly Report (CQWR)* is absolutely essential for every researcher. It comes to your library every week, is indexed, and is bound by volume every year. This source contains useful information on members of Congress, issues, scandals, political action committees, legislation, international affairs, and other material related to Congress. Tables and charts are excellent sources of information.

The *National Journal* covers material similar to the *CQWR.*

The *Supreme Court Reporter* (West Publishing) is one of the best-annotated sources of Supreme Court cases. It provides detailed information about the case and background as well as reference to other relevant cases.

The *Book of the States* is the authoritative source on the structure of state government, statistics, finances, and other information about the fifty states. This is published every two years.

The *Encyclopedia of Associations* is a multivolume source of information on organizations. You will be amazed at the number and diversity of organized groups, associations, and other organizations that exist. The *Encyclopedia* tells you the objectives, organizations, budget, membership, names of officers, address, and telephone numbers.

V. Using Government Publications

One of the best sources of information for research is the U.S. government, the largest publisher in the world. There are federal government publications for virtually every research topic. Because of the sheer volume, only specially designated *depository libraries* receive most of these publications. Ask your librarian where the nearest one is located. Remember that you can obtain this material through interlibrary loan.

Federal publications include statistics; congressional material including hearings, pamphlets, and bulletins; technical reports; presidential statements and documents; court rulings; and agency-specific publications. To find this material, you may want to use the following:

The *CIS* (Congressional Information Service) *Index.* This is published monthly and bound into a volume each year. It covers congressional hearings, reports, and special publications. Each item listed includes an abstract.

The *Congressional Monitor* is the best source of information on congressional hearings, which are listed by subject area for each House and Senate committee.

The *American Statistics Index* covers over five hundred federal government sources of information including numerical data.

The *Guide to U.S. Government Publications,* by John L. Andriot, is an annual guide to the reports and regular publications (magazines, for example) that are produced by more than 2,000 government agencies.

The following are selected United States government publications by topic:

Foreign Policy: *United States Foreign Policy: A Report of the Secretary of State.* This annual report reviews U.S. foreign policy, military and technical assistance, and other international activities country by country.

Federalism: *Catalog of Federal Domestic Assistance.* This publication is compiled by the Office of Management and Budget and lists virtually all federal grant programs to state and local governments. *Intergovernmental Perspective* is published by the Advisory Commission on Intergovernmental Relations four times a year and contains statistical information, analysis, and listings on all aspects of intergovernmental relations.

Voting/Elections: The *Journal of Election Administration* is published by the Federal Election Commission (FEC), which also publishes an array of statistical information on campaigns, voting, and related matters (call toll free, 800-424-9530).

Congress: The *Congressional Record* is published every day Congress is in session and contains the proceedings as well as supplemental documents inserted by members of Congress.

Presidency: The *Weekly Compilation of Presidential Documents* is issued every week and compiled annually as *Public Powers of the President of the United States*. It contains the speeches, messages, statements, and press conferences of the president.

The Supreme Court: The *United States Reports,* published since 1790, is the official publication of Supreme Court decisions. Citation of a case is usually to the *Reports.* For example Miranda v. Arizona, 348 U.S. 436 (1966) means volume 348 of the U.S. Reports, page 436 in the year 1966.

Domestic Policy: One of the best sources of information is the *Budget of the United States* and its appendices or the *United States Budget in Brief,* which contain the specific spending plans and revenue sources of the federal government.

Public Welfare Policy: The book *Characteristics of General Assistance in the United States* provides state-by-state data on federal and state assistance programs for the needy.

Education: data are found in the *Digest of Educational Statistics* published by the Department of Education each year.

The Economy and the Society: Statistics on general aspects of the society and the economy can be found in *Social Indicators: Selected Statistics on Social Conditions and Trends in the U.S.,* published by the Office of Management and Budget.

The U.S. Federal Government: The *United States Government Manual,* describes the agencies of the executive branch, their activities and the names and addresses of key officials. This book can be considered the "official" directory of U.S. government agencies. Government publication can also be obtained from your representative and senators. Find their nearest office in the government section of your local phone book. Ask for the publication by title, date, publication number, and issuing agency. (Have as much of this information as possible.) You can also write or call their office and tell them what general topic you are researching; they will send you material. However, be aware that this will be a random selection from publications they have in their office. You will still need to do further research to make certain you've covered the subject fully.

VI. Computerized Research Sources

Computerized searching capabilities are rather recent. The *Logging On* features at the end of the chapters in this text can serve as a guide to the types of sources that can be accessed through the Internet. The following sources are also useful for students doing research in American government:

The *Social Science Index* is available on CD-ROM floppy disks and also on-line through various library services.

DIALOG Information Service Inc. contains over 350 databases with more than 200 million individual records (units of information generally citations to sources). A typical ten-minute search costs from $5 to $15. It is available twenty-four-hours a day except from 3 A.M. to 1 P.M. EST on Sundays.

One of the most useful files is *U.S. Political Science Documents #93.* This contains 48,970 records starting in 1975 and consisting of detailed abstracts and indexes from roughly 150 of the major American scholarly journals in political science.

Social Science #7 contains over 2.5 million records indexed from the 1,500 most important social science journals throughout the world. It covers every area of the social and behavioral sciences.

PAIS International #49 has 338,817 records with bibliographic information on the public policy literature in a range of disciplines.

Another separate computerized source is the *Monthly Catalog of Government Publications,* which is available on CD-ROM disks under the name MARCIVE, GPO CAT/PAC.

The research librarian at your library is an excellent source for other and computerized sources of information for research projects and papers.

VII. More on Research

For a more detailed discussion of how to do research in political science, the following are excellent: Carl Kalvelage, Albert P. Melone, and Morley Segal, *Bridges to Knowledge in Political Science: A Handbook for Research,* (Pacific Palisades, CA: Palisades Publishers, 1984), or Robert Weissberg, *Politics: A Handbook for Students* (New York: Harcourt Brace Jovanovich, Publishers, 1985).

Jay M. Shafritz, *The Dorsey Dictionary of American Government and Politics* (Chicago: The Dorsey Press, 1988) is a 661-page treasure of detailed information and reference that you should consider owning. It is richly illustrated and very easy to use.

Chief Justices

NAME	YEARS OF SERVICE	STATE APP'T FROM	APPOINTING PRESIDENT	AGE APP'T	POLITICAL AFFILIATION	EDUCATIONAL* BACKGROUND
Jay, John	1789–1795	New York	Washington	44	Federalist	King's College (Columbia)
Rutledge, John	1795 Aug.–Dec.	South Carolina	Washington	56	Federalist	Middle Temple, England
Ellsworth, Oliver	1796–1800	Connecticut	Washington	51	Federalist	Princeton
Marshall, John	1801–1835	Virginia	John Adams	46	Federalist	Self-taught in law
Taney, Roger Brooke	1836–1864	Maryland	Jackson	59	Democrat	Dickinson College
Chase, Salmon Portland	1864–1873	Ohio	Lincoln	56	Republican	Dartmouth College
Waite, Morrison Remick	1874–1888	Ohio	Grant	58	Republican	Yale College
Fuller, Melville Weston	1888–1910	Illinois	Cleveland	55	Democrat	Bowdoin College; studied at Harvard Law School
White, Edward Douglass	1910–1921	Louisiana	Taft	65	Democrat	Mount St. Mary's College; Georgetown College (now University)
Taft, William Howard	1921–1930	Connecticut	Harding	64	Republican	Yale; Cincinnati Law School
Hughes, Charles Evans	1930–1941	New York	Hoover	68	Republican	Colgate University; Brown; Columbia Law School
Stone, Harlan Fiske	1941–1946	New York	Roosevelt, F.	69	Republican	Amherst College; Columbia
Vinson, Frederick Moore	1946–1953	Kentucky	Truman	56	Democrat	Centre College
Warren, Earl	1953–1969	California	Eisenhower	62	Republican	University of California, Berkeley
Burger, Warren Earl	1969–1986	Virginia	Nixon	62	Republican	University of Minnesota; St. Paul College of Law (Mitchell College)
Rehnquist, William Hubbs	1986–	Virginia	Reagan	62	Republican	Stanford; Harvard; Stanford University Law School

* SOURCE: Educational background information derived from Elder Witt, *Guide to the U.S. Supreme Court*, 2d ed. (Washington, D.C.: Congressional Quarterly Press, Inc., 1990) Reprinted with the permission of the publisher.

Associate Justices

Name	Years of Service	State App't from	Appointing President	Age App't	Political Affiliation	Educational Background
Rutledge, John	1790–1791	South Carolina	Washington	51	Federalist	Middle Temple, England
Cushing, William	1790–1810	Massachusetts	Washington	58	Federalist	Harvard College
Wilson, James	1789–1798	Pennsylvania	Washington	47	Federalist	University of St. Andrews, Scotland
Blair, John	1790–1795	Virginia	Washington	48	Federalist	College of William and Mary; Middle Temple, England
Iredell, James	1790–1799	North Carolina	Washington	49	Federalist	Educated in England; read law under Samuel Johnston
Johnson, Thomas	1792–1793	Maryland	Washington	60	Federalist	Educated at home; read law under Stephen Bordley
Paterson, William	1793–1806	New Jersey	Washington	48	Federalist	College of New Jersey (Princeton)
Chase, Samuel	1796–1811	Maryland	Washington	55	Federalist	Tutored by father; read law in Annapolis
Washington, Bushrod	1799–1829	Virginia	Adams, John	37	Federalist	College of William and Mary
Moore, Alfred	1800–1804	North Carolina	Adams, John	45	Federalist	Educated in Boston; read law under father
Johnson, William	1804–1834	South Carolina	Jefferson	33	Democratic-Republican	College of New Jersey (Princeton)
Livingston, Henry Brockholst	1807–1823	New York	Jefferson	50	Democratic-Republican	College of New Jersey (Princeton)
Todd, Thomas	1807–1826	Kentucky	Jefferson	42	Democratic-Republican	Liberty Hall (Washington and Lee University)
Duvall, Gabriel	1811–1835	Maryland	Madison	59	Democratic-Republican	Self-taught in law
Story, Joseph	1812–1845	Massachusetts	Madison	33	Democratic-Republican	Harvard
Thompson, Smith	1823–1843	New York	Monroe	55	Democratic-Republican	College of New Jersey (Princeton)
Trimble, Robert	1826–1828	Kentucky	Adams, J. Q.	50	Democratic-Republican	Kentucky Academy (Transylvania University)
McLean, John	1830–1861	Ohio	Jackson	45	Democrat	Read law under Arthur St. Clair, Jr.
Baldwin, Henry	1830–1844	Pennsylvania	Jackson	50	Democrat	Yale College
Wayne, James Moore	1835–1867	Georgia	Jackson	45	Democrat	Princeton
Barbour, Philip Pendleton	1836–1841	Virginia	Jackson	53	Democrat	Read on his own; attended one session at College of William and Mary
Catron, John	1837–1865	Tennessee	Van Buren	51	Democrat	Self-taught in law
McKinley, John	1838–1852	Alabama	Van Buren	58	Democrat	Self-taught in law
Daniel, Peter Vivian	1842–1860	Virginia	Van Buren	58	Democrat	Attended one year at Princeton
Nelson, Samuel	1845–1872	New York	Tyler	53	Democrat	Middlebury College
Woodbury, Levi	1845–1851	New Hampshire	Polk	56	Democrat	Dartmouth College; Tapping Reeve Law School
Grier, Robert Cooper	1846–1870	Pennsylvania	Polk	52	Democrat	Dickinson College

Associate Justices (continued)

Name	Years of Service	State App't From	Appointing President	Age App't	Political Affiliation	Educational Background
Curtis, Benjamin Robbins	1851–1857	Massachusetts	Fillmore	42	Whig	Harvard; Harvard Law School
Campbell, John Archibald	1853–1861	Alabama	Pierce	42	Democrat	Franklin College; U.S. Military Academy at West Point
Clifford, Nathan	1858–1881	Maine	Buchanan	55	Democrat	Read law in offices of Josiah Quincy
Swayne, Noah Haynes	1862–1881	Ohio	Lincoln	58	Republican	Read law privately
Miller, Samuel Freeman	1862–1890	Iowa	Lincoln	46	Republican	Transylvania University Medical School; read law privately
Davis, David	1862–1877	Illinois	Lincoln	47	Republican	Kenyon College; Yale Law School
Field, Stephen Johnson	1863–1897	California	Lincoln	47	Democrat	Williams College; read law privately
Strong, William	1870–1880	Pennsylvania	Grant	62	Republican	Yale College
Bradley, Joseph P.	1870–1892	New Jersey	Grant	57	Republican	Rutgers
Hunt, Ward	1873–1882	New York	Grant	63	Republican	Union College; read law privately
Harlan, John Marshall	1877–1911	Kentucky	Hayes	61	Republican	Centre College; studied law at Transylvania University
Woods, William Burnham	1881–1887	Georgia	Hayes	57	Republican	Yale
Matthews, Stanley	1881–1889	Ohio	Garfield	57	Republican	Kenyon College
Gray, Horace	1882–1902	Massachusetts	Arthur	54	Republican	Harvard College; Harvard Law School
Blatchford, Samuel	1882–1893	New York	Arthur	62	Republican	Columbia College
Lamar, Lucius Quintus C.	1888–1893	Mississippi	Cleveland	63	Democrat	Emory College
Brewer, David Josiah	1890–1910	Kansas	Harrison	53	Republican	Wesleyan University; Yale; Albany Law School
Brown, Henry Billings	1891–1906	Michigan	Harrison	55	Republican	Yale; studied at Yale Law School and Harvard Law School
Shiras, George, Jr.	1892–1903	Pennsylvania	Harrison	61	Republican	Ohio University; Yale; studied law at Yale and privately
Jackson, Howell Edmunds	1893–1895	Tennessee	Harrison	61	Democrat	West Tennessee College; University of Virginia; one year in Legal Dept. of Cumberland University
White, Edward Douglass	1894–1910	Louisiana	Cleveland	49	Democrat	Mount St. Mary's College; Georgetown College (now University)
Peckham, Rufus Wheeler	1896–1909	New York	Cleveland	58	Democrat	Read law in father's firm
McKenna, Joseph	1898–1925	California	McKinley	55	Republican	Benicia Collegiate Institute, Law Dept.

Associate Justices (continued)

Name	Years of Service	State App't From	Appointing President	Age App't	Political Affiliation	Educational Background
Holmes, Oliver Wendell, Jr.	1902–1932	Massachusetts	Roosevelt, T.	61	Republican	Harvard College; studied law at Harvard Law School
Day, William Rufus	1903–1922	Ohio	Roosevelt, T.	54	Republican	University of Michigan; University of Michigan Law School
Moody, William Henry	1906–1910	Massachusetts	Roosevelt, T.	53	Republican	Harvard; Harvard Law School
Lurton, Horace Harmon	1910–1914	Tennessee	Taft	66	Democrat	University of Chicago; Cumberland Law School
Hughes, Charles Evans	1910–1916	New York	Taft	48	Republican	Colgate University; Brown University; Columbia Law School
Van Devanter, Willis	1911–1937	Wyoming	Taft	52	Republican	Indiana Asbury University; University of Cincinnati Law School
Lamar, Joseph Rucker	1911–1916	Georgia	Taft	54	Democrat	University of Georgia; Bethany College; Washington and Lee University
Pitney, Mahlon	1912–1922	New Jersey	Taft	54	Republican	College of New Jersey (Princeton); read law under father
McReynolds, James Clark	1914–1941	Tennessee	Wilson	52	Democrat	Vanderbilt University; University of Virginia
Brandeis, Louis Dembitz	1916–1939	Massachusetts	Wilson	60	Democrat	Harvard Law School
Clarke, John Hessin	1916–1922	Ohio	Wilson	59	Democrat	Western Reserve University; read law under father
Sutherland, George	1922–1938	Utah	Harding	60	Republican	Brigham Young Academy; one year at University of Michigan Law School
Butler, Pierce	1923–1939	Minnesota	Harding	57	Democrat	Carleton College
Sanford, Edward Terry	1923–1930	Tennessee	Harding	58	Republican	University of Tennessee; Harvard; Harvard Law School
Stone, Harlan Fiske	1925–1941	New York	Coolidge	53	Republican	Amherst College; Columbia University Law School
Roberts, Owen Josephus	1930–1945	Pennsylvania	Hoover	55	Republican	University of Pennsylvania; University of Pennsylvania Law School
Cardozo, Benjamin Nathan	1932–1938	New York	Hoover	62	Democrat	Columbia University; two years at Columbia Law School
Black, Hugo Lafayette	1937–1971	Alabama	Roosevelt, F.	51	Democrat	Birmingham Medical College; University of Alabama Law School
Reed, Stanley Forman	1938–1957	Kentucky	Roosevelt, F.	54	Democrat	Kentucky Wesleyan University; Yale; studied law at University of Virginia and Columbia University; University of Paris
Frankfurter, Felix	1939–1962	Massachusetts	Roosevelt, F.	57	Independent	College of the City of New York; Harvard Law School
Douglas, William Orville	1939–1975	Connecticut	Roosevelt, F.	41	Democrat	Whitman College; Columbia University Law School
Murphy, Frank	1940–1949	Michigan	Roosevelt, F.	50	Democrat	University of Michigan; Lincoln's Inn, London; Trinity College

Associate Justices (continued)

Name	Years of Service	State App't from	Appointing President	Age App't	Political Affiliation	Educational Background
Byrnes, James Francis	1941–1942	South Carolina	Roosevelt, F.	62	Democrat	Read law privately
Jackson, Robert Houghwout	1941–1954	New York	Roosevelt, F.	49	Democrat	Albany Law School
Rutledge, Wiley Blount	1943–1949	Iowa	Roosevelt, F.	49	Democrat	University of Wisconsin; University of Colorado
Burton, Harold Hitz	1945–1958	Ohio	Truman	57	Republican	Bowdoin College; Harvard University Law School
Clark, Thomas Campbell	1949–1967	Texas	Truman	50	Democrat	University of Texas
Minton, Sherman	1949–1956	Indiana	Truman	59	Democrat	Indiana University College of Law; Yale Law School
Harlan, John Marshall	1955–1971	New York	Eisenhower	56	Republican	Princeton; Oxford University; New York Law School
Brennan, William J., Jr.	1956–1990	New Jersey	Eisenhower	50	Democrat	University of Pennsylvania; Harvard Law School
Whittaker, Charles Evans	1957–1962	Missouri	Eisenhower	56	Republican	University of Kansas City Law School
Stewart, Potter	1958–1981	Ohio	Eisenhower	43	Republican	Yale; Yale Law School
White, Byron Raymond	1962–1993	Colorado	Kennedy	45	Democrat	University of Colorado; Oxford University; Yale Law School
Goldberg, Arthur Joseph	1962–1965	Illinois	Kennedy	54	Democrat	Northwestern University
Fortas, Abe	1965–1969	Tennessee	Johnson, L.	55	Democrat	Southwestern College; Yale Law School
Marshall, Thurgood	1967–1991	New York	Johnson, L.	59	Democrat	Lincoln University; Howard University Law School
Blackmun, Harry A.	1970–1994	Minnesota	Nixon	62	Republican	Harvard; Harvard Law School
Powell, Lewis F., Jr.	1972–1987	Virginia	Nixon	65	Democrat	Washington and Lee University; Washington and Lee University Law School; Harvard Law School
Rehnquist, William H.	1972–1986	Arizona	Nixon	48	Republican	Stanford; Harvard; Stanford University Law School
Stevens, John Paul	1975	Illinois	Ford	55	Republican	University of Colorado; Northwestern University Law School
O'Connor, Sandra Day	1981–	Arizona	Reagan	51	Republican	Stanford; Stanford University Law School
Scalia, Antonin	1986–	Virginia	Reagan	50	Republican	Georgetown University; Harvard Law School
Kennedy, Anthony M.	1988–	California	Reagan	52	Republican	Stanford; London School of Economics; Harvard Law School
Souter, David Hackett	1990–	New Hampshire	Bush	51	Republican	Harvard; Oxford University
Thomas, Clarence	1991–	District of Columbia	Bush	43	Republican	Holy Cross College; Yale Law School
Ginsburg, Ruth Bader	1993–	District of Columbia	Clinton	60	Democrat	Cornell University; Columbia Law School
Breyer, Stephen, G.	1994–	Massachusetts	Clinton	55	Democrat	Stanford University; Oxford University; Harvard Law School

Acid Rain: Lluvia Acida
Acquisitive Model: Modelo Adquisitivo
Actionable: Procesable, Enjuiciable
Action-reaction Syndrome: Sídrome de Acción y Reacción
Actual Malice: Malicia Expresa
Administrative Agency: Agencia Administrativa
Advice and Consent: Consejo y Consentimiento
Affirmative Action: Acción Afirmativa
Affirm: Afirmar
Agenda Setting: Agenda Establecida
Aid to Families with Dependent Children (AFDC): Ayuda para Familias con Niños Dependientes
AMICUS CURIAE Brief: Tercer persona o grupo no involucrado en el caso, admitido en un juicio para hacer valer el intéres público o el de un grupo social importante.
Anarchy: Anarquía
Anti-Federalists: Anti-Federalistas
Anti-Federalist: Anti-Federalista
Appellate Court: Corte de Apelación
Appointment Power: Poder de Apuntamiento
Appropriation: Apropiación
Aristocracy: Aristocracia
Attentive Public: Público Atento
Australian Ballot: Voto Australiano
Authority: Autoridad
Authorization: Autorización

Bad-Tendency Rule: Regla de Tendencia-mala
"Beauty Contest": Concurso de Belleza

Bicameralism: Bicameralismo
Bicameral Legislature: Legislatura Bicameral
Bill of Rights: Declaración de Derechos
Blanket Primary: Primaria Comprensiva
Block Grants: Concesiones de Bloque
Bureaucracy: Burocracia
Busing in Boston: Transporte público

Cabinet: Gabinete, Consejo de Ministros
Cabinet Department: Departamento del Gabinete
Cadre: El núcleo de activistas de partidos políticos encargados de cumplir las funciones importantes de los partidos políticos americanos.
Canvassing Board: Consejo encargado con la encuesta de una violación.
Capture: Captura, toma
Casework: Trabajo de Caso
Categorical Grants-in-Aid: Concesiones Categóricas de Ayuda
Caucus: Reunión de Dirigentes
Challenge: Reto
Checks and Balances: Chequeos y Equilibrio
Chief Diplomat: Jefe Diplomático
Chief Executive: Jefe Ejecutivo
Chief Legislator: Jefe Legislador
Chief of Staff: Jefe de Personal
Chief of State: Jefe de Estado
Civil Law: Derecho Civil
Civil Liberties: Libertades Civiles
Civil Rights: Derechos Civiles
Civil Service Commission: Comisión de Servicio Civil
Civil Service: Servicio Civil

Class-action Suit: Demanda en representación de un grupo o clase.
Class Politics: Política de Clase
Clear and Present Danger Test: Prueba de Peligro Claro y Presente
Climate Control: Control de Clima
Closed Primary: Primaria Cerrada
Cloture: Cierre al voto
Coattail Effect: Effecto de Cola de Chaqueta
Cold War: Guerra Fría
Commander in Chief: Comandante en Jefe
Commerce Clause: Clausula de Comercio
Commercial Speech: Discurso Comercial
Common Law: Ley Comú, Derecho Consuetudinario
Comparable Worth: Valor Comparable
Compliance: De acuerdo
Concurrent Majority: Mayoría Concurrente
Concurring Opinion: Opinión Concurrente
Confederal System: Sistema Confederal
Confederation: Confederación
Conference Committee: Comité de Conferencia
Consensus: Concenso
Consent of the People: Consentimiento de la Gente
Conservatism: Calidad de Conservador
Conservative Coalition: Coalición Conservadora
Consolidation: Consolidación
Constant Dollars: Dólares Constantes
Constitutional

Initiative: Iniciativa Constitucional
Constitutional Power: Poder Constitucional
Containment: Contenimiento
Continuing Resolution: Resolución Contíua
Cooley's Rule: Régla de Cooley
Cooperative Federalism: Federalismo Cooperativo
Corrupt Practices Acts: Leyes Contra Acciones Corruptas
Council of Economic Advisers (CEA): Consejo de Asesores Económicos
Council of Government (COG): Consejo de Gobierno
County: Condado
Credentials Committee: Comité de Credenciales
Criminal Law: Ley Criminal

DE FACTO Segregation: Segregación de Hecho
DE JURE Segregation: Segregación Cotidiana
Defamation of Character: Defamación de Carácter
Democracy: Democracia
Democratic Party: Partido Democratico
Dillon's Rule: Régla de Dillon
Diplomacy: Diplomácia
Direct Democracy: Democracia Directa
Direct Primary: Primaria Directa
Direct Technique: Técnica Directa
Discharge Petition: Petición de Descargo
Dissenting Opinion: Opinión Disidente
Divisive Opinion: Opinión Divisiva
Domestic Policy: Principio Político Doméstico
Dual Citizenship: Ciudadanía Dual
Dual Federalism: Federalismo Dual
Détente: No Spanish equivalent.

Economic Aid: Ayuda Económica
Economic Regulation: Regulación Económica
Elastic Clause, or Necessary and

Proper Clause: Cláusula Flexible o Cláusula Propia Necesaria
Electoral College: Colegio Electoral
Elector: Elector
Electronic Media: Media Electronica
Elite: Elite (el selecto)
Elite Theory: Teoría Elitista (de lo selecto)
Emergency Power: Poder de Emergencia
Enumerated Power: Poder Enumerado
Environmental Impact Statement (EIS): Afirmación de Impacto Ambiental
Equality: Igualdad
Equalization: Igualación
Equal Employment Opportunity Commission (EEOC): Comisión de Igualdad de Oportunidad en el Empleo
Era of Good Feeling: Era de Buen Sentimiento
Era of Personal Politics: Era de Política Personal
Establishment Clause: Cláusula de Establecimiento
Euthanasia: Eutanasia
Exclusionary Rule: Regla de Exclusión
Executive Agreement: Acuerdo Ejecutivo
Executive Budget: Presupuesto Ejecutivo
Executive Office of the President (EOP): Oficina Ejecutiva del Presidente
Executive Order: Orden Ejecutiva
Executive Privilege: Privilegio Ejecutivo
Expressed Power: Poder Expresado
Extradite: Entregar por Extradición

Faction: Facción
Fairness Doctrine: Doctrina de Justicia
Fall Review: Revision de Otoño
Federalists: Federalistas
Federalist: Federalista
Federal Mandate: Mandato Federal

Federal Open Market Committee (FOMC): Comité Federal de Libre Mercado
Federal Register: Registro Federal
Federal System: Sistema Federal
Fighting Words: Palabras de Provocación
Filibustering: Obstrucción de Propuesta
Filibuster: Obstrucción de iniciativas de ley
Fireside Chat: Charla de Hogar
First Budget Resolution: Resolución Primera Presupuesta
First Continental Congress: Primér Congreso Continental
Fiscal Policy: Poliza Fiscal
Fiscal Year (FY): Año Fiscal
Fluidity: Fluidez
Food Stamps: Estampillas para Comida
Foreign Policy: Póliza Extranjera
Foreign Policy Process: Proceso de Poliza Extranjera
Franking: Franqueando
Fraternity: Fraternidad
Free Exercise Clause: Cláusula de Ejercicio Libre
Full Faith and Credit Clause: Cláusula de Completa Fé y Crédito
Functional Consolidation: Consolidación Funcional

Gag Order: Orden de Silencio
Garbage Can Model: Modelo Bote de Basura
Gender Gap: Brecha de Géero
General Law City: Regla General Urbana
General Sales Tax: Impuesto General de Ventas
Generational Effect: Efecto Generacional
Gerrymandering: División arbitraria de los distritos electorales con fines políticos.
Government Corporation: Corporación Gubernamental
Government: Gobierno
Government in the Sunshine

Act: Gobierno en la acta: Luz del Sol
Grandfather Clause: Clausula del Abuelo
Grand Jury: Gran Jurado
Great Compromise: Grá Acuerdo de Negociación

Hatch Act (Political Activities Act): Acta Hatch (acta de actividades politicas)
Hecklers' Veto: Veto de Abuchamiento
Home Rule City: Regla Urbana
Horizontal Federalism: Federalismo Horizontal
Hyperpluralism: Hiperpluralismo

Ideologue: Ideólogo
Ideology: Ideología
Image Building: Construcción de Imágen
Impeachment: Acción Penal Contra un Funcionario Público
Inalienable Rights: Derechos Inalienables
Income Transfer: Transferencia de Ingresos
Incorporation Theory: Teoría de Incorporación
Independent Candidate: Candidato Independiente
Independent: Independiente
Independent Executive Agency: Agencia Ejecutiva Independiente
Independent Regulatory Agency: Agencia Regulatoria Independiente
Indirect Technique: Técnica Indirecta
Inherent Power: Poder Inherente
Initiative: Iniciativa
Injunction: Injunción, Prohibición Judicial
Institution: Institución
Instructed Delegate: Delegado con Instrucciones
Intelligence Community: Comunidad de Inteligencia
Intensity: Intensidad
Interest Group: Grupo de Interés
Interposition: Interposición

Interstate Compact: Compacto Interestatal
In-kind Subsidy: Subsidio de Clase
Iron Curtain: Cortina de Acero
Iron Triangle: Triágulo de Acero
Isolationist Foreign Policy: Póliza Extranjera de Aislamiento
Issue Voting: Voto Temático
Item Veto: Artículo de Veto

Jim Crow Laws: No Spanish equivalent.
Joint Committee: Comité Mancomunado
Judicial Activism: Activismo Judicial
Judicial Implementation: Implementacion Judicial
Judicial Restraint: Restricción Judicial
Judicial Review: Revisión Judicial
Jurisdiction: Jurisdicción
Justiciable Dispute: Disputa Judiciaria
Justiciable Question: Pregunta Justiciable

Keynesian Economics: Economía Keynesiana
Kitchen Cabinet: Gabinete de Cocina

Labor Movement: Movimiento Laboral
Latent Public Opinion: Opinión Pública Latente
Lawmaking: Hacedores de Ley
Legislative History: Historia Legislativa
Legislative Initiative: Iniciativa de legislación
Legislative Veto: Veto Legislativo
Legislature: Legislatura
Legitimacy: Legitimidad
Libel: Libelo, Difamación Escrita
Liberalism: Liberalismo
Liberty: Libertad
Limited Government: Gobierno Limitado
Line Organization: Organización de Linea
Literacy Test: Exámen de alfabetización

Litigate: Litigar
Lobbying: Cabildeo
Logrolling: Práctica legislativa que consiste en incluir en un mismo proyecto de ley temas de diversa ídole.
Loophole: Hueco Legal, escapatoria

Madisonian Model: Modelo Madisóico
Majority: Mayoría
Majority Floor Leader: Líder Mayoritario de Piso
Majority Leader of the House: Líder Mayoritario de la Casa
Majority Opinion: Opinión Mayoritaria
Majority Rule: Regla de Mayoría
Managed News: Noticias Manipuladas
Mandatory Retirement: Retiro Mandatorio
Matching Funds: Fondos Combinados
Material Incentive: Incentivo Material
Media Access: Acceso de Media
Media: Media
Merit System: Sistema de Mérito
Military-Industrial Complex: Complejo Industriomilitar
Minority Floor Leader: Líder Minoritario de Piso
Minority Leader of the House: Líder Minorial del Cuerpo Legislativo
Monetary Policy: Poliza Monetaria
Monopolistic Model: Modelo Monopólico
Monroe Doctrine: Doctrina Monroe
Moral Idealism: Idealismo Moral
Municipal Home Rule: Regla Municipal

Narrow Casting: Mensaje Dirigído
National Committee: Comité Nacional
National Convention: Convención Nacional

National Politics: Politica Nacional

National Security Council (NSC): Concilio de Seguridad Nacional

National Security Policy: Póliza de Seguridad Nacional

Natural Aristocracy: Aristocracia Natural

Natural Rights: Derechos Naturales

Necessaries: Necesidades

Negative Constituents: Constituyentes Negativos

New England Town: Pueblo de Nueva Inglaterra

New Federalism: Federalismo Nuevo

Nullification: Nulidad, Anulación

Office-Block, or Massachusetts, Ballot: Cuadro-Oficina, o Massachusetts, Voto

Office of Management and Budget (OMB): Oficina de Administración y Presupuesto

Oligarchy: Oligarquía

Ombudsman: Funcionario que representa al ciudadano ante el gobierno.

Open Primary: Primaria Abierta

Opinion: Opinión

Opinion Leader: Líder de Opinión

Opinion Poll: Encuesta, Conjunto de Opinión

Oral Arguments: Argumentos Orales

Oversight: Inadvertencia, Omisión

Paid-for-Political Announcement: Anuncios Politicos Pagados

Pardon: Perdón

Party-Column, or Indiana, Ballot: Partido-Columna, o Indiana, Voto

Party Identification: Identificación de Partido

Party Identifier: Identificador de Partido

Party-in-Electorate: Partido Electoral

Party-in-Government: Partido en Gobierno

Party Organization: Organización de Partido

Party Platform: Plataforma de Partido

Patronage: Patrocinio

Peer Group: Grupo de Contemporáeos

Pendleton Act (Civil Service Reform Act): Acta Pendleton (Acta de Reforma al Servicio Civil)

Personal Attack Rule: Regla de Ataque Personal

Petit Jury: Jurado Ordinario

Pluralism: Pluralismo

Plurality: Pluralidad

Pocket Veto: Veto de Bolsillo

Police Power: Poder Policiaco

Policy Trade-offs: Intercambio de Pólizas

Political Action Committee (PAC): Comité de Acción Política

Political Consultant: Consultante Político

Political Culture: Cultura Politica

Political Party: Partido Político

Political Question: Pregunta Politica

Political Realism: Realismo Político

Political Socialization: Socialización Politica

Political Tolerance: Tolerancia Política

Political Trust: Confianza Política

Politico: Político

Politics: Politica

Poll Tax: Impuesto sobre el sufragio

Poll Watcher: Observador de Encuesta

Popular Sovereignty: Soberanía Popular

Power: Poder

Precedent: Precedente

Preferred-Position Test: Prueba de Posición Preferida

Presidential Primary: Primaria Presidencial

President Pro Tempore: Presidente Provisoriamente

Press Secretary: Secretaría de Prensa

Prior Restraint: Restricción Anterior

Privileges and

Immunities: Privilégios e Imunidades

Privitization, or Contracting Out: Privatización

Property: Propiedad

Property Tax: Impuesto de Propiedad

Public Agenda: Agenda Pública

Public Debt Financing: Financiamiento de Deuda Pública

Public Debt, or National Debt: Deuda Pública o Nacional

Public Interest: Interes Público

Public Opinion: Opinión Pública

Purposive Incentive: Incentivo de Propósito

Ratification: Ratificación

Rational Ignorance Effect: Effecto de Ignorancia Racional

Reapportionment: Redistribución

Recall: Suspender

Recognition Power: Poder de Reconocimiento

Recycling: Reciclaje

Redistricting: Redistrictificación

Referendum: Referédum

Registration: Registración

Regressive Tax: Impuestos Regresivos

Relevance: Pertinencia

Remand: Reenviar

Representation: Representación

Representative Assembly: Asamblea Representativa

Representative Democracy: Democracia Representativa

Reprieve: Trequa, Suspensión

Republican Party: Partido Republicano

Republic: República

Resulting Powers: Poderes Resultados

Reverse: Cambiarse a lo contrario

Reverse Discrimination: Discriminación Reversiva

Rules Committee: Comité Regulador

Rule of Four: Regla de Cuatro

Run-off Primary: Primaria Residual

Safe Seat: Asiento Seguro
Sampling Error: Error de Encuesta
Secession: Secesión
Second Budget Resolution: Resolución Segunda Presupuestal
Second Continental Congress: Segundo Congreso Continental
Sectional Politics: Política Seccional
Segregation: Segregación
Selectperson: Persona Selecta
Select Committee: Comité Selecto
Senatorial Courtesy: Cortesia Senatorial
Seniority System: Sistema Señiorial
Separate-but-Equal Doctrine: Separados pero iguales
Separation of Powers: Separación de Poderes
Service Sector: Sector de Servicio
Sexual Harassment: Acosamiento Sexual
Sex Discrimination: Discriminacion Sexual
Slander: Difamación Oral, Calumnia
Sliding-Scale Test: Prueba Escalonada
Social Movement: Movimiento Social
Social Security: Seguridad Social
Socioeconomic Status: Estado Socioeconómico
Solidary Incentive: Incentivo de Solideridad
Solid South: Súr Sólido
Sound Bite: Mordida de Sonido
Soviet Bloc: Bloque Soviético
Speaker of the House: Vocero de la Casa
Spin: Girar/Giro
Spin Doctor: Doctor en Giro
Spin-off Party: Partido Estático
Spoils System: Sistema de Despojos
Spring Review: Revisión de Primavera
STARE DECISIS: El principio característico del ley comú por el cual los precedentes jurisprudenciales tienen fuerza obligatoria, no sólo entre las partes, sino tambien para casos sucesivos análogos.
Stability: Estabilidad
Standing Committee: Comité de Sostenimiento
State Central Committee: Comité Central del Estado
State: Estado
State of the Union Message: Mensaje Sobre el Estado de la Unión
Statutory Power: Poder Estatorial
Strategic Arms Limitation Treaty (SALT I): Tratado de Limitación de Armas Estratégicas
Subpoena: Orden de Testificación
Subsidy: Subsidio
Suffrage: Sufrágio
Sunset Legislation: Legislación Sunset
Superdelegate: Líder de partido o oficial elegido quien tiene el derecho de votar.
Supplemental Security Income (SSI): Ingresos de Seguridad Suplementaria
Supremacy Clause: Cláusula de Supremacia
Supremacy Doctrine: Doctrina de Supremacia
Symbolic Speech: Discurso Simbólico

Technical Assistance: Asistencia Técnica
Third Party: Tercer Partido
Third-party Candidate: Candidato de Tercer Partido
Ticket Splitting: División de Boletos
Totalitarian Regime: Régimen Totalitario
Township: Municipio
Town Manager System: Sistema de Manejador Municipal
Town Meeting: Junta Municipal
Tracking Poll: Seguimiento de Encuesta
Trial Court: Tribunal de Primera
Truman Doctrine: Doctrina Truman
Trustee: Depositario
Twelfth Amendment: Doceava Enmienda
Twenty-fifth Amendment: Veinticincoava Enmienda
Two-party System: Sistema de Dos Partidos

Unanimous Opinion: Opinión Unáime
Underground Economy: Economía Subterráea
Unicameral Legislature: Legislatura Unicameral
Unincorporated Area: Area no Incorporada
Unitary System: Sistema Unitario
Unit Rule: Regla de Unidad
Universal Suffrage: Sufragio Universal
U.S. Treasury Bond: Bono de la Tesoreria de E.U.A.

Veto Message: Comunicado de Veto
Voter Turnout: Renaimiento de Votantes

War Powers Act: Acta de Poderes de Guerra
Washington Community: Comunidad de Washington
Weberian Model: Modelo Weberiano
Whip: Látigo
Whistleblower: Privatización o Contratista
White House Office: Oficina de la Casa Blanca
White House Press Corps: Cuerpo de Prensa de la Casa Blanca
White Primary: Sufragio en Elección Primaria/Blancos Solamente
Writ of CERTIORARI: Prueba de certeza; orden emitida por el tribunal de apelaciones para que el tribunal inferior dé lugar a la apelación.
Writ of HABEAS CORPUS: Prueba de Evidencia Concreta
Writ of MANDAMUS: Un mandato por la corte para que un acto se lleve a cabo.

Yellow Journalism: Amarillismo Periodístico

We cannot foresee every situation that you are likely to confront during your career as a college student. This guide, however, will provide you with information about several topics that may interest you or problems that you may face as a college or university student.

YOU AND THE POLITICAL SYSTEM

Any person, providing that he or she fulfills certain minimal requirements, can participate in the American political system. Here we provide information on how you can register to vote; how to obtain information about political candidates, as well as events occurring in state legislatures and the U.S. Congress; and what to do if you wish to become a political candidate.

How Do I Register to Vote?

In most states, you must register before you go to the polls on election day.

Who May Register?   In general, you are eligible to vote if you are a citizen of the United States, will be eighteen years old on election day, and are a resident of the state in which you wish to register.

How Do I Register?   You may register to vote at the appropriate county office in your state, or you may complete a postcard registration form and return it to the correct official. To find out which county official or office you need to contact (whether the appropriate official or office is the county clerk, county auditor, or county board of elections, for example), check the information pages of your local telephone directory.

Registration forms are available throughout your county in places such as banks, union halls, city halls, savings and loans, utility offices, libraries, and political party headquarters. If you cannot register by one of the above methods, call your county clerk, political party headquarters, or the League of Women Voters.

For How Long Is My Registration Valid?   In general, your registration will be valid indefinitely if you vote at least once every four calendar years and if you remain in the county in which you are registered. These rules vary somewhat from state to state, because some states have regular "purges" of their voter registration lists and others do this less routinely.

When May I Register?   In states that require pre-voting registration, you must register no later than 5:00 P.M. on the tenth calendar day prior to the primary and general elections, or the eleventh calendar day prior to any other election in which you wish to vote. Postcard registration forms must be postmarked no later than fifteen days prior to the election in which you wish to vote.

If I Move, How Do I Record My Change of Address?   If you move within a county, write a letter to the appropriate county official. State the full name under which you are registered, your old address, your new address, and any other information to assist the county official in identifying you. The letter must include a signature from each affected voter. You may also record the change at the county offices in person, at the polls on election day, or by completing a postcard registration form. If you move to a different county, you must register as a new voter.

May I Vote Using an Absentee Ballot?   Yes. If you are properly registered and you expect to be out of your precinct on election day, or if you are ill or physically disabled, you may vote by sending in an absentee ballot. Incidentally, if you are voting via an absentee ballot from another state, check with a local notary public; a notary public's signature may be required for the out-of-state absentee ballot to be acceptable back home. If you are using an absentee ballot within your state, you can have it notarized at the county auditor's office during regular office hours.

You may request a ballot by mail not more than seventy days prior to an election. If the request is for a primary election ballot and you are in a state that requires party registration, you must include your party preference. Persons who are residents of health-care facilities or patients in hospitals may have a ballot delivered to them upon request to the registration official. Your completed absentee ballot must be postmarked no later than one day before the election. An absentee ballot must be returned, regardless of whether it is completed.

Where Do I Get Information about the Candidates?

Apart from paying attention to political and election news on television and radio, take the time to read a national newspaper (such as the *New York Times*) or a news magazine (such as *Time* or *Newsweek*). Also, watch C-Span or CNN on cable television, or contact interested groups. Local election headquarters for a candidate are probably the most direct source of information, but you should also contact the county or state party headquarters, look in your local public library for campaign material, or rely on nonpartisan activist groups, such the League of Women Voters, for unbiased information.

How Can I Find Out What's Going on in Congress or in My State Legislature?

To find out what is happening in Congress, you can call the offices of a U.S. senator or congressional representative from your state. To obtain information about events in your state legislature, you can call the legislature and leave a message for an individual state senator or representative, or you can ask for information about upcoming votes or events in the legislature. Most legislatures have a number with a recorded message describing the day's events in the legislature and a separate number with information on the status of bills, public hearings, and legislative agendas.

How Can I Become a Candidate?

If you want to be a candidate, contact one of the following offices:

- For county positions, contact the county clerk's office.
- For state and federal positions, contact the secretary of state's office.
- For municipal positions, contact the city clerk's office in your city.
- For school district positions, contact the secretary of the school district in your district.

Note that candidates must also file campaign finance disclosure reports. Federal candidates should write or call the Federal Election Commission, 999 E Street N.W., Washington, DC 20463 (800–424–9530). All other candidates should write or call the Campaign Finance Disclosure Commission for their state.

YOU AND THE JUSTICE SYSTEM

One of the essential "survival skills" in today's world is knowing what to do if you are a victim of a crime or have an encounter with the police. The following sections provide information on how to deal with such situations. Additionally, any American citizen has a chance of being called up for jury duty. If you should be called, you should know what jury duty entails.

What If I Am the Victim of a Crime?

If you are the victim of a crime, you should, of course, report the crime to the proper authorities. At a college or university, this may involve contacting the campus security office, the local municipal police, or both. Many campus security personnel have powers of arrest, as well as training comparable to local police, and they probably can respond more quickly than the local police if the crime occurred on campus. Help with legal services is available through many student governments or university administrations.

Beyond that, many states have crime-victim compensation programs that help victims with costs related to injuries resulting from criminal acts. In general, you may be eligible for this form of assistance if you have been physically or emotionally injured in a violent crime; if you are the victim of drunk driving, hit-and-run driving, reckless driving, or driving in which a car is used as a weapon; or if you are the survivor of a homicide victim. To qualify for such financial compensation, generally you must report the crime to local law-enforcement officers within a specified amount of time (for example, seventy-two hours), unless there is an explanation of why you could not do so; file an application with the program within a time limit (for example, two years) from the date of the crime; cooperate with the reasonable requests of law-enforcement officers in their investigation or prosecution of the crime; not have consented to, provoked, or incited the crime; and not have been assisting in, or committing, the criminal act causing your injuries. Payments generally will be made when all required information is received.

Within established limits, you may be compensated for medical or nursing care needed for crime injuries, crime-related counseling, wages lost due to crime injuries, loss of support (for dependents of deceased victims or victims who cannot work), funeral and burial costs for homicide victims, grief counseling for survivors of homicide victims, cleaning the homicide location in a home, or replacing clothing and bedding held as evidence by law-enforcement officials. Depending on particular state legislation, you may not be eligible under these programs to be compensated for property loss or repair, legal fees, travel, telephone bills, meals, or pain and suffering.

What Happens If I Have an Encounter with the Police?

Let's say that you are involved in a traffic accident, and the police start asking questions. Then again, you might be stopped as you leave a store at the mall and be charged with shoplifting. What kinds of things do you need to know to help you get through experiences such as these?

We will assume in what follows that you will be dealing with state law-enforcement and court authorities rather than federal officials, because by far the greatest number of violations of the law involve transgressions against state laws or local ordinances.

Criminal laws are passed to protect the public from conduct that is dangerous or offensive. When a criminal law is broken, the city, county, or state brings criminal charges against an individual. Criminal law is divided into two classifications: felonies and misdemeanors. A *felony* is a major crime (such as murder, robbery, or sexual assault) and may be punishable by an imprisonment for anywhere from one year to life (or death, for that matter, in states that provide for capital punishment), depending on the severity and classification of the felony. In contrast, a *misdemeanor* is a comparatively minor offense that is punishable by a fine, imprisonment for up to one year, or both.

Criminal Procedures. Most arrests are for misdemeanors, and in such situations, the arresting officers often release the suspect with a citation rather than taking him or her to the police station. The *citation* instructs the person to appear in court at some later date to respond to the charges. If, after arrest, the suspect is not released with a citation, he or she will be taken into custody. Within twenty-four hours, the suspect will be brought before a magistrate or a judge. At this time, the suspect is informed of the charges against him or her, and bail or conditions of release are set. In some serious cases, state law may prohibit a release on bail. Within a relatively short time (twenty days, for example), the accused person may receive a preliminary hearing before a district judge or a district associate judge. The purpose of this hearing is to determine if there is enough evidence ("probable cause") to continue to prosecute the case. If a preliminary hearing is held and the court finds probable cause, the defendant will be held for further proceedings.

Depending on state law or other factors, the case may be presented to a grand jury. A *grand jury* is a panel consisting of six to twenty-three citizens who decide whether to return an indictment against the defendant. If a specified number of the grand jurors feel that there is enough evidence to bring the accused person to trial, they *indict* the defendant, which means that the case is presented to the court for filing. Few criminal cases are heard by grand juries. Usually, the county attorney will file an *information,* which is a statement of the charges and the evidence in the case. After the indictment or the filing of an information, the defendant appears before a judge or magistrate for arraignment, generally within forty-five days of the preliminary hearing. At the arraignment, the defendant hears the charges and enters a plea, which is usually either "guilty" or "not guilty." The judge will either dismiss the case, accept the not guilty plea, or accept the guilty plea. If the guilty plea is accepted, the judge will announce the sentence, which may be a fine, confinement in a jail or prison, probation, and/or other treatment. Sometimes, if a judge is not convinced that a defendant is guilty, he or she may require that a trial be held.

If the defendant pleads not guilty, a trial date is set. The defendant has the right to a trial by jury. If a jury is not requested, a *bench trial* is scheduled. In a bench trial, the judge will hear the evidence and render a verdict. If a jury is requested, the jury will hear and weigh the evidence and render a verdict. If the jury is not convinced beyond a reasonable doubt of the defendant's guilt, a not guilty verdict must be returned. In a criminal trial, the jurors' decision as to whether the defendant is guilty or not guilty must be unanimous. If the jury cannot reach a unanimous verdict, the judge will declare a *mistrial.* The state then will decide whether to retry the case before another jury or to dismiss the charges. If the jury returns a guilty verdict, a sentencing date will be set. The judge will also order a complete investigation of the defendant's background and the circumstances of the case.

After weighing the information from the investigation, the judge at a sentencing hearing may sentence the defendant to a fine, confinement in a jail or prison, probation, other form of special correctional treatment, or a combination of these punishments. If the sentence is a fine or confinement, the judge may suspend the sentence. If the sentence is suspended, the fine or confinement does not have to be paid or served, and the defendant is placed on probation. If the defendant fails to follow the rules and conditions of the probation, it may be revoked and the original sentence reinstated.

Traffic Violations. For traffic-related matters, a somewhat different pattern is followed. Fines and costs are listed on tickets when they are issued for minor violations, such as parking and most moving violations (speeding violations, for example). These costs are usually paid by mail but can be paid at the traffic clerk's or district clerk's office. Usually, a court appearance is not required for a minor violation. Some jurisdictions, though, may require you to go through a "shock" session before a judge. If damages from an accident exceed a specified amount, a court appearance may be required. More serious traffic violations—such as reckless driving, operating a motor vehicle while intoxicated, or driving when your license is suspended—require a court appearance before a judge or magistrate.

What If I Am Called for Jury Duty?

Eligibility to serve on a jury is a basic obligation of citizenship. In general, any registered voter (and, in many locations, people who are registered as owning motor vehicles or whose names appear on other publicly available lists) may be called up periodically (the frequency varies) to show up at the county courthouse for possible selection to serve on a jury. Jurors may be excused from service for reasons of serious hardship, inconvenience, or public necessity. The United States Supreme Court has stated that, during the jury-selection process, potential jurors may not be excluded because of their race or gender. In general, to "qualify" for jury duty, you must be at least eighteen years old, be a citizen of the United States, and be able to understand spoken and written English (those with hearing disabilities will be accommodated).

In many states, there are few, if any, blanket exemptions from jury duty for students or others whose lives or jobs might be disrupted by having to take the time to sit on a jury. It may be possible, however, to ask that your period of eligibility for jury duty be delayed to a later date. Whether you will be allowed to delay jury duty often depends on the cooperation of the local judge and, possibly, of the court clerks. One situation that normally would excuse you from jury duty is if you were solely responsible for the daily care of a permanently disabled person living in your own household.

Although many trials may last no more than one or two days and many potential juries are dissolved before they actually meet (because defendants plea-bargain for a lesser sentence from the judge), you will have no control over the length of time you must serve on the jury. It is quite possible that you might be required to participate for a week or longer, during which time you may not be permitted to watch or listen to certain broadcasted news reports or to read certain printed news articles. There is no guarantee that you will not be chosen on more than one occasion to serve on a jury.

If you or any member of your immediate family has been a party to a lawsuit involving the principal persons involved in the trial or has had any other significant interaction with those principals or the law-enforcement officers participating in the case, or if you feel that physical or mental circumstances would make it difficult for you to make an informed and impartial decision, then you may be excused by the judge.

YOU AND YOUR PERSONAL PROTECTION

Being a victim of crimes against persons is not inevitable, but these crimes are certainly commonplace. An important survival skill today is knowing what you can do to avoid becoming a victim of crime. You should also be aware of what steps you can take if you are the victim of a sexual assault or battering.

Suggestions for Guaranteeing Your Personal Safety

Anticrime experts have a number of tips that can help you avoid being a victim. Here are some of them:

1. Always park your car near a light and as close to a gate or to a security booth as you can. When possible, use valet parking. Only give the valet your ignition key. Otherwise, a simple wax impression of your home keys can easily be made by an enterprising valet.

2. Never stop on the street to look at your watch if someone asks the time. While you are looking at your watch, you are extremely vulnerable. Simply approximate the time, and give the person the approximate time while you continue walking.

3. If you are traveling or simply worried about a robbery at your house or hotel room, do the following: Leave a $20 bill about four feet inside the entry door. Few criminals will walk past that money without pocketing it. Thus, when you return and open the door, if you notice that the $20 bill has disappeared, you should immediately close the door and not return until you are with a police officer or a security guard.

4. According to many self-defense experts and police personnel, meekness often invites aggression. An alternative to meekness is "cerebral self-defense." This is the state of being mentally prepared for trouble. One of the first things to do when accosted by a criminal is to use "choice speech." Most attackers, if made to speak, will become somewhat distracted. The attacker's talking buys you time either to make an escape or to signal for help. In some situations, it even changes the attacker's mind. Some examples of choice speech are "You don't want to hurt me. After all, I hate the same people you do," or "I'll bet you were probably abused as a child."*

What Can I Do If I Am the Victim of a Sexual Assault or Battering?

Many cities, counties, and towns have assault care shelters and telephone hotlines for reporting serious crises that happen to you in your relationships. Local facilities often provide some or all of the following services: a twenty-four-hour crisis telephone line for listening, support, information, and advocacy; a shelter to provide safe, temporary housing for women and their children; children's programs for counseling, advocacy, outings, and therapeutic play groups; free, short-term individual counseling provided to adult survivors of child sexual abuse, rape, and battering; support groups for battered women or victims of sexual assault, with child care; and education programs for community groups and public agencies.

You may be a victim of battering if your partner hits, kicks, or shoves you; uses his or her temper, jealous rages, or anger to frighten you; isolates you from your social support system; calls you names, puts you down, or plays mind games; threatens to commit suicide; threatens to report you to the authorities; controls access to money, food, and necessities; or forces sex on you against your will.

Many colleges and universities have affirmative action offices, sexual-harassment offices, or both that you may contact if these or related events occur to you while you are a student. Particular rules and guidelines may apply in your institution. To find out about those rules, contact your student

---

*These suggestions come from Tony Blauer, a self-defense instructor in Montreal, as reported in *Forbes*, March 14, 1994, p. 122.

government, the campus affirmative action office, or the campus women's center. Some universities and colleges have a sexual-harassment hotline.

Protecting Yourself on the Electronic Superhighway

To protect yourself against huge phone bills and the ability of others to get into your electronic mail, (*E-mail*), it is important that you choose a password that cannot be easily discovered by others. Here are some rules for choosing a password and keeping your password secret:

- Do not use any words that are in any dictionary.
- Use at least eight characters.
- Do not use obvious passwords, such as sports teams or your birthday.
- Mix up numbers, special characters, and letters. Mix upper and lower case.
- Never write your password anyplace where people can find it.
- Change passwords frequently.
- Do not "lend" your password to anyone else.
- Do not tell your password to someone over the phone.

YOU AND YOUR EMPLOYER

Finding and keeping a job is clearly important to your future well-being. In the past, an employer could hire and fire workers with virtually no legal restrictions. Today, many laws restrict the employer's discretion in hiring and firing employees and ensure that employees are treated more fairly. These laws do not guarantee fairness in the workplace, but they do prevent certain specific forms of unfairness.

Legislation Prohibiting Employment Discrimination

Until the early 1960s, private employers were free to discriminate openly against minorities, women, or any other group. Title VII of the Civil Rights Act of 1964 prohibited employment discrimination based on race, color, national origin, religion, or gender. The Equal Employment Opportunity Commission (EEOC) was created to help resolve or prosecute discrimination cases for employees. Two other federal acts—the Age Discrimination in Employment Act of 1967 and the Americans with Disabilities Act of 1990—prohibited employment discrimination on the basis of age and disability, respectively.

These laws prohibit employment discrimination at any stage of employment. A business may not discriminate on the basis of race, color, national origin, religion, gender, age, or disability in hiring new employees, in setting pay scales, in granting promotions, or in firing employees. The law also prohibits discrimination regarding the "terms and conditions of employment." This means that an employer cannot expect a person who falls into one of the categories, or groups, protected by the laws mentioned above to work longer hours or suffer less desirable working conditions than other employees. Indeed, employers must be very careful about giving preferential treatment to the members of any protected class. Sexual or racial harassment is a prohibited act, as is discrimination on the basis of pregnancy. An employer cannot refuse to hire a pregnant woman, fire her because of her pregnancy, or force her to take maternity leave. Pregnancy must be treated the same as any other temporary disability. For example, pregnancy must be covered under health insurance if other temporary disabilities are covered.

Under the Family and Medical Leave Act of 1993, employers with fifty or more workers must provide up to twelve weeks of leave during any twelve-month period to employees for family or medical reasons, which include caring for a newborn baby. During the leave, the employer must continue the worker's health-care coverage and guarantee employment in the same position or a comparable position when the employee returns to work.

Intentional and Unintentional Discrimination

The initial focus of Title VII of the Civil Rights Act of 1964 was on intentional discrimination against the classes of employees designated by the act. As the law evolved, courts began to recognize the presence of discriminatory practices (such as certain educational requirements) that had a discriminatory effect, or *disparate impact*. For example, suppose that a fire department had a rule requiring all job applicants to be at least 6 feet tall and weigh at least 175 pounds. Although this rule is applied equally to everyone, the requirements exclude a disproportionate number of women who might want to become firefighters. This rule has a disparate impact.

An employer may justify a rule or policy having a discriminatory impact by claiming that the rule or policy is a *business necessity*. If the fire department were sued for discriminating against women, for example, the fire department might respond that firefighters need to be strong, and therefore the rule is necessary to perform the job. The plaintiff could rebut (counter) this claim by showing that an alternative test of strength or other measure—one that does not have a discriminatory impact—could serve the fire department's needs. An employer may also justify a rule by claiming that the rule is a *bona fide occupational qualification* (BFOQ). The BFOQ exception is very limited, however, and it generally applies only in obvious situations, such as those involving fashion models or actors.

Affirmative Action Programs

To make up for past discriminatory practices against certain groups, many employers have instituted *affirmative action programs*. For such a program to be lawful, the employer must show a reason, or need, for affirmative action. Such a reason might be that the company has an extremely low number of minority employees relative to the number of qualified workers in the community. Any affirmative action program must be temporary and limited to correcting the need to create a balanced workforce. Affirmative action programs cannot unduly restrict the opportunities of groups, such as white males, that are not protected under employment-discrimination laws. Courts have upheld affirmative action programs in hiring but have been very reluctant to accept affirmative action programs that result in the firing of white workers from their positions.

What Can I Do If I Am a Victim of Employment Discrimination?

If you believe that you have suffered unlawful discrimination, you should first file a claim with your state government human rights agency, which will investigate and pursue your case if it is deemed meritorious. If you receive no relief at the state level, you can file a claim with the EEOC. You must file a claim with the EEOC within 180 days of suffering the discrimination. The EEOC will try to reach a voluntary settlement with your employer that protects your interests. If no settlement can be reached, the EEOC will determine whether there is reasonable cause to suspect unlawful discrimination. If it finds reasonable cause, the EEOC will take the case to court for you. If it does not find reasonable cause, the EEOC will give you a "right-to-sue" letter, and you can initiate a lawsuit against your employer for illegal employment discrimination. You must file your lawsuit within 90 days of obtaining a right-to-sue letter. If your claim is successful, you may be awarded back pay (wages for up to two years), compensatory damages, attorneys' fees, and job reinstatement.

Other Laws Protecting Employees

In addition to the discrimination laws discussed above, a number of statutes provide a variety of protections to workers. Many of these laws protect the economic and safety interests of workers and are summarized below.

Fair Labor Standards Act. The Fair Labor Standards Act (FLSA) of 1938 governs the hours and wages of work. The coverage of the FLSA is very broad and reaches virtually every employer in the country. This law establishes a minimum wage, which is now set at $4.25 per hour. Some states have a higher minimum wage. Employers must pay the applicable minimum-wage rate for the first forty hours worked in a week. If you work more than forty hours a week, you are entitled to one-and-one-half times your regular wage rate (usually called "overtime" wages) for the hours worked beyond the first forty.

Not every worker is protected by the FLSA. For example, agricultural workers, many salespeople, and professional, managerial, and supervisory employees are exempted from the law. The FLSA also has child-labor provisions that generally prevent the employment of persons younger than fourteen years of age and that restrict the terms of employment of persons between the ages of fourteen and seventeen.

Worker Safety. The Occupational Safety and Health Act of 1970 was enacted to help ensure safe and healthful working conditions on the job. Numerous standards have been set under this law, including limits on exposures to harmful chemicals and various workplace standards to avert accidents. In addition, the law obligates employers to keep the workplace free of recognized hazards to health, even in the absence of a standard. Employees can file complaints about unsafe conditions and cannot be required to work when they have reason to fear that their safety is in jeopardy.

When an on-the-job accident does occur, the employee may apply for *workers' compensation.* Each state has a workers' compensation system that pays benefits for accidents or diseases that arise out of or during the course of normal employment. A worker may recover even if his or her own negligence contributed to the injury, but there is no recovery for intentionally self-inflicted harms. The injured worker may not file suit against the employer but may be able to bring a case against a manufacturer of the product that caused the injury. Some workers have been afraid to file for compensation, lest they be fired. In most states, a person cannot be discharged in retaliation for filing a legitimate workers' compensation claim.

Unemployment Compensation.   The United States has an unemployment compensation system, in which employers pay taxes into a fund, and the proceeds are paid out to workers who qualify for such compensation. Each state has authority to set rules determining which workers are entitled to unemployment benefits. Some typical state requirements are as follows:

The employee must have been fired without good cause or have quit the job with good cause.

The employee must be unemployed for some minimum amount of time, such as a week.

The employee must have worked on a reasonably regular basis prior to unemployment.

The employee must register with a state-operated employment agency, seek a new job, and accept any reasonably suitable new job offer.

The employee must be able to work and not be a striker.

If the worker qualifies for unemployment compensation, he or she will receive regular, but temporary, benefits based on a formula. The formula is generally based on a fraction of the worker's average wages during a recent period up to a certain maximum. Benefits are available for up to twenty-six weeks, and this time period has been extended during times of serious unemployment. This income may be taxable.

Employee Privacy

Employee privacy rights are a major new concern of the law. In general, employees have little on-the-job privacy protection under the common law. Some statutes have been passed to provide a measure of privacy protection to workers, but this protection is still quite limited.

Lie Detector Tests.   In most occupations, you cannot be forced to take a lie detector test and therefore cannot be fired for refusing to take the test. There are some exceptions when such testing is allowed. Workers holding certain sensitive jobs, such as security personnel, may be subjected to lie detector testing. An employer may also force an employee to take such a test if the company is conducting an ongoing investigation of losses and has a reasonable suspicion that the employee was involved in the losses.

Even if you are lawfully subject to testing, federal law contains further protections. You cannot be asked needlessly intrusive or degrading questions. You must be informed of the purpose of the testing, and disclosure of the test results is limited to those who have a need to know them. The testing must follow accepted standards for accuracy.

Drug Testing.   Recent years have seen a significant increase in the use of employer drug testing, as the costs to employers of drug abuse are increasingly recognized. With the exception of a few states, such drug tests are legal. Although drug tests plainly intrude upon your privacy, the tests are generally held to be a reasonable exercise of the employer's rights. Courts may require that steps be taken to ensure the tests' accuracy and that the privacy invasion resulting from drug testing be no greater than necessary.

Employee Monitoring.   With the advance of new technologies, employers are increasingly able to monitor the work of their employees. Companies may monitor your telephone calls or your computer work. Closed-circuit monitors may be installed in the workplace to observe your work habits. Like drug testing, such monitoring is considered to be a private matter between employer and employee and is generally legal. A few states have laws restricting such monitoring in certain areas, such as nonwork areas.

Personnel Records.   Federal law provides no right for workers to see their personnel records, though a number of states grant such a right, as do many employers' voluntary policies. Moreover, an employer may lawfully disclose the contents of your personnel file to individuals either inside or outside the company. If the revealed information is false, you may sue for *defamation.*

Glossary

ACID RAIN Rain that has picked up pollutants, usually sulfur dioxides, from industrial areas of the earth that are often hundreds of miles distant from where the rain falls.

ACQUISITIVE MODEL A model of bureaucracy that views top-level bureaucrats as seeking constantly to expand the size of their budgets and the staffs of their departments or agencies so as to gain greater power and influence in the public sector.

ACTIONABLE Furnishing grounds for a lawsuit. Actionable words, for example, in the law of libel are such words that naturally imply damage to the individual in question.

ACTION-REACTION SYNDROME For every action on the part of government, there is a reaction on the part of the affected public. Then the government attempts to counter the reaction with another action, which starts the cycle all over again.

ACTUAL MALICE Actual desire and intent to see another suffer by one's actions. Actual malice involves a condition of mind that prompts a person to do a wrongful act willfully (that is, on purpose) to the injury of another, or to do intentionally a wrongful act toward another without justification or excuse. Actual malice in libel cases generally consists of intentionally publishing, without justifiable cause, any written or printed matter that is injurious to the character of another.

ADMINISTRATIVE AGENCY An agency that forms part of the executive branch, an independent regulatory agency, or an independent agency (for example, the Federal Trade Commission, the Securities and Exchange Commission, and the Federal Communications Commission). State and local governments also have administrative agencies.

ADVICE AND CONSENT The power vested in the U.S. Senate by the Constitution (Article II, Section 2) to give its advice and consent to the president concerning treaties and presidential appointments.

AFFIRMATIVE ACTION A policy in job hiring that gives special consideration or compensatory treatment to traditionally disadvantaged groups in an effort to overcome present effects of past discrimination.

AFFIRM To declare that a judgment is valid and must stand.

AGENDA SETTING Determining which public policy questions will be debated or considered by Congress.

AID TO FAMILIES WITH DEPENDENT CHILDREN (AFDC) A state-administered program that furnishes assistance for families in which dependent children do not have the financial support of the father, owing to the father's desertion, disability, or death. The program is financed partially by federal grants.

AMICUS CURIAE BRIEF Latin for "friend of the court"; refers here to a brief filed by a third party (a party not directly involved in the litigation) who has an interest in the outcome of the case. These briefs are documents filed with the court that contain legal arguments supporting a particular desired outcome in a case.

ANARCHY The condition of having no government and no laws. Each member of the society governs himself or herself.

ANTI-FEDERALISTS Those who opposed the adoption of the Constitution because of its centralist tendencies and attacked the failure of the Constitution's framers to include a bill of rights.

APPELLATE COURT A court having jurisdiction to review cases and issues that were originally tried in lower courts.

APPOINTMENT POWER The authority vested in the president to fill a government office or position. Positions filled by presidential appointment include those in the executive branch, the federal judiciary, commissioned officers in the armed forces, and members of the independent regulatory commissions.

APPROPRIATION The passage, by Congress, of a spending bill, specifying the amount of authorized funds that actually will be allocated for an agency's use.

ARISTOCRACY Rule by the best suited, through virtue, talent, or education; in later usage, rule by the upper class.

ATTENTIVE PUBLIC That portion of the general public that pays attention to foreign policy issues.

AUSTRALIAN BALLOT A secret ballot prepared, distributed, and tabulated by government officials at public expense. Since 1888, all states have used the Australian ballot rather than an open, public ballot.

AUTHORITY The features of a leader or an institution that compel obedience, usually because of ascribed legitimacy. For most societies, government is the ultimate authority in the allocation of values.

AUTHORIZATION A formal declaration by a legislative committee that a certain amount of funding may be available to an agency. Some authorizations terminate in a year; others are renewable automatically without further congressional authorization.

BAD-TENDENCY RULE A rule stating that speech or other First Amendment freedoms may be curtailed if there is a possibility that such expression might lead to some "evil."

"BEAUTY CONTEST" A presidential primary in which contending candidates compete for popular votes but the results have little or no impact on the selection of delegates to the national convention, which is made by the party elite.

BICAMERALISM The division of a legislature into two separate assemblies.

BICAMERAL LEGISLATURE A legislature made up of two chambers, or parts. The U.S. Congress, composed of the House of Representatives and the Senate, is a bicameral legislature.

BILL OF RIGHTS The first ten amendments to the U.S. Constitution. They contain a listing of the freedoms that a person enjoys and that cannot be infringed upon by the government, such as the freedoms of speech, press, and religion.

BLANKET PRIMARY A primary in which all candidates' names are printed on the same ballot, regardless of party affiliation. The voter may vote for candidates of more than one party.

BLOCK GRANTS Federal programs that provide funding to the state and local governments for general functional areas, such as criminal justice or mental-health programs.

BUREAUCRACY A large organization that is structured hierarchically to carry out specific functions.

BUSING The transportation of public school students from areas where they live to schools in other areas to eliminate school segregation based on residential patterns.

CABINET An advisory group selected by the president to aid in making decisions. The cabinet presently numbers thirteen department secretaries and the attorney general. Depending on the president, the cabinet may be highly influential or relatively insignificant in its advisory role.

CABINET DEPARTMENT One of the fourteen departments of the executive branch (State, Treasury, Defense, Justice, Interior, Agriculture, Commerce, Labor, Health and Human Services, Housing and Urban Development, Education, Energy, Transportation, and Veterans Affairs).

CADRE The nucleus of political party activists carrying out the major functions of American political parties.

CANVASSING BOARD An official group at the county, city, or state level that receives vote counts from every precinct in the area, tabulates the figures, and sends them to the state canvassing authority, which certifies the winners.

CAPTURE The act of gaining direct or indirect control over agency personnel and decision makers by the industry that is being regulated.

CASEWORK Personal work for constituents by members of Congress.

CATEGORICAL GRANTS-IN-AID Federal grants-in-aid to states or local governments that are for very specific programs or projects.

CAUCUS A closed meeting of party leaders to select party candidates or to decide on policy; also, a meeting of party members designed to select candidates and propose policies.

CHALLENGE An allegation by a poll watcher that a potential voter is unqualified to vote or that a vote is invalid; designed to prevent fraud in elections.

CHECKS AND BALANCES A major principle of the American governmental system whereby each branch of the government exercises a check on the actions of the others.

CHIEF DIPLOMAT The role of the president in recognizing foreign governments, making treaties, and making executive agreements.

CHIEF EXECUTIVE The role of the president as head of the executive branch of the government.

CHIEF LEGISLATOR The role of the president in influencing the making of laws.

CHIEF OF STAFF The person who is named to direct the White House Office and advise the president.

CHIEF OF STATE The role of the president as ceremonial head of the government.

CIVIL LAW The law regulating conduct between private persons over noncriminal matters. Under civil law, the government provides the forum for the settlement of disputes between private parties in such matters as contracts, domestic relations, and business relations.

CIVIL LIBERTIES Those personal freedoms that are protected for all individuals and generally that deal with individual freedom. Civil liberties typically involve restraining the government's actions against individuals.

CIVIL RIGHTS Those powers or privileges that are guaranteed to individuals or protected groups and that are protected from arbitrary removal by government or by individuals.

CIVIL SERVICE A collective term for the body of employees working for the government. Generally, civil service is understood to apply to all those who gain government employment through a merit system.

CIVIL SERVICE COMMISSION The initial central personnel agency of the national government; created in 1883.

CLASS-ACTION SUIT A lawsuit filed by an individual seeking damages for "all persons similarly situated."

CLASS POLITICS Political preferences based on income level, social status, or both.

CLEAR AND PRESENT DANGER TEST The test proposed by Justice Holmes for determining when government may restrict free speech. Restrictions are permissible, he argued, only when speech provokes a "clear and present danger" to the public order.

CLIMATE CONTROL The use of public relations techniques to create favorable public opinion toward an interest group, industry, or corporation.

CLOSED PRIMARY The most widely used primary, in which voters may participate only in the primary of the party with which they are registered.

CLOTURE A method invoked to close off debate and to bring the matter under consideration to a vote in the Senate.

COATTAIL EFFECT The influence of a popular or unpopular candidate on the electoral success or failure of other candidates on the same party ticket. The effect is increased by the party-column ballot, which encourages straight-ticket voting.

COLD WAR The ideological, political, and economic impasse that existed between the United States and the Soviet Union following World War II.

COMMANDER IN CHIEF The role of the president as supreme commander of the military forces of the United States and of the state national guard units when they are called into federal service.

COMMERCE CLAUSE The section of the Constitution in which Congress is given the power to regulate trade among the states and with foreign countries.

COMMERCIAL SPEECH Advertising statements, which have increasingly been given First Amendment protection.

COMMON LAW Judge-made law that originated in England from decisions shaped according to prevailing customs. Decisions were applied to similar situations and thus gradually became common to the nation. Common law forms the basis of legal procedures in the United States.

COMPARABLE WORTH The idea that compensation should be based on the worth of the job to an employer and that factors unrelated to the worth of a job, such as the sex of the employee, should not affect compensation. Supporters of the comparable-worth doctrine argue that women should be entitled to comparable wages for doing work that is different from, but of comparable worth and value to, work done by higher-paid men.

COMPLIANCE Accepting and carrying out authorities' decisions.

CONCURRENT MAJORITY A principle advanced by John C. Calhoun whereby democratic decisions could be made only with the concurrence of all segments of society affected by the decision. Without their concurrence, a decision should not be binding on those whose interests it violates.

CONCURRENT POWERS Powers held jointly by the national and state governments.

CONCURRING OPINION A separate opinion, prepared by a judge who supports the decision of the majority of the court but who wants to make or clarify a particular point or to voice disapproval of the grounds on which the decision was made.

CONFEDERAL SYSTEM A system of government consisting of a league of independent states, each having essentially sovereign powers. The central government created by such a league has only limited powers over the states.

CONFEDERATION A political system in which states or regional governments retain ultimate authority except for those powers they expressly delegate to a central government. A voluntary association of independent states, in which the member states agree to limited restraints on their freedom of action.

CONFERENCE COMMITTEE A special joint committee appointed to reconcile differences when bills pass the two chambers of Congress in different forms.

CONSENSUS General agreement among the citizenry on an issue.

CONSENT OF THE PEOPLE The idea that governments and laws derive their legitimacy from the consent of the governed.

CONSERVATISM A set of beliefs that includes a limited role for the national government in helping individuals, support for traditional values and lifestyles, and a cautious response to change.

CONSERVATIVE COALITION An alliance of Republicans and southern Democrats that can form in the House or the Senate to oppose liberal legislation and support conservative legislation.

CONSTANT DOLLARS Dollars corrected for inflation; dollars expressed in terms of purchasing power for a given year.

CONSTITUTIONAL POWER A power vested in the president by Article II of the Constitution.

CONTAINMENT A U.S. diplomatic policy adopted by the Truman administration to "build situations of strength" around the globe to contain communist power within its existing boundaries.

CONTINUING RESOLUTION A temporary law that Congress passes when an appropriations bill has not been decided by the beginning of the new fiscal year on October 1.

COOPERATIVE FEDERALISM The theory that the states and the national government should cooperate in solving problems.

CORRUPT PRACTICES ACTS A series of acts passed by Congress in an attempt to limit and regulate the size and sources of contributions and expenditures in political campaigns.

COUNCIL OF ECONOMIC ADVISERS (CEA) A staff agency in the Executive Office of the President that advises the president on measures to maintain stability in the nation's economy; established in 1946.

CREDENTIALS COMMITTEE A committee used by political parties at their national conventions to determine which delegates may participate. The committee inspects the claim of each prospective delegate to be seated as a legitimate representative of his or her state.

CRIMINAL LAW The law that defines crimes and provides punishment for violations. In criminal cases, the government is the prosecutor, because crimes are against the public order.

DE FACTO SEGREGATION Racial segregation that occurs not as a result of laws but because of past social and economic conditions and residential patterns.

DEFAMATION OF CHARACTER Wrongfully hurting a person's good reputation. The law has imposed a general duty on all persons to refrain from making false, defamatory statements about others.

DE JURE SEGREGATION Racial segregation that occurs because of laws or administrative decisions by public agencies.

DEMOCRACY A system of government in which ultimate

political authority is vested in the people. Derived from the Greek words *demos* ("the people") and *kratos* ("authority").

DEMOCRATIC PARTY   One of the two major American political parties evolving out of the Democratic (Jeffersonian) Republican group supporting Thomas Jefferson.

DIPLOMACY   The total process by which states carry on political relations with each other; settling conflicts among nations by peaceful means.

DIRECT DEMOCRACY   A system of government in which political decisions are made by the people directly, rather than by their elected representatives; probably possible only in small political communities.

DIRECT PRIMARY   An intraparty election in which the voters select the candidates who will run on a party's ticket in the subsequent general election.

DIRECT TECHNIQUE   An interest group activity that involves interaction with government officials to further the group's goals.

DISCHARGE PETITION   A procedure by which a bill in the House of Representatives may be forced out of a committee (discharged) that has refused to report it for consideration by the House. The discharge petition must be signed by an absolute majority (218) of representatives and is used only on rare occasions.

DISSENTING OPINION   A separate opinion in which a judge dissents from the conclusion reached by the majority of the court and expounds his or her own views about the case.

DIVISIVE OPINION   Public opinion that is polarized between two quite different positions.

DOMESTIC POLICY   Those public plans or courses of action that concern issues of national importance, such as poverty, crime, and the environment, in contrast to economic policies that normally relate only to issues of inflation, interest rates, and unemployment.

DUAL CITIZENSHIP   The condition of being a citizen of two sovereign political units; being a citizen of both a state and the nation.

DUAL FEDERALISM   A system of government in which the states and the national government each remain supreme within their own spheres. The doctrine looks on nation and state as coequal sovereign powers. It holds that acts of states within their reserved powers could be legitimate limitations on the powers of the national government.

DÉTENTE   A French word meaning the relaxation of tension. The term characterizes U.S.–Soviet policy as it developed under President Richard Nixon and Secretary of State Henry Kissinger. Détente stresses direct cooperative dealings with Cold War rivals but avoids ideological accommodation.

ECONOMIC AID   Assistance to other nations in the form of grants, loans, or credits to buy the assisting nation's products.

ECONOMIC REGULATION   The regulation of business practices by government agencies.

ELASTIC CLAUSE, OR NECESSARY AND PROPER CLAUSE   The clause in Article I, Section 8, that grants Congress the power to do whatever is necessary to execute its specifically delegated powers.

ELECTOR   A person on the partisan slate that is selected early in the presidential election year according to state laws and the applicable political party apparatus. Electors cast ballots for president and vice president. The number of electors in each state is equal to that state's number of representatives in both houses of Congress.

ELECTORAL COLLEGE   A group of persons called electors who are selected by the voters in each state. This group officially elects the president and the vice president of the United States. The number of electors in each state is equal to the number of each state's representatives in both houses of Congress.

ELITE   An upper socioeconomic class that controls political and economic affairs.

ELITE THEORY   A perspective holding that society is ruled by a small number of people who exercise power in their self-interest.

EMERGENCY POWER   An inherent power exercised by the president during a period of national crisis, particularly in foreign affairs.

ENUMERATED POWER   A power specifically granted to the national government by the Constitution. The first seventeen clauses of Article I, Section 8, specify most of the enumerated powers of Congress.

ENVIRONMENTAL IMPACT STATEMENT (EIS)   As a requirement mandated by the National Environmental Policy Act, a report that must show the costs and benefits of major federal actions that could significantly affect the quality of the environment.

EQUALITY   A concept that all people are of equal worth.

EQUALIZATION   A method for adjusting the amount of money that a state must put up to receive federal funds. The formula used takes into account the wealth of the state or its ability to tax its citizens.

EQUAL EMPLOYMENT OPPORTUNITY COMMISSION (EEOC)   A commission established by the 1964 Civil Rights Act to (1) end discrimination based on race, color, religion, gender, or national origin in conditions of employment and (2) promote voluntary action programs by employers, unions, and community organizations to foster equal job opportunities.

ERA OF GOOD FEELING   The years from 1817 to 1825, when James Monroe was president and there was, in effect, no political opposition.

ERA OF PERSONAL POLITICS   An era when attention centered on the character of individual candidates rather than on party identification.

ESTABLISHMENT CLAUSE   The part of the First Amendment prohibiting the establishment of a church officially supported by the national government. It is applied to questions of state and local government aid to religious organizations and schools, questions of the legality of allowing or requiring school prayers, and questions of the teaching of evolution versus fundamentalist theories of creation.

EUTHANASIA Killing incurably ill people for reasons of mercy.

EXCLUSIONARY RULE A policy forbidding the admission at trial of illegally seized evidence.

EXECUTIVE AGREEMENT An international agreement made by the president, without senatorial ratification, with the head of a foreign state.

EXECUTIVE BUDGET The budget prepared by the president and submitted to Congress.

EXECUTIVE OFFICE OF THE PRESIDENT (EOP) Established by President Franklin Roosevelt by executive order under the Reorganization Act of 1939, the EOP currently consists of ten staff agencies that assist the president in carrying out major duties.

EXECUTIVE ORDER A rule or regulation issued by the president that has the effect of law. Executive orders can implement and give administrative effect to provisions in the Constitution, to treaties, and to statutes.

EXECUTIVE PRIVILEGE The right of executive officials to refuse to appear before, or to withhold information from, a legislative committee. Executive privilege is enjoyed by the president and by those executive officials accorded that right by the president.

EXPRESSED POWER A constitutional or statutory power of the president, which is expressly written into the Constitution or into congressional law.

EXTRADITE To surrender an accused or convicted criminal to the authorities of the state from which he or she has fled; to return a fugitive criminal to the jurisdiction of the accusing state.

FACTION A group or bloc in a legislature or a political party acting together in pursuit of some special interest or position.

FAIRNESS DOCTRINE A Federal Communications Commission regulation affecting broadcasting media, which required that fair or equal opportunity be given to legitimate opposing political groups or individuals to broadcast their views.

FALL REVIEW The time every year when, after receiving formal federal agency requests for funding for the next fiscal year, the Office of Management and Budget reviews the requests, makes changes, and submits its recommendations to the president.

FEDERAL MANDATE A requirement in federal legislation that forces states and municipalities to comply with certain rules.

FEDERAL OPEN MARKET COMMITTEE (FOMC) The most important body within the Federal Reserve System. The FOMC decides how monetary policy should be carried out by the Federal Reserve.

FEDERAL REGISTER A publication of the executive branch of the U.S. government that prints executive orders, rules, and regulations.

FEDERAL SYSTEM A system of government in which power is divided by a written constitution between a central government and regional, or subdivisional, governments. Each level must have some domain in which its policies are dominant and some genuine political or constitutional guarantee of its authority.

FIGHTING WORDS Words that, when uttered by a public speaker, are so inflammatory that they could provoke the average listener to violence; the words are usually of a racial, religious, or ethnic type.

FEDERALISTS The first American political party, led by Alexander Hamilton and John Adams. Many of its members had strongly supported the adoption of the new Constitution and the creation of the federal union.

FILIBUSTER In the Senate, unlimited debate to halt action on a particular bill.

FIRESIDE CHAT One of the warm, informal talks by Franklin D. Roosevelt to a few million of his intimate friends— via the radio. Roosevelt's fireside chats were so effective that succeeding presidents have been urged by their advisers to emulate him by giving more radio and television reports to the nation.

FIRST BUDGET RESOLUTION A resolution passed by Congress in May that sets overall revenue and spending goals and hence, by definition, the size of the budget deficit for the following fiscal year.

FIRST CONTINENTAL CONGRESS The first gathering of delegates from twelve of the thirteen colonies, held in 1774.

FISCAL POLICY The use of changes in government spending or taxes to alter national economic variables, such as the rate of unemployment.

FISCAL YEAR (FY) The twelve-month period that is used for bookkeeping, or accounting, purposes. Usually, the fiscal year does not coincide with the calendar year. For example, the federal government's fiscal year runs from October 1 through September 30.

FLUIDITY The extent to which public opinion changes over time.

FOOD STAMPS Coupons issued by the federal government to low-income individuals to be used for the purchase of food.

FOREIGN POLICY A nation's external goals and the techniques and strategies used to achieve them.

FOREIGN POLICY PROCESS The steps by which external goals are decided and acted on.

FRATERNITY From the Latin fraternus (brother), a term that came to mean, in the political philosophy of the eighteenth century, the condition in which each individual considers the needs of all others; a brotherhood. In the

French Revolution of 1789, the popular cry was "liberty, equality, and fraternity."

FREE EXERCISE CLAUSE   The provision of the First Amendment guaranteeing the free exercise of religion.

FULL FAITH AND CREDIT CLAUSE   A section of the Constitution that requires states to recognize one another's laws and court decisions. It ensures that rights established under deeds, wills, contracts, and other civil matters in one state will be honored by other states.

GAG ORDER   An order issued by a judge restricting the publication of news about a trial in progress or a pretrial hearing in order to protect the accused's right to a fair trial.

GARBAGE CAN MODEL   A model of bureaucracy that characterizes bureaucracies as rudderless entities with little formal organization in which solutions to problems are based on trial and error rather than rational policy planning.

GENDER GAP   Most often used to describe the difference between the percentage of votes a candidate receives from women and the percentage the candidate receives from men. The term was widely used after the 1980 presidential election.

GENERATIONAL EFFECT   A long-lasting effect of events of a particular time period on the political opinions or preferences of those who came of political age at that time.

GERRYMANDERING   The drawing of legislative district boundary lines for the purpose of obtaining partisan or factional advantage. A district is said to be gerrymandered when its shape is manipulated by the dominant party in the state legislature to maximize electoral strength at the expense of the minority party.

GOVERNMENT   A permanent structure (institution) composed of decision makers who make society's rules about conflict resolution and the allocation of resources and who possess the power to enforce them.

GOVERNMENT CORPORATION   An agency of government that administers a quasi-business enterprise. These corporations are used when an activity is primarily commercial. They produce revenue for their continued existence, and they require greater flexibility than is permitted for departments and agencies.

GOVERNMENT IN THE SUNSHINE ACT   A law that requires all multiheaded federal agencies to conduct their business regularly in public session.

GRAND JURY   A jury called to hear evidence and determine whether indictments should be issued against persons suspected of having committed crimes.

GRANDFATHER CLAUSE   A device used by southern states to exempt whites from state taxes and literacy laws originally intended to disenfranchise African-American voters. It restricted the voting franchise to those who could prove that their grandfathers had voted before 1867.

GREAT COMPROMISE   The compromise between the New Jersey and the Virginia plans that created one chamber of the Congress based on population and one chamber that represented each state equally; also called the Connecticut Compromise.

HATCH ACT (POLITICAL ACTIVITIES ACT)   An act passed in 1939 that prohibited a political committee from spending more than $3 million in any campaign and limited individual contributions to a committee to $5,000. The act was designed to control political influence buying.

HECKLERS' VETO   Boisterous and generally disruptive behavior by listeners of public speakers that, in effect, vetoes the public speakers' right to speak.

HORIZONTAL FEDERALISM   Activities, problems, and policies that require state governments to interact with one another.

HYPERPLURALISM   A situation that arises when interest groups become so powerful that they dominate the political decision-making structures, rendering any consideration of the greater public interest impossible.

IDEOLOGUE   An individual whose political opinions are carefully thought out and relatively consistent with one another. Ideologues are often described as having a comprehensive world view.

IDEOLOGY   A comprehensive and logically ordered set of beliefs about the nature of people and about the institutions and role of government.

IMAGE BUILDING   Using public and private opinion polls to mold the candidate's image to meet the particular needs of the campaign. Image building is done primarily through the media.

IMPEACHMENT   As authorized by Article I of the Constitution, an action by the House of Representatives and the Senate to remove the president, vice president, or civil officers of the United States from office for crimes of "Treason, Bribery, or other high Crimes and Misdemeanors."

INALIENABLE RIGHTS   Rights held to be inherent in natural law and not dependent on government; as asserted in the Declaration of Independence, the rights to "life, liberty, and the pursuit of happiness."

INCOME TRANSFER   A transfer of income from some individuals in the economy to others. This is generally done by way of the government. It is a transfer in the sense that no current services are rendered by the recipients.

INCORPORATION THEORY   The view that most of the protections of the Bill of Rights are incorporated into the Fourteenth Amendment's protection against state governments.

INDEPENDENT   A voter or candidate who does not identify with a political party.

INDEPENDENT CANDIDATE   A political candidate who is not affiliated with a political party.

INDEPENDENT EXECUTIVE AGENCY   A federal agency that is not part of a cabinet department but reports directly to the president.

INDEPENDENT REGULATORY AGENCY   An agency outside the major executive departments charged with making and implementing rules and regulations to protect the public interest.

INDIRECT TECHNIQUE A strategy employed by interest groups that uses third parties to influence government officials.

INHERENT POWER A power of the president derived from the loosely worded statement in the Constitution that "the executive Power shall be vested in a President" and that the president should "take Care that the Laws be faithfully executed"; defined through practice rather than through constitutional or statutory law.

INITIATIVE A procedure by which voters can propose a law or a constitutional amendment.

INJUNCTION An order issued by a court to compel or restrain the performance of an act by an individual or government official.

INSTITUTION A long-standing, identifiable structure or association that performs functions for society.

INSTRUCTED DELEGATE A legislator who is an agent of the voters who elected him or her and who votes according to the views of constituents regardless of personal assessments.

INTELLIGENCE COMMUNITY The government agencies involved in gathering information about the capabilities and intentions of foreign governments and that engages in covert activities to further U.S. foreign policy aims.

INTENSITY The strength of a position for or against a public policy or an issue. Intensity is often critical in generating public action; an intense minority can often win on an issue of public policy over a less intense majority.

INTEREST GROUP An organized group of individuals sharing common objectives who actively attempt to influence policymakers (in all three branches of the government and at all levels) through direct and indirect methods, including the marshalling of public opinion, lobbying, and electioneering. Also called *pressure group* or *lobby*.

INTERPOSITION The act in which a state places itself between its citizens and the national government as a protector, shielding its citizens from any national legislation that may be harmful to them. The doctrine of interposition has been rejected by the federal courts as contrary to the supremacy clause in Article VI of the Constitution.

INTERSTATE COMPACT An agreement between two or more states. Agreements on minor matters are made without congressional consent, but any compact that tends to increase the power of the contracting states relative to other states or relative to the national government generally requires the consent of Congress. Such compacts serve as a means by which states can solve regional problems.

IN-KIND SUBSIDY A good or service—such as food stamps, housing, or medical care—provided by the government to lower-income groups.

IRON CURTAIN The term used to describe the division of Europe between the Soviet Union and the West; popularized by Winston Churchill in a speech portraying Europe as being divided by an iron curtain, with the nations of Eastern Europe behind the curtain and increasingly under Soviet control.

IRON TRIANGLE The three-way alliance among legislators, bureaucrats, and interest groups to make or preserve policies that benefit their respective interests.

ISOLATIONIST FOREIGN POLICY Abstaining from an active role in international affairs or alliances, which characterized U.S. foreign policy toward Europe during most of the nineteenth century.

ISSUE VOTING Voting for a candidate based on how he or she stands on a particular issue.

JOINT COMMITTEE A legislative committee composed of members from both chambers of Congress.

JUDICIABLE DISPUTE A dispute that raises questions about the law and that is appropriate for resolution before a court of law.

JUDICIAL ACTIVISM A doctrine advocating an active role for the Supreme Court in enforcing the Constitution and in using judicial review.

JUDICIAL IMPLEMENTATION The way in which court decisions are translated into policy.

JUDICIAL RESTRAINT A doctrine holding that the Court should rarely use its power of judicial review or otherwise intervene in the political process.

JUDICIAL REVIEW The power of the courts to declare acts of the executive and legislative branches unconstitutional; first established in *Marbury v. Madison.*

JURISDICTION The authority of a court to decide certain cases. Not all courts have the authority to decide all cases. Where a case arises and what its subject matter is are two jurisdictional factors.

JUSTICIABLE QUESTION A question that may be raised and reviewed in court.

KEYNESIAN ECONOMICS An economic theory, named after English economist John Maynard Keynes, that gained prominence during the Great Depression of the 1930s. It is typically associated with the use of fiscal policy to alter national economic variables—for example, increased government spending during times of economic downturns.

KITCHEN CABINET The informal advisers to the president.

LABOR MOVEMENT Generally, the full range of economic and political expression of working-class interests; politically, the organization of working-class interests.

LATENT PUBLIC OPINION Unexpressed political opinions that have the potential to become manifest attitudes or beliefs.

LAWMAKING The process of deciding the legal rules that govern our society. Such laws may regulate minor affairs or establish broad national policies.

LEGISLATIVE HISTORY The background and events leading up to the enactment of a law. This may include legislative committee reports, hearings, and floor debates.

LEGISLATIVE VETO   A provision in a bill reserving to Congress or to a congressional committee the power to reject an act or regulation of a national agency by majority vote; declared unconstitutional by the Supreme Court in 1983.

LEGISLATURE   A government body primarily responsible for the making of laws.

LEGITIMACY   A status conferred by the people on the government's officials, acts, and institutions through their belief that the government's actions are an appropriate use of power by a legally constituted governmental authority following correct decision-making procedures. These actions are regarded as rightful and entitled to compliance and obedience on the part of citizens.

LIBEL   A written defamation of a person's character, reputation, business, or property rights. To a limited degree, the First Amendment protects the press from libel actions.

LIBERALISM   A set of beliefs that includes the advocacy of positive government action to improve the welfare of individuals, support for civil rights, and tolerance for political and social change.

LIBERTY   The greatest freedom of individuals that is consistent with the freedom of other individuals in the society.

LIMITED GOVERNMENT   A form of government based on the principle that the powers of government should be clearly limited either through a written document or through wide public understanding; characterized by institutional checks to ensure that government serves the public rather than private interests.

LINE ORGANIZATION   Government or corporate units that provide direct services or products for the public.

LITERACY TEST   A test administered as a precondition for voting, often used to prevent African Americans from exercising their right to vote.

LITIGATE   To engage in a legal proceeding or seek relief in a court of law; to carry on a lawsuit.

LOBBYING   The attempt by organizations or by individuals to influence the passage, defeat, or contents of legislation and the administrative decisions of government. The derivation of the term may be traced back to over a century ago, when certain private citizens regularly congregated in the lobby outside the legislative chambers before a session to petition legislators.

LOGROLLING   An arrangement by which two or more members of Congress agree in advance to support each other's bills.

LOOPHOLE   A legal method by which individuals and businesses are allowed to reduce the tax liabilities owed to the government.

MADISONIAN MODEL   The model of government devised by James Madison in which the powers of the government are separated into three branches: executive, legislative, and judicial.

MAJORITY   More than 50 percent. In regard to age, the term means the age at which a person is entitled by law to the management of his or her own affairs and to the full enjoyment of civil rights.

MAJORITY FLOOR LEADER   The chief spokesperson of the majority party in the Senate who directs the legislative program and party strategy.

MAJORITY LEADER OF THE HOUSE   A legislative position held by an important party member in the House of Representatives. The majority leader is selected by the majority party in caucus or conference to foster cohesion among party members and to act as a spokesperson for the majority party in the House.

MAJORITY OPINION   The views of the majority of the judges.

MAJORITY RULE   A basic principle of democracy asserting that a numerical majority (usually 51 percent) in a political unit has the power to make decisions binding on the unit.

MANDATORY RETIREMENT   Forced retirement when a person reaches a certain age.

MATCHING FUNDS   For many categorical grant programs, money with which the state must "match" the federal funds. Some programs require the state to raise only 10 percent of the funds, whereas others approach an even share.

MATERIAL INCENTIVE   A reason or motive having to do with economic benefits or opportunities.

MEDIA   The technical means of communication with mass audiences.

MERIT SYSTEM   The selection, retention, and promotion of government employees on the basis of competitive examinations.

MILITARY-INDUSTRIAL COMPLEX   The mutually beneficial relationship between the armed forces and defense contractors.

MINORITY FLOOR LEADER   The party officer in the Senate who commands the minority party's opposition to the policies of the majority party and directs the legislative program and strategy of his or her party.

MINORITY LEADER OF THE HOUSE   The party leader elected by the minority party in the House.

MONETARY POLICY   The use of changes in the amount of money in circulation to alter credit markets, employment, and the rate of inflation.

MONOPOLISTIC MODEL   A model of bureaucracy that compares bureaucracies to monopolistic business firms. Lack of competition within a bureaucracy leads to inefficient and costly operations, just as it does within monopolistic firms. Because bureaucracies are not penalized for inefficiency, there is no incentive to save costs or use resources more productively.

MONROE DOCTRINE   The policy statement included in President James Monroe's 1823 annual message to Congress that set out three principles: (1) European nations should not establish new colonies in the Western Hemisphere, (2) European nations should not intervene in the affairs of independent nations of the Western Hemisphere, and (3) the United States would not interfere in the affairs of European nations.

MORAL IDEALISM A philosophy that sees all nations as willing to cooperate and agree on moral standards of conduct.

NATIONAL COMMITTEE A standing committee of a national political party established to direct and coordinate party activities during the four-year period between national party conventions.

NATIONAL CONVENTION The meeting held every four years by each major party to select presidential and vice presidential candidates, to write a platform, to choose a national committee, and to conduct party business. In theory, the national convention is at the top of a hierarchy of party conventions (the local and state conventions are below it) that consider candidates and issues.

NATIONAL POLITICS The pursuit of interests that are of concern to the nation as a whole.

NATIONAL SECURITY COUNCIL (NSC) A staff agency in the Executive Office of the President established by the National Security Act of 1947. The NSC advises the president on domestic and foreign matters involving national security.

NATIONAL SECURITY POLICY Foreign and domestic policy designed to protect the independence and political and economic integrity of the United States; policy that is concerned with the safety and defense of the nation.

NATURAL ARISTOCRACY A small ruling clique of the state's "best" citizens, whose membership is based on birth, wealth, and ability. The Jeffersonian era emphasized government rule by such a group.

NATURAL RIGHTS Rights held to be inherent in natural law, not dependent on governments. John Locke stated that natural law, being superior to human law, specifies certain rights of "life, liberty, and property." These rights, altered to become "life, liberty, and the pursuit of happiness," are asserted in the Declaration of Independence.

NECESSARIES In contract law, necessaries include whatever is reasonably necessary for suitable subsistence as measured by age, state, condition in life, and so on.

NEGATIVE CONSTITUENTS Citizens who openly oppose government foreign policies.

NEW FEDERALISM A plan to limit the national government's power to regulate, as well as to restore power to state governments. Essentially, the new federalism was designed to give the states greater ability to decide for themselves how government revenues should be spent.

NULLIFICATION The act of nullifying, or rendering void. John C. Calhoun asserted that a state had the right to declare a national law to be null and void and therefore not binding on its citizens, on the assumption that ultimate sovereign authority rested with the several states.

OFFICE-BLOCK, OR MASSACHUSETTS, BALLOT A form of general election ballot in which candidates for elective office are grouped together under the title of each office. It emphasizes voting for the office and the individual, rather than for the party.

OFFICE OF MANAGEMENT AND BUDGET (OMB) A division of the Executive Office of the President created by executive order in 1970 to replace the Bureau of the Budget. The OMB's main functions are to assist the president in preparing the annual budget, to clear and coordinate all departmental agency budgets, to help set fiscal policy, and to supervise the administration of the federal budget.

OLIGARCHY Rule by a few members of the elite, who generally make decisions to benefit their own group.

OMBUDSMAN An individual in the role of hearing and investigating complaints by private individuals against public officials or agencies.

OPEN PRIMARY A direct primary in which voters may cast ballots in the primary of either party without having to declare their party registration. Once voters choose which party primary they will vote in, they must select among only the candidates of that party.

OPINION The statement by a judge or a court of the decision reached in a case tried or argued before it. The opinion sets forth the law that applies to the case and details the legal reasoning on which the judgment was based.

OPINION LEADER One who is able to influence the opinions of others because of position, expertise, or personality. Such leaders help to shape public opinion either formally or informally.

OPINION POLL A method of systematically questioning a small, selected sample of respondents who are deemed representative of the total population. These polls are widely used by government, business, university scholars, political candidates, and volunteer groups to provide reasonably accurate data on public attitudes, beliefs, expectations, and behavior.

ORAL ARGUMENTS The verbal arguments presented in person by attorneys to an appellate court. Each attorney presents reasons to the court why the court should rule in his or her client's favor.

OVERSIGHT The responsibility Congress has for following up on laws it has enacted to ensure that they are being enforced and administered in the way in which they were intended.

PAID-FOR POLITICAL ANNOUNCEMENT A message about a political candidate conveyed through the media and designed to elicit positive public opinion.

PARDON The granting of a release from the punishment or legal consequences of crime; a pardon can be granted by the president before or after a conviction.

PARTY-COLUMN, OR INDIANA, BALLOT A form of general election ballot in which candidates for elective office are arranged in one column under their respective party labels and symbols. It emphasizes voting for the party, rather than for the office or individual.

PARTY IDENTIFICATION Linking oneself to a particular political party.

PARTY IDENTIFIER A person who identifies himself or herself with a political party.

PARTY-IN-ELECTORATE Those members of the general public who identify with a political party or who express a preference for one party over the other.

PARTY-IN-GOVERNMENT All of the elected and appointed officials who identify with a political party.

PARTY ORGANIZATION The formal structure and leadership of a political party, including election committees; local, state, and national executives; and paid professional staff.

PARTY PLATFORM A document drawn up by the platform committee at each national convention, outlining the policies, positions, and principles of the party; it is then submitted to the entire convention for approval.

PATRONAGE Rewarding faithful party workers and followers with government employment and contracts.

PEER GROUP A group consisting of members sharing common relevant social characteristics. These groups play an important part in the socialization process, helping to shape attitudes and beliefs.

PENDLETON ACT (CIVIL SERVICE REFORM ACT) The law, as amended over the years, that remains the basic statute regulating federal employment personnel policies. It established the principle of employment on the basis of merit and created the Civil Service Commission to administer the personnel service.

PLURALISM A theory that views politics as a conflict among interest groups. Political decision making is characterized by bargaining and compromise.

PLURALITY The total votes cast for a candidate who receives more votes than any other candidate but not necessarily a majority. Most national, state, and local electoral laws provide for winning elections by a plurality vote.

POCKET VETO A special veto power exercised by the chief executive after a legislative body has adjourned. Bills not signed by the chief executive die after a specified period of time. If Congress wishes to reconsider such a bill, it must be reintroduced in the following session of Congress.

POLICE POWER The authority to legislate for the protection of the health, morals, safety, and welfare of the people. In the United States, most police power is a reserved power of the states.

POLICY TRADE-OFFS The cost to the nation of undertaking any one policy in terms of all of the other policies that could have been undertaken. For example, an increase in the expenditures on one federal program means either a reduction in expenditures on another program or an increase in federal taxes (or the deficit).

POLITICAL ACTION COMMITTEE (PAC) A committee set up by and representing a corporation, labor union, or special interest group. PACs raise and give campaign dona-

tions on behalf of the organizations or groups they represent.

POLITICAL CONSULTANT A paid professional hired to devise a campaign strategy and manage a campaign. Image building is the crucial task of the political consultant.

POLITICAL CULTURE That set of beliefs and values regarding the political system that are widely shared by the citizens of a nation.

POLITICAL PARTY A group of political activists who organize to win elections, to operate the government, and to determine public policy.

POLITICAL QUESTION An issue that a court believes should be decided by the executive or legislative branches.

POLITICAL REALISM A philosophy that sees each nation acting principally in its own interest.

POLITICAL SOCIALIZATION The process through which individuals learn a set of political attitudes and form opinions about social issues. The family and the educational system are two of the most important forces in the political socialization process.

POLITICAL TOLERANCE The degree to which individuals are willing to grant civil liberties to groups that have opinions differing strongly from their own.

POLITICAL TRUST The degree to which individuals express trust in the government and political institutions. This concept is usually measured through a specific series of survey questions.

POLITICO The legislative role that combines the trustee and instructed-delegate trustee concepts. The legislator varies the role according to the issue under consideration.

POLITICS According to David Easton, the "authoritative allocation of values" for a society; according to Harold Lasswell, "who gets what, when, and how" in a society.

POLL TAX A special tax that must be paid as a qualification for voting. The Twenty-fourth Amendment to the Constitution outlawed the poll tax in national elections, and in 1966 the Supreme Court declared it unconstitutional in all elections.

POLL WATCHER An individual appointed by a political party to scrutinize the voting process on election day. Usually, there are two poll watchers at every voting place, representing the Democratic and the Republican parties, both attempting to ensure the honesty of the election.

POPULAR SOVEREIGNTY The concept that ultimate political authority rests with the people.

POWER The ability to cause others to modify their behavior and to conform to what the power holder wants.

PRECEDENT A court rule bearing on subsequent legal decisions in similar cases. Judges rely on precedents in deciding cases.

PREFERRED-POSITION TEST A court test used in determining the limits of free expression guaranteed by the First Amendment. Under this test, limitations on speech are permissible if they are necessary to avoid imminent, serious, and important evils.

PRESIDENTIAL PRIMARY A statewide primary election of

delegates to a political party's national convention to help a party determine its presidential nominee. Such delegates are either pledged to a particular candidate or unpledged.

PRESIDENT PRO TEMPORE The temporary presiding officer of the Senate in the absence of the vice president.

PRESS SECRETARY The individual responsible for representing the White House before the media. The press secretary writes news releases, provides background information, sets up press conferences, and so on.

PRIOR RESTRAINT Restraining an action before the activity has actually occurred. It involves censorship, as opposed to subsequent punishment.

PRIVATIZATION, OR CONTRACTING OUT The replacement of government services with services provided by private firms.

PRIVILEGES AND IMMUNITIES Special rights and exceptions provided by law. Article IV, Section 2, of the Constitution requires states not to discriminate against one another's citizens. A resident of one state cannot be treated as an alien when in another state; he or she may not be denied such privileges and immunities as legal protection, access to courts, travel rights, or property rights.

PROPERTY Anything that is or may be subject to ownership. As conceived by the political philosopher John Locke, the right to property is a natural right superior to human law (laws made by government).

PUBLIC AGENDA Issues that commonly are perceived by members of the political community as meriting public attention and governmental action. The media play an important role in setting the public agenda by focusing attention on certain topics.

PUBLIC DEBT, OR NATIONAL DEBT The total amount of debt carried by the federal government.

PUBLIC DEBT FINANCING The government's spending more than it receives in taxes and paying for the difference by issuing U.S. Treasury bonds, thereby adding to the public debt.

PUBLIC INTEREST The best interests of the collective, overall community; the national good, rather than the narrow interests of a self-serving group.

PUBLIC OPINION The aggregate of individual attitudes or beliefs shared by some portion of adults. There is no one public opinion, because there are many different "publics."

PURPOSIVE INCENTIVE A reason or motive having to do with ethical beliefs or ideological principles.

RATIFICATION Formal approval.

REAPPORTIONMENT The allocation of seats in the House to each state after each census.

RECALL A procedure allowing the people to vote to dismiss an elected official from state office before his or her term has expired.

RECOGNITION POWER The president's power, as chief diplomat, to extend diplomatic recognition to foreign governments.

RECYCLING The reuse of raw materials derived from already manufactured products.

REDISTRICTING The redrawing of the boundaries of the districts within each state.

REFERENDUM An act of referring legislative (statutory) or constitutional measures to the voters for approval or disapproval.

REGISTRATION The entry of a person's name onto the list of eligible voters for elections. Registration requires meeting certain legal requirements relating to age, citizenship, and residency.

RELEVANCE The extent to which an issue is of concern at a particular time. Issues become relevant when the public views them as pressing or of direct concern to daily life.

REMAND To send a case back to the court that originally heard it.

REPRESENTATION The function of members of Congress as elected officials to represent the views of their constituents.

REPRESENTATIVE ASSEMBLY A legislature composed of individuals who represent the population.

REPRESENTATIVE DEMOCRACY A form of government in which representatives elected by the people make and enforce laws and policies.

REPRIEVE The presidential power to postpone the execution of a sentence imposed by a court of law; usually done for humanitarian reasons or to await new evidence.

REPUBLIC The form of government in which sovereignty rests with the people, who elect agents to represent them in lawmaking and other decisions.

REPUBLICAN PARTY One of the two major American political parties, which emerged in the 1850s as an antislavery party. It was created to fill the vacuum caused by the disintegration of the Whig party. The Republican party traces its name—but not its ideology—to Jefferson's Democratic Republican party.

RESULTING POWERS The accumulation of several expressed powers that results in a specific power of the federal government.

REVERSE To annul or make void a judgment on account of some error or irregularity.

REVERSE DISCRIMINATION The charge that affirmative action programs requiring preferential treatment or quotas discriminate against those who do not have minority status.

RULE OF FOUR A United States Supreme Court procedure requiring four affirmative votes to hear the case before the full Court.

RULES COMMITTEE A standing committee of the House of Representatives that provides special rules under which specific bills can be debated, amended, and considered by the House.

RUN-OFF PRIMARY An election that is held to nominate candidates within the party if no candidate receives a majority of the votes in the first primary election.

SAFE SEAT A district that returns the legislator with 55 percent of the vote or more.

SAMPLING ERROR The difference between a sample's results and the true result if the entire population had been interviewed.

SECESSION The act of formally withdrawing from membership in an alliance; the withdrawal of a state from the federal union.

SECOND BUDGET RESOLUTION A resolution passed by Congress in September that sets "binding" limits on taxes and spending for the next fiscal year beginning October 1.

SECOND CONTINENTAL CONGRESS The 1775 congress of the colonies that established an army.

SECTIONAL POLITICS The pursuit of interests that are of special concern to a region or section of the country.

SELECT COMMITTEE A temporary legislative committee established for a limited time period and for a special purpose.

SENATORIAL COURTESY In regard to federal district court judgeship nominations, a Senate tradition allowing a senator of the president's political party to veto a judgeship appointment in his or her state simply by indicating that the appointment is personally not acceptable. At that point, the Senate may reject the nomination, or the president may withdraw consideration of the nominee.

SENIORITY SYSTEM A custom followed in both chambers of Congress specifying that members with longer terms of continuous service will be given preference when committee chairpersons and holders of other significant posts are selected.

SEPARATE-BUT-EQUAL DOCTRINE The doctrine holding that segregation in schools and public accommodations does not imply that one race is superior to another; rather, it implies that each race is entitled to separate-but-equal facilities.

SEPARATION OF POWERS The principle of dividing governmental powers among the executive, the legislative, and the judicial branches of government.

SERVICE SECTOR The sector of the economy that provides services—such as food services, insurance, and education—in contrast to the sector of the economy that produces goods.

SEXUAL HARASSMENT Harassment on the basis of sex, in violation of Title VII of the Civil Rights Act of 1964. This includes unwanted physical or verbal conduct or abuse of a sexual nature that interferes with a recipient's job performance or carries with it an implicit or explicit threat of adverse employment consequences.

SEX DISCRIMINATION Overt behavior in which people are given differential or unfavorable treatment on the basis of sex; any practice, policy, or procedure that denies equality of treatment to an individual or to a group because of gender.

SLANDER The public uttering of a statement that holds a person up for contempt, ridicule, or hatred. This means that the defamatory statement is made to, or within the hearing of, persons other than the defamed party.

SLIDING-SCALE TEST A test that requires the courts to examine the facts of each individual case carefully before restricting expression.

SOCIAL MOVEMENT A movement that represents the demands of a large segment of the public for political, economic, or social change.

SOCIAL SECURITY A federal program that provides monthly payments to millions of people who are retired or unable to work.

SOCIOECONOMIC STATUS The position held in society by virtue of one's level of income or type of occupation.

SOLIDARY INCENTIVE A reason or motive having to do with the desire to associate with others and to share with others a particular interest or hobby.

SOLID SOUTH A term describing the tendency of the post–Civil War southern states to vote for the Democratic party. (Voting patterns in the South have changed, though.)

SOUND BITE A brief, memorable comment that can easily be fit into news broadcasts.

SOVIET BLOC The Eastern European countries that installed communist regimes after World War II.

SPEAKER OF THE HOUSE The presiding officer in the House of Representatives. The speaker is always a member of the majority party and is the most powerful and influential member of the House.

SPIN An interpretation of campaign events or election results that is most favorable to the candidate's campaign strategy.

SPIN DOCTOR A political campaign adviser who tries to convince journalists of the truth of a particular interpretation of events.

SPIN-OFF PARTY A new party formed by a dissident faction within a major political party. Usually, spin-off parties have emerged when a particular personality was at odds with the major party.

SPOILS SYSTEM The awarding of government jobs to political supporters and friends; generally associated with President Andrew Jackson.

SPRING REVIEW The time every year when the Office of Management and Budget requires federal agencies to review their programs, activities, and goals and submit their requests for funding for the next year.

STABILITY The extent to which public opinion remains constant over time.

STANDING COMMITTEE A permanent committee within the House or Senate that considers bills within a certain subject area.

STARE DECISIS To stand on decided cases; the policy of courts to follow precedents established by past decisions.

STATE A group of people occupying a specific area and organized under one government; may be either a nation or a subunit of a nation.

STATE CENTRAL COMMITTEE The principal organized structure of each political party within each state. This committee is responsible for carrying out policy decisions of the party's state convention.

STATE OF THE UNION MESSAGE An annual message to

Congress in which the president proposes a legislative program. The message is addressed not only to Congress but also to the American people and to the world. It offers the opportunity to dramatize policies and objectives and to gain public support.

STATUTORY POWER A power created for the president through laws established by Congress.

STRATEGIC ARMS LIMITATION TREATY (SALT I) A treaty between the United States and the Soviet Union to stabilize the nuclear arms competition between the two countries. SALT I talks began in 1969, and agreements were signed on May 26, 1972.

SUBPOENA To serve with a legal writ requiring a person's appearance in court to give testimony.

SUBSIDY A negative tax; usually a payment to a producer given on a per-unit basis according to the amount of production of a particular commodity.

SUFFRAGE The right to vote; the franchise.

SUNSET LEGISLATION A law requiring that an existing program be reviewed regularly for its effectiveness and be terminated unless specifically extended as a result of this review.

SUPERDELEGATE A party leader or elected official who is given the right to vote at the party's national convention. Superdelegates are not elected at the state level.

SUPPLEMENTAL SECURITY INCOME (SSI) A federal program established to provide assistance to elderly persons and persons with disabilities.

SUPREMACY CLAUSE The constitutional provision that makes the Constitution and federal laws superior to all conflicting state and local legislation.

SUPREMACY DOCTRINE A doctrine that asserts the superiority of national law over state or regional laws. This principle is rooted in Article VI of the Constitution, which provides that the Constitution, the laws passed by the national government under its constitutional powers, and all treaties constitute the supreme law of the land.

SYMBOLIC SPEECH Nonverbal expression of beliefs, which is given substantial protection by the courts.

TECHNICAL ASSISTANCE The sending of experts with technical skills in agriculture, engineering, or business to aid other nations.

THIRD PARTY A political party other than the two major political parties (Republican and Democratic). Usually, third parties are composed of dissatisfied groups that have split from the major parties. They act as indicators of political trends and as safety valves for dissident groups.

THIRD-PARTY CANDIDATE A political candidate running under the banner of a party other than the two major political parties.

TICKET SPLITTING Voting for candidates of two or more parties for different offices. For example, a voter splits her ticket if she votes for a Republican presidential candidate and for a Democratic congressional candidate.

TOTALITARIAN REGIME A form of government that controls all aspects of the political and social life of a nation. All power resides with the government. The citizens have no power to choose the leadership or policies of the country.

TRACKING POLL A poll taken for the candidate on a nearly daily basis as election day approaches.

TRIAL COURT The court in which most cases usually begin and in which questions of fact are examined.

TRUMAN DOCTRINE The policy adopted by President Harry Truman in 1947 to halt communist expansion in southeastern Europe.

TRUSTEE In regard to a legislator, one who acts according to his or her conscience and the broad interests of the entire society.

TWELFTH AMENDMENT An amendment to the Constitution, adopted in 1804, that specifies the separate election of the president and vice president by the electoral college.

TWENTY-FIFTH AMENDMENT An amendment to the Constitution, adopted in 1967, that establishes procedures for filling vacancies in the two top executive offices and that makes provisions for situations involving presidential disability.

TWO-PARTY SYSTEM A political system in which only two parties have a reasonable chance of winning.

UNANIMOUS OPINION An opinion or determination on which all judges agree.

UNDERGROUND ECONOMY The part of the economy that does not pay taxes and so is not directly measured by government statisticians; also called the *subterranean economy* or *unreported economy.*

UNICAMERAL LEGISLATURE A legislature with only one legislative body, as compared with a bicameral (two-house) legislature, such as the U.S. Congress. Nebraska is the only state in the union with a unicameral legislature.

UNIT RULE All of most states' electoral votes are cast for the presidential candidate receiving a plurality of the popular vote.

UNITARY SYSTEM A centralized governmental system in which local or subdivisional governments exercise only those powers given to them by the central government.

UNIVERSAL SUFFRAGE The right of all adults to vote for their representatives.

U.S. TREASURY BOND Evidence of debt issued by the federal government; similar to corporate bonds but issued by the U.S. Treasury.

VETO MESSAGE The president's formal explanation of a veto when legislation is returned to the Congress.

VOTER TURNOUT The percentage of citizens taking part in the election process; the number of eligible voters that actually "turn out" on election day to cast their ballots.

WAR POWERS ACT A law passed in 1973 spelling out the conditions under which the president can commit troops without congressional approval.

WASHINGTON COMMUNITY Individuals regularly involved with politics in Washington, D.C.

WATERGATE BREAK-IN The 1972 illegal entry into the Democratic Campaign offices engineered by participants in Richard Nixon's reelection campaign.

WEBERIAN MODEL A model of bureaucracy developed by the German sociologist Max Weber, who viewed bureaucracies as rational, hierarchical organizations in which power flows from the top downward and decisions are based on logical reasoning and data analysis.

WHIG PARTY One of the foremost political organizations in the United States during the first half of the nineteenth century, formally established in 1836. The Whig party was dominated by the same anti-Jackson elements that organized the National Republican faction within the Jeffersonian Republicans and represented a variety of regional interests. It fell apart as a national party in the early 1850s.

WHIP An assistant who aids the majority or minority leader of the House or the majority or minority floor leader of the Senate.

WHISTLEBLOWER Someone who brings to public attention gross governmental inefficiency or an illegal action.

WHITE HOUSE OFFICE The personal office of the president, which tends to presidential political needs and manages the media.

WHITE HOUSE PRESS CORPS A group of reporters assigned full time to cover the presidency.

WHITE PRIMARY A state primary election that restricts voting to whites only; outlawed by the Supreme Court in 1944.

WRIT OF *HABEAS CORPUS* *Habeas corpus* means, literally, "you have the body." A writ of *habeas corpus* is an order that requires jailers to bring a person before a court or judge and explain why the person is being held in prison.

WRIT OF *CERTIORARI* An order issued by a higher court to a lower court to send up the record of a case for review. It is the principal vehicle for United States Supreme Court review.

WRIT OF *MANDAMUS* An order issued by a court to compel the performance of an act.

Index

Photo Credits

ix © Ira Wyman, Sygma; **xi** © Sandra Baker, Liaison International; **xiii** © Bob Daemmrich, Black Star; **xiv** © Flip Schulke, Black Star: **xvii** © Allan Tannenbaum, Sygma; **xviii** © Cynthia Johnson, Gamma Liaison; **xx** © Brad Markel, Gamma Liaison; **xxii** © J. L. Atlan, Sygma; **xxv** © Larry Downing, Sygma; **xxviii** © David Weintraub; **xxxi** © William Johnson, Stock, Boston; **xlviii** all eleven photos on page © AP/Wide World Photos; **il** all photos on page © AP/Wide World except photo of Nancy Kassebaum which is © Frank Fisher, Gamma Liaison and the photos of Olympia Snowe and J. C. Watts which are © NYT Pictures—New York Times News Service; **1** © Peter Gridley, FPG International; **3** © Peter Miller, Photo Researchers, Inc.; **5** © Brooks Kraft, Sygma; **10** © Rick Friedman, Black Star; **12** © Bettman; **13** © Lisa Quinones, Black Star; **15** © Rob Nelson, Stock, Boston; **17** © Brooks Kraft, Sygma; **19** © Ira Wyman, Sygma; **23** © Joe Sohn/Chromosohn, Stock, Boston; **31** © Sandra Baker, Liaison International; **33** © The Granger Collection; **34** © The Granger Collection; **36** From the Studio of A. Ramsay, © 1767, Courtesy of the National Portrait Gallery, London; **38** © Photo Researchers; **42** © The Granger Collection; **44** © The Granger Collection; **45** The Library of Congress; **47** © Bettmann; **65** © Jim Pickerell, Stock, Boston; **70** © Bettmann; **74** © David Burton, Black Star; **76** © Eunice Harris, Photo Researchers; **78** © Burrows, Gamma Liaison; **80** The Library of Congress; **82** The Library of Congress; **85** The Library of Congress; **86** © Ellis Herwig, Stock, Boston; **88** Richard Pasley, Stock, Boston; **99** © Dennis Brack, Black Star; **101** © 1994 Erica Lansner, Black Star; **106** © Bob Nelson, Picture Group; **108** © Bruce Flynn, Picture Group; **113** © UPI/Bettmann; **114** © Andrew Holbroke, Black Star: **120** © Bill Swersey, Gamma Liaison; **121** AP/Wide World Photos; **122** © Paul Miller, Black Star; **124** (left) © Dennis Brack, Black Star; **124** (right) © Rick Friedman, Black Star; **125** Al Schaben, Sygma; **127** © Bob Daemmrich, Black Star; **128** © Flip Schulke, Black Star; **130** © Phil Huber, Black Star: **137** © Lynn Johnson, Black Star; **139** © Missouri Historical Society; **140** © The Granger Collection; **143** From the Dorthy Sterling Collection at the Amistad Research Center; **144** © Burt Glinn, Magnum; **145** © Ellis Herwig, Stock, Boston; **148** UPI/Bettmann; **149** © Flip Schulke, Black Star; **155** © Ira Wyman, Sygma; **157** © Donald Dietz, Stock, Boston; **160** © J. P. Laffont, Sygma; **163** (top) © Bettmann; **163** (bottom) © Paul Conklin, Monkmeyer; **164** © Bettmann; **168** © Cynthia Johnson, Gamma Liaison; **169** © Donna Ferrato, Black Star; **170** © Minneapolis Star and Tribune; **172** © Bob Daemmrich, Stock, Boston; **173** (top) © P. F. Gero, Sygma; **173** (bottom) © Ron Sachs, Sygma; **176** © Dennis Brack, Black Star; **178** © Burt Bartholomew, Black Star; **179** © Steve Berman, Gamma Liaison; **187** © Bob Daemmrich, Stock, Boston; **189** © Bob Daemmrich, Stock, Boston; **191** © Allan Tannenbaum, Sygma; **192** © Arthur Grace, Stock, Boston; **198** © Bob Daemmrich, Stock, Boston; **199** © Andy Levin, Photo Researchers; **201** UPI/Bettmann; **204** AP/Wide World Photos; **205** © Cynthia Johnson, Gamma Liaison; **209** © Wide World Photos; **214** (left) © Rob Crandall, Picture Group; **214** (right) © Allan Tannenbaum; **216** © Dennis Brack, Black Star; **221** © Dennis Brack, Black Star; **223** © Dennis Brack, Black Star; **224** © The Bettmann Archive; **226** © Halstead, Gamma Liaison; **229** © Renee Lynn, Photo Researchers; **230** © David Sutton, Picture Group; **233** © Mark D. Phillips, Photo Researchers; **234** © Brad Markel, Gamma Liaison; **235** © Lisa Quinones, Black Star; **236** © A. Berliner, Gamma Liaison; **238** © Stacy Pick, Stock, Boston; **242** © Lisa